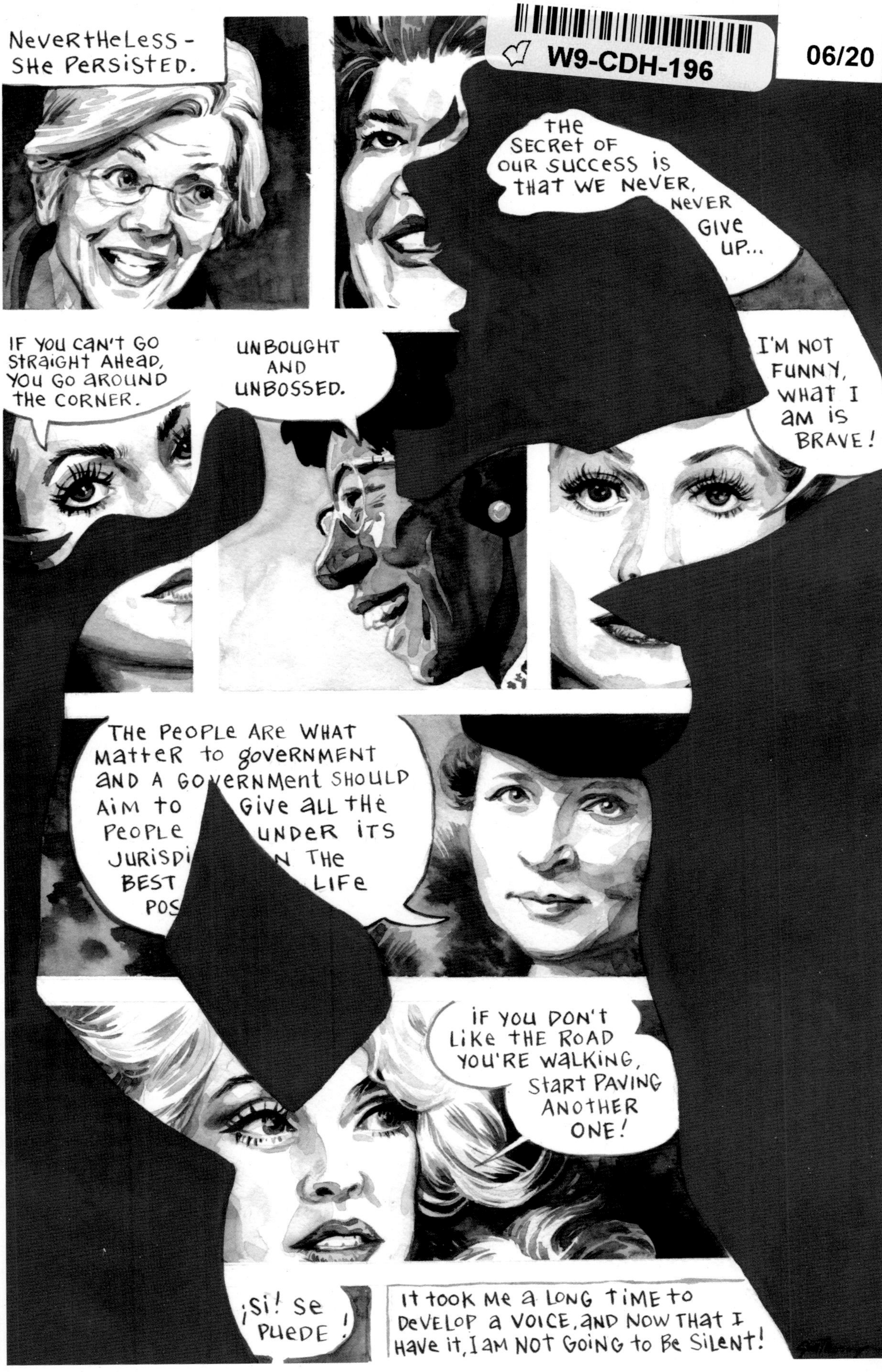
NEVERTHELESS - SHE PERSISTED.
THE SECRET OF OUR SUCCESS IS THAT WE NEVER, NEVER GIVE UP...
IF YOU CAN'T GO STRAIGHT AHEAD, YOU GO AROUND THE CORNER.
UNBOUGHT AND UNBOSSED.
I'M NOT FUNNY, WHAT I AM IS BRAVE!
THE PEOPLE ARE WHAT MATTER TO GOVERNMENT AND A GOVERNMENT SHOULD AIM TO GIVE ALL THE PEOPLE UNDER ITS JURISDI N THE BEST LIFE POS
IF YOU DON'T LIKE THE ROAD YOU'RE WALKING, START PAVING ANOTHER ONE!
¡SI! SE PUEDE!
IT TOOK ME A LONG TIME TO DEVELOP A VOICE, AND NOW THAT I HAVE IT, I AM NOT GOING TO BE SILENT!

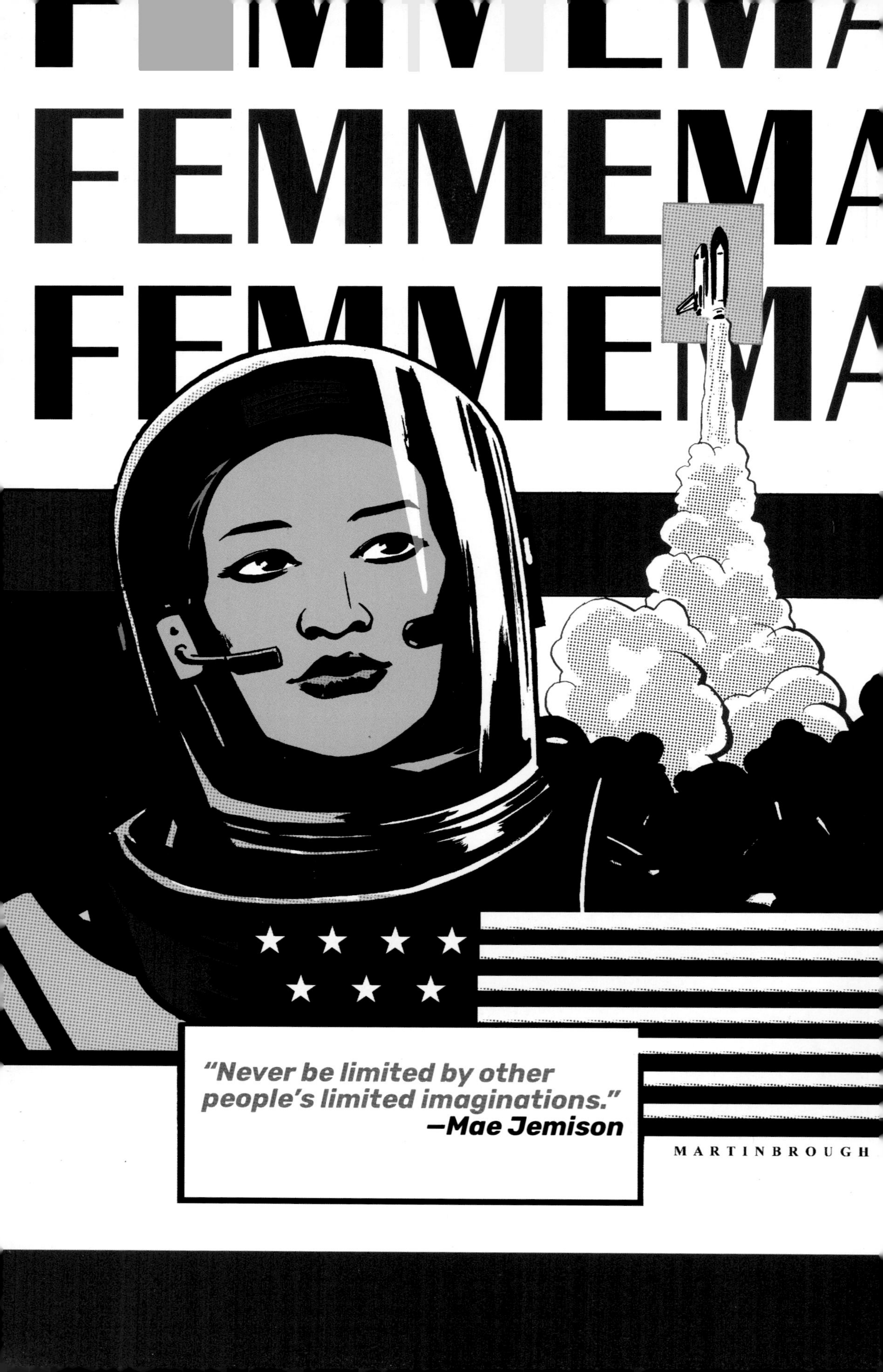
"Never be limited by other people's limited imaginations."
—Mae Jemison
MARTINBROUGH

GNIFIQUE

GNIFIQUE

GNIFIQUE

**A comic book anthology salute
to 50 magnificent women from
pop
politics
art &
science**

> *"Somebody must show that the Afro-American race is more sinned against than sinning, and it seems to have fallen upon me to do so."*
> **—Ida B. Wells**

LEGAL CONSULTING & CONTRACTS by Lillian Laserson

PROOFREAD by Arlene Lo

LETTERING by Aditya Bidikar

COLORS by Claudia Aguirre, Jordie Bellaire, Tamra Bonvillain, Kelly Fitzpatrick, Irma Kniivila, Lee Loughridge, Fabi Marques, Rick Taylor, and Hi-Fi

DESIGN by Hi-Fi with Megan Hutchison and Philip Bond

STORIES CURATED by Shelly Bond, Kristy Miller, and Brian Miller

EDITED by Shelly Bond with Editorial Assistance by Megan Hutchison and Chase Marotz

SPECIAL THANKS TO:
Elsa Charretier for illustrating the Femme Magnifique cover icon.
Jill Thompson for the page one painted illustration.
Shawn Martinbrough for the title page illustrations.
Tess Fowler for providing the main image on the front cover art.
Philip Bond for wraparound cover design.

FOR HI-FI:
Flats: Chris Canibano, Rebekah Cleveland, Bernie Fritts, Stephanie Letterson, Marcia Patricio, and Jana Siefkas
Colors: Michael Birkhofer, Owen Jollands, Brian Miller, Melinda Timpone, Sapphire Trickett, and Dustin Yee
Layout & Design: Bernie Fritts and Brian Miller
Production Coordination & Accounting: Kristy Miller

For international rights, contact **licensing@idwpublishing.com**

ISBN: 978-1-68405-320-9

21 20 19 18   1 2 3 4

IDW

www.IDWPUBLISHING.com

Greg Goldstein, President & Publisher • **John Barber**, Editor-in-Chief • **Robbie Robbins**, EVP/Sr. Art Director • **Cara Morrison**, Chief Financial Officer • **Matthew Ruzicka**, Chief Accounting Officer • **Anita Frazier**, SVP of Sales and Marketing • **David Hedgecock**, Associate Publisher • **Jerry Bennington**, VP of New Product Development • **Lorelei Bunjes**, VP of Digital Services • **Justin Eisinger**, Editorial Director, Graphic Novels and Collections • **Eric Moss**, Sr. Director, Licensing & Business Development

Ted Adams, Founder & CEO of IDW Media Holdings

Facebook: facebook.com/idwpublishing • Twitter: @idwpublishing • YouTube: youtube.com/idwpublishing
Tumblr: tumblr.idwpublishing.com • Instagram: instagram.com/idwpublishing

FEMME MAGNIFIQUE: 50 MAGNIFICENT WOMEN WHO CHANGED THE WORLD. SEPTEMBER 2018. FIRST PRINTING. Copyright © 2018 by Shelly Bond, Kristy Miller, & Brian Miller. IDW Publishing, a division of Idea and Design Works, LLC. Editorial offices: 2765 Truxtun Road, San Diego, CA 92106. The IDW logo is registered in the U.S. Patent and Trademark Office. Any similarities to persons living or dead are purely coincidental. With the exception of artwork used for review purposes, none of the contents of this publication may be reprinted without the permission of Idea and Design Works, LLC. Printed in Korea.
IDW Publishing does not read or accept unsolicited submissions of ideas, stories, or artwork.

TABLE OF CONTENTS

BONUS MATERIAL

Introduction by Cindy Whitehead

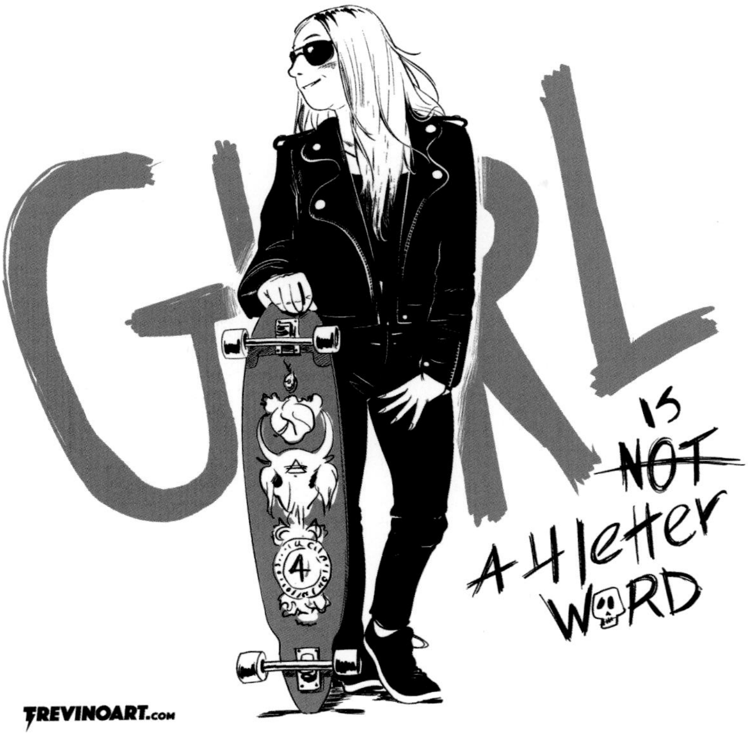
GIRL
IS
NOT
A 4 letter
WORD
TREVINOART.com

When Shelly Bond, editor and co-founder of *Femme Magnifique*, approached me about this book, it was to let me know that *Street Angel* artist Jim Rugg had selected me to be his "Femme Magnifique" subject. Needless to say, I was completely honored to have been selected by Jim, and I knew immediately from Shelly's e-mail detailing the project that this was something I felt strongly about and really wanted to be a part of.

It was less than a month after our world changed dramatically and women and men were marching in the streets to assert themselves and protest the government's having control of our bodies and our hard-won rights. We had all been coasting a bit up until now, and we got hit with the cold, hard reality that there was so much more to be done. The timing of Shelly's e-mail couldn't have been any more perfect.

At this point, I hadn't met Shelly, but I knew from her trailblazing history in the male-dominated comic book world that she believes in what I believe in. Strong women as role models. Women who make a difference in the world and who aren't afraid to show the next generation what that looks like. Women willing to take risks and live their lives full throttle, not giving in to what society deems acceptable.

Sometimes creating change is chaotic, messy, and downright hard. There are times we move five steps ahead and then get pushed three steps back, but we keep moving onward towards goals, dreams, and most of all, equality.

This book is filled with fifty unbelievably strong women who have done just that. Their backgrounds are diverse, and they come from the world of art, science, politics, pop, and sports. These badass women don't waste their time taking selfies and waiting for Internet adoration on social media; they are too busy standing up, speaking out, and making things happen.

Speaking of female trailblazers, I need to mention that my personal Femme Magnifique is Bree Newsome. After the racially motivated killing of nine black church members, this courageous woman, who is no stranger to being an activist, scaled a 30-foot flagpole on June 27, 2015 to remove a Confederate flag from South Carolina Statehouse grounds. This act of civil disobedience (as they call it) led to the permanent removal of that flag less than a month later, proving that one person *can* make a big difference in the world.

The collective history in this book is meant to inspire you, and to remind you that you can be anything you want to be. All you have to do is take that first step and know that there are some seriously rad women standing right there beside you.

Cindy Whitehead

OG Pro Vert Skateboarder inducted into the 2016 Skateboard Hall of Fame, Sports Stylist & Founder of Girl is NOT a 4 Letter Word

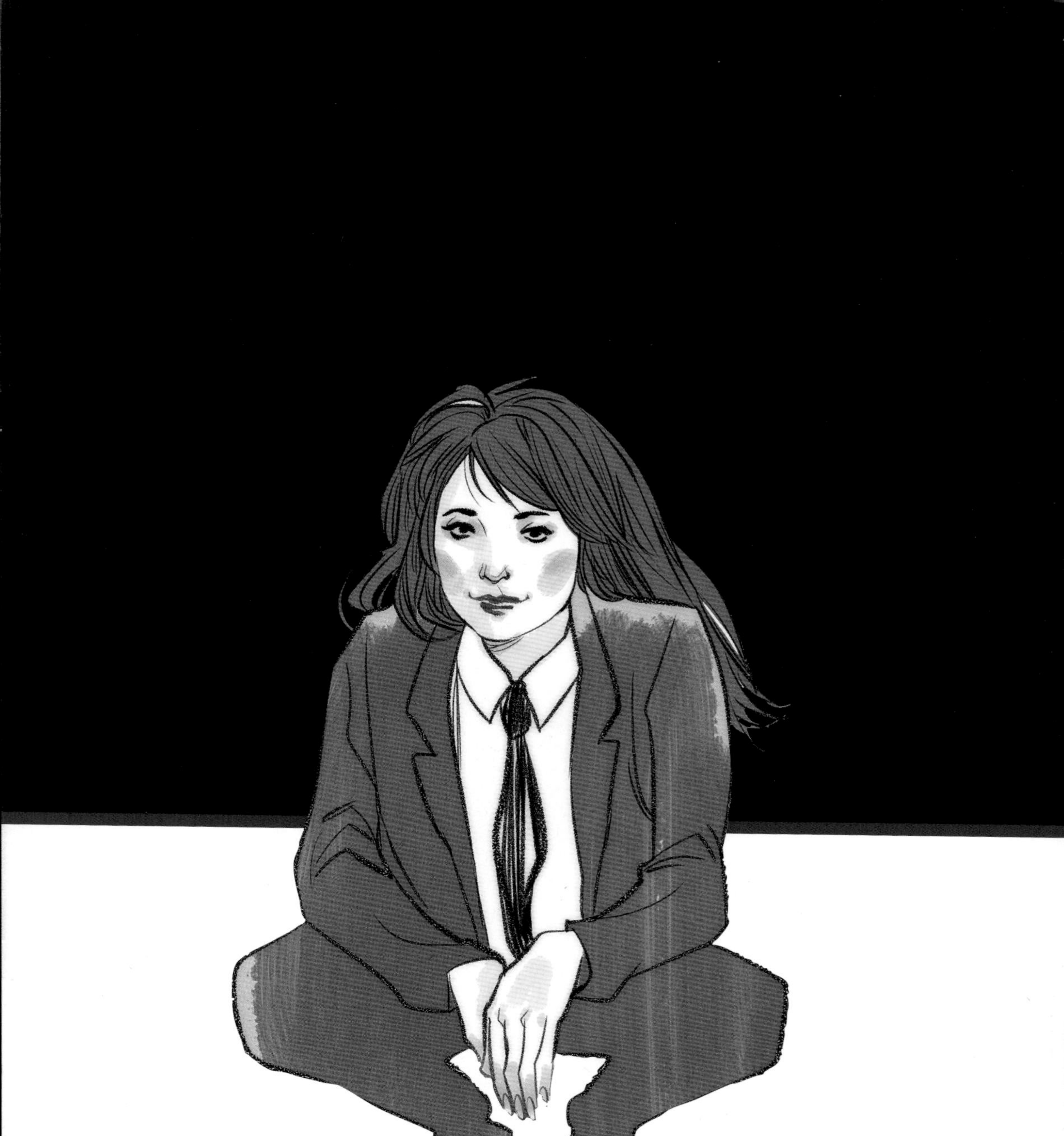

"Quite often, lyrics get misunderstood — and I never mind that. I guess what all artists want is for their work to touch someone or for it to be thought-provoking."

—Kate Bush

THE KICK INSIDE

GAIL SIMONE
WRITER

MARGUERITE SAUVAGE
ARTIST

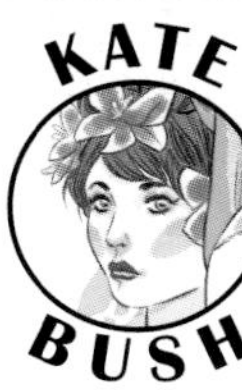

KATE
BUSH

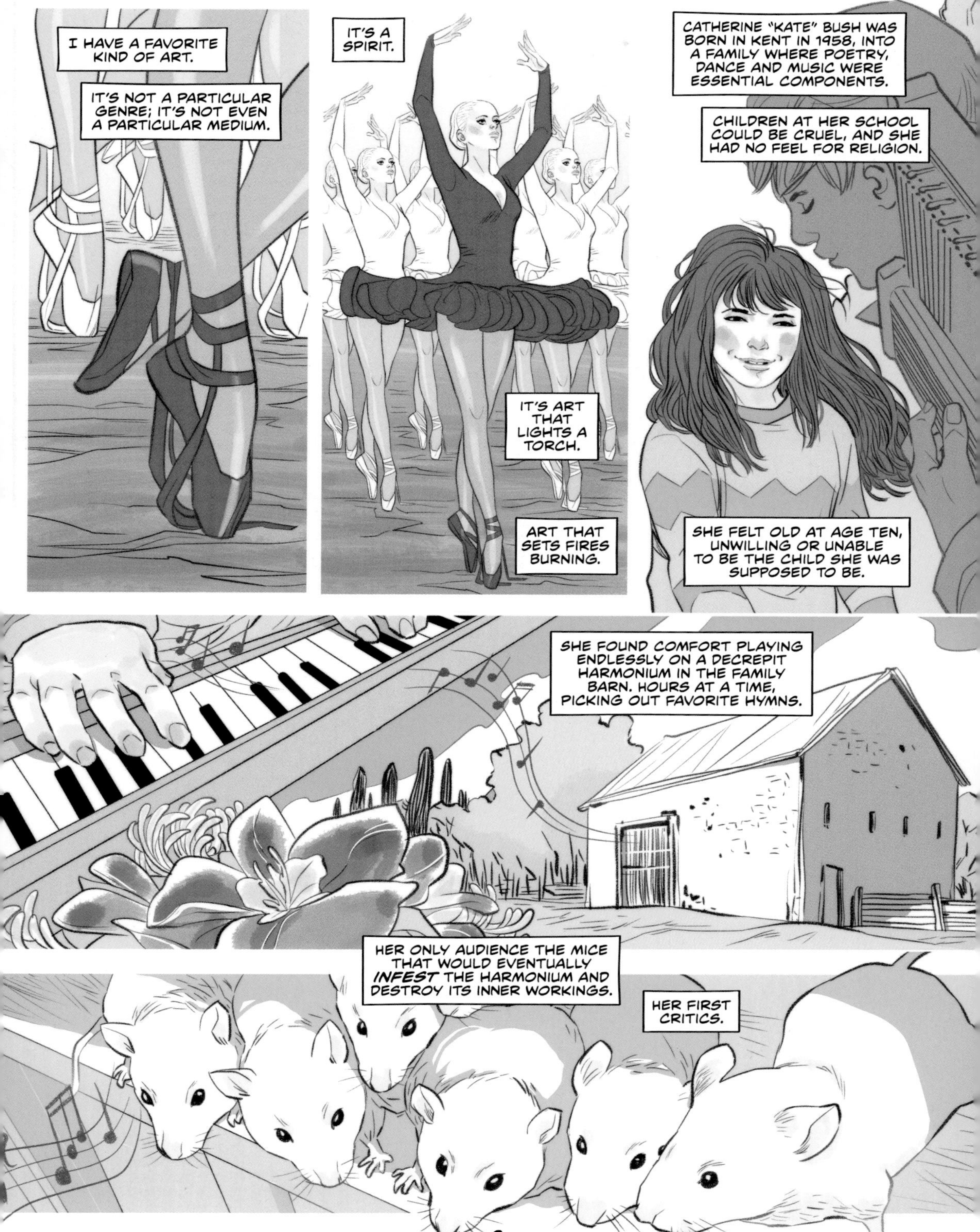

I HAVE A FAVORITE KIND OF ART.
IT'S NOT A PARTICULAR GENRE; IT'S NOT EVEN A PARTICULAR MEDIUM.
IT'S A SPIRIT.
IT'S ART THAT LIGHTS A TORCH.
ART THAT SETS FIRES BURNING.
CATHERINE "KATE" BUSH WAS BORN IN KENT IN 1958, INTO A FAMILY WHERE POETRY, DANCE AND MUSIC WERE ESSENTIAL COMPONENTS.
CHILDREN AT HER SCHOOL COULD BE CRUEL, AND SHE HAD NO FEEL FOR RELIGION.
SHE FELT OLD AT AGE TEN, UNWILLING OR UNABLE TO BE THE CHILD SHE WAS SUPPOSED TO BE.
SHE FOUND COMFORT PLAYING ENDLESSLY ON A DECREPIT HARMONIUM IN THE FAMILY BARN. HOURS AT A TIME, PICKING OUT FAVORITE HYMNS.
HER ONLY AUDIENCE THE MICE THAT WOULD EVENTUALLY *INFEST* THE HARMONIUM AND DESTROY ITS INNER WORKINGS.
HER FIRST CRITICS.

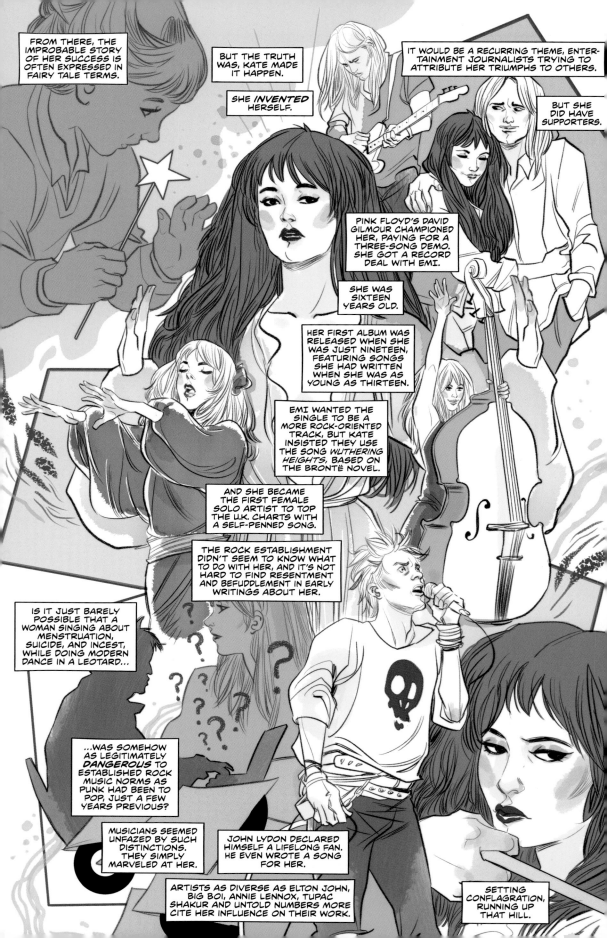

FROM THERE, THE IMPROBABLE STORY OF HER SUCCESS IS OFTEN EXPRESSED IN FAIRY TALE TERMS.

BUT THE TRUTH WAS, KATE MADE IT HAPPEN.

SHE *INVENTED* HERSELF.

IT WOULD BE A RECURRING THEME, ENTERTAINMENT JOURNALISTS TRYING TO ATTRIBUTE HER TRIUMPHS TO OTHERS.

BUT SHE DID HAVE SUPPORTERS.

PINK FLOYD'S DAVID GILMOUR CHAMPIONED HER, PAYING FOR A THREE-SONG DEMO. SHE GOT A RECORD DEAL WITH EMI.

SHE WAS SIXTEEN YEARS OLD.

HER FIRST ALBUM WAS RELEASED WHEN SHE WAS JUST NINETEEN, FEATURING SONGS SHE HAD WRITTEN WHEN SHE WAS AS YOUNG AS THIRTEEN.

EMI WANTED THE SINGLE TO BE A MORE ROCK-ORIENTED TRACK, BUT KATE INSISTED THEY USE THE SONG *WUTHERING HEIGHTS*, BASED ON THE BRONTË NOVEL.

AND SHE BECAME THE FIRST FEMALE SOLO ARTIST TO TOP THE U.K. CHARTS WITH A SELF-PENNED SONG.

THE ROCK ESTABLISHMENT DIDN'T SEEM TO KNOW WHAT TO DO WITH HER, AND IT'S NOT HARD TO FIND RESENTMENT AND BEFUDDLEMENT IN EARLY WRITINGS ABOUT HER.

IS IT JUST BARELY POSSIBLE THAT A WOMAN SINGING ABOUT MENSTRUATION, SUICIDE, AND INCEST, WHILE DOING MODERN DANCE IN A LEOTARD...

...WAS SOMEHOW AS LEGITIMATELY *DANGEROUS* TO ESTABLISHED ROCK MUSIC NORMS AS PUNK HAD BEEN TO POP, JUST A FEW YEARS PREVIOUS?

MUSICIANS SEEMED UNFAZED BY SUCH DISTINCTIONS. THEY SIMPLY MARVELED AT HER.

JOHN LYDON DECLARED HIMSELF A LIFELONG FAN. HE EVEN WROTE A SONG FOR HER.

ARTISTS AS DIVERSE AS ELTON JOHN, BIG BOI, ANNIE LENNOX, TUPAC SHAKUR AND UNTOLD NUMBERS MORE CITE HER INFLUENCE ON THEIR WORK.

SETTING CONFLAGRATION, RUNNING UP THAT HILL.

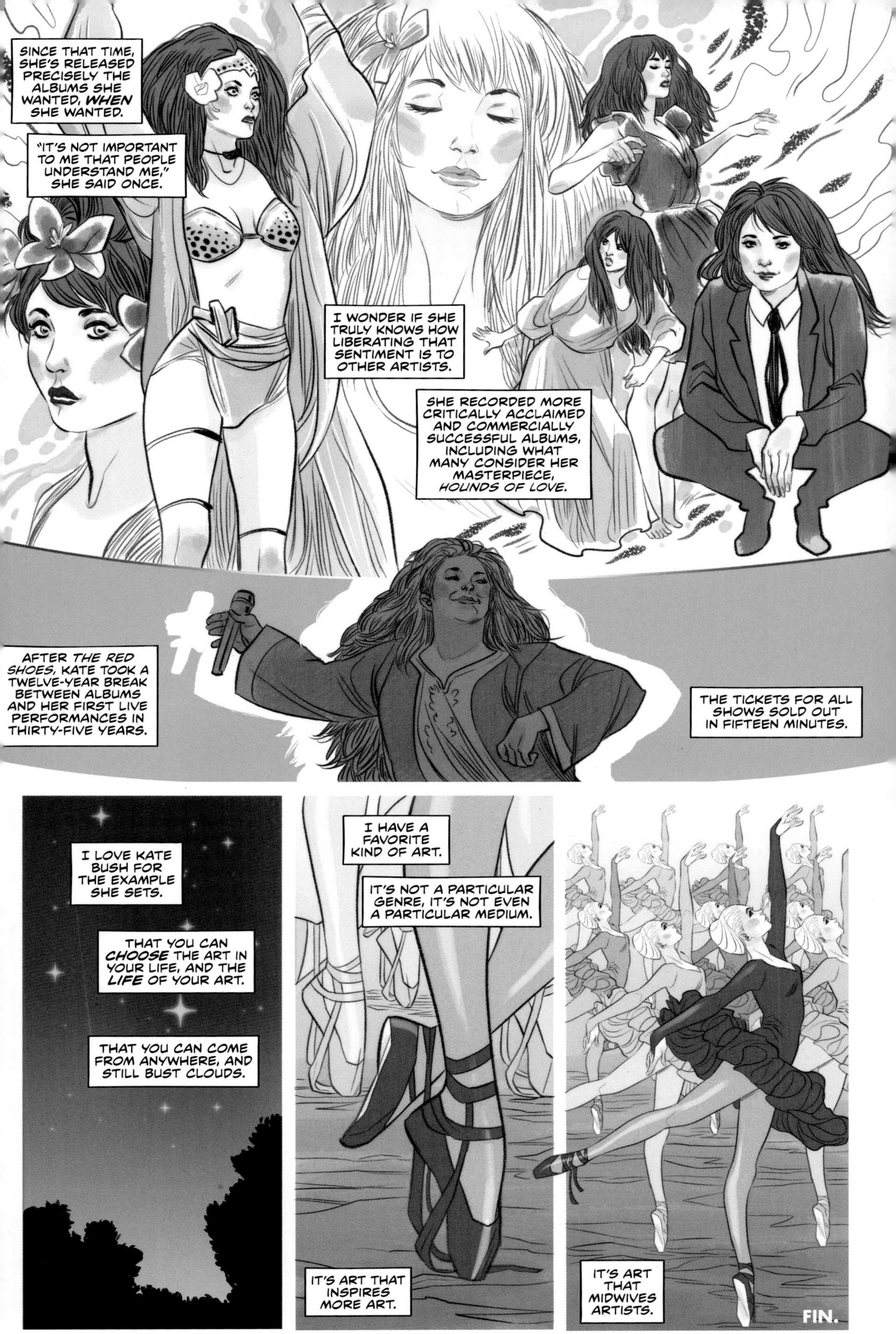
SINCE THAT TIME, SHE'S RELEASED PRECISELY THE ALBUMS SHE WANTED, WHEN SHE WANTED.
"IT'S NOT IMPORTANT TO ME THAT PEOPLE UNDERSTAND ME," SHE SAID ONCE.
I WONDER IF SHE TRULY KNOWS HOW LIBERATING THAT SENTIMENT IS TO OTHER ARTISTS.
SHE RECORDED MORE CRITICALLY ACCLAIMED AND COMMERCIALLY SUCCESSFUL ALBUMS, INCLUDING WHAT MANY CONSIDER HER MASTERPIECE, HOUNDS OF LOVE.
AFTER THE RED SHOES, KATE TOOK A TWELVE-YEAR BREAK BETWEEN ALBUMS AND HER FIRST LIVE PERFORMANCES IN THIRTY-FIVE YEARS.
THE TICKETS FOR ALL SHOWS SOLD OUT IN FIFTEEN MINUTES.
I LOVE KATE BUSH FOR THE EXAMPLE SHE SETS.
THAT YOU CAN CHOOSE THE ART IN YOUR LIFE, AND THE LIFE OF YOUR ART.
THAT YOU CAN COME FROM ANYWHERE, AND STILL BUST CLOUDS.
I HAVE A FAVORITE KIND OF ART.
IT'S NOT A PARTICULAR GENRE, IT'S NOT EVEN A PARTICULAR MEDIUM.
IT'S ART THAT INSPIRES MORE ART.
IT'S ART THAT MIDWIVES ARTISTS.
FIN.

"I beg your pardon for distrusting your friendship. The world has used me so unkindly, I fear it has made me suspicious of everyone."

—Mary Anning
referring to the fact that she was rarely given credit for her work.

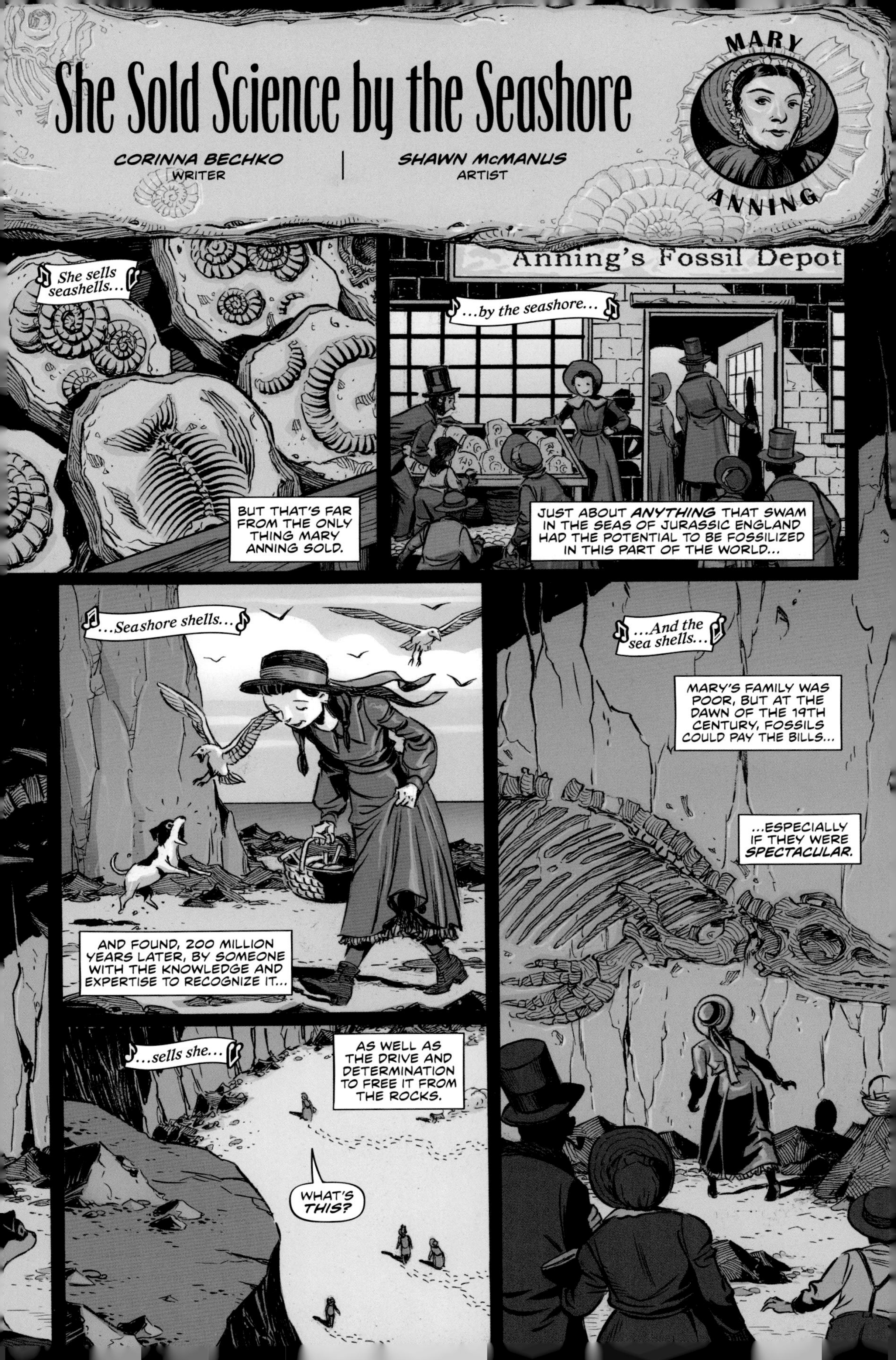
She Sold Science by the Seashore
CORINNA BECHKO
WRITER
SHAWN McMANUS
ARTIST
MARY ANNING
She sells seashells...
BUT THAT'S FAR FROM THE ONLY THING MARY ANNING SOLD.
Anning's Fossil Depot
...by the seashore...
JUST ABOUT *ANYTHING* THAT SWAM IN THE SEAS OF JURASSIC ENGLAND HAD THE POTENTIAL TO BE FOSSILIZED IN THIS PART OF THE WORLD...
...Seashore shells...
AND FOUND, 200 MILLION YEARS LATER, BY SOMEONE WITH THE KNOWLEDGE AND EXPERTISE TO RECOGNIZE IT...
...sells she...
AS WELL AS THE DRIVE AND DETERMINATION TO FREE IT FROM THE ROCKS.
WHAT'S *THIS?*
...And the sea shells...
MARY'S FAMILY WAS POOR, BUT AT THE DAWN OF THE 19TH CENTURY, FOSSILS COULD PAY THE BILLS...
...ESPECIALLY IF THEY WERE *SPECTACULAR*.

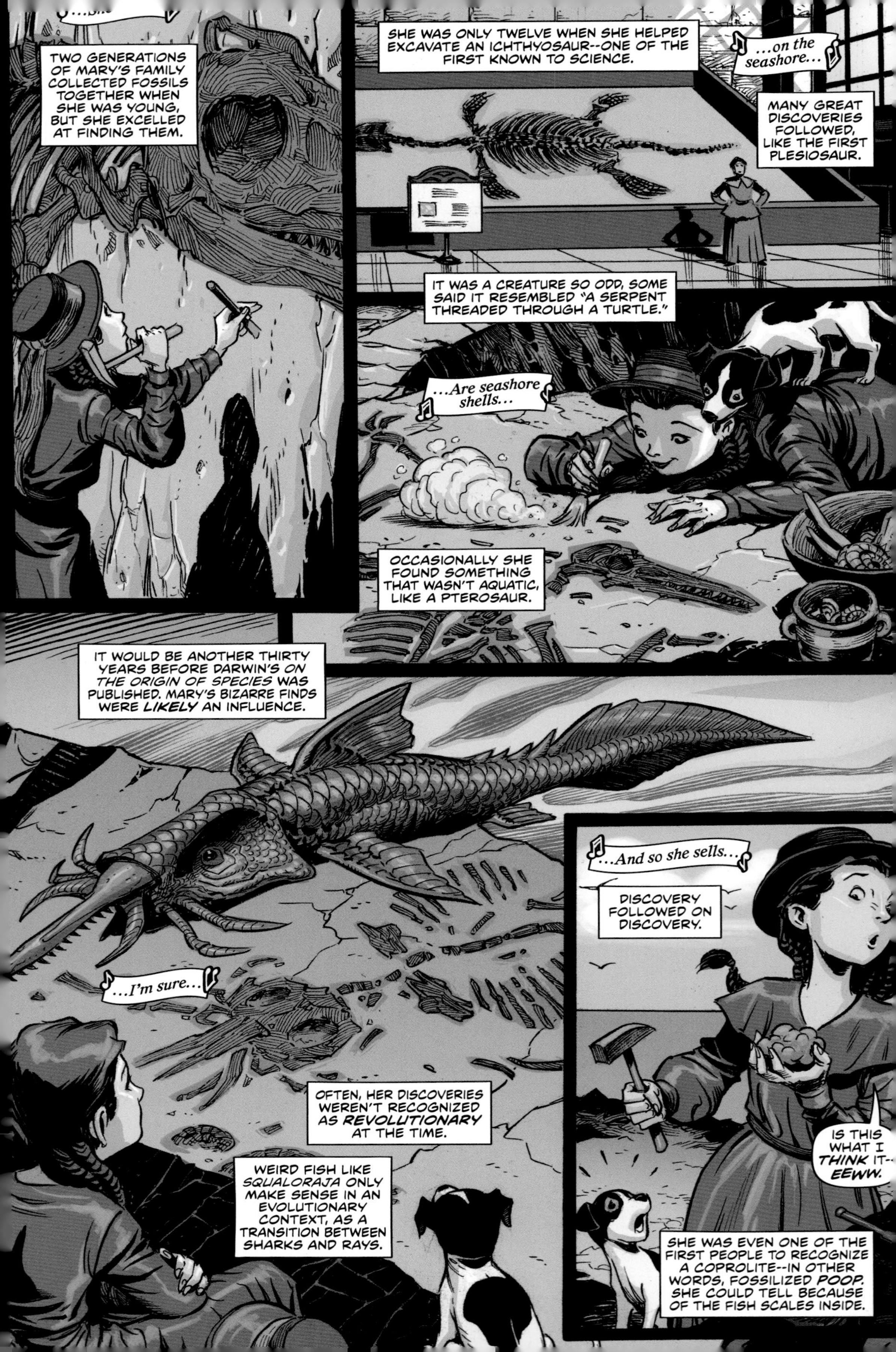

TWO GENERATIONS OF MARY'S FAMILY COLLECTED FOSSILS TOGETHER WHEN SHE WAS YOUNG, BUT SHE EXCELLED AT FINDING THEM.
SHE WAS ONLY TWELVE WHEN SHE HELPED EXCAVATE AN ICHTHYOSAUR--ONE OF THE FIRST KNOWN TO SCIENCE.
...on the seashore...
MANY GREAT DISCOVERIES FOLLOWED, LIKE THE FIRST PLESIOSAUR.
IT WAS A CREATURE SO ODD, SOME SAID IT RESEMBLED "A SERPENT THREADED THROUGH A TURTLE."
...Are seashore shells...
OCCASIONALLY SHE FOUND SOMETHING THAT WASN'T AQUATIC, LIKE A PTEROSAUR.
IT WOULD BE ANOTHER THIRTY YEARS BEFORE DARWIN'S *ON THE ORIGIN OF SPECIES* WAS PUBLISHED. MARY'S BIZARRE FINDS WERE ***LIKELY*** AN INFLUENCE.
...I'm sure...
OFTEN, HER DISCOVERIES WEREN'T RECOGNIZED AS ***REVOLUTIONARY*** AT THE TIME.
WEIRD FISH LIKE *SQUALORAJA* ONLY MAKE SENSE IN AN EVOLUTIONARY CONTEXT, AS A TRANSITION BETWEEN SHARKS AND RAYS.
...And so she sells...
DISCOVERY FOLLOWED ON DISCOVERY.
IS THIS WHAT I ***THINK*** IT-- ***EEWW.***
SHE WAS EVEN ONE OF THE FIRST PEOPLE TO RECOGNIZE A COPROLITE--IN OTHER WORDS, FOSSILIZED ***POOP.*** SHE COULD TELL BECAUSE OF THE FISH SCALES INSIDE.

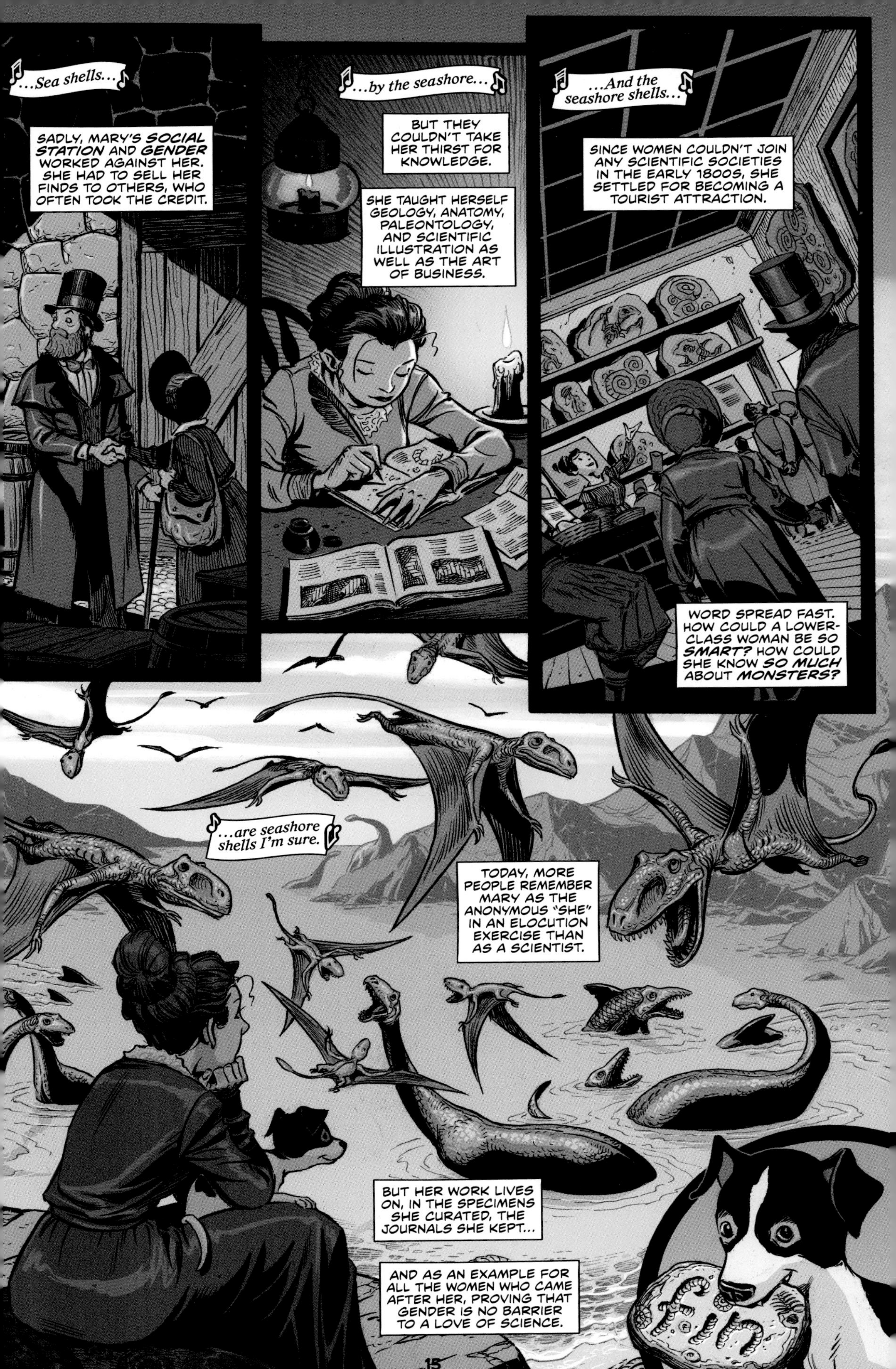

…Sea shells…
SADLY, MARY'S SOCIAL STATION AND GENDER WORKED AGAINST HER. SHE HAD TO SELL HER FINDS TO OTHERS, WHO OFTEN TOOK THE CREDIT.
…by the seashore…
BUT THEY COULDN'T TAKE HER THIRST FOR KNOWLEDGE.
SHE TAUGHT HERSELF GEOLOGY, ANATOMY, PALEONTOLOGY, AND SCIENTIFIC ILLUSTRATION AS WELL AS THE ART OF BUSINESS.
…And the seashore shells…
SINCE WOMEN COULDN'T JOIN ANY SCIENTIFIC SOCIETIES IN THE EARLY 1800S, SHE SETTLED FOR BECOMING A TOURIST ATTRACTION.
WORD SPREAD FAST. HOW COULD A LOWER-CLASS WOMAN BE SO SMART? HOW COULD SHE KNOW SO MUCH ABOUT MONSTERS?
…are seashore shells I'm sure.
TODAY, MORE PEOPLE REMEMBER MARY AS THE ANONYMOUS "SHE" IN AN ELOCUTION EXERCISE THAN AS A SCIENTIST.
BUT HER WORK LIVES ON, IN THE SPECIMENS SHE CURATED, THE JOURNALS SHE KEPT…
AND AS AN EXAMPLE FOR ALL THE WOMEN WHO CAME AFTER HER, PROVING THAT GENDER IS NO BARRIER TO A LOVE OF SCIENCE.

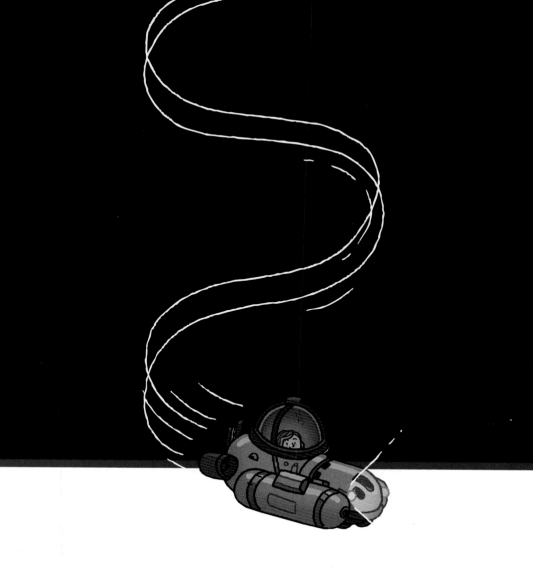

"We need to respect the oceans and take care of them as if our lives depended on it. Because they do."

—Sylvia Earle

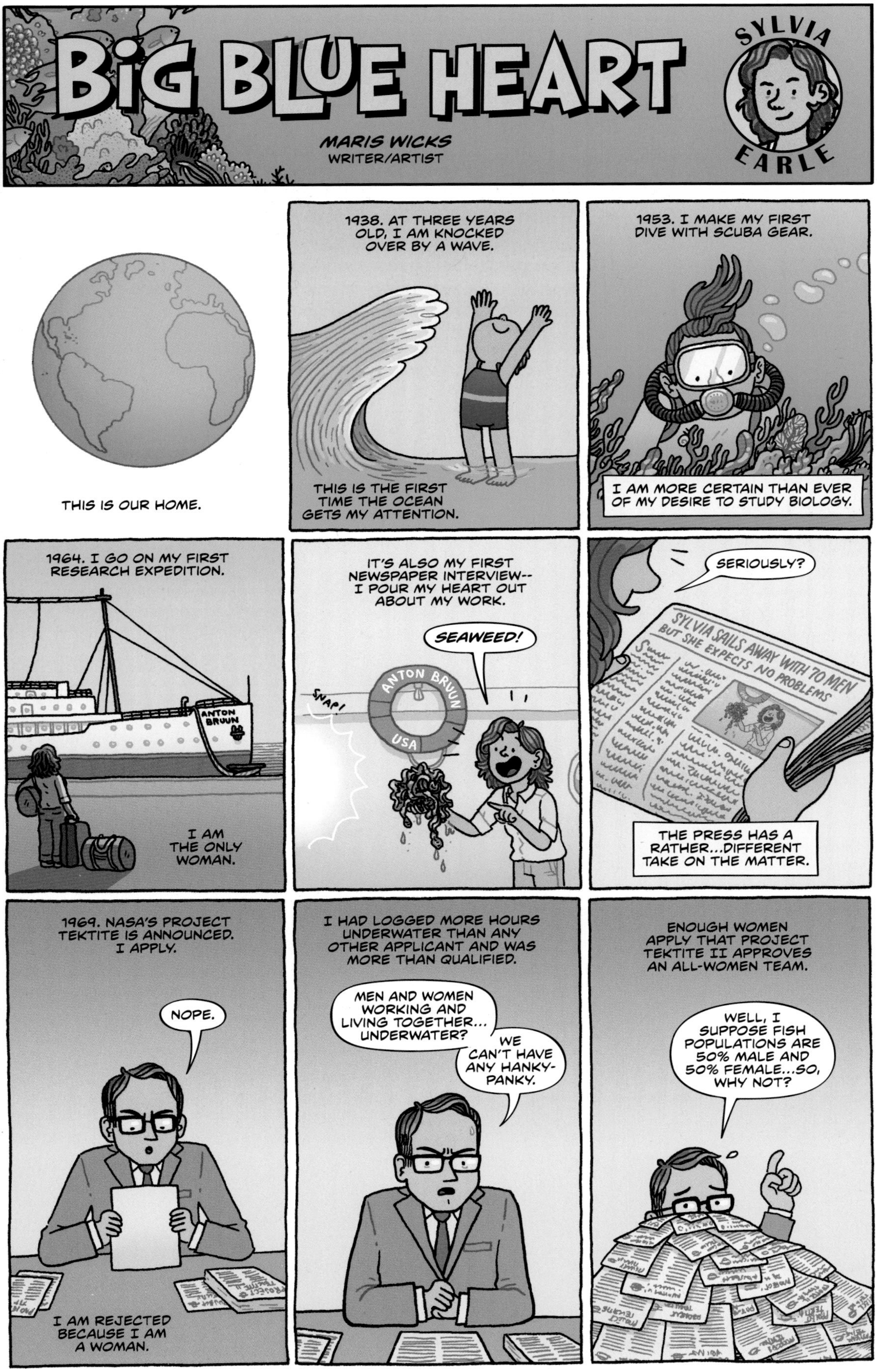
BIG BLUE HEART
MARIS WICKS
WRITER/ARTIST
SYLVIA EARLE
THIS IS OUR HOME.
1938. AT THREE YEARS OLD, I AM KNOCKED OVER BY A WAVE.
THIS IS THE FIRST TIME THE OCEAN GETS MY ATTENTION.
1953. I MAKE MY FIRST DIVE WITH SCUBA GEAR.
I AM MORE CERTAIN THAN EVER OF MY DESIRE TO STUDY BIOLOGY.
1964. I GO ON MY FIRST RESEARCH EXPEDITION.
ANTON BRUUN
I AM THE ONLY WOMAN.
IT'S ALSO MY FIRST NEWSPAPER INTERVIEW-- I POUR MY HEART OUT ABOUT MY WORK.
SNAP!
ANTON BRUUN USA
SEAWEED!
SERIOUSLY?
SYLVIA SAILS AWAY WITH 70 MEN
BUT SHE EXPECTS NO PROBLEMS
THE PRESS HAS A RATHER...DIFFERENT TAKE ON THE MATTER.
1969. NASA'S PROJECT TEKTITE IS ANNOUNCED. I APPLY.
NOPE.
I AM REJECTED BECAUSE I AM A WOMAN.
I HAD LOGGED MORE HOURS UNDERWATER THAN ANY OTHER APPLICANT AND WAS MORE THAN QUALIFIED.
MEN AND WOMEN WORKING AND LIVING TOGETHER... UNDERWATER?
WE CAN'T HAVE ANY HANKY-PANKY.
ENOUGH WOMEN APPLY THAT PROJECT TEKTITE II APPROVES AN ALL-WOMEN TEAM.
WELL, I SUPPOSE FISH POPULATIONS ARE 50% MALE AND 50% FEMALE...SO, WHY NOT?

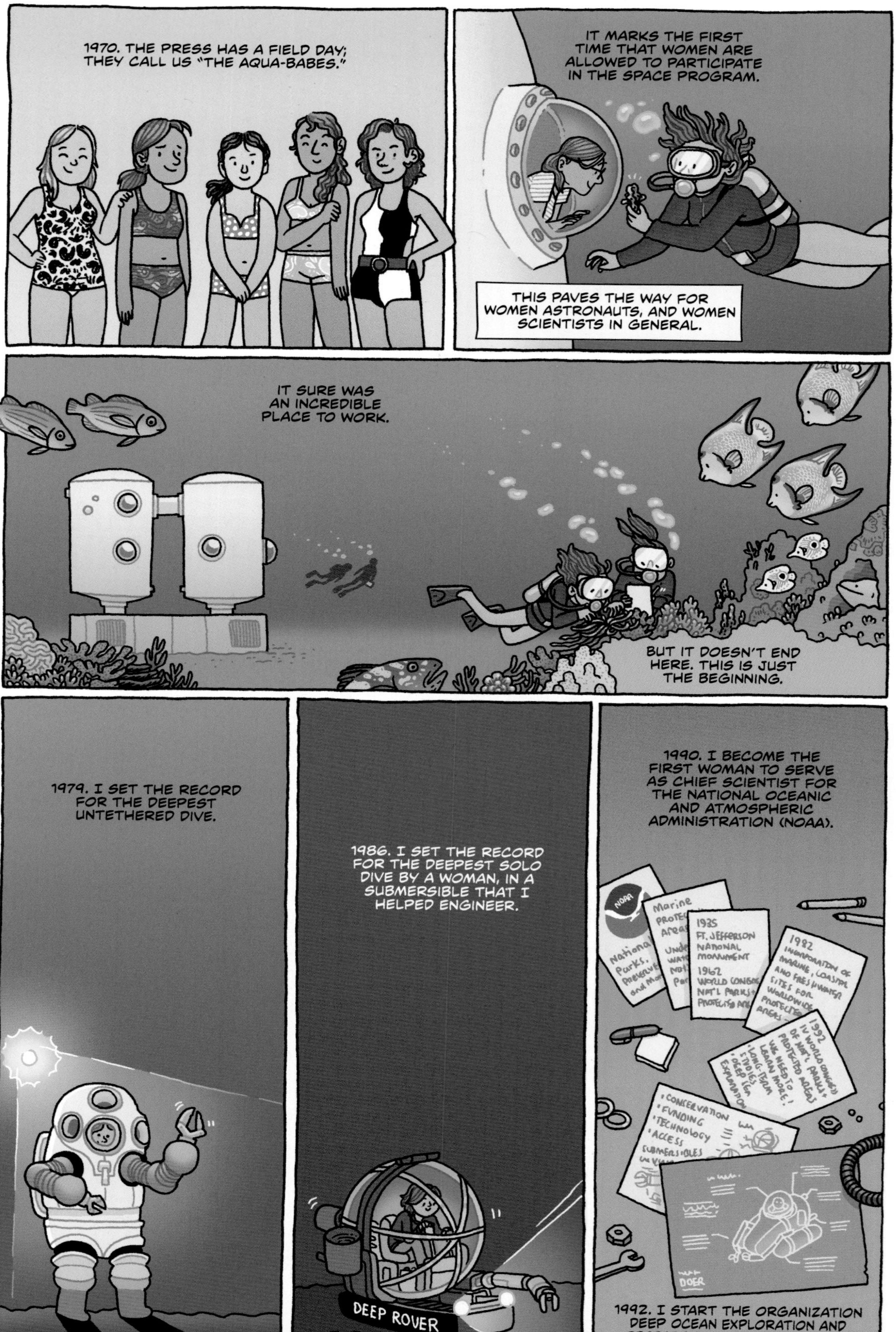
1970. THE PRESS HAS A FIELD DAY; THEY CALL US "THE AQUA-BABES."
IT MARKS THE FIRST TIME THAT WOMEN ARE ALLOWED TO PARTICIPATE IN THE SPACE PROGRAM.
THIS PAVES THE WAY FOR WOMEN ASTRONAUTS, AND WOMEN SCIENTISTS IN GENERAL.
IT SURE WAS AN INCREDIBLE PLACE TO WORK.
BUT IT DOESN'T END HERE. THIS IS JUST THE BEGINNING.
1979. I SET THE RECORD FOR THE DEEPEST UNTETHERED DIVE.
1,250 FT.
1986. I SET THE RECORD FOR THE DEEPEST SOLO DIVE BY A WOMAN, IN A SUBMERSIBLE THAT I HELPED ENGINEER.
DEEP ROVER
3,281 FT.
1990. I BECOME THE FIRST WOMAN TO SERVE AS CHIEF SCIENTIST FOR THE NATIONAL OCEANIC AND ATMOSPHERIC ADMINISTRATION (NOAA).
NOAA
DOER
1992. I START THE ORGANIZATION DEEP OCEAN EXPLORATION AND RESEARCH (DOER) TO DEVELOP ROVs AND SUBMERSIBLES THAT PROVIDE EVEN MORE ACCESS TO STUDYING THE OCEAN.

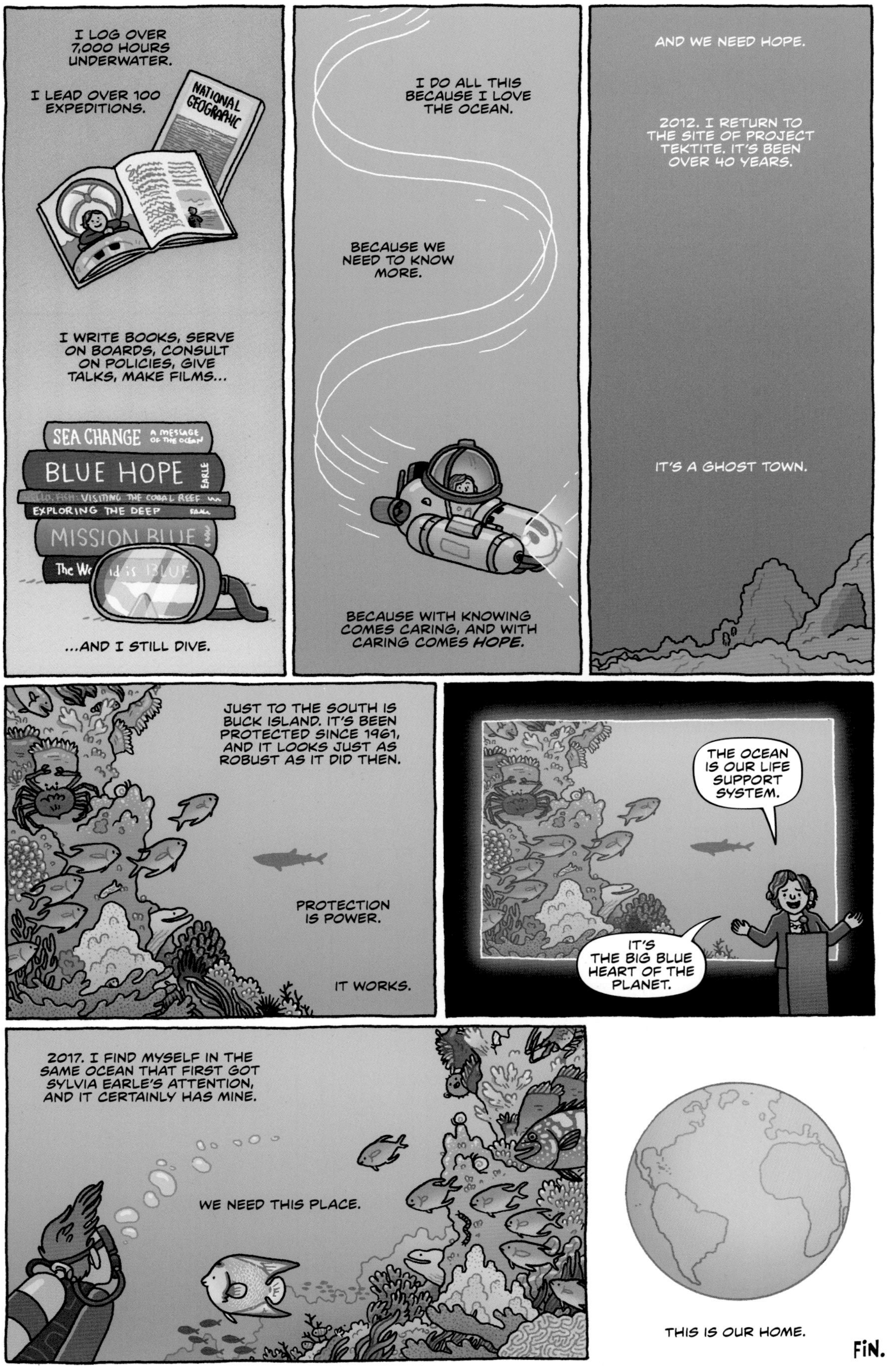

I LOG OVER 7,000 HOURS UNDERWATER.
I LEAD OVER 100 EXPEDITIONS.
NATIONAL GEOGRAPHIC
I WRITE BOOKS, SERVE ON BOARDS, CONSULT ON POLICIES, GIVE TALKS, MAKE FILMS...
SEA CHANGE A MESSAGE OF THE OCEAN
BLUE HOPE EARLE
VISITING THE CORAL REEF
EXPLORING THE DEEP
MISSION BLUE
...AND I STILL DIVE.
I DO ALL THIS BECAUSE I LOVE THE OCEAN.
BECAUSE WE NEED TO KNOW MORE.
BECAUSE WITH KNOWING COMES CARING, AND WITH CARING COMES *HOPE*.
AND WE NEED HOPE.
2012. I RETURN TO THE SITE OF PROJECT TEKTITE. IT'S BEEN OVER 40 YEARS.
IT'S A GHOST TOWN.
JUST TO THE SOUTH IS BUCK ISLAND. IT'S BEEN PROTECTED SINCE 1961, AND IT LOOKS JUST AS ROBUST AS IT DID THEN.
PROTECTION IS POWER.
IT WORKS.
THE OCEAN IS OUR LIFE SUPPORT SYSTEM.
IT'S THE BIG BLUE HEART OF THE PLANET.
2017. I FIND MYSELF IN THE SAME OCEAN THAT FIRST GOT SYLVIA EARLE'S ATTENTION, AND IT CERTAINLY HAS MINE.
WE NEED THIS PLACE.
THIS IS OUR HOME.
FIN.

If We Do Not Lose Heart

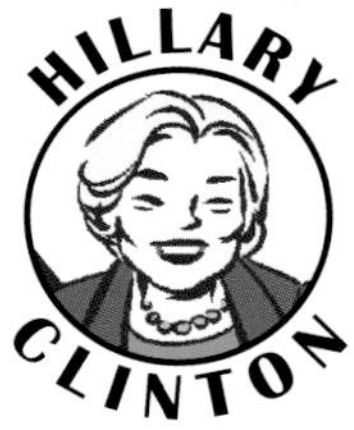
HILLARY
CLINTON

KELLY SUE DECONNICK WRITER | **ELSA CHARRETIER** ARTIST | **HI-FI** COLORIST

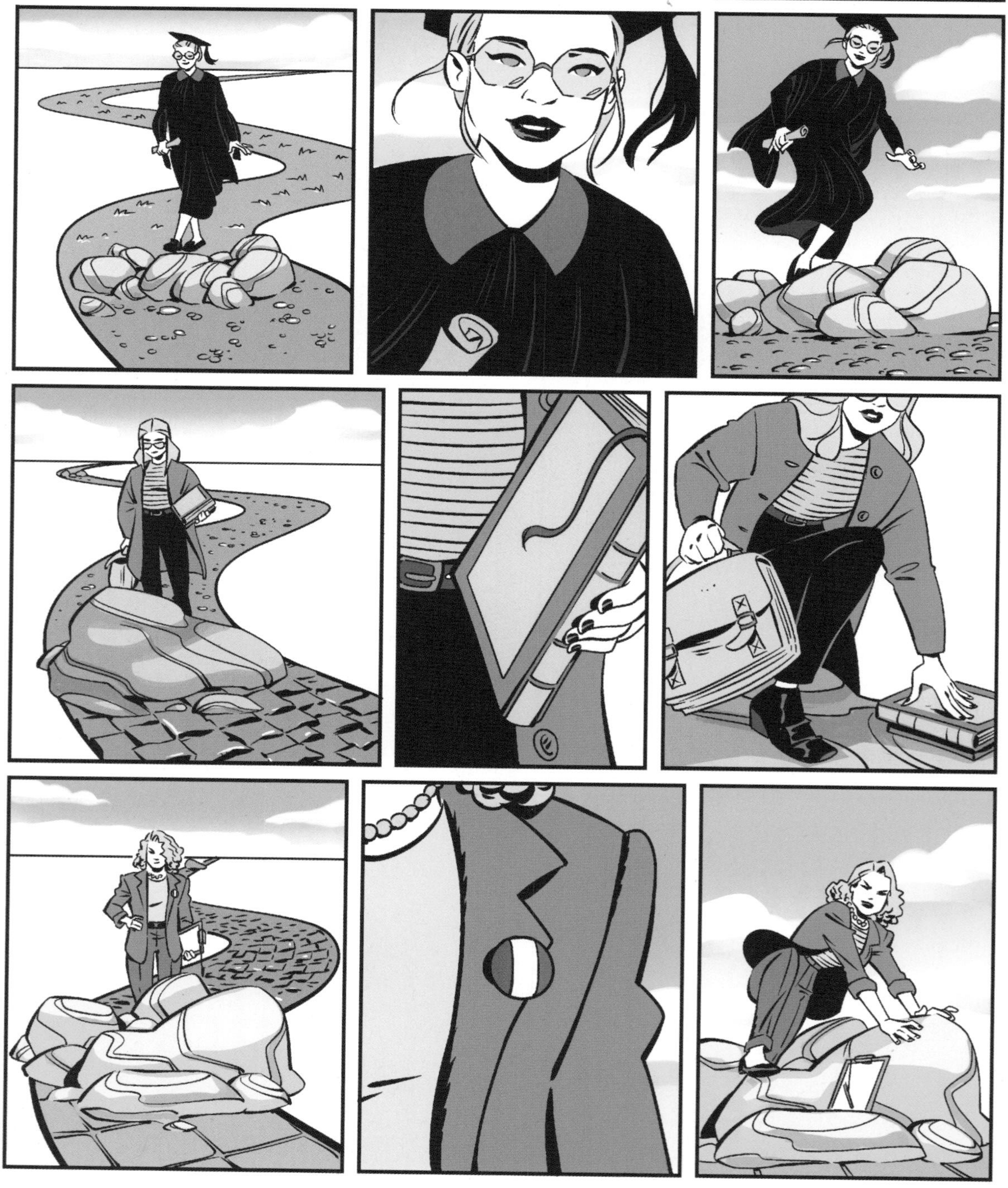

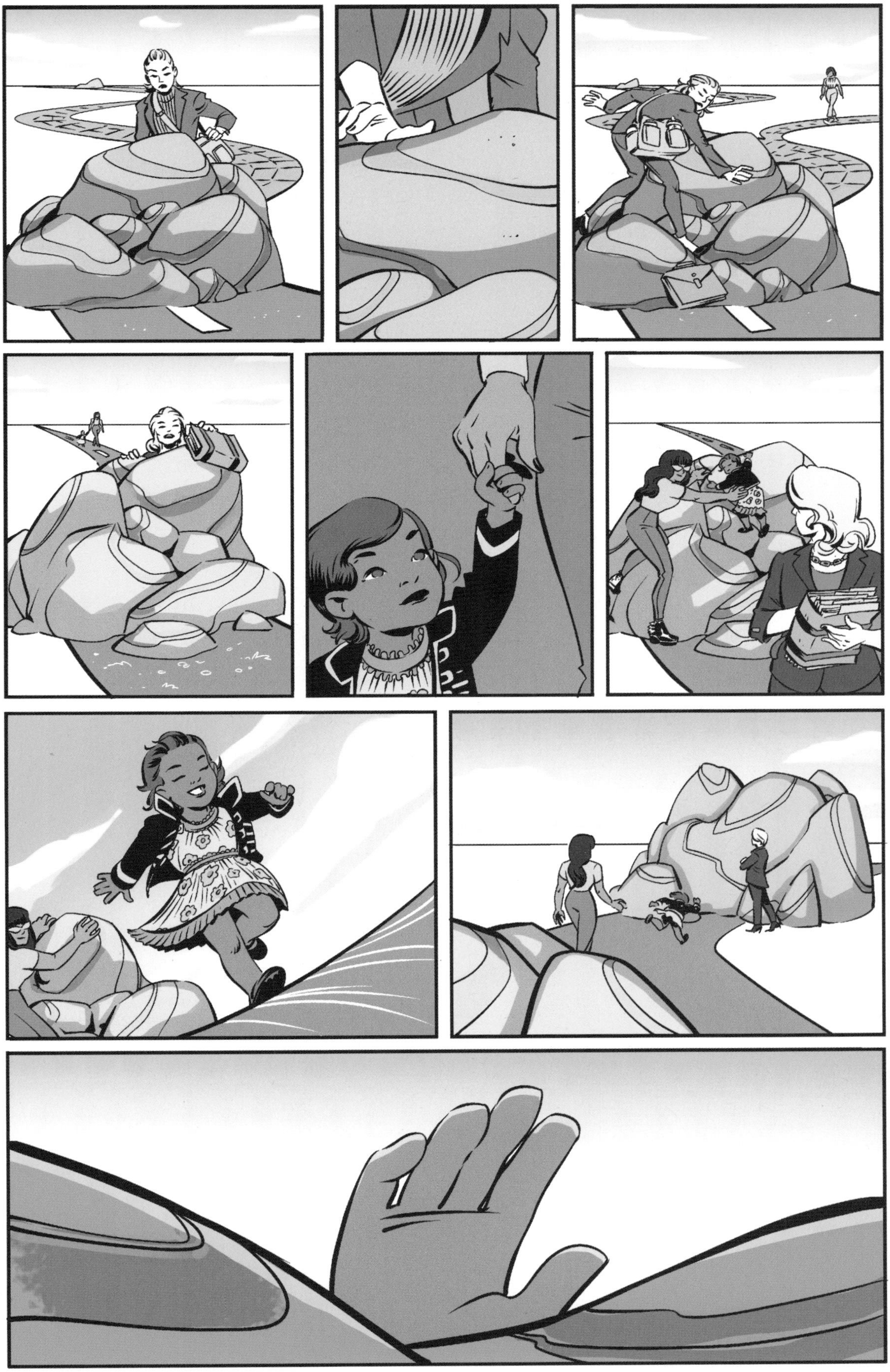

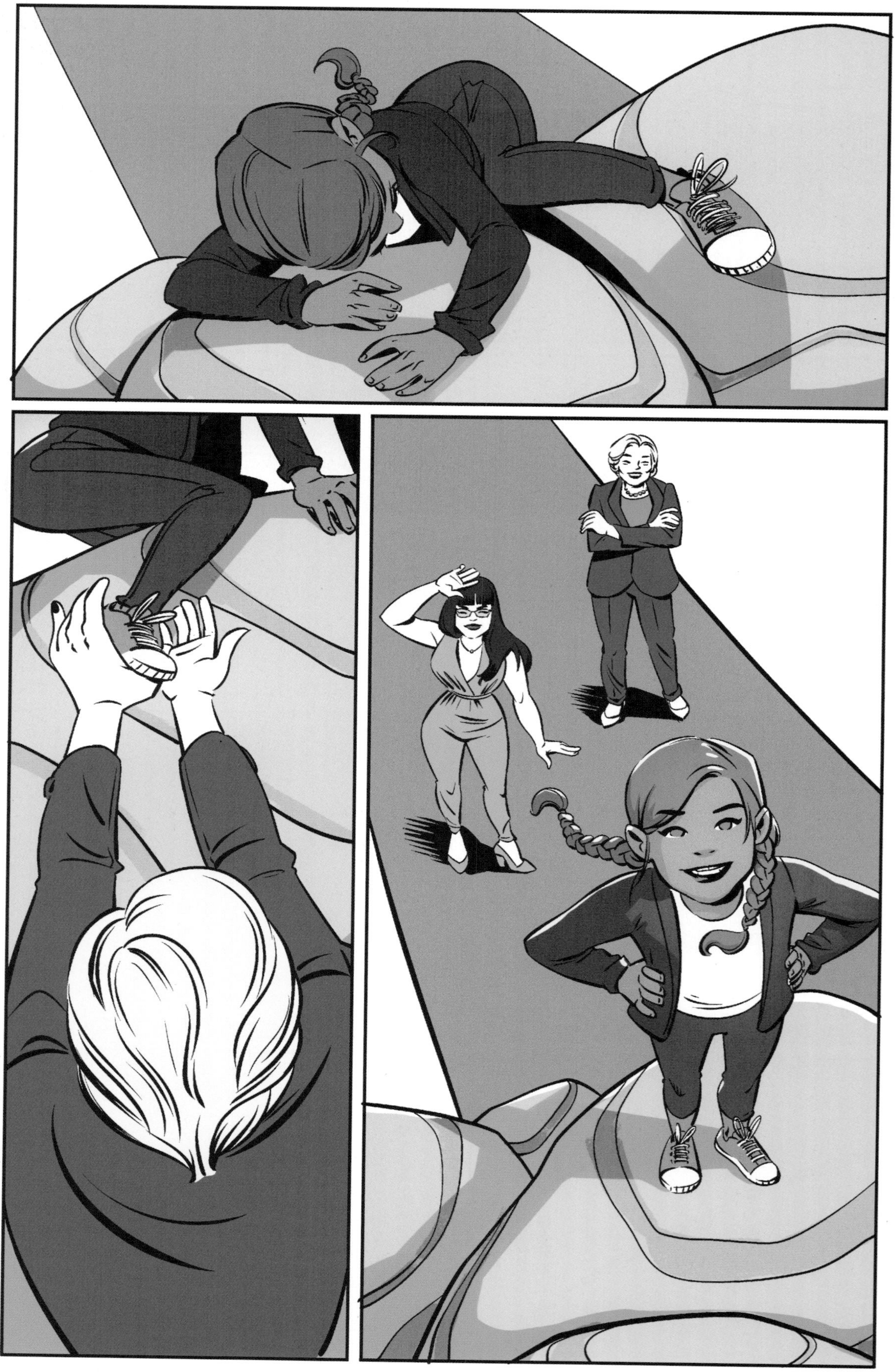

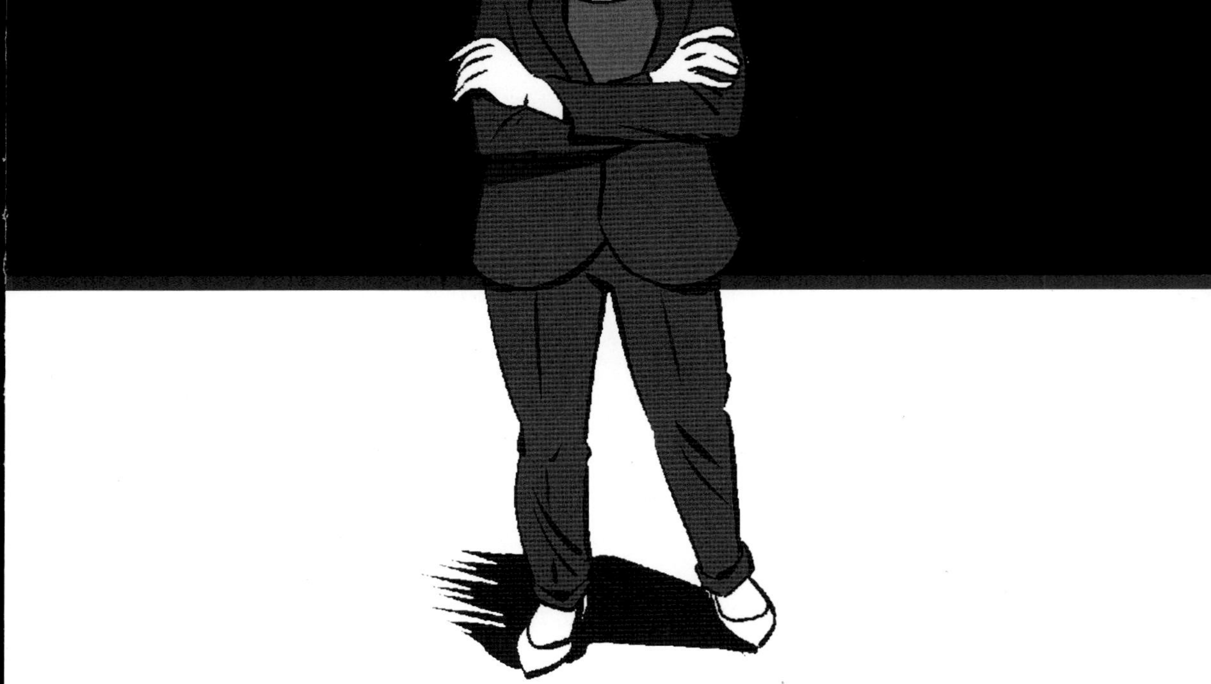

"We need to understand that there is no formula for how women should lead their lives. That is why we must respect the choices that each woman makes for herself and her family. Every woman deserves the chance to realize her God-given potential."

—Hillary Clinton

"I've always had the feeling that nothing is impossible if one applies a certain amount of energy in the right direction. If you want to do it, you can do it."

—Nellie Bly

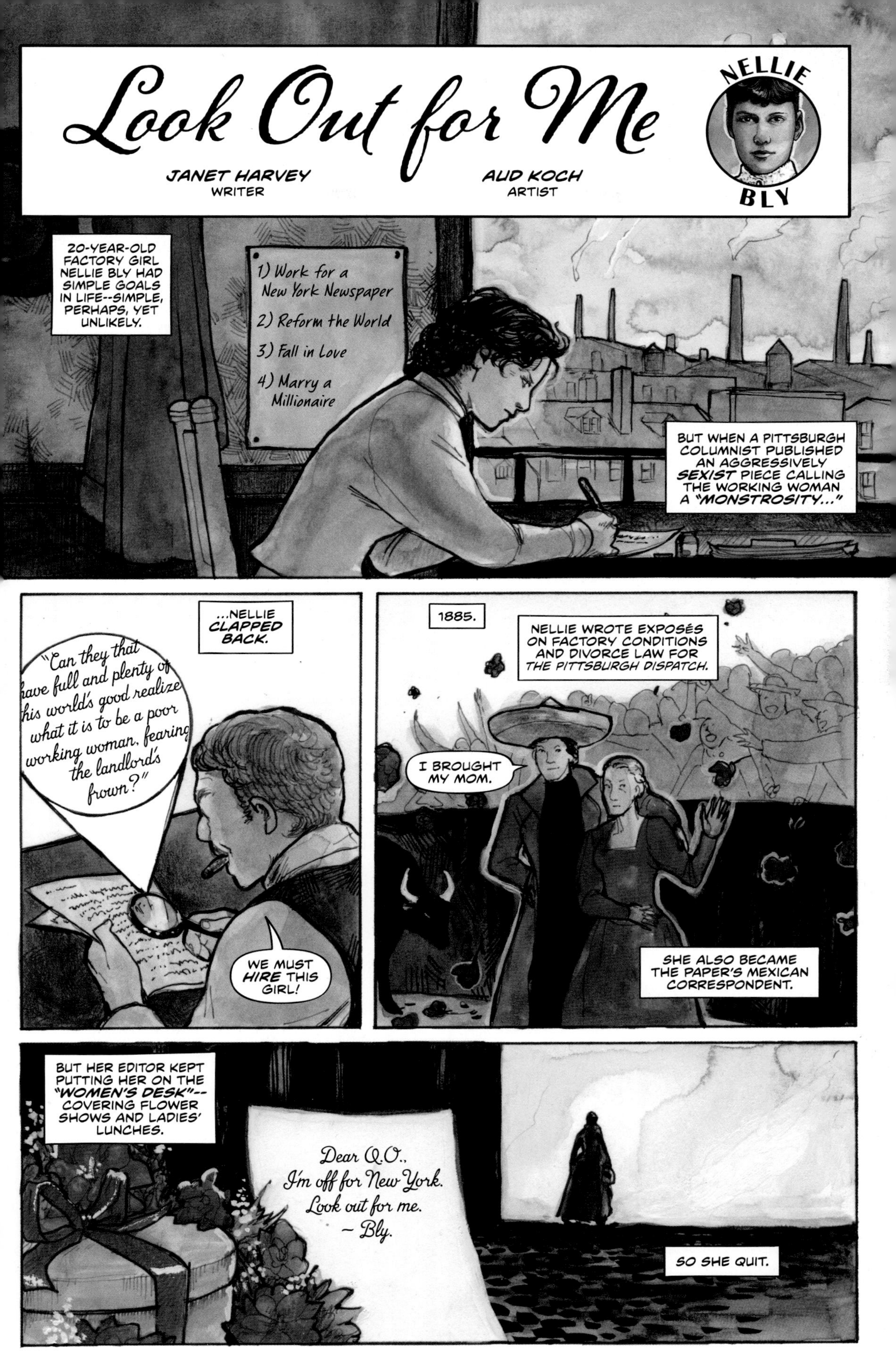
Look Out for Me
JANET HARVEY
WRITER
AUD KOCH
ARTIST
NELLIE BLY
20-YEAR-OLD FACTORY GIRL NELLIE BLY HAD SIMPLE GOALS IN LIFE--SIMPLE, PERHAPS, YET UNLIKELY.
1) Work for a New York Newspaper
2) Reform the World
3) Fall in Love
4) Marry a Millionaire
BUT WHEN A PITTSBURGH COLUMNIST PUBLISHED AN AGGRESSIVELY SEXIST PIECE CALLING THE WORKING WOMAN A "MONSTROSITY..."
...NELLIE CLAPPED BACK.
"Can they that have full and plenty of this world's good realize what it is to be a poor working woman, fearing the landlord's frown?"
WE MUST HIRE THIS GIRL!
1885.
NELLIE WROTE EXPOSÉS ON FACTORY CONDITIONS AND DIVORCE LAW FOR THE PITTSBURGH DISPATCH.
I BROUGHT MY MOM.
SHE ALSO BECAME THE PAPER'S MEXICAN CORRESPONDENT.
BUT HER EDITOR KEPT PUTTING HER ON THE "WOMEN'S DESK"--COVERING FLOWER SHOWS AND LADIES' LUNCHES.
Dear Q.O., I'm off for New York. Look out for me. ~ Bly.
SO SHE QUIT.

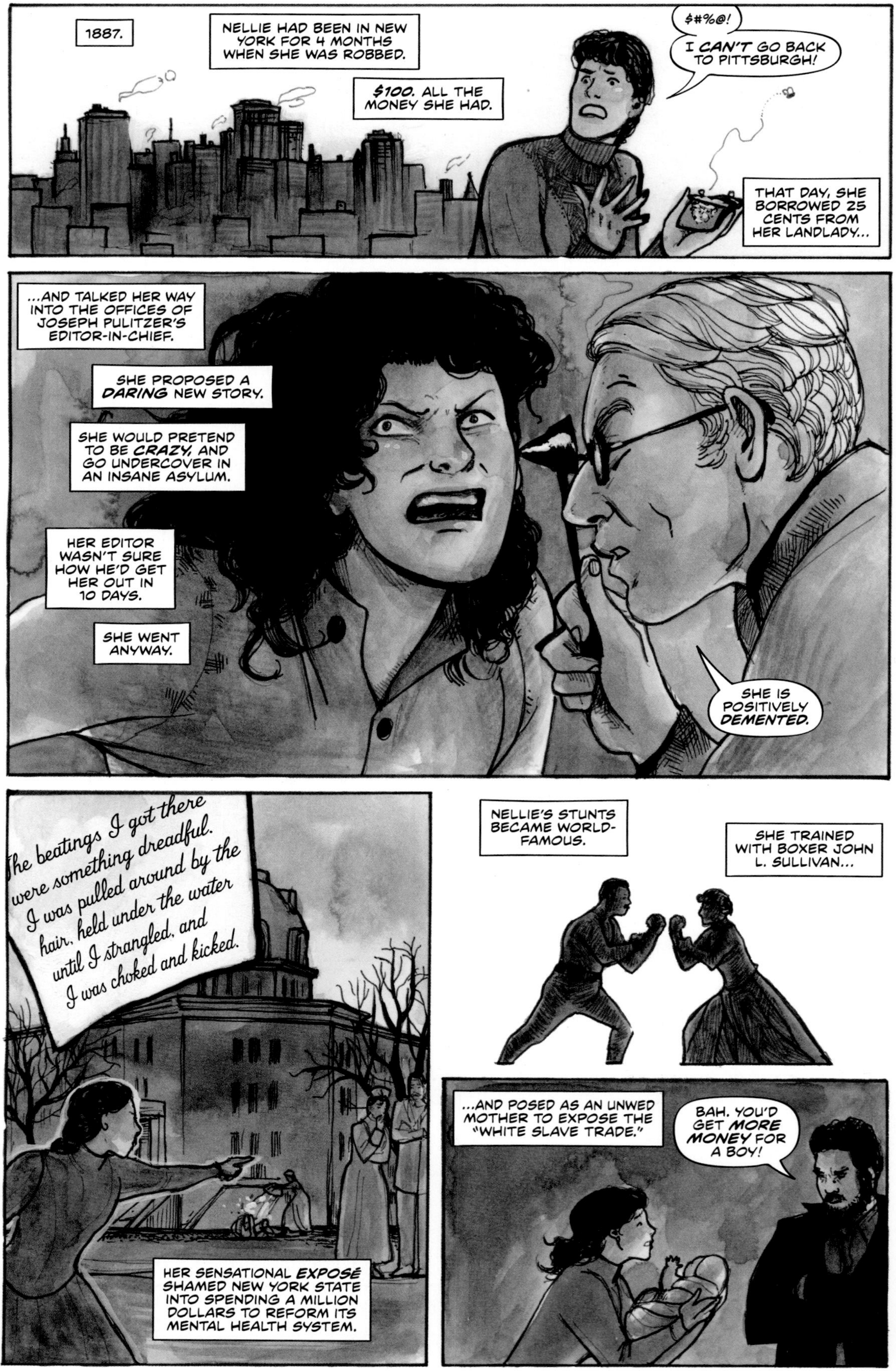

1887.
NELLIE HAD BEEN IN NEW YORK FOR 4 MONTHS WHEN SHE WAS ROBBED.
$100. ALL THE MONEY SHE HAD.
$#%@!
I CAN'T GO BACK TO PITTSBURGH!
THAT DAY, SHE BORROWED 25 CENTS FROM HER LANDLADY...
...AND TALKED HER WAY INTO THE OFFICES OF JOSEPH PULITZER'S EDITOR-IN-CHIEF.
SHE PROPOSED A DARING NEW STORY.
SHE WOULD PRETEND TO BE CRAZY, AND GO UNDERCOVER IN AN INSANE ASYLUM.
HER EDITOR WASN'T SURE HOW HE'D GET HER OUT IN 10 DAYS.
SHE WENT ANYWAY.
SHE IS POSITIVELY DEMENTED.
The beatings I got there were something dreadful. I was pulled around by the hair, held under the water until I strangled, and I was choked and kicked.
HER SENSATIONAL EXPOSE SHAMED NEW YORK STATE INTO SPENDING A MILLION DOLLARS TO REFORM ITS MENTAL HEALTH SYSTEM.
NELLIE'S STUNTS BECAME WORLD-FAMOUS.
SHE TRAINED WITH BOXER JOHN L. SULLIVAN...
...AND POSED AS AN UNWED MOTHER TO EXPOSE THE "WHITE SLAVE TRADE."
BAH. YOU'D GET MORE MONEY FOR A BOY!

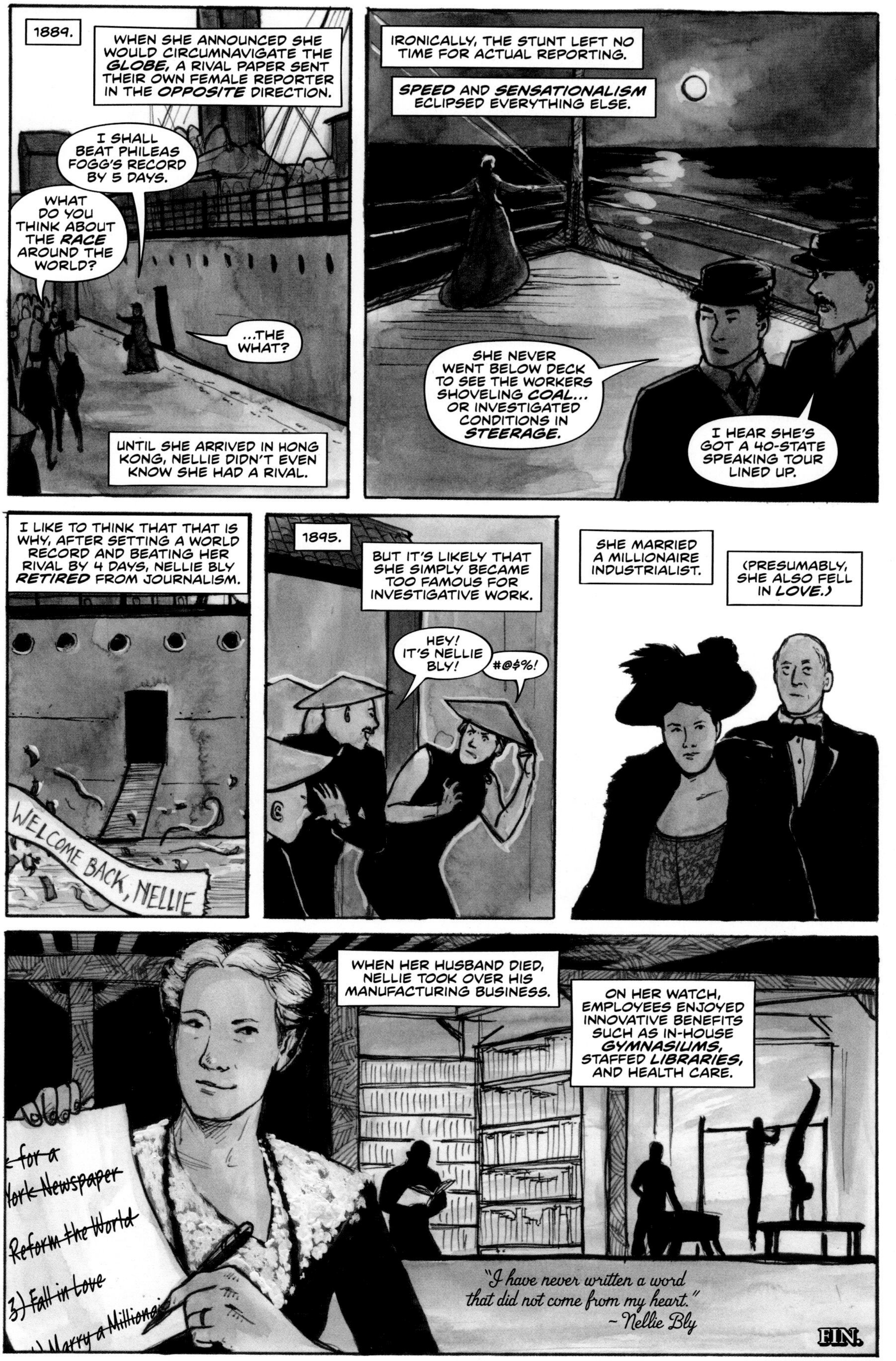
1889.
WHEN SHE ANNOUNCED SHE WOULD CIRCUMNAVIGATE THE *GLOBE*, A RIVAL PAPER SENT THEIR OWN FEMALE REPORTER IN THE *OPPOSITE* DIRECTION.
I SHALL BEAT PHILEAS FOGG'S RECORD BY 5 DAYS.
WHAT DO YOU THINK ABOUT THE *RACE* AROUND THE WORLD?
...THE WHAT?
UNTIL SHE ARRIVED IN HONG KONG, NELLIE DIDN'T EVEN KNOW SHE HAD A RIVAL.
IRONICALLY, THE STUNT LEFT NO TIME FOR ACTUAL REPORTING.
SPEED AND *SENSATIONALISM* ECLIPSED EVERYTHING ELSE.
SHE NEVER WENT BELOW DECK TO SEE THE WORKERS SHOVELING *COAL*... OR INVESTIGATED CONDITIONS IN *STEERAGE*.
I HEAR SHE'S GOT A 40-STATE SPEAKING TOUR LINED UP.
I LIKE TO THINK THAT THAT IS WHY, AFTER SETTING A WORLD RECORD AND BEATING HER RIVAL BY 4 DAYS, NELLIE BLY *RETIRED* FROM JOURNALISM.
WELCOME BACK, NELLIE
1895.
BUT IT'S LIKELY THAT SHE SIMPLY BECAME TOO FAMOUS FOR INVESTIGATIVE WORK.
HEY! IT'S NELLIE BLY!
#@$%!
SHE MARRIED A MILLIONAIRE INDUSTRIALIST.
(PRESUMABLY, SHE ALSO FELL IN *LOVE.*)
WHEN HER HUSBAND DIED, NELLIE TOOK OVER HIS MANUFACTURING BUSINESS.
ON HER WATCH, EMPLOYEES ENJOYED INNOVATIVE BENEFITS SUCH AS IN-HOUSE *GYMNASIUMS*, STAFFED *LIBRARIES*, AND HEALTH CARE.
Reform the World
3) Fall in Love
"I have never written a word that did not come from my heart."
~ Nellie Bly
FIN.

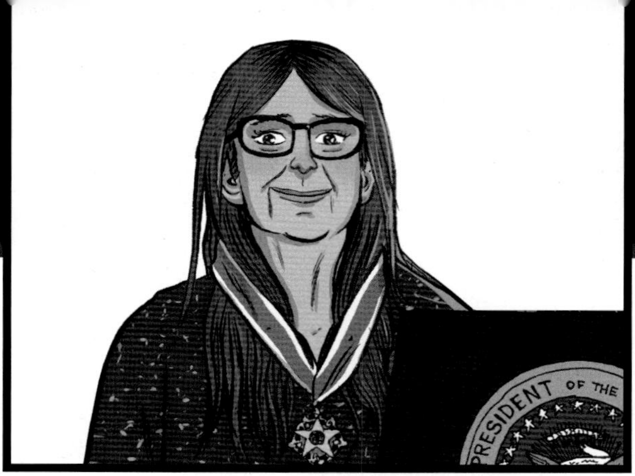
PRESIDENT OF THE

"One should not be afraid to say 'I don't know' or 'I don't understand,' or to ask 'dumb' questions, since no question is a dumb question. To continue even when things appear to be impossible, even when the so-called experts say it is impossible; to stand alone or to be different; and not to be afraid to be wrong or to make and admit mistakes, for only those who dare to fail greatly can ever achieve greatly."

—Margaret Hamilton

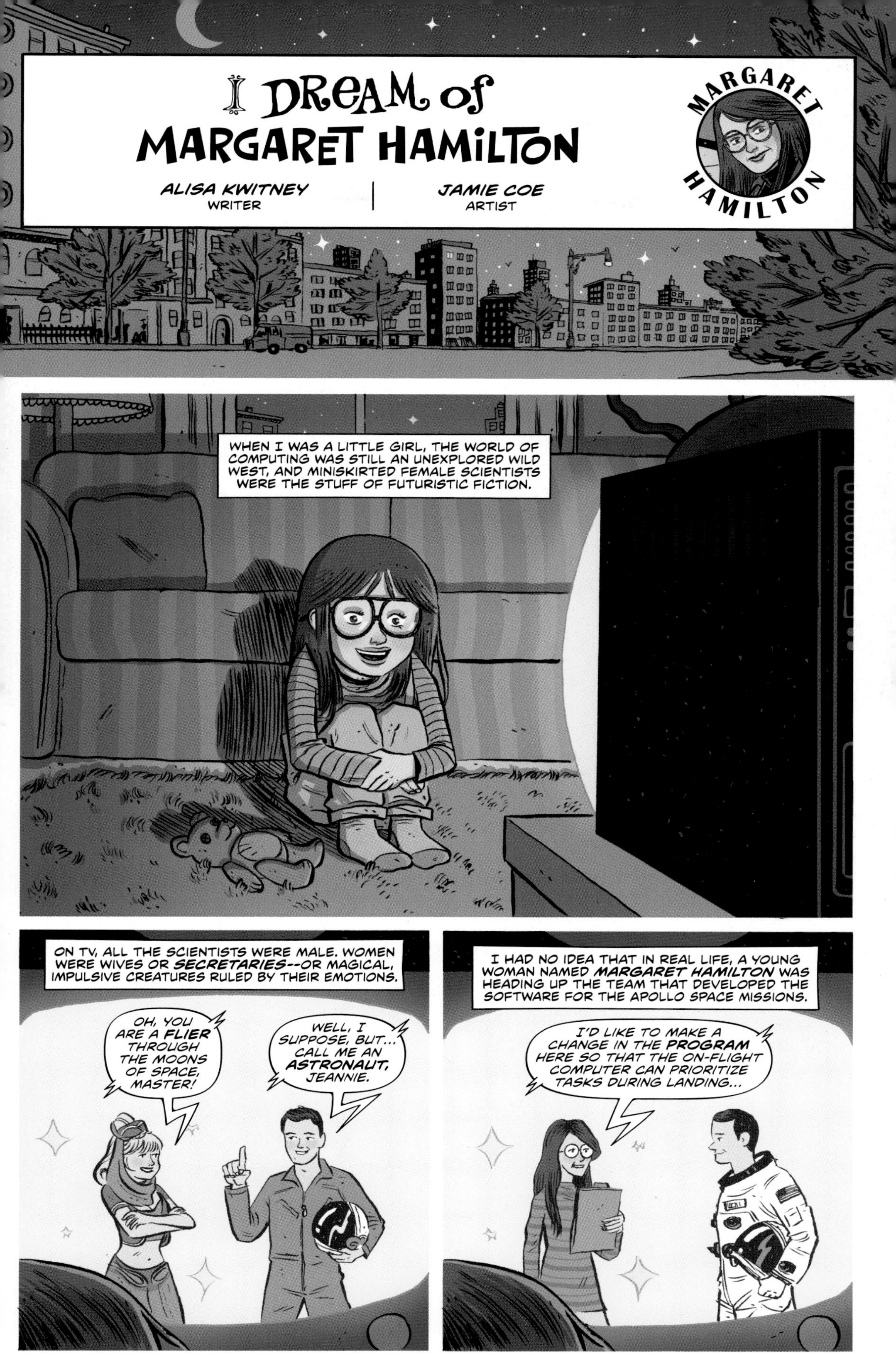
I DREAM OF MARGARET HAMILTON
ALISA KWITNEY
WRITER
JAMIE COE
ARTIST
MARGARET HAMILTON
WHEN I WAS A LITTLE GIRL, THE WORLD OF COMPUTING WAS STILL AN UNEXPLORED WILD WEST, AND MINISKIRTED FEMALE SCIENTISTS WERE THE STUFF OF FUTURISTIC FICTION.
ON TV, ALL THE SCIENTISTS WERE MALE. WOMEN WERE WIVES OR SECRETARIES--OR MAGICAL, IMPULSIVE CREATURES RULED BY THEIR EMOTIONS.
OH, YOU ARE A FLIER THROUGH THE MOONS OF SPACE, MASTER!
WELL, I SUPPOSE, BUT... CALL ME AN ASTRONAUT, JEANNIE.
I HAD NO IDEA THAT IN REAL LIFE, A YOUNG WOMAN NAMED MARGARET HAMILTON WAS HEADING UP THE TEAM THAT DEVELOPED THE SOFTWARE FOR THE APOLLO SPACE MISSIONS.
I'D LIKE TO MAKE A CHANGE IN THE PROGRAM HERE SO THAT THE ON-FLIGHT COMPUTER CAN PRIORITIZE TASKS DURING LANDING...

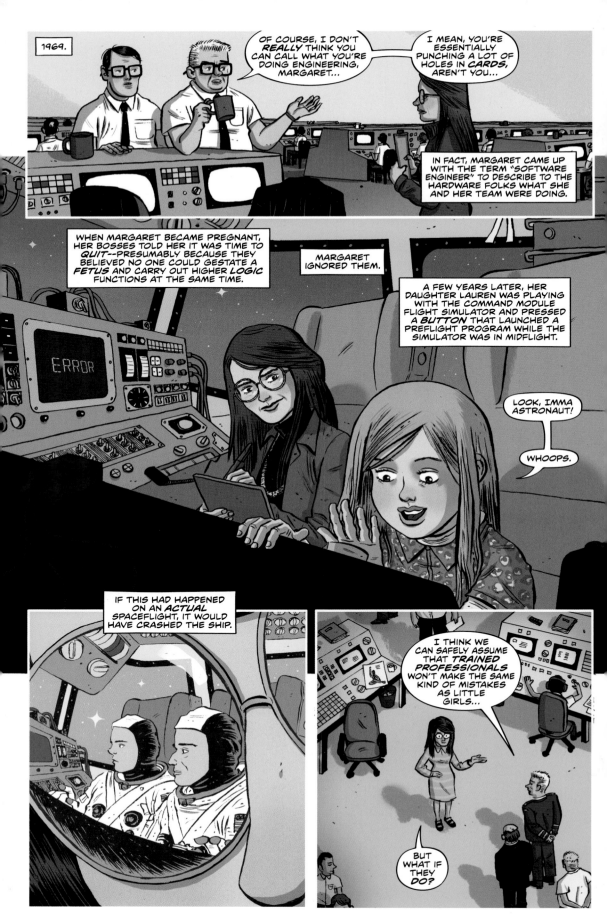

1969.

OF COURSE, I DON'T *REALLY* THINK YOU CAN CALL WHAT YOU'RE DOING ENGINEERING, MARGARET...

I MEAN, YOU'RE ESSENTIALLY PUNCHING A LOT OF HOLES IN *CARDS*, AREN'T YOU...

IN FACT, MARGARET CAME UP WITH THE TERM "SOFTWARE ENGINEER" TO DESCRIBE TO THE HARDWARE FOLKS WHAT SHE AND HER TEAM WERE DOING.

WHEN MARGARET BECAME PREGNANT, HER BOSSES TOLD HER IT WAS TIME TO *QUIT*--PRESUMABLY BECAUSE THEY BELIEVED NO ONE COULD GESTATE A *FETUS* AND CARRY OUT HIGHER *LOGIC* FUNCTIONS AT THE SAME TIME.

MARGARET IGNORED THEM.

A FEW YEARS LATER, HER DAUGHTER LAUREN WAS PLAYING WITH THE *COMMAND MODULE* FLIGHT SIMULATOR AND PRESSED A *BUTTON* THAT LAUNCHED A PREFLIGHT PROGRAM WHILE THE SIMULATOR WAS IN MIDFLIGHT.

ERROR

LOOK, IMMA ASTRONAUT!

WHOOPS.

IF THIS HAD HAPPENED ON AN *ACTUAL* SPACEFLIGHT, IT WOULD HAVE CRASHED THE SHIP.

I THINK WE CAN SAFELY ASSUME THAT *TRAINED PROFESSIONALS* WON'T MAKE THE SAME KIND OF MISTAKES AS LITTLE GIRLS...

BUT WHAT IF THEY *DO*?

30

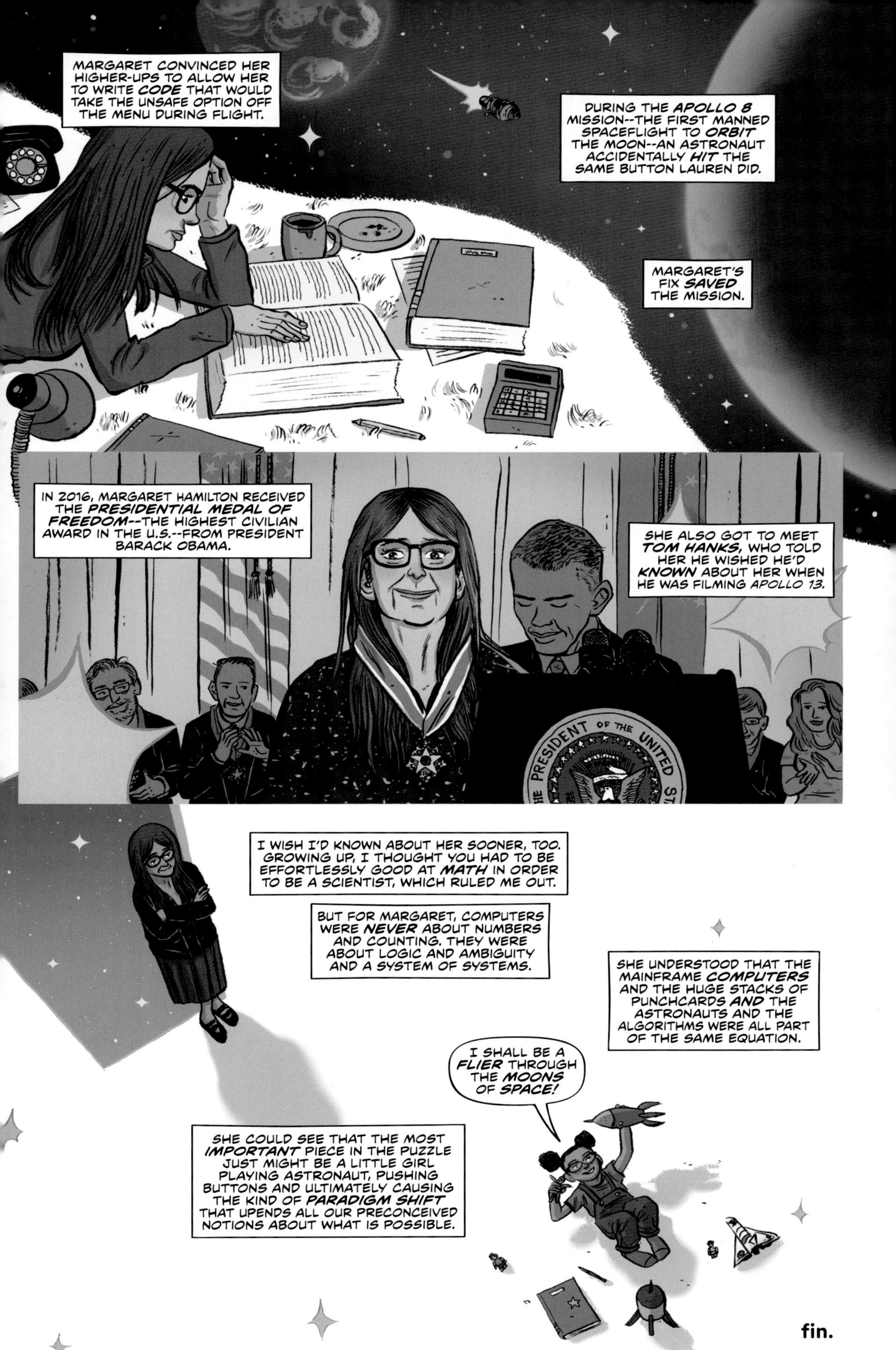
MARGARET CONVINCED HER HIGHER-UPS TO ALLOW HER TO WRITE CODE THAT WOULD TAKE THE UNSAFE OPTION OFF THE MENU DURING FLIGHT.
DURING THE APOLLO 8 MISSION--THE FIRST MANNED SPACEFLIGHT TO ORBIT THE MOON--AN ASTRONAUT ACCIDENTALLY HIT THE SAME BUTTON LAUREN DID.
MARGARET'S FIX SAVED THE MISSION.
IN 2016, MARGARET HAMILTON RECEIVED THE PRESIDENTIAL MEDAL OF FREEDOM--THE HIGHEST CIVILIAN AWARD IN THE U.S.--FROM PRESIDENT BARACK OBAMA.
SHE ALSO GOT TO MEET TOM HANKS, WHO TOLD HER HE WISHED HE'D KNOWN ABOUT HER WHEN HE WAS FILMING APOLLO 13.
I WISH I'D KNOWN ABOUT HER SOONER, TOO. GROWING UP, I THOUGHT YOU HAD TO BE EFFORTLESSLY GOOD AT MATH IN ORDER TO BE A SCIENTIST, WHICH RULED ME OUT.
BUT FOR MARGARET, COMPUTERS WERE NEVER ABOUT NUMBERS AND COUNTING. THEY WERE ABOUT LOGIC AND AMBIGUITY AND A SYSTEM OF SYSTEMS.
SHE UNDERSTOOD THAT THE MAINFRAME COMPUTERS AND THE HUGE STACKS OF PUNCHCARDS AND THE ASTRONAUTS AND THE ALGORITHMS WERE ALL PART OF THE SAME EQUATION.
I SHALL BE A FLIER THROUGH THE MOONS OF SPACE!
SHE COULD SEE THAT THE MOST IMPORTANT PIECE IN THE PUZZLE JUST MIGHT BE A LITTLE GIRL PLAYING ASTRONAUT, PUSHING BUTTONS AND ULTIMATELY CAUSING THE KIND OF PARADIGM SHIFT THAT UPENDS ALL OUR PRECONCEIVED NOTIONS ABOUT WHAT IS POSSIBLE.
fin.

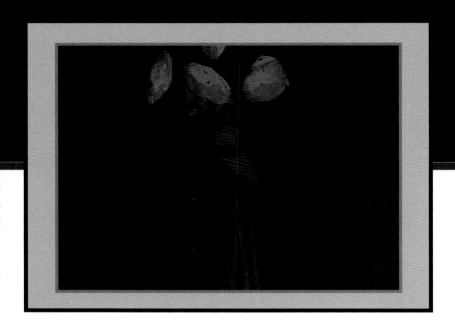

"I took advice from none but the best. I listened, how I listened! That's how I finally became my own expert."
—Peggy Guggenheim

PEGGY

GUGGENHEIM

Steven T. Seagle
WRITER

Teddy H. Kristiansen
ARTIST

MY FATHER WENT DOWN WITH THE *TITANIC*.

I INHERITED PART OF HIS ESTATE--A SMALL FORTUNE--ON MY 21ST BIRTHDAY.

THE FOLLOWING YEAR I EMIGRATED TO FRANCE WHERE I WAS PHOTOGRAPHED BY *MAN RAY*, WHOM I LATER REPRESENTED.

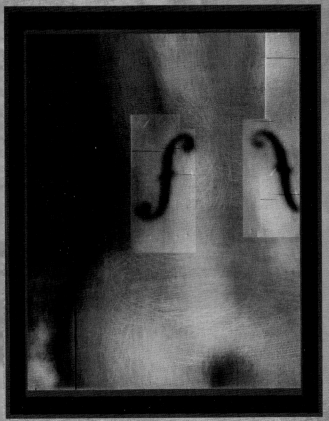

I HAD TWO CHILDREN WITH MY FIRST HUSBAND, THE DADAIST SCULPTOR LAURENCE VAIL.

MY SECOND HUSBAND WAS THE SURREALIST MAX ERNST.

RUMOR HAS IT I SLEPT WITH 1,000 OTHER MEN. I WAS ALWAYS UNDER-ESTIMATED BY INNUENDO.

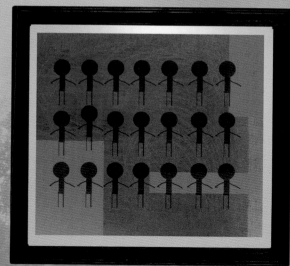

ONE LOVER, THE PLAYWRIGHT SAMUEL BECKETT, ENCOURAGED ME TO PATRONIZE ONLY MODERN ART.

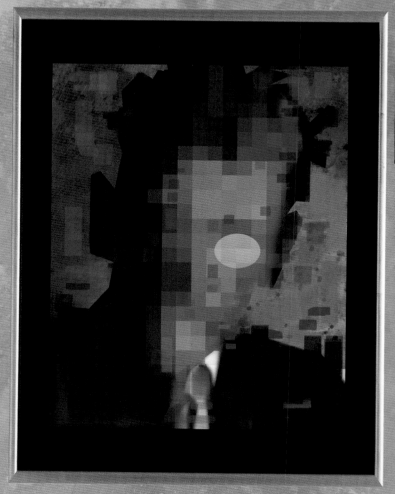

AFTER I BROKE UP WITH HIM, I AMASSED A STUNNING COLLECTION, BUYING, AT TIMES, A PAINTING A DAY.

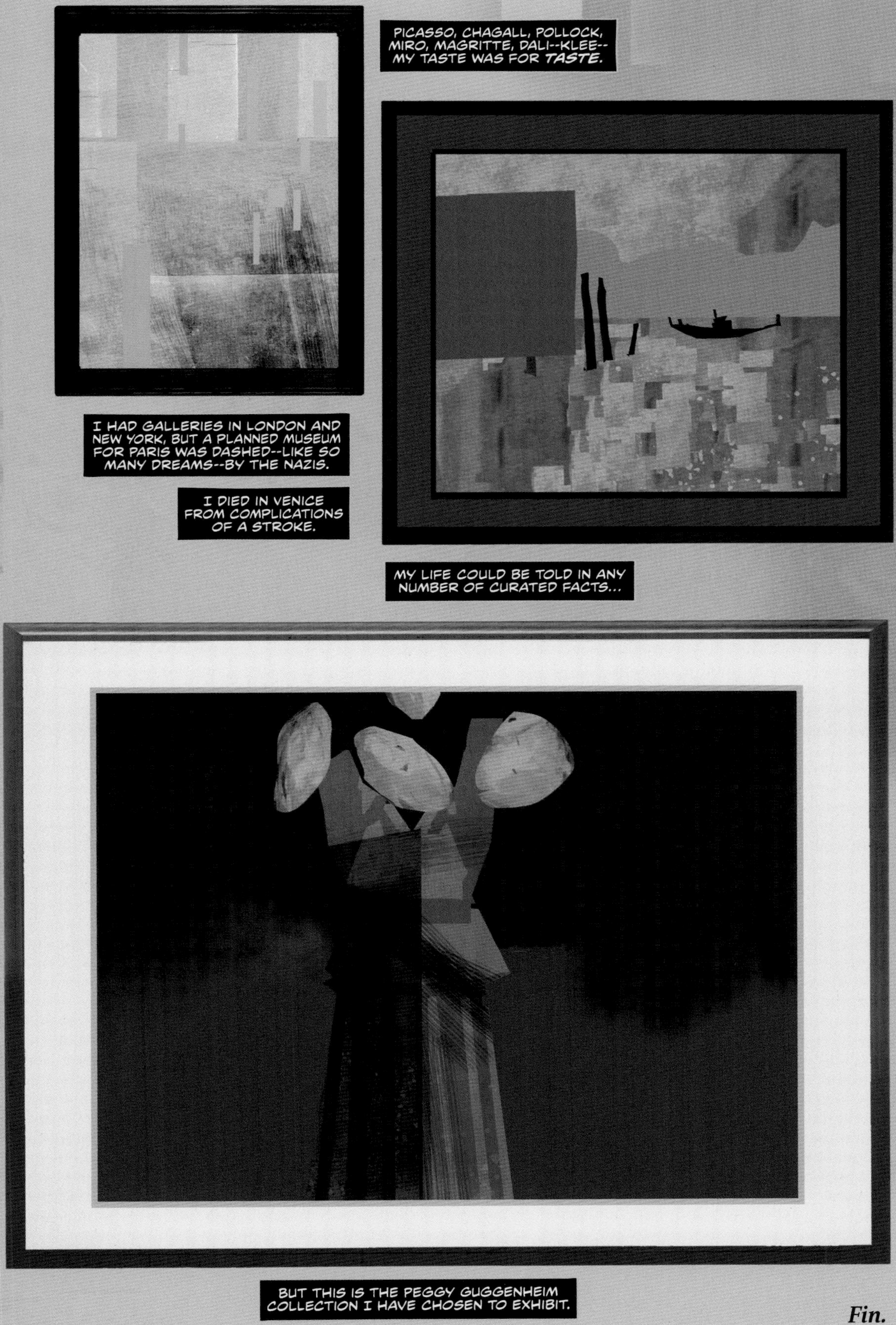
PICASSO, CHAGALL, POLLOCK, MIRO, MAGRITTE, DALI--KLEE-- MY TASTE WAS FOR *TASTE.*
I HAD GALLERIES IN LONDON AND NEW YORK, BUT A PLANNED MUSEUM FOR PARIS WAS DASHED--LIKE SO MANY DREAMS--BY THE NAZIS.
I DIED IN VENICE FROM COMPLICATIONS OF A STROKE.
MY LIFE COULD BE TOLD IN ANY NUMBER OF CURATED FACTS...
BUT THIS IS THE PEGGY GUGGENHEIM COLLECTION I HAVE CHOSEN TO EXHIBIT.

Fin.

HYPOBALLAD

KIERON GILLEN
WRITER

ANNIE WU
ARTIST

HI-FI
COLORIST

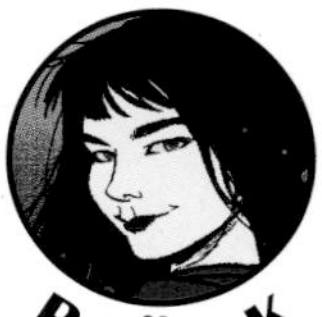

BJÖRK

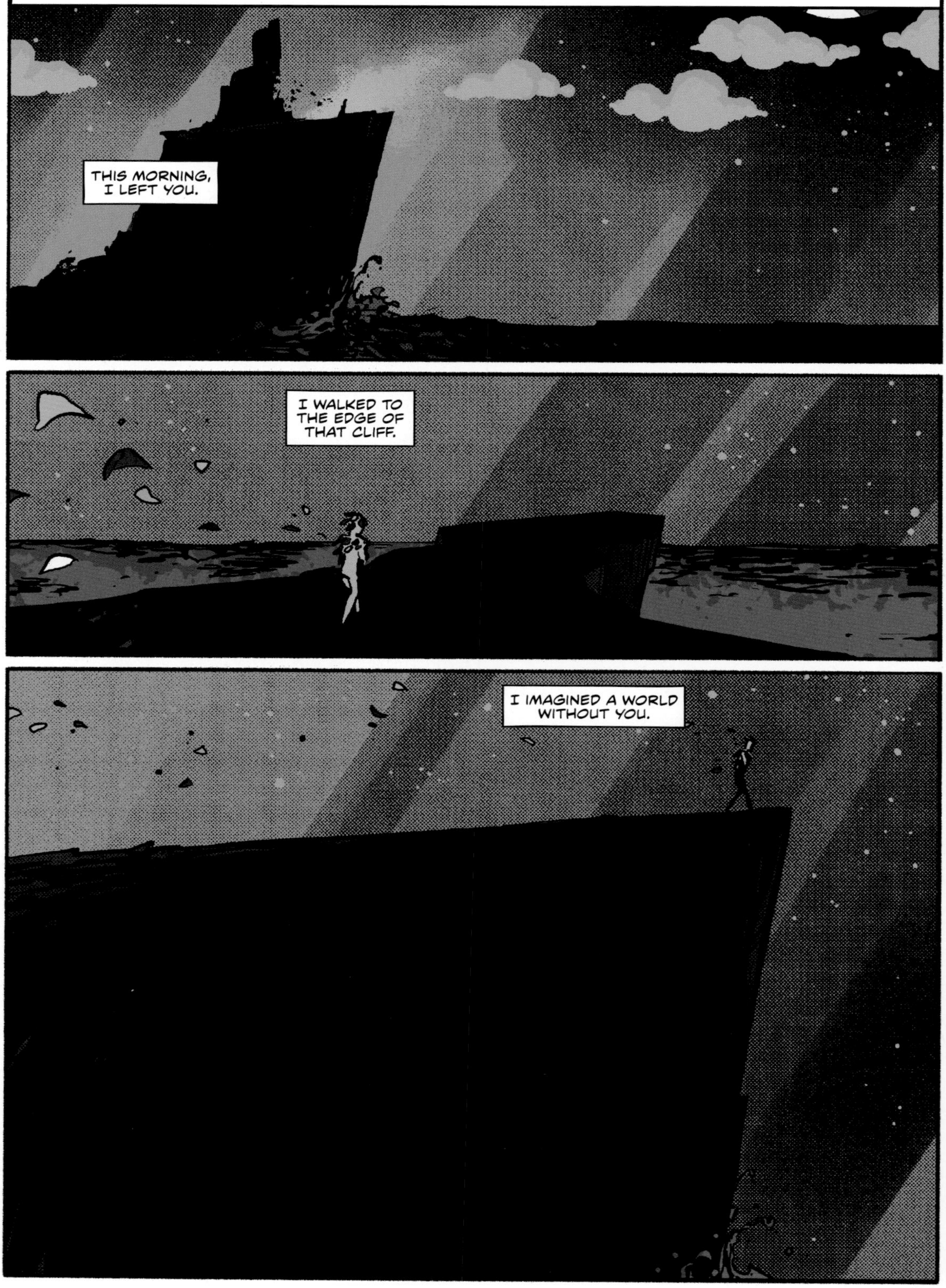

THIS MORNING, I LEFT YOU.
I WALKED TO THE EDGE OF THAT CLIFF.
I IMAGINED A WORLD WITHOUT YOU.

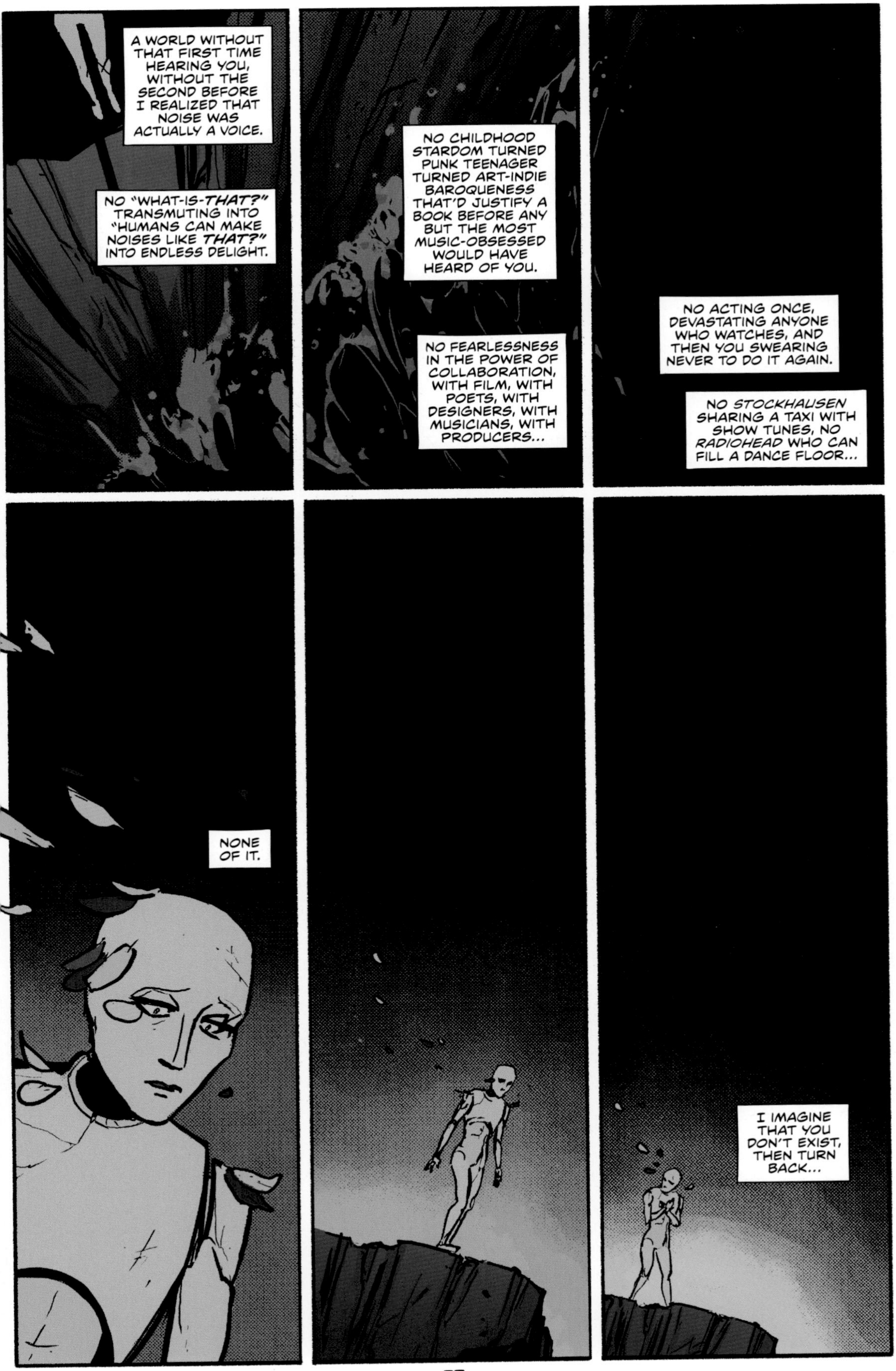
A WORLD WITHOUT THAT FIRST TIME HEARING YOU, WITHOUT THE SECOND BEFORE I REALIZED THAT NOISE WAS ACTUALLY A VOICE.
NO "WHAT-IS-*THAT?*" TRANSMUTING INTO "HUMANS CAN MAKE NOISES LIKE *THAT?*" INTO ENDLESS DELIGHT.
NO CHILDHOOD STARDOM TURNED PUNK TEENAGER TURNED ART-INDIE BAROQUENESS THAT'D JUSTIFY A BOOK BEFORE ANY BUT THE MOST MUSIC-OBSESSED WOULD HAVE HEARD OF YOU.
NO FEARLESSNESS IN THE POWER OF COLLABORATION, WITH FILM, WITH POETS, WITH DESIGNERS, WITH MUSICIANS, WITH PRODUCERS...
NO ACTING ONCE, DEVASTATING ANYONE WHO WATCHES, AND THEN YOU SWEARING NEVER TO DO IT AGAIN.
NO *STOCKHAUSEN* SHARING A TAXI WITH SHOW TUNES, NO *RADIOHEAD* WHO CAN FILL A DANCE FLOOR...
NONE OF IT.
I IMAGINE THAT YOU DON'T EXIST, THEN TURN BACK...

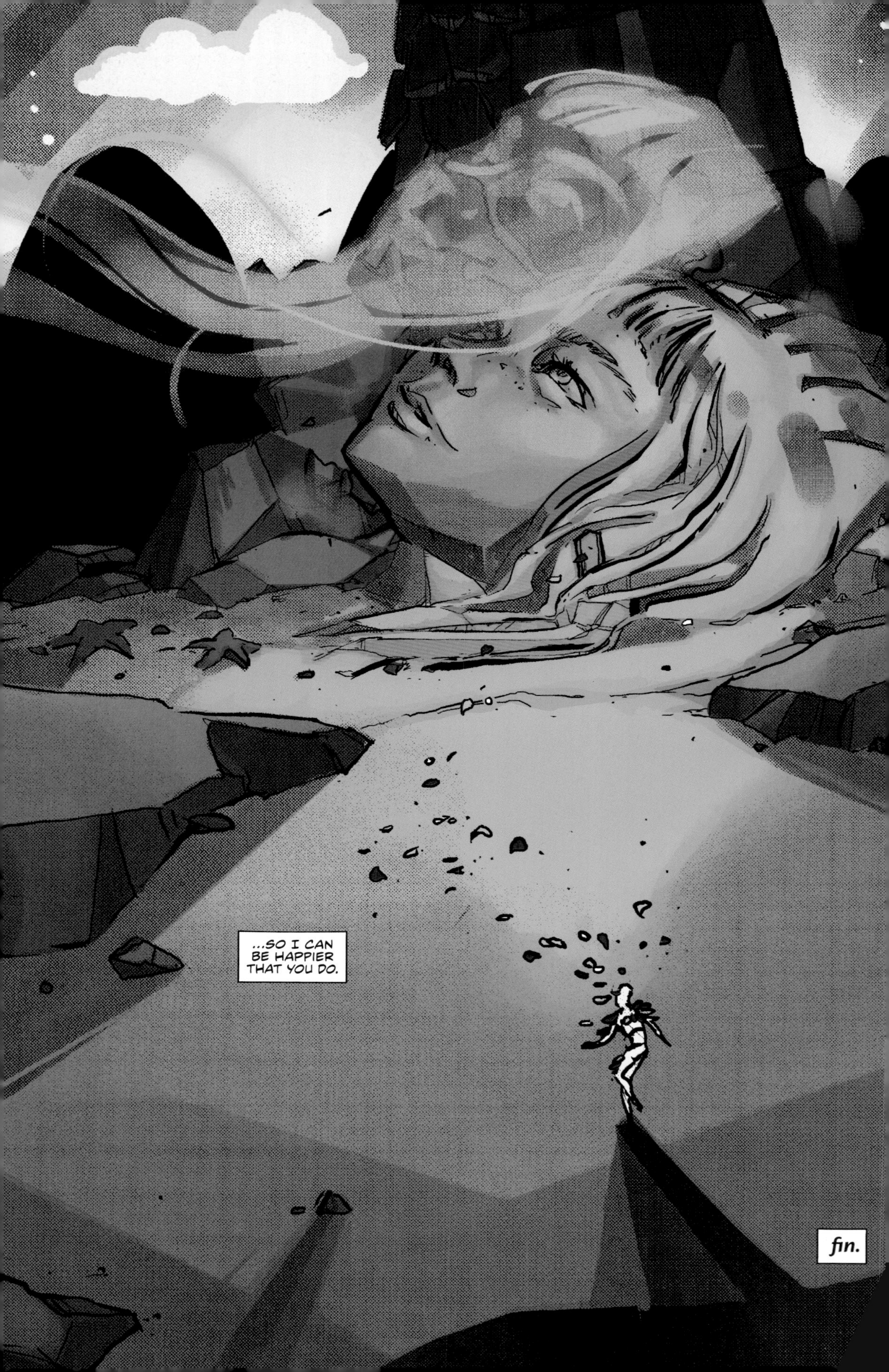
...SO I CAN BE HAPPIER THAT YOU DO.
fin.

"I don't expect people to get me. That would be quite arrogant. I think there are a lot of people out there in the world that nobody gets."

— Björk

"No woman can call herself free who does not own and control her body. No woman can call herself free until she can choose consciously whether she will or will not be a mother."

—Margaret Sanger

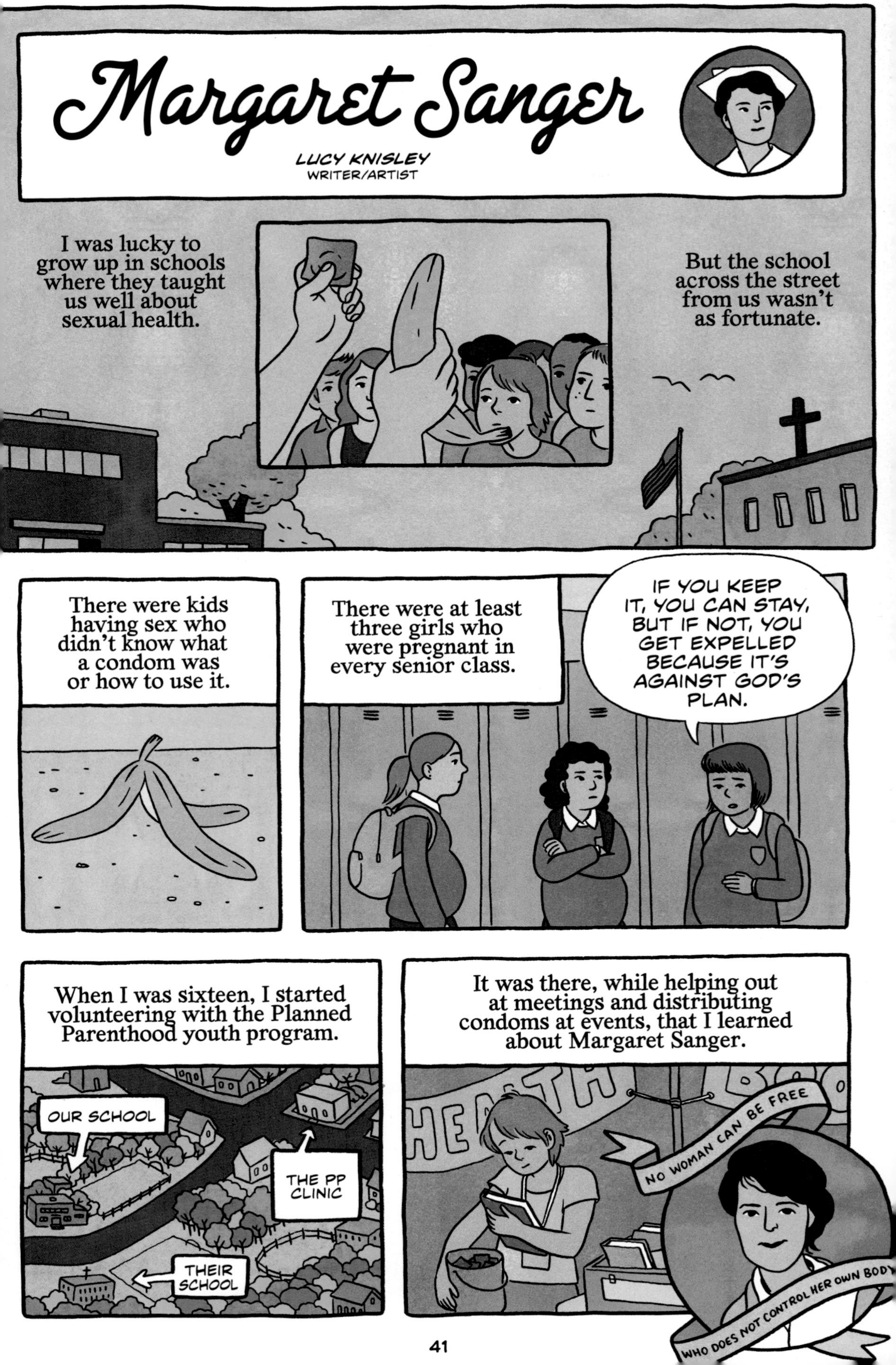
Margaret Sanger
LUCY KNISLEY
WRITER/ARTIST
I was lucky to grow up in schools where they taught us well about sexual health.
But the school across the street from us wasn't as fortunate.
There were kids having sex who didn't know what a condom was or how to use it.
There were at least three girls who were pregnant in every senior class.
IF YOU KEEP IT, YOU CAN STAY, BUT IF NOT, YOU GET EXPELLED BECAUSE IT'S AGAINST GOD'S PLAN.
When I was sixteen, I started volunteering with the Planned Parenthood youth program.
OUR SCHOOL
THE PP CLINIC
THEIR SCHOOL
It was there, while helping out at meetings and distributing condoms at events, that I learned about Margaret Sanger.
NO WOMAN CAN BE FREE
WHO DOES NOT CONTROL HER OWN BODY

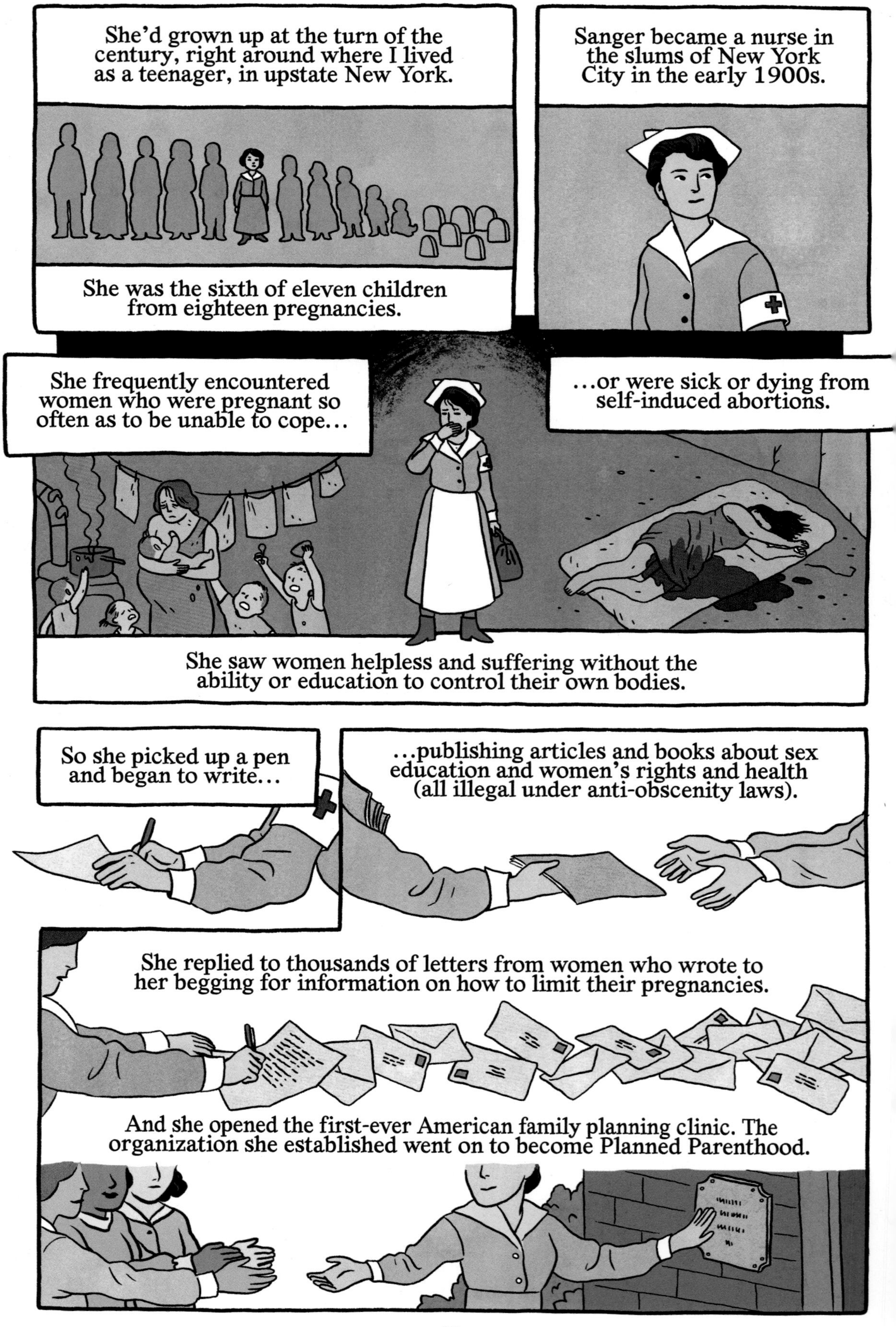
She'd grown up at the turn of the century, right around where I lived as a teenager, in upstate New York.
She was the sixth of eleven children from eighteen pregnancies.
Sanger became a nurse in the slums of New York City in the early 1900s.
She frequently encountered women who were pregnant so often as to be unable to cope…
…or were sick or dying from self-induced abortions.
She saw women helpless and suffering without the ability or education to control their own bodies.
So she picked up a pen and began to write…
…publishing articles and books about sex education and women's rights and health (all illegal under anti-obscenity laws).
She replied to thousands of letters from women who wrote to her begging for information on how to limit their pregnancies.
And she opened the first-ever American family planning clinic. The organization she established went on to become Planned Parenthood.

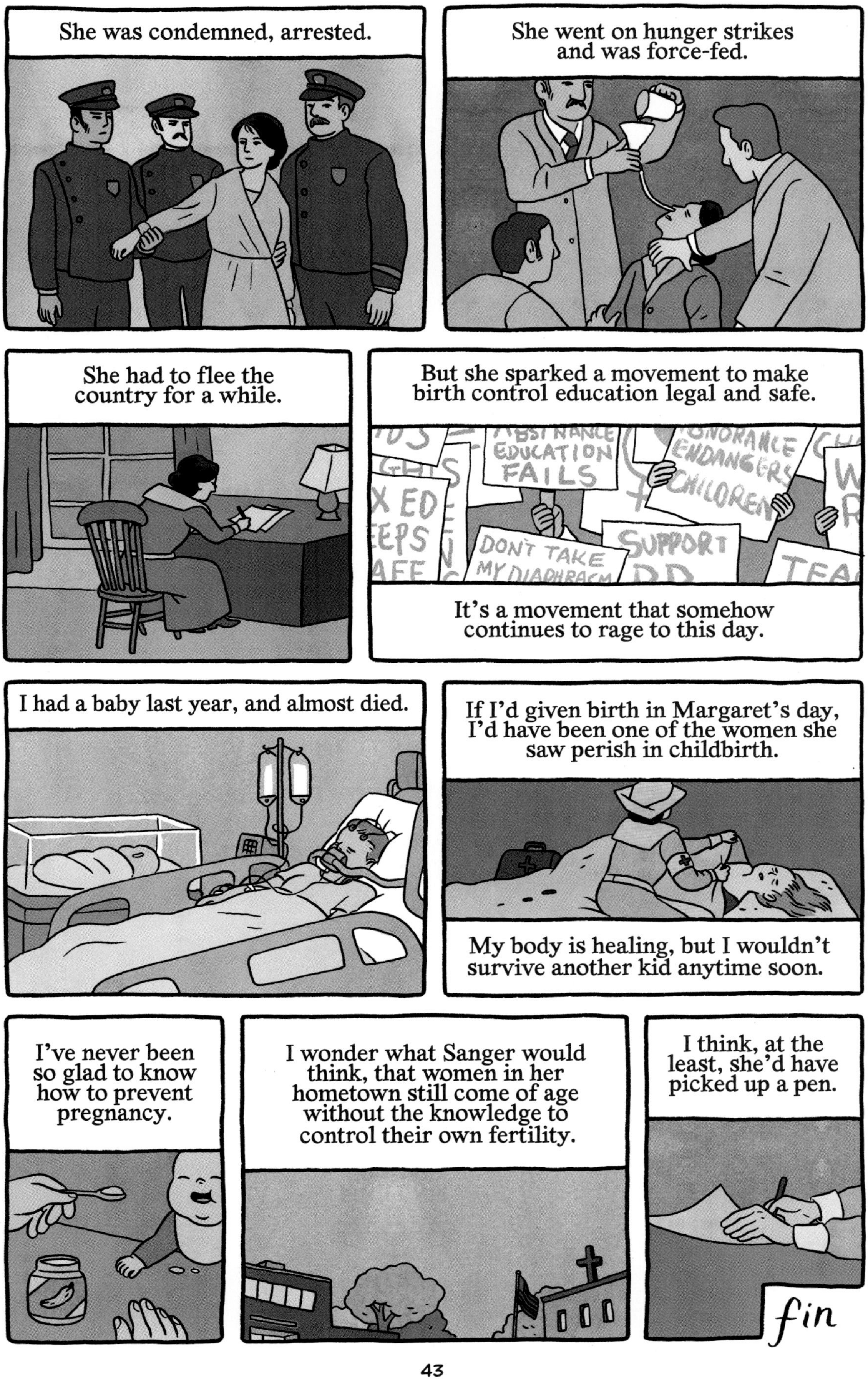
She was condemned, arrested.
She went on hunger strikes and was force-fed.
She had to flee the country for a while.
But she sparked a movement to make birth control education legal and safe.
EDUCATION FAILS
ENDANGERS CHILDREN
DON'T TAKE
SUPPORT
It's a movement that somehow continues to rage to this day.
I had a baby last year, and almost died.
If I'd given birth in Margaret's day, I'd have been one of the women she saw perish in childbirth.
My body is healing, but I wouldn't survive another kid anytime soon.
I've never been so glad to know how to prevent pregnancy.
I wonder what Sanger would think, that women in her hometown still come of age without the knowledge to control their own fertility.
I think, at the least, she'd have picked up a pen.
fin

"Never were such things brought to any king since the world was."

—Hatshepsut
from a relief where Hatshepsut talks about her vast trading expeditions.

The Forgotten PHARAOH

KRISTY MILLER WRITER | EVA CABRERA ARTIST | HI-FI COLORIST

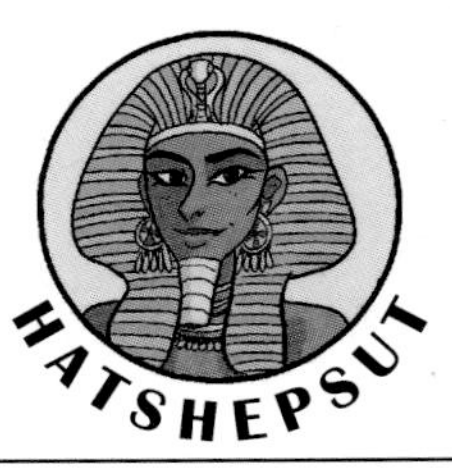

HATSHEPSUT

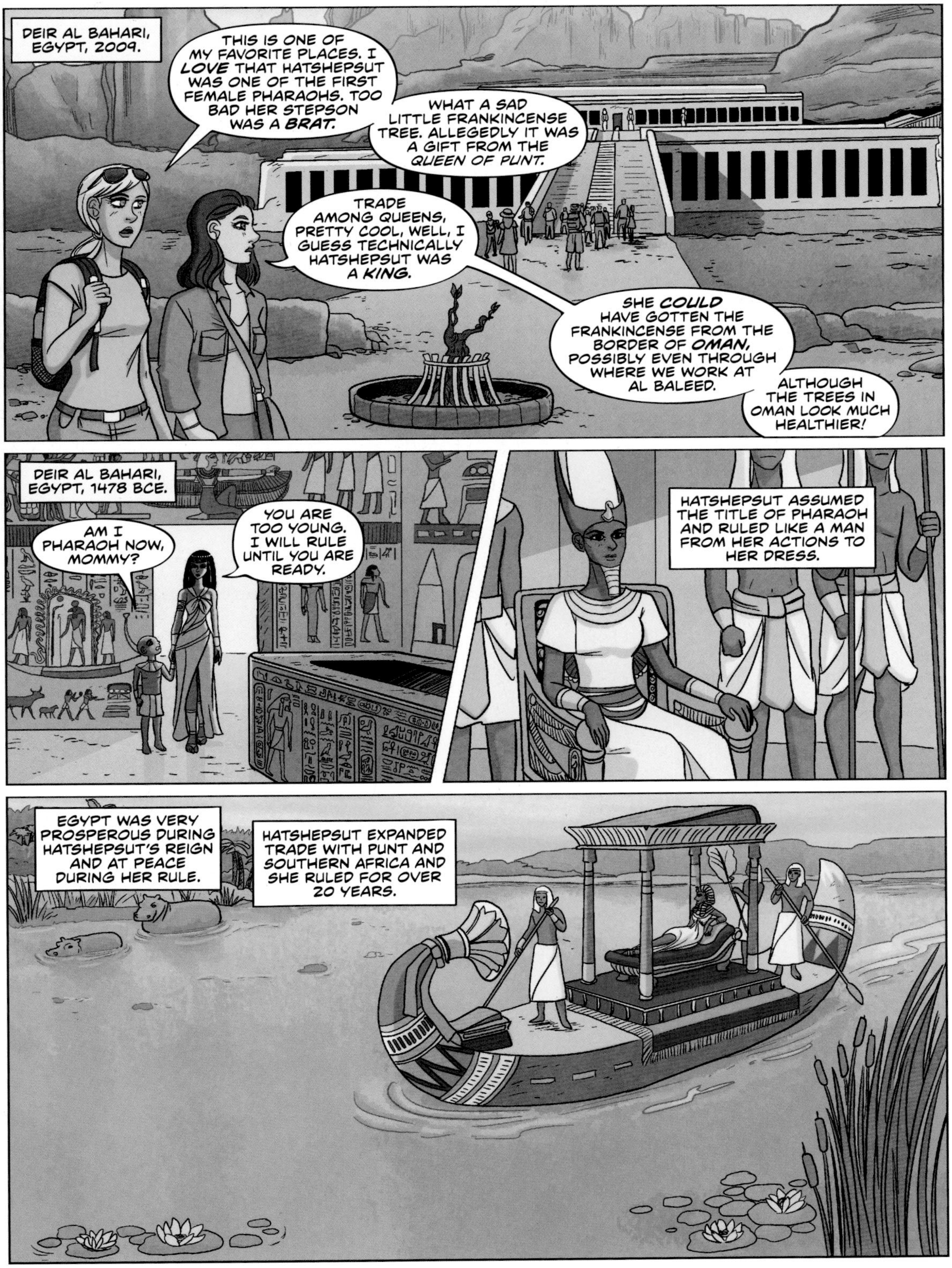

DEIR AL BAHARI, EGYPT, 2009.
THIS IS ONE OF MY FAVORITE PLACES. I LOVE THAT HATSHEPSUT WAS ONE OF THE FIRST FEMALE PHARAOHS. TOO BAD HER STEPSON WAS A BRAT.
WHAT A SAD LITTLE FRANKINCENSE TREE. ALLEGEDLY IT WAS A GIFT FROM THE QUEEN OF PUNT.
TRADE AMONG QUEENS, PRETTY COOL, WELL, I GUESS TECHNICALLY HATSHEPSUT WAS A KING.
SHE COULD HAVE GOTTEN THE FRANKINCENSE FROM THE BORDER OF OMAN, POSSIBLY EVEN THROUGH WHERE WE WORK AT AL BALEED.
ALTHOUGH THE TREES IN OMAN LOOK MUCH HEALTHIER!
DEIR AL BAHARI, EGYPT, 1478 BCE.
AM I PHARAOH NOW, MOMMY?
YOU ARE TOO YOUNG. I WILL RULE UNTIL YOU ARE READY.
HATSHEPSUT ASSUMED THE TITLE OF PHARAOH AND RULED LIKE A MAN FROM HER ACTIONS TO HER DRESS.
EGYPT WAS VERY PROSPEROUS DURING HATSHEPSUT'S REIGN AND AT PEACE DURING HER RULE.
HATSHEPSUT EXPANDED TRADE WITH PUNT AND SOUTHERN AFRICA AND SHE RULED FOR OVER 20 YEARS.

SENENMUT WAS A ROYAL ADVISOR, ARCHITECT, AND CLOSE FRIEND OF HATSHEPSUT.

NOW IS IT TIME FOR ME TO BECOME PHARAOH?

NO, SON, NOT YET. WHEN YOU ARE OLDER. AND DO NOT BE DISRESPECTFUL TO SENENMUT.

HE HOLDS A RESPECTED PLACE IN OUR KINGDOM.

NOW IS THE TIME FOR ME TO RULE.

IT'S MY RIGHTFUL PLACE. I SHOULD BE PHARAOH, NOT HER!

HATSHEPSUT DIED UNDER MYSTERIOUS CIRCUMSTANCES.

MOTHER IS FINALLY DEAD, SENENMUT. I AM PHARAOH AND YOU ARE NO LONGER NEEDED.

SENENMUT WAS LOST IN HISTORY FOR YEARS. RECENTLY HIS TOMB WAS FOUND NEXT TO HATSHEPSUT'S.

IT IS POSSIBLE HE WAS THE FATHER OF HATSHEPSUT'S DAUGHTER, WHO WAS BORN DURING HER TIME AS PHARAOH.

I WANT EVERYTHING THAT RESEMBLES MY MOTHER DESTROYED!

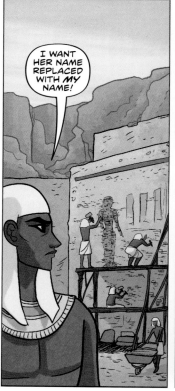

I WANT HER NAME REPLACED WITH MY NAME!

I AM PHARAOH. NO ONE WILL MENTION THE NAME HATSHEPSUT AGAIN!

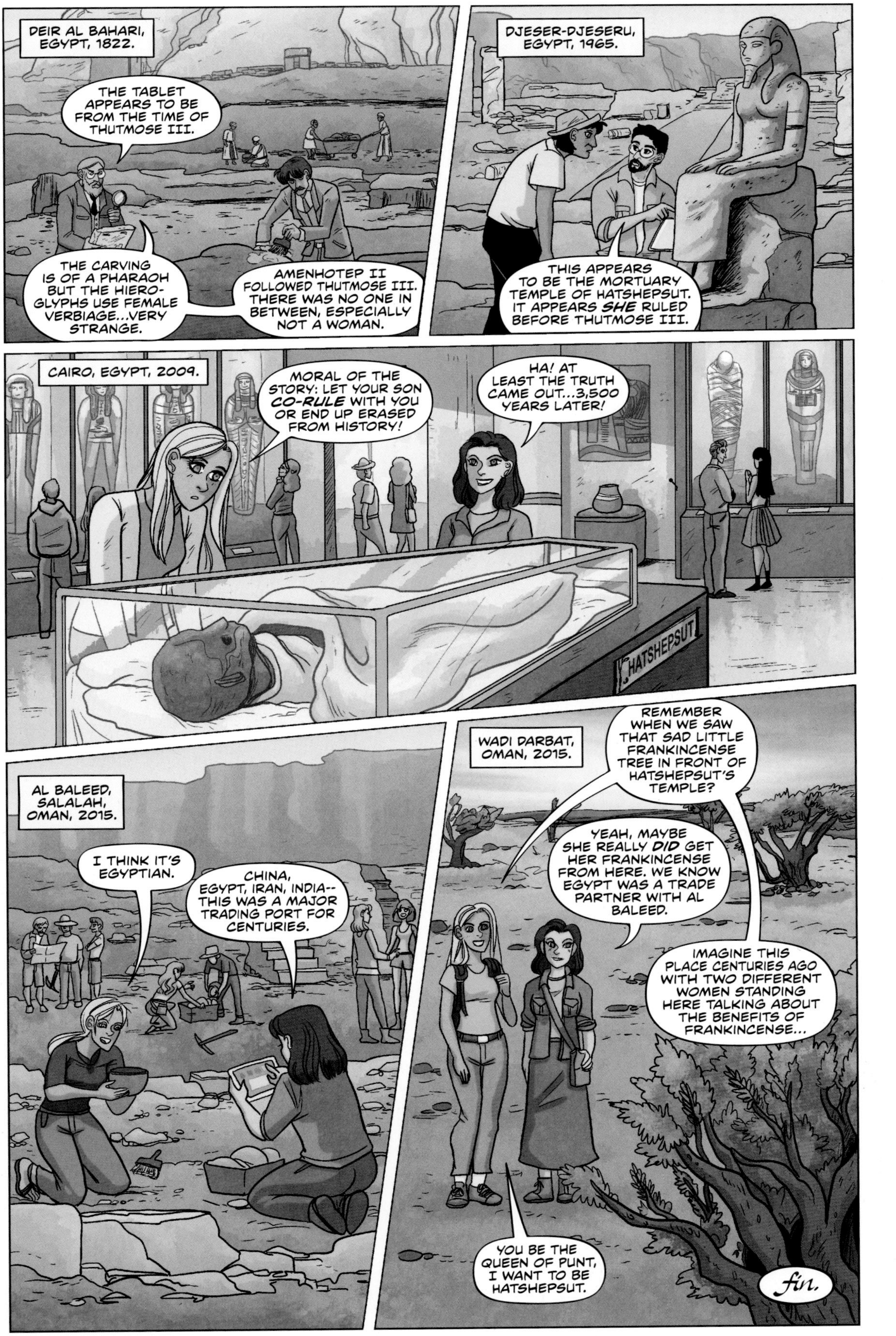
DEIR AL BAHARI, EGYPT, 1822.
THE TABLET APPEARS TO BE FROM THE TIME OF THUTMOSE III.
THE CARVING IS OF A PHARAOH BUT THE HIERO-GLYPHS USE FEMALE VERBIAGE...VERY STRANGE.
AMENHOTEP II FOLLOWED THUTMOSE III. THERE WAS NO ONE IN BETWEEN, ESPECIALLY NOT A WOMAN.
DJESER-DJESERU, EGYPT, 1965.
THIS APPEARS TO BE THE MORTUARY TEMPLE OF HATSHEPSUT. IT APPEARS *SHE* RULED BEFORE THUTMOSE III.
CAIRO, EGYPT, 2009.
MORAL OF THE STORY: LET YOUR SON *CO-RULE* WITH YOU OR END UP ERASED FROM HISTORY!
HA! AT LEAST THE TRUTH CAME OUT...3,500 YEARS LATER!
HATSHEPSUT
AL BALEED, SALALAH, OMAN, 2015.
I THINK IT'S EGYPTIAN.
CHINA, EGYPT, IRAN, INDIA-- THIS WAS A MAJOR TRADING PORT FOR CENTURIES.
WADI DARBAT, OMAN, 2015.
REMEMBER WHEN WE SAW THAT SAD LITTLE FRANKINCENSE TREE IN FRONT OF HATSHEPSUT'S TEMPLE?
YEAH, MAYBE SHE REALLY *DID* GET HER FRANKINCENSE FROM HERE. WE KNOW EGYPT WAS A TRADE PARTNER WITH AL BALEED.
IMAGINE THIS PLACE CENTURIES AGO WITH TWO DIFFERENT WOMEN STANDING HERE TALKING ABOUT THE BENEFITS OF FRANKINCENSE...
YOU BE THE QUEEN OF PUNT, I WANT TO BE HATSHEPSUT.
fin.

AND THEN THEY WERE UPON HER

MATT WAGNER
WRITER

CHRISTINE NORRIE
ARTIST

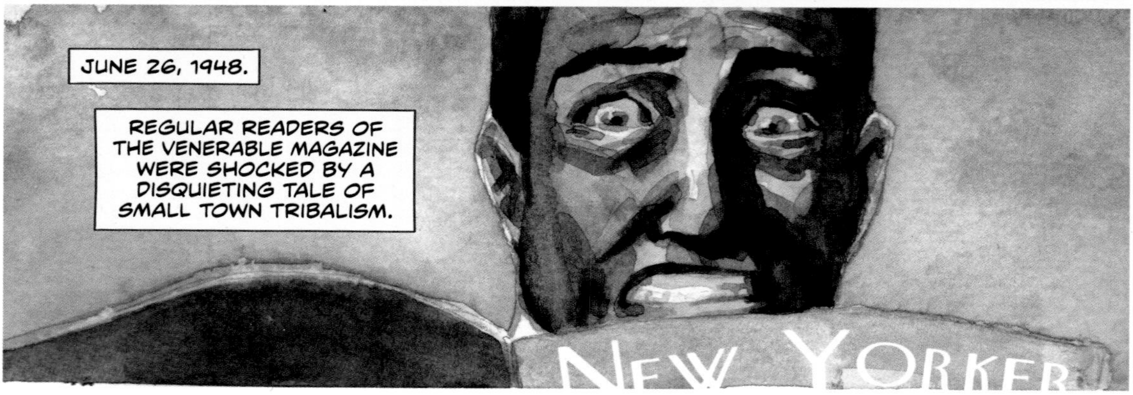
JUNE 26, 1948.
REGULAR READERS OF THE VENERABLE MAGAZINE WERE SHOCKED BY A DISQUIETING TALE OF SMALL TOWN TRIBALISM.
NEW YORKER

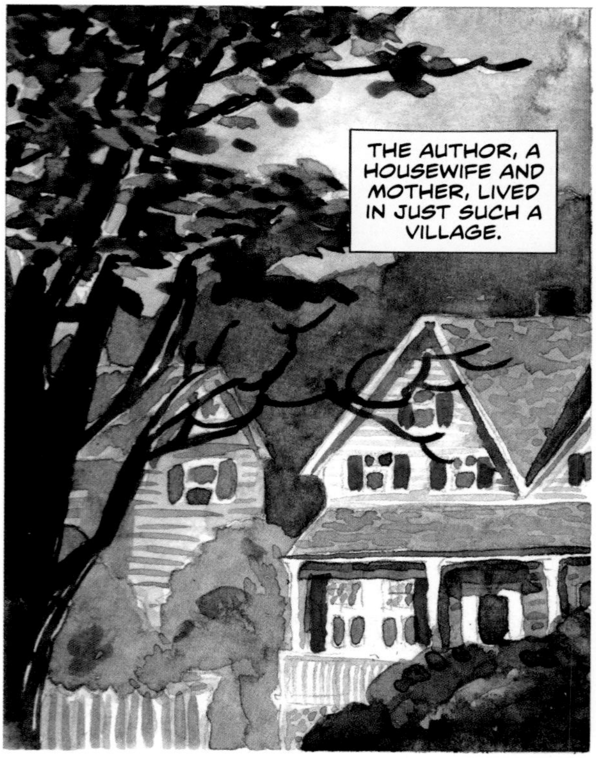
THE AUTHOR, A HOUSEWIFE AND MOTHER, LIVED IN JUST SUCH A VILLAGE.

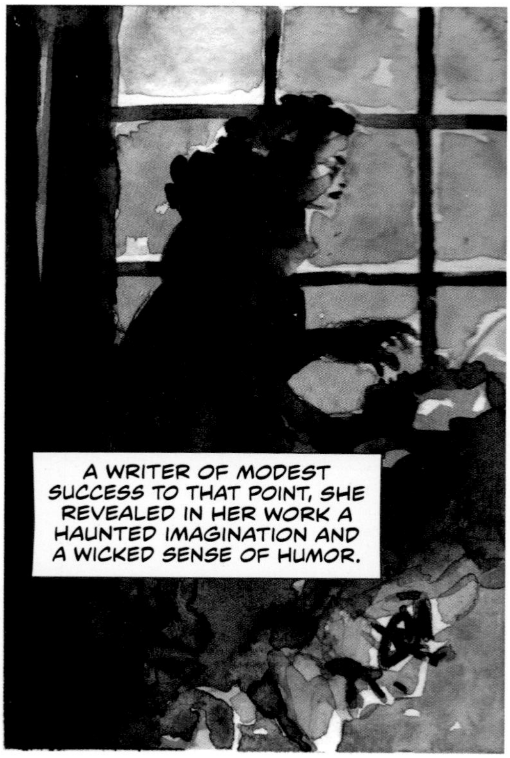
A WRITER OF MODEST SUCCESS TO THAT POINT, SHE REVEALED IN HER WORK A HAUNTED IMAGINATION AND A WICKED SENSE OF HUMOR.

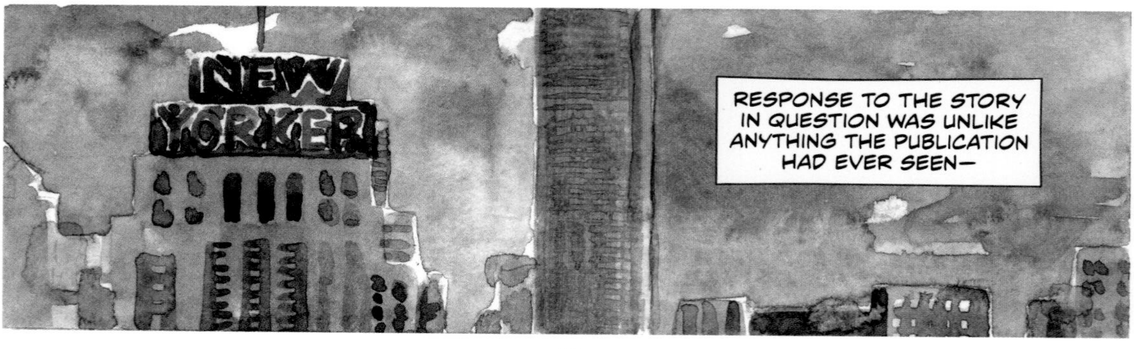
NEW YORKER
RESPONSE TO THE STORY IN QUESTION WAS UNLIKE ANYTHING THE PUBLICATION HAD EVER SEEN—

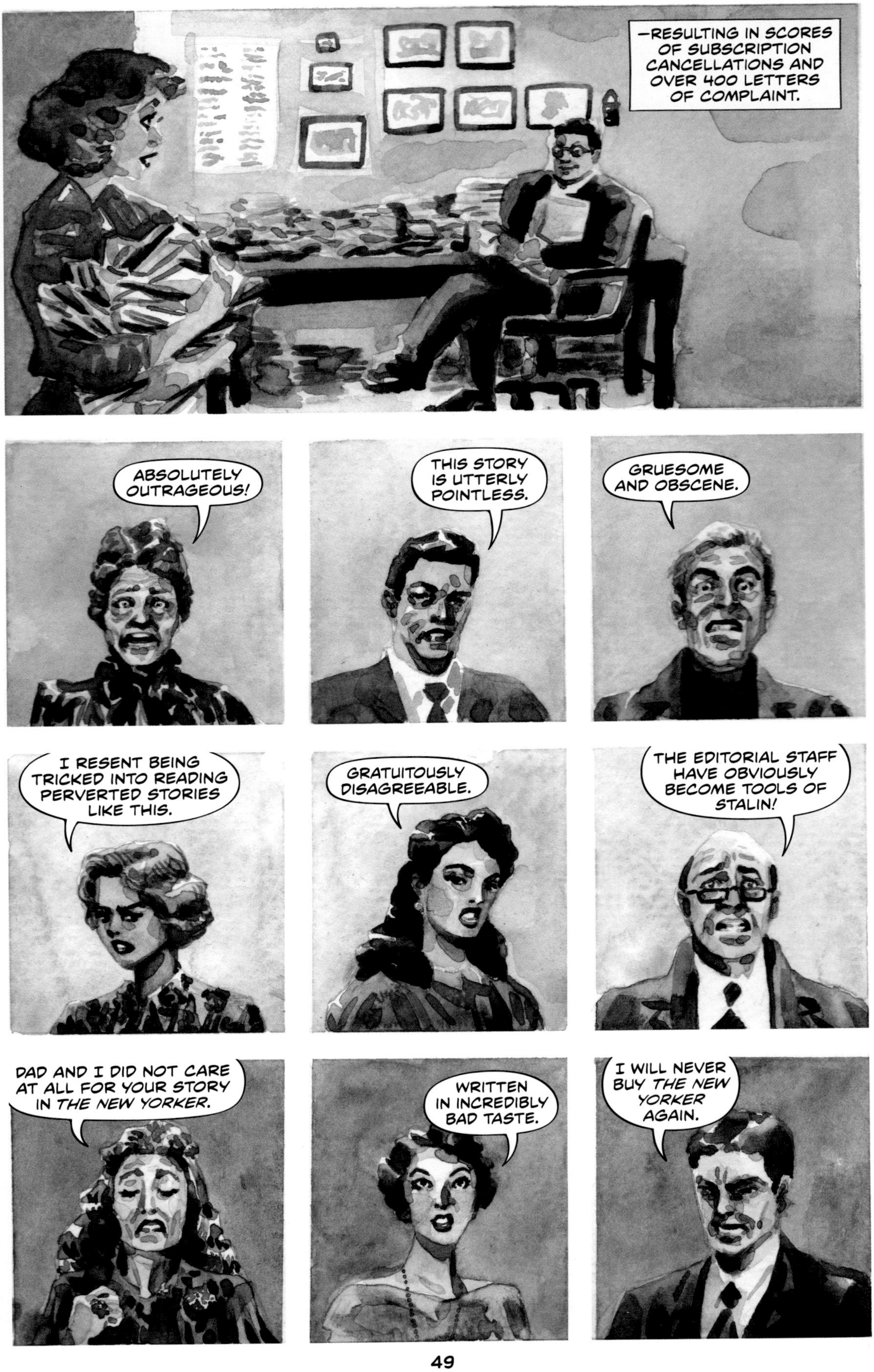
—RESULTING IN SCORES OF SUBSCRIPTION CANCELLATIONS AND OVER 400 LETTERS OF COMPLAINT.
ABSOLUTELY OUTRAGEOUS!
THIS STORY IS UTTERLY POINTLESS.
GRUESOME AND OBSCENE.
I RESENT BEING TRICKED INTO READING PERVERTED STORIES LIKE THIS.
GRATUITOUSLY DISAGREEABLE.
THE EDITORIAL STAFF HAVE OBVIOUSLY BECOME TOOLS OF STALIN!
DAD AND I DID NOT CARE AT ALL FOR YOUR STORY IN *THE NEW YORKER*.
WRITTEN IN INCREDIBLY BAD TASTE.
I WILL NEVER BUY *THE NEW YORKER* AGAIN.

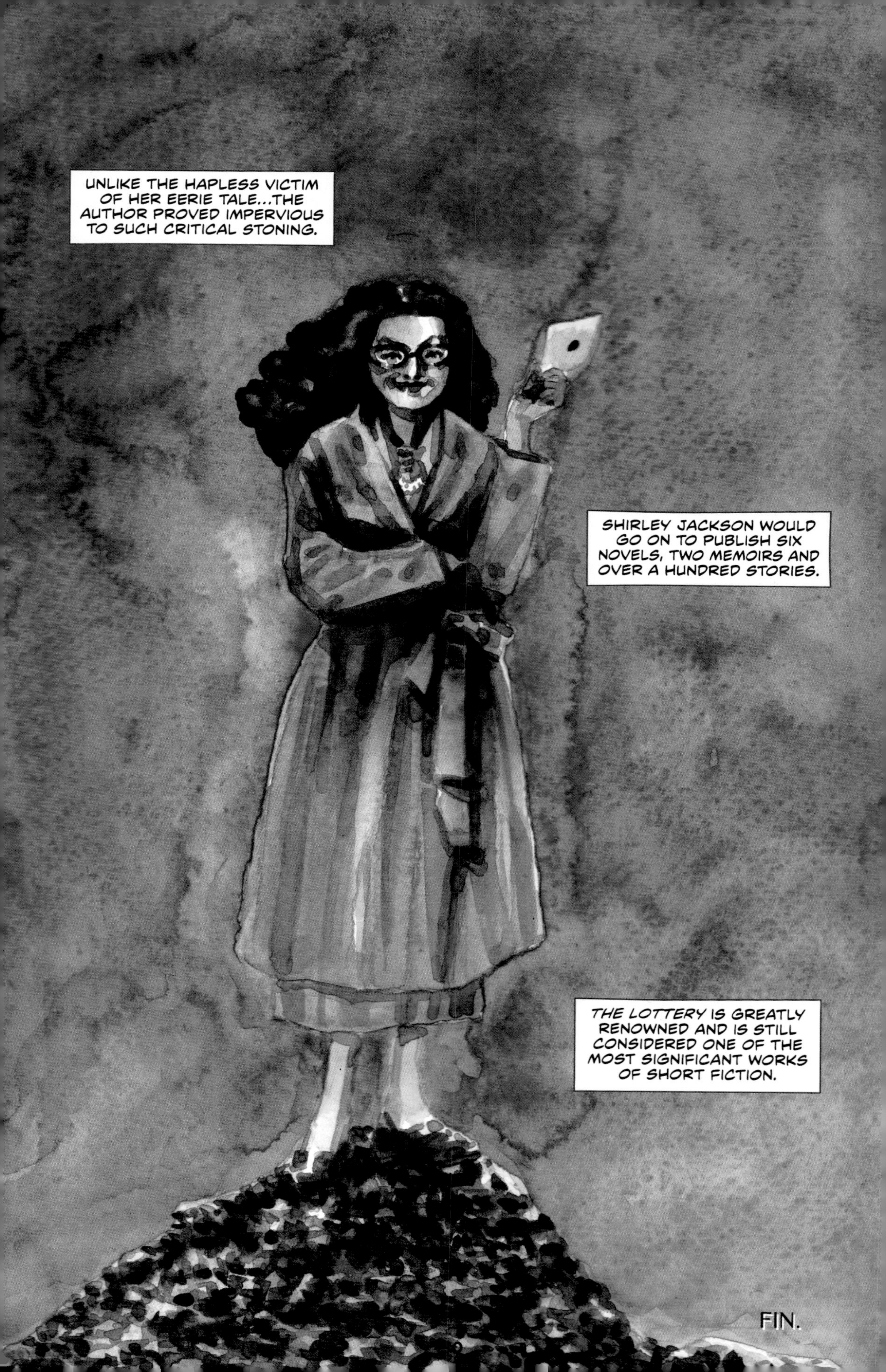
UNLIKE THE HAPLESS VICTIM OF HER EERIE TALE...THE AUTHOR PROVED IMPERVIOUS TO SUCH CRITICAL STONING.
SHIRLEY JACKSON WOULD GO ON TO PUBLISH SIX NOVELS, TWO MEMOIRS AND OVER A HUNDRED STORIES.
THE LOTTERY IS GREATLY RENOWNED AND IS STILL CONSIDERED ONE OF THE MOST SIGNIFICANT WORKS OF SHORT FICTION.
FIN.

"I suppose, I hoped, by setting a particularly brutal ancient rite in the present and in my own village, to shock the story's readers with a graphic dramatization of the pointless violence and general inhumanity in their own lives."

—Shirley Jackson
discussing her book The Lottery.

"I never went into physics or the astronaut corps to become a role model. But after my first flight, it became clear to me that I was one. And I began to understand the importance of that to people. Young girls need to see role models in whatever careers they may choose, just so they can picture themselves doing those jobs someday. You can't be what you can't see."

—Sally Ride

THE RIGHT STUFF

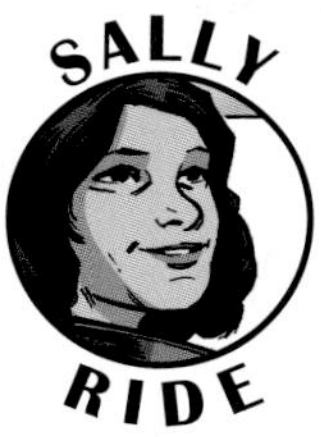
SALLY
RIDE

CECIL CASTELLUCCI
WRITER

PHILIP BOND
ARTIST

HI-FI
COLORIST

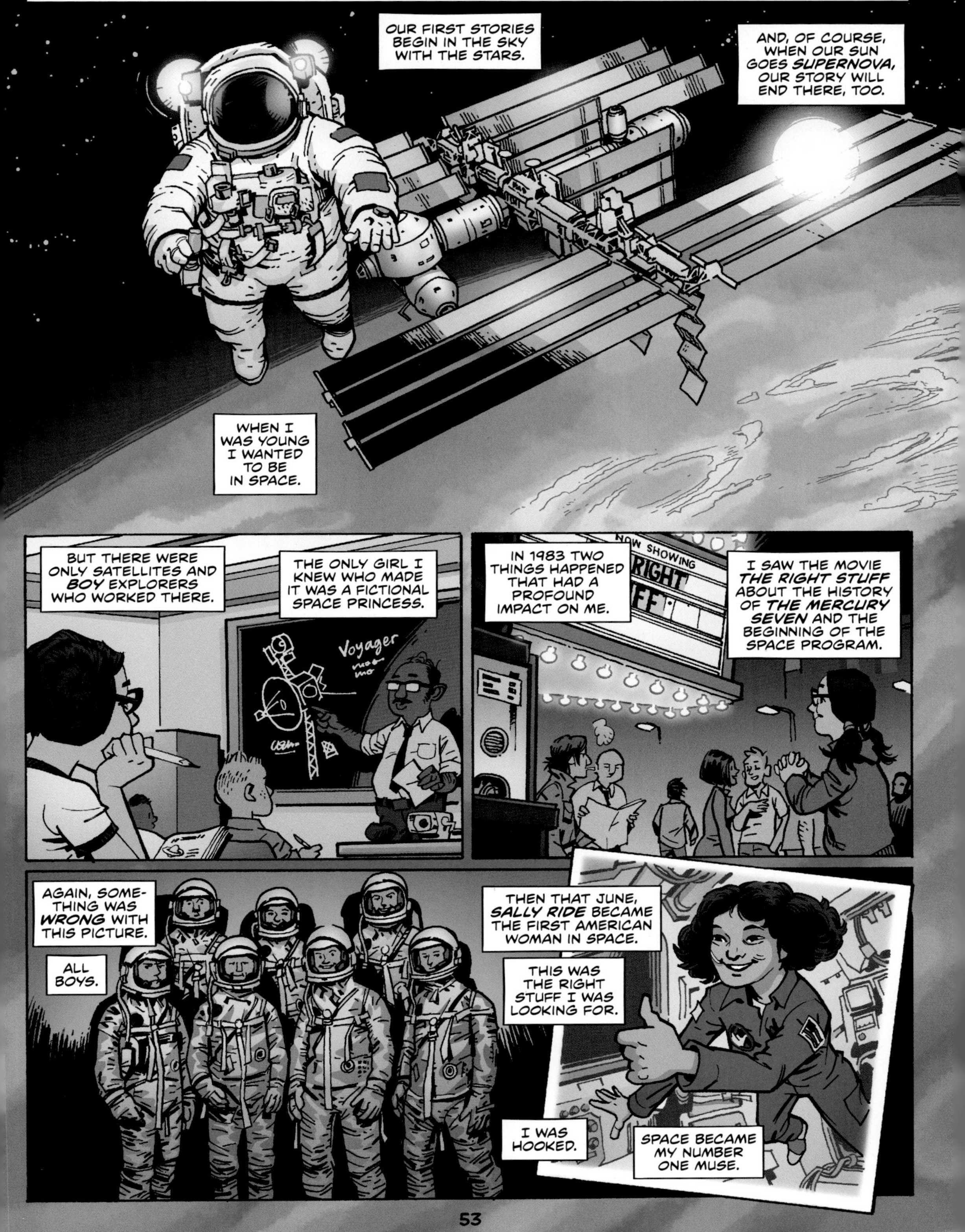
OUR FIRST STORIES BEGIN IN THE SKY WITH THE STARS.
AND, OF COURSE, WHEN OUR SUN GOES *SUPERNOVA*, OUR STORY WILL END THERE, TOO.
WHEN I WAS YOUNG I WANTED TO BE IN SPACE.
BUT THERE WERE ONLY SATELLITES AND *BOY* EXPLORERS WHO WORKED THERE.
THE ONLY GIRL I KNEW WHO MADE IT WAS A FICTIONAL SPACE PRINCESS.
Voyager
IN 1983 TWO THINGS HAPPENED THAT HAD A PROFOUND IMPACT ON ME.
NOW SHOWING
I SAW THE MOVIE *THE RIGHT STUFF* ABOUT THE HISTORY OF *THE MERCURY SEVEN* AND THE BEGINNING OF THE SPACE PROGRAM.
AGAIN, SOMETHING WAS *WRONG* WITH THIS PICTURE.
ALL BOYS.
THEN THAT JUNE, *SALLY RIDE* BECAME THE FIRST AMERICAN WOMAN IN SPACE.
THIS WAS THE RIGHT STUFF I WAS LOOKING FOR.
I WAS HOOKED.
SPACE BECAME MY NUMBER ONE MUSE.

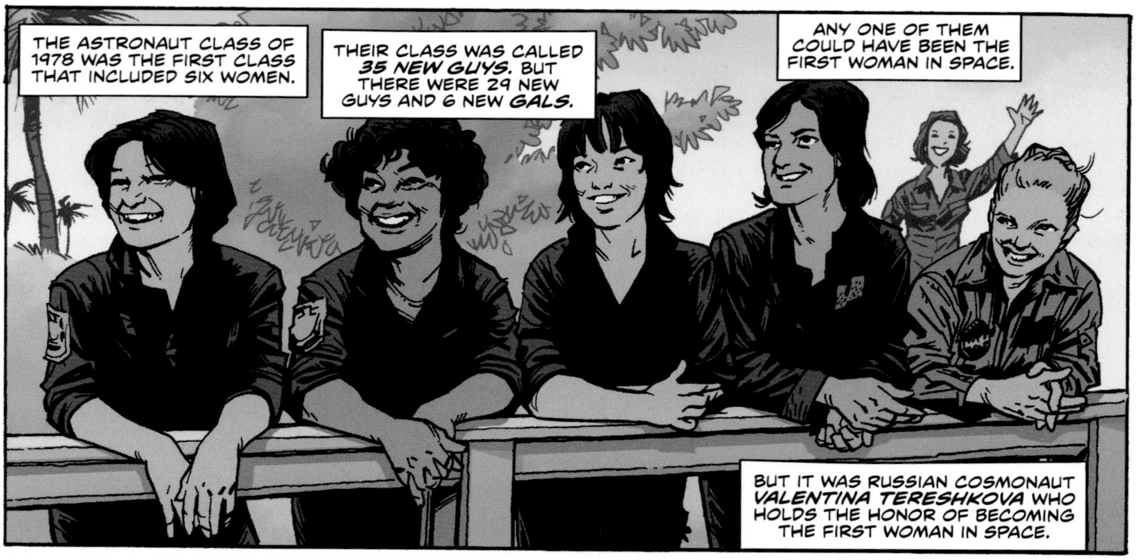
THE ASTRONAUT CLASS OF 1978 WAS THE FIRST CLASS THAT INCLUDED SIX WOMEN.
THEIR CLASS WAS CALLED *35 NEW GUYS.* BUT THERE WERE 29 NEW GUYS AND 6 NEW *GALS.*
ANY ONE OF THEM COULD HAVE BEEN THE FIRST WOMAN IN SPACE.
BUT IT WAS RUSSIAN COSMONAUT *VALENTINA TERESHKOVA* WHO HOLDS THE HONOR OF BECOMING THE FIRST WOMAN IN SPACE.

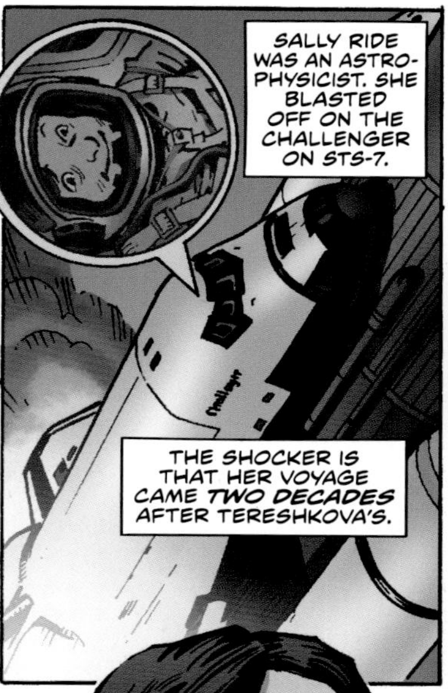
SALLY RIDE WAS AN ASTRO-PHYSICIST. SHE BLASTED OFF ON THE CHALLENGER ON STS-7.
THE SHOCKER IS THAT HER VOYAGE CAME *TWO DECADES* AFTER TERESHKOVA'S.

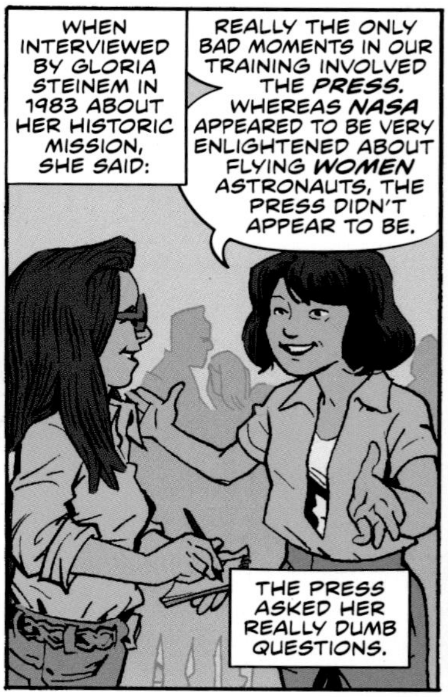
WHEN INTERVIEWED BY GLORIA STEINEM IN 1983 ABOUT HER HISTORIC MISSION, SHE SAID:
REALLY THE ONLY BAD MOMENTS IN OUR TRAINING INVOLVED THE *PRESS.* WHEREAS *NASA* APPEARED TO BE VERY ENLIGHTENED ABOUT FLYING *WOMEN* ASTRONAUTS, THE PRESS DIDN'T APPEAR TO BE.
THE PRESS ASKED HER REALLY DUMB QUESTIONS.

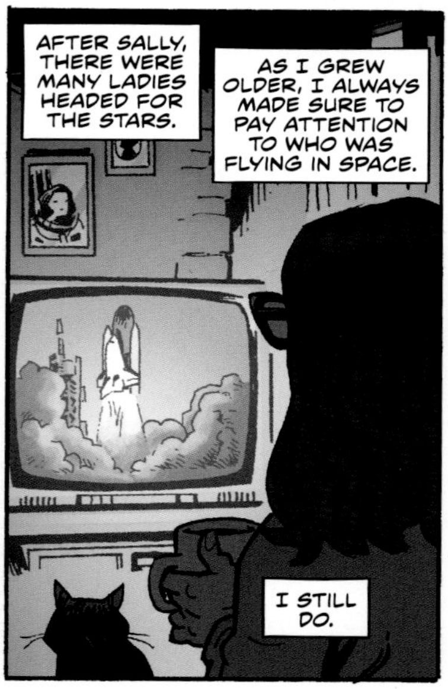
AFTER SALLY, THERE WERE MANY LADIES HEADED FOR THE STARS.
AS I GREW OLDER, I ALWAYS MADE SURE TO PAY ATTENTION TO WHO WAS FLYING IN SPACE.
I STILL DO.

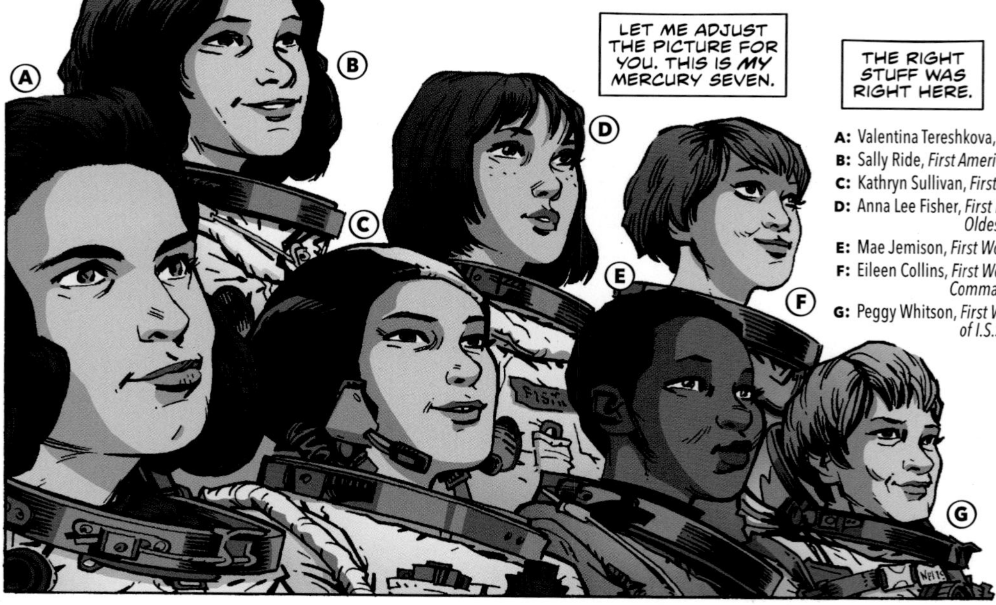
LET ME ADJUST THE PICTURE FOR YOU. THIS IS *MY* MERCURY SEVEN.
THE RIGHT STUFF WAS RIGHT HERE.
A
B
C
D
E
F
G

A: Valentina Tereshkova, *First Woman in Space*
B: Sally Ride, *First American Woman in Space*
C: Kathryn Sullivan, *First Female E.V.A.*
D: Anna Lee Fisher, *First Mother in Space and Oldest Active Astronaut*
E: Mae Jemison, *First Woman of Color in Space*
F: Eileen Collins, *First Woman Pilot and Commander in Space*
G: Peggy Whitson, *First Woman Commander of I.S.S. in 2007*

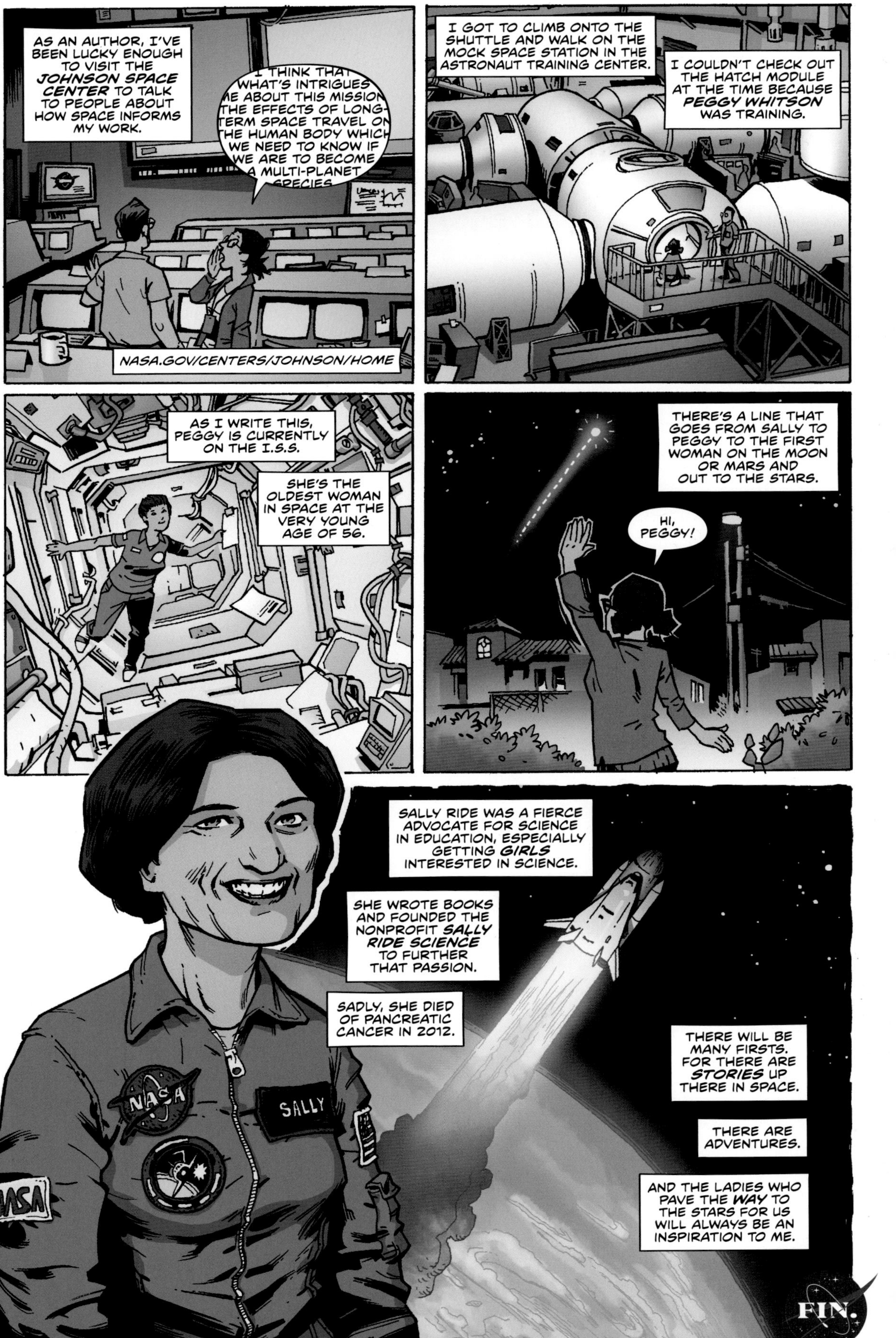
AS AN AUTHOR, I'VE BEEN LUCKY ENOUGH TO VISIT THE JOHNSON SPACE CENTER TO TALK TO PEOPLE ABOUT HOW SPACE INFORMS MY WORK.
I THINK THAT WHAT'S INTRIGUES ME ABOUT THIS MISSION THE EFFECTS OF LONG-TERM SPACE TRAVEL ON THE HUMAN BODY WHICH WE NEED TO KNOW IF WE ARE TO BECOME A MULTI-PLANET SPECIES
NASA.GOV/CENTERS/JOHNSON/HOME
I GOT TO CLIMB ONTO THE SHUTTLE AND WALK ON THE MOCK SPACE STATION IN THE ASTRONAUT TRAINING CENTER.
I COULDN'T CHECK OUT THE HATCH MODULE AT THE TIME BECAUSE PEGGY WHITSON WAS TRAINING.
AS I WRITE THIS, PEGGY IS CURRENTLY ON THE I.S.S.
SHE'S THE OLDEST WOMAN IN SPACE AT THE VERY YOUNG AGE OF 56.
THERE'S A LINE THAT GOES FROM SALLY TO PEGGY TO THE FIRST WOMAN ON THE MOON OR MARS AND OUT TO THE STARS.
HI, PEGGY!
SALLY RIDE WAS A FIERCE ADVOCATE FOR SCIENCE IN EDUCATION, ESPECIALLY GETTING GIRLS INTERESTED IN SCIENCE.
SHE WROTE BOOKS AND FOUNDED THE NONPROFIT SALLY RIDE SCIENCE TO FURTHER THAT PASSION.
SADLY, SHE DIED OF PANCREATIC CANCER IN 2012.
NASA
SALLY
NASA
THERE WILL BE MANY FIRSTS. FOR THERE ARE STORIES UP THERE IN SPACE.
THERE ARE ADVENTURES.
AND THE LADIES WHO PAVE THE WAY TO THE STARS FOR US WILL ALWAYS BE AN INSPIRATION TO ME.
FIN.

"After covering big-time trials for fifteen years or more, I'm pretty sure I don't act like celluloid newspaper women."
—Agness Underwood

The FIRST with the LATEST

CHRISTINA RICE WRITER | ***JON DAVIS-HUNT*** ARTIST | ***HI-FI*** COLORIST

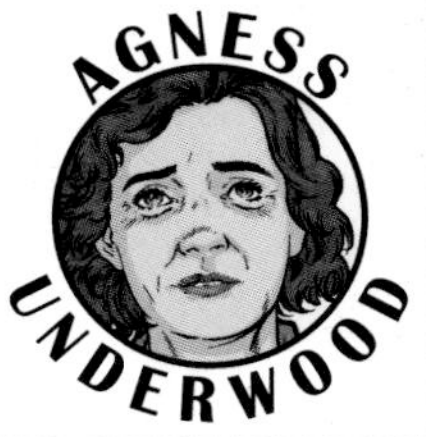

AGNESS UNDERWOOD

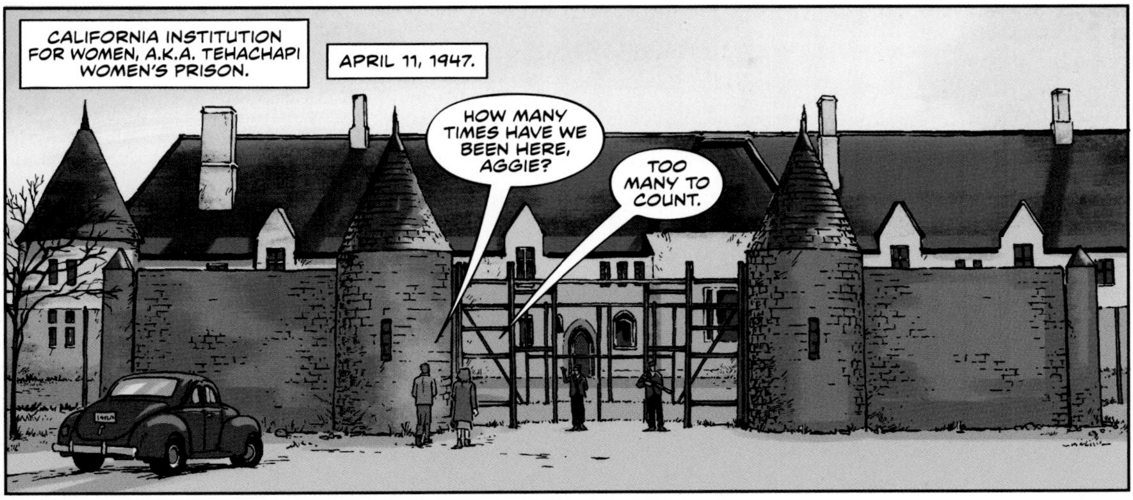

CALIFORNIA INSTITUTION FOR WOMEN, A.K.A. TEHACHAPI WOMEN'S PRISON.
APRIL 11, 1947.
HOW MANY TIMES HAVE WE BEEN HERE, AGGIE?
TOO MANY TO COUNT.

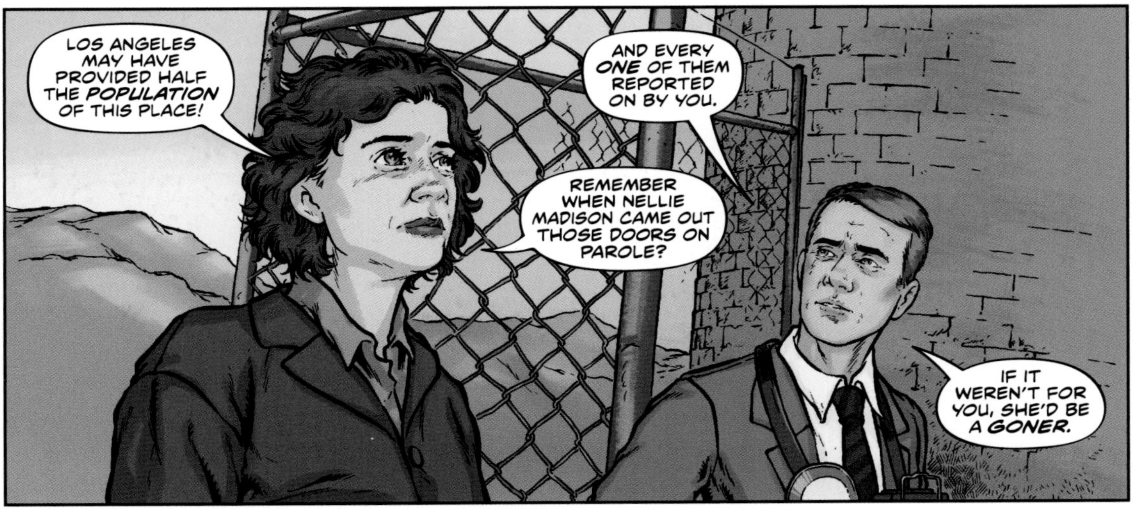

LOS ANGELES MAY HAVE PROVIDED HALF THE *POPULATION* OF THIS PLACE!
AND EVERY *ONE* OF THEM REPORTED ON BY YOU.
REMEMBER WHEN NELLIE MADISON CAME OUT THOSE DOORS ON PAROLE?
IF IT WEREN'T FOR YOU, SHE'D BE A *GONER.*

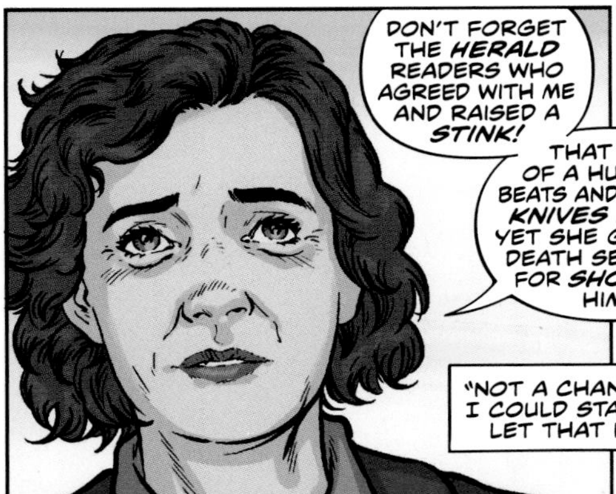

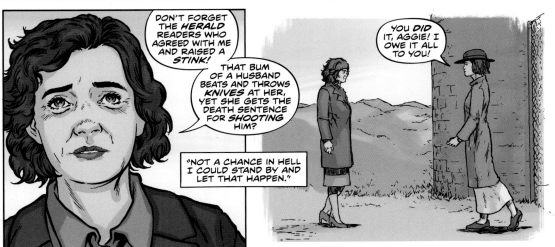

DON'T FORGET THE *HERALD* READERS WHO AGREED WITH ME AND RAISED A *STINK!*
THAT BUM OF A HUSBAND BEATS AND THROWS *KNIVES* AT HER, YET SHE GETS THE DEATH SENTENCE FOR *SHOOTING* HIM?
"NOT A CHANCE IN HELL I COULD STAND BY AND LET THAT HAPPEN."

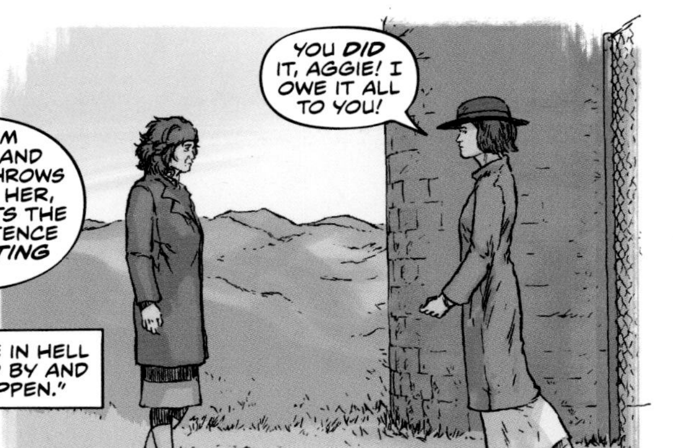

YOU *DID* IT, AGGIE! I OWE IT ALL TO YOU!

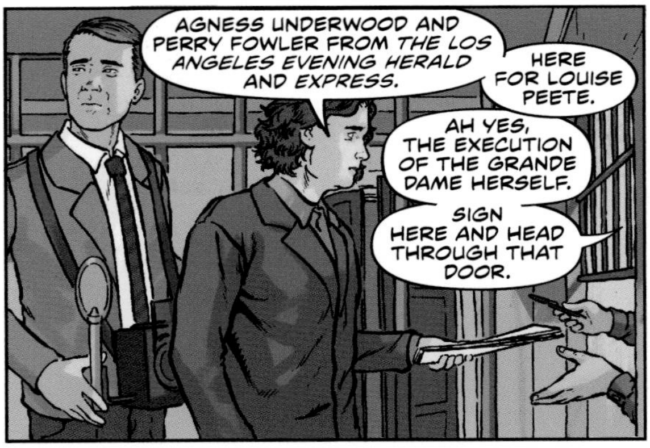
AGNESS UNDERWOOD AND PERRY FOWLER FROM THE LOS ANGELES EVENING HERALD AND EXPRESS.
HERE FOR LOUISE PEETE.
AH YES, THE EXECUTION OF THE GRANDE DAME HERSELF.
SIGN HERE AND HEAD THROUGH THAT DOOR.
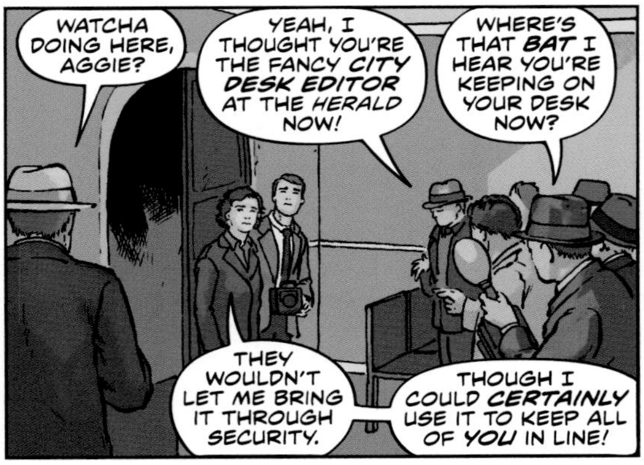
WATCHA DOING HERE, AGGIE?
YEAH, I THOUGHT YOU'RE THE FANCY CITY DESK EDITOR AT THE HERALD NOW!
WHERE'S THAT BAT I HEAR YOU'RE KEEPING ON YOUR DESK NOW?
THEY WOULDN'T LET ME BRING IT THROUGH SECURITY.
THOUGH I COULD CERTAINLY USE IT TO KEEP ALL OF YOU IN LINE!
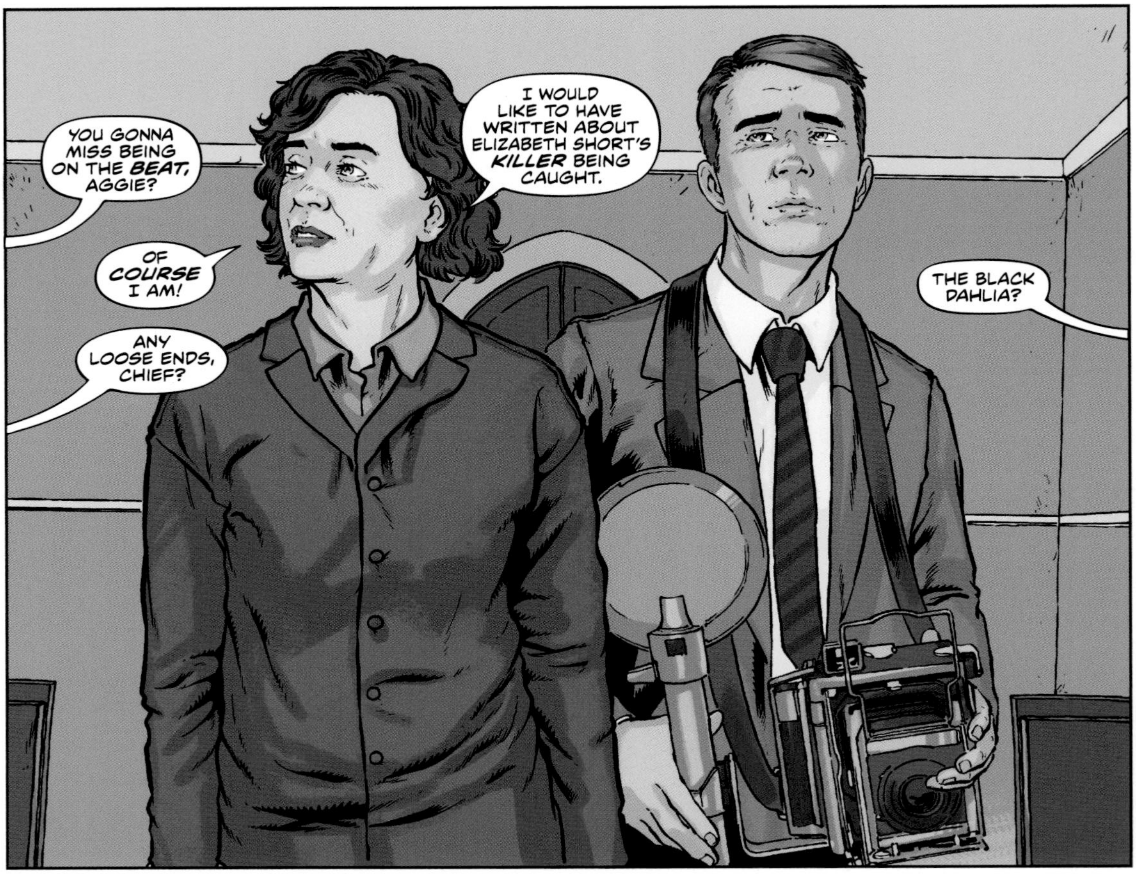
YOU GONNA MISS BEING ON THE BEAT, AGGIE?
OF COURSE I AM!
ANY LOOSE ENDS, CHIEF?
I WOULD LIKE TO HAVE WRITTEN ABOUT ELIZABETH SHORT'S KILLER BEING CAUGHT.
THE BLACK DAHLIA?
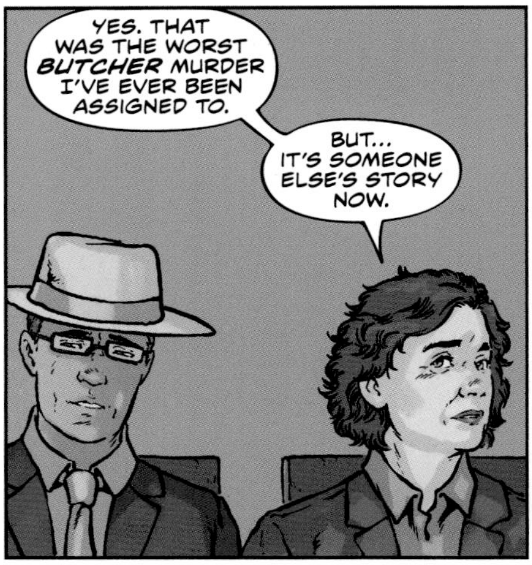
YES. THAT WAS THE WORST BUTCHER MURDER I'VE EVER BEEN ASSIGNED TO.
BUT... IT'S SOMEONE ELSE'S STORY NOW.
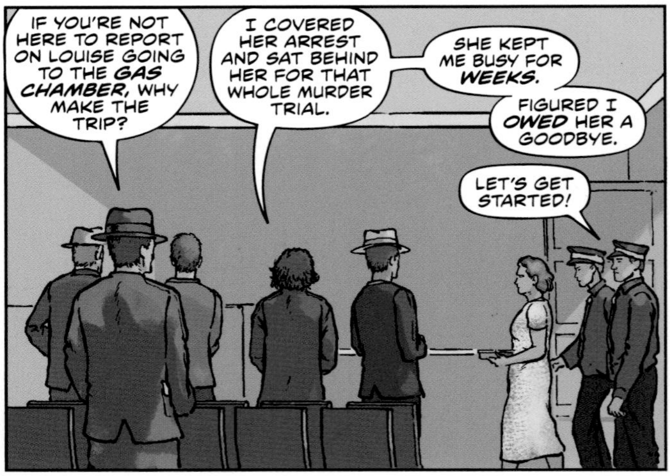
IF YOU'RE NOT HERE TO REPORT ON LOUISE GOING TO THE GAS CHAMBER, WHY MAKE THE TRIP?
I COVERED HER ARREST AND SAT BEHIND HER FOR THAT WHOLE MURDER TRIAL.
SHE KEPT ME BUSY FOR WEEKS.
FIGURED I OWED HER A GOODBYE.
LET'S GET STARTED!

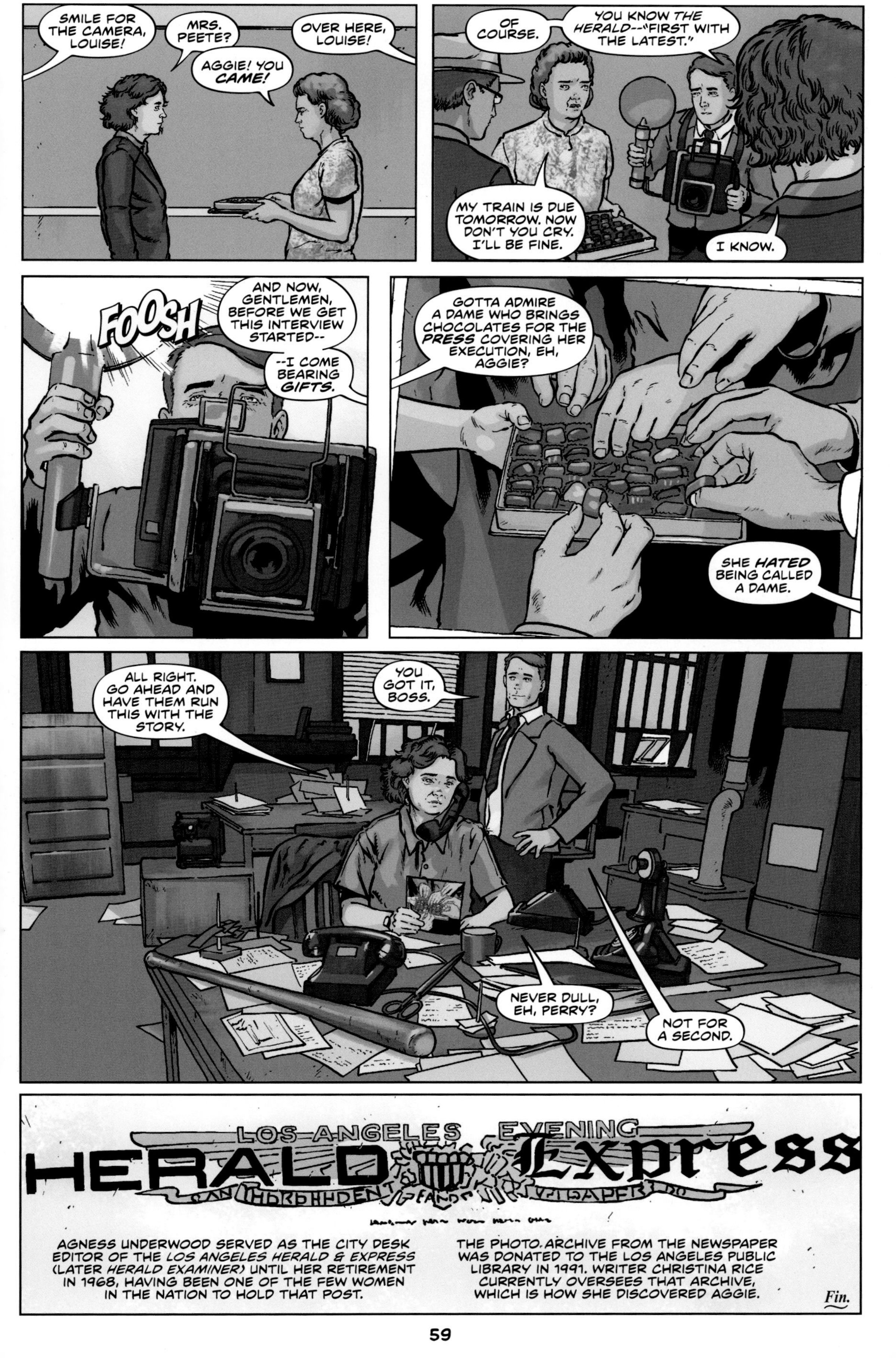
SMILE FOR THE CAMERA, LOUISE!
MRS. PEETE?
AGGIE! YOU *CAME!*
OVER HERE, LOUISE!
OF COURSE.
YOU KNOW *THE HERALD*--"FIRST WITH THE LATEST."
MY TRAIN IS DUE TOMORROW. NOW DON'T YOU CRY. I'LL BE FINE.
I KNOW.
FOOSH
AND NOW, GENTLEMEN, BEFORE WE GET THIS INTERVIEW STARTED--
--I COME BEARING *GIFTS.*
GOTTA ADMIRE A DAME WHO BRINGS CHOCOLATES FOR THE *PRESS* COVERING HER EXECUTION, EH, AGGIE?
SHE *HATED* BEING CALLED A DAME.
ALL RIGHT. GO AHEAD AND HAVE THEM RUN THIS WITH THE STORY.
YOU GOT IT, BOSS.
NEVER DULL, EH, PERRY?
NOT FOR A SECOND.

LOS ANGELES EVENING HERALD Express

AGNESS UNDERWOOD SERVED AS THE CITY DESK EDITOR OF THE *LOS ANGELES HERALD & EXPRESS* (LATER *HERALD EXAMINER*) UNTIL HER RETIREMENT IN 1968, HAVING BEEN ONE OF THE FEW WOMEN IN THE NATION TO HOLD THAT POST.

THE PHOTO ARCHIVE FROM THE NEWSPAPER WAS DONATED TO THE LOS ANGELES PUBLIC LIBRARY IN 1991. WRITER CHRISTINA RICE CURRENTLY OVERSEES THAT ARCHIVE, WHICH IS HOW SHE DISCOVERED AGGIE.

Fin.

"Well, dear, when you think about La MaMa embracing the global consciousness, we have been doing that since our first tour to Europe in 1965. We've just always been global. Hasn't been any different. Can you imagine in '66 we were playing in Yugoslavia?"

—Ellen Stewart

Within the Dimensions of Love

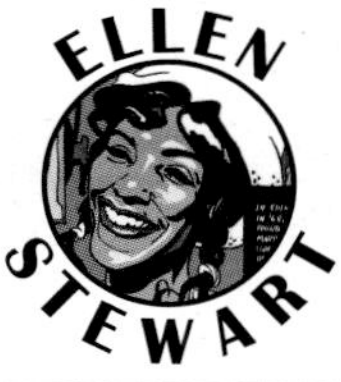
ELLEN
STEWART

RONALD WIMBERLY
WRITER/ARTIST

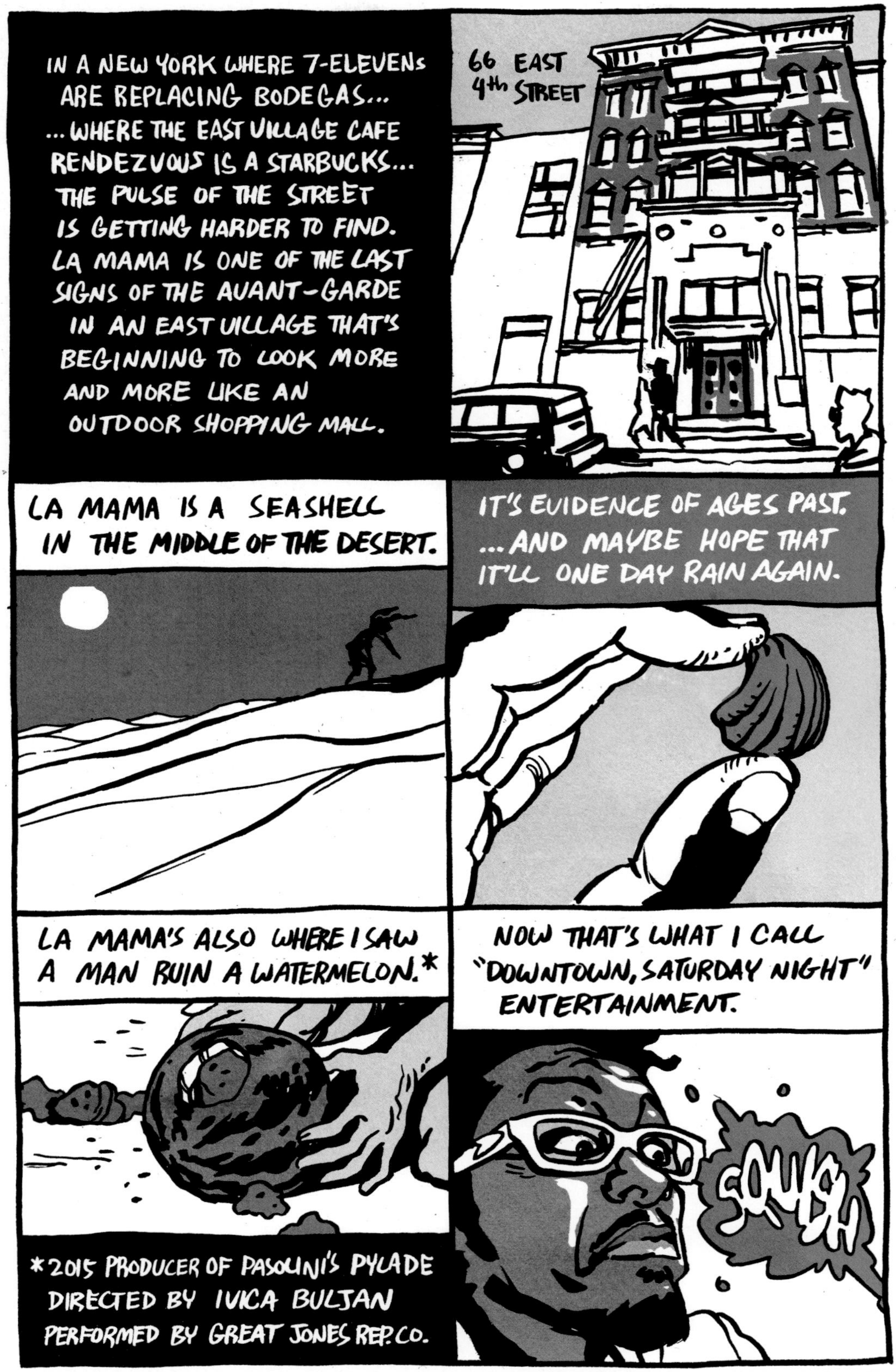
IN A NEW YORK WHERE 7-ELEVENS ARE REPLACING BODEGAS... ...WHERE THE EAST VILLAGE CAFE RENDEZVOUS IS A STARBUCKS... THE PULSE OF THE STREET IS GETTING HARDER TO FIND. LA MAMA IS ONE OF THE LAST SIGNS OF THE AVANT-GARDE IN AN EAST VILLAGE THAT'S BEGINNING TO LOOK MORE AND MORE LIKE AN OUTDOOR SHOPPING MALL.
66 EAST 4th STREET
LA MAMA IS A SEASHELL IN THE MIDDLE OF THE DESERT.
IT'S EVIDENCE OF AGES PAST. ...AND MAYBE HOPE THAT IT'LL ONE DAY RAIN AGAIN.
LA MAMA'S ALSO WHERE I SAW A MAN RUIN A WATERMELON.*
*2015 PRODUCER OF PASOLINI'S PYLADE DIRECTED BY IVICA BULJAN PERFORMED BY GREAT JONES REP. CO.
NOW THAT'S WHAT I CALL "DOWNTOWN, SATURDAY NIGHT" ENTERTAINMENT.
SQUISH

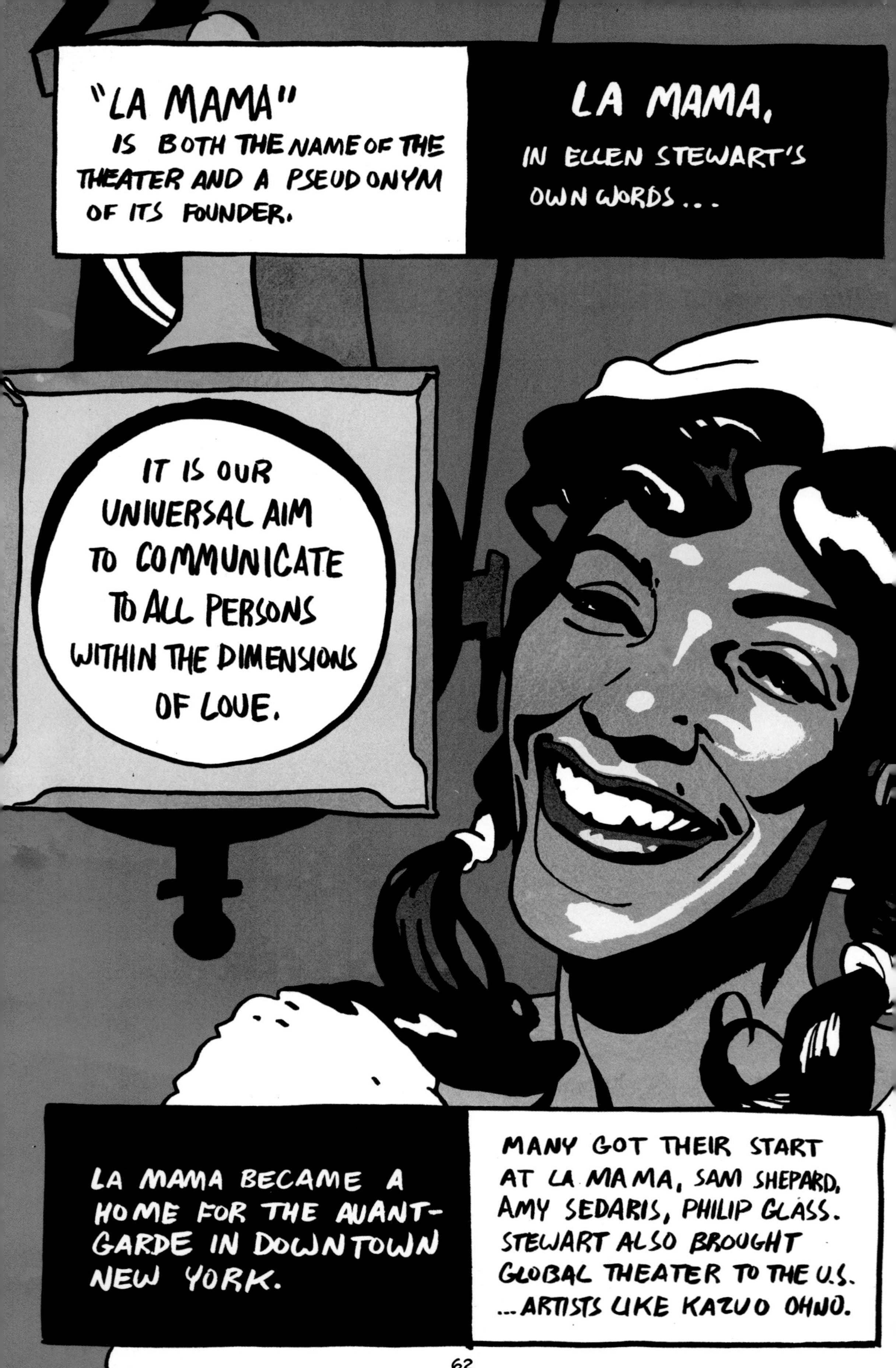

"LA MAMA" IS BOTH THE NAME OF THE THEATER AND A PSEUDONYM OF ITS FOUNDER.
LA MAMA, IN ELLEN STEWART'S OWN WORDS...
IT IS OUR UNIVERSAL AIM TO COMMUNICATE TO ALL PERSONS WITHIN THE DIMENSIONS OF LOVE.
LA MAMA BECAME A HOME FOR THE AVANT-GARDE IN DOWNTOWN NEW YORK.
MANY GOT THEIR START AT LA MAMA, SAM SHEPARD, AMY SEDARIS, PHILIP GLASS. STEWART ALSO BROUGHT GLOBAL THEATER TO THE U.S. ...ARTISTS LIKE KAZUO OHNO.

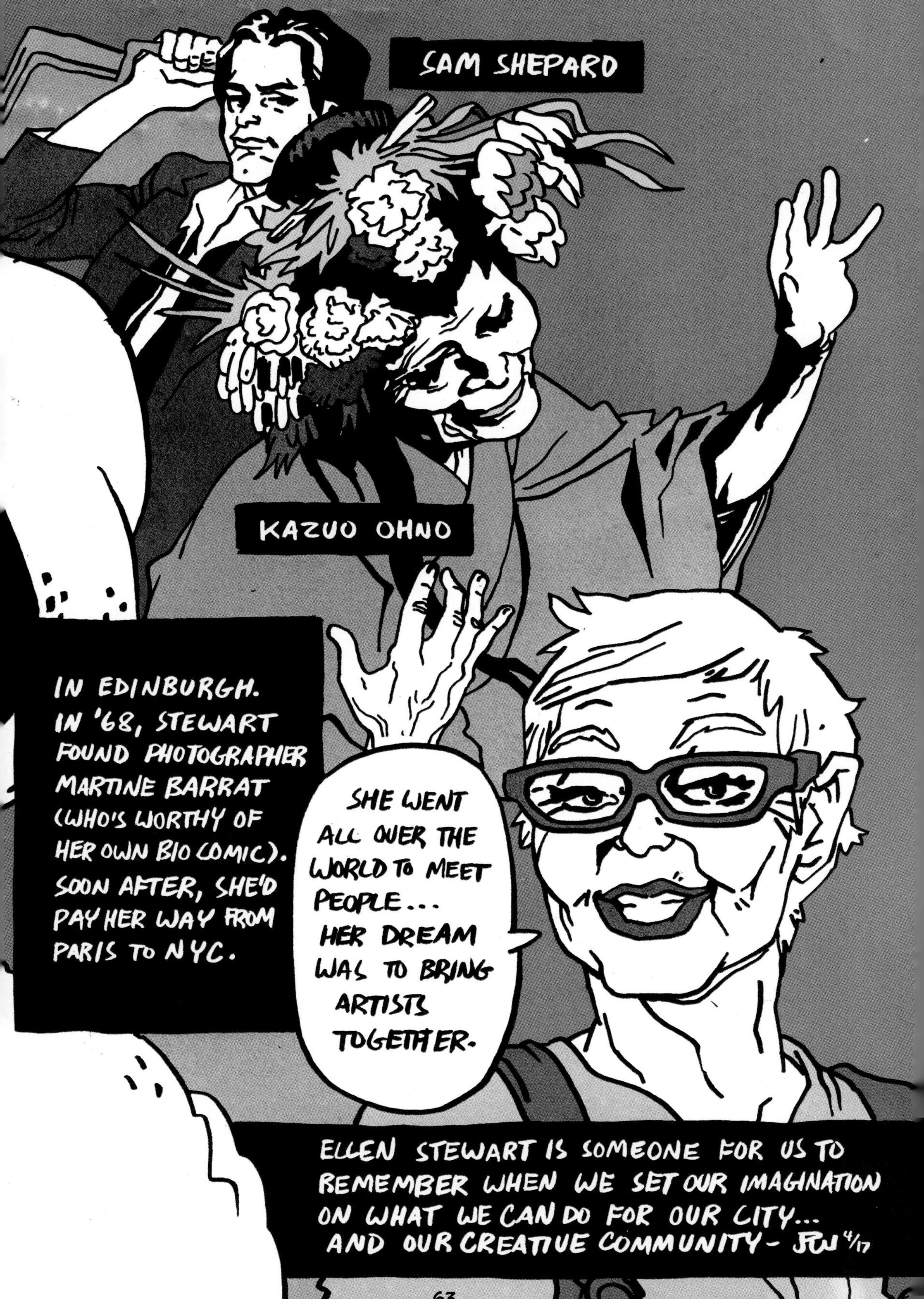
SAM SHEPARD
KAZUO OHNO
IN EDINBURGH. IN '68, STEWART FOUND PHOTOGRAPHER MARTINE BARRAT (WHO'S WORTHY OF HER OWN BIO COMIC). SOON AFTER, SHE'D PAY HER WAY FROM PARIS TO NYC.
SHE WENT ALL OVER THE WORLD TO MEET PEOPLE... HER DREAM WAS TO BRING ARTISTS TOGETHER.
ELLEN STEWART IS SOMEONE FOR US TO REMEMBER WHEN WE SET OUR IMAGINATION ON WHAT WE CAN DO FOR OUR CITY... AND OUR CREATIVE COMMUNITY - JCW 4/17

"Brenda was already a reporter when the strip started, but she was sick and tired of covering nothing but ice-cream socials. She wanted a job with action, like the men reporters had."

—Dale Messick

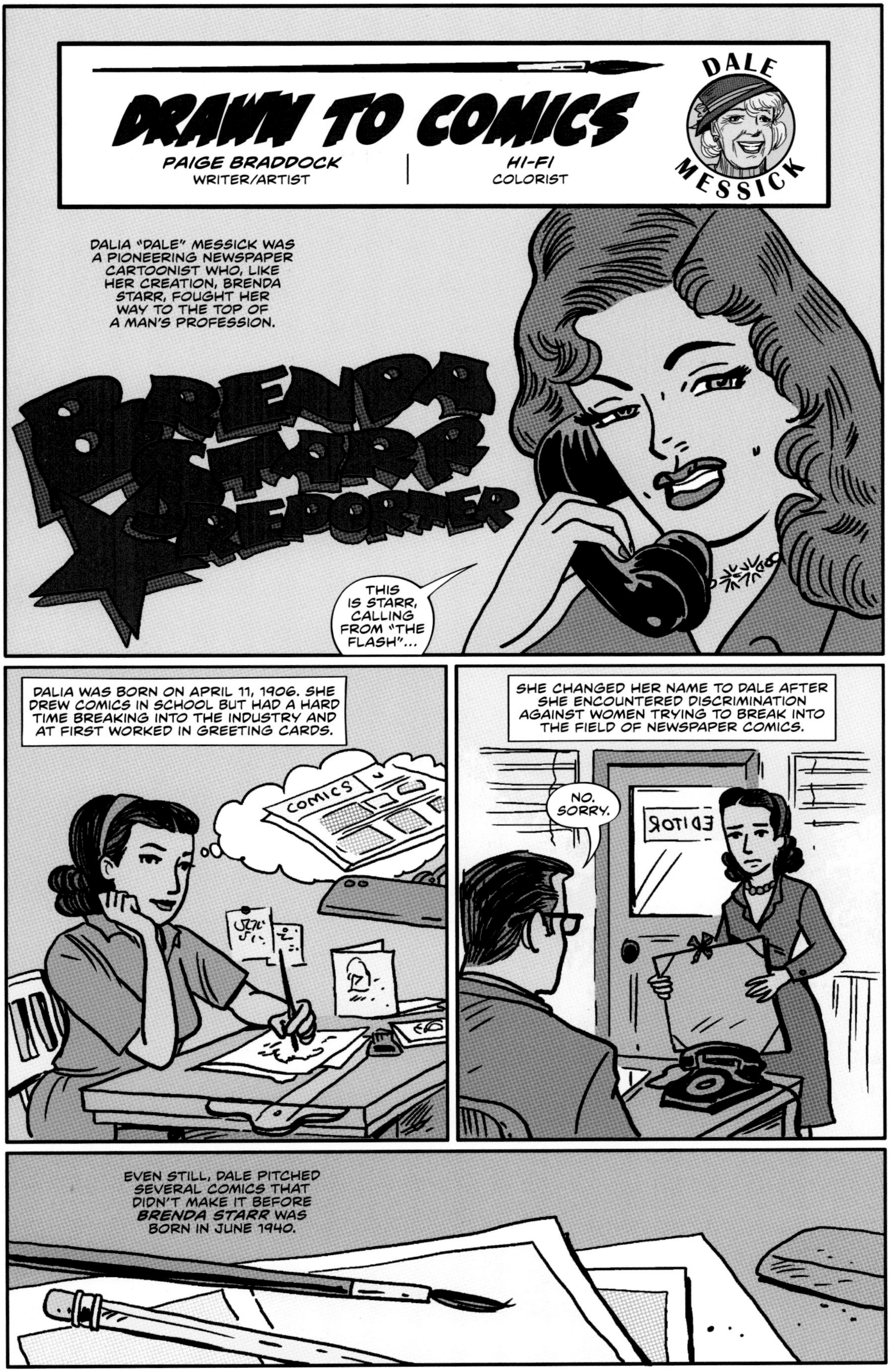
DRAWN TO COMICS
PAIGE BRADDOCK
WRITER/ARTIST
HI-FI
COLORIST
DALE MESSICK
DALIA "DALE" MESSICK WAS A PIONEERING NEWSPAPER CARTOONIST WHO, LIKE HER CREATION, BRENDA STARR, FOUGHT HER WAY TO THE TOP OF A MAN'S PROFESSION.
BRENDA STARR REPORTER
THIS IS STARR, CALLING FROM "THE FLASH"...
DALIA WAS BORN ON APRIL 11, 1906. SHE DREW COMICS IN SCHOOL BUT HAD A HARD TIME BREAKING INTO THE INDUSTRY AND AT FIRST WORKED IN GREETING CARDS.
COMICS
SHE CHANGED HER NAME TO DALE AFTER SHE ENCOUNTERED DISCRIMINATION AGAINST WOMEN TRYING TO BREAK INTO THE FIELD OF NEWSPAPER COMICS.
NO. SORRY.
EVEN STILL, DALE PITCHED SEVERAL COMICS THAT DIDN'T MAKE IT BEFORE *BRENDA STARR* WAS BORN IN JUNE 1940.

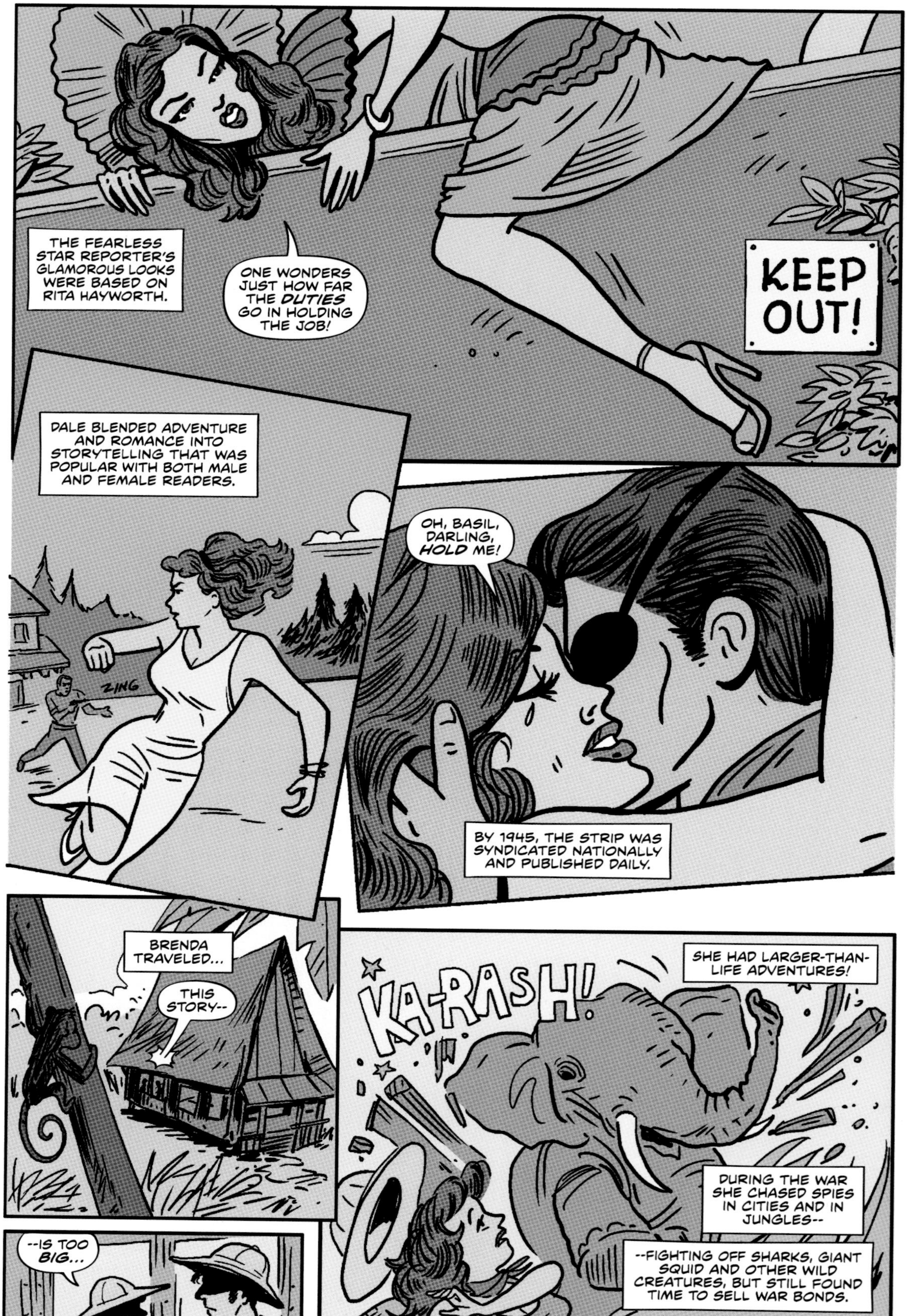
THE FEARLESS STAR REPORTER'S GLAMOROUS LOOKS WERE BASED ON RITA HAYWORTH.
ONE WONDERS JUST HOW FAR THE *DUTIES* GO IN HOLDING THE JOB!
KEEP OUT!
DALE BLENDED ADVENTURE AND ROMANCE INTO STORYTELLING THAT WAS POPULAR WITH BOTH MALE AND FEMALE READERS.
ZING
OH, BASIL, DARLING, ***HOLD*** ME!
BY 1945, THE STRIP WAS SYNDICATED NATIONALLY AND PUBLISHED DAILY.
BRENDA TRAVELED...
THIS STORY--
--IS TOO *BIG*...
KA-RASH!
SHE HAD LARGER-THAN-LIFE ADVENTURES!
DURING THE WAR SHE CHASED SPIES IN CITIES AND IN JUNGLES--
--FIGHTING OFF SHARKS, GIANT SQUID AND OTHER WILD CREATURES, BUT STILL FOUND TIME TO SELL WAR BONDS.
AND SHE DID IT ALL WITH PERFECT HAIR AND SPARKLES IN HER EYES.

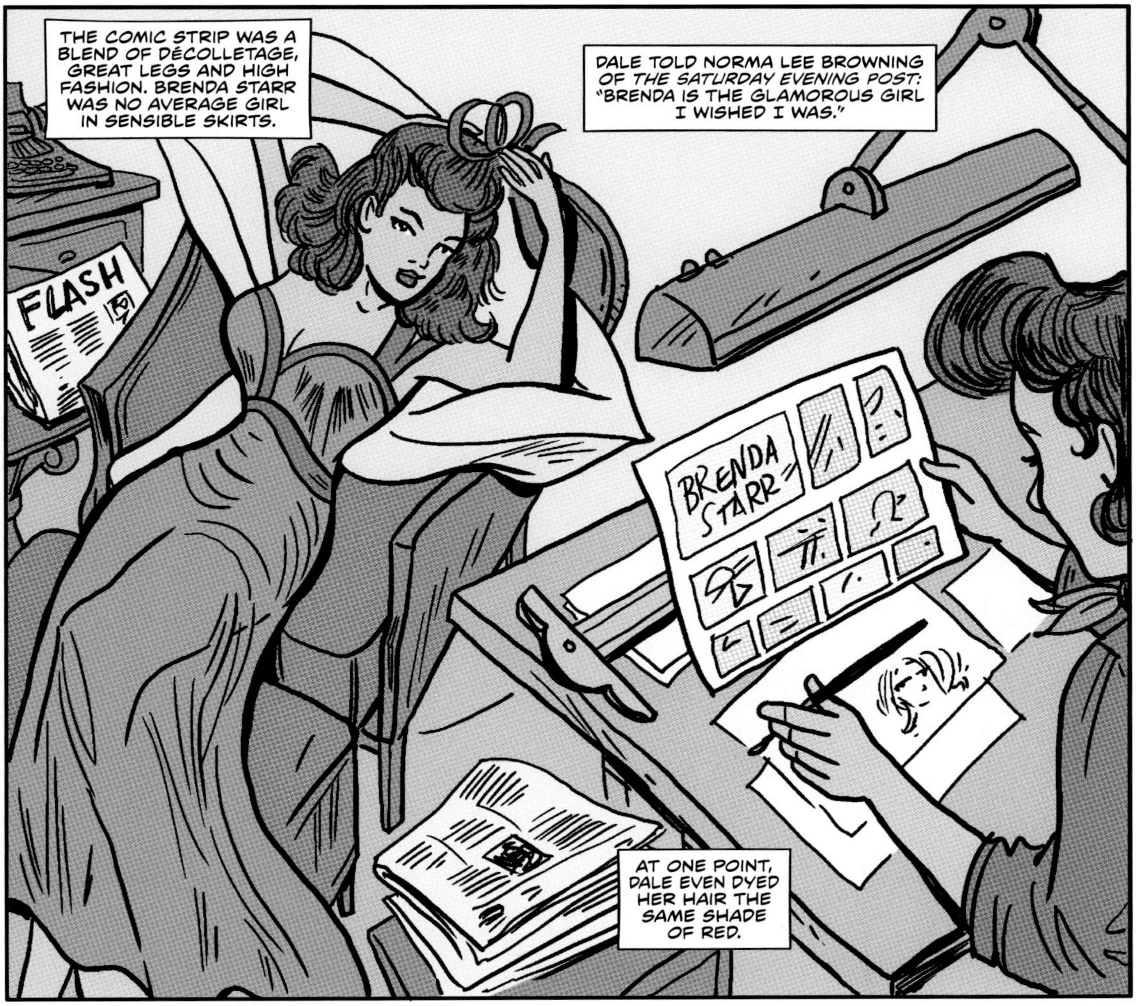
THE COMIC STRIP WAS A BLEND OF DÉCOLLETAGE, GREAT LEGS AND HIGH FASHION. BRENDA STARR WAS NO AVERAGE GIRL IN SENSIBLE SKIRTS.
DALE TOLD NORMA LEE BROWNING OF *THE SATURDAY EVENING POST*: "BRENDA IS THE GLAMOROUS GIRL I WISHED I WAS."
FLASH
BRENDA STARR
AT ONE POINT, DALE EVEN DYED HER HAIR THE SAME SHADE OF RED.

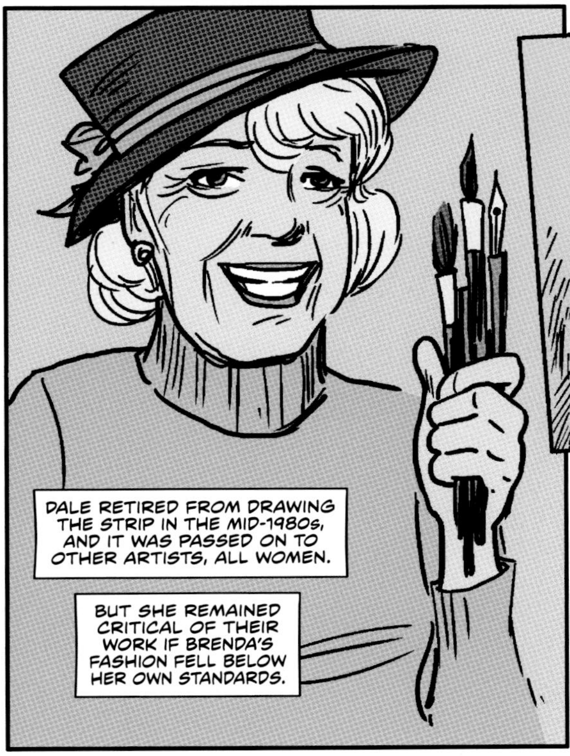
DALE RETIRED FROM DRAWING THE STRIP IN THE MID-1980s, AND IT WAS PASSED ON TO OTHER ARTISTS, ALL WOMEN.
BUT SHE REMAINED CRITICAL OF THEIR WORK IF BRENDA'S FASHION FELL BELOW HER OWN STANDARDS.

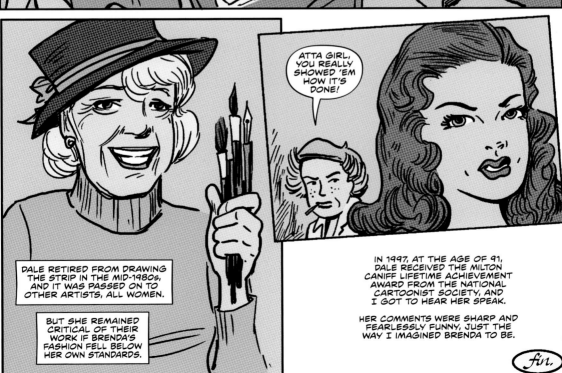

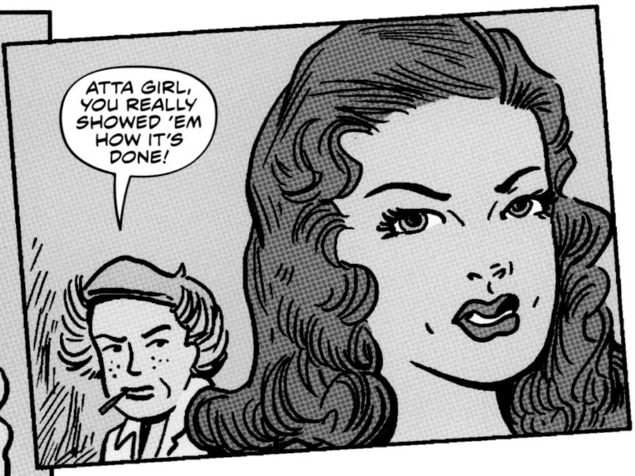
ATTA GIRL, YOU REALLY SHOWED 'EM HOW IT'S DONE!

IN 1997, AT THE AGE OF 91, DALE RECEIVED THE MILTON CANIFF LIFETIME ACHIEVEMENT AWARD FROM THE NATIONAL CARTOONIST SOCIETY, AND I GOT TO HEAR HER SPEAK.

HER COMMENTS WERE SHARP AND FEARLESSLY FUNNY, JUST THE WAY I IMAGINED BRENDA TO BE.

fin.

"I'm a woman, I'm black, I'm curvy and I'm trans. There are a lot of things that I deal with. When I talk about those things, I am literally talking about my embodiment of these intersections."
—Kat Blaque

THANK YOU

TESS FOWLER
WRITER/ARTIST

HI-FI
COLORIST

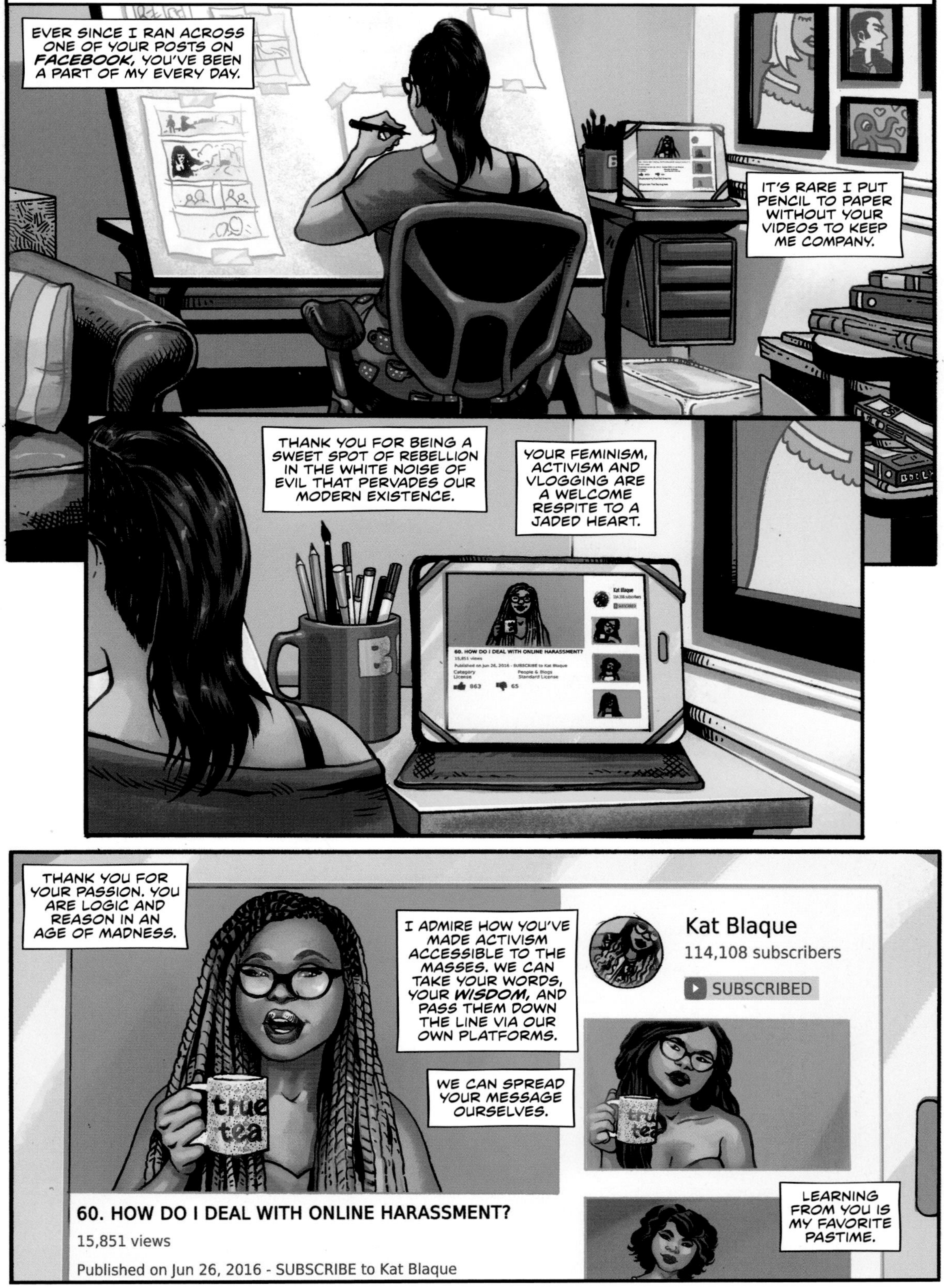

EVER SINCE I RAN ACROSS ONE OF YOUR POSTS ON ***FACEBOOK***, YOU'VE BEEN A PART OF MY EVERY DAY.
IT'S RARE I PUT PENCIL TO PAPER WITHOUT YOUR VIDEOS TO KEEP ME COMPANY.
THANK YOU FOR BEING A SWEET SPOT OF REBELLION IN THE WHITE NOISE OF EVIL THAT PERVADES OUR MODERN EXISTENCE.
YOUR FEMINISM, ACTIVISM AND VLOGGING ARE A WELCOME RESPITE TO A JADED HEART.
THANK YOU FOR YOUR PASSION. YOU ARE LOGIC AND REASON IN AN AGE OF MADNESS.
I ADMIRE HOW YOU'VE MADE ACTIVISM ACCESSIBLE TO THE MASSES. WE CAN TAKE YOUR WORDS, YOUR ***WISDOM***, AND PASS THEM DOWN THE LINE VIA OUR OWN PLATFORMS.
WE CAN SPREAD YOUR MESSAGE OURSELVES.
Kat Blaque
114,108 subscribers
SUBSCRIBED
true tea
60. HOW DO I DEAL WITH ONLINE HARASSMENT?
15,851 views
Published on Jun 26, 2016 - SUBSCRIBE to Kat Blaque
LEARNING FROM YOU IS MY FAVORITE PASTIME.

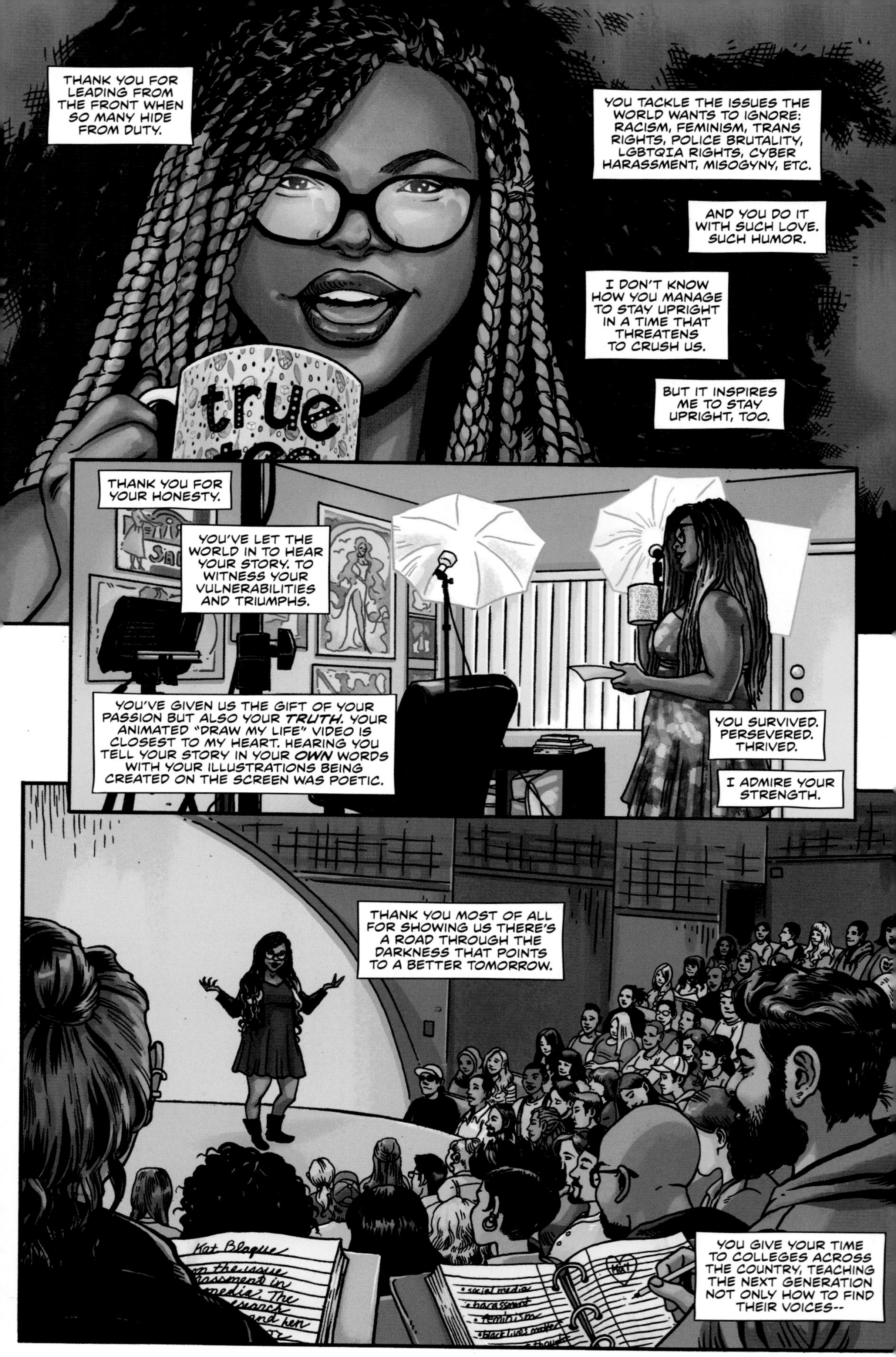
THANK YOU FOR LEADING FROM THE FRONT WHEN SO MANY HIDE FROM DUTY.
true
YOU TACKLE THE ISSUES THE WORLD WANTS TO IGNORE: RACISM, FEMINISM, TRANS RIGHTS, POLICE BRUTALITY, LGBTQIA RIGHTS, CYBER HARASSMENT, MISOGYNY, ETC.
AND YOU DO IT WITH SUCH LOVE. SUCH HUMOR.
I DON'T KNOW HOW YOU MANAGE TO STAY UPRIGHT IN A TIME THAT THREATENS TO CRUSH US.
BUT IT INSPIRES ME TO STAY UPRIGHT, TOO.
THANK YOU FOR YOUR HONESTY.
YOU'VE LET THE WORLD IN TO HEAR YOUR STORY. TO WITNESS YOUR VULNERABILITIES AND TRIUMPHS.
YOU'VE GIVEN US THE GIFT OF YOUR PASSION BUT ALSO YOUR *TRUTH.* YOUR ANIMATED "DRAW MY LIFE" VIDEO IS CLOSEST TO MY HEART. HEARING YOU TELL YOUR STORY IN YOUR *OWN* WORDS WITH YOUR ILLUSTRATIONS BEING CREATED ON THE SCREEN WAS POETIC.
YOU SURVIVED. PERSEVERED. THRIVED.
I ADMIRE YOUR STRENGTH.
THANK YOU MOST OF ALL FOR SHOWING US THERE'S A ROAD THROUGH THE DARKNESS THAT POINTS TO A BETTER TOMORROW.
Kat Blaque
Kat
• social media
• harassment
• feminism
• black lives matter
YOU GIVE YOUR TIME TO COLLEGES ACROSS THE COUNTRY, TEACHING THE NEXT GENERATION NOT ONLY HOW TO FIND THEIR VOICES--

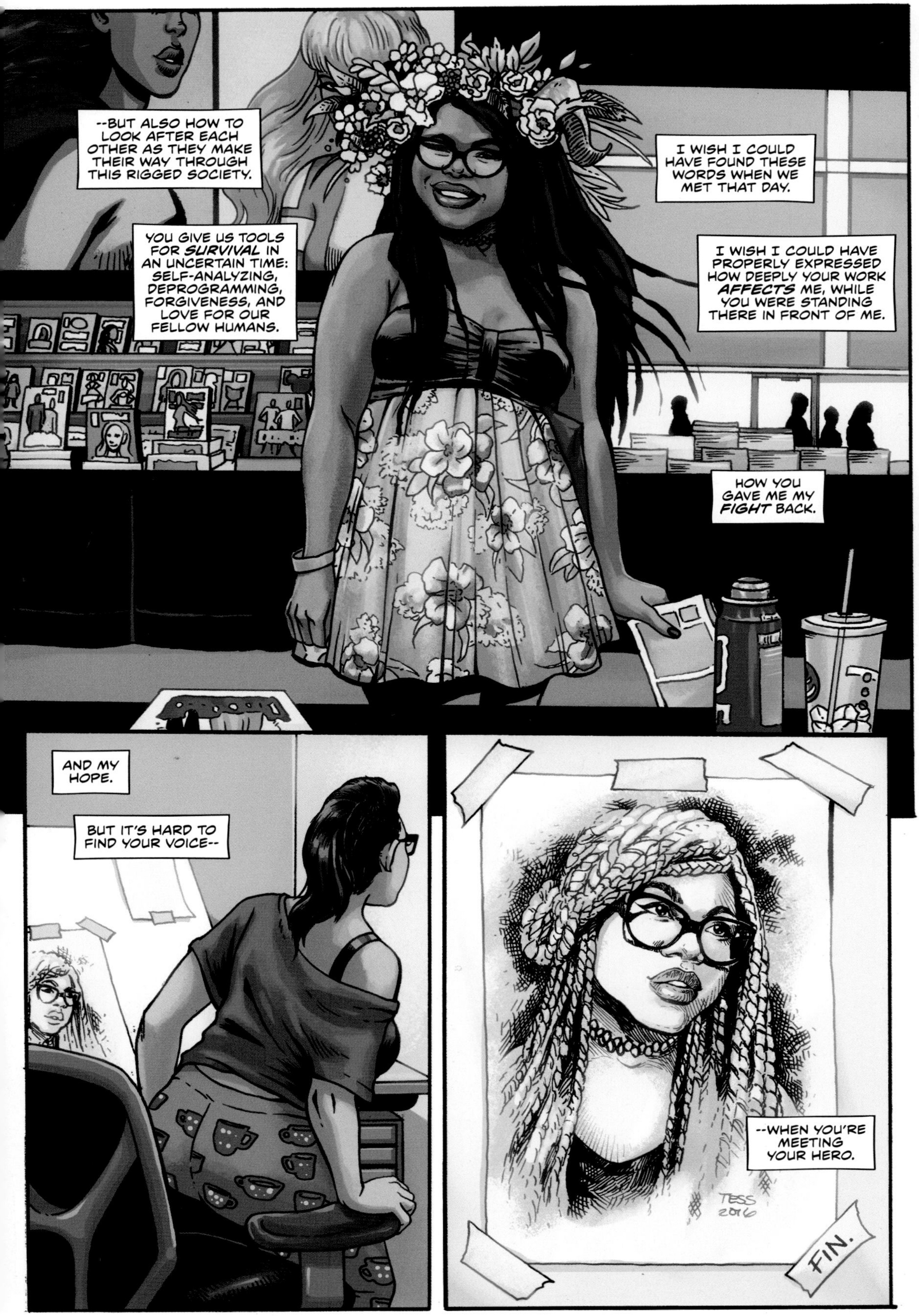
--BUT ALSO HOW TO LOOK AFTER EACH OTHER AS THEY MAKE THEIR WAY THROUGH THIS RIGGED SOCIETY.
YOU GIVE US TOOLS FOR ***SURVIVAL*** IN AN UNCERTAIN TIME: SELF-ANALYZING, DEPROGRAMMING, FORGIVENESS, AND LOVE FOR OUR FELLOW HUMANS.
I WISH I COULD HAVE FOUND THESE WORDS WHEN WE MET THAT DAY.
I WISH I COULD HAVE PROPERLY EXPRESSED HOW DEEPLY YOUR WORK ***AFFECTS*** ME, WHILE YOU WERE STANDING THERE IN FRONT OF ME.
HOW YOU GAVE ME MY ***FIGHT*** BACK.
AND MY HOPE.
BUT IT'S HARD TO FIND YOUR VOICE--
--WHEN YOU'RE MEETING YOUR HERO.
TESS 2016
FIN.

"We are volcanoes. When we women offer our experience as our truth, as human truth, all the maps change. There are new mountains."

—Ursula K. Le Guin

THE WALL

ROBIN FURTH WRITER | *DEVAKI NEOGI* ARTIST | *HI-FI* COLORIST

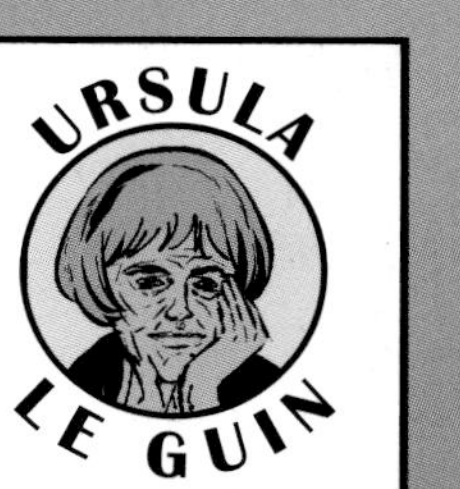
URSULA
LE GUIN

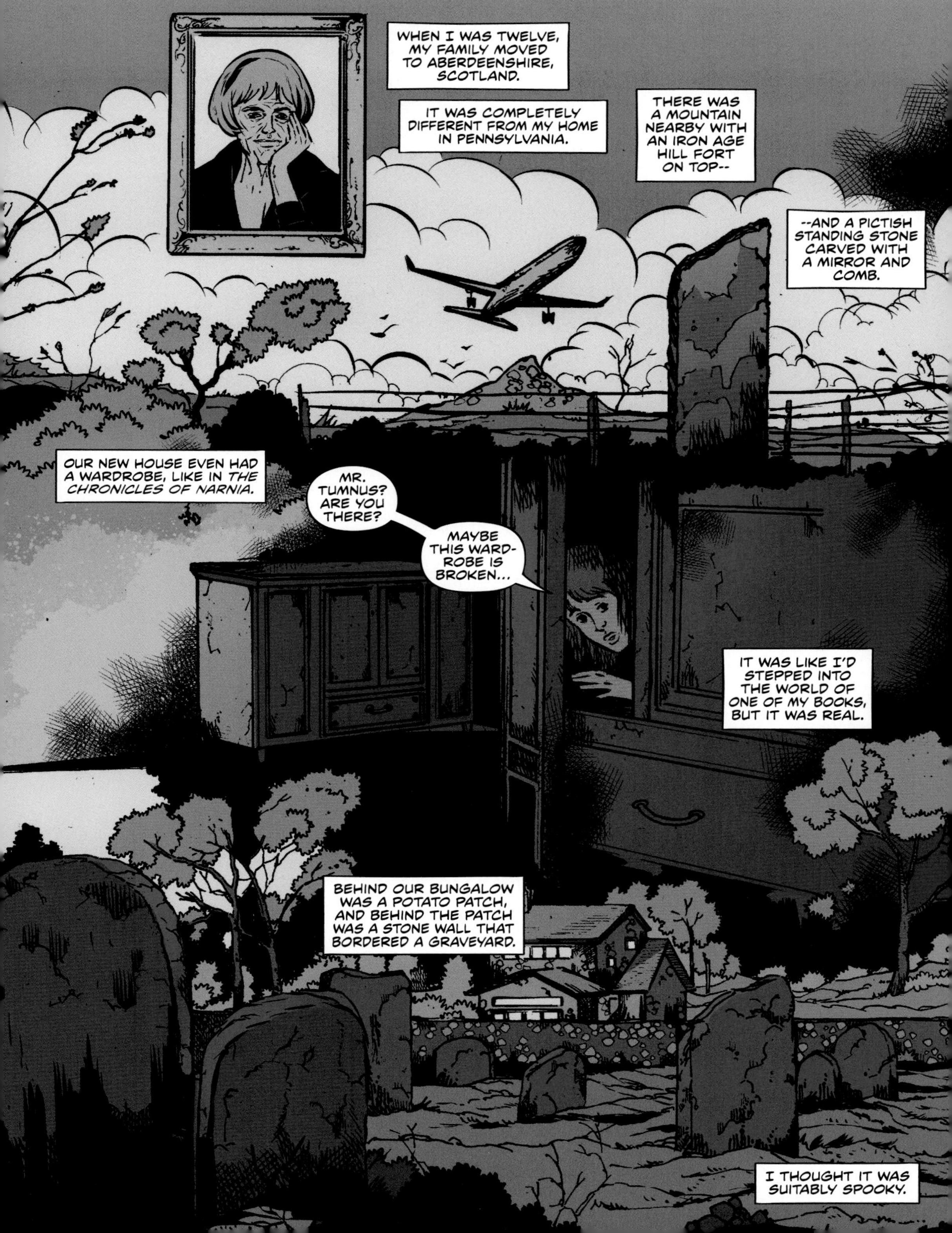
WHEN I WAS TWELVE, MY FAMILY MOVED TO ABERDEENSHIRE, SCOTLAND.
IT WAS COMPLETELY DIFFERENT FROM MY HOME IN PENNSYLVANIA.
THERE WAS A MOUNTAIN NEARBY WITH AN IRON AGE HILL FORT ON TOP--
--AND A PICTISH STANDING STONE CARVED WITH A MIRROR AND COMB.
OUR NEW HOUSE EVEN HAD A WARDROBE, LIKE IN *THE CHRONICLES OF NARNIA*.
MR. TUMNUS? ARE YOU THERE?
MAYBE THIS WARD-ROBE IS BROKEN...
IT WAS LIKE I'D STEPPED INTO THE WORLD OF ONE OF MY BOOKS, BUT IT WAS REAL.
BEHIND OUR BUNGALOW WAS A POTATO PATCH, AND BEHIND THE PATCH WAS A STONE WALL THAT BORDERED A GRAVEYARD.
I THOUGHT IT WAS SUITABLY SPOOKY.

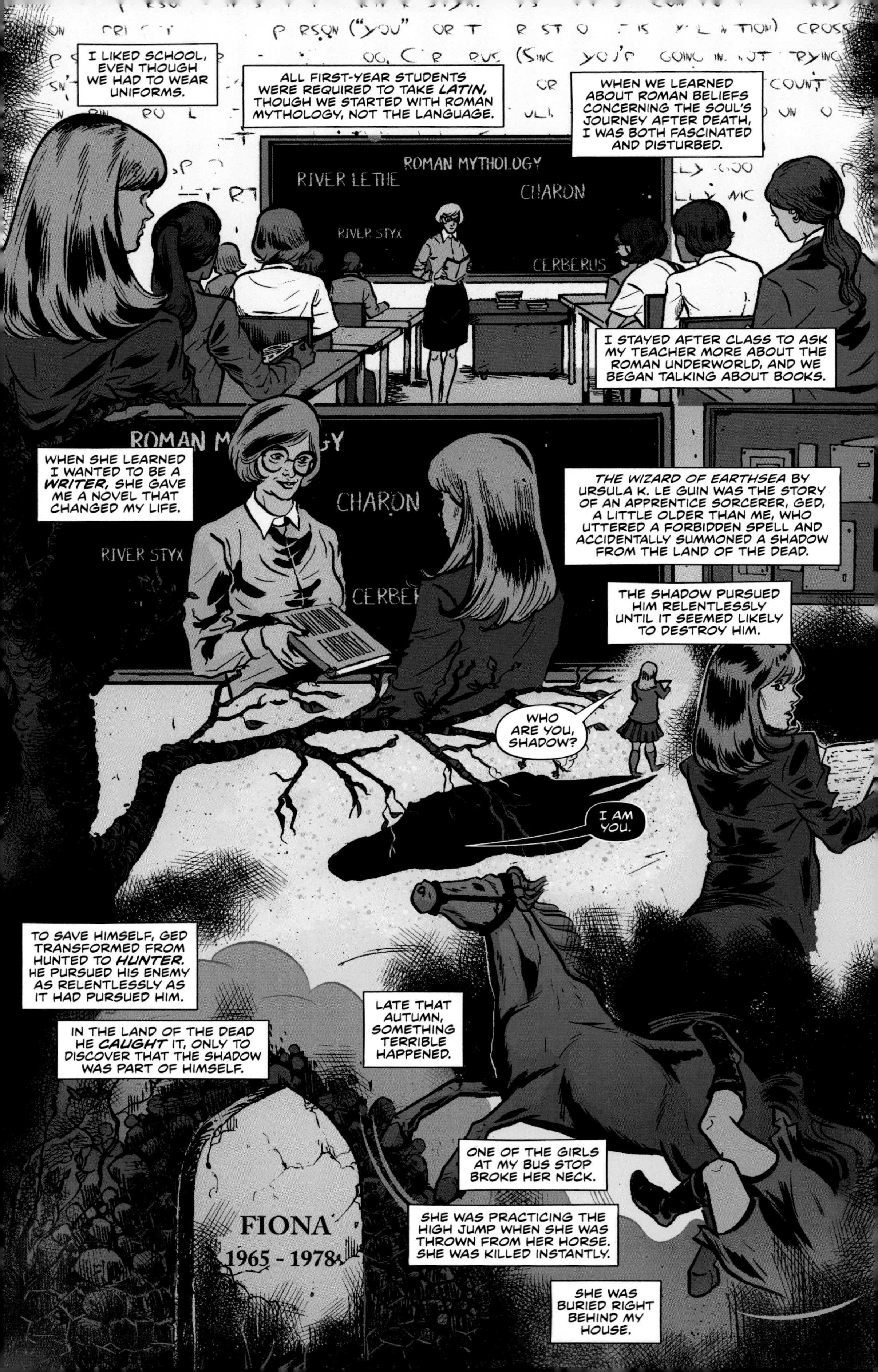
I LIKED SCHOOL, EVEN THOUGH WE HAD TO WEAR UNIFORMS.
ALL FIRST-YEAR STUDENTS WERE REQUIRED TO TAKE *LATIN,* THOUGH WE STARTED WITH ROMAN MYTHOLOGY, NOT THE LANGUAGE.
WHEN WE LEARNED ABOUT ROMAN BELIEFS CONCERNING THE SOUL'S JOURNEY AFTER DEATH, I WAS BOTH FASCINATED AND DISTURBED.
ROMAN MYTHOLOGY
RIVER LETHE
CHARON
RIVER STYX
CERBERUS
I STAYED AFTER CLASS TO ASK MY TEACHER MORE ABOUT THE ROMAN UNDERWORLD, AND WE BEGAN TALKING ABOUT BOOKS.
WHEN SHE LEARNED I WANTED TO BE A ***WRITER,*** SHE GAVE ME A NOVEL THAT CHANGED MY LIFE.
CHARON
RIVER STYX
THE WIZARD OF EARTHSEA BY URSULA K. LE GUIN WAS THE STORY OF AN APPRENTICE SORCERER, GED, A LITTLE OLDER THAN ME, WHO UTTERED A FORBIDDEN SPELL AND ACCIDENTALLY SUMMONED A SHADOW FROM THE LAND OF THE DEAD.
THE SHADOW PURSUED HIM RELENTLESSLY UNTIL IT SEEMED LIKELY TO DESTROY HIM.
WHO ARE YOU, SHADOW?
I AM YOU.
TO SAVE HIMSELF, GED TRANSFORMED FROM HUNTED TO ***HUNTER.*** HE PURSUED HIS ENEMY AS RELENTLESSLY AS IT HAD PURSUED HIM.
IN THE LAND OF THE DEAD HE ***CAUGHT*** IT, ONLY TO DISCOVER THAT THE SHADOW WAS PART OF HIMSELF.
LATE THAT AUTUMN, SOMETHING TERRIBLE HAPPENED.
ONE OF THE GIRLS AT MY BUS STOP BROKE HER NECK.
FIONA
1965 - 1978
SHE WAS PRACTICING THE HIGH JUMP WHEN SHE WAS THROWN FROM HER HORSE. SHE WAS KILLED INSTANTLY.
SHE WAS BURIED RIGHT BEHIND MY HOUSE.

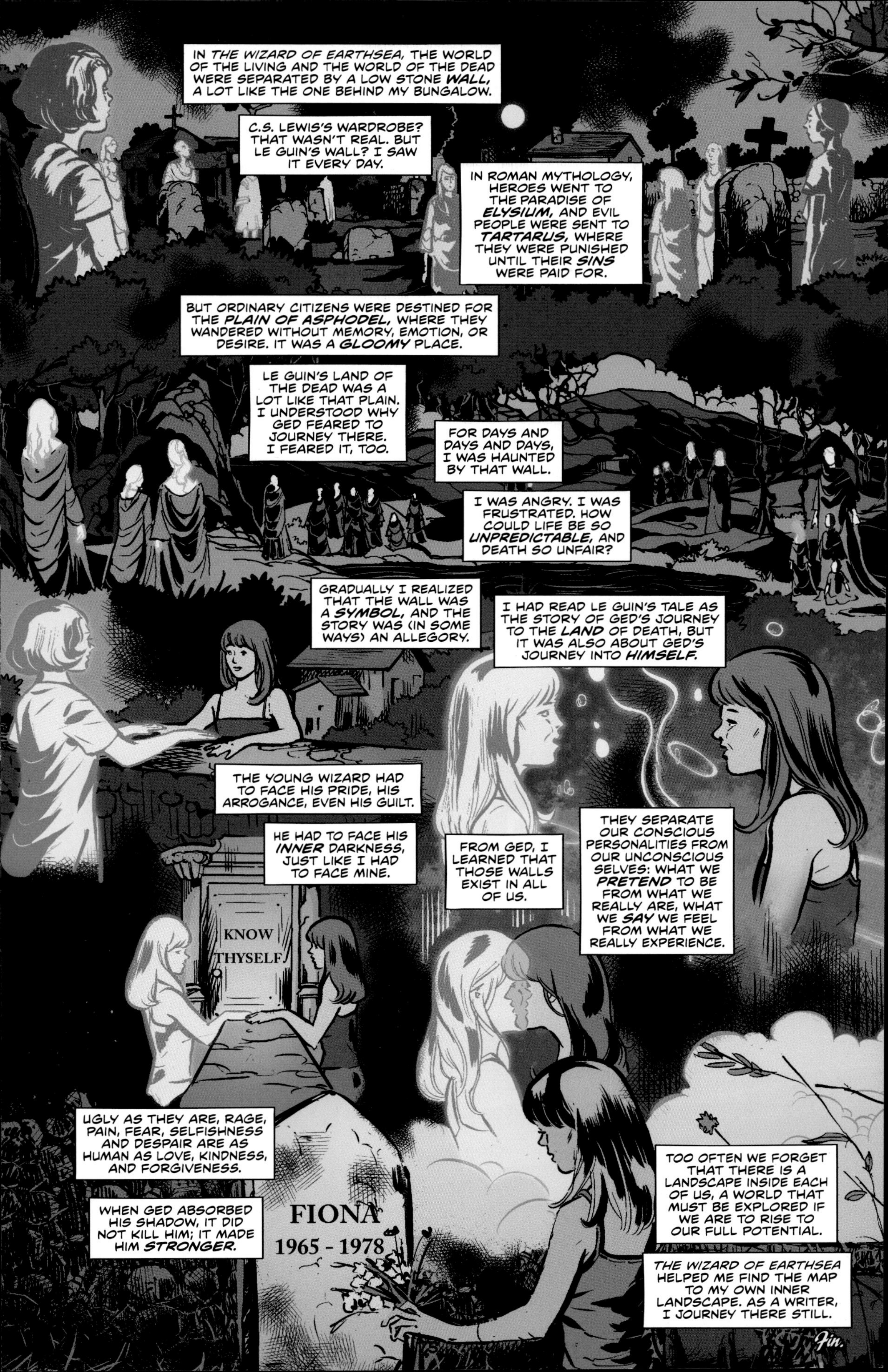
IN *THE WIZARD OF EARTHSEA*, THE WORLD OF THE LIVING AND THE WORLD OF THE DEAD WERE SEPARATED BY A LOW STONE **WALL**, A LOT LIKE THE ONE BEHIND MY BUNGALOW.
C.S. LEWIS'S WARDROBE? THAT WASN'T REAL. BUT LE GUIN'S WALL? I SAW IT EVERY DAY.
IN ROMAN MYTHOLOGY, HEROES WENT TO THE PARADISE OF ***ELYSIUM,*** AND EVIL PEOPLE WERE SENT TO ***TARTARUS,*** WHERE THEY WERE PUNISHED UNTIL THEIR ***SINS*** WERE PAID FOR.
BUT ORDINARY CITIZENS WERE DESTINED FOR THE ***PLAIN OF ASPHODEL,*** WHERE THEY WANDERED WITHOUT MEMORY, EMOTION, OR DESIRE. IT WAS A ***GLOOMY*** PLACE.
LE GUIN'S LAND OF THE DEAD WAS A LOT LIKE THAT PLAIN. I UNDERSTOOD WHY GED FEARED TO JOURNEY THERE. I FEARED IT, TOO.
FOR DAYS AND DAYS AND DAYS, I WAS HAUNTED BY THAT WALL.
I WAS ANGRY. I WAS FRUSTRATED. HOW COULD LIFE BE SO ***UNPREDICTABLE,*** AND DEATH SO UNFAIR?
GRADUALLY I REALIZED THAT THE WALL WAS A ***SYMBOL,*** AND THE STORY WAS (IN SOME WAYS) AN ALLEGORY.
I HAD READ LE GUIN'S TALE AS THE STORY OF GED'S JOURNEY TO THE ***LAND*** OF DEATH, BUT IT WAS ALSO ABOUT GED'S JOURNEY INTO ***HIMSELF.***
THE YOUNG WIZARD HAD TO FACE HIS PRIDE, HIS ARROGANCE, EVEN HIS GUILT.
HE HAD TO FACE HIS ***INNER*** DARKNESS, JUST LIKE I HAD TO FACE MINE.
FROM GED, I LEARNED THAT THOSE WALLS EXIST IN ALL OF US.
THEY SEPARATE OUR CONSCIOUS PERSONALITIES FROM OUR UNCONSCIOUS SELVES: WHAT WE ***PRETEND*** TO BE FROM WHAT WE REALLY ARE, WHAT WE ***SAY*** WE FEEL FROM WHAT WE REALLY EXPERIENCE.
KNOW THYSELF
UGLY AS THEY ARE, RAGE, PAIN, FEAR, SELFISHNESS AND DESPAIR ARE AS HUMAN AS LOVE, KINDNESS, AND FORGIVENESS.
WHEN GED ABSORBED HIS SHADOW, IT DID NOT KILL HIM; IT MADE HIM ***STRONGER.***
FIONA
1965 - 1978
TOO OFTEN WE FORGET THAT THERE IS A LANDSCAPE INSIDE EACH OF US, A WORLD THAT MUST BE EXPLORED IF WE ARE TO RISE TO OUR FULL POTENTIAL.
THE WIZARD OF EARTHSEA HELPED ME FIND THE MAP TO MY OWN INNER LANDSCAPE. AS A WRITER, I JOURNEY THERE STILL.
Fin.

"I remembered that you can find joy in work and life, and if you do it right, they fuel each other — like dueling drummers, better and better, one after the other."

—Abbi Jacobson
Carry This Book

YAS, AND... QUEEN

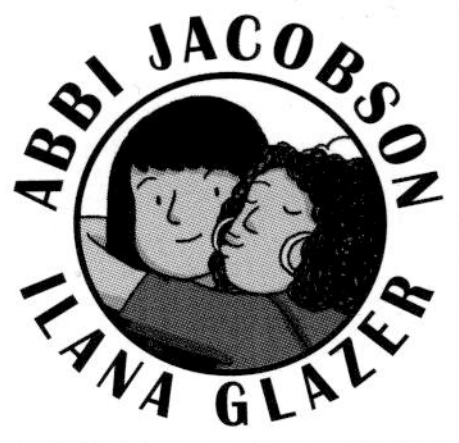
ABBI JACOBSON
ILANA GLAZER

LIZ PRINCE
WRITER/ARTIST

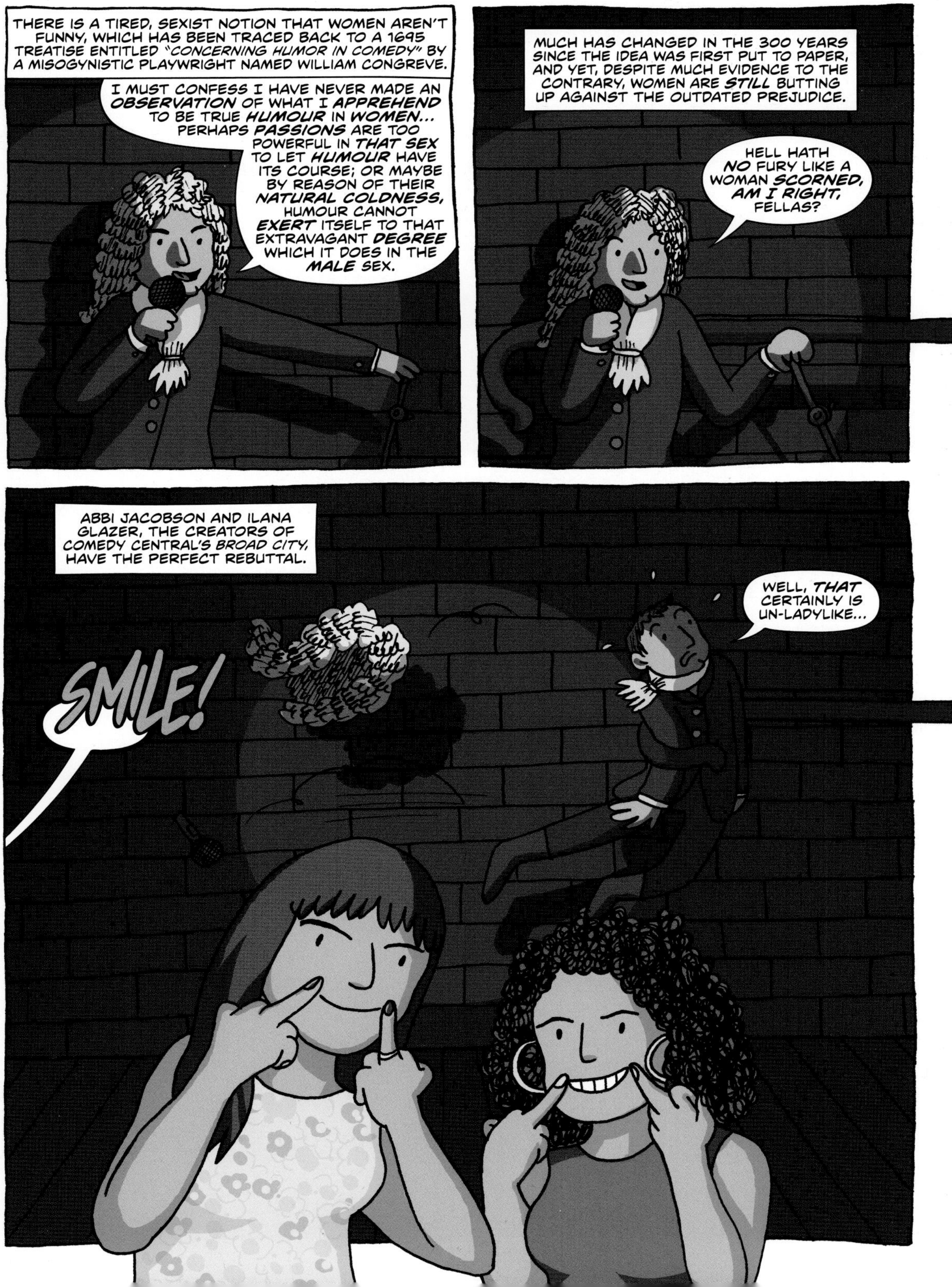
THERE IS A TIRED, SEXIST NOTION THAT WOMEN AREN'T FUNNY, WHICH HAS BEEN TRACED BACK TO A 1695 TREATISE ENTITLED "CONCERNING HUMOR IN COMEDY" BY A MISOGYNISTIC PLAYWRIGHT NAMED WILLIAM CONGREVE.
I MUST CONFESS I HAVE NEVER MADE AN OBSERVATION OF WHAT I APPREHEND TO BE TRUE HUMOUR IN WOMEN... PERHAPS PASSIONS ARE TOO POWERFUL IN THAT SEX TO LET HUMOUR HAVE ITS COURSE; OR MAYBE BY REASON OF THEIR NATURAL COLDNESS, HUMOUR CANNOT EXERT ITSELF TO THAT EXTRAVAGANT DEGREE WHICH IT DOES IN THE MALE SEX.
MUCH HAS CHANGED IN THE 300 YEARS SINCE THE IDEA WAS FIRST PUT TO PAPER, AND YET, DESPITE MUCH EVIDENCE TO THE CONTRARY, WOMEN ARE STILL BUTTING UP AGAINST THE OUTDATED PREJUDICE.
HELL HATH NO FURY LIKE A WOMAN SCORNED, AM I RIGHT, FELLAS?
ABBI JACOBSON AND ILANA GLAZER, THE CREATORS OF COMEDY CENTRAL'S BROAD CITY, HAVE THE PERFECT REBUTTAL.
SMILE!
WELL, THAT CERTAINLY IS UN-LADYLIKE...

THE TWO FRIENDS MET WHILE TAKING IMPROV CLASSES AT UPRIGHT CITIZENS BRIGADE IN NYC, AND IN 2009 STARTED *BROAD CITY* AS A WEB SERIES COMPOSED OF SHORT SEMI-AUTOBIOGRAPHICAL COMEDY SKETCHES.

DESCRIBED BY JACOBSON AND GLAZER AS BEING INSPIRED BY SHOWS LIKE *SEINFELD* AND *CURB YOUR ENTHUSIASM*, IT WASN'T LONG BEFORE *BROAD CITY* WAS NOTICED BY AMY POEHLER, WHO SIGNED ON AS EXECUTIVE PRODUCER WHEN THE SHOW WAS PITCHED TO COMEDY CENTRAL.

WHEN THE FIRST SEASON OF *BROAD CITY* AIRED IN 2014 ON COMEDY CENTRAL, A NOTORIOUSLY MALE-CENTRIC TELEVISION NETWORK, IT WAS ONE OF THE FEW SHOWS IN THEIR *HISTORY* OF ORIGINAL PROGRAMMING THAT WAS CREATED, WRITTEN, PRODUCED BY, AND STARRING WOMEN.

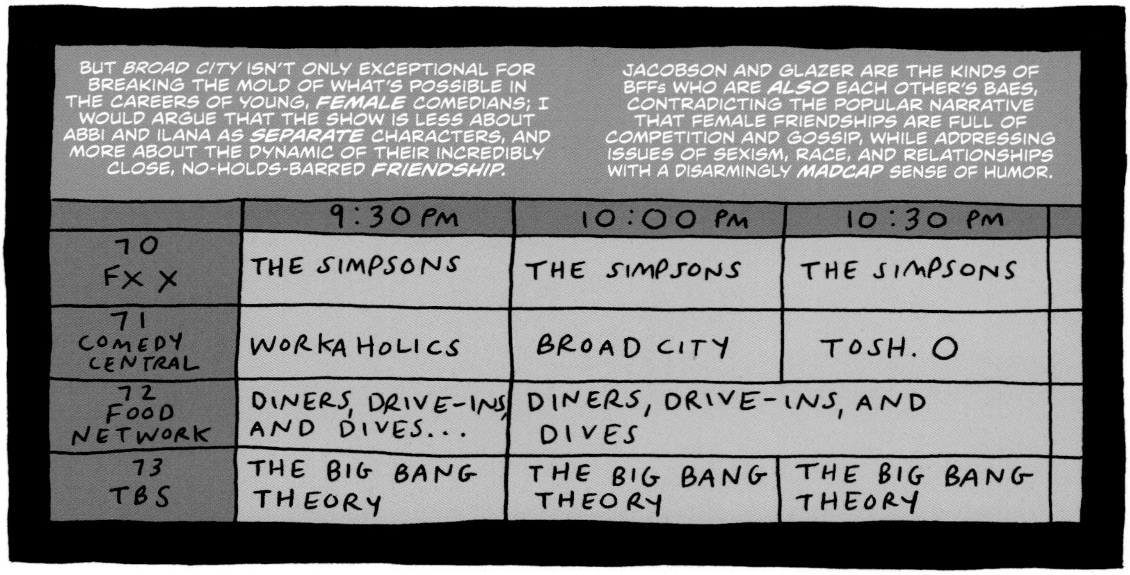

BUT *BROAD CITY* ISN'T ONLY EXCEPTIONAL FOR BREAKING THE MOLD OF WHAT'S POSSIBLE IN THE CAREERS OF YOUNG, *FEMALE* COMEDIANS; I WOULD ARGUE THAT THE SHOW IS LESS ABOUT ABBI AND ILANA AS *SEPARATE* CHARACTERS, AND MORE ABOUT THE DYNAMIC OF THEIR INCREDIBLY CLOSE, NO-HOLDS-BARRED *FRIENDSHIP*.

JACOBSON AND GLAZER ARE THE KINDS OF BFFs WHO ARE *ALSO* EACH OTHER'S BAES, CONTRADICTING THE POPULAR NARRATIVE THAT FEMALE FRIENDSHIPS ARE FULL OF COMPETITION AND GOSSIP, WHILE ADDRESSING ISSUES OF SEXISM, RACE, AND RELATIONSHIPS WITH A DISARMINGLY *MADCAP* SENSE OF HUMOR.

	9:30 PM	10:00 PM	10:30 PM	
70 FX X	THE SIMPSONS	THE SIMPSONS	THE SIMPSONS	
71 COMEDY CENTRAL	WORKAHOLICS	BROAD CITY	TOSH.O	
72 FOOD NETWORK	DINERS, DRIVE-INS, AND DIVES...	DINERS, DRIVE-INS, AND DIVES		
73 TBS	THE BIG BANG THEORY	THE BIG BANG THEORY	THE BIG BANG THEORY	

AND THE WOMEN ARE BEST FRIENDS OFF-SCREEN TOO--

--PROVING THAT THERE'S NO FAKE-IT-TIL-YOU-MAKE-IT ASPECT TO THEIR CLIMB UP THE COMEDY LADDER.

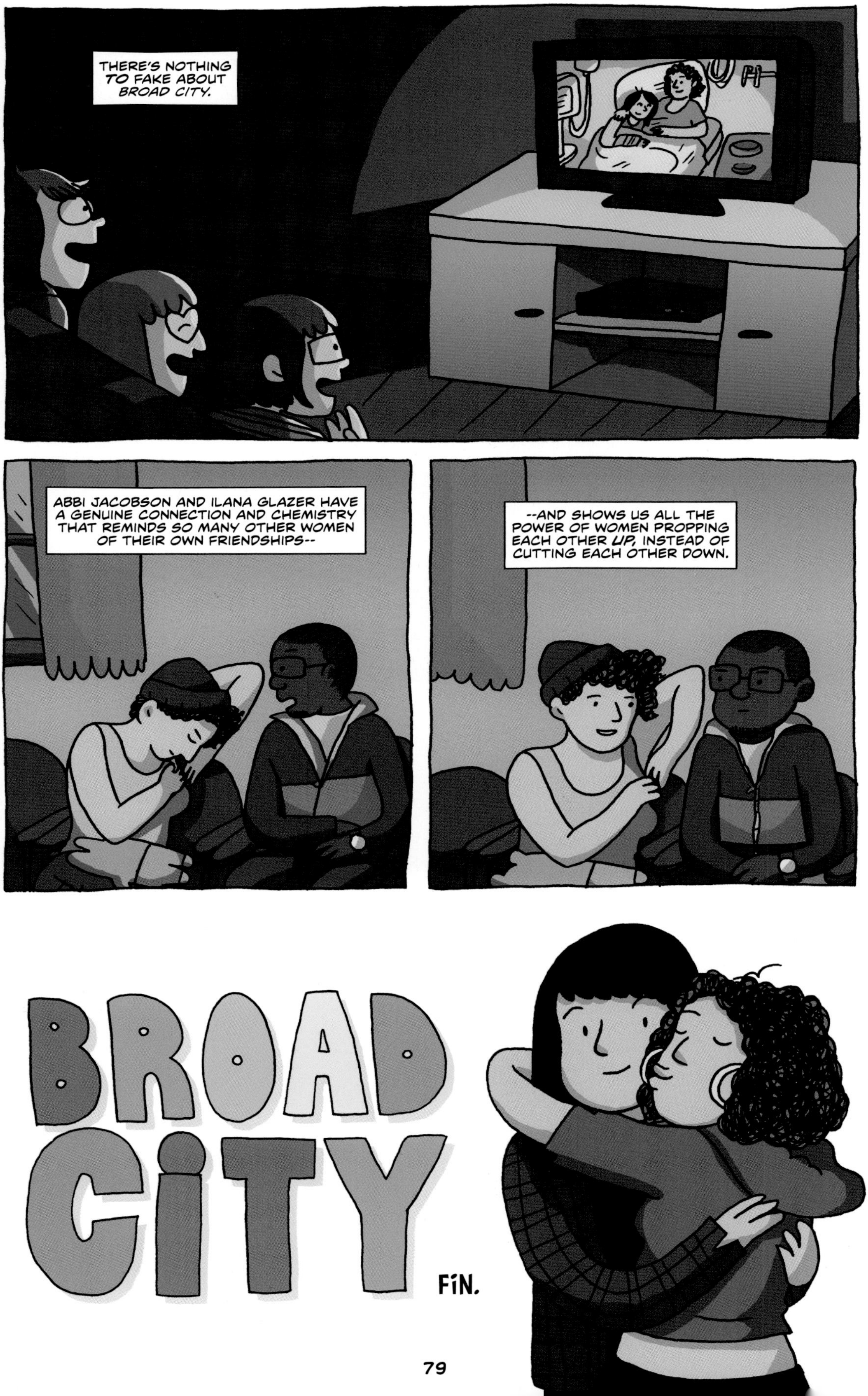
THERE'S NOTHING *TO* FAKE ABOUT *BROAD CITY.*
ABBI JACOBSON AND ILANA GLAZER HAVE A GENUINE CONNECTION AND CHEMISTRY THAT REMINDS SO MANY OTHER WOMEN OF THEIR OWN FRIENDSHIPS--
--AND SHOWS US ALL THE POWER OF WOMEN PROPPING EACH OTHER *UP,* INSTEAD OF CUTTING EACH OTHER DOWN.
BROAD CiTY
FiN.

"You want me to spy for you, right?"

—Margery Booth
from the screenplay
The Spy in the Eagle's Nest.

Secrets in Her Knickers

DAVID BARNETT
WRITER

RACHAEL STOTT
ARTIST

HI-FI
COLORIST

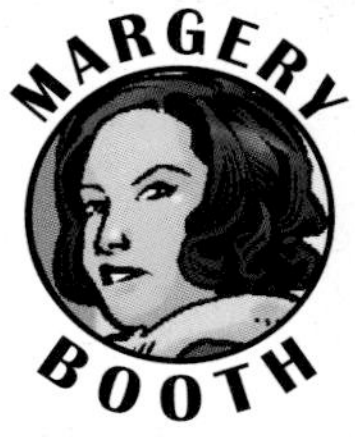
MARGERY
BOOTH

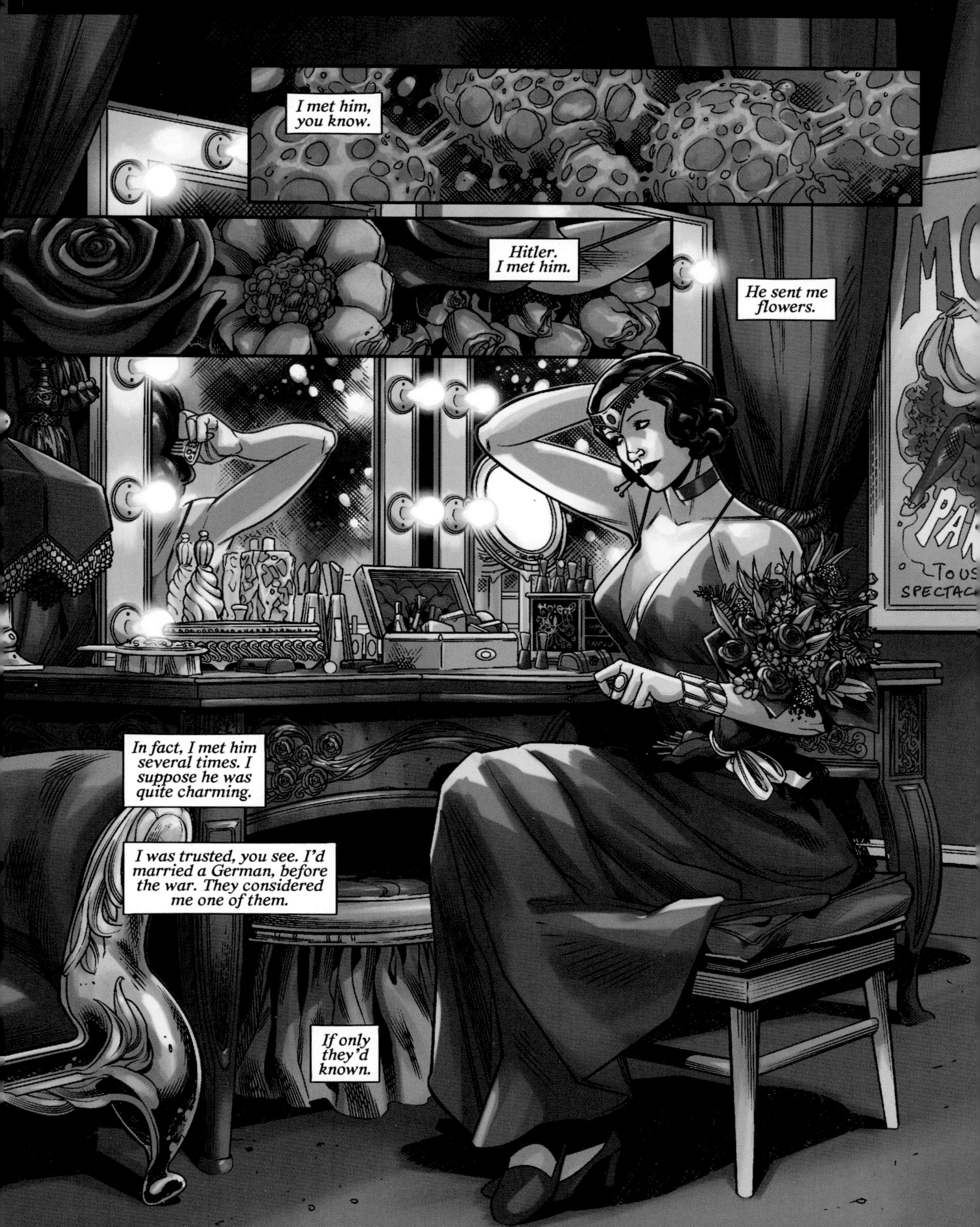
I met him, you know.
Hitler. I met him.
He sent me flowers.
In fact, I met him several times. I suppose he was quite charming.
I was trusted, you see. I'd married a German, before the war. They considered me one of them.
If only they'd known.

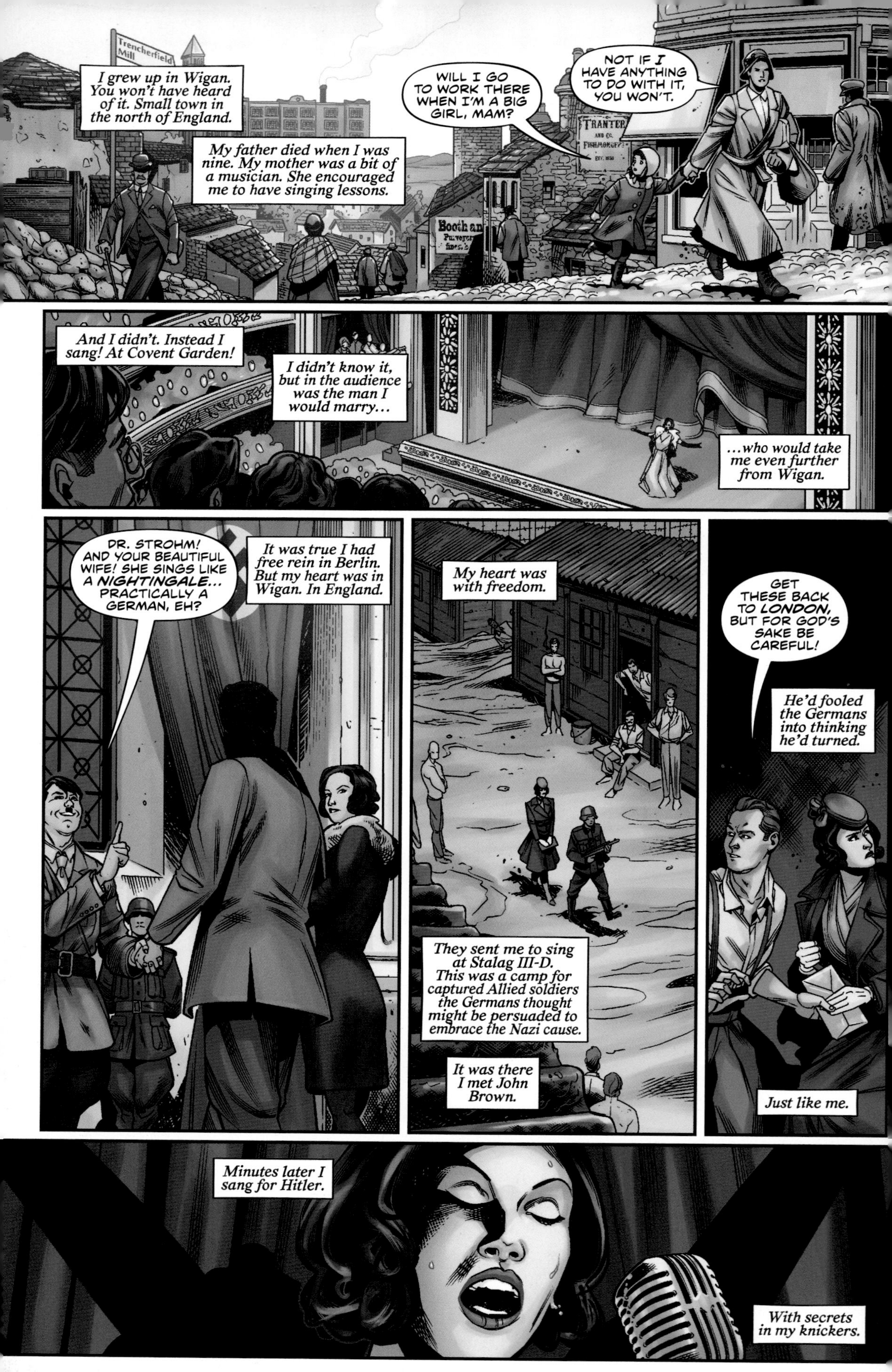
Trencherfield Mill
I grew up in Wigan. You won't have heard of it. Small town in the north of England.
My father died when I was nine. My mother was a bit of a musician. She encouraged me to have singing lessons.
WILL I GO TO WORK THERE WHEN I'M A BIG GIRL, MAM?
NOT IF I HAVE ANYTHING TO DO WITH IT, YOU WON'T.
TRANTER
And I didn't. Instead I sang! At Covent Garden!
I didn't know it, but in the audience was the man I would marry...
...who would take me even further from Wigan.
DR. STROHM! AND YOUR BEAUTIFUL WIFE! SHE SINGS LIKE A NIGHTINGALE... PRACTICALLY A GERMAN, EH?
It was true I had free rein in Berlin. But my heart was in Wigan. In England.
My heart was with freedom.
They sent me to sing at Stalag III-D. This was a camp for captured Allied soldiers the Germans thought might be persuaded to embrace the Nazi cause.
It was there I met John Brown.
GET THESE BACK TO LONDON, BUT FOR GOD'S SAKE BE CAREFUL!
He'd fooled the Germans into thinking he'd turned.
Just like me.
Minutes later I sang for Hitler.
With secrets in my knickers.

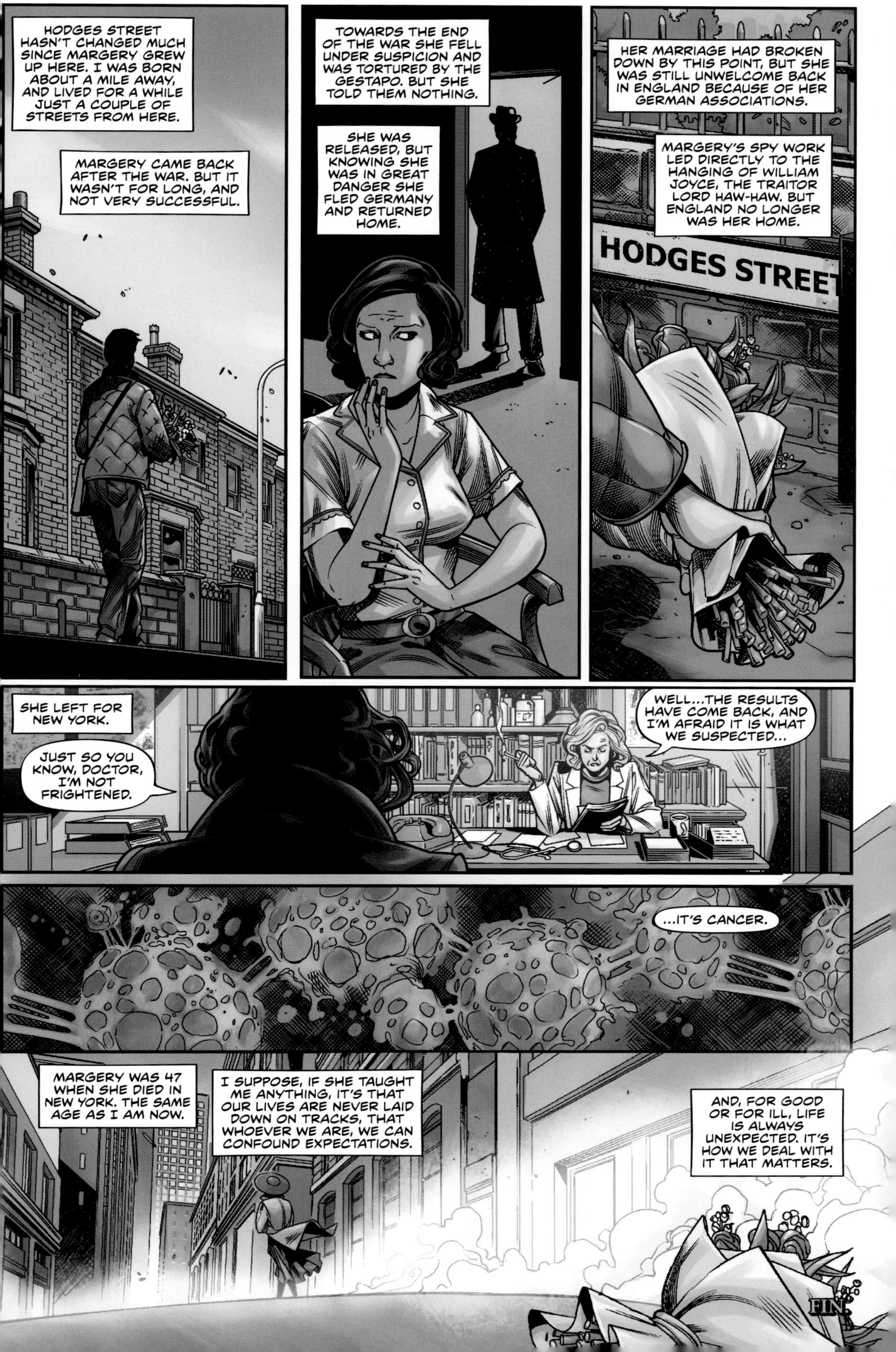
HODGES STREET HASN'T CHANGED MUCH SINCE MARGERY GREW UP HERE. I WAS BORN ABOUT A MILE AWAY, AND LIVED FOR A WHILE JUST A COUPLE OF STREETS FROM HERE.
MARGERY CAME BACK AFTER THE WAR. BUT IT WASN'T FOR LONG, AND NOT VERY SUCCESSFUL.
TOWARDS THE END OF THE WAR SHE FELL UNDER SUSPICION AND WAS TORTURED BY THE GESTAPO. BUT SHE TOLD THEM NOTHING.
SHE WAS RELEASED, BUT KNOWING SHE WAS IN GREAT DANGER SHE FLED GERMANY AND RETURNED HOME.
HER MARRIAGE HAD BROKEN DOWN BY THIS POINT, BUT SHE WAS STILL UNWELCOME BACK IN ENGLAND BECAUSE OF HER GERMAN ASSOCIATIONS.
MARGERY'S SPY WORK LED DIRECTLY TO THE HANGING OF WILLIAM JOYCE, THE TRAITOR LORD HAW-HAW. BUT ENGLAND NO LONGER WAS HER HOME.
HODGES STREET
SHE LEFT FOR NEW YORK.
JUST SO YOU KNOW, DOCTOR, I'M NOT FRIGHTENED.
WELL...THE RESULTS HAVE COME BACK, AND I'M AFRAID IT IS WHAT WE SUSPECTED...
...IT'S CANCER.
MARGERY WAS 47 WHEN SHE DIED IN NEW YORK. THE SAME AGE AS I AM NOW.
I SUPPOSE, IF SHE TAUGHT ME ANYTHING, IT'S THAT OUR LIVES ARE NEVER LAID DOWN ON TRACKS, THAT WHOEVER WE ARE, WE CAN CONFOUND EXPECTATIONS.
AND, FOR GOOD OR FOR ILL, LIFE IS ALWAYS UNEXPECTED. IT'S HOW WE DEAL WITH IT THAT MATTERS.
FIN.

"My body is very different from most of the dancers I dance with. My hair is different than most I dance with. But I didn't let that stop me. Black girls rock and can be ballerinas."

—Misty Copeland

Aberration

LAUREN MOYER
WRITER

CARA McGEE
ARTIST

HI-FI
COLORIST

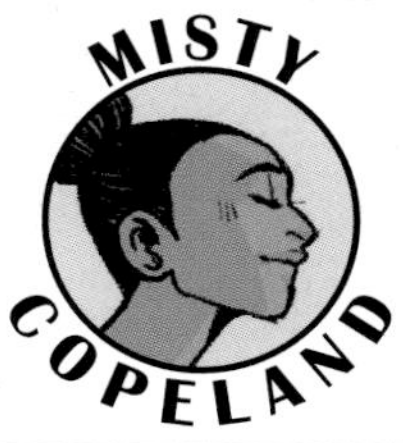
MISTY
COPELAND

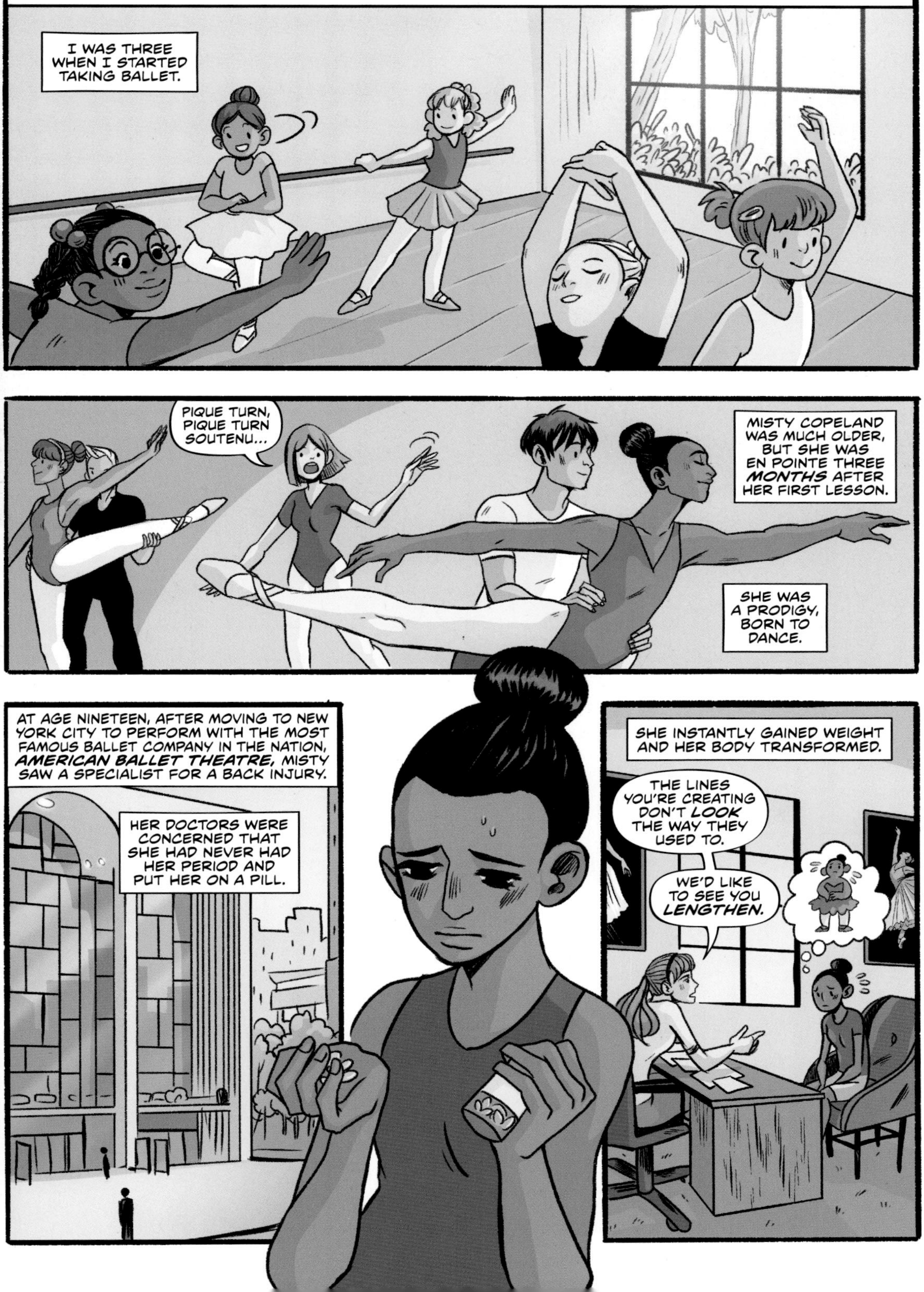
I WAS THREE WHEN I STARTED TAKING BALLET.
PIQUE TURN, PIQUE TURN SOUTENU...
MISTY COPELAND WAS MUCH OLDER, BUT SHE WAS EN POINTE THREE MONTHS AFTER HER FIRST LESSON.
SHE WAS A PRODIGY, BORN TO DANCE.
AT AGE NINETEEN, AFTER MOVING TO NEW YORK CITY TO PERFORM WITH THE MOST FAMOUS BALLET COMPANY IN THE NATION, AMERICAN BALLET THEATRE, MISTY SAW A SPECIALIST FOR A BACK INJURY.
HER DOCTORS WERE CONCERNED THAT SHE HAD NEVER HAD HER PERIOD AND PUT HER ON A PILL.
SHE INSTANTLY GAINED WEIGHT AND HER BODY TRANSFORMED.
THE LINES YOU'RE CREATING DON'T LOOK THE WAY THEY USED TO.
WE'D LIKE TO SEE YOU LENGTHEN.

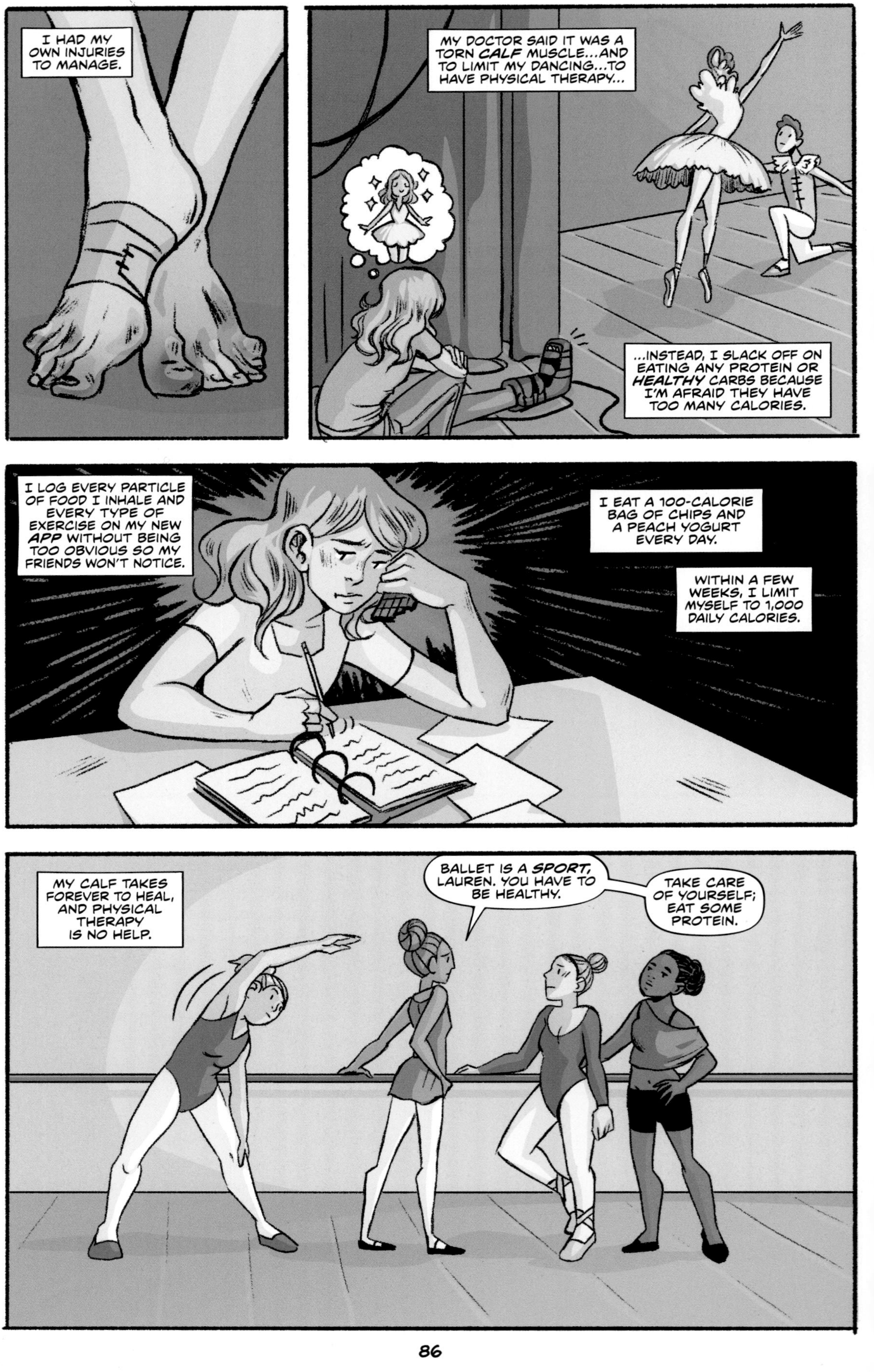
I HAD MY OWN INJURIES TO MANAGE.
MY DOCTOR SAID IT WAS A TORN CALF MUSCLE...AND TO LIMIT MY DANCING...TO HAVE PHYSICAL THERAPY...
...INSTEAD, I SLACK OFF ON EATING ANY PROTEIN OR HEALTHY CARBS BECAUSE I'M AFRAID THEY HAVE TOO MANY CALORIES.
I LOG EVERY PARTICLE OF FOOD I INHALE AND EVERY TYPE OF EXERCISE ON MY NEW APP WITHOUT BEING TOO OBVIOUS SO MY FRIENDS WON'T NOTICE.
I EAT A 100-CALORIE BAG OF CHIPS AND A PEACH YOGURT EVERY DAY.
WITHIN A FEW WEEKS, I LIMIT MYSELF TO 1,000 DAILY CALORIES.
MY CALF TAKES FOREVER TO HEAL, AND PHYSICAL THERAPY IS NO HELP.
BALLET IS A SPORT, LAUREN. YOU HAVE TO BE HEALTHY.
TAKE CARE OF YOURSELF; EAT SOME PROTEIN.

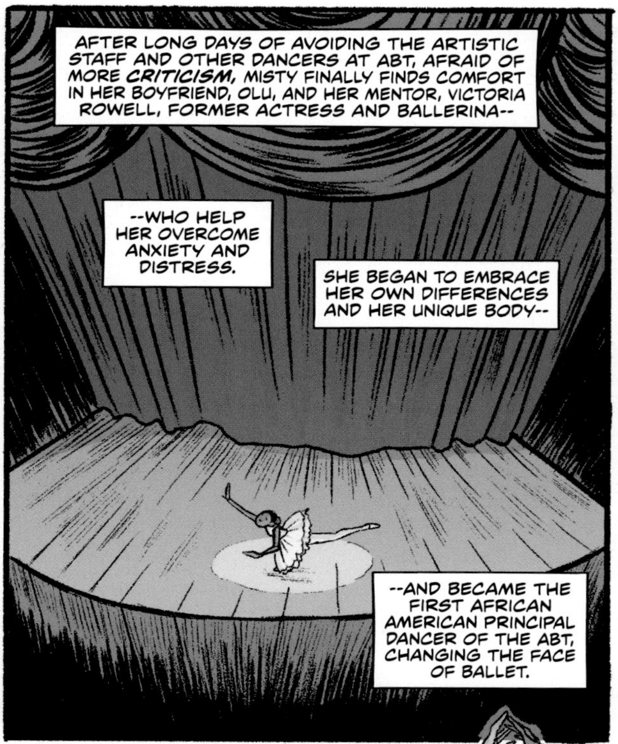
AFTER LONG DAYS OF AVOIDING THE ARTISTIC STAFF AND OTHER DANCERS AT ABT, AFRAID OF MORE ***CRITICISM,*** MISTY FINALLY FINDS COMFORT IN HER BOYFRIEND, OLU, AND HER MENTOR, VICTORIA ROWELL, FORMER ACTRESS AND BALLERINA--
--WHO HELP HER OVERCOME ANXIETY AND DISTRESS.
SHE BEGAN TO EMBRACE HER OWN DIFFERENCES AND HER UNIQUE BODY--
--AND BECAME THE FIRST AFRICAN AMERICAN PRINCIPAL DANCER OF THE ABT, CHANGING THE FACE OF BALLET.

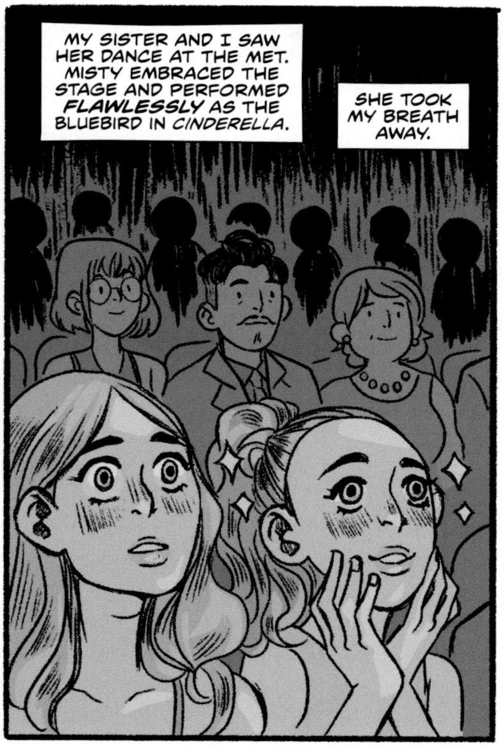
MY SISTER AND I SAW HER DANCE AT THE MET. MISTY EMBRACED THE STAGE AND PERFORMED ***FLAWLESSLY*** AS THE BLUEBIRD IN *CINDERELLA*.
SHE TOOK MY BREATH AWAY.

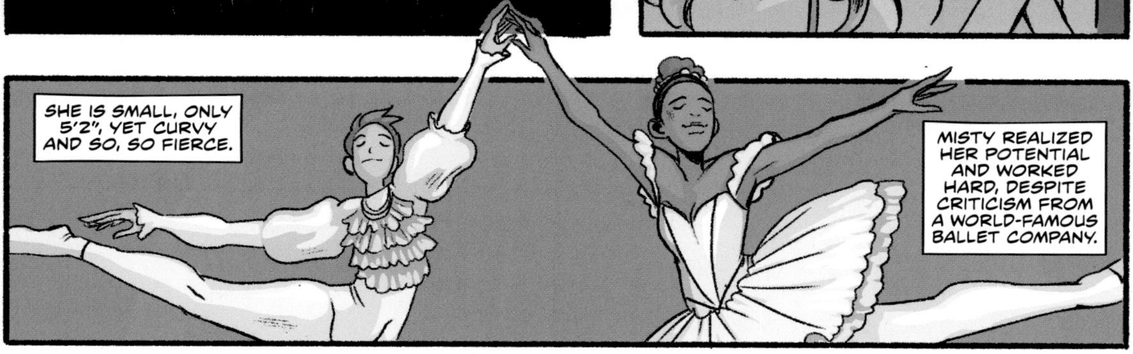
SHE IS SMALL, ONLY 5'2", YET CURVY AND SO, SO FIERCE.
MISTY REALIZED HER POTENTIAL AND WORKED HARD, DESPITE CRITICISM FROM A WORLD-FAMOUS BALLET COMPANY.

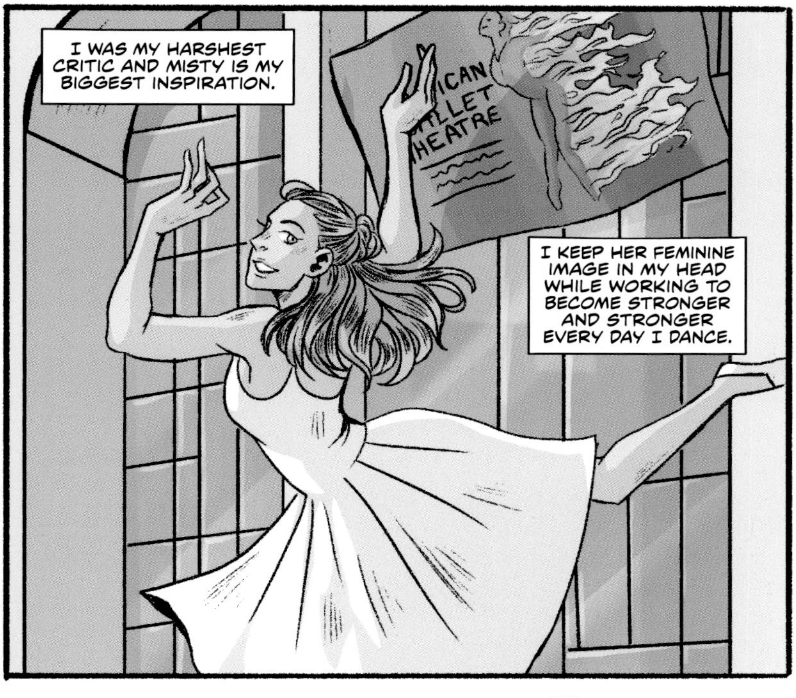
I WAS MY HARSHEST CRITIC AND MISTY IS MY BIGGEST INSPIRATION.
I KEEP HER FEMININE IMAGE IN MY HEAD WHILE WORKING TO BECOME STRONGER AND STRONGER EVERY DAY I DANCE.

"When I turned onto the sidewalk, I saw it: a huge billboard on the front of the Metropolitan Opera House with my picture on it. I was in profile, wearing a red leotard, with my chest and back arched so you could see my full, feminine breasts and my round butt. It was everything that people don't expect in a ballerina. I stood completely still for five minutes, just crying. It was beauty. It was power.
'It was a woman. It was me."

– Misty Copeland

"As an historian, I'm fascinated by the past and the small stories that are encapsulated within big events. Aida's story is one of many, but it has always captivated and inspired me to be strong and courageous even during dark times."

—Irma Page
Aida's great niece

MEDALS AND MEMORIES
(or One Life Lived Many Times)

IRMA PAGE WRITER | ***MARK BUCKINGHAM*** ARTIST | ***HI-FI*** COLORIST

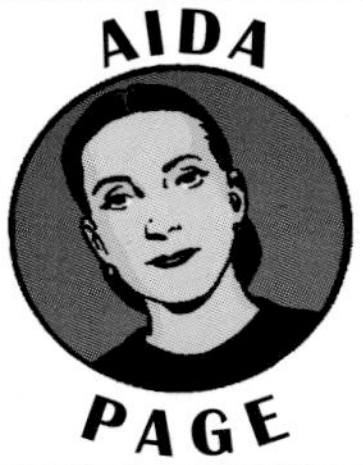

AIDA
PAGE

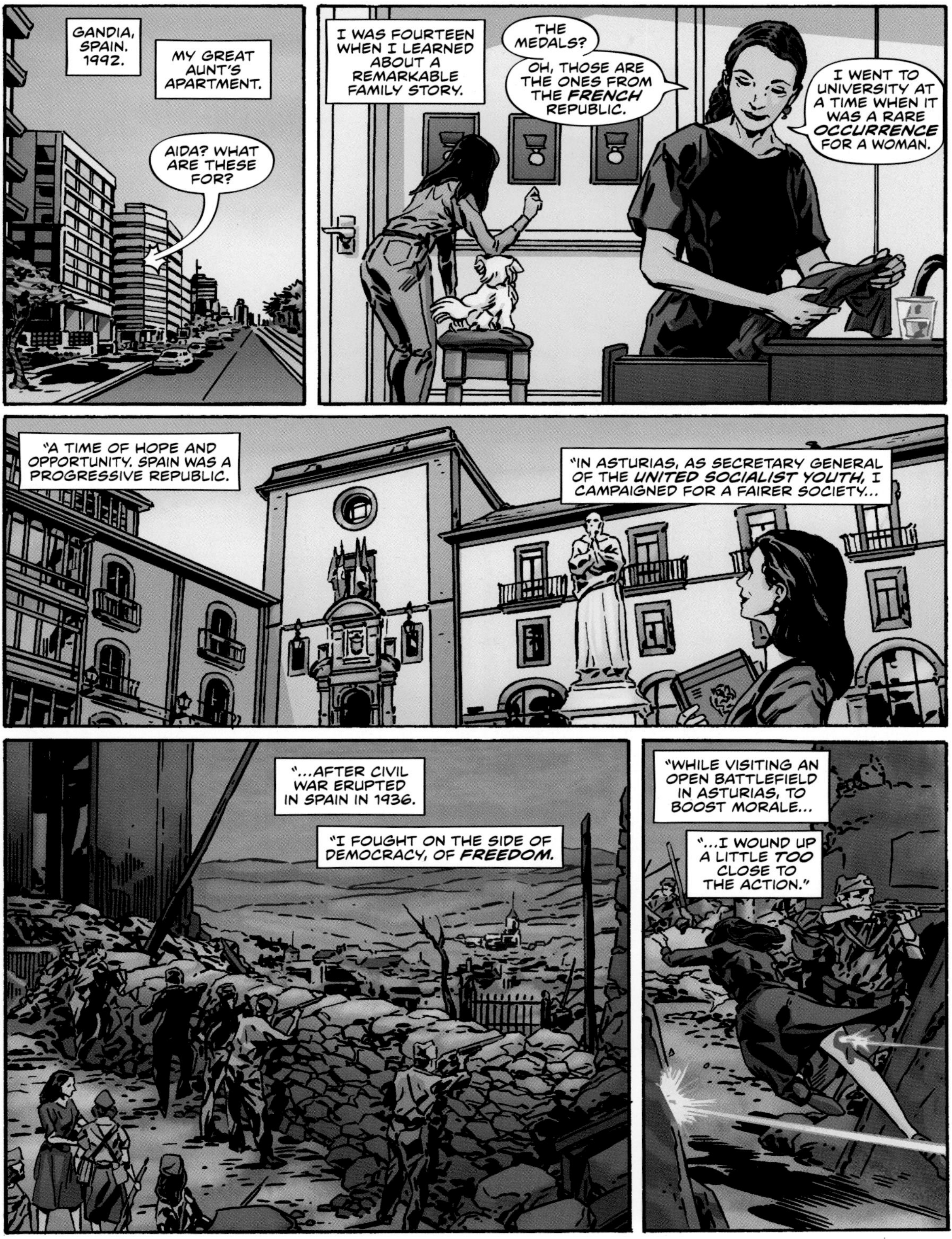

GANDIA, SPAIN. 1992.
MY GREAT AUNT'S APARTMENT.
AIDA? WHAT ARE THESE FOR?
I WAS FOURTEEN WHEN I LEARNED ABOUT A REMARKABLE FAMILY STORY.
THE MEDALS?
OH, THOSE ARE THE ONES FROM THE *FRENCH* REPUBLIC.
I WENT TO UNIVERSITY AT A TIME WHEN IT WAS A RARE *OCCURRENCE* FOR A WOMAN.
"A TIME OF HOPE AND OPPORTUNITY. SPAIN WAS A PROGRESSIVE REPUBLIC.
"IN ASTURIAS, AS SECRETARY GENERAL OF THE *UNITED SOCIALIST YOUTH,* I CAMPAIGNED FOR A FAIRER SOCIETY...
"...AFTER CIVIL WAR ERUPTED IN SPAIN IN 1936.
"I FOUGHT ON THE SIDE OF DEMOCRACY, OF *FREEDOM.*
"WHILE VISITING AN OPEN BATTLEFIELD IN ASTURIAS, TO BOOST MORALE...
"...I WOUND UP A LITTLE *TOO* CLOSE TO THE ACTION."

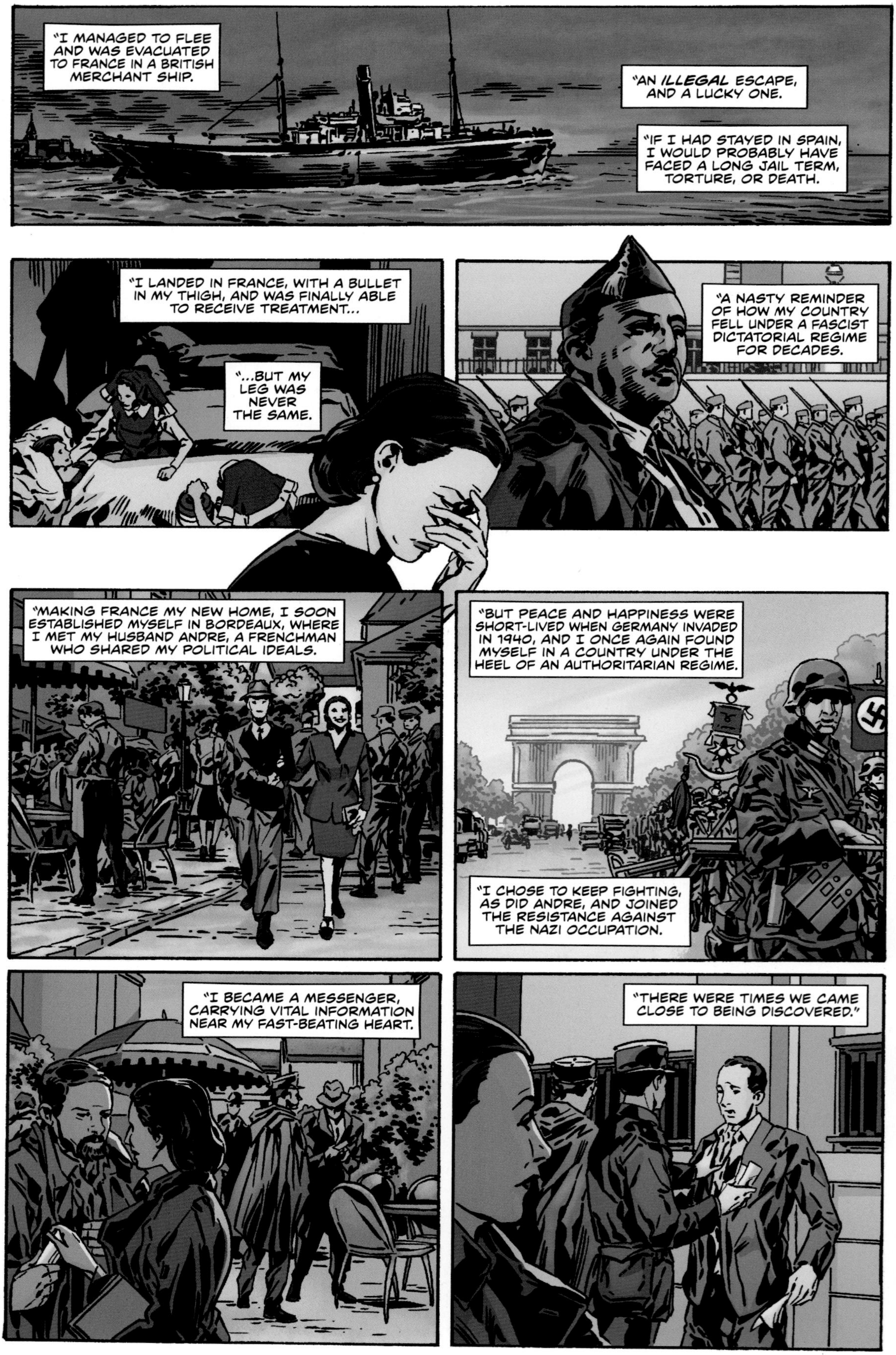
"I MANAGED TO FLEE AND WAS EVACUATED TO FRANCE IN A BRITISH MERCHANT SHIP.
"AN *ILLEGAL* ESCAPE, AND A LUCKY ONE.
"IF I HAD STAYED IN SPAIN, I WOULD PROBABLY HAVE FACED A LONG JAIL TERM, TORTURE, OR DEATH.
"I LANDED IN FRANCE, WITH A BULLET IN MY THIGH, AND WAS FINALLY ABLE TO RECEIVE TREATMENT...
"...BUT MY LEG WAS NEVER THE SAME.
"A NASTY REMINDER OF HOW MY COUNTRY FELL UNDER A FASCIST DICTATORIAL REGIME FOR DECADES.
"MAKING FRANCE MY NEW HOME, I SOON ESTABLISHED MYSELF IN BORDEAUX, WHERE I MET MY HUSBAND ANDRE, A FRENCHMAN WHO SHARED MY POLITICAL IDEALS.
"BUT PEACE AND HAPPINESS WERE SHORT-LIVED WHEN GERMANY INVADED IN 1940, AND I ONCE AGAIN FOUND MYSELF IN A COUNTRY UNDER THE HEEL OF AN AUTHORITARIAN REGIME.
"I CHOSE TO KEEP FIGHTING, AS DID ANDRE, AND JOINED THE RESISTANCE AGAINST THE NAZI OCCUPATION.
"I BECAME A MESSENGER, CARRYING VITAL INFORMATION NEAR MY FAST-BEATING HEART.
"THERE WERE TIMES WE CAME CLOSE TO BEING DISCOVERED."

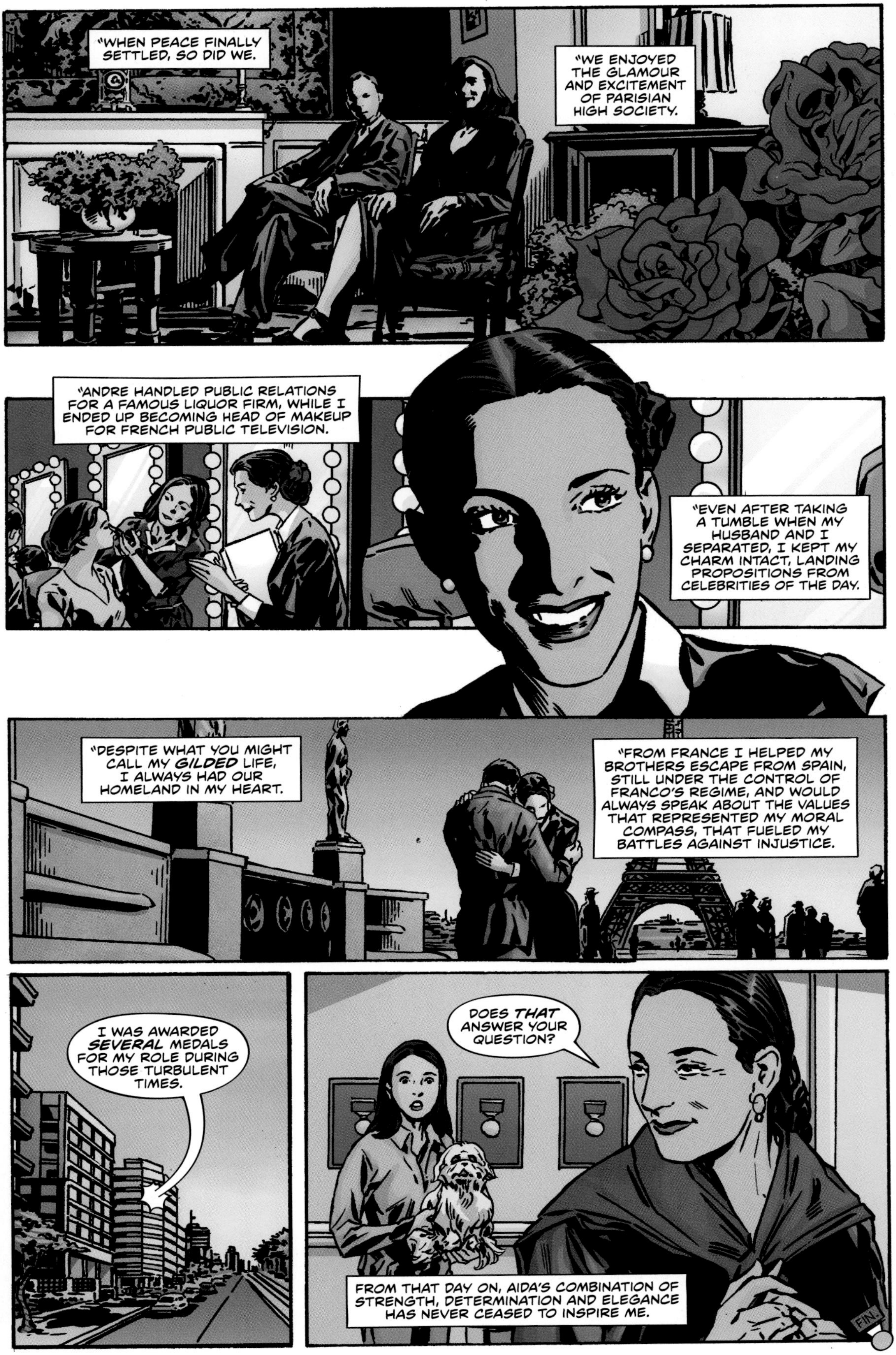
"WHEN PEACE FINALLY SETTLED, SO DID WE.
"WE ENJOYED THE GLAMOUR AND EXCITEMENT OF PARISIAN HIGH SOCIETY.
"ANDRE HANDLED PUBLIC RELATIONS FOR A FAMOUS LIQUOR FIRM, WHILE I ENDED UP BECOMING HEAD OF MAKEUP FOR FRENCH PUBLIC TELEVISION.
"EVEN AFTER TAKING A TUMBLE WHEN MY HUSBAND AND I SEPARATED, I KEPT MY CHARM INTACT, LANDING PROPOSITIONS FROM CELEBRITIES OF THE DAY.
"DESPITE WHAT YOU MIGHT CALL MY *GILDED* LIFE, I ALWAYS HAD OUR HOMELAND IN MY HEART.
"FROM FRANCE I HELPED MY BROTHERS ESCAPE FROM SPAIN, STILL UNDER THE CONTROL OF FRANCO'S REGIME, AND WOULD ALWAYS SPEAK ABOUT THE VALUES THAT REPRESENTED MY MORAL COMPASS, THAT FUELED MY BATTLES AGAINST INJUSTICE.
I WAS AWARDED *SEVERAL* MEDALS FOR MY ROLE DURING THOSE TURBULENT TIMES.
DOES *THAT* ANSWER YOUR QUESTION?
FROM THAT DAY ON, AIDA'S COMBINATION OF STRENGTH, DETERMINATION AND ELEGANCE HAS NEVER CEASED TO INSPIRE ME.
FIN.

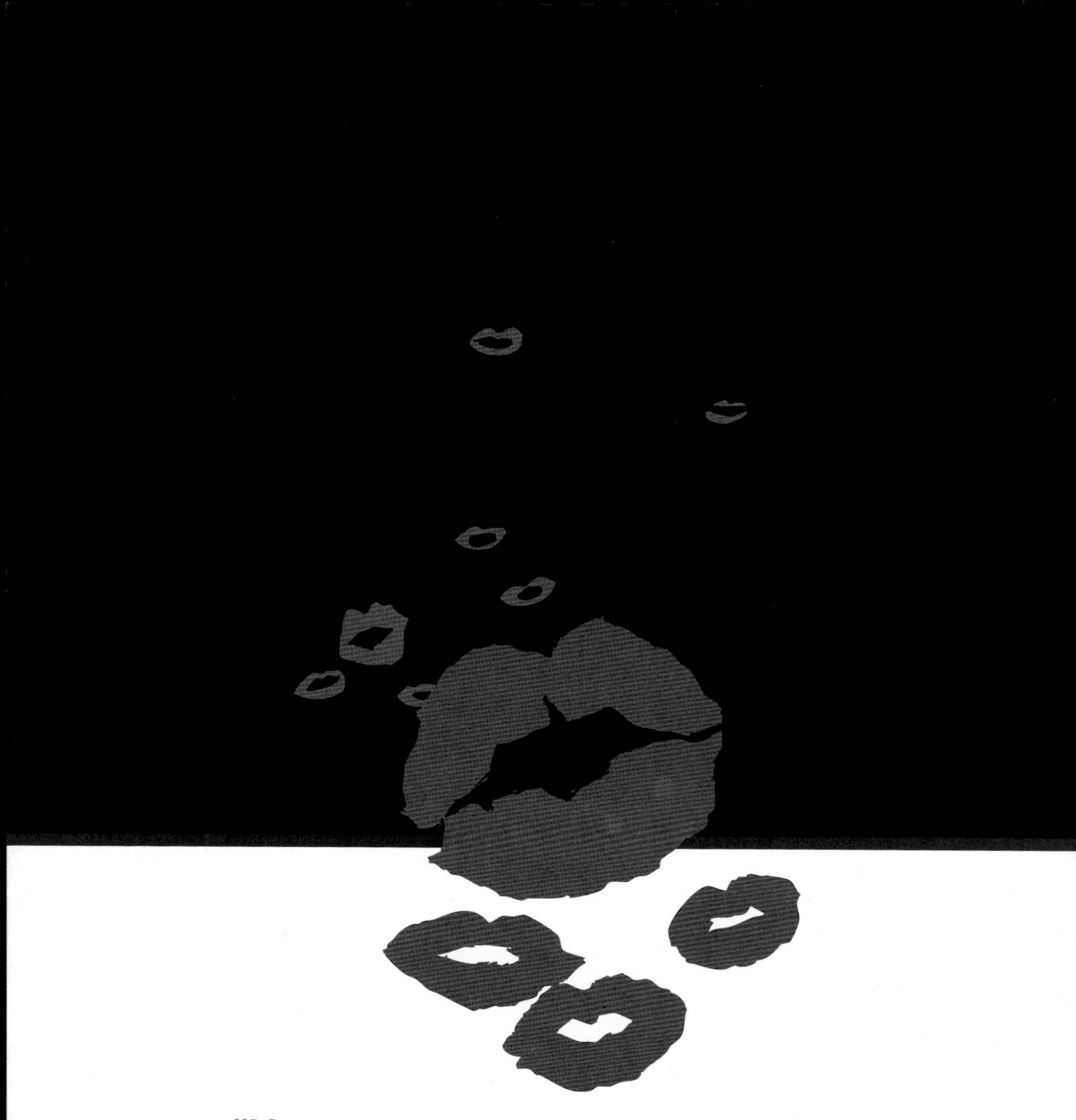

"I have no control over what people think of me but I have 100% control of what I think of myself, and that is so important. And not just about your body, but so many ways of confidence. You're constantly learning how to be confident, aren't you?"

—Beth Ditto

STANDING IN THE WAY OF CONTROL

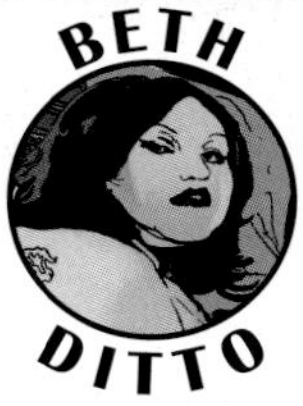
BETH
DITTO

LEAH MOORE WRITER | ***ALISON SAMPSON*** ARTIST | ***IRMA KNIIVILA*** COLORIST

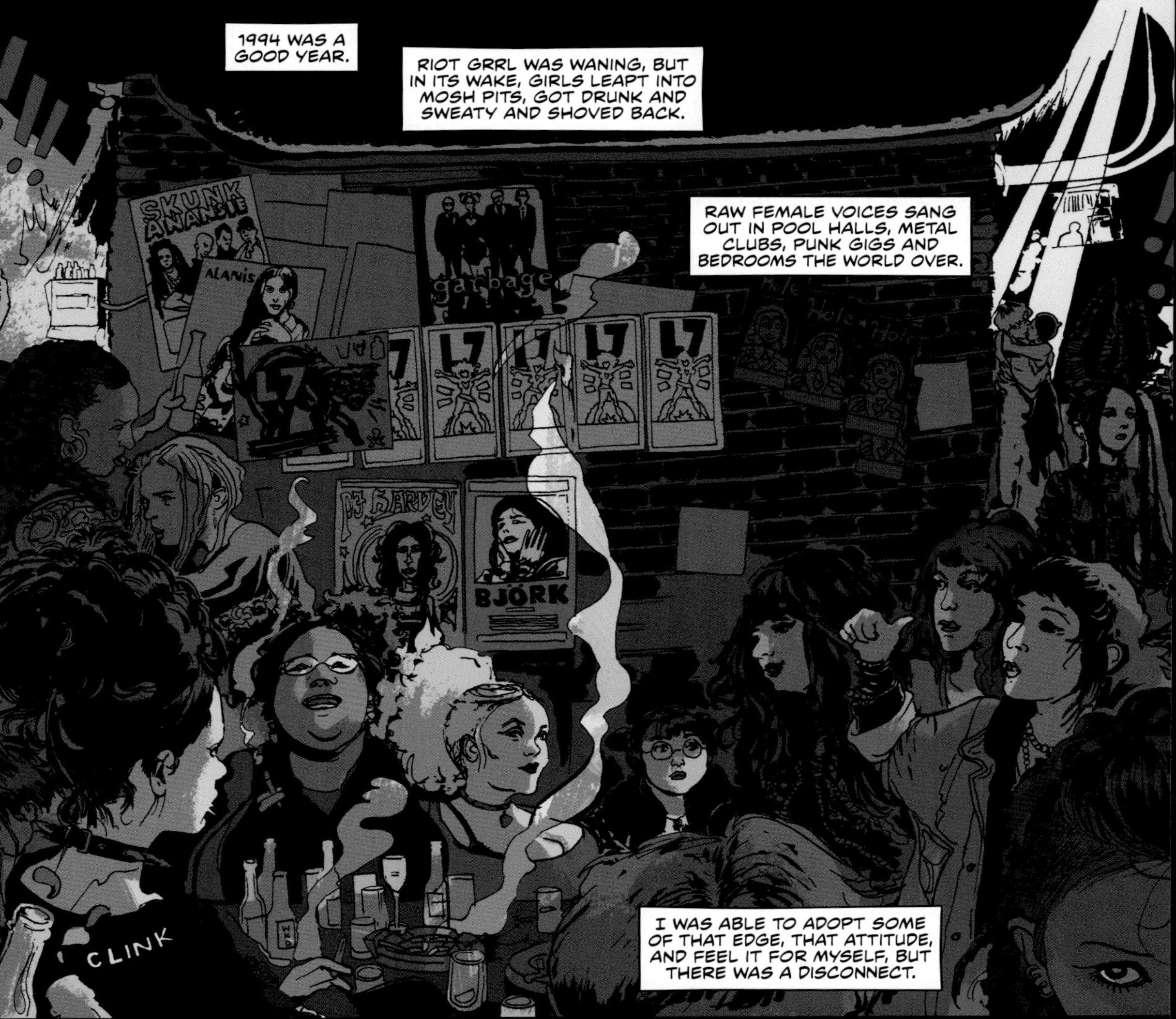
1994 WAS A GOOD YEAR.
RIOT GRRL WAS WANING, BUT IN ITS WAKE, GIRLS LEAPT INTO MOSH PITS, GOT DRUNK AND SWEATY AND SHOVED BACK.
SKUNK ANANSIE
ALANIS
garbage
L7
RAW FEMALE VOICES SANG OUT IN POOL HALLS, METAL CLUBS, PUNK GIGS AND BEDROOMS THE WORLD OVER.
BJÖRK
CLINK
I WAS ABLE TO ADOPT SOME OF THAT EDGE, THAT ATTITUDE, AND FEEL IT FOR MYSELF, BUT THERE WAS A DISCONNECT.

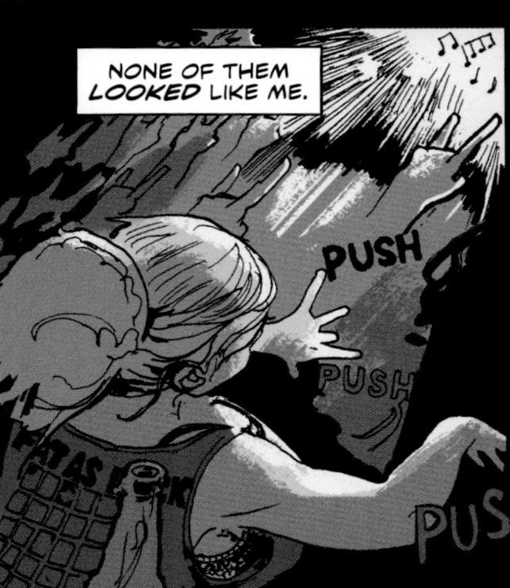
NONE OF THEM *LOOKED* LIKE ME.
PUSH
PUSH
PUSH

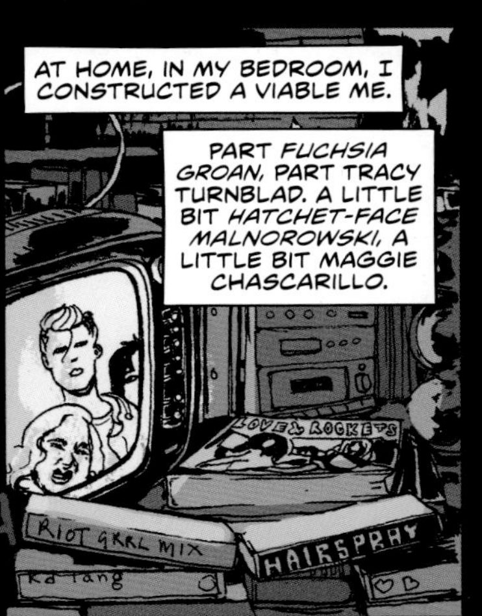
AT HOME, IN MY BEDROOM, I CONSTRUCTED A VIABLE ME.
PART *FUCHSIA GROAN*, PART TRACY TURNBLAD. A LITTLE BIT *HATCHET-FACE MALNOROWSKI*, A LITTLE BIT MAGGIE CHASCARILLO.
LOVE & ROCKETS
RIOT GRRL MIX
HAIRSPRAY

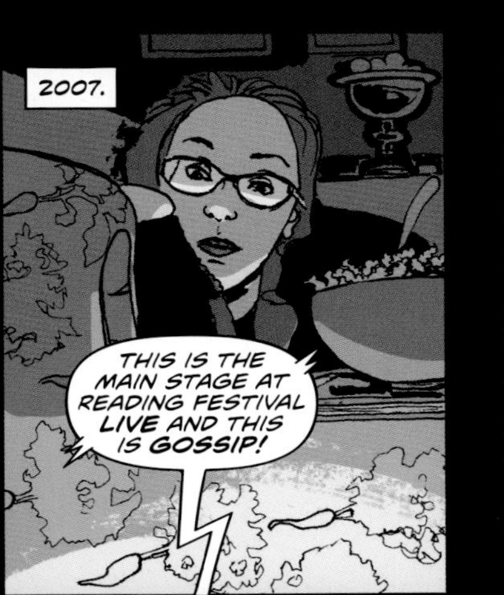
2007.
*THIS IS THE MAIN STAGE AT READING FESTIVAL **LIVE** AND THIS IS **GOSSIP!***

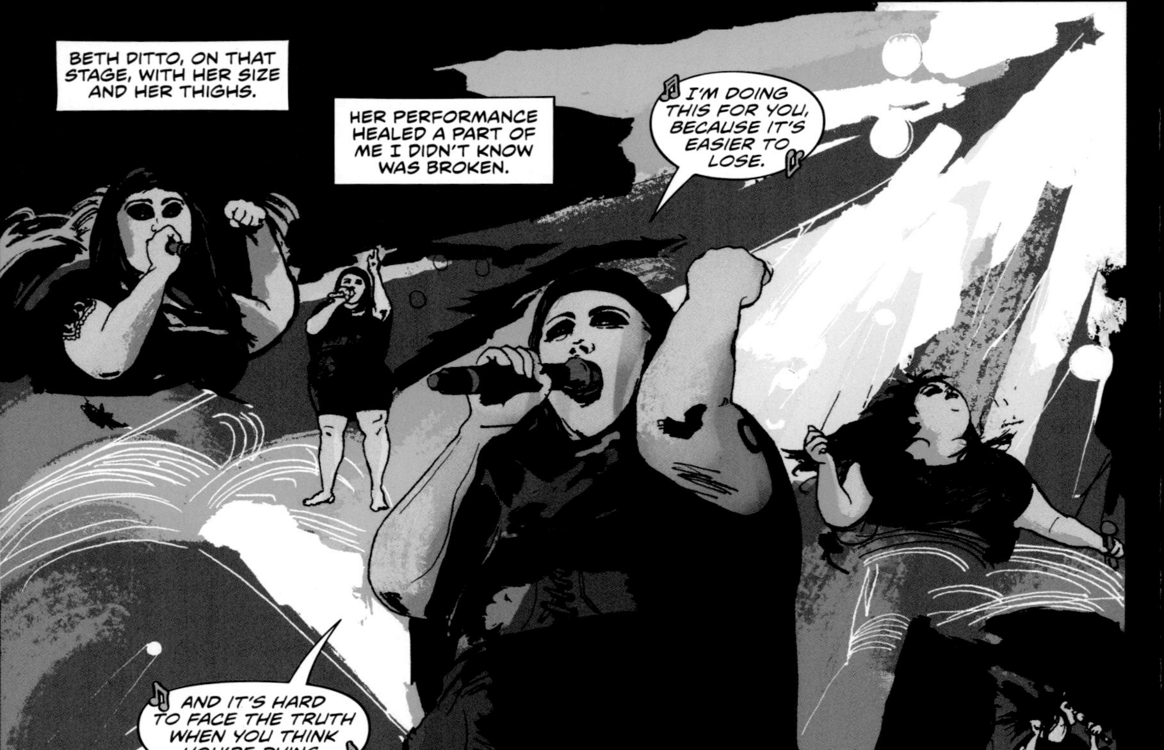
BETH DITTO, ON THAT STAGE, WITH HER SIZE AND HER THIGHS.
HER PERFORMANCE HEALED A PART OF ME I DIDN'T KNOW WAS BROKEN.
I'M DOING THIS FOR YOU, BECAUSE IT'S EASIER TO LOSE.
AND IT'S HARD TO FACE THE TRUTH WHEN YOU THINK YOU'RE DYING.
IT'S PART NOT GIVING IN, AND PART TRUSTING YOUR FRIENDS.
YOU DO IT ALL AGAIN, BUT YOU **DON'T STOP TRYING!**

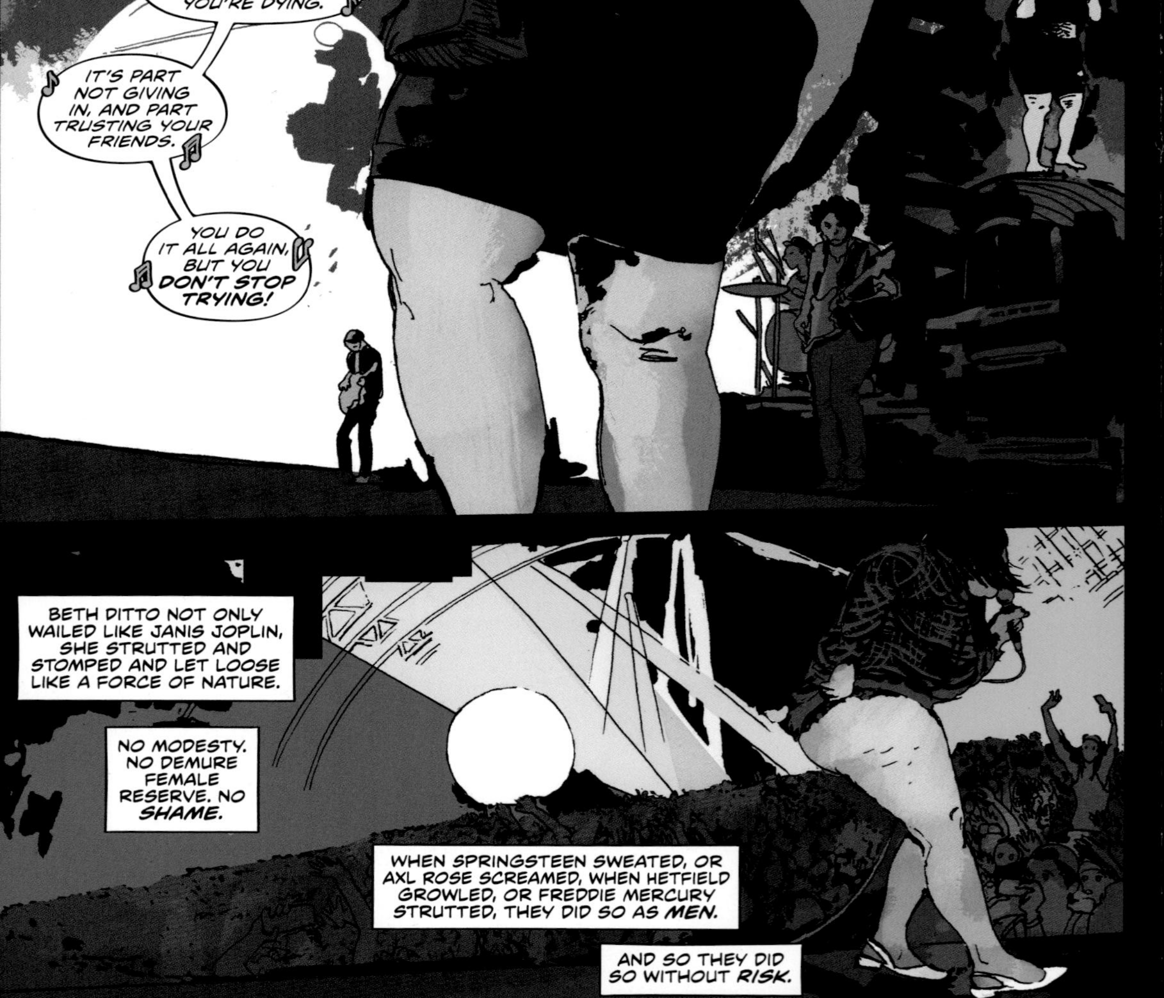
BETH DITTO NOT ONLY WAILED LIKE JANIS JOPLIN, SHE STRUTTED AND STOMPED AND LET LOOSE LIKE A FORCE OF NATURE.
NO MODESTY. NO DEMURE FEMALE RESERVE. NO ***SHAME.***
WHEN SPRINGSTEEN SWEATED, OR AXL ROSE SCREAMED, WHEN HETFIELD GROWLED, OR FREDDIE MERCURY STRUTTED, THEY DID SO AS ***MEN.***
AND SO THEY DID SO WITHOUT ***RISK.***

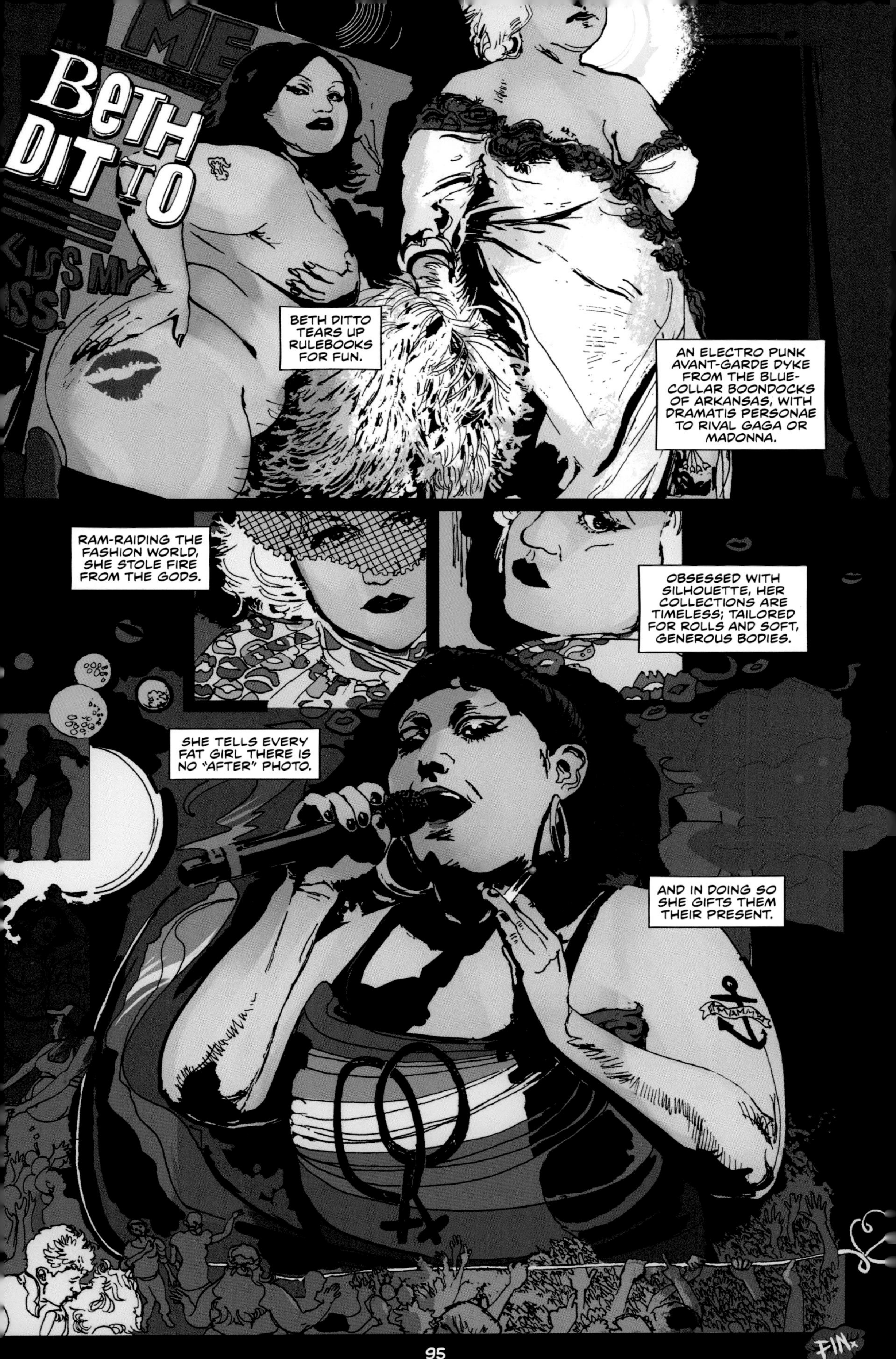
BETH DITTO
ME
KISS MY ASS!
BETH DITTO TEARS UP RULEBOOKS FOR FUN.
AN ELECTRO PUNK AVANT-GARDE DYKE FROM THE BLUE-COLLAR BOONDOCKS OF ARKANSAS, WITH DRAMATIS PERSONAE TO RIVAL GAGA OR MADONNA.
RAM-RAIDING THE FASHION WORLD, SHE STOLE FIRE FROM THE GODS.
OBSESSED WITH SILHOUETTE, HER COLLECTIONS ARE TIMELESS; TAILORED FOR ROLLS AND SOFT, GENEROUS BODIES.
SHE TELLS EVERY FAT GIRL THERE IS NO "AFTER" PHOTO.
AND IN DOING SO SHE GIFTS THEM THEIR PRESENT.
MAMA
FIN

"Understand well as I may, my comprehension can only be an infinitesimal fraction of all I want to understand."

—Ada Lovelace

Enchantress of Number

MEGAN HUTCHISON
WRITER/ARTIST

HI-FI
COLORIST

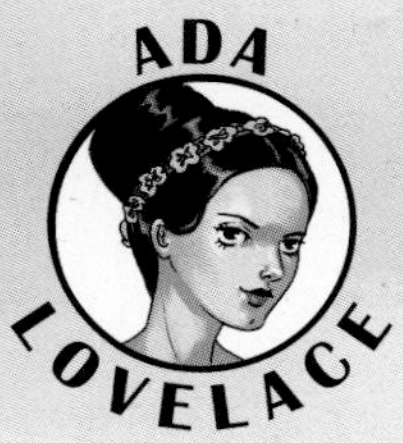
ADA
LOVELACE

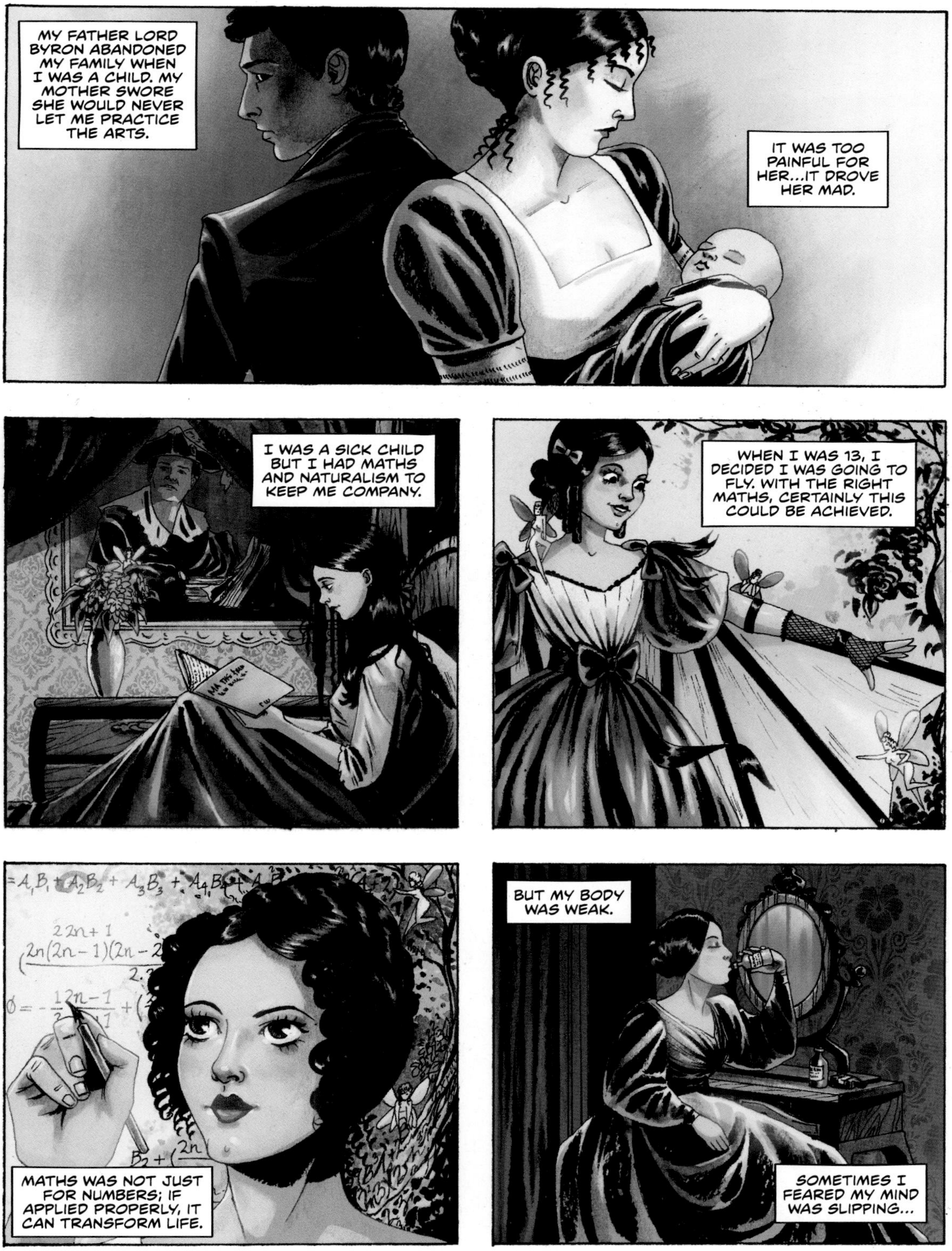
MY FATHER LORD BYRON ABANDONED MY FAMILY WHEN I WAS A CHILD. MY MOTHER SWORE SHE WOULD NEVER LET ME PRACTICE THE ARTS.
IT WAS TOO PAINFUL FOR HER...IT DROVE HER MAD.
I WAS A SICK CHILD BUT I HAD MATHS AND NATURALISM TO KEEP ME COMPANY.
WHEN I WAS 13, I DECIDED I WAS GOING TO FLY. WITH THE RIGHT MATHS, CERTAINLY THIS COULD BE ACHIEVED.
MATHS WAS NOT JUST FOR NUMBERS; IF APPLIED PROPERLY, IT CAN TRANSFORM LIFE.
BUT MY BODY WAS WEAK.
SOMETIMES I FEARED MY MIND WAS SLIPPING...

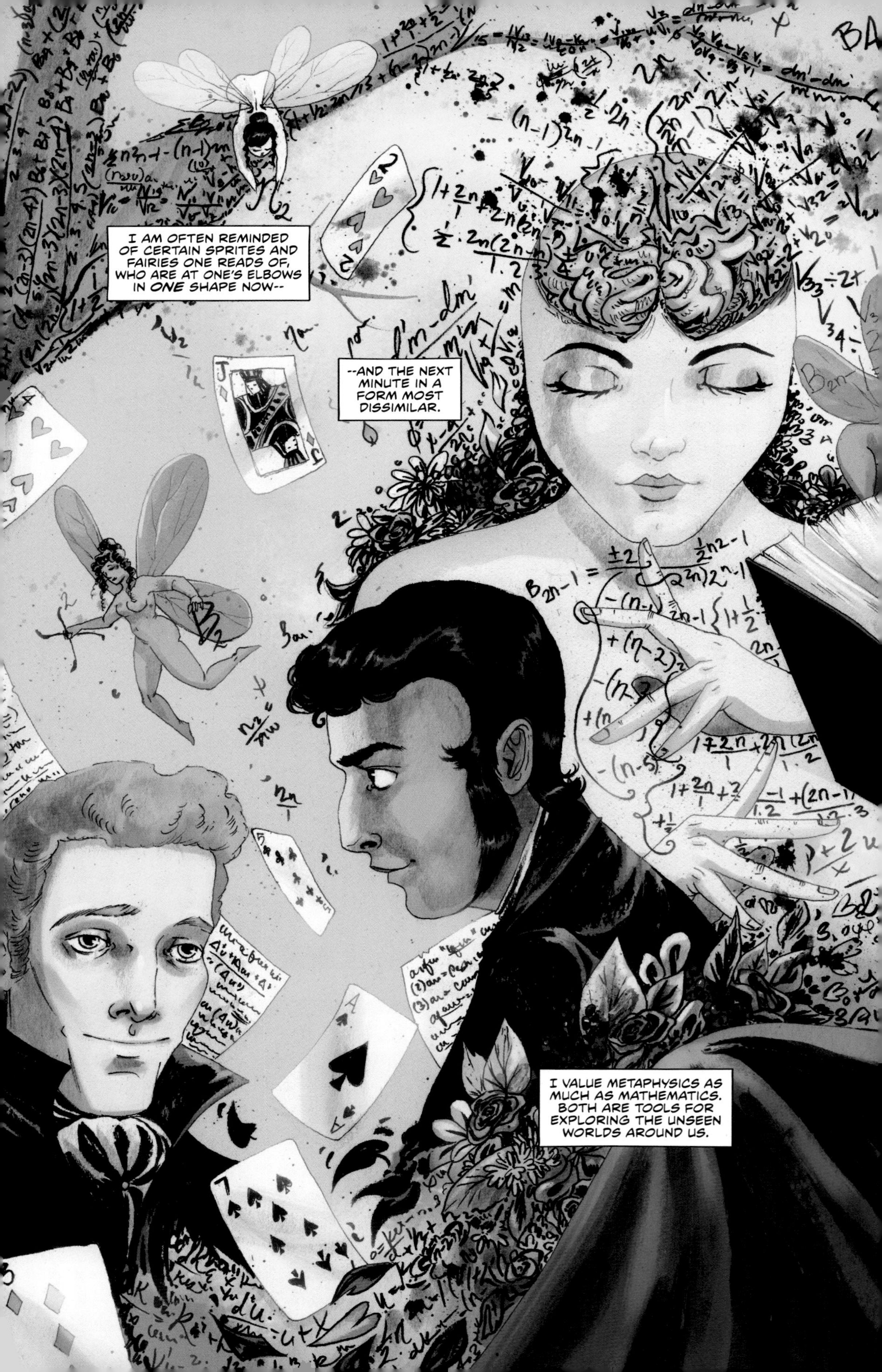
I AM OFTEN REMINDED OF CERTAIN SPRITES AND FAIRIES ONE READS OF, WHO ARE AT ONE'S ELBOWS IN *ONE* SHAPE NOW--
--AND THE NEXT MINUTE IN A FORM MOST DISSIMILAR.
I VALUE METAPHYSICS AS MUCH AS MATHEMATICS. BOTH ARE TOOLS FOR EXPLORING THE UNSEEN WORLDS AROUND US.

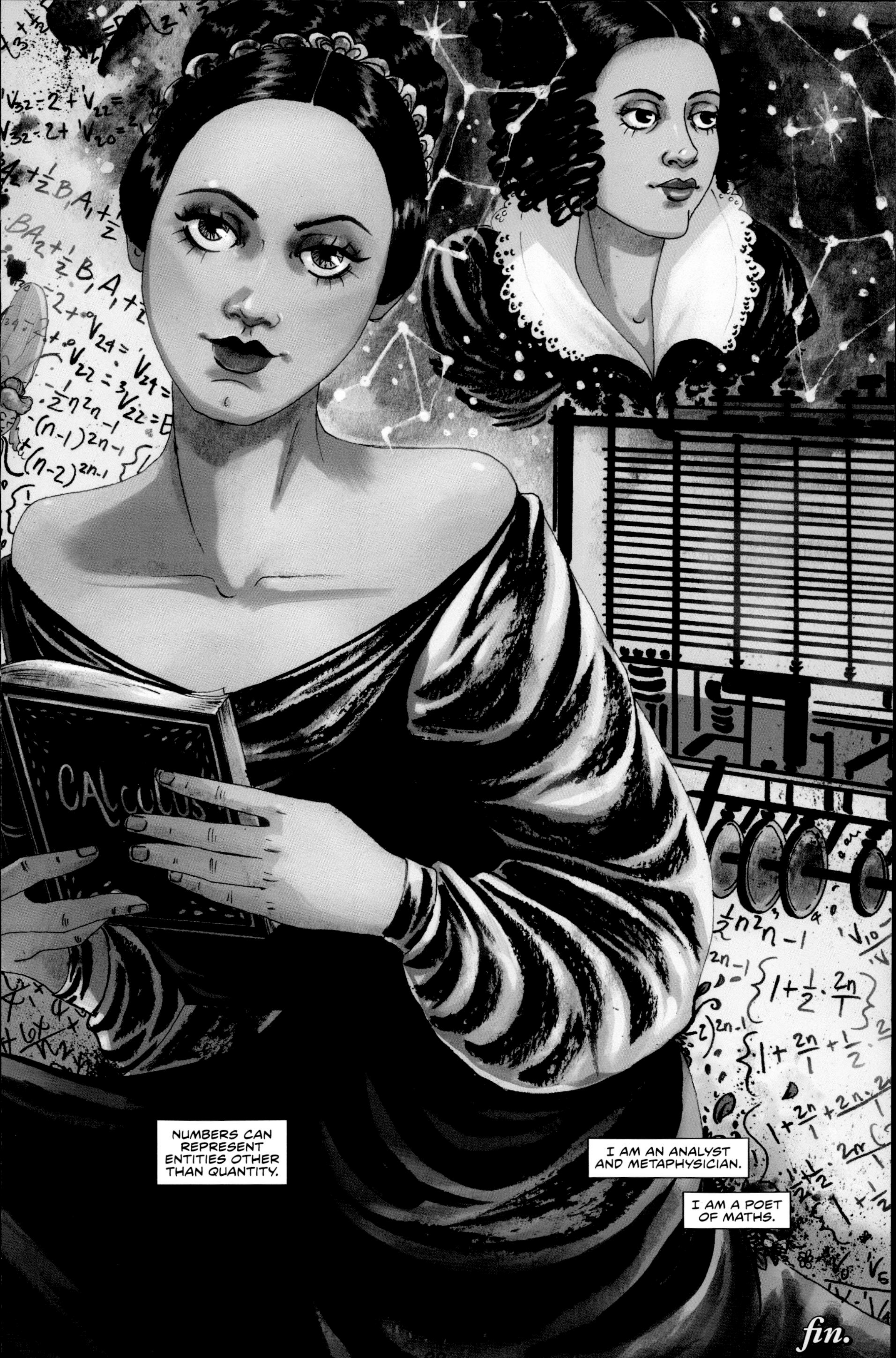
NUMBERS CAN REPRESENT ENTITIES OTHER THAN QUANTITY.
I AM AN ANALYST AND METAPHYSICIAN.
I AM A POET OF MATHS.
fin.

"You get an education in school and in college. And then you start to work, and that's when you learn!"

—Mary Blair

my small world

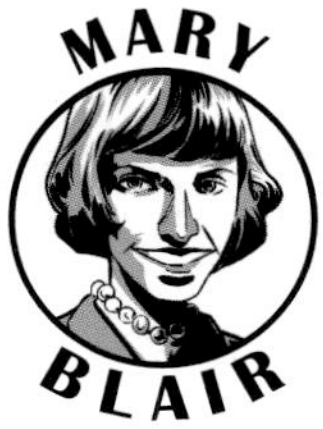

MARY
BLAIR

CASEY GILLY
WRITER

JEN HICKMAN
ARTIST/COLORIST

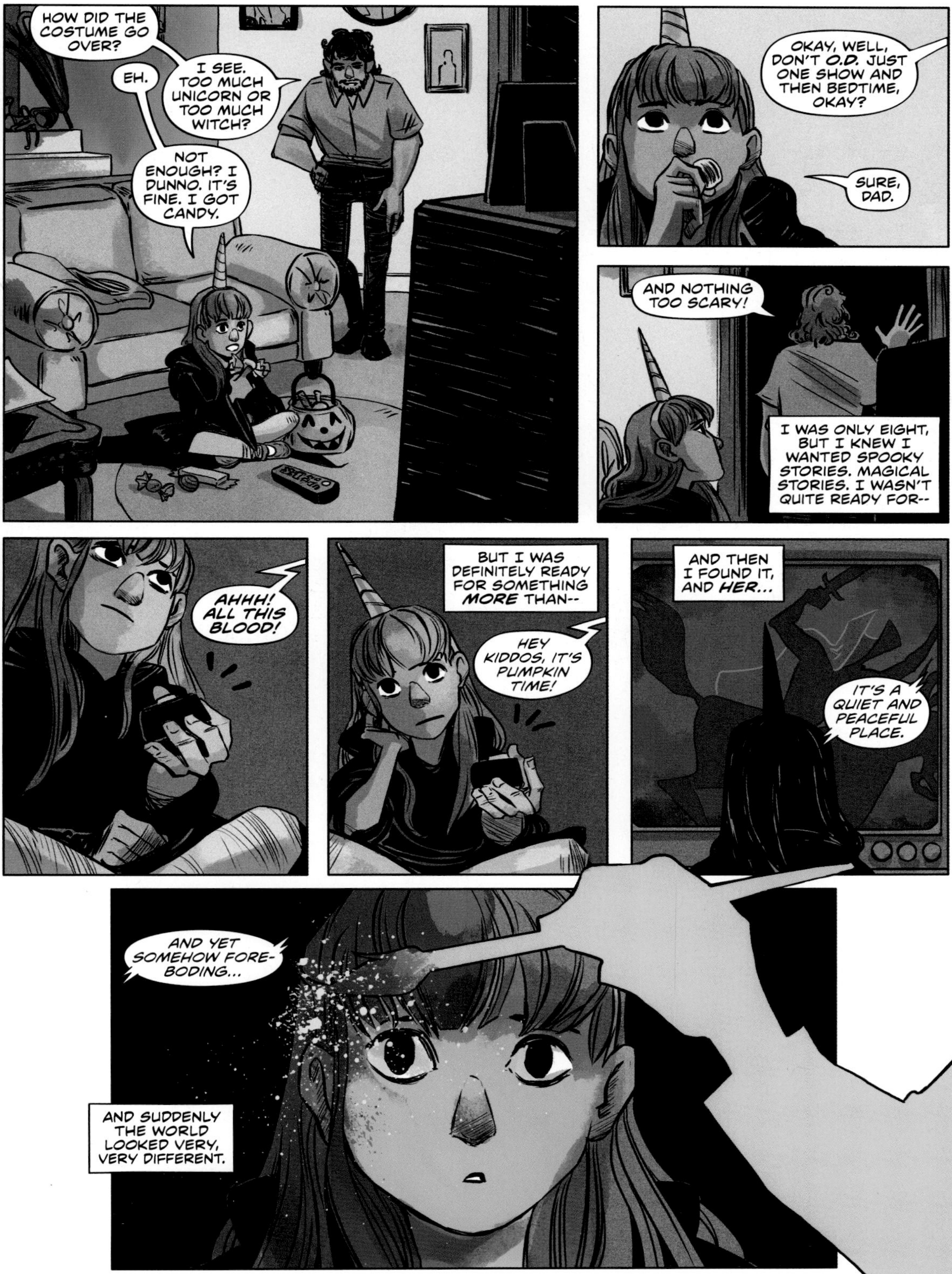

HOW DID THE COSTUME GO OVER?
EH.
I SEE. TOO MUCH UNICORN OR TOO MUCH WITCH?
NOT ENOUGH? I DUNNO. IT'S FINE. I GOT CANDY.
OKAY, WELL, DON'T O.D. JUST ONE SHOW AND THEN BEDTIME, OKAY?
SURE, DAD.
AND NOTHING TOO SCARY!
I WAS ONLY EIGHT, BUT I KNEW I WANTED SPOOKY STORIES. MAGICAL STORIES. I WASN'T QUITE READY FOR--
AHHH! ALL THIS BLOOD!
BUT I WAS DEFINITELY READY FOR SOMETHING MORE THAN--
HEY KIDDOS, IT'S PUMPKIN TIME!
AND THEN I FOUND IT, AND HER...
IT'S A QUIET AND PEACEFUL PLACE.
AND YET SOMEHOW FORE-BODING...
AND SUDDENLY THE WORLD LOOKED VERY, VERY DIFFERENT.

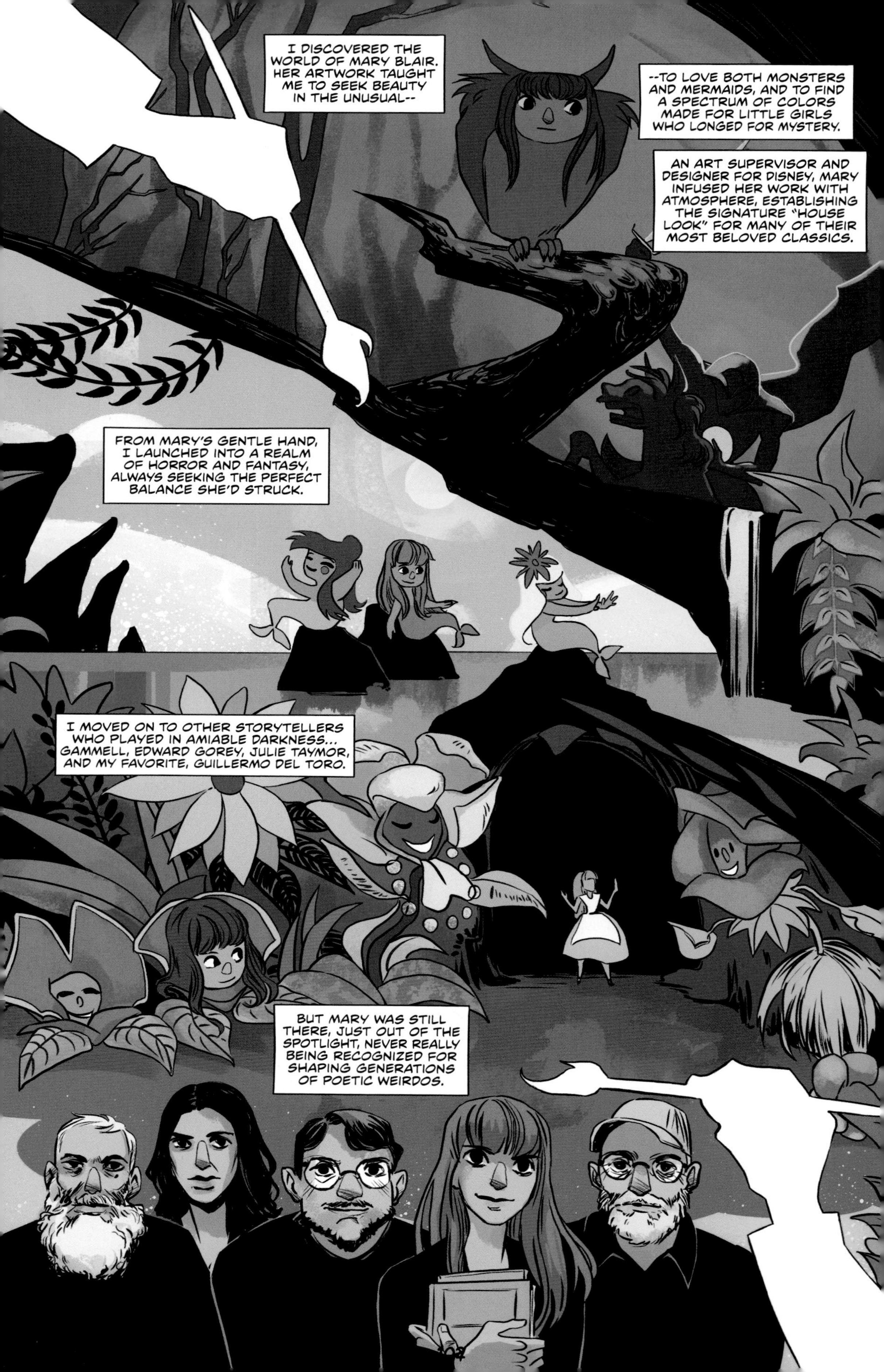
I DISCOVERED THE WORLD OF MARY BLAIR. HER ARTWORK TAUGHT ME TO SEEK BEAUTY IN THE UNUSUAL--
--TO LOVE BOTH MONSTERS AND MERMAIDS, AND TO FIND A SPECTRUM OF COLORS MADE FOR LITTLE GIRLS WHO LONGED FOR MYSTERY.
AN ART SUPERVISOR AND DESIGNER FOR DISNEY, MARY INFUSED HER WORK WITH ATMOSPHERE, ESTABLISHING THE SIGNATURE "HOUSE LOOK" FOR MANY OF THEIR MOST BELOVED CLASSICS.
FROM MARY'S GENTLE HAND, I LAUNCHED INTO A REALM OF HORROR AND FANTASY, ALWAYS SEEKING THE PERFECT BALANCE SHE'D STRUCK.
I MOVED ON TO OTHER STORYTELLERS WHO PLAYED IN AMIABLE DARKNESS... GAMMELL, EDWARD GOREY, JULIE TAYMOR, AND MY FAVORITE, GUILLERMO DEL TORO.
BUT MARY WAS STILL THERE, JUST OUT OF THE SPOTLIGHT, NEVER REALLY BEING RECOGNIZED FOR SHAPING GENERATIONS OF POETIC WEIRDOS.

TWENTY-SOMETHING YEARS LATER, I'M STILL THAT SAME LITTLE GIRL, IN LOVE WITH BEAUTIFUL, SCARY THINGS.

SO OF COURSE WHEN I HEARD ABOUT THE DEL TORO EXHIBIT AT LACMA, LOS ANGELES COUNTY MUSEUM OF ART, I HAD TO GO.

BUT I DIDN'T EXPECT TO FIND MARY THERE, TOO.

COME ON! I'VE BEEN WAITING TO SEE THIS FOR AGES!

ALTHOUGH HER INFLUENCE SPARKED MY LOVE OF MAGICAL REALISM...

...I'D NEVER KNOWN HOW MUCH SHE INSPIRED SOME OTHER CREATORS I ADMIRED.

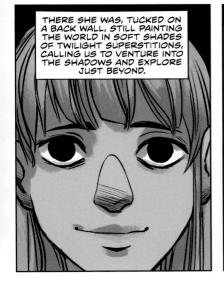

THERE SHE WAS, TUCKED ON A BACK WALL, STILL PAINTING THE WORLD IN SOFT SHADES OF TWILIGHT SUPERSTITIONS, CALLING US TO VENTURE INTO THE SHADOWS AND EXPLORE JUST BEYOND.

NOW I SIT HERE TRACING MY CREATIVE PATH BACK, KNOWING SHE IS HOW I ARRIVED AT A PLACE WHERE I WRITE STORIES MEANT TO CAPTURE THE HEARTS OF LITTLE GIRLS WHO WANT TO BE UNICORNS AND WITCHES.

AND I WILL ALWAYS BE GRATEFUL.

MARY B

fin.

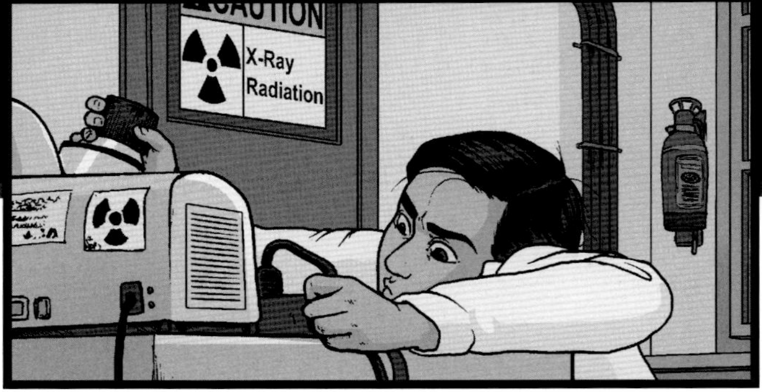
CAUTION
X-Ray
Radiation

"You look at science (or at least talk of it) as some sort of demoralizing invention of man, something apart from real life, and which must be cautiously guarded and kept separate from everyday existence. But science and everyday life cannot and should not be separated."

—Rosalind Franklin

A Doubly Twisted String With a Million Knots

MIKE CAREY
WRITER

EUGENIA KOUMAKI
ARTIST

HI-FI
COLORIST

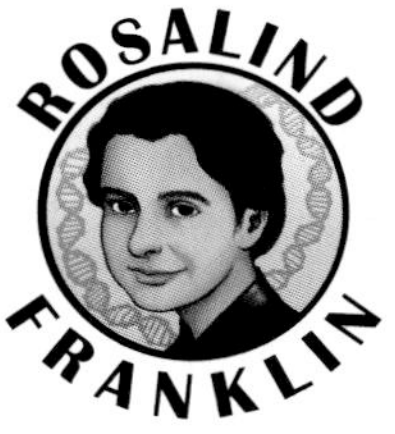
ROSALIND
FRANKLIN

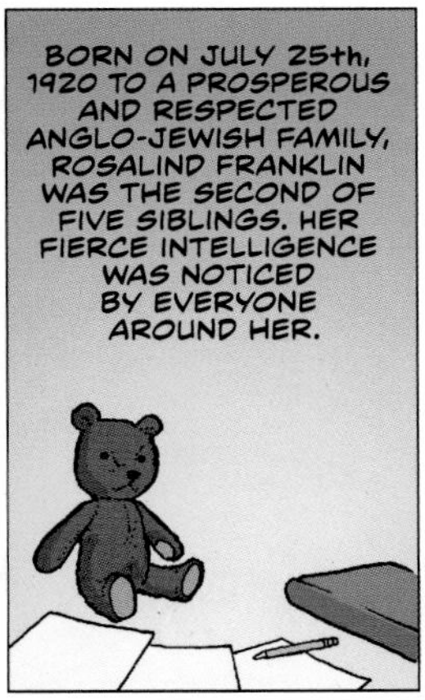
BORN ON JULY 25th, 1920 TO A PROSPEROUS AND RESPECTED ANGLO-JEWISH FAMILY, ROSALIND FRANKLIN WAS THE SECOND OF FIVE SIBLINGS. HER FIERCE INTELLIGENCE WAS NOTICED BY EVERYONE AROUND HER.

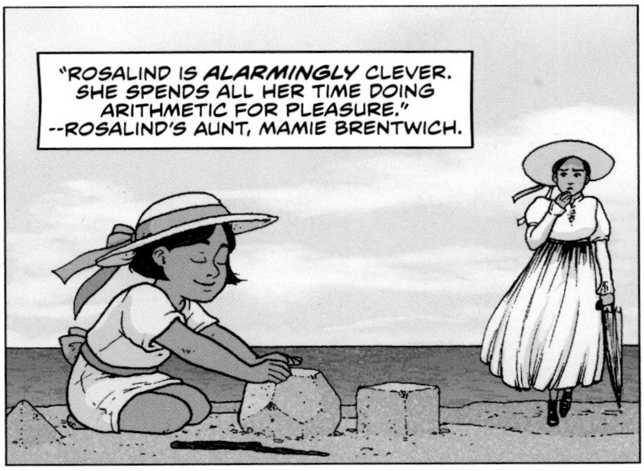
"ROSALIND IS ALARMINGLY CLEVER. SHE SPENDS ALL HER TIME DOING ARITHMETIC FOR PLEASURE." --ROSALIND'S AUNT, MAMIE BRENTWICH.

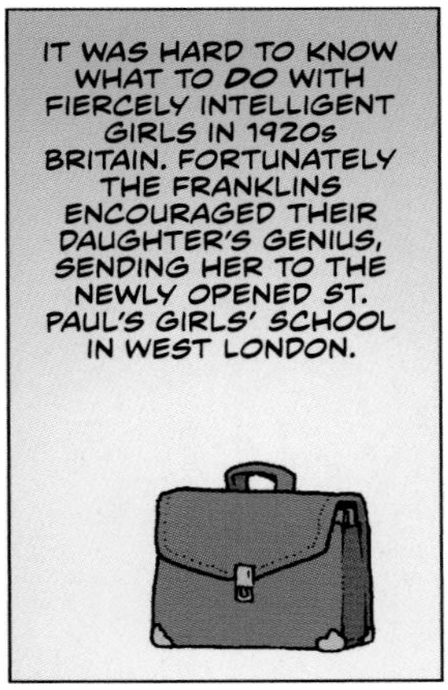
IT WAS HARD TO KNOW WHAT TO DO WITH FIERCELY INTELLIGENT GIRLS IN 1920s BRITAIN. FORTUNATELY THE FRANKLINS ENCOURAGED THEIR DAUGHTER'S GENIUS, SENDING HER TO THE NEWLY OPENED ST. PAUL'S GIRLS' SCHOOL IN WEST LONDON.

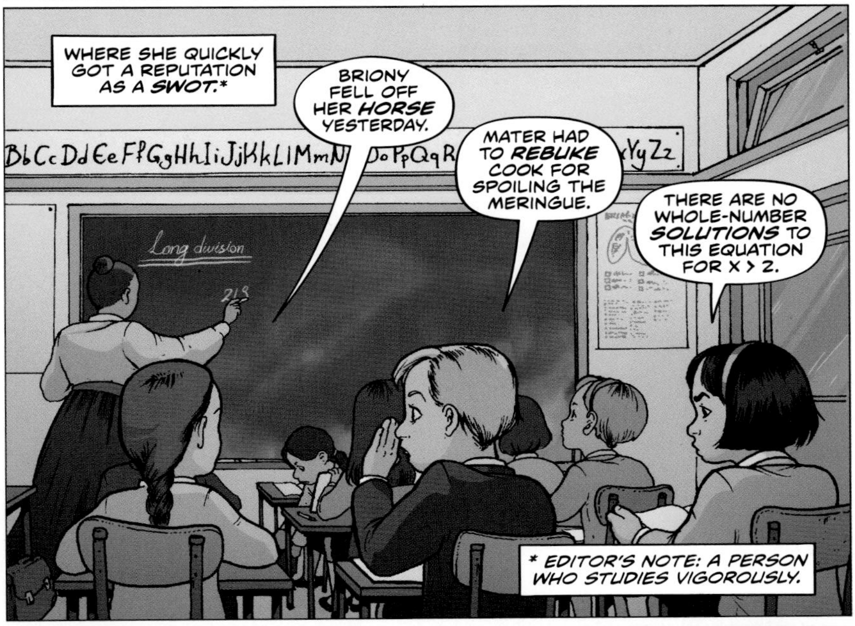
WHERE SHE QUICKLY GOT A REPUTATION AS A SWOT.*
Long division
BRIONY FELL OFF HER HORSE YESTERDAY.
MATER HAD TO REBUKE COOK FOR SPOILING THE MERINGUE.
THERE ARE NO WHOLE-NUMBER SOLUTIONS TO THIS EQUATION FOR X > 2.
* EDITOR'S NOTE: A PERSON WHO STUDIES VIGOROUSLY.

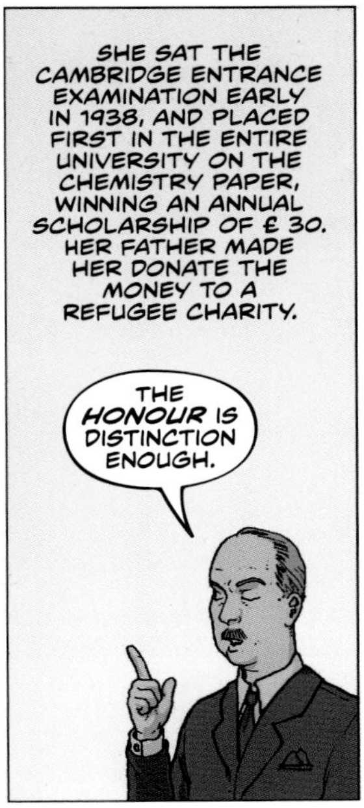
SHE SAT THE CAMBRIDGE ENTRANCE EXAMINATION EARLY IN 1938, AND PLACED FIRST IN THE ENTIRE UNIVERSITY ON THE CHEMISTRY PAPER, WINNING AN ANNUAL SCHOLARSHIP OF £ 30. HER FATHER MADE HER DONATE THE MONEY TO A REFUGEE CHARITY.
THE HONOUR IS DISTINCTION ENOUGH.

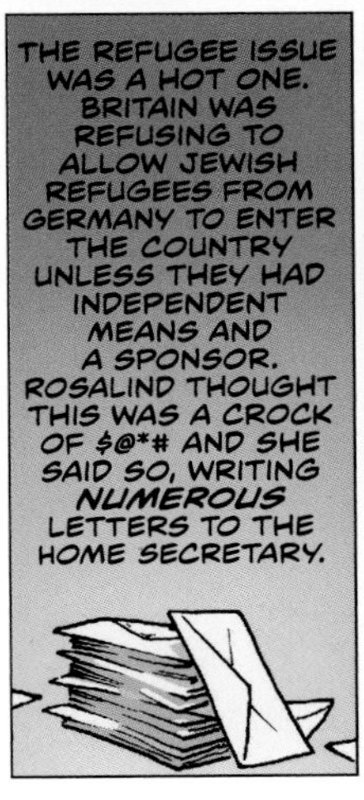
THE REFUGEE ISSUE WAS A HOT ONE. BRITAIN WAS REFUSING TO ALLOW JEWISH REFUGEES FROM GERMANY TO ENTER THE COUNTRY UNLESS THEY HAD INDEPENDENT MEANS AND A SPONSOR. ROSALIND THOUGHT THIS WAS A CROCK OF $@*# AND SHE SAID SO, WRITING NUMEROUS LETTERS TO THE HOME SECRETARY.

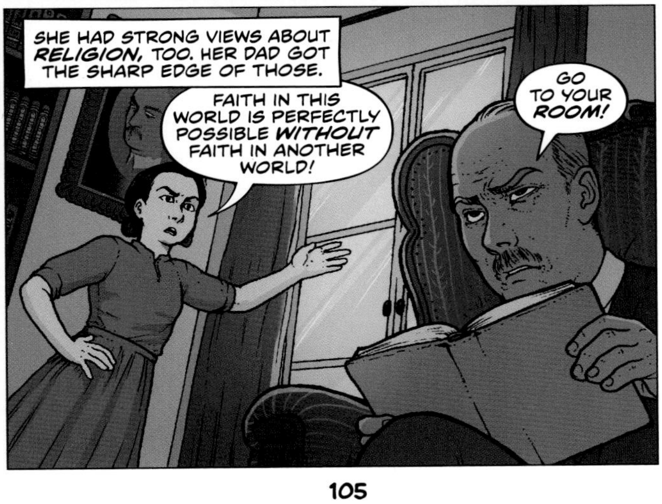
SHE HAD STRONG VIEWS ABOUT RELIGION, TOO. HER DAD GOT THE SHARP EDGE OF THOSE.
FAITH IN THIS WORLD IS PERFECTLY POSSIBLE WITHOUT FAITH IN ANOTHER WORLD!
GO TO YOUR ROOM!

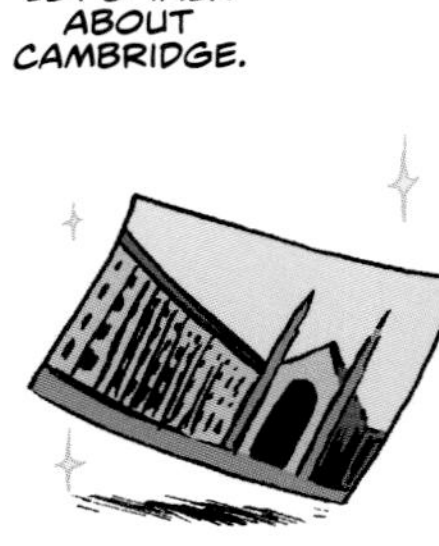
BUT YEAH. CAMBRIDGE.
LET'S TALK ABOUT CAMBRIDGE.

IN 1938, FEMALE UNDERGRADUATES COULDN'T SIT FOR A REGULAR BACHELOR'S DEGREE. THEY COULD ONLY GET WHAT WAS CALLED A DEGREE TITULAR. THEY COULDN'T OFFICIALLY GRADUATE, WEAR UNIVERSITY GOWNS OR TAKE ANY UNIVERSITY OFFICE.
STILL, FRANKLIN WAS OVER THE MOON JUST TO *BE* THERE. A FEW GENERATIONS EARLIER SHE WOULD HAVE BEEN BARRED *TWICE,* FOR BEING BOTH A WOMAN AND A JEW.
THE *WAR* HAD BROKEN OUT BY THIS POINT. LESSONS WERE FREQUENTLY INTERRUPTED BY AIR RAID SIRENS, WHICH MEANT EVERYONE HAD TO RUN TO THE NEAREST UNDERGROUND SHELTER.
BUT FRANKLIN DIDN'T LET THAT SLOW HER DOWN MUCH.
THIS MOLECULE REQUIRES AN ADDITIONAL *HYDROGEN* BOND AT LOCUS 3.
AFTER SHE GRADUATED, FRANKLIN WENT TO PARIS.
WHERE SHE STUDIED *COAL.*
HMM.
SHE WAS EMPLOYED AT THE *LABORATOIRE CENTRAL* TO STUDY THE IMPERFECT CRYSTALLINE STRUCTURES OF CARBON MOLECULES. SHE PERFECTED TECHNIQUES FOR PHOTOGRAPHING THEM USING X-RAYS, WHICH WAS WHAT ULTIMATELY LED BOTH TO THE BIGGEST TRIUMPH OF HER CAREER AND [SPOILER ALERT] TO HER TRAGICALLY EARLY DEATH.
HAVING MADE A BREAKTHROUGH IN MAPPING THE FORMATION OF GRAPHITE—WHICH HAD IMMEDIATE AND FAR-REACHING INDUSTRIAL APPLICATIONS—SHE WAS HEADHUNTED BY JAMES RANDALL OF KING'S COLLEGE LONDON. HE WANTED HER TO APPLY HER X-RAY MICROSCOPY TECHNIQUES TO THE STUDY OF THE DNA MOLECULE.
EVERYONE KNEW HOW IMPORTANT *DNA* WAS, AND THERE WAS A THREE-WAY RACE TO BE THE FIRST TO MAP ITS STRUCTURE.
LINUS PAULING IN THE USA. FRANCIS CRICK AND JAMES WATSON AT CAMBRIDGE. AND MAURICE WILKINS AT KING'S.
CAUTION
X-Ray Radiation
NOBODY EXPECTED AN *OUTSIDER* TO ENTER THE RACE.
WAIT. WHAT ARE YOU...? NO. *STOP* THAT.
LET ALONE AN OUTSIDER WITH A *CHEMISTRY* DOCTORATE AND HER OWN HOMEMADE X-RAY-POWERED CAMERA.
CRICK AND WATSON DIDN'T HAVE A CHEMISTRY DEGREE BETWEEN THEM. THEY WERE *BIOLOGISTS,* WITH A LITTLE BIT OF PHYSICS.
THEIR FIRST ATTEMPT AT A 3-D MODEL OF DNA WAS A *CAR CRASH.*
HAND ME ANOTHER *SPOON.*
THEY SHOWED IT TO ROSALIND FRANKLIN. WHO STRAIGHT-UP MARKED THEIR HOMEWORK.
MAGNESIUM IONS? SERIOUSLY?
WHAT ABOUT THE *TOOTH FAIRY?* IS SHE IN THERE, TOO?
MAYBE THAT, RIGHT THERE, WAS ONE REASON FOR WHAT HAPPENED.

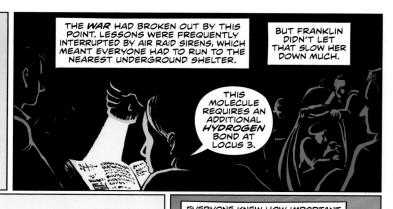

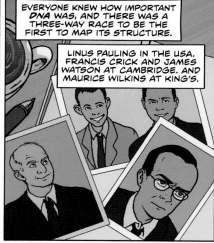

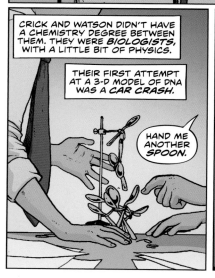

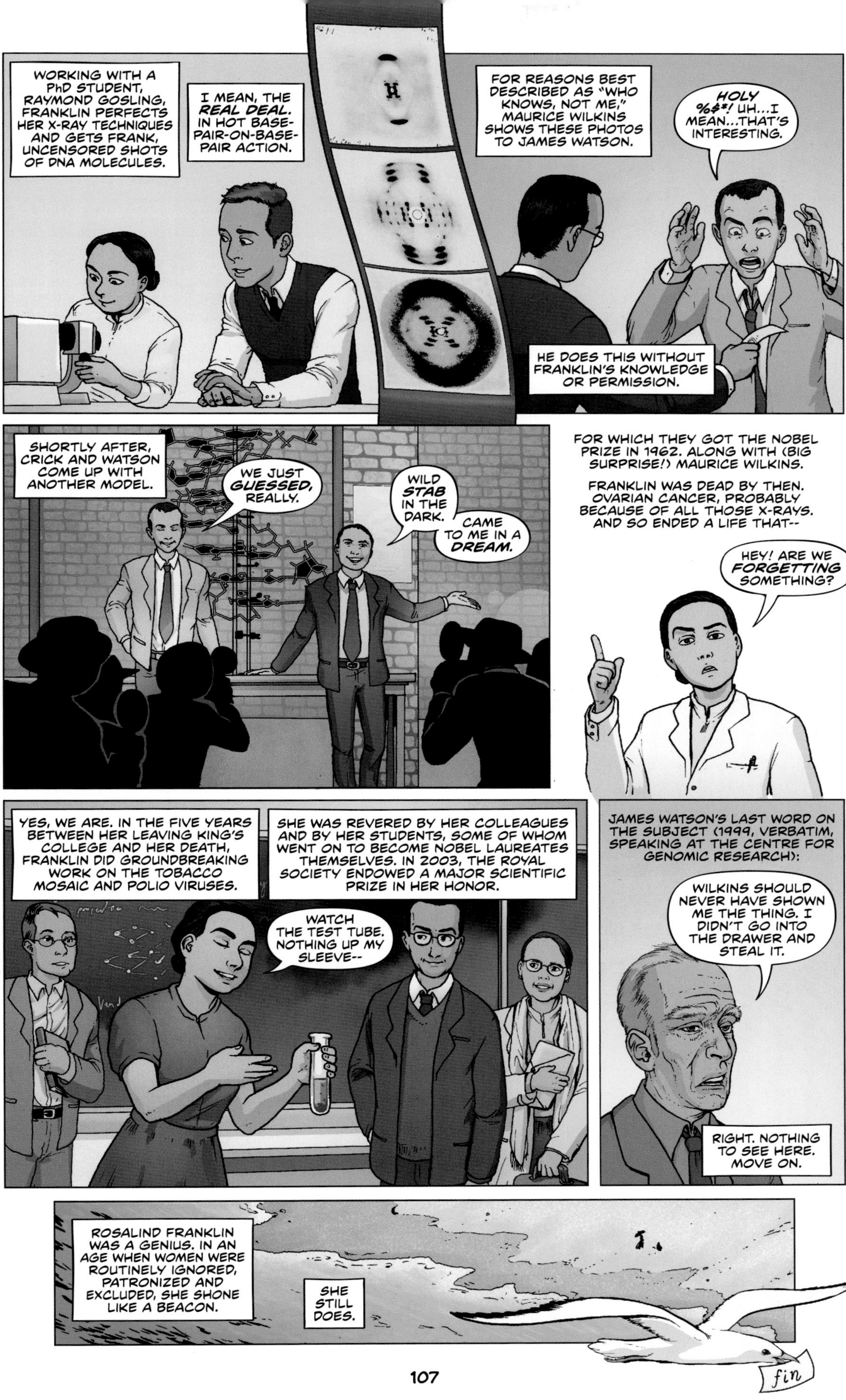
WORKING WITH A PhD STUDENT, RAYMOND GOSLING, FRANKLIN PERFECTS HER X-RAY TECHNIQUES AND GETS FRANK, UNCENSORED SHOTS OF DNA MOLECULES.
I MEAN, THE *REAL DEAL.* IN HOT BASE-PAIR-ON-BASE-PAIR ACTION.
FOR REASONS BEST DESCRIBED AS "WHO KNOWS, NOT ME," MAURICE WILKINS SHOWS THESE PHOTOS TO JAMES WATSON.
HOLY %$!* UH...I MEAN...THAT'S INTERESTING.
HE DOES THIS WITHOUT FRANKLIN'S KNOWLEDGE OR PERMISSION.
SHORTLY AFTER, CRICK AND WATSON COME UP WITH ANOTHER MODEL.
WE JUST *GUESSED,* REALLY.
WILD *STAB* IN THE DARK.
CAME TO ME IN A *DREAM.*
FOR WHICH THEY GOT THE NOBEL PRIZE IN 1962. ALONG WITH (BIG SURPRISE!) MAURICE WILKINS.
FRANKLIN WAS DEAD BY THEN. OVARIAN CANCER, PROBABLY BECAUSE OF ALL THOSE X-RAYS. AND SO ENDED A LIFE THAT--
HEY! ARE WE *FORGETTING* SOMETHING?
YES, WE ARE. IN THE FIVE YEARS BETWEEN HER LEAVING KING'S COLLEGE AND HER DEATH, FRANKLIN DID GROUNDBREAKING WORK ON THE TOBACCO MOSAIC AND POLIO VIRUSES.
SHE WAS REVERED BY HER COLLEAGUES AND BY HER STUDENTS, SOME OF WHOM WENT ON TO BECOME NOBEL LAUREATES THEMSELVES. IN 2003, THE ROYAL SOCIETY ENDOWED A MAJOR SCIENTIFIC PRIZE IN HER HONOR.
WATCH THE TEST TUBE. NOTHING UP MY SLEEVE--
JAMES WATSON'S LAST WORD ON THE SUBJECT (1999, VERBATIM, SPEAKING AT THE CENTRE FOR GENOMIC RESEARCH):
WILKINS SHOULD NEVER HAVE SHOWN ME THE THING. I DIDN'T GO INTO THE DRAWER AND STEAL IT.
RIGHT. NOTHING TO SEE HERE. MOVE ON.
ROSALIND FRANKLIN WAS A GENIUS. IN AN AGE WHEN WOMEN WERE ROUTINELY IGNORED, PATRONIZED AND EXCLUDED, SHE SHONE LIKE A BEACON.
SHE STILL DOES.
fin

*"I'm not usually where I think I am.
It's kind of spooky."*
—Laurie Anderson

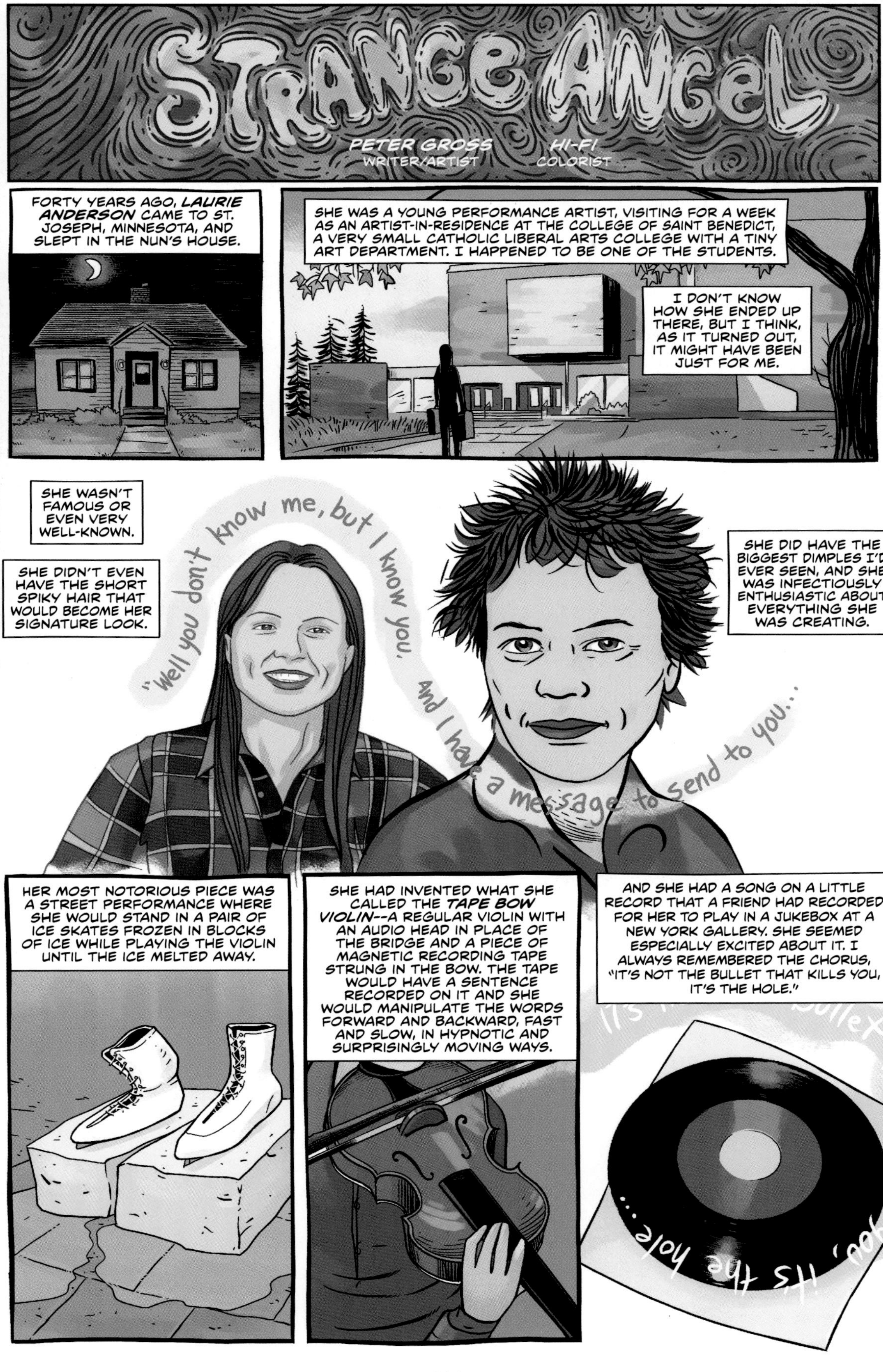
STRANGE ANGEL
PETER GROSS
WRITER/ARTIST
HI-FI
COLORIST
FORTY YEARS AGO, LAURIE ANDERSON CAME TO ST. JOSEPH, MINNESOTA, AND SLEPT IN THE NUN'S HOUSE.
SHE WAS A YOUNG PERFORMANCE ARTIST, VISITING FOR A WEEK AS AN ARTIST-IN-RESIDENCE AT THE COLLEGE OF SAINT BENEDICT, A VERY SMALL CATHOLIC LIBERAL ARTS COLLEGE WITH A TINY ART DEPARTMENT. I HAPPENED TO BE ONE OF THE STUDENTS.
I DON'T KNOW HOW SHE ENDED UP THERE, BUT I THINK, AS IT TURNED OUT, IT MIGHT HAVE BEEN JUST FOR ME.
SHE WASN'T FAMOUS OR EVEN VERY WELL-KNOWN.
SHE DIDN'T EVEN HAVE THE SHORT SPIKY HAIR THAT WOULD BECOME HER SIGNATURE LOOK.
"well you don't know me, but I know you. and I have a message to send to you...
SHE DID HAVE THE BIGGEST DIMPLES I'D EVER SEEN, AND SHE WAS INFECTIOUSLY ENTHUSIASTIC ABOUT EVERYTHING SHE WAS CREATING.
HER MOST NOTORIOUS PIECE WAS A STREET PERFORMANCE WHERE SHE WOULD STAND IN A PAIR OF ICE SKATES FROZEN IN BLOCKS OF ICE WHILE PLAYING THE VIOLIN UNTIL THE ICE MELTED AWAY.
SHE HAD INVENTED WHAT SHE CALLED THE TAPE BOW VIOLIN--A REGULAR VIOLIN WITH AN AUDIO HEAD IN PLACE OF THE BRIDGE AND A PIECE OF MAGNETIC RECORDING TAPE STRUNG IN THE BOW. THE TAPE WOULD HAVE A SENTENCE RECORDED ON IT AND SHE WOULD MANIPULATE THE WORDS FORWARD AND BACKWARD, FAST AND SLOW, IN HYPNOTIC AND SURPRISINGLY MOVING WAYS.
AND SHE HAD A SONG ON A LITTLE RECORD THAT A FRIEND HAD RECORDED FOR HER TO PLAY IN A JUKEBOX AT A NEW YORK GALLERY. SHE SEEMED ESPECIALLY EXCITED ABOUT IT. I ALWAYS REMEMBERED THE CHORUS, "IT'S NOT THE BULLET THAT KILLS YOU, IT'S THE HOLE."
it's
bullet that kills you, it's the hole...

SHE HELD A NUMBER OF SMALL TALKS AND PERFORMANCES FOR THE FEW OF US WHO SHOWED UP. THEY WERE IN A LOUNGE OFF THE ART STUDIOS, NOT EVEN IN A THEATER OR WITH A STAGE, BUT SHE SEEMED TO LIKE IT THAT WAY.

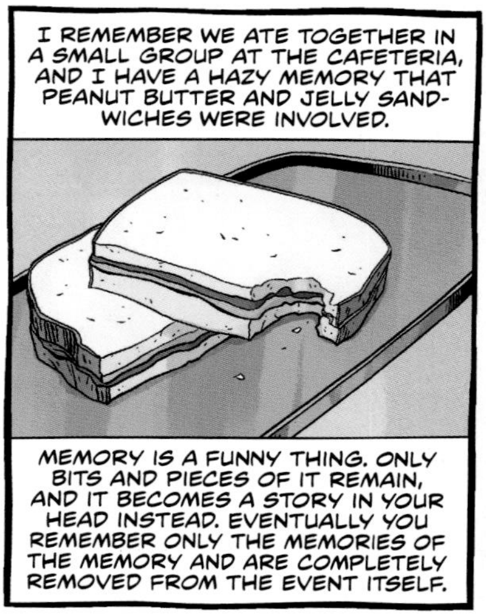
I REMEMBER WE ATE TOGETHER IN A SMALL GROUP AT THE CAFETERIA, AND I HAVE A HAZY MEMORY THAT PEANUT BUTTER AND JELLY SANDWICHES WERE INVOLVED.
MEMORY IS A FUNNY THING. ONLY BITS AND PIECES OF IT REMAIN, AND IT BECOMES A STORY IN YOUR HEAD INSTEAD. EVENTUALLY YOU REMEMBER ONLY THE MEMORIES OF THE MEMORY AND ARE COMPLETELY REMOVED FROM THE EVENT ITSELF.

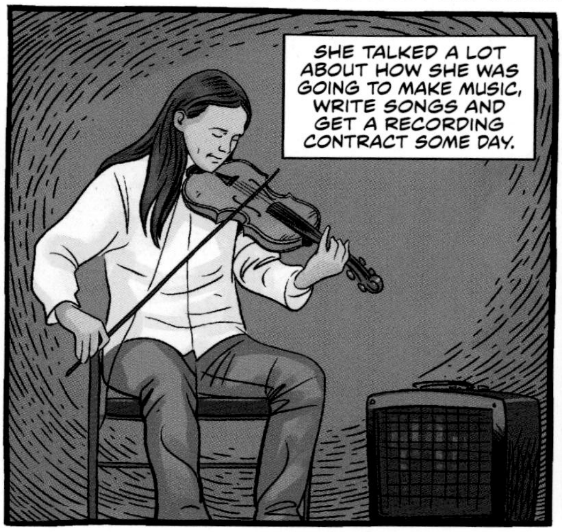
SHE TALKED A LOT ABOUT HOW SHE WAS GOING TO MAKE MUSIC, WRITE SONGS AND GET A RECORDING CONTRACT SOME DAY.

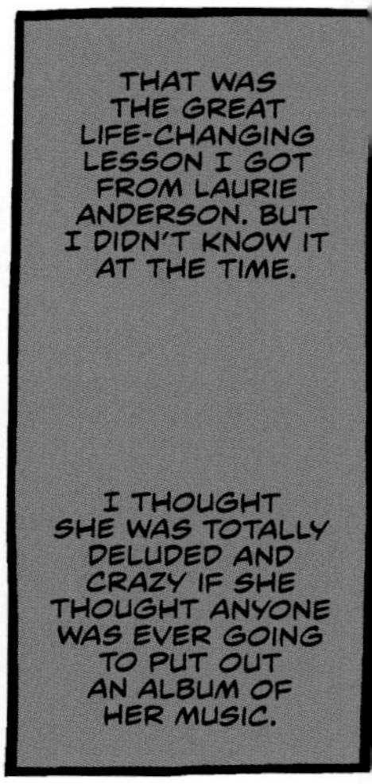
THAT WAS THE GREAT LIFE-CHANGING LESSON I GOT FROM LAURIE ANDERSON. BUT I DIDN'T KNOW IT AT THE TIME.
I THOUGHT SHE WAS TOTALLY DELUDED AND CRAZY IF SHE THOUGHT ANYONE WAS EVER GOING TO PUT OUT AN ALBUM OF HER MUSIC.

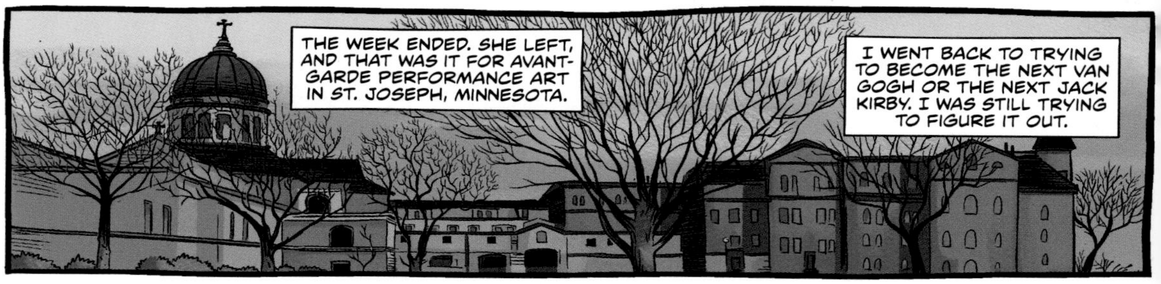
THE WEEK ENDED. SHE LEFT, AND THAT WAS IT FOR AVANT-GARDE PERFORMANCE ART IN ST. JOSEPH, MINNESOTA.
I WENT BACK TO TRYING TO BECOME THE NEXT VAN GOGH OR THE NEXT JACK KIRBY. I WAS STILL TRYING TO FIGURE IT OUT.

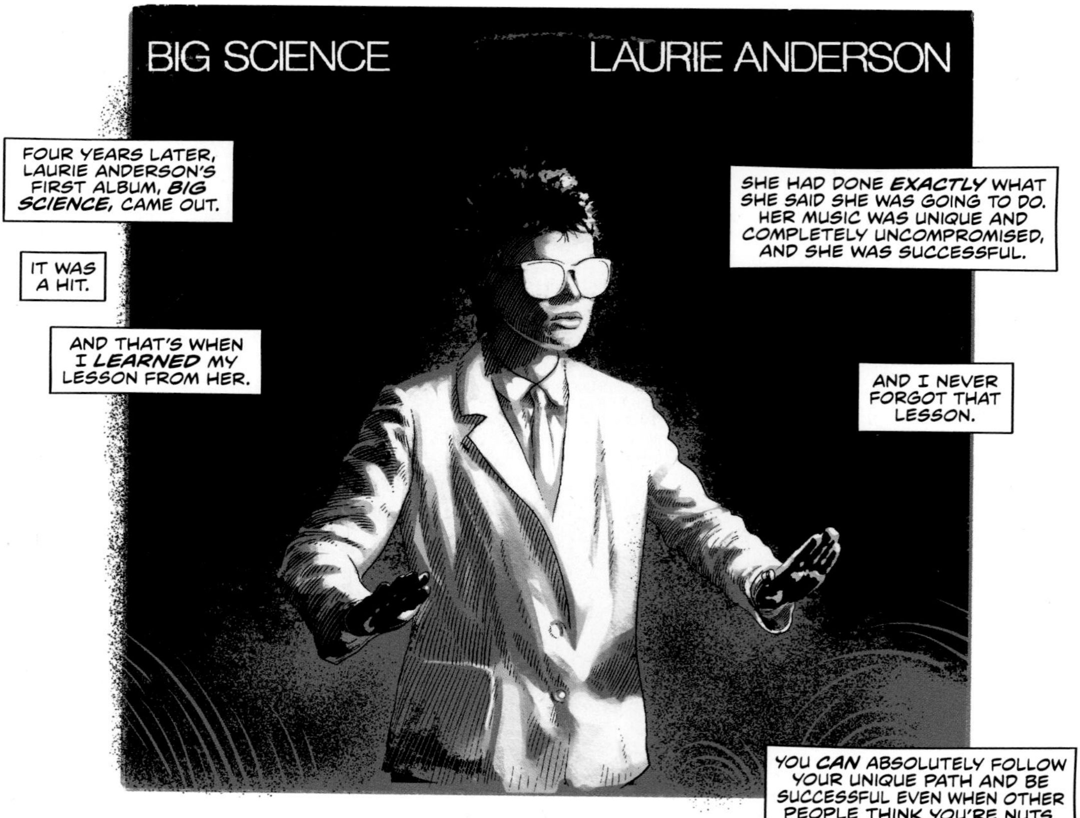
BIG SCIENCE
LAURIE ANDERSON
FOUR YEARS LATER, LAURIE ANDERSON'S FIRST ALBUM, ***BIG SCIENCE,*** CAME OUT.
IT WAS A HIT.
AND THAT'S WHEN I ***LEARNED*** MY LESSON FROM HER.
SHE HAD DONE ***EXACTLY*** WHAT SHE SAID SHE WAS GOING TO DO. HER MUSIC WAS UNIQUE AND COMPLETELY UNCOMPROMISED, AND SHE WAS SUCCESSFUL.
AND I NEVER FORGOT THAT LESSON.
YOU ***CAN*** ABSOLUTELY FOLLOW YOUR UNIQUE PATH AND BE SUCCESSFUL EVEN WHEN OTHER PEOPLE THINK YOU'RE NUTS.

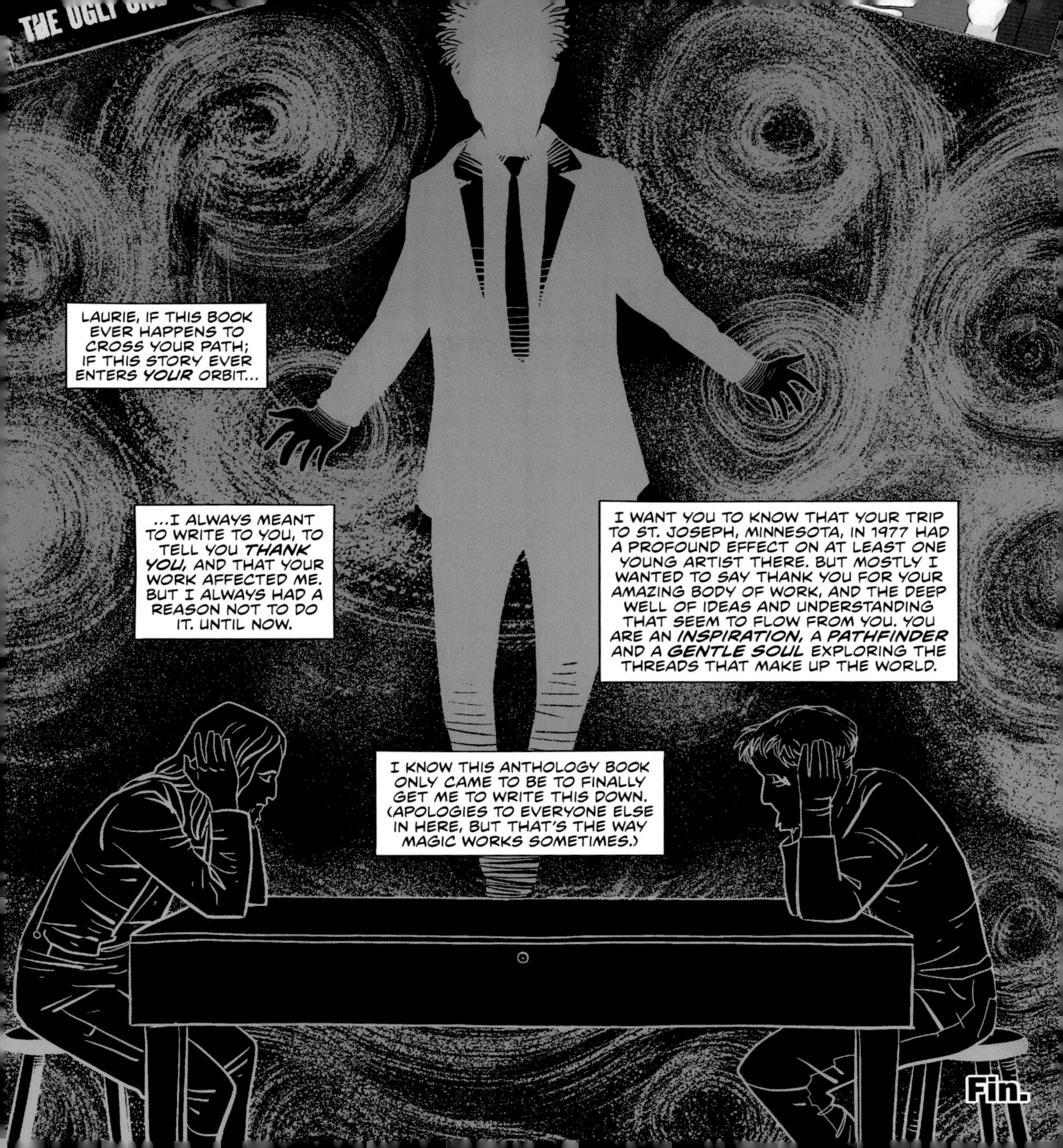
LAURIE, IF THIS BOOK EVER HAPPENS TO CROSS YOUR PATH; IF THIS STORY EVER ENTERS *YOUR* ORBIT...
...I ALWAYS MEANT TO WRITE TO YOU, TO TELL YOU *THANK YOU,* AND THAT YOUR WORK AFFECTED ME. BUT I ALWAYS HAD A REASON NOT TO DO IT. UNTIL NOW.
I WANT YOU TO KNOW THAT YOUR TRIP TO ST. JOSEPH, MINNESOTA, IN 1977 HAD A PROFOUND EFFECT ON AT LEAST ONE YOUNG ARTIST THERE. BUT MOSTLY I WANTED TO SAY THANK YOU FOR YOUR AMAZING BODY OF WORK, AND THE DEEP WELL OF IDEAS AND UNDERSTANDING THAT SEEM TO FLOW FROM YOU. YOU ARE AN *INSPIRATION,* A *PATHFINDER* AND A *GENTLE SOUL* EXPLORING THE THREADS THAT MAKE UP THE WORLD.
I KNOW THIS ANTHOLOGY BOOK ONLY CAME TO BE TO FINALLY GET ME TO WRITE THIS DOWN. (APOLOGIES TO EVERYONE ELSE IN HERE, BUT THAT'S THE WAY MAGIC WORKS SOMETIMES.)
Fin.

"Your strength does not depend on numbers, nor your might on the powerful. But you are the God of the lowly, helper of the oppressed, upholder of the weak, protector of the forsaken, savior of those without hope."

—Judith
9:11 New Revised
Standard Version

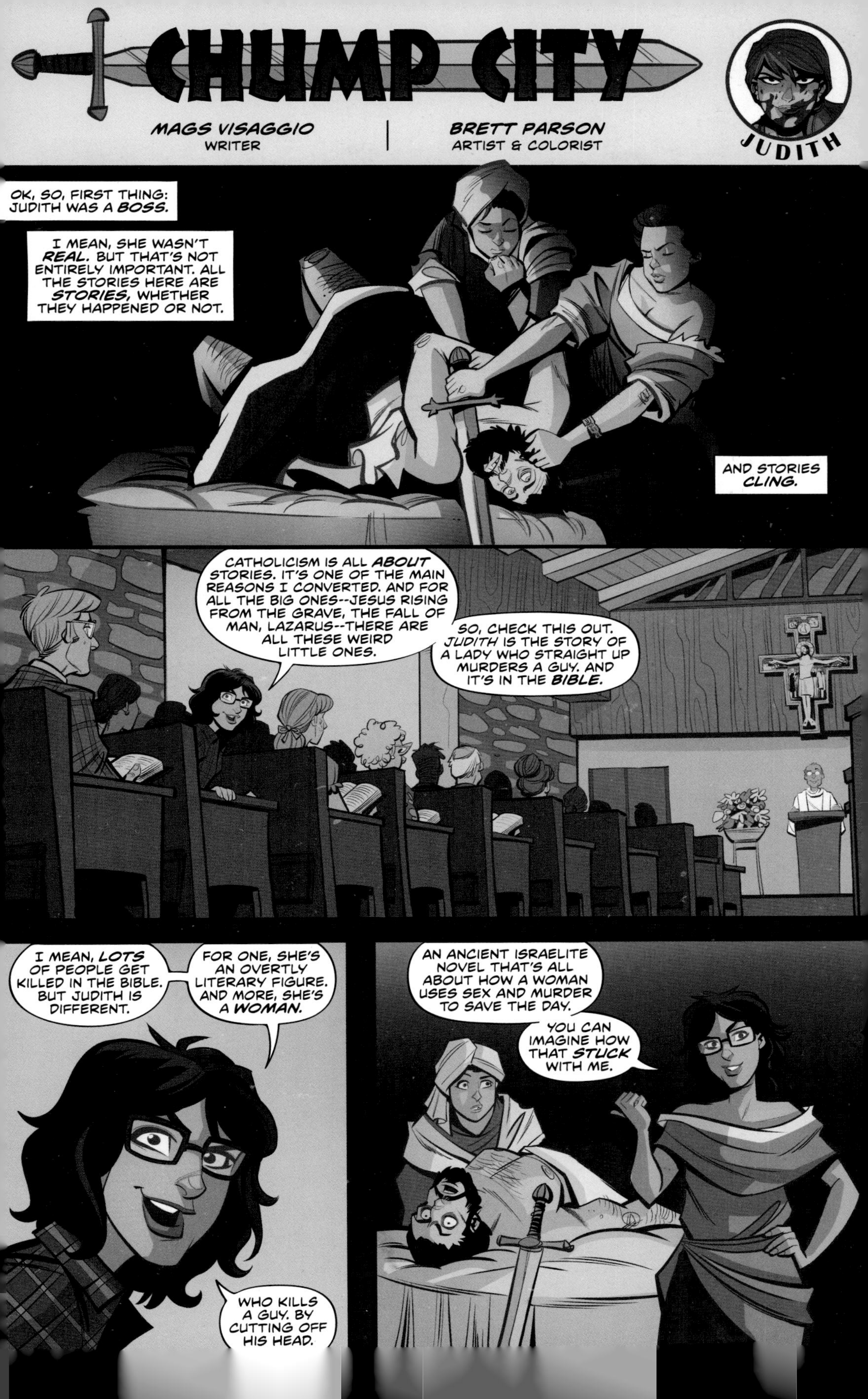
CHUMP CITY
JUDITH
MAGS VISAGGIO
WRITER
BRETT PARSON
ARTIST & COLORIST
OK, SO, FIRST THING: JUDITH WAS A BOSS.
I MEAN, SHE WASN'T REAL. BUT THAT'S NOT ENTIRELY IMPORTANT. ALL THE STORIES HERE ARE STORIES, WHETHER THEY HAPPENED OR NOT.
AND STORIES CLING.
CATHOLICISM IS ALL ABOUT STORIES. IT'S ONE OF THE MAIN REASONS I CONVERTED. AND FOR ALL THE BIG ONES--JESUS RISING FROM THE GRAVE, THE FALL OF MAN, LAZARUS--THERE ARE ALL THESE WEIRD LITTLE ONES.
SO, CHECK THIS OUT. JUDITH IS THE STORY OF A LADY WHO STRAIGHT UP MURDERS A GUY. AND IT'S IN THE BIBLE.
I MEAN, LOTS OF PEOPLE GET KILLED IN THE BIBLE. BUT JUDITH IS DIFFERENT.
FOR ONE, SHE'S AN OVERTLY LITERARY FIGURE. AND MORE, SHE'S A WOMAN.
WHO KILLS A GUY. BY CUTTING OFF HIS HEAD.
AN ANCIENT ISRAELITE NOVEL THAT'S ALL ABOUT HOW A WOMAN USES SEX AND MURDER TO SAVE THE DAY.
YOU CAN IMAGINE HOW THAT STUCK WITH ME.

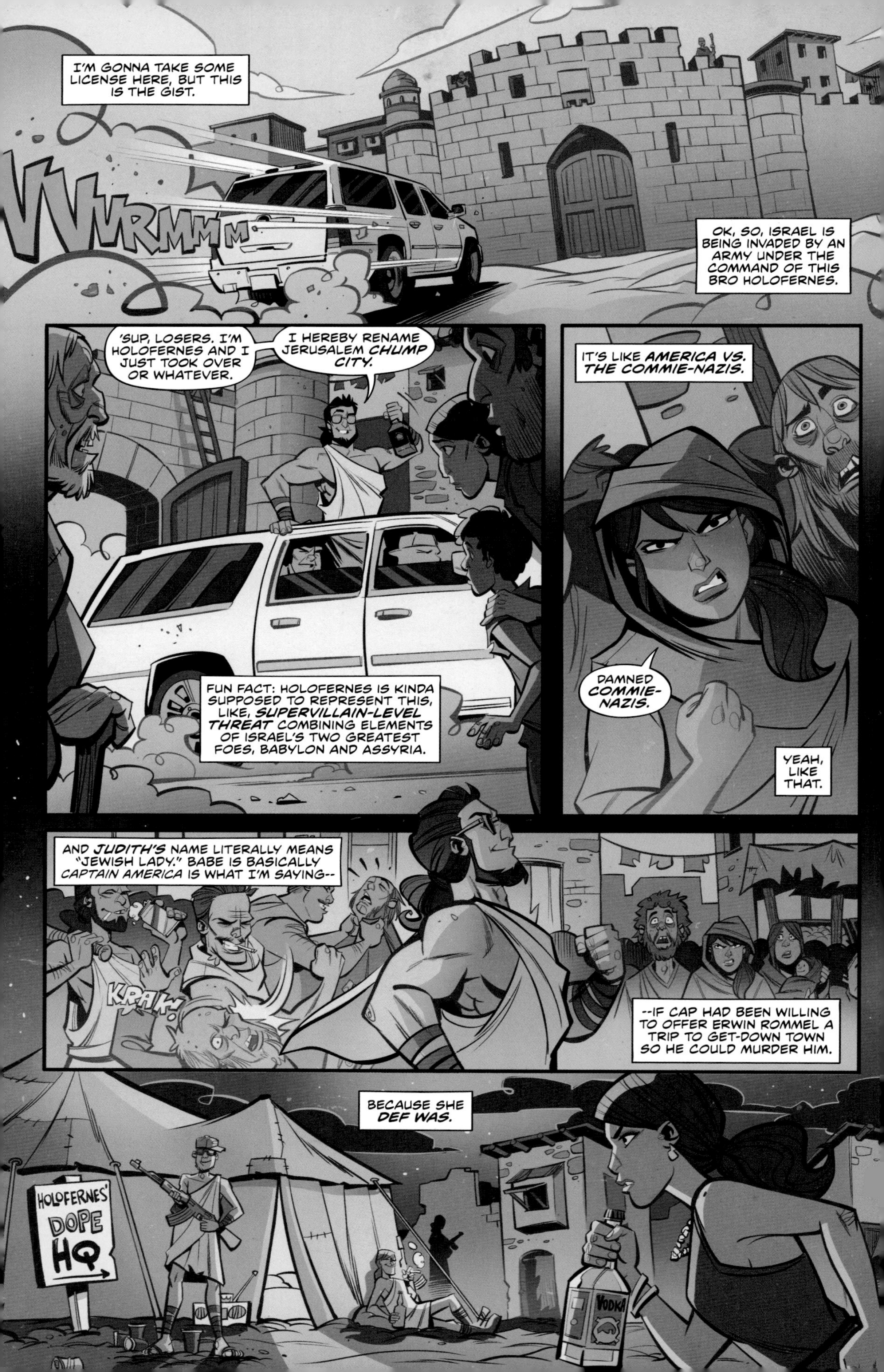
I'M GONNA TAKE SOME LICENSE HERE, BUT THIS IS THE GIST.
VVVRMMMM
OK, SO, ISRAEL IS BEING INVADED BY AN ARMY UNDER THE COMMAND OF THIS BRO HOLOFERNES.
'SUP, LOSERS. I'M HOLOFERNES AND I JUST TOOK OVER OR WHATEVER.
I HEREBY RENAME JERUSALEM CHUMP CITY.
FUN FACT: HOLOFERNES IS KINDA SUPPOSED TO REPRESENT THIS, LIKE, SUPERVILLAIN-LEVEL THREAT COMBINING ELEMENTS OF ISRAEL'S TWO GREATEST FOES, BABYLON AND ASSYRIA.
IT'S LIKE AMERICA VS. THE COMMIE-NAZIS.
DAMNED COMMIE-NAZIS.
YEAH, LIKE THAT.
AND JUDITH'S NAME LITERALLY MEANS "JEWISH LADY." BABE IS BASICALLY CAPTAIN AMERICA IS WHAT I'M SAYING--
KRAK!
--IF CAP HAD BEEN WILLING TO OFFER ERWIN ROMMEL A TRIP TO GET-DOWN TOWN SO HE COULD MURDER HIM.
BECAUSE SHE DEF WAS.
HOLOFERNES' DOPE HQ
VODKA

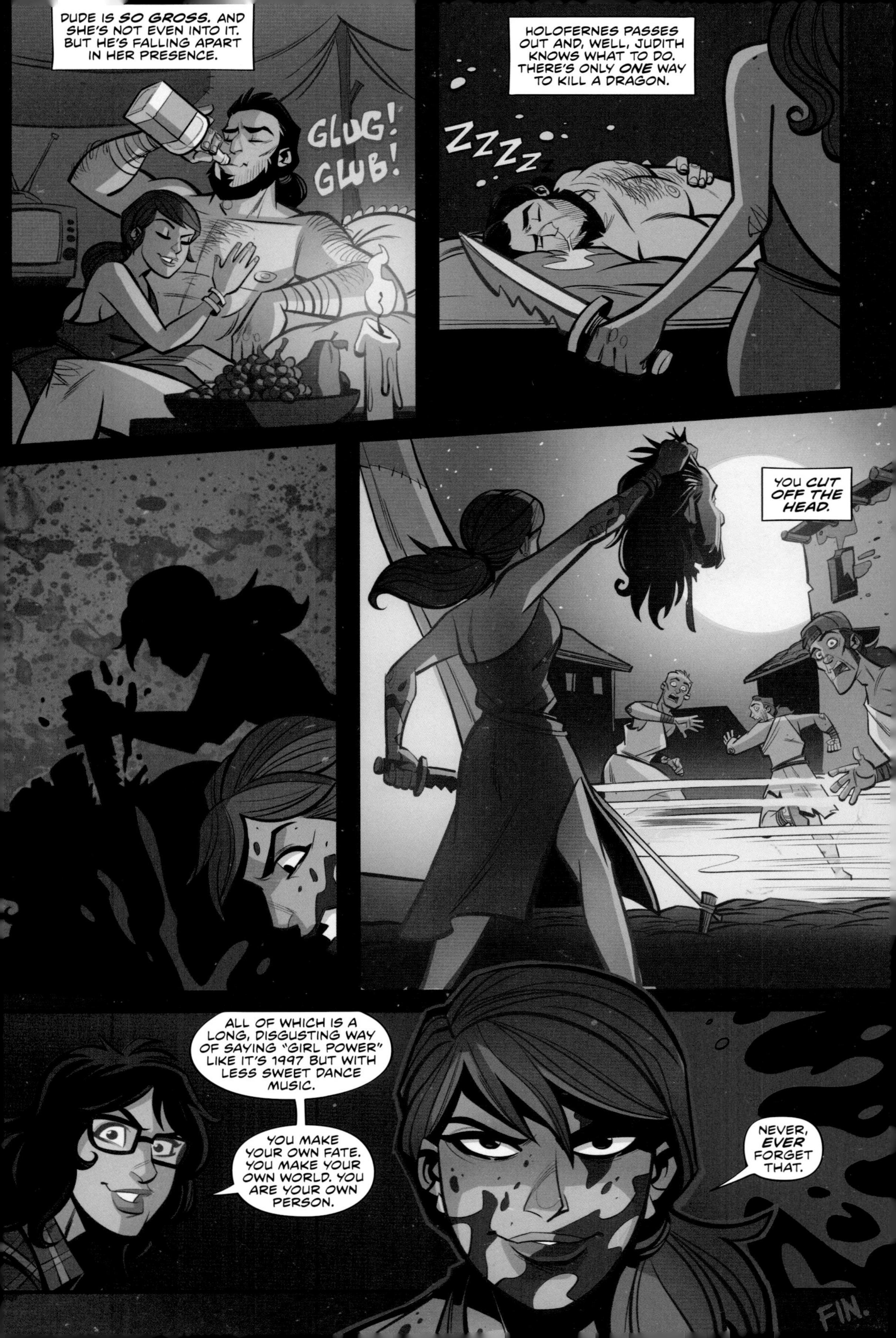
DUDE IS ***SO GROSS.*** AND SHE'S NOT EVEN INTO IT. BUT HE'S FALLING APART IN HER PRESENCE.
GLUG! GLUB!
HOLOFERNES PASSES OUT AND, WELL, JUDITH KNOWS WHAT TO DO. THERE'S ONLY ***ONE*** WAY TO KILL A DRAGON.
ZZZZ
YOU ***CUT OFF THE HEAD.***
ALL OF WHICH IS A LONG, DISGUSTING WAY OF SAYING "GIRL POWER" LIKE IT'S 1997 BUT WITH LESS SWEET DANCE MUSIC.
YOU MAKE YOUR OWN FATE. YOU MAKE YOUR OWN WORLD. YOU ARE YOUR OWN PERSON.
NEVER, ***EVER*** FORGET THAT.
FIN.

"If not for war, they would be just like me. They would be at home with their family, doing just ordinary things and peaceful work. Let us pray that there will be no more war."

—Elizabeth Choy

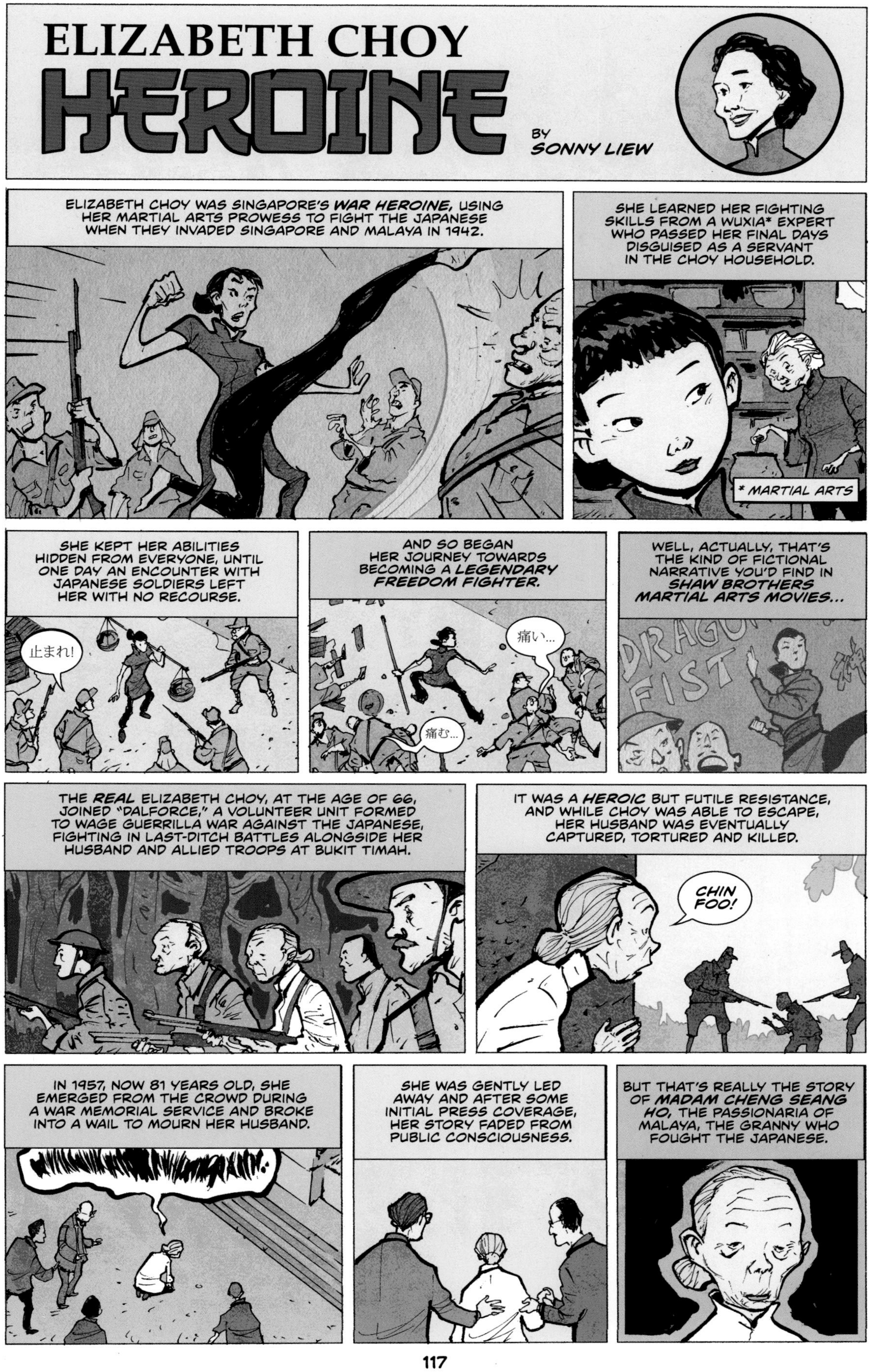
ELIZABETH CHOY
HEROINE
BY
SONNY LIEW
ELIZABETH CHOY WAS SINGAPORE'S WAR HEROINE, USING HER MARTIAL ARTS PROWESS TO FIGHT THE JAPANESE WHEN THEY INVADED SINGAPORE AND MALAYA IN 1942.
SHE LEARNED HER FIGHTING SKILLS FROM A WUXIA* EXPERT WHO PASSED HER FINAL DAYS DISGUISED AS A SERVANT IN THE CHOY HOUSEHOLD.
* MARTIAL ARTS
SHE KEPT HER ABILITIES HIDDEN FROM EVERYONE, UNTIL ONE DAY AN ENCOUNTER WITH JAPANESE SOLDIERS LEFT HER WITH NO RECOURSE.
止まれ!
AND SO BEGAN HER JOURNEY TOWARDS BECOMING A LEGENDARY FREEDOM FIGHTER.
痛い…
痛む…
WELL, ACTUALLY, THAT'S THE KIND OF FICTIONAL NARRATIVE YOU'D FIND IN SHAW BROTHERS MARTIAL ARTS MOVIES...
DRAGON FIST
THE REAL ELIZABETH CHOY, AT THE AGE OF 66, JOINED "DALFORCE," A VOLUNTEER UNIT FORMED TO WAGE GUERRILLA WAR AGAINST THE JAPANESE, FIGHTING IN LAST-DITCH BATTLES ALONGSIDE HER HUSBAND AND ALLIED TROOPS AT BUKIT TIMAH.
IT WAS A HEROIC BUT FUTILE RESISTANCE, AND WHILE CHOY WAS ABLE TO ESCAPE, HER HUSBAND WAS EVENTUALLY CAPTURED, TORTURED AND KILLED.
CHIN FOO!
IN 1957, NOW 81 YEARS OLD, SHE EMERGED FROM THE CROWD DURING A WAR MEMORIAL SERVICE AND BROKE INTO A WAIL TO MOURN HER HUSBAND.
SHE WAS GENTLY LED AWAY AND AFTER SOME INITIAL PRESS COVERAGE, HER STORY FADED FROM PUBLIC CONSCIOUSNESS.
BUT THAT'S REALLY THE STORY OF MADAM CHENG SEANG HO, THE PASSIONARIA OF MALAYA, THE GRANNY WHO FOUGHT THE JAPANESE.

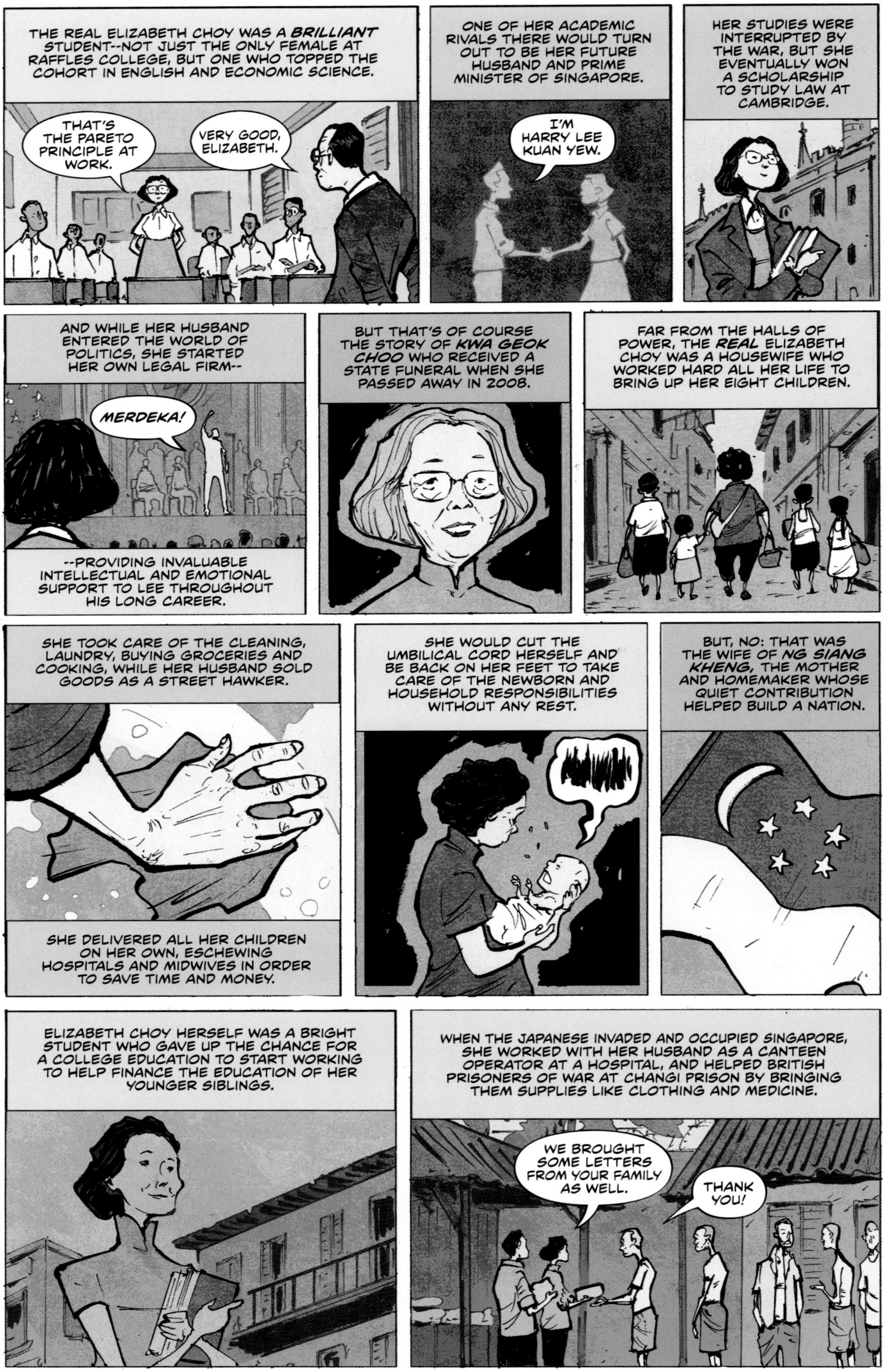
THE REAL ELIZABETH CHOY WAS A *BRILLIANT* STUDENT--NOT JUST THE ONLY FEMALE AT RAFFLES COLLEGE, BUT ONE WHO TOPPED THE COHORT IN ENGLISH AND ECONOMIC SCIENCE.
THAT'S THE PARETO PRINCIPLE AT WORK.
VERY GOOD, ELIZABETH.
ONE OF HER ACADEMIC RIVALS THERE WOULD TURN OUT TO BE HER FUTURE HUSBAND AND PRIME MINISTER OF SINGAPORE.
I'M HARRY LEE KUAN YEW.
HER STUDIES WERE INTERRUPTED BY THE WAR, BUT SHE EVENTUALLY WON A SCHOLARSHIP TO STUDY LAW AT CAMBRIDGE.
AND WHILE HER HUSBAND ENTERED THE WORLD OF POLITICS, SHE STARTED HER OWN LEGAL FIRM--
MERDEKA!
--PROVIDING INVALUABLE INTELLECTUAL AND EMOTIONAL SUPPORT TO LEE THROUGHOUT HIS LONG CAREER.
BUT THAT'S OF COURSE THE STORY OF *KWA GEOK CHOO* WHO RECEIVED A STATE FUNERAL WHEN SHE PASSED AWAY IN 2008.
FAR FROM THE HALLS OF POWER, THE *REAL* ELIZABETH CHOY WAS A HOUSEWIFE WHO WORKED HARD ALL HER LIFE TO BRING UP HER EIGHT CHILDREN.
SHE TOOK CARE OF THE CLEANING, LAUNDRY, BUYING GROCERIES AND COOKING, WHILE HER HUSBAND SOLD GOODS AS A STREET HAWKER.
SHE DELIVERED ALL HER CHILDREN ON HER OWN, ESCHEWING HOSPITALS AND MIDWIVES IN ORDER TO SAVE TIME AND MONEY.
SHE WOULD CUT THE UMBILICAL CORD HERSELF AND BE BACK ON HER FEET TO TAKE CARE OF THE NEWBORN AND HOUSEHOLD RESPONSIBILITIES WITHOUT ANY REST.
BUT, NO: THAT WAS THE WIFE OF *NG SIANG KHENG*, THE MOTHER AND HOMEMAKER WHOSE QUIET CONTRIBUTION HELPED BUILD A NATION.
ELIZABETH CHOY HERSELF WAS A BRIGHT STUDENT WHO GAVE UP THE CHANCE FOR A COLLEGE EDUCATION TO START WORKING TO HELP FINANCE THE EDUCATION OF HER YOUNGER SIBLINGS.
WHEN THE JAPANESE INVADED AND OCCUPIED SINGAPORE, SHE WORKED WITH HER HUSBAND AS A CANTEEN OPERATOR AT A HOSPITAL, AND HELPED BRITISH PRISONERS OF WAR AT CHANGI PRISON BY BRINGING THEM SUPPLIES LIKE CLOTHING AND MEDICINE.
WE BROUGHT SOME LETTERS FROM YOUR FAMILY AS WELL.
THANK YOU!

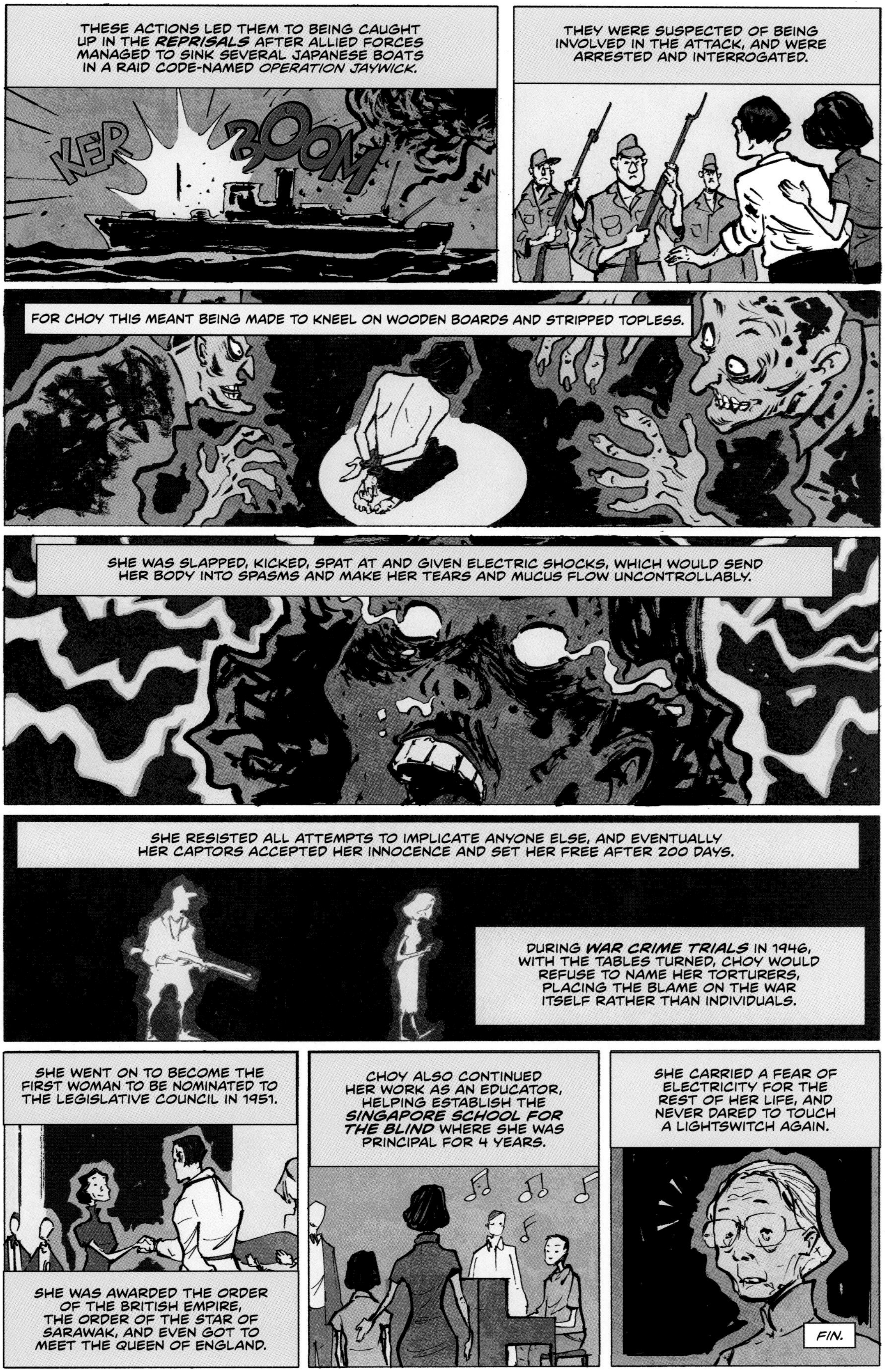
THESE ACTIONS LED THEM TO BEING CAUGHT UP IN THE *REPRISALS* AFTER ALLIED FORCES MANAGED TO SINK SEVERAL JAPANESE BOATS IN A RAID CODE-NAMED *OPERATION JAYWICK.*
KER BOOM
THEY WERE SUSPECTED OF BEING INVOLVED IN THE ATTACK, AND WERE ARRESTED AND INTERROGATED.
FOR CHOY THIS MEANT BEING MADE TO KNEEL ON WOODEN BOARDS AND STRIPPED TOPLESS.
SHE WAS SLAPPED, KICKED, SPAT AT AND GIVEN ELECTRIC SHOCKS, WHICH WOULD SEND HER BODY INTO SPASMS AND MAKE HER TEARS AND MUCUS FLOW UNCONTROLLABLY.
SHE RESISTED ALL ATTEMPTS TO IMPLICATE ANYONE ELSE, AND EVENTUALLY HER CAPTORS ACCEPTED HER INNOCENCE AND SET HER FREE AFTER 200 DAYS.
DURING ***WAR CRIME TRIALS*** IN 1946, WITH THE TABLES TURNED, CHOY WOULD REFUSE TO NAME HER TORTURERS, PLACING THE BLAME ON THE WAR ITSELF RATHER THAN INDIVIDUALS.
SHE WENT ON TO BECOME THE FIRST WOMAN TO BE NOMINATED TO THE LEGISLATIVE COUNCIL IN 1951.
SHE WAS AWARDED THE ORDER OF THE BRITISH EMPIRE, THE ORDER OF THE STAR OF SARAWAK, AND EVEN GOT TO MEET THE QUEEN OF ENGLAND.
CHOY ALSO CONTINUED HER WORK AS AN EDUCATOR, HELPING ESTABLISH THE ***SINGAPORE SCHOOL FOR THE BLIND*** WHERE SHE WAS PRINCIPAL FOR 4 YEARS.
SHE CARRIED A FEAR OF ELECTRICITY FOR THE REST OF HER LIFE, AND NEVER DARED TO TOUCH A LIGHTSWITCH AGAIN.
FIN.

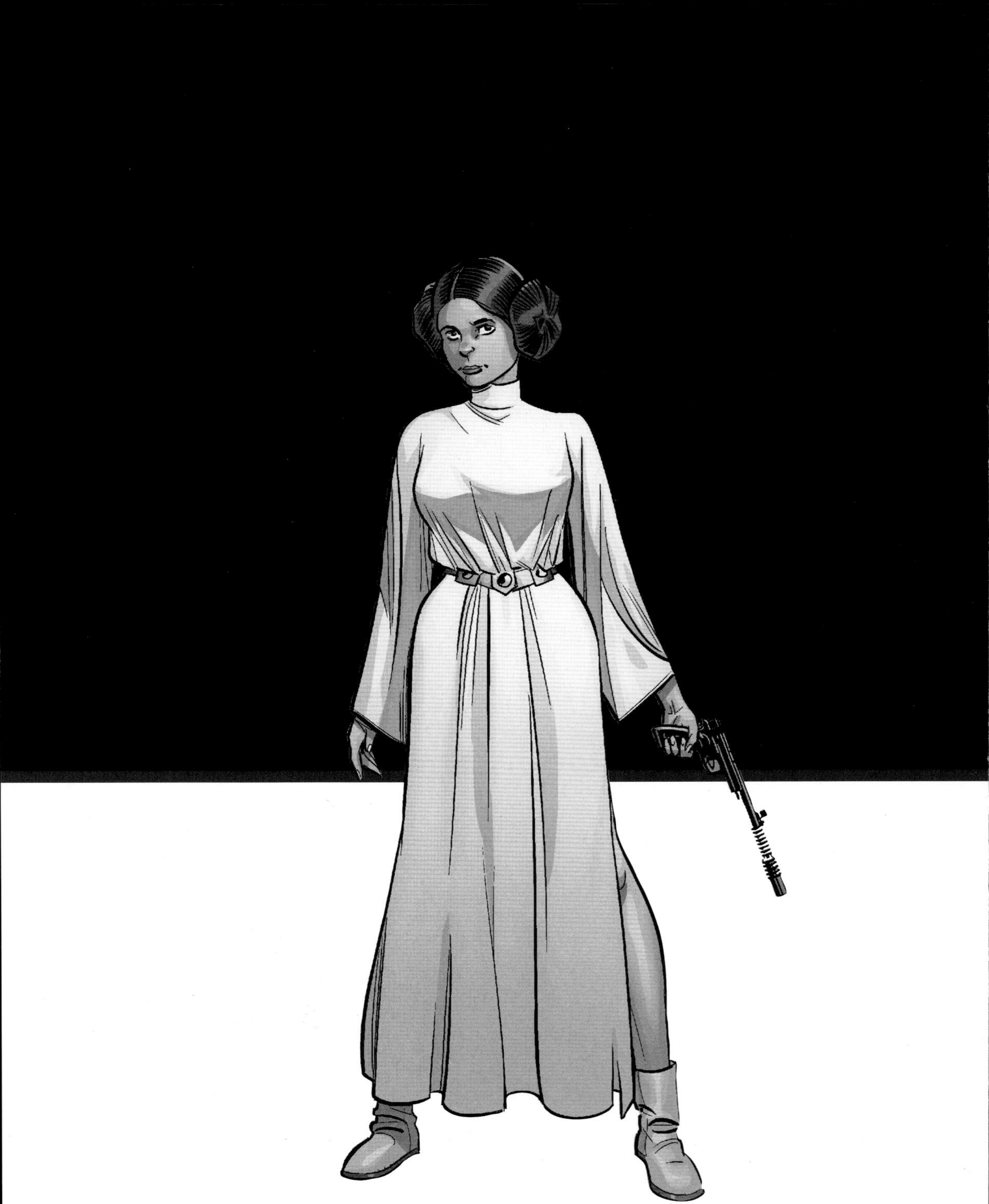

"Even in space there's a double standard for women."

—Carrie Fisher

TRIPLE GEEK GODDESS

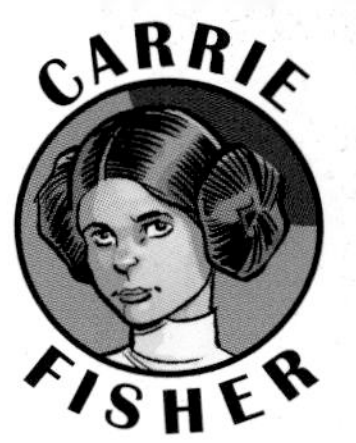
CARRIE
FISHER

ALISA KWITNEY WRITER | *ALAIN MAURICET* ARTIST | *HI-FI* COLORIST

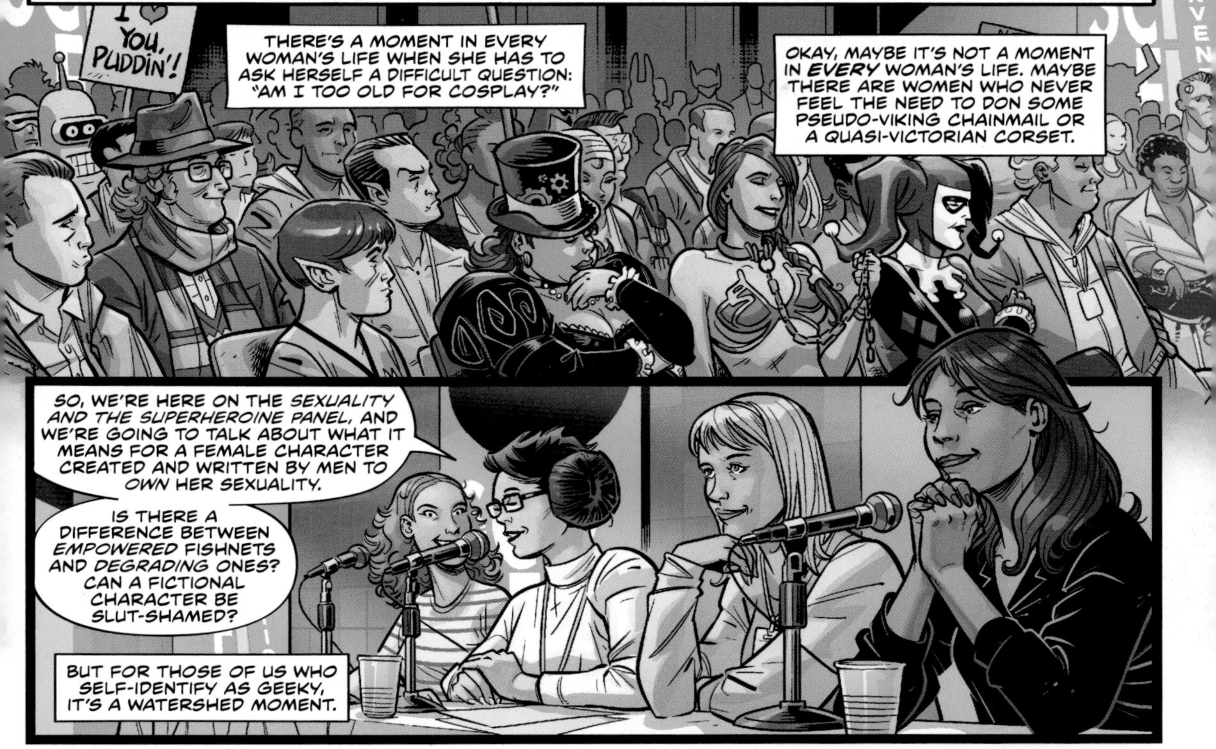
I ♥ YOU, PUDDIN'!
THERE'S A MOMENT IN EVERY WOMAN'S LIFE WHEN SHE HAS TO ASK HERSELF A DIFFICULT QUESTION: "AM I TOO OLD FOR COSPLAY?"
OKAY, MAYBE IT'S NOT A MOMENT IN *EVERY* WOMAN'S LIFE. MAYBE THERE ARE WOMEN WHO NEVER FEEL THE NEED TO DON SOME PSEUDO-VIKING CHAINMAIL OR A QUASI-VICTORIAN CORSET.
SO, WE'RE HERE ON THE *SEXUALITY AND THE SUPERHEROINE PANEL*, AND WE'RE GOING TO TALK ABOUT WHAT IT MEANS FOR A FEMALE CHARACTER CREATED AND WRITTEN BY MEN TO *OWN* HER SEXUALITY.
IS THERE A DIFFERENCE BETWEEN *EMPOWERED* FISHNETS AND *DEGRADING* ONES? CAN A FICTIONAL CHARACTER BE SLUT-SHAMED?
BUT FOR THOSE OF US WHO SELF-IDENTIFY AS GEEKY, IT'S A WATERSHED MOMENT.

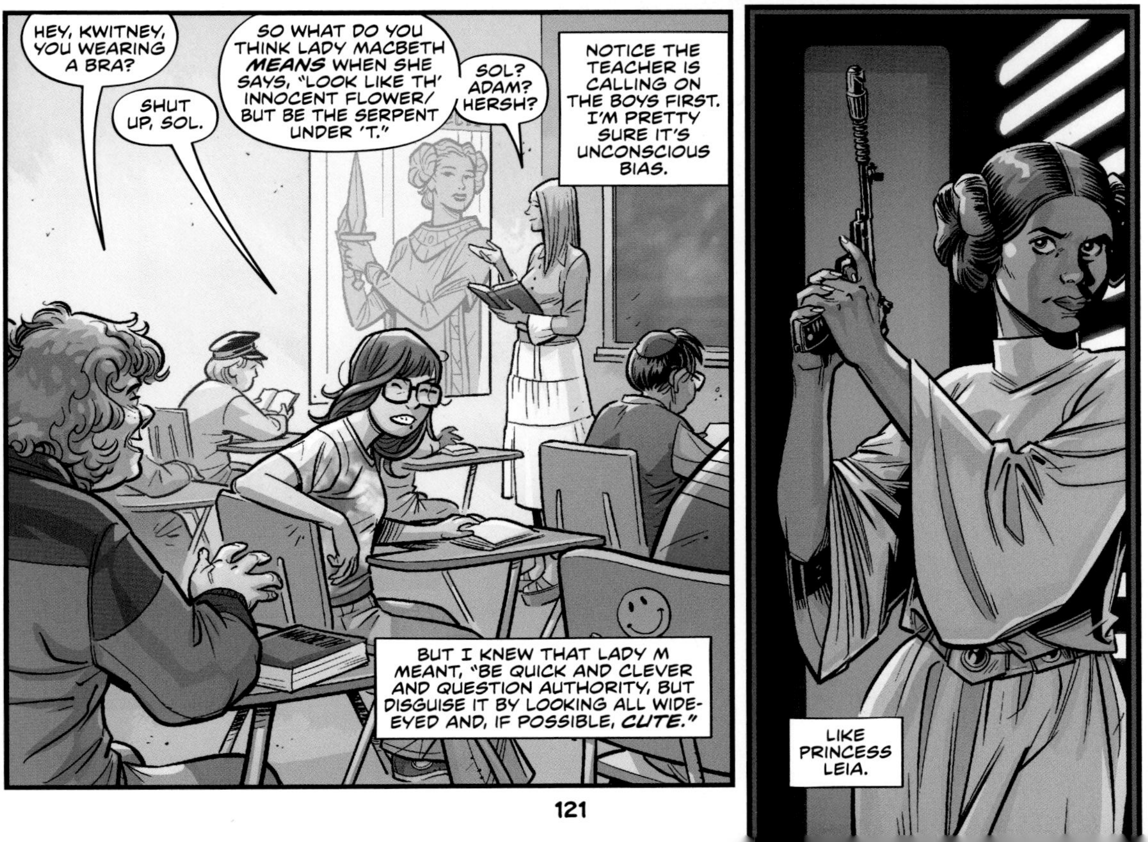
HEY, KWITNEY, YOU WEARING A BRA?
SHUT UP, SOL.
SO WHAT DO YOU THINK LADY MACBETH *MEANS* WHEN SHE SAYS, "LOOK LIKE TH' INNOCENT FLOWER/ BUT BE THE SERPENT UNDER 'T."
SOL? ADAM? HERSH?
NOTICE THE TEACHER IS CALLING ON THE BOYS FIRST. I'M PRETTY SURE IT'S UNCONSCIOUS BIAS.
BUT I KNEW THAT LADY M MEANT, "BE QUICK AND CLEVER AND QUESTION AUTHORITY, BUT DISGUISE IT BY LOOKING ALL WIDE-EYED AND, IF POSSIBLE, *CUTE.*"
LIKE PRINCESS LEIA.

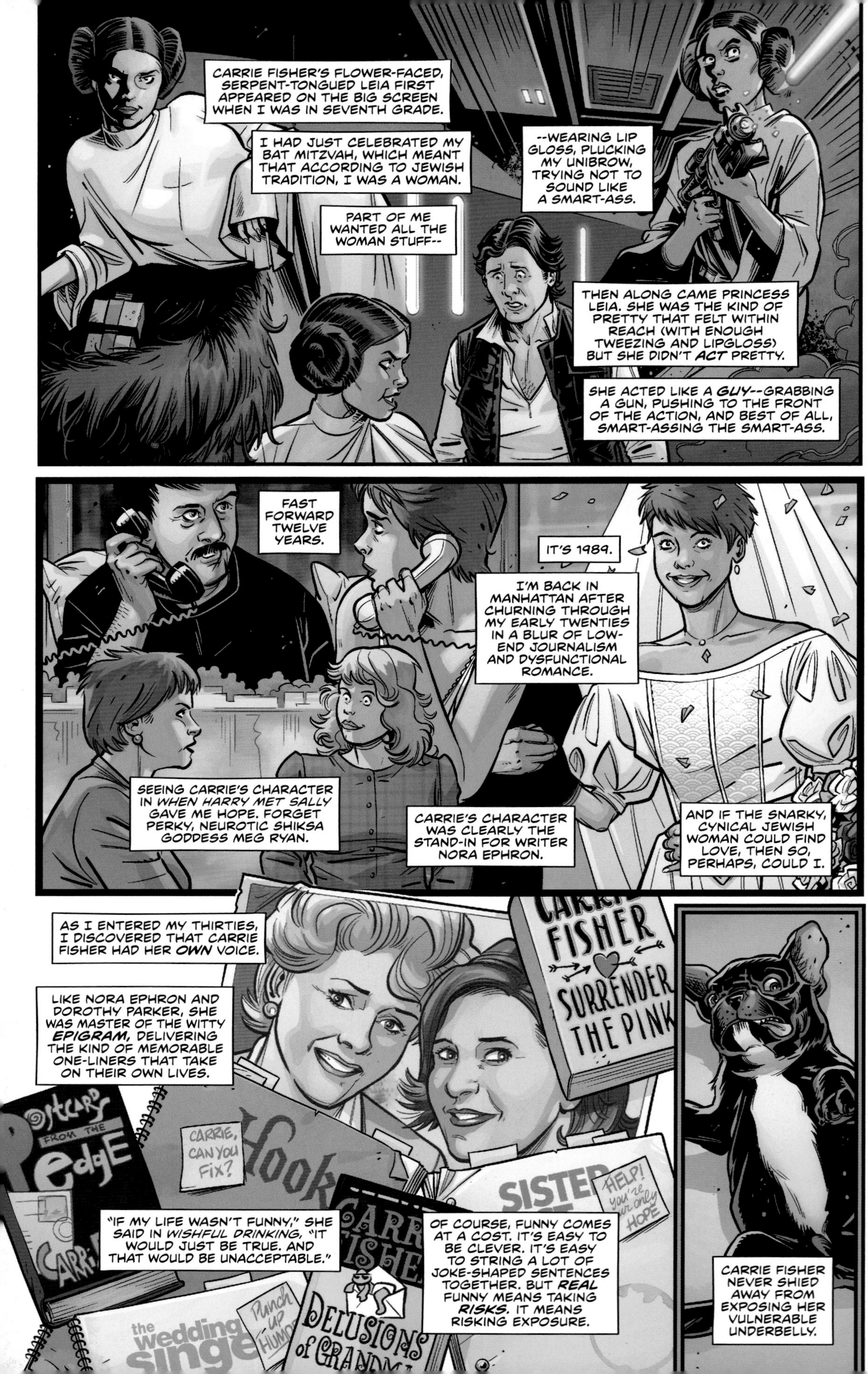
CARRIE FISHER'S FLOWER-FACED, SERPENT-TONGUED LEIA FIRST APPEARED ON THE BIG SCREEN WHEN I WAS IN SEVENTH GRADE.
I HAD JUST CELEBRATED MY BAT MITZVAH, WHICH MEANT THAT ACCORDING TO JEWISH TRADITION, I WAS A WOMAN.
PART OF ME WANTED ALL THE WOMAN STUFF--
--WEARING LIP GLOSS, PLUCKING MY UNIBROW, TRYING NOT TO SOUND LIKE A SMART-ASS.
THEN ALONG CAME PRINCESS LEIA. SHE WAS THE KIND OF PRETTY THAT FELT WITHIN REACH (WITH ENOUGH TWEEZING AND LIPGLOSS) BUT SHE DIDN'T *ACT* PRETTY.
SHE ACTED LIKE A *GUY*--GRABBING A GUN, PUSHING TO THE FRONT OF THE ACTION, AND BEST OF ALL, SMART-ASSING THE SMART-ASS.
FAST FORWARD TWELVE YEARS.
IT'S 1989.
I'M BACK IN MANHATTAN AFTER CHURNING THROUGH MY EARLY TWENTIES IN A BLUR OF LOW-END JOURNALISM AND DYSFUNCTIONAL ROMANCE.
SEEING CARRIE'S CHARACTER IN *WHEN HARRY MET SALLY* GAVE ME HOPE. FORGET PERKY, NEUROTIC SHIKSA GODDESS MEG RYAN.
CARRIE'S CHARACTER WAS CLEARLY THE STAND-IN FOR WRITER NORA EPHRON.
AND IF THE SNARKY, CYNICAL JEWISH WOMAN COULD FIND LOVE, THEN SO, PERHAPS, COULD I.
AS I ENTERED MY THIRTIES, I DISCOVERED THAT CARRIE FISHER HAD HER *OWN* VOICE.
LIKE NORA EPHRON AND DOROTHY PARKER, SHE WAS MASTER OF THE WITTY *EPIGRAM,* DELIVERING THE KIND OF MEMORABLE ONE-LINERS THAT TAKE ON THEIR OWN LIVES.
FISHER
SURRENDER THE PINK
Postcards FROM THE Edge
CARRIE, CAN YOU FIX?
Hook
HELP! you're our only HOPE
"IF MY LIFE WASN'T FUNNY," SHE SAID IN *WISHFUL DRINKING,* "IT WOULD JUST BE TRUE. AND THAT WOULD BE UNACCEPTABLE."
OF COURSE, FUNNY COMES AT A COST. IT'S EASY TO BE CLEVER. IT'S EASY TO STRING A LOT OF JOKE-SHAPED SENTENCES TOGETHER. BUT *REAL* FUNNY MEANS TAKING *RISKS.* IT MEANS RISKING EXPOSURE.
DELUSIONS
the wedding
CARRIE FISHER NEVER SHIED AWAY FROM EXPOSING HER VULNERABLE UNDERBELLY.

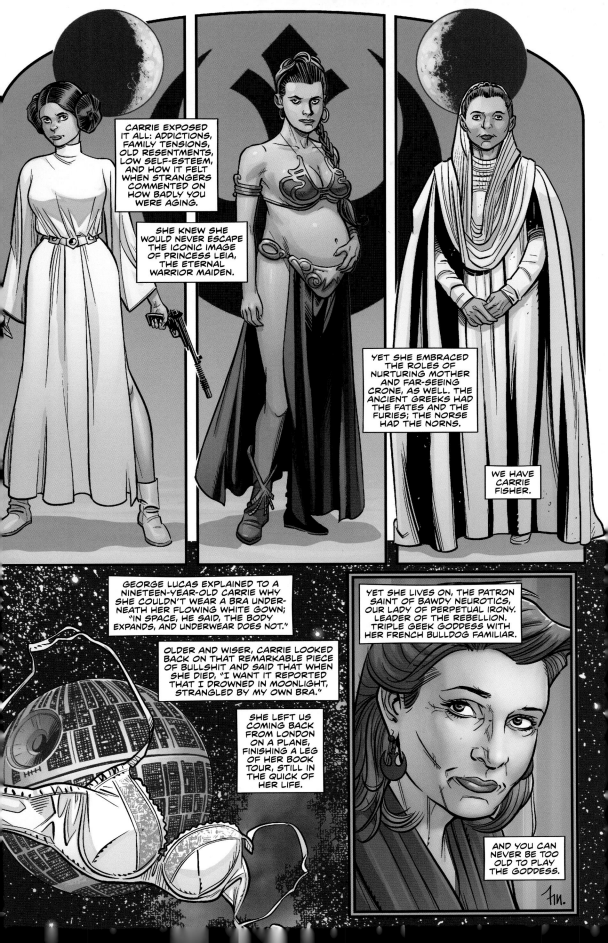

CARRIE EXPOSED IT ALL: ADDICTIONS, FAMILY TENSIONS, OLD RESENTMENTS, LOW SELF-ESTEEM, AND HOW IT FELT WHEN STRANGERS COMMENTED ON HOW BADLY YOU WERE AGING.

SHE KNEW SHE WOULD NEVER ESCAPE THE ICONIC IMAGE OF PRINCESS LEIA, THE ETERNAL WARRIOR MAIDEN.

YET SHE EMBRACED THE ROLES OF NURTURING MOTHER AND FAR-SEEING CRONE, AS WELL. THE ANCIENT GREEKS HAD THE FATES AND THE FURIES; THE NORSE HAD THE NORNS.

WE HAVE CARRIE FISHER.

GEORGE LUCAS EXPLAINED TO A NINETEEN-YEAR-OLD CARRIE WHY SHE COULDN'T WEAR A BRA UNDERNEATH HER FLOWING WHITE GOWN; "IN SPACE, HE SAID, THE BODY EXPANDS, AND UNDERWEAR DOES NOT."

OLDER AND WISER, CARRIE LOOKED BACK ON THAT REMARKABLE PIECE OF BULLSHIT AND SAID THAT WHEN SHE DIED, "I WANT IT REPORTED THAT I DROWNED IN MOONLIGHT, STRANGLED BY MY OWN BRA."

SHE LEFT US COMING BACK FROM LONDON ON A PLANE, FINISHING A LEG OF HER BOOK TOUR, STILL IN THE QUICK OF HER LIFE.

YET SHE LIVES ON, THE PATRON SAINT OF BAWDY NEUROTICS, OUR LADY OF PERPETUAL IRONY. LEADER OF THE REBELLION. TRIPLE GEEK GODDESS WITH HER FRENCH BULLDOG FAMILIAR.

AND YOU CAN NEVER BE TOO OLD TO PLAY THE GODDESS.

"You don't make progress by standing on the sidelines, whimpering and complaining. You make progress by implementing ideas."

—Shirley Chisholm

UNBOUGHT and UNBOSSED

GIBSON TWIST
WRITER

RORI!
ARTIST

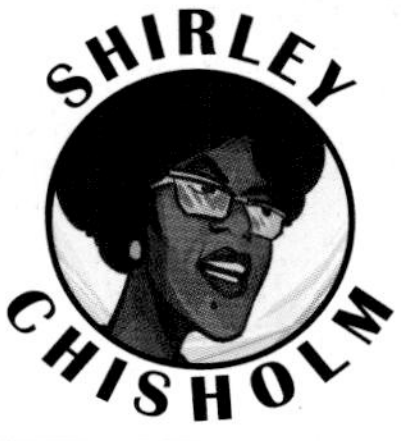
SHIRLEY
CHISHOLM

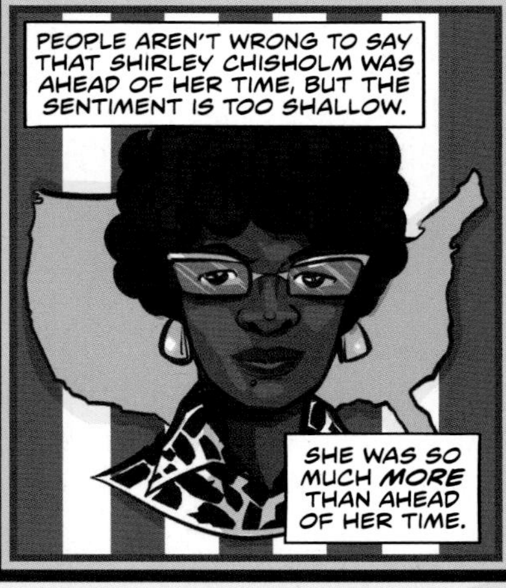
PEOPLE AREN'T WRONG TO SAY THAT SHIRLEY CHISHOLM WAS AHEAD OF HER TIME, BUT THE SENTIMENT IS TOO SHALLOW.
SHE WAS SO MUCH ***MORE*** THAN AHEAD OF HER TIME.

- ✩ Volunteered with the Bedford-Stuyvesant Political League and The League of Women Voters.
- ✩ Served in NY State Assembly.
- ✩ First black woman elected to Congress.
- ✩ Founding member of the Congressional Black Caucus and National Political Women's Caucus.
- ✩ Helped found the African-American Women for Reproductive Freedom (in retirement!).

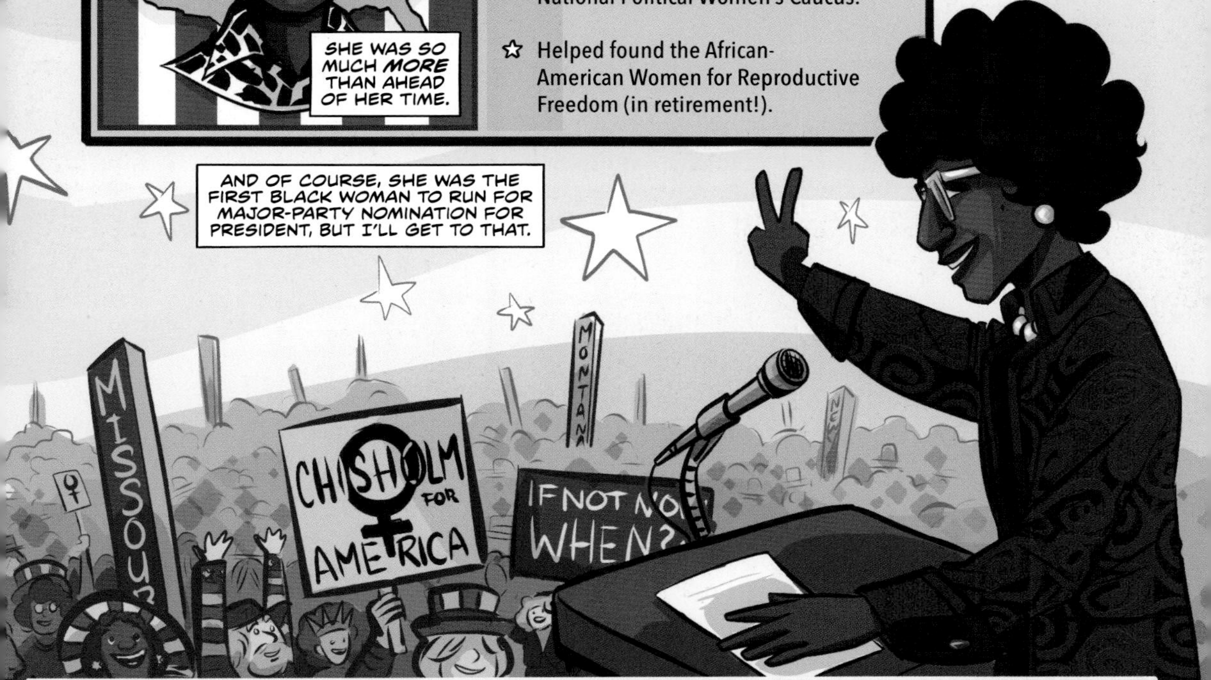
AND OF COURSE, SHE WAS THE FIRST BLACK WOMAN TO RUN FOR MAJOR-PARTY NOMINATION FOR PRESIDENT, BUT I'LL GET TO THAT.
MISSOU
MONTANA
CHISHOLM FOR AMERICA
IF NOT
WHEN?

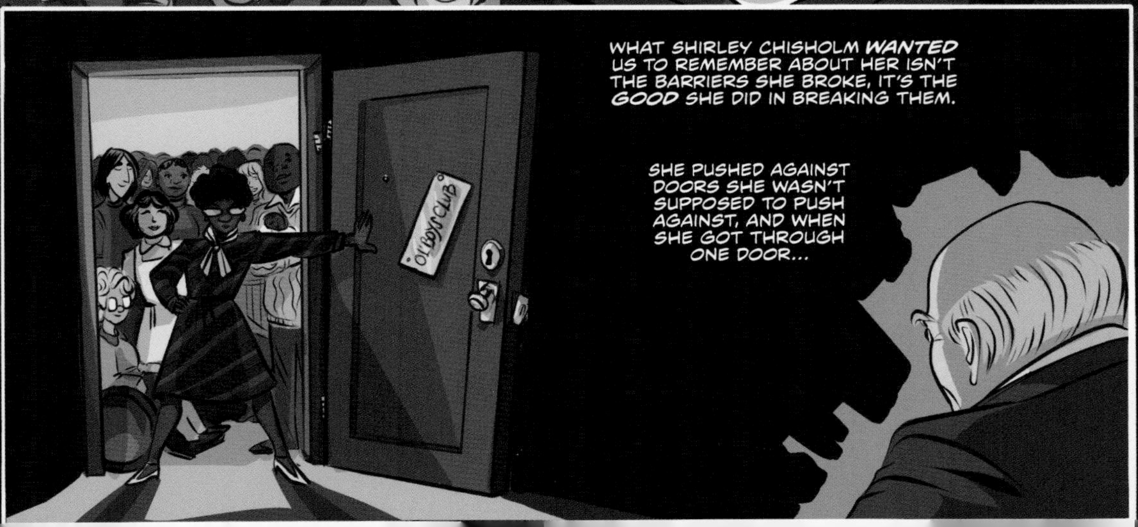
OL' BOYS CLUB
WHAT SHIRLEY CHISHOLM ***WANTED*** US TO REMEMBER ABOUT HER ISN'T THE BARRIERS SHE BROKE, IT'S THE ***GOOD*** SHE DID IN BREAKING THEM.
SHE PUSHED AGAINST DOORS SHE WASN'T SUPPOSED TO PUSH AGAINST, AND WHEN SHE GOT THROUGH ONE DOOR...

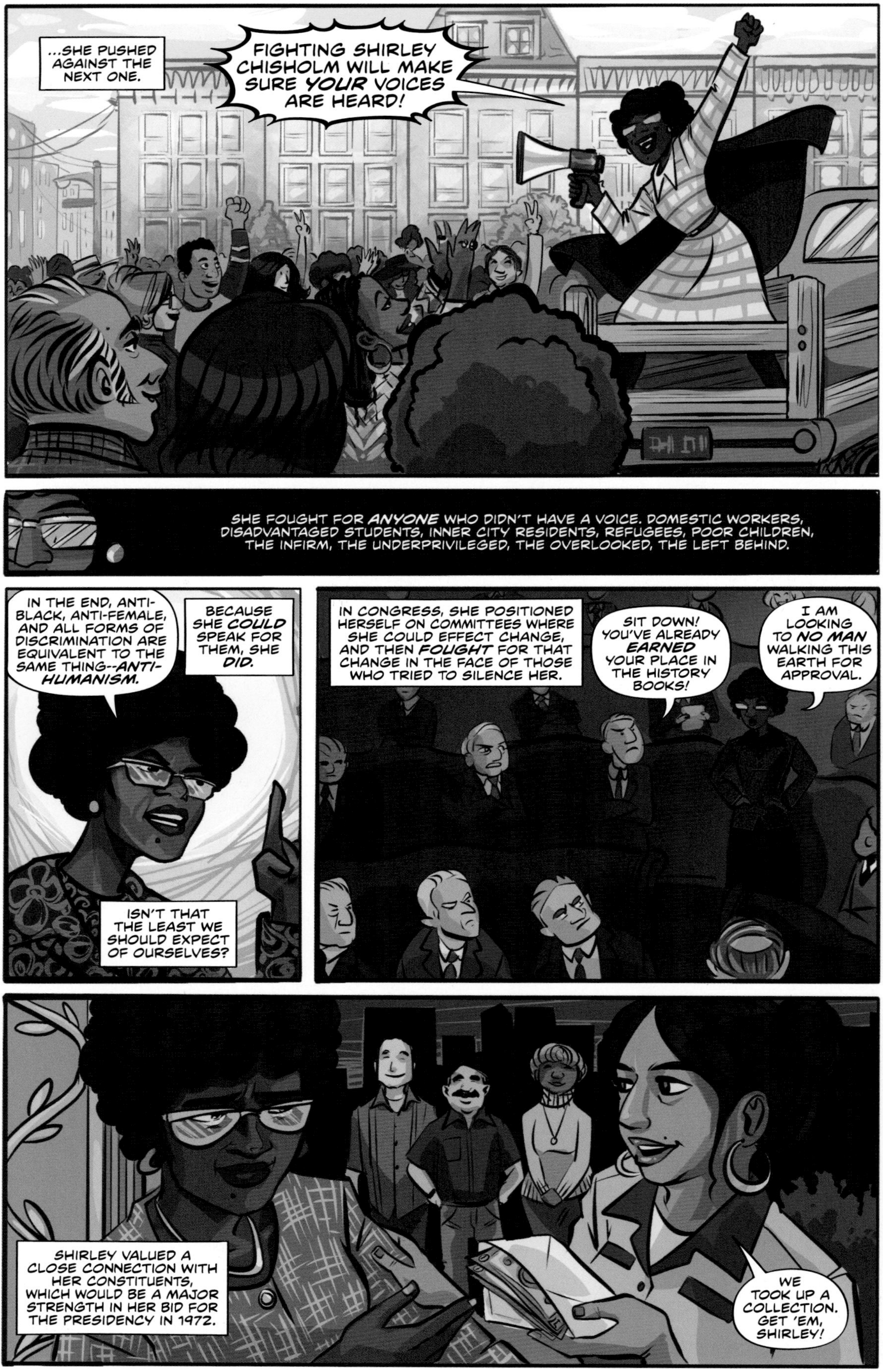
...SHE PUSHED AGAINST THE NEXT ONE.
FIGHTING SHIRLEY CHISHOLM WILL MAKE SURE *YOUR* VOICES ARE HEARD!
SHE FOUGHT FOR *ANYONE* WHO DIDN'T HAVE A VOICE. DOMESTIC WORKERS, DISADVANTAGED STUDENTS, INNER CITY RESIDENTS, REFUGEES, POOR CHILDREN, THE INFIRM, THE UNDERPRIVILEGED, THE OVERLOOKED, THE LEFT BEHIND.
IN THE END, ANTI-BLACK, ANTI-FEMALE, AND ALL FORMS OF DISCRIMINATION ARE EQUIVALENT TO THE SAME THING--*ANTI-HUMANISM.*
BECAUSE SHE *COULD* SPEAK FOR THEM, SHE *DID.*
ISN'T THAT THE LEAST WE SHOULD EXPECT OF OURSELVES?
IN CONGRESS, SHE POSITIONED HERSELF ON COMMITTEES WHERE SHE COULD EFFECT CHANGE, AND THEN *FOUGHT* FOR THAT CHANGE IN THE FACE OF THOSE WHO TRIED TO SILENCE HER.
SIT DOWN! YOU'VE ALREADY *EARNED* YOUR PLACE IN THE HISTORY BOOKS!
I AM LOOKING TO *NO MAN* WALKING THIS EARTH FOR APPROVAL.
SHIRLEY VALUED A CLOSE CONNECTION WITH HER CONSTITUENTS, WHICH WOULD BE A MAJOR STRENGTH IN HER BID FOR THE PRESIDENCY IN 1972.
WE TOOK UP A COLLECTION. GET 'EM, SHIRLEY!

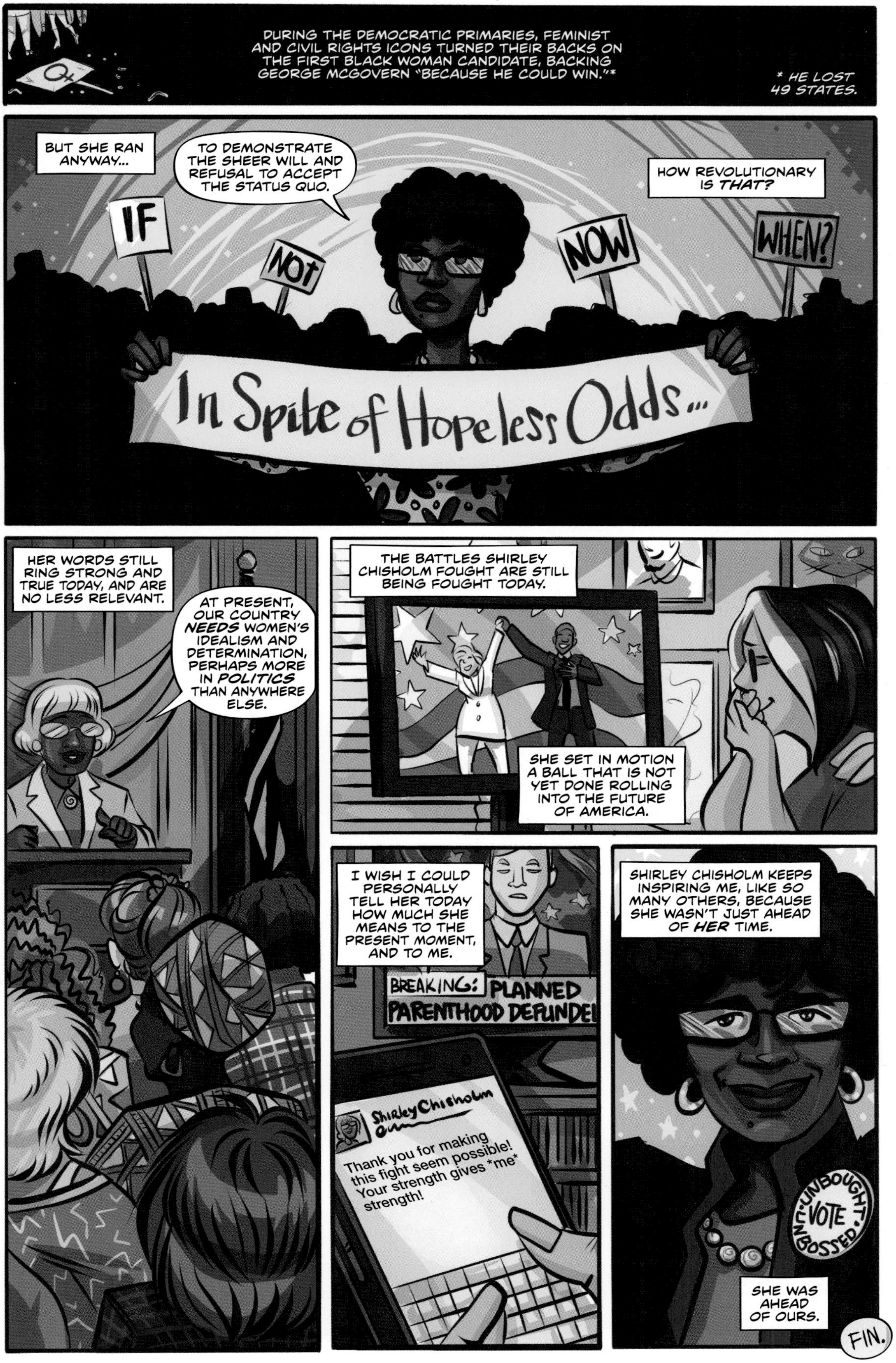
DURING THE DEMOCRATIC PRIMARIES, FEMINIST AND CIVIL RIGHTS ICONS TURNED THEIR BACKS ON THE FIRST BLACK WOMAN CANDIDATE, BACKING GEORGE MCGOVERN "BECAUSE HE COULD WIN."*
* HE LOST 49 STATES.
BUT SHE RAN ANYWAY...
TO DEMONSTRATE THE SHEER WILL AND REFUSAL TO ACCEPT THE STATUS QUO.
HOW REVOLUTIONARY IS *THAT?*
IF
NOT
NOW
WHEN?
In Spite of Hopeless Odds...
HER WORDS STILL RING STRONG AND TRUE TODAY, AND ARE NO LESS RELEVANT.
AT PRESENT, OUR COUNTRY ***NEEDS*** WOMEN'S IDEALISM AND DETERMINATION, PERHAPS MORE IN ***POLITICS*** THAN ANYWHERE ELSE.
THE BATTLES SHIRLEY CHISHOLM FOUGHT ARE STILL BEING FOUGHT TODAY.
SHE SET IN MOTION A BALL THAT IS NOT YET DONE ROLLING INTO THE FUTURE OF AMERICA.
I WISH I COULD PERSONALLY TELL HER TODAY HOW MUCH SHE MEANS TO THE PRESENT MOMENT, AND TO ME.
BREAKING: PLANNED PARENTHOOD DEFUNDE
ShirleyChisholm
Thank you for making this fight seem possible! Your strength gives *me* strength!
SHIRLEY CHISHOLM KEEPS INSPIRING ME, LIKE SO MANY OTHERS, BECAUSE SHE WASN'T JUST AHEAD OF ***HER*** TIME.
UNBOUGHT VOTE UNBOSSED
SHE WAS AHEAD OF OURS.
FIN.

"I'm not going to start justifying my character. The way I am is the way I am, so take me as I am. If I want to do anything, anywhere with anybody, that's what I want to do and that's nobody's business."

—Brenda Fassie

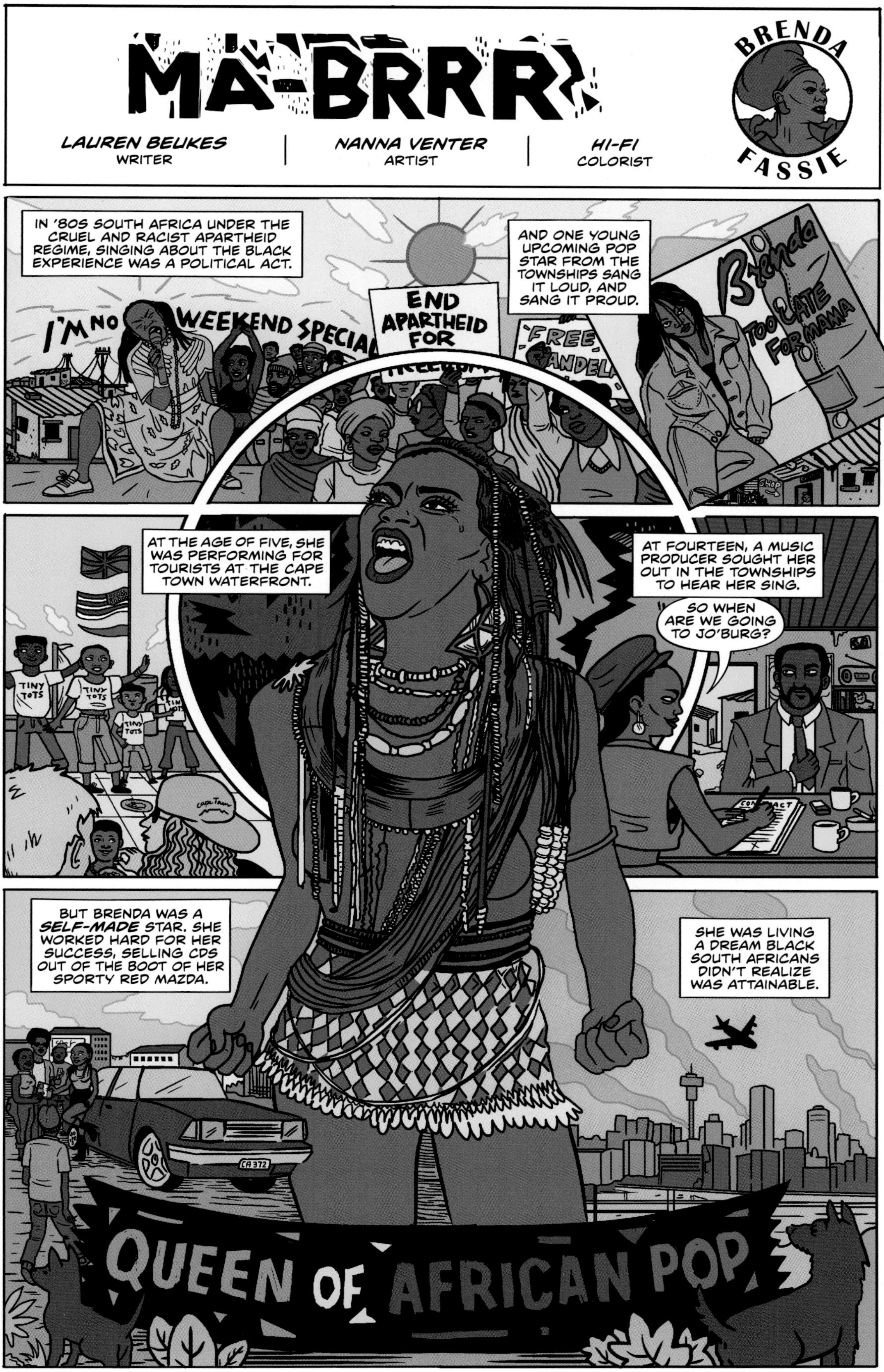
MA-BRRR
LAUREN BEUKES
WRITER
NANNA VENTER
ARTIST
HI-FI
COLORIST
BRENDA FASSIE
IN '80S SOUTH AFRICA UNDER THE CRUEL AND RACIST APARTHEID REGIME, SINGING ABOUT THE BLACK EXPERIENCE WAS A POLITICAL ACT.
I'M NO WEEKEND SPECIAL
END APARTHEID FOR
AND ONE YOUNG UPCOMING POP STAR FROM THE TOWNSHIPS SANG IT LOUD, AND SANG IT PROUD.
FREE MANDELA
Brenda
TOO LATE FOR MAMA
SHOP
AT THE AGE OF FIVE, SHE WAS PERFORMING FOR TOURISTS AT THE CAPE TOWN WATERFRONT.
TINY TOTS
AT FOURTEEN, A MUSIC PRODUCER SOUGHT HER OUT IN THE TOWNSHIPS TO HEAR HER SING.
SO WHEN ARE WE GOING TO JO'BURG?
CONTRACT
BUT BRENDA WAS A *SELF-MADE* STAR. SHE WORKED HARD FOR HER SUCCESS, SELLING CDS OUT OF THE BOOT OF HER SPORTY RED MAZDA.
SHE WAS LIVING A DREAM BLACK SOUTH AFRICANS DIDN'T REALIZE WAS ATTAINABLE.
CA 372
QUEEN OF AFRICAN POP

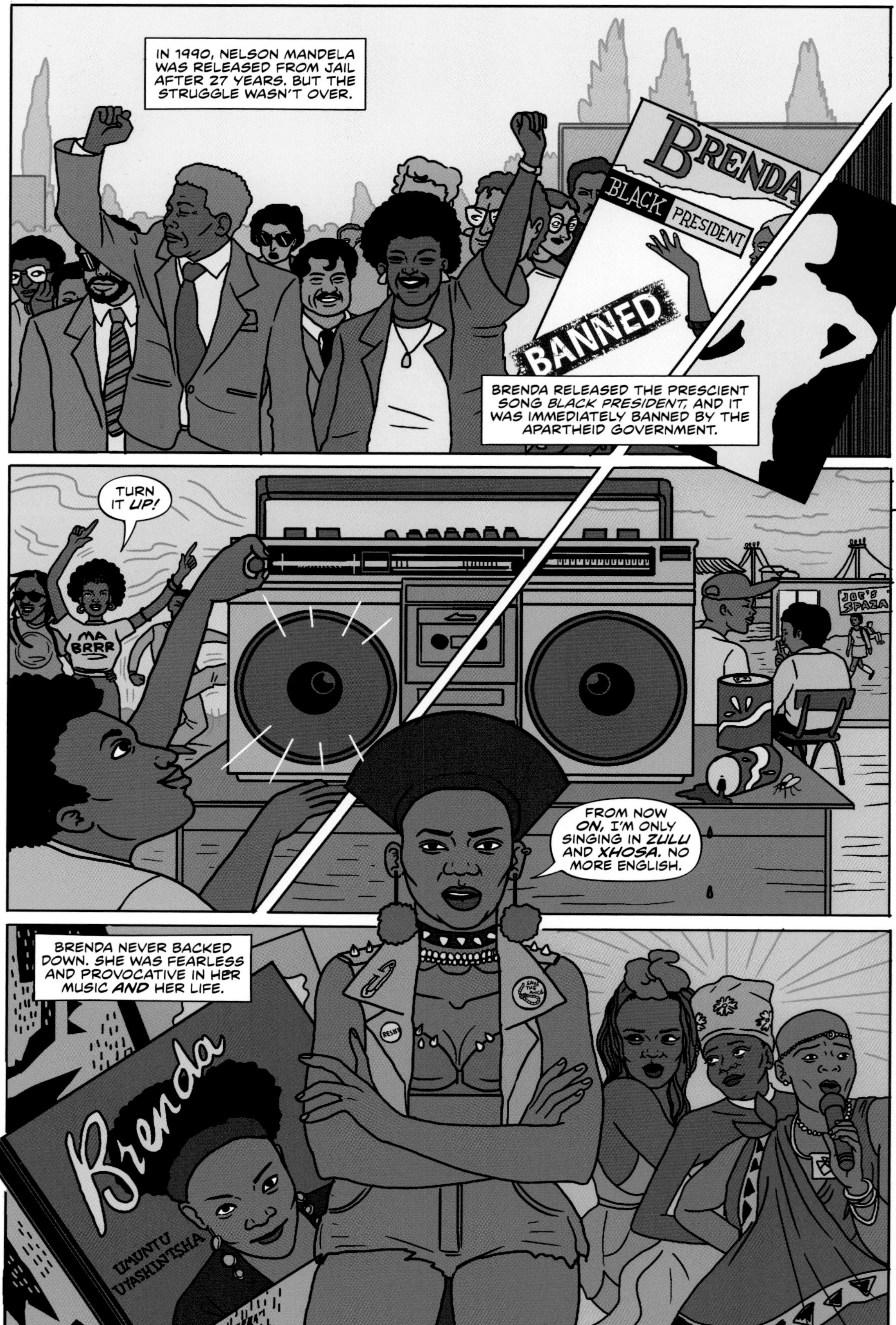
IN 1990, NELSON MANDELA WAS RELEASED FROM JAIL AFTER 27 YEARS. BUT THE STRUGGLE WASN'T OVER.
BRENDA
BLACK PRESIDENT
BANNED
BRENDA RELEASED THE PRESCIENT SONG *BLACK PRESIDENT*, AND IT WAS IMMEDIATELY BANNED BY THE APARTHEID GOVERNMENT.
TURN IT *UP!*
MA BRRR
JOE'S SPAZA
FROM NOW *ON*, I'M ONLY SINGING IN *ZULU* AND *XHOSA*. NO MORE ENGLISH.
BRENDA NEVER BACKED DOWN. SHE WAS FEARLESS AND PROVOCATIVE IN HER MUSIC *AND* HER LIFE.
Brenda
UMUNTU UYASHINTSHA

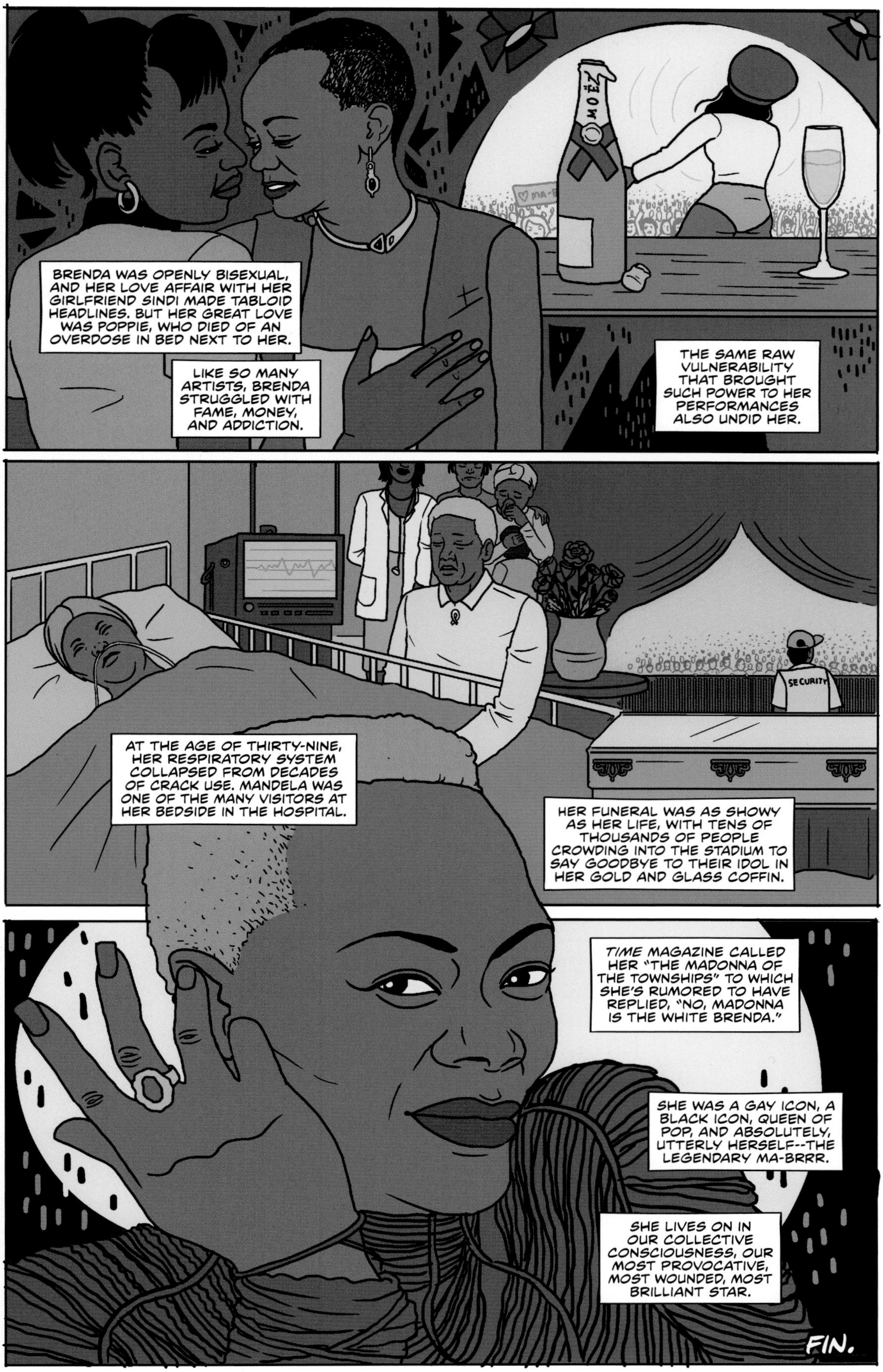
BRENDA WAS OPENLY BISEXUAL, AND HER LOVE AFFAIR WITH HER GIRLFRIEND SINDI MADE TABLOID HEADLINES. BUT HER GREAT LOVE WAS POPPIE, WHO DIED OF AN OVERDOSE IN BED NEXT TO HER.
LIKE SO MANY ARTISTS, BRENDA STRUGGLED WITH FAME, MONEY, AND ADDICTION.
THE SAME RAW VULNERABILITY THAT BROUGHT SUCH POWER TO HER PERFORMANCES ALSO UNDID HER.
AT THE AGE OF THIRTY-NINE, HER RESPIRATORY SYSTEM COLLAPSED FROM DECADES OF CRACK USE. MANDELA WAS ONE OF THE MANY VISITORS AT HER BEDSIDE IN THE HOSPITAL.
SECURITY
HER FUNERAL WAS AS SHOWY AS HER LIFE, WITH TENS OF THOUSANDS OF PEOPLE CROWDING INTO THE STADIUM TO SAY GOODBYE TO THEIR IDOL IN HER GOLD AND GLASS COFFIN.
TIME MAGAZINE CALLED HER "THE MADONNA OF THE TOWNSHIPS" TO WHICH SHE'S RUMORED TO HAVE REPLIED, "NO, MADONNA IS THE WHITE BRENDA."
SHE WAS A GAY ICON, A BLACK ICON, QUEEN OF POP, AND ABSOLUTELY, UTTERLY HERSELF--THE LEGENDARY MA-BRRR.
SHE LIVES ON IN OUR COLLECTIVE CONSCIOUSNESS, OUR MOST PROVOCATIVE, MOST WOUNDED, MOST BRILLIANT STAR.
FIN.

"*I think the poet is the last person who is still speaking the truth when no one else dares to. I think the poet is the first person to begin the shaping and visioning of the new forms and the new consciousness when no one else has begun to sense it; I think these are two of the most essential human functions.*"

—Diane di Prima

A RARE KIND OF BIRD

DIANE di PRIMA

TINI HOWARD WRITER | *MING DOYLE* ARTIST | *KELLY FITZPATRICK* COLORIST

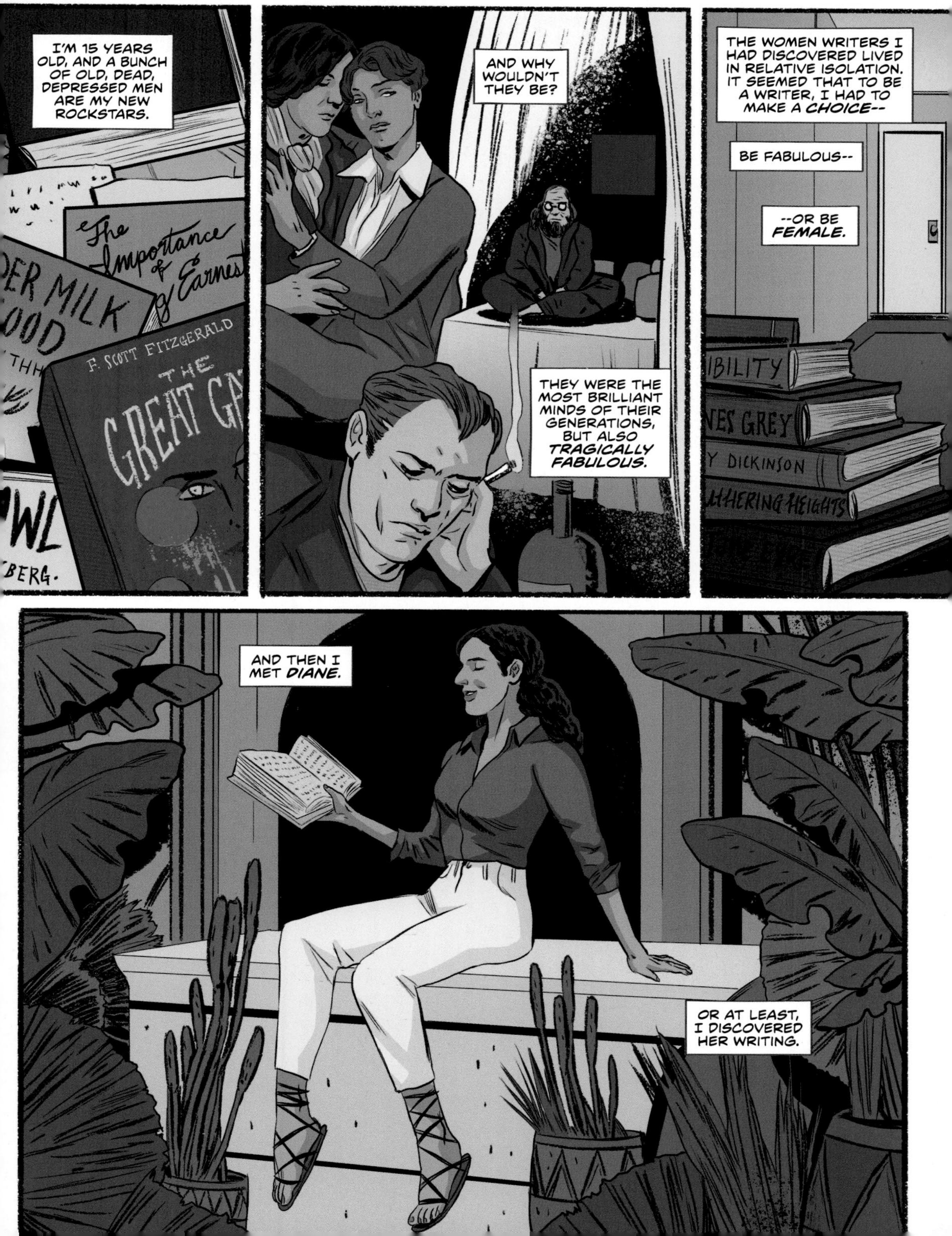

I'M 15 YEARS OLD, AND A BUNCH OF OLD, DEAD, DEPRESSED MEN ARE MY NEW ROCKSTARS.
F. SCOTT FITZGERALD
AND WHY WOULDN'T THEY BE?
THEY WERE THE MOST BRILLIANT MINDS OF THEIR GENERATIONS, BUT ALSO *TRAGICALLY FABULOUS.*
THE WOMEN WRITERS I HAD DISCOVERED LIVED IN RELATIVE ISOLATION. IT SEEMED THAT TO BE A WRITER, I HAD TO MAKE A *CHOICE*--
BE FABULOUS--
--OR BE *FEMALE.*
AND THEN I MET *DIANE.*
OR AT LEAST, I DISCOVERED HER WRITING.

DIANE di PRIMA DROPPED OUT OF SWARTHMORE COLLEGE TO BE A POET IN 1953.

NOW, POETS TEND TO *LOVE* COLLEGE, USING IT AS SHELTER FROM THE *REAL* WORLD, BUT DIANE WASN'T LIKE THAT.

SHE PUBLISHED HER FIRST BOOK OF POETRY, *THIS KIND OF BIRD FLIES BACKWARD*, IN 1958.

Gaslight CAFE

SHE WENT TO PARTIES ALONGSIDE GINSBERG AND KEROUAC, GIVING VOICE TO THE INFAMOUS 'GIRLS WHO SAY NOTHING AND WEAR BLACK.'*

* JACK KEROUAC, INFAMOUSLY SPEAKING ABOUT THE WOMEN OF THE BEAT GENERATION.

I DISCOVERED HER BOOK *MEMOIRS OF A BEATNIK* AS A TEENAGER, BUT IT WAS WRITTEN IN 1969.

IT IS... *VERY* ADULT.

BUT IT WASN'T THE HOT NIGHTS THAT GOT ME READING THAT BOOK; IT WAS HER COOL DAYS.

IN BETWEEN STEAMY ENCOUNTERS, DIANE WROTE ABOUT HER LIFE *LIKE THIS*--

--SPINNING JAZZ RECORDS WHILE SHE WROTE POETRY FOR HOURS AND LIVED ON CHEAP FOODS LIKE SCRAMBLED EGGS AND CUPS OF MILKY, SUGARY COFFEE.

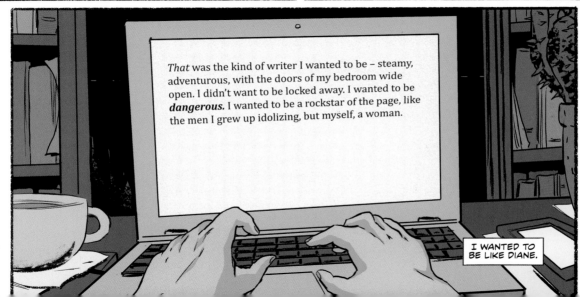

That was the kind of writer I wanted to be – steamy, adventurous, with the doors of my bedroom wide open. I didn't want to be locked away. I wanted to be *dangerous.* I wanted to be a rockstar of the page, like the men I grew up idolizing, but myself, a woman.

I WANTED TO BE LIKE DIANE.

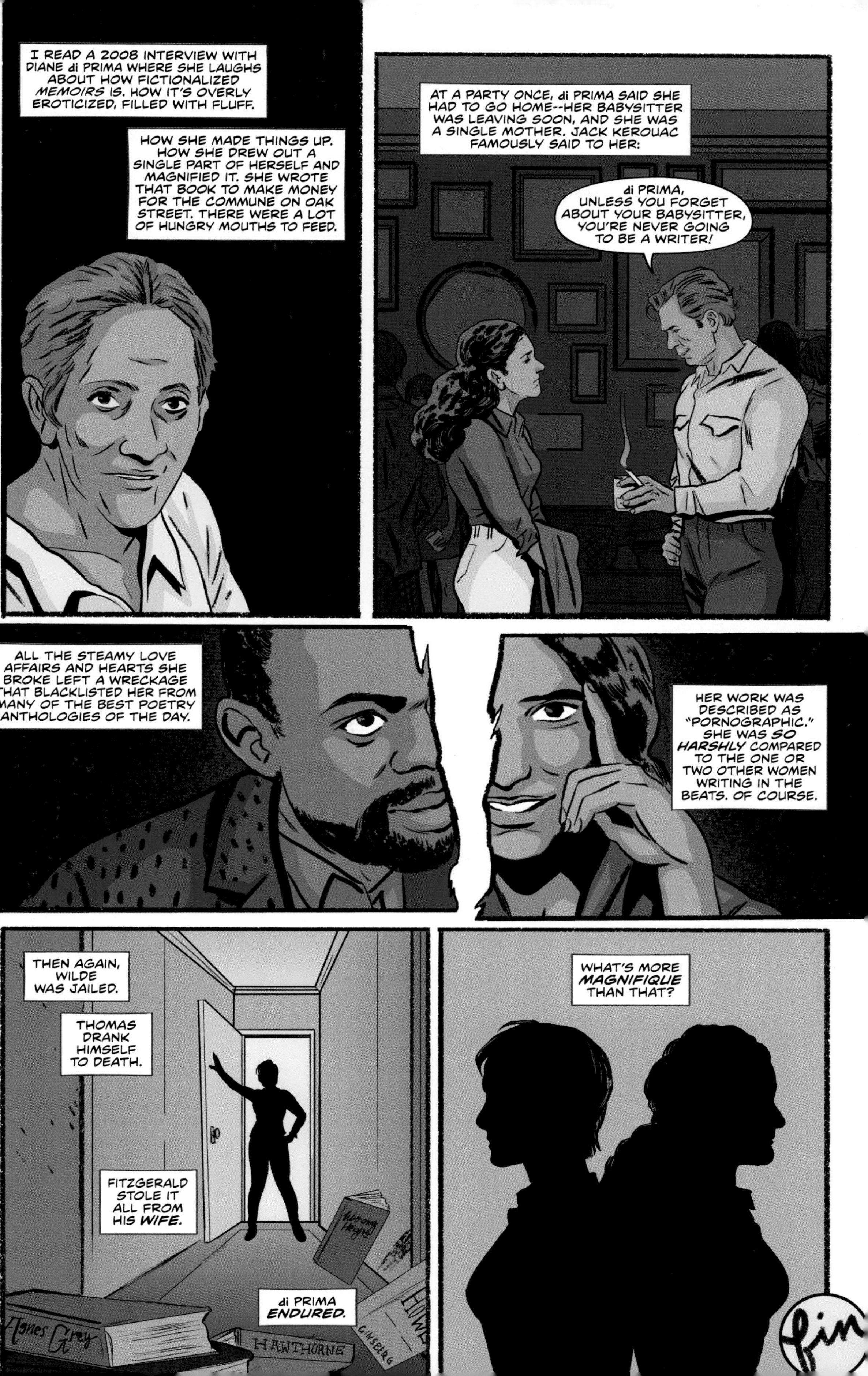
I READ A 2008 INTERVIEW WITH DIANE di PRIMA WHERE SHE LAUGHS ABOUT HOW FICTIONALIZED *MEMOIRS* IS. HOW IT'S OVERLY EROTICIZED, FILLED WITH FLUFF.
HOW SHE MADE THINGS UP. HOW SHE DREW OUT A SINGLE PART OF HERSELF AND MAGNIFIED IT. SHE WROTE THAT BOOK TO MAKE MONEY FOR THE COMMUNE ON OAK STREET. THERE WERE A LOT OF HUNGRY MOUTHS TO FEED.
AT A PARTY ONCE, di PRIMA SAID SHE HAD TO GO HOME--HER BABYSITTER WAS LEAVING SOON, AND SHE WAS A SINGLE MOTHER. JACK KEROUAC FAMOUSLY SAID TO HER:
di PRIMA, UNLESS YOU FORGET ABOUT YOUR BABYSITTER, YOU'RE NEVER GOING TO BE A WRITER!
ALL THE STEAMY LOVE AFFAIRS AND HEARTS SHE BROKE LEFT A WRECKAGE THAT BLACKLISTED HER FROM MANY OF THE BEST POETRY ANTHOLOGIES OF THE DAY.
HER WORK WAS DESCRIBED AS "PORNOGRAPHIC." SHE WAS ***SO HARSHLY*** COMPARED TO THE ONE OR TWO OTHER WOMEN WRITING IN THE BEATS. OF COURSE.
THEN AGAIN, WILDE WAS JAILED.
THOMAS DRANK HIMSELF TO DEATH.
FITZGERALD STOLE IT ALL FROM HIS ***WIFE***.
Wuthering Heights
di PRIMA ***ENDURED***.
Agnes Grey
HAWTHORNE
GINSBERG
WHAT'S MORE ***MAGNIFIQUE*** THAN THAT?
fin

"If laughing hurts you... stay at home!"

—Ellen Armstrong

from a handbill promoting her show.

ALL THUMBS

DANI COLMAN WRITER | **SARAH GORDON** ARTIST | **HI-FI** COLORIST

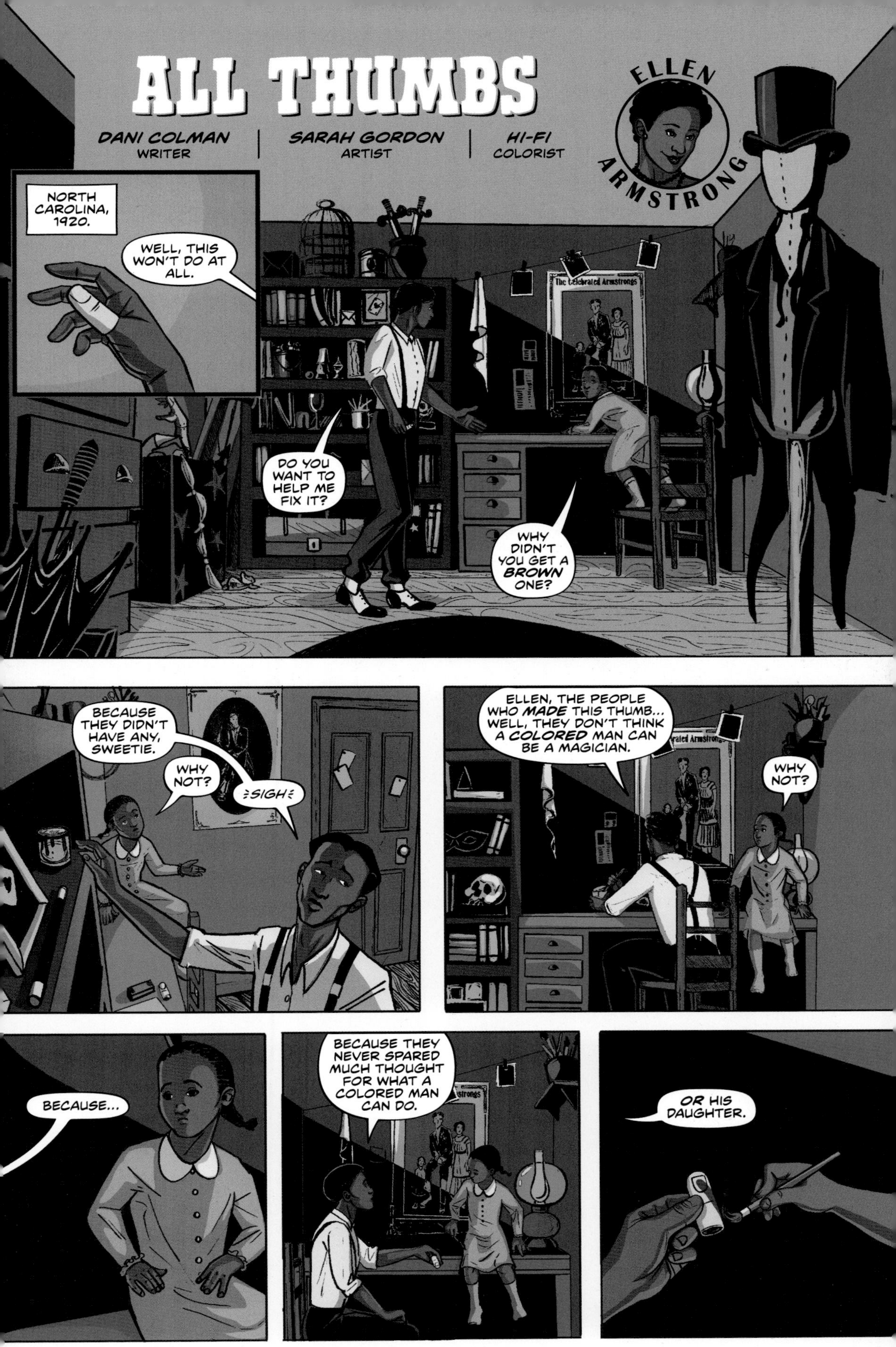
ELLEN ARMSTRONG
NORTH CAROLINA, 1920.
WELL, THIS WON'T DO AT ALL.
The Celebrated Armstrongs
DO YOU WANT TO HELP ME FIX IT?
WHY DIDN'T YOU GET A ***BROWN*** ONE?
BECAUSE THEY DIDN'T HAVE ANY, SWEETIE.
WHY NOT?
SIGH
ELLEN, THE PEOPLE WHO ***MADE*** THIS THUMB... WELL, THEY DON'T THINK A ***COLORED*** MAN CAN BE A MAGICIAN.
WHY NOT?
BECAUSE...
BECAUSE THEY NEVER SPARED MUCH THOUGHT FOR WHAT A COLORED MAN CAN DO.
OR HIS DAUGHTER.

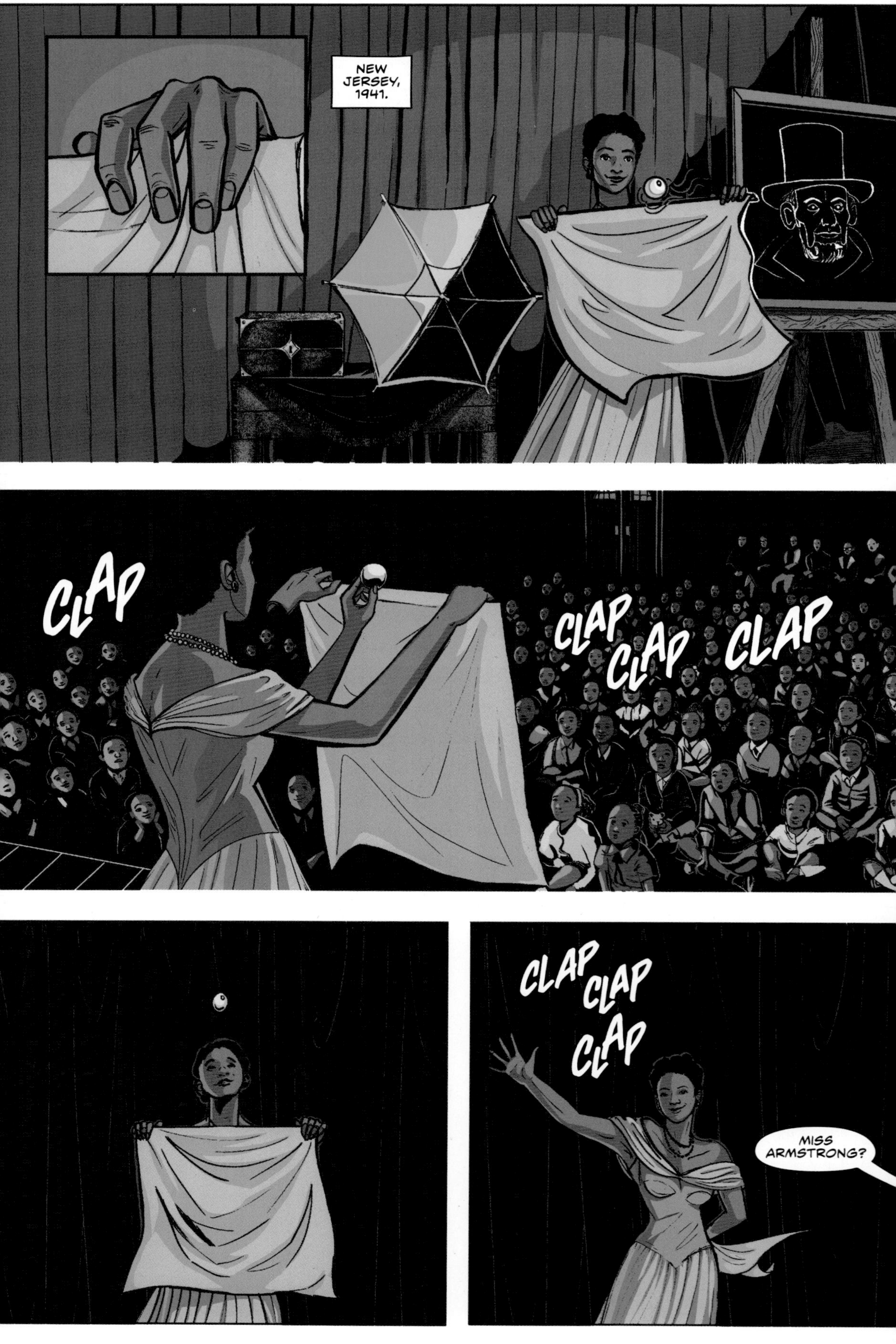
NEW JERSEY, 1941.
CLAP
CLAP
CLAP
CLAP
CLAP
CLAP
CLAP
MISS ARMSTRONG?

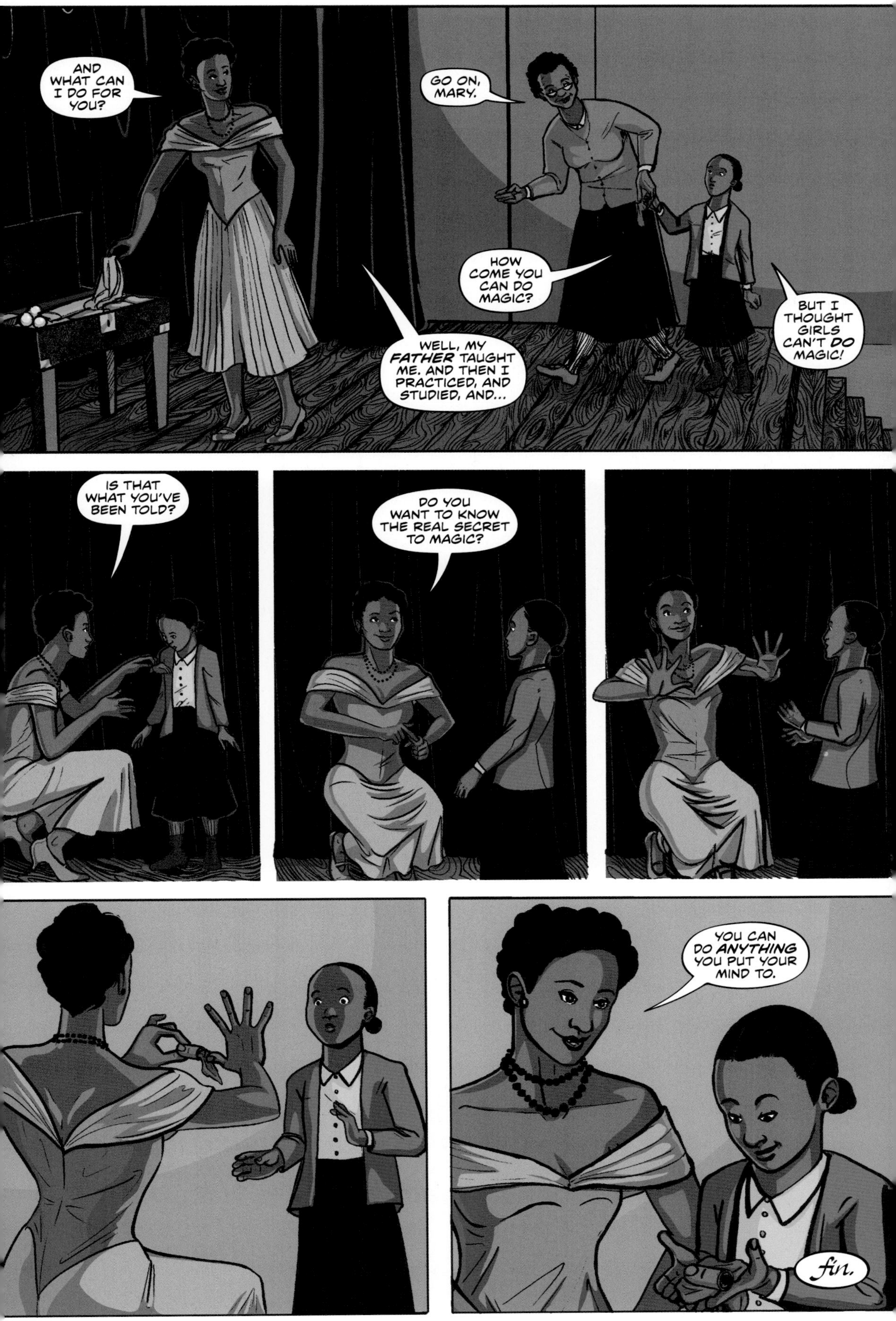
AND WHAT CAN I DO FOR YOU?
GO ON, MARY.
HOW COME YOU CAN DO MAGIC?
WELL, MY FATHER TAUGHT ME. AND THEN I PRACTICED, AND STUDIED, AND...
BUT I THOUGHT GIRLS CAN'T DO MAGIC!
IS THAT WHAT YOU'VE BEEN TOLD?
DO YOU WANT TO KNOW THE REAL SECRET TO MAGIC?
YOU CAN DO ANYTHING YOU PUT YOUR MIND TO.
fin.

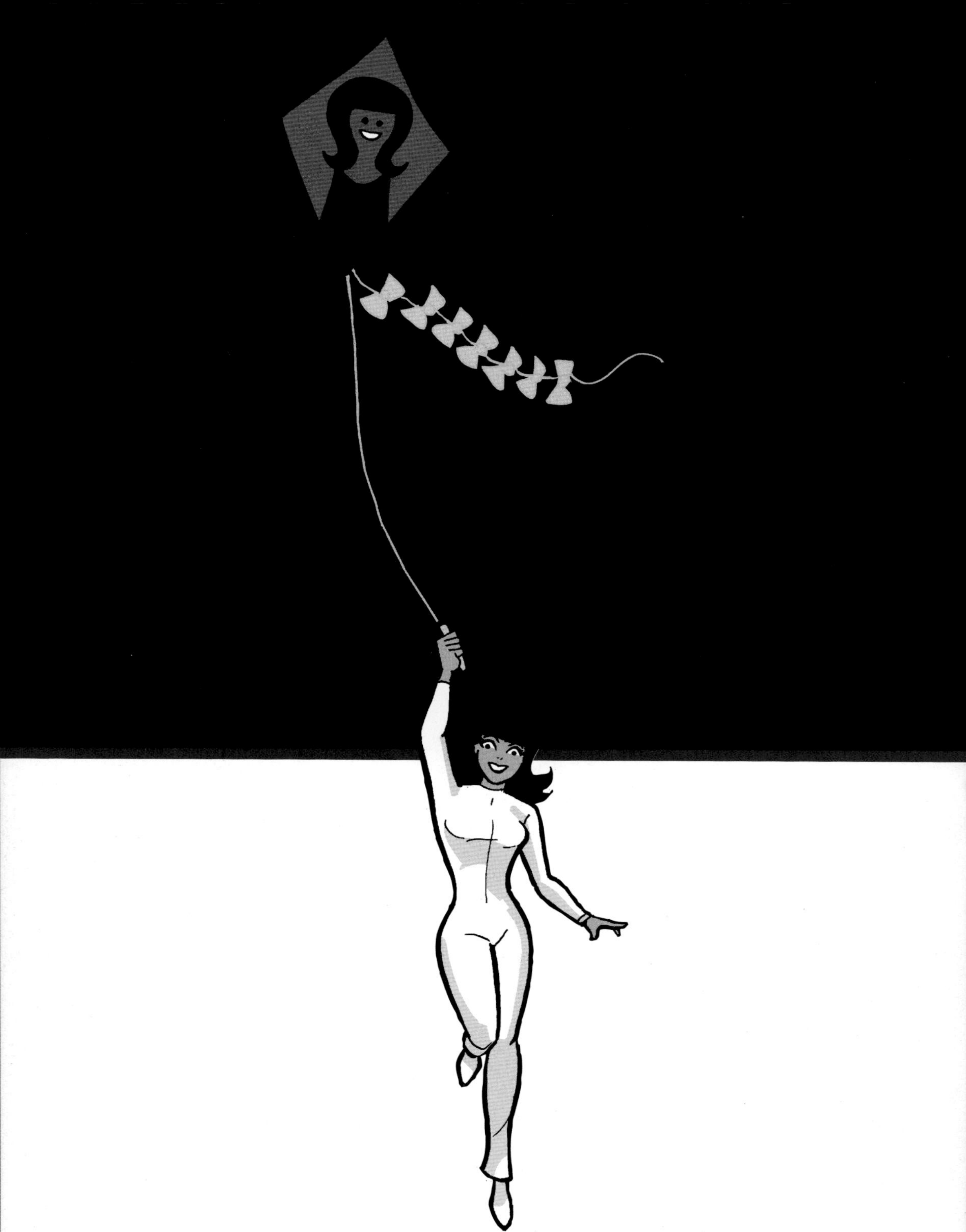

"One of the things about equality is not just that you be treated equally to a man, but that you treat yourself equally to the way you treat a man."

—Marlo Thomas

That Amazing Girl

DAN PARENT WRITER/ARTIST | **RICK TAYLOR** COLORIST

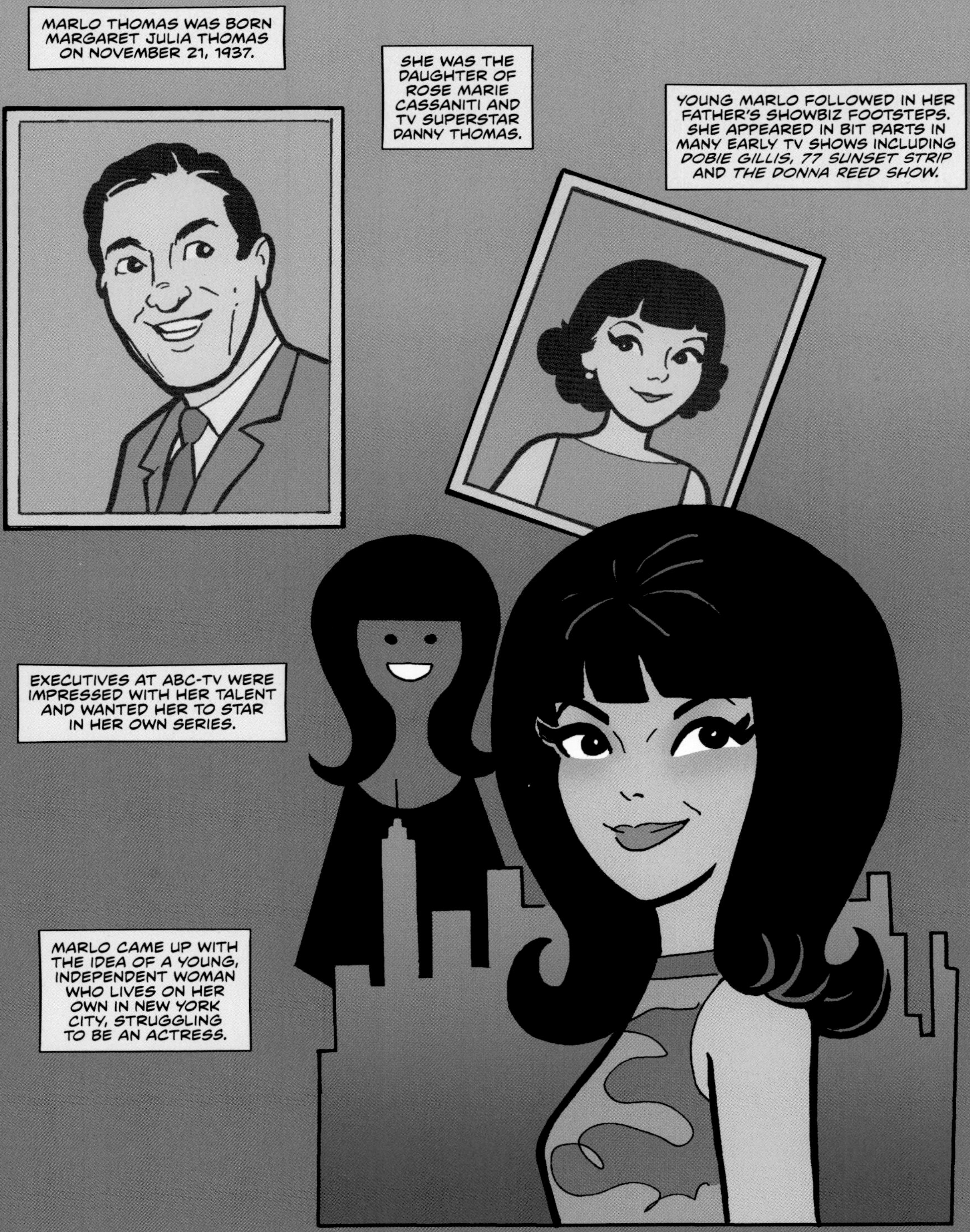
MARLO THOMAS WAS BORN MARGARET JULIA THOMAS ON NOVEMBER 21, 1937.
SHE WAS THE DAUGHTER OF ROSE MARIE CASSANITI AND TV SUPERSTAR DANNY THOMAS.
YOUNG MARLO FOLLOWED IN HER FATHER'S SHOWBIZ FOOTSTEPS. SHE APPEARED IN BIT PARTS IN MANY EARLY TV SHOWS INCLUDING *DOBIE GILLIS, 77 SUNSET STRIP* AND *THE DONNA REED SHOW.*
EXECUTIVES AT ABC-TV WERE IMPRESSED WITH HER TALENT AND WANTED HER TO STAR IN HER OWN SERIES.
MARLO CAME UP WITH THE IDEA OF A YOUNG, INDEPENDENT WOMAN WHO LIVES ON HER OWN IN NEW YORK CITY, STRUGGLING TO BE AN ACTRESS.

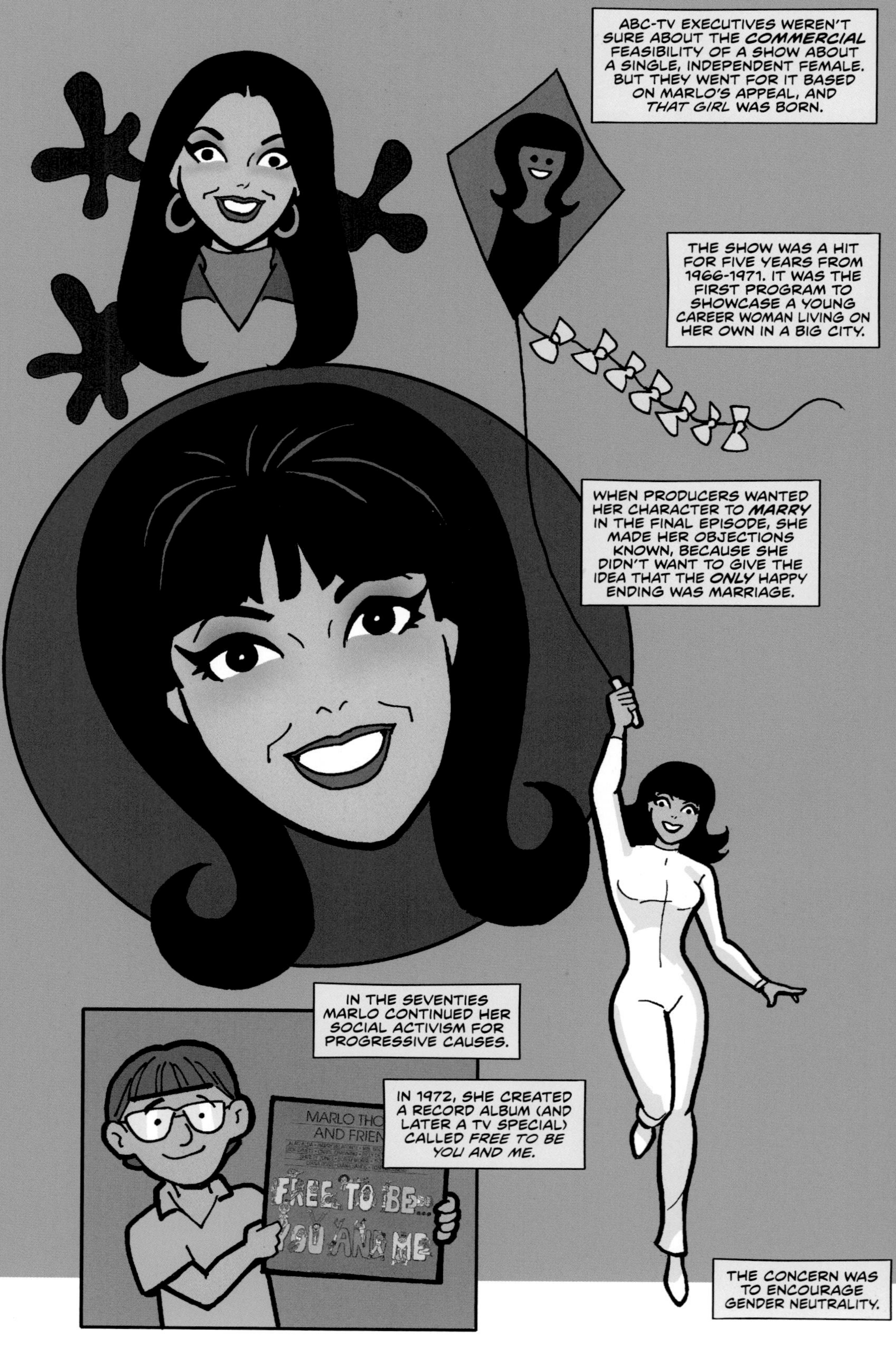
ABC-TV EXECUTIVES WEREN'T SURE ABOUT THE *COMMERCIAL* FEASIBILITY OF A SHOW ABOUT A SINGLE, INDEPENDENT FEMALE. BUT THEY WENT FOR IT BASED ON MARLO'S APPEAL, AND *THAT GIRL* WAS BORN.
THE SHOW WAS A HIT FOR FIVE YEARS FROM 1966-1971. IT WAS THE FIRST PROGRAM TO SHOWCASE A YOUNG CAREER WOMAN LIVING ON HER OWN IN A BIG CITY.
WHEN PRODUCERS WANTED HER CHARACTER TO *MARRY* IN THE FINAL EPISODE, SHE MADE HER OBJECTIONS KNOWN, BECAUSE SHE DIDN'T WANT TO GIVE THE IDEA THAT THE *ONLY* HAPPY ENDING WAS MARRIAGE.
IN THE SEVENTIES MARLO CONTINUED HER SOCIAL ACTIVISM FOR PROGRESSIVE CAUSES.
IN 1972, SHE CREATED A RECORD ALBUM (AND LATER A TV SPECIAL) CALLED *FREE TO BE YOU AND ME.*
FREE TO BE... YOU AND ME
THE CONCERN WAS TO ENCOURAGE GENDER NEUTRALITY.

THE THEME PROMOTED INDIVIDUALITY, TOLERANCE AND COMFORT WITH ONE'S IDENTITY.
THE MAJOR THEME: YOU CAN ACHIEVE ***ANYTHING***--WHETHER YOU'RE A BOY OR A GIRL!

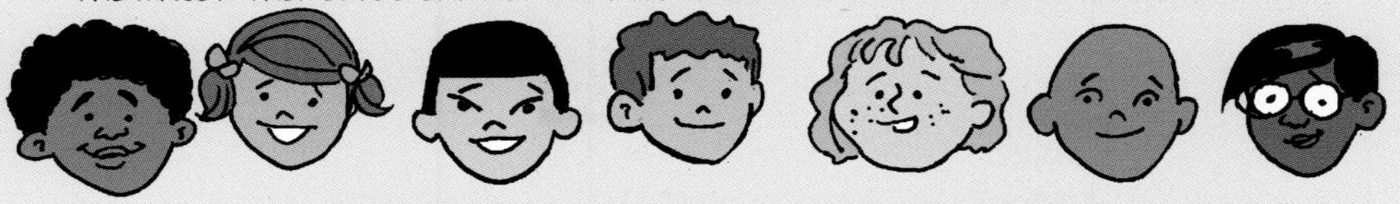

THE SHOW AND RELATED BOOKS AND SPECIALS WON AN EMMY AND A PEABODY AWARD...
AND MILLIONS OF CHILDREN EMBRACED THEMSELVES FOR WHO THEY WERE.

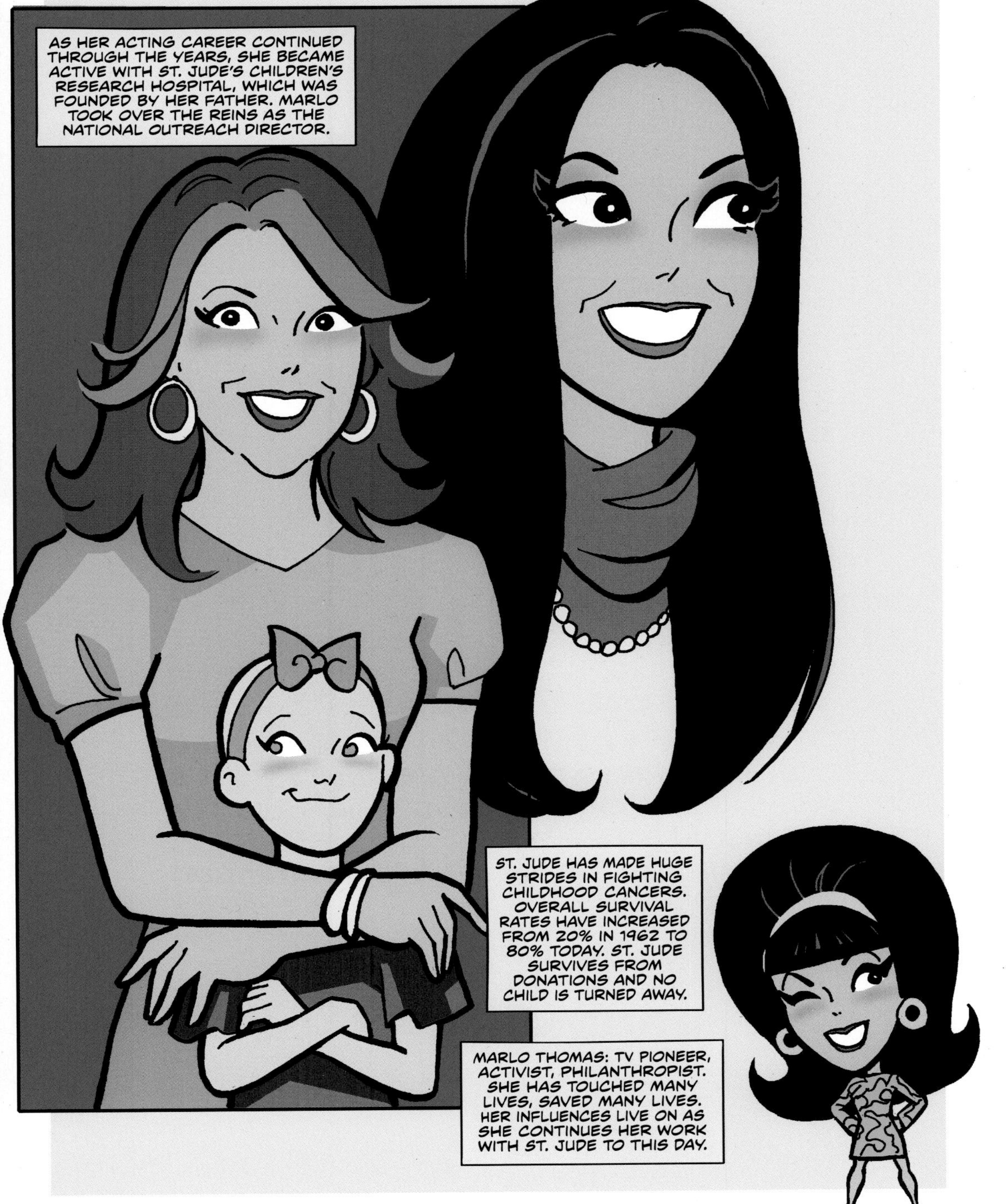
AS HER ACTING CAREER CONTINUED THROUGH THE YEARS, SHE BECAME ACTIVE WITH ST. JUDE'S CHILDREN'S RESEARCH HOSPITAL, WHICH WAS FOUNDED BY HER FATHER. MARLO TOOK OVER THE REINS AS THE NATIONAL OUTREACH DIRECTOR.
ST. JUDE HAS MADE HUGE STRIDES IN FIGHTING CHILDHOOD CANCERS. OVERALL SURVIVAL RATES HAVE INCREASED FROM 20% IN 1962 TO 80% TODAY. ST. JUDE SURVIVES FROM DONATIONS AND NO CHILD IS TURNED AWAY.
MARLO THOMAS: TV PIONEER, ACTIVIST, PHILANTHROPIST. SHE HAS TOUCHED MANY LIVES, SAVED MANY LIVES. HER INFLUENCES LIVE ON AS SHE CONTINUES HER WORK WITH ST. JUDE TO THIS DAY.

Fin.

"You know what? You're an individual, and that makes people nervous. And it's gonna keep making people nervous for the rest of your life."

— Louise Fitzhugh
Harriet the Spy

SPIES LIKE US

GILLIAN GOERZ
WRITER/ARTIST

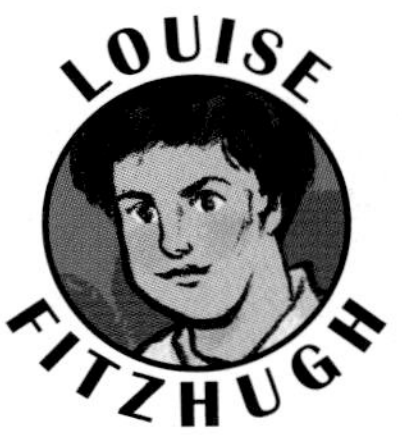
LOUISE
FITZHUGH

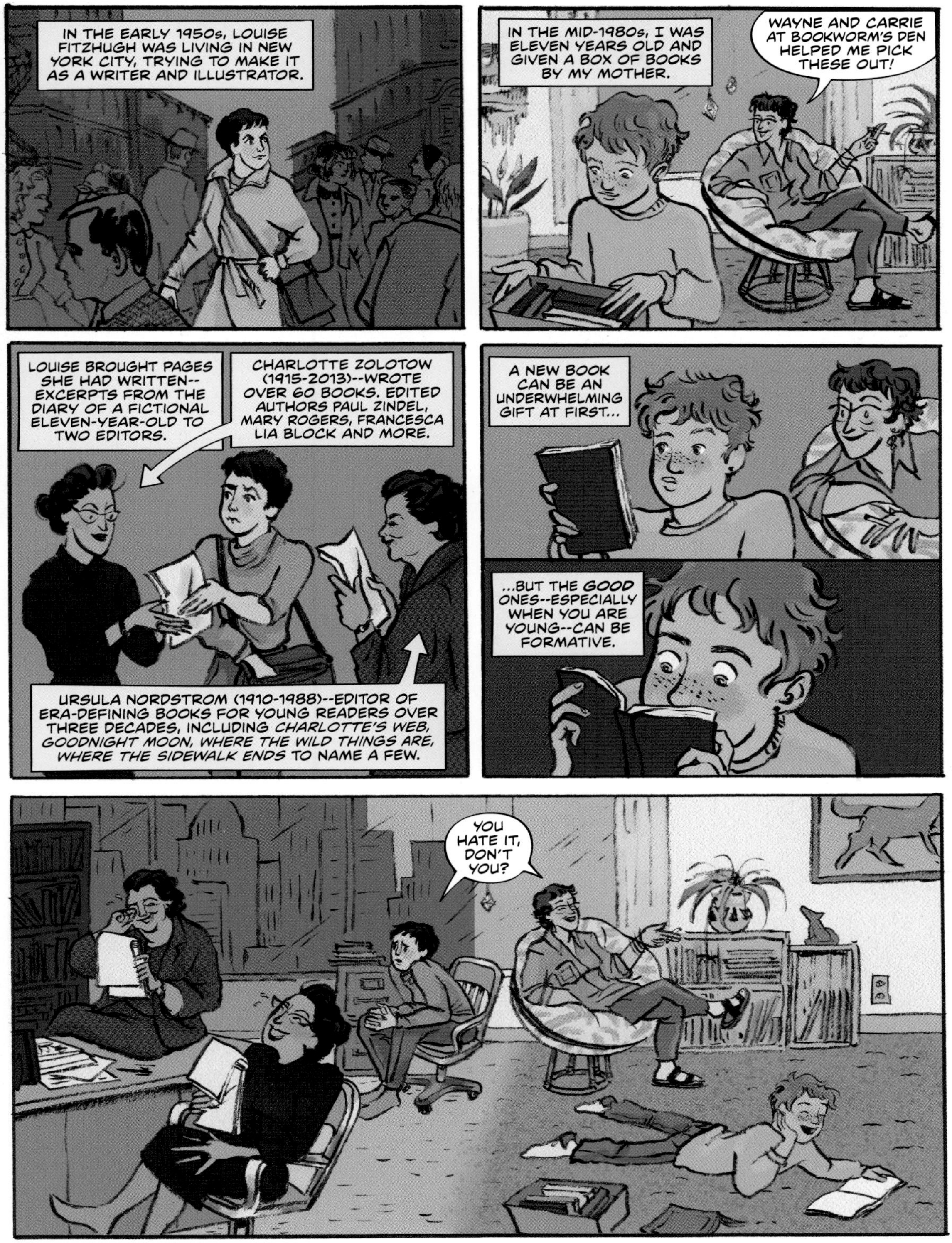
IN THE EARLY 1950s, LOUISE FITZHUGH WAS LIVING IN NEW YORK CITY, TRYING TO MAKE IT AS A WRITER AND ILLUSTRATOR.
IN THE MID-1980s, I WAS ELEVEN YEARS OLD AND GIVEN A BOX OF BOOKS BY MY MOTHER.
WAYNE AND CARRIE AT BOOKWORM'S DEN HELPED ME PICK THESE OUT!
LOUISE BROUGHT PAGES SHE HAD WRITTEN-- EXCERPTS FROM THE DIARY OF A FICTIONAL ELEVEN-YEAR-OLD TO TWO EDITORS.
CHARLOTTE ZOLOTOW (1915-2013)--WROTE OVER 60 BOOKS. EDITED AUTHORS PAUL ZINDEL, MARY ROGERS, FRANCESCA LIA BLOCK AND MORE.
URSULA NORDSTROM (1910-1988)--EDITOR OF ERA-DEFINING BOOKS FOR YOUNG READERS OVER THREE DECADES, INCLUDING *CHARLOTTE'S WEB, GOODNIGHT MOON, WHERE THE WILD THINGS ARE, WHERE THE SIDEWALK ENDS* TO NAME A FEW.
A NEW BOOK CAN BE AN UNDERWHELMING GIFT AT FIRST...
...BUT THE *GOOD* ONES--ESPECIALLY WHEN YOU ARE YOUNG--CAN BE FORMATIVE.
YOU HATE IT, DON'T YOU?

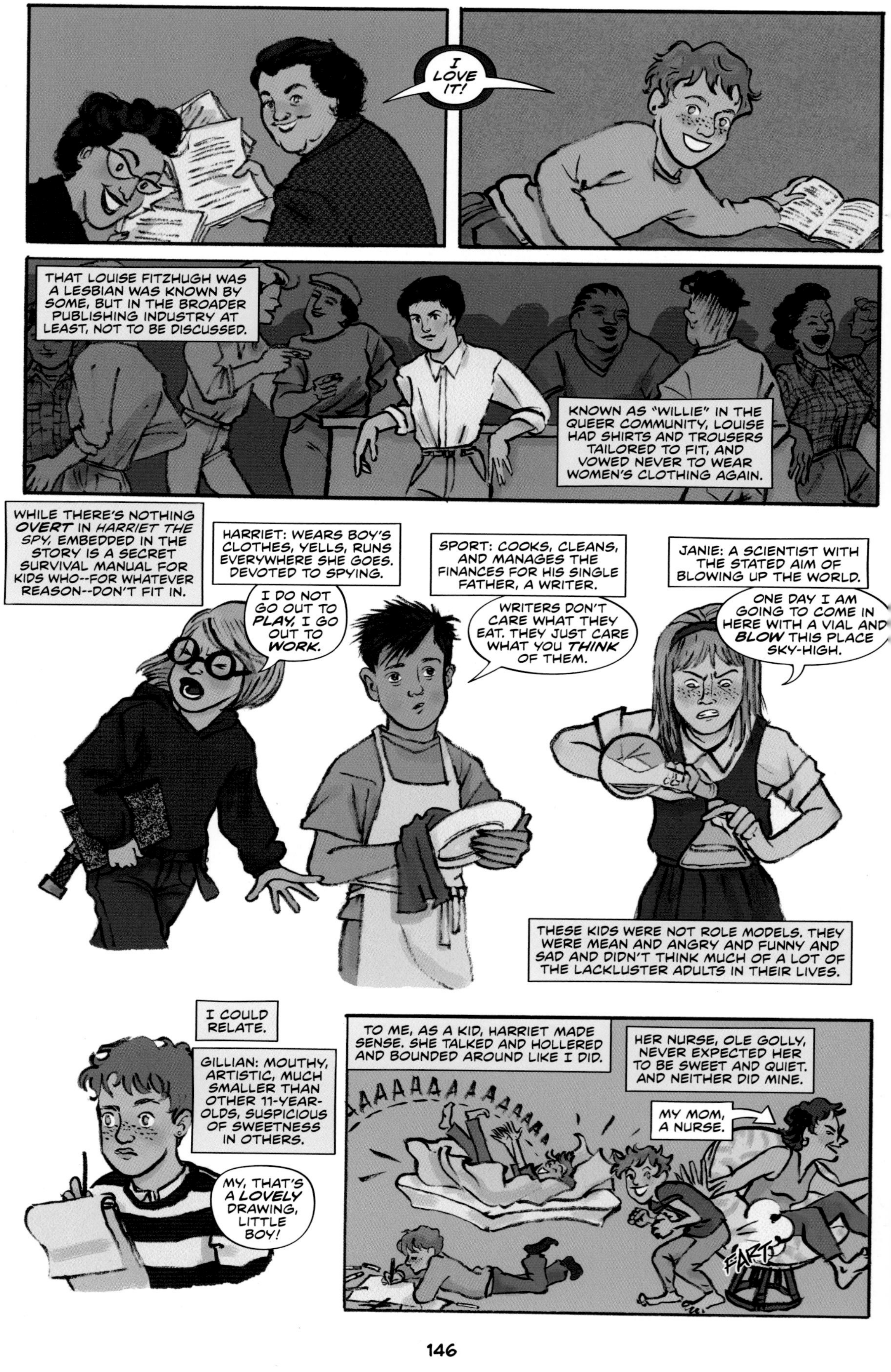
I LOVE IT!
THAT LOUISE FITZHUGH WAS A LESBIAN WAS KNOWN BY SOME, BUT IN THE BROADER PUBLISHING INDUSTRY AT LEAST, NOT TO BE DISCUSSED.
KNOWN AS "WILLIE" IN THE QUEER COMMUNITY, LOUISE HAD SHIRTS AND TROUSERS TAILORED TO FIT, AND VOWED NEVER TO WEAR WOMEN'S CLOTHING AGAIN.
WHILE THERE'S NOTHING ***OVERT*** IN *HARRIET THE SPY*, EMBEDDED IN THE STORY IS A SECRET SURVIVAL MANUAL FOR KIDS WHO--FOR WHATEVER REASON--DON'T FIT IN.
HARRIET: WEARS BOY'S CLOTHES, YELLS, RUNS EVERYWHERE SHE GOES. DEVOTED TO SPYING.
I DO NOT GO OUT TO ***PLAY***, I GO OUT TO ***WORK***.
SPORT: COOKS, CLEANS, AND MANAGES THE FINANCES FOR HIS SINGLE FATHER, A WRITER.
WRITERS DON'T CARE WHAT THEY EAT. THEY JUST CARE WHAT YOU ***THINK*** OF THEM.
JANIE: A SCIENTIST WITH THE STATED AIM OF BLOWING UP THE WORLD.
ONE DAY I AM GOING TO COME IN HERE WITH A VIAL AND ***BLOW*** THIS PLACE SKY-HIGH.
THESE KIDS WERE NOT ROLE MODELS. THEY WERE MEAN AND ANGRY AND FUNNY AND SAD AND DIDN'T THINK MUCH OF A LOT OF THE LACKLUSTER ADULTS IN THEIR LIVES.
I COULD RELATE.
GILLIAN: MOUTHY, ARTISTIC, MUCH SMALLER THAN OTHER 11-YEAR-OLDS, SUSPICIOUS OF SWEETNESS IN OTHERS.
MY, THAT'S A ***LOVELY*** DRAWING, LITTLE BOY!
TO ME, AS A KID, HARRIET MADE SENSE. SHE TALKED AND HOLLERED AND BOUNDED AROUND LIKE I DID.
HER NURSE, OLE GOLLY, NEVER EXPECTED HER TO BE SWEET AND QUIET. AND NEITHER DID MINE.
MY MOM, A NURSE.
FART!

AROUND MY VERY RELIGIOUS EXTENDED FAMILY, THERE WERE DIFFERENT RULES THAN AT HOME WITH JUST MY MOM AND ME.

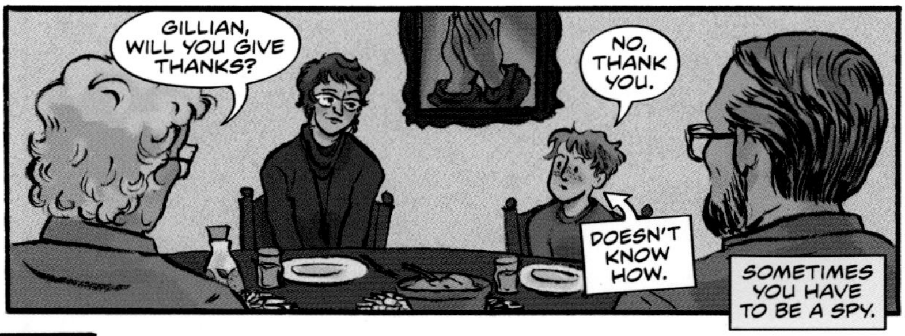
GILLIAN, WILL YOU GIVE THANKS?
NO, THANK YOU.
DOESN'T KNOW HOW.
SOMETIMES YOU HAVE TO BE A SPY.

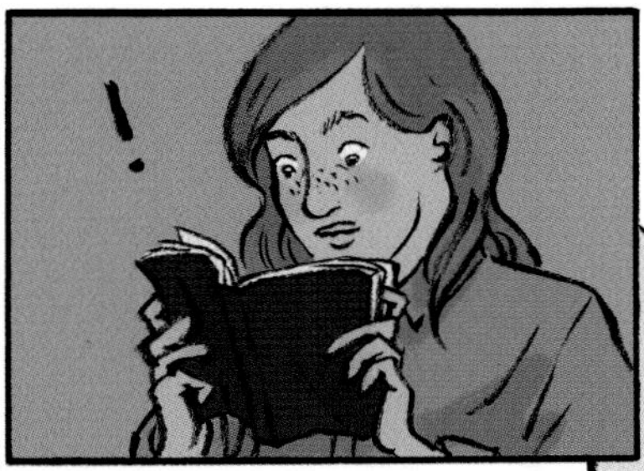

AS AN ADULT, THE INSTRUCTIONS OF LOUISE'S SURVIVAL MANUAL POP OUT IN NEON.

"Don't give up," Harriet whispered as she left.
"Never," Janie whispered back.

"OLE GOLLY SAYS THERE ARE AS MANY WAYS TO LIVE AS THERE ARE PEOPLE ON THE EARTH AND I SHOULDN'T GO ROUND WITH BLINDERS BUT SHOULD SEE EVERY WAY I CAN. THEN I'LL KNOW WHAT WAY I WANT TO LIVE AND NOT JUST LIVE LIKE MY FAMILY."

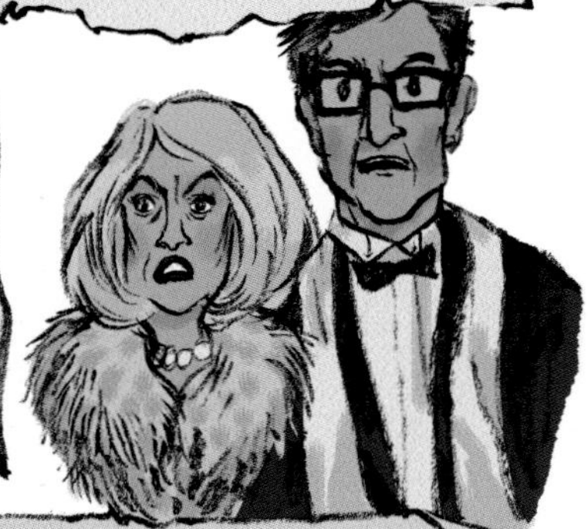

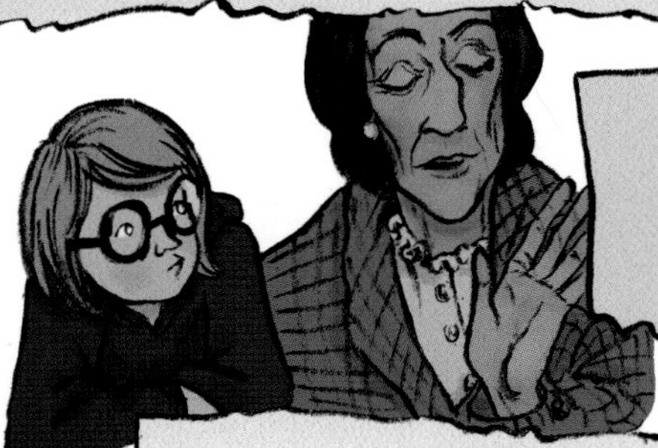

"[I]f... everyone knows you're a spy... what have you gained? No, You have to look like everyone else, then you'll get by and no one will suspect you."

"You have to lie... But to yourself you must always tell the truth."

BY THE 1960S, LOUISE'S REALISTIC APPROACH WAS AN UNSTOPPABLE TREND. URSULA NORDSTROM, HER EDITOR, WHO WAS ALSO A LESBIAN, QUIETLY FOSTERED QUEER AUTHORS LIKE FITZHUGH, MAURICE SENDAK AND MARGARET WISE BROWN, WHOSE BOOKS SHAPED CHILDREN'S LITERATURE INTO SOMETHING MORE HONEST. NANCY DREW AND HER KINDRED GAVE WAY TO HARRIET, GILLY HOPKINS, RAMONA QUIMBY, GEORGIA NICOLSON, AND A HOPEFULLY ENDLESS LINE OF COMPLICATED YOUNG CHARACTERS.

LOUISE UNDERSTOOD THE TRUTH THAT MY MOTHER KNEW GROWING UP IN A RELIGIOUS HOME, THAT I KNEW AS A LOUD-MOUTHED RUNT, AND THAT *ALL* CHILDREN IN AN ADULT'S WORLD KNOW:

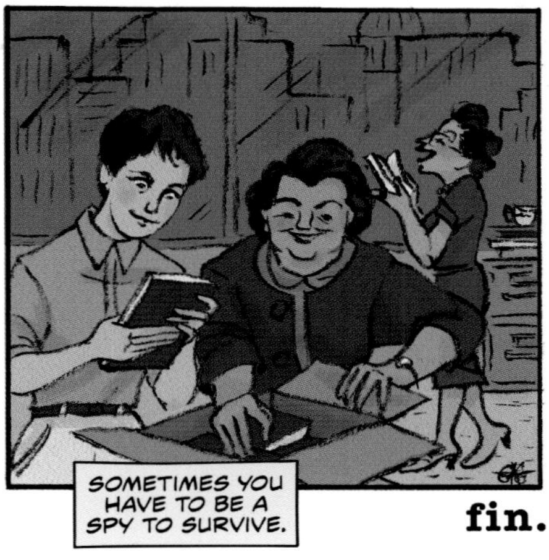
SOMETIMES YOU HAVE TO BE A SPY TO SURVIVE.

fin.

"Maria Bonita is considered by many to be the first feminist of Brazil. She brought equality to the cangaço and became an inspiration for many courageous women who have come after."

—Thedy Corrêa, writer

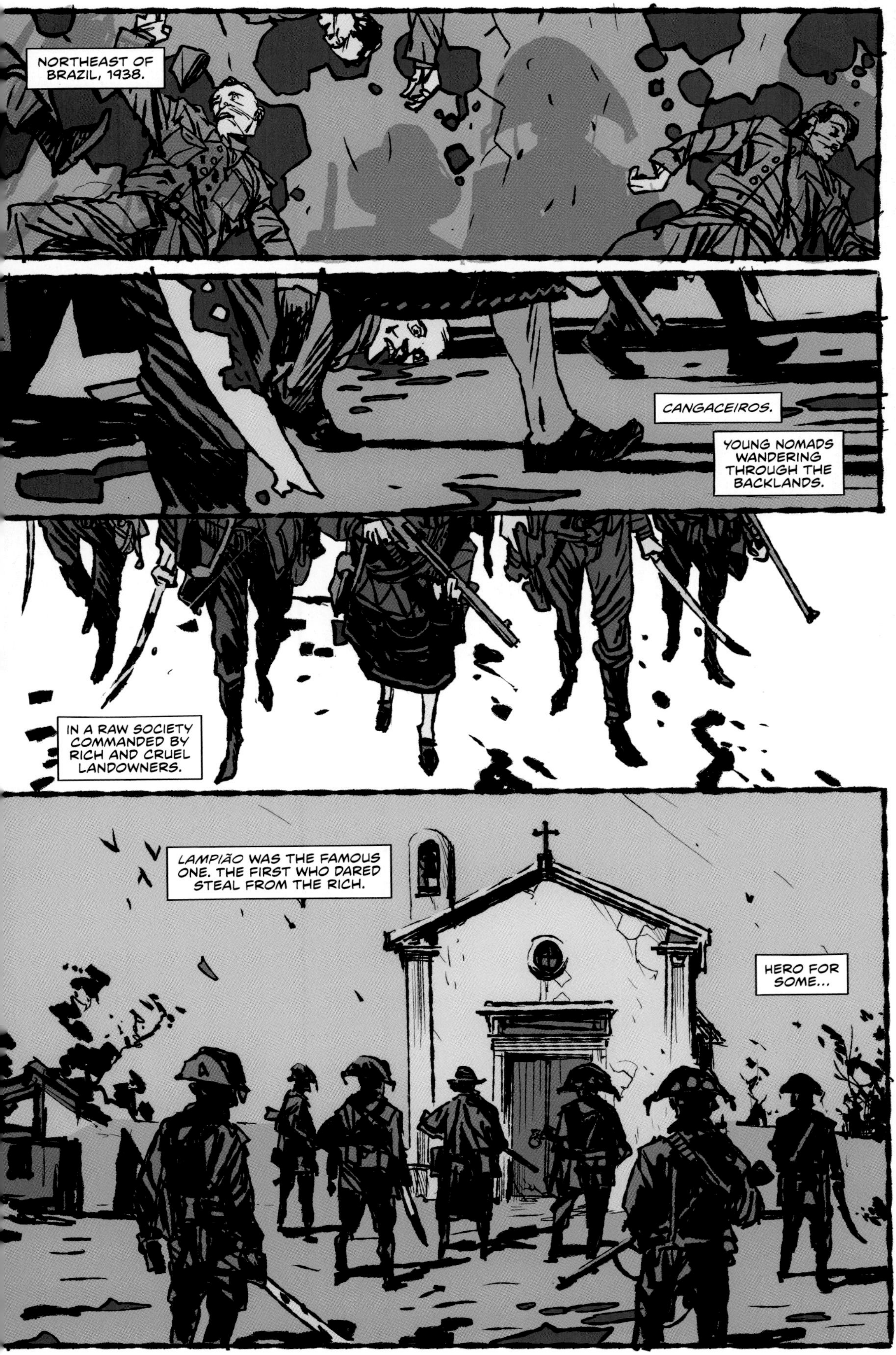
NORTHEAST OF BRAZIL, 1938.
CANGACEIROS.
YOUNG NOMADS WANDERING THROUGH THE BACKLANDS.
IN A RAW SOCIETY COMMANDED BY RICH AND CRUEL LANDOWNERS.
LAMPIÃO WAS THE FAMOUS ONE. THE FIRST WHO DARED STEAL FROM THE RICH.
HERO FOR SOME...

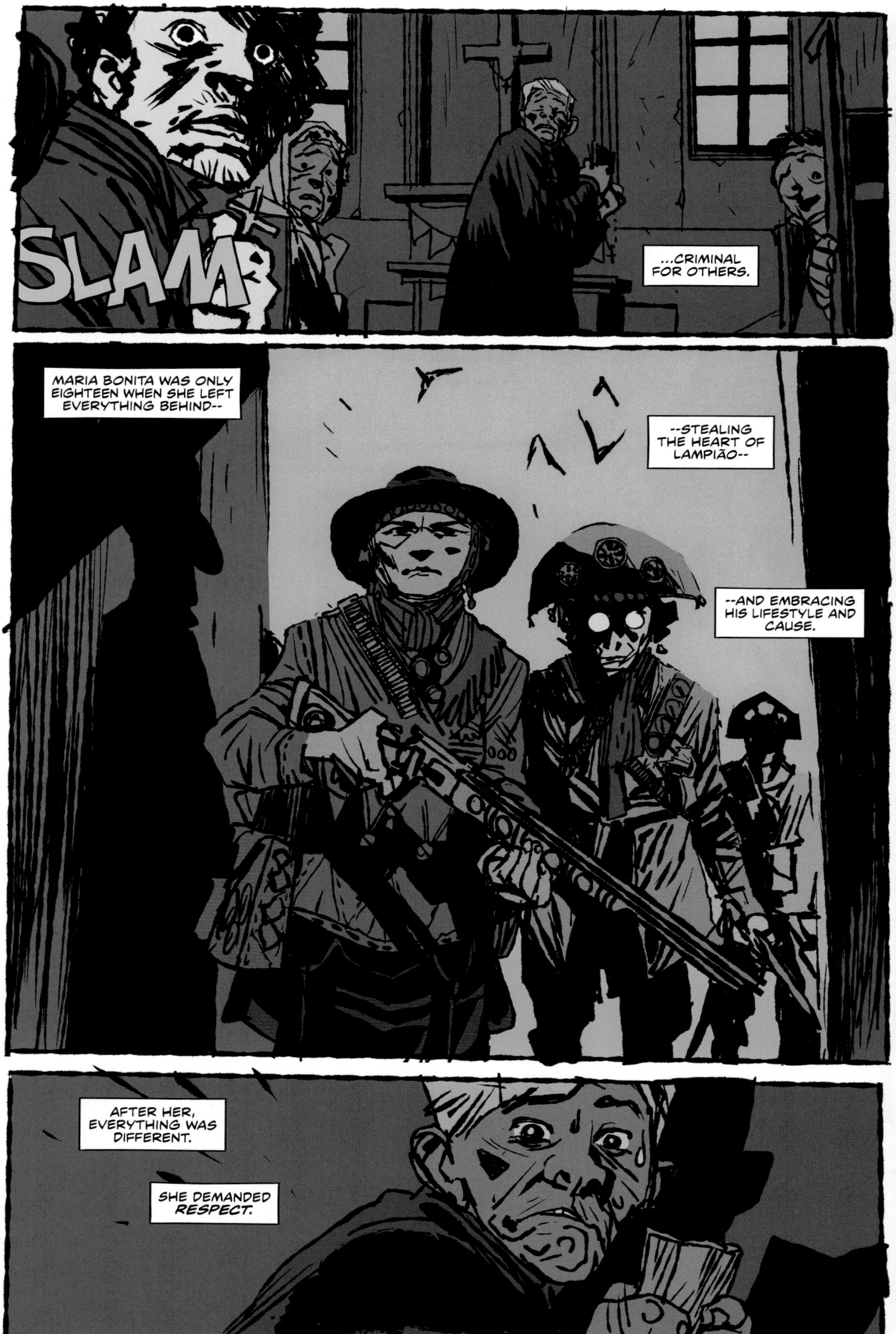
SLAM
...CRIMINAL FOR OTHERS.
MARIA BONITA WAS ONLY EIGHTEEN WHEN SHE LEFT EVERYTHING BEHIND--
--STEALING THE HEART OF LAMPIÃO--
--AND EMBRACING HIS LIFESTYLE AND CAUSE.
AFTER HER, EVERYTHING WAS DIFFERENT.
SHE DEMANDED *RESPECT.*

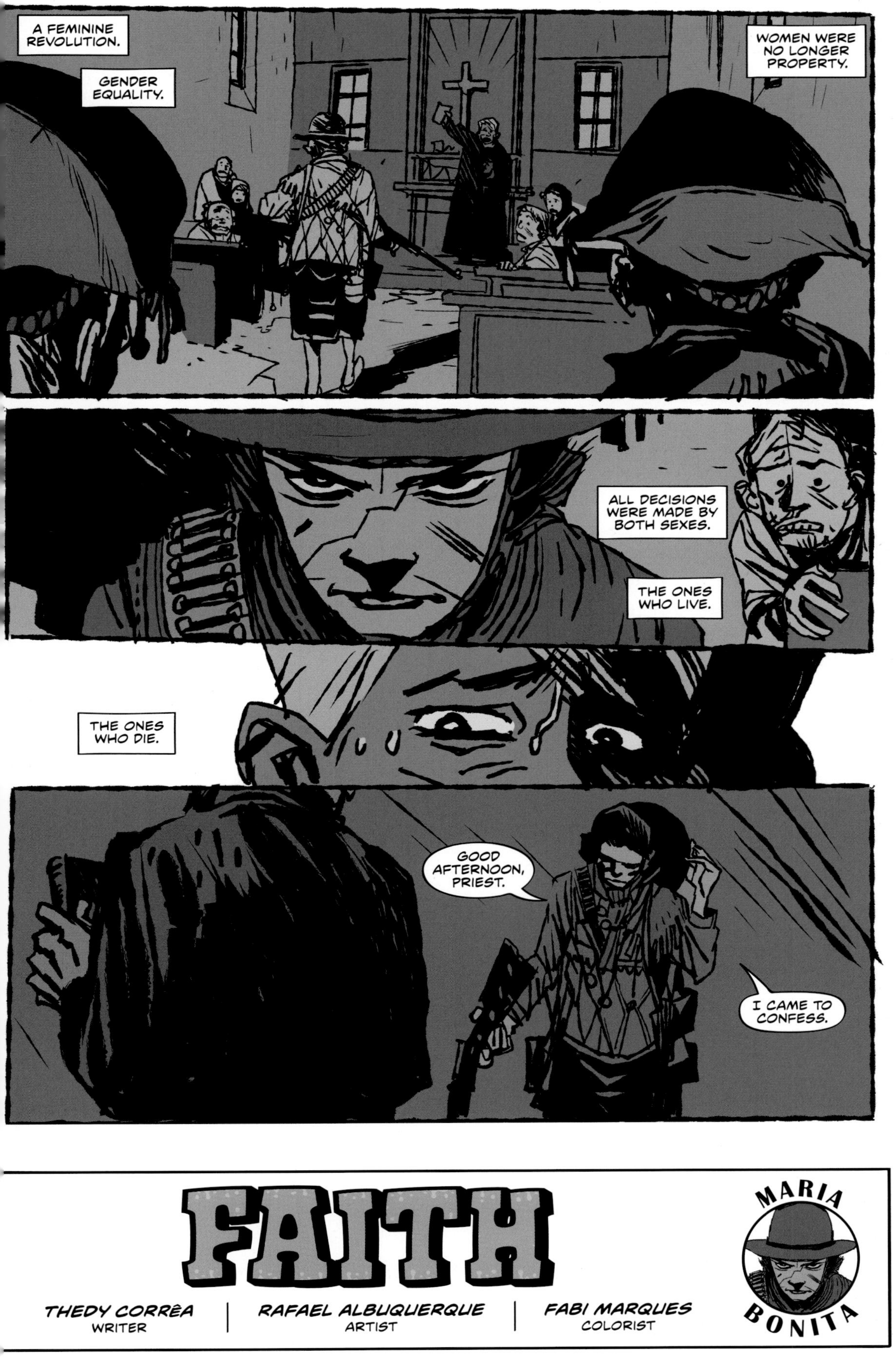
A FEMININE REVOLUTION.
GENDER EQUALITY.
WOMEN WERE NO LONGER PROPERTY.
ALL DECISIONS WERE MADE BY BOTH SEXES.
THE ONES WHO LIVE.
THE ONES WHO DIE.
GOOD AFTERNOON, PRIEST.
I CAME TO CONFESS.

FAITH

MARIA BONITA

THEDY CORRÊA WRITER | *RAFAEL ALBUQUERQUE* ARTIST | *FABI MARQUES* COLORIST

"In the eyes of science we are not related, but to us and due to everything we have been through together we are sisters."

—Karly

ABOVE WATER

ANONYMOUS

KARRIE FRANSMAN
WRITER

ROB DAVIS
ARTIST

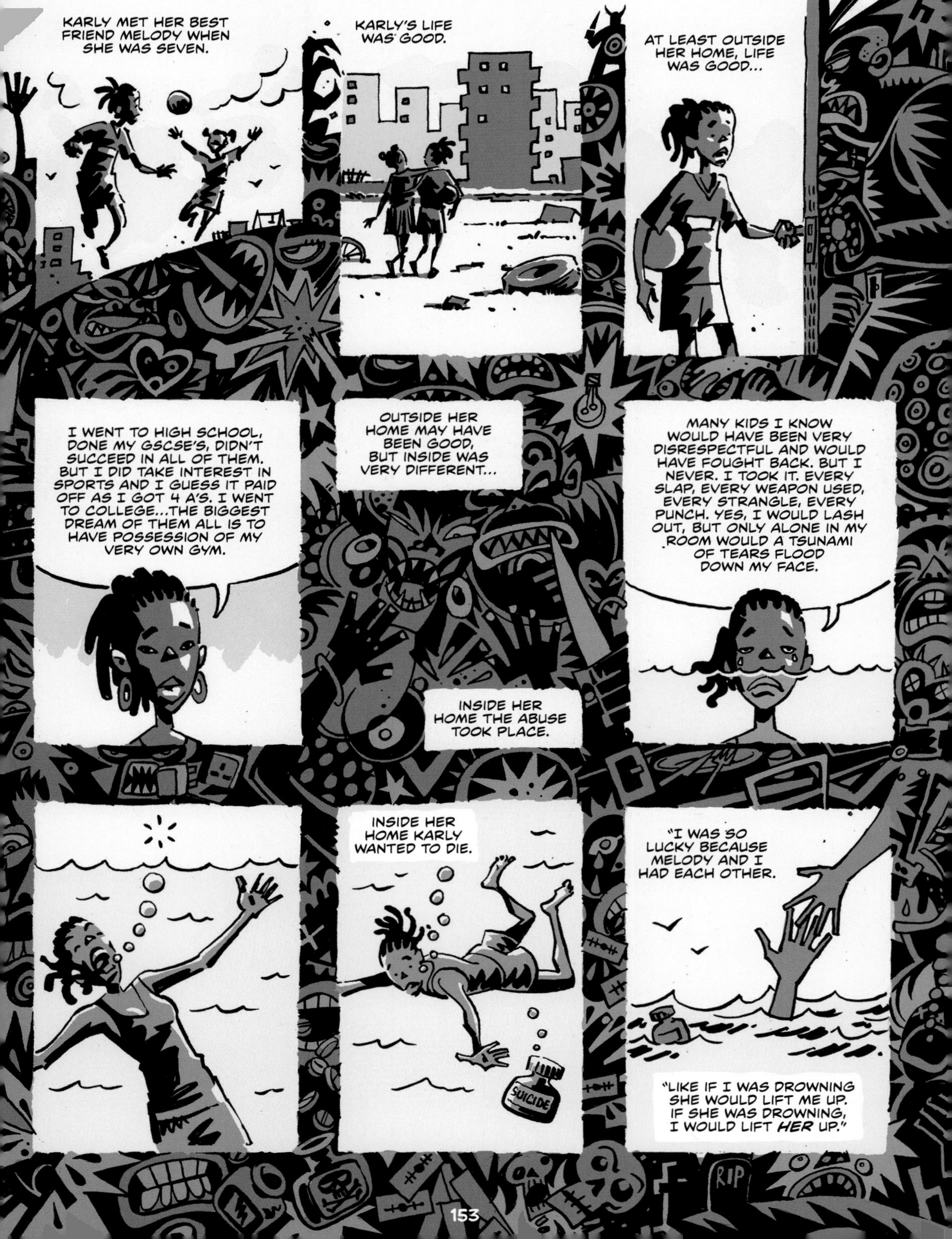
KARLY MET HER BEST FRIEND MELODY WHEN SHE WAS SEVEN.
KARLY'S LIFE WAS GOOD.
AT LEAST OUTSIDE HER HOME, LIFE WAS GOOD...
I WENT TO HIGH SCHOOL, DONE MY GSCSE'S, DIDN'T SUCCEED IN ALL OF THEM. BUT I DID TAKE INTEREST IN SPORTS AND I GUESS IT PAID OFF AS I GOT 4 A'S. I WENT TO COLLEGE...THE BIGGEST DREAM OF THEM ALL IS TO HAVE POSSESSION OF MY VERY OWN GYM.
OUTSIDE HER HOME MAY HAVE BEEN GOOD, BUT INSIDE WAS VERY DIFFERENT...
INSIDE HER HOME THE ABUSE TOOK PLACE.
MANY KIDS I KNOW WOULD HAVE BEEN VERY DISRESPECTFUL AND WOULD HAVE FOUGHT BACK. BUT I NEVER. I TOOK IT. EVERY SLAP, EVERY WEAPON USED, EVERY STRANGLE, EVERY PUNCH. YES, I WOULD LASH OUT, BUT ONLY ALONE IN MY ROOM WOULD A TSUNAMI OF TEARS FLOOD DOWN MY FACE.
INSIDE HER HOME KARLY WANTED TO DIE.
SUICIDE
"I WAS SO LUCKY BECAUSE MELODY AND I HAD EACH OTHER.
"LIKE IF I WAS DROWNING SHE WOULD LIFT ME UP. IF SHE WAS DROWNING, I WOULD LIFT *HER* UP."
RIP

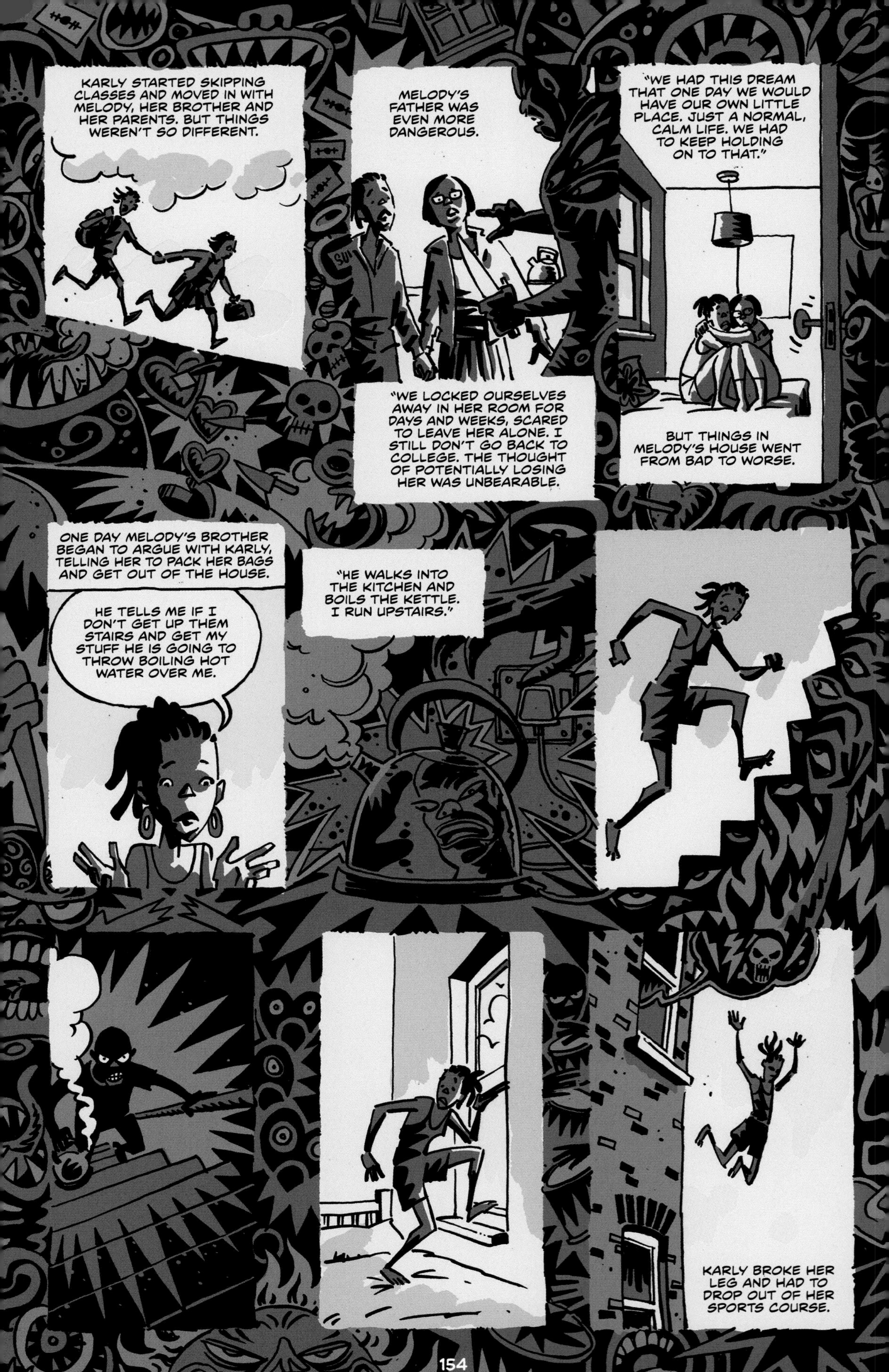
KARLY STARTED SKIPPING CLASSES AND MOVED IN WITH MELODY, HER BROTHER AND HER PARENTS. BUT THINGS WEREN'T SO DIFFERENT.
MELODY'S FATHER WAS EVEN MORE DANGEROUS.
"WE LOCKED OURSELVES AWAY IN HER ROOM FOR DAYS AND WEEKS, SCARED TO LEAVE HER ALONE. I STILL DON'T GO BACK TO COLLEGE. THE THOUGHT OF POTENTIALLY LOSING HER WAS UNBEARABLE.
"WE HAD THIS DREAM THAT ONE DAY WE WOULD HAVE OUR OWN LITTLE PLACE. JUST A NORMAL, CALM LIFE. WE HAD TO KEEP HOLDING ON TO THAT."
BUT THINGS IN MELODY'S HOUSE WENT FROM BAD TO WORSE.
ONE DAY MELODY'S BROTHER BEGAN TO ARGUE WITH KARLY, TELLING HER TO PACK HER BAGS AND GET OUT OF THE HOUSE.
HE TELLS ME IF I DON'T GET UP THEM STAIRS AND GET MY STUFF HE IS GOING TO THROW BOILING HOT WATER OVER ME.
"HE WALKS INTO THE KITCHEN AND BOILS THE KETTLE. I RUN UPSTAIRS."
KARLY BROKE HER LEG AND HAD TO DROP OUT OF HER SPORTS COURSE.

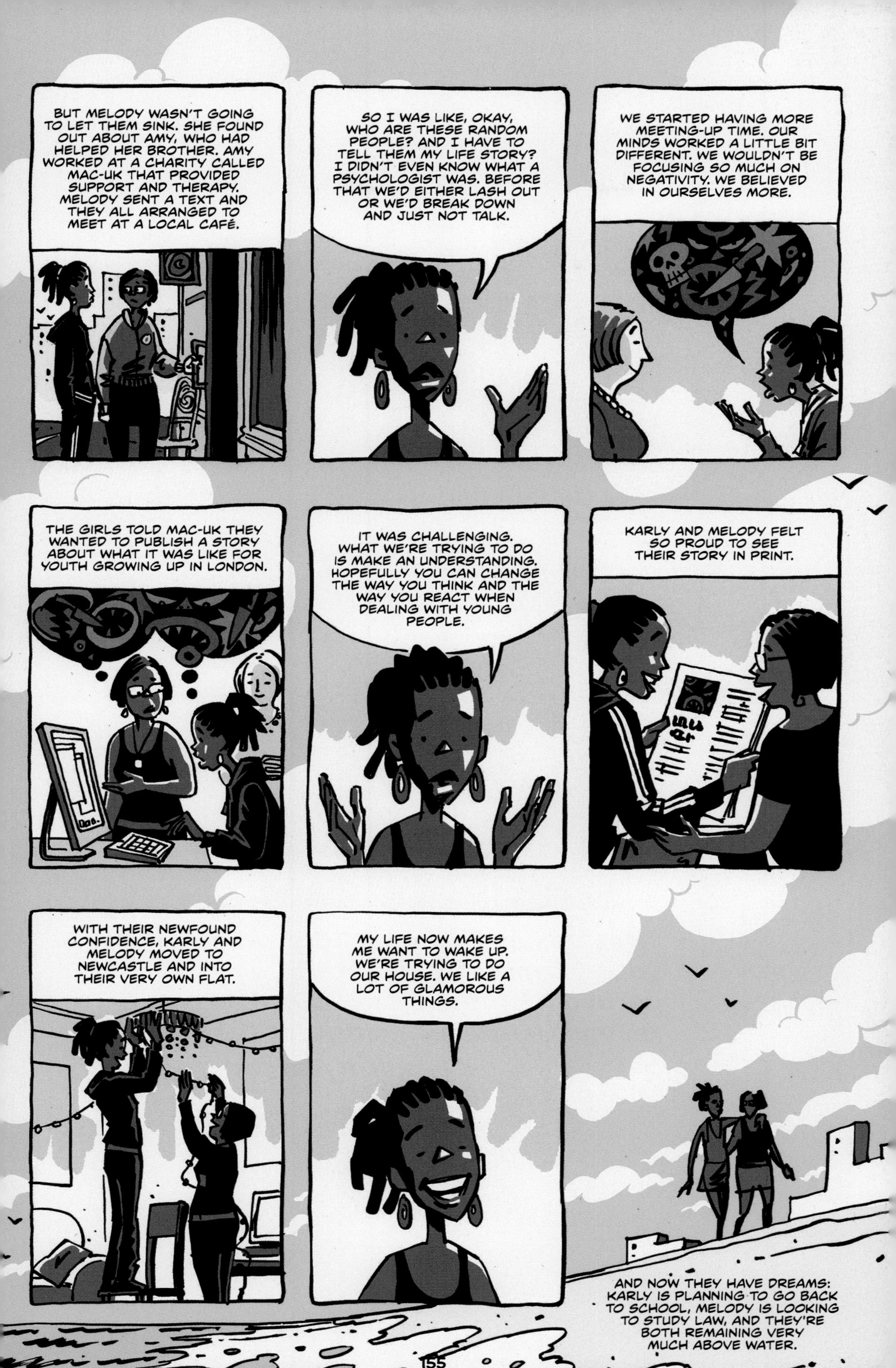
BUT MELODY WASN'T GOING TO LET THEM SINK. SHE FOUND OUT ABOUT AMY, WHO HAD HELPED HER BROTHER. AMY WORKED AT A CHARITY CALLED MAC-UK THAT PROVIDED SUPPORT AND THERAPY. MELODY SENT A TEXT AND THEY ALL ARRANGED TO MEET AT A LOCAL CAFÉ.
SO I WAS LIKE, OKAY, WHO ARE THESE RANDOM PEOPLE? AND I HAVE TO TELL THEM MY LIFE STORY? I DIDN'T EVEN KNOW WHAT A PSYCHOLOGIST WAS. BEFORE THAT WE'D EITHER LASH OUT OR WE'D BREAK DOWN AND JUST NOT TALK.
WE STARTED HAVING MORE MEETING-UP TIME. OUR MINDS WORKED A LITTLE BIT DIFFERENT. WE WOULDN'T BE FOCUSING SO MUCH ON NEGATIVITY. WE BELIEVED IN OURSELVES MORE.
THE GIRLS TOLD MAC-UK THEY WANTED TO PUBLISH A STORY ABOUT WHAT IT WAS LIKE FOR YOUTH GROWING UP IN LONDON.
IT WAS CHALLENGING. WHAT WE'RE TRYING TO DO IS MAKE AN UNDERSTANDING. HOPEFULLY YOU CAN CHANGE THE WAY YOU THINK AND THE WAY YOU REACT WHEN DEALING WITH YOUNG PEOPLE.
KARLY AND MELODY FELT SO PROUD TO SEE THEIR STORY IN PRINT.
WITH THEIR NEWFOUND CONFIDENCE, KARLY AND MELODY MOVED TO NEWCASTLE AND INTO THEIR VERY OWN FLAT.
MY LIFE NOW MAKES ME WANT TO WAKE UP. WE'RE TRYING TO DO OUR HOUSE. WE LIKE A LOT OF GLAMOROUS THINGS.
AND NOW THEY HAVE DREAMS: KARLY IS PLANNING TO GO BACK TO SCHOOL, MELODY IS LOOKING TO STUDY LAW, AND THEY'RE BOTH REMAINING VERY MUCH ABOVE WATER.

"Men often ask me, 'Why are your female characters so paranoid?' It's not paranoia. It's recognition of their situation."

—Margaret Atwood

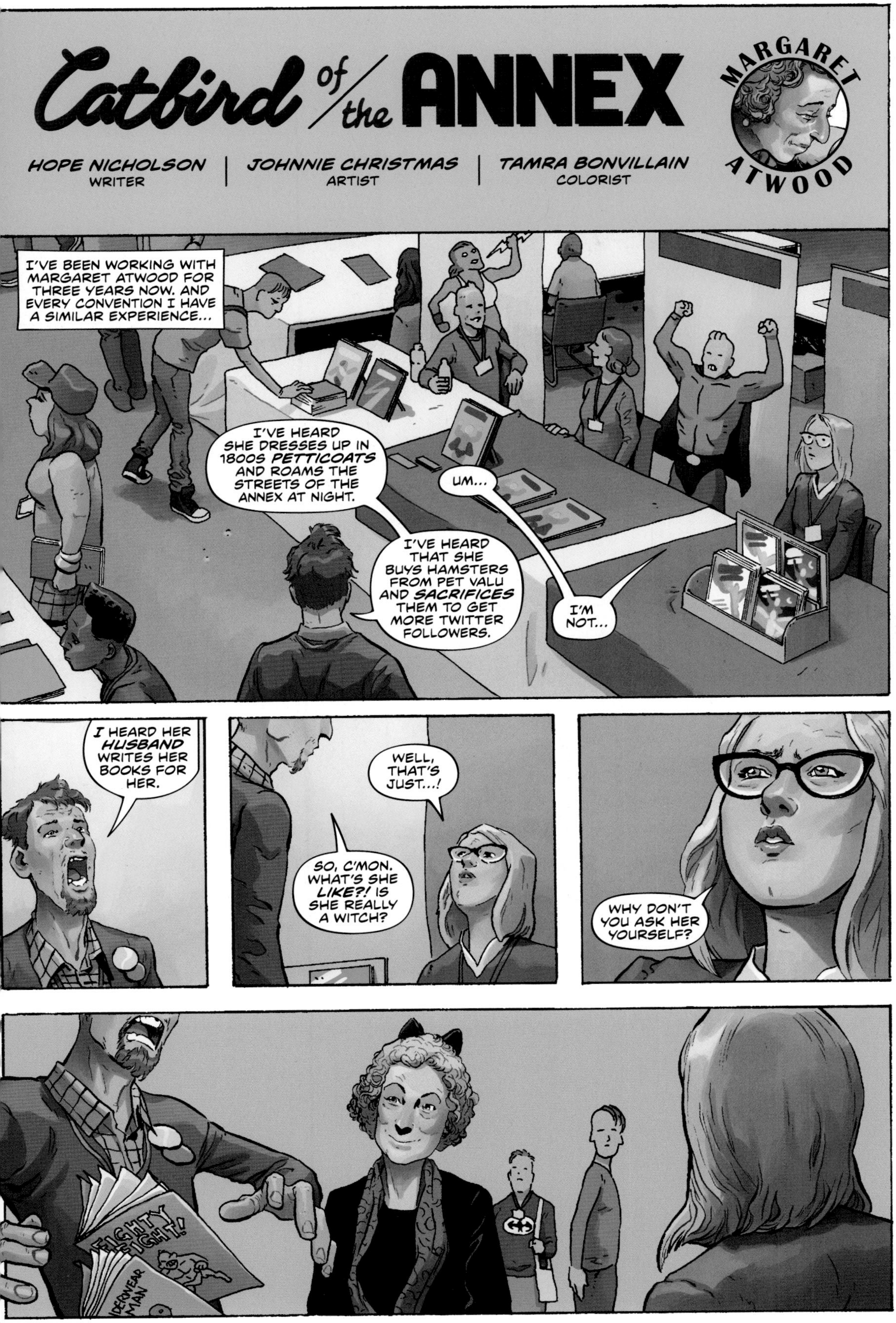
Catbird of the ANNEX
MARGARET ATWOOD
HOPE NICHOLSON
WRITER
JOHNNIE CHRISTMAS
ARTIST
TAMRA BONVILLAIN
COLORIST
I'VE BEEN WORKING WITH MARGARET ATWOOD FOR THREE YEARS NOW. AND EVERY CONVENTION I HAVE A SIMILAR EXPERIENCE...
I'VE HEARD SHE DRESSES UP IN 1800S PETTICOATS AND ROAMS THE STREETS OF THE ANNEX AT NIGHT.
UM...
I'VE HEARD THAT SHE BUYS HAMSTERS FROM PET VALU AND SACRIFICES THEM TO GET MORE TWITTER FOLLOWERS.
I'M NOT...
I HEARD HER HUSBAND WRITES HER BOOKS FOR HER.
WELL, THAT'S JUST...!
SO, C'MON. WHAT'S SHE LIKE?! IS SHE REALLY A WITCH?
WHY DON'T YOU ASK HER YOURSELF?

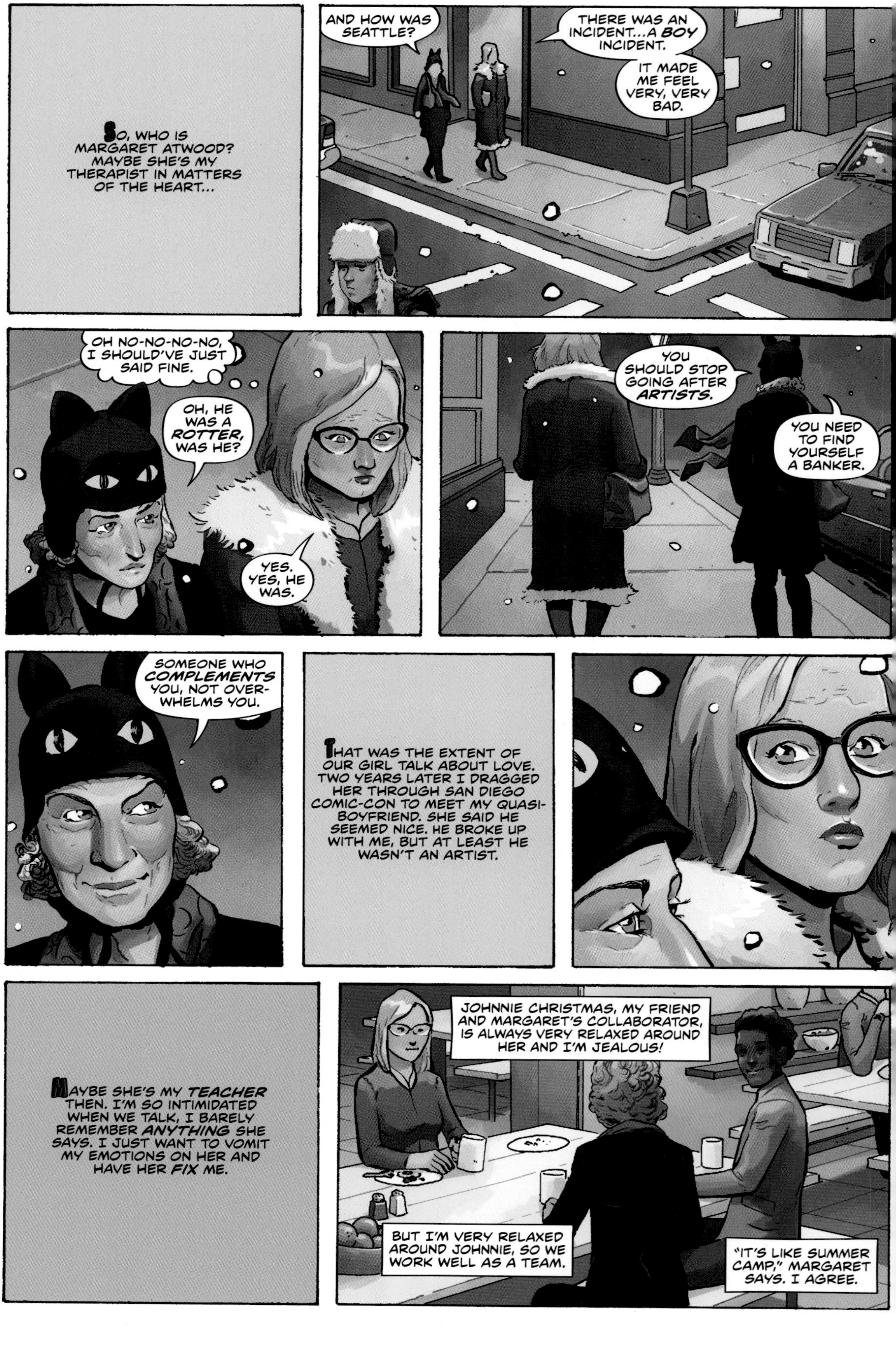
SO, WHO IS MARGARET ATWOOD? MAYBE SHE'S MY THERAPIST IN MATTERS OF THE HEART...
AND HOW WAS SEATTLE?
THERE WAS AN INCIDENT...A *BOY* INCIDENT.
IT MADE ME FEEL VERY, VERY BAD.
OH NO-NO-NO-NO, I SHOULD'VE JUST SAID FINE.
OH, HE WAS A *ROTTER,* WAS HE?
YES. YES, HE WAS.
YOU SHOULD STOP GOING AFTER *ARTISTS.*
YOU NEED TO FIND YOURSELF A BANKER.
SOMEONE WHO *COMPLEMENTS* YOU, NOT OVER-WHELMS YOU.
THAT WAS THE EXTENT OF OUR GIRL TALK ABOUT LOVE. TWO YEARS LATER I DRAGGED HER THROUGH SAN DIEGO COMIC-CON TO MEET MY QUASI-BOYFRIEND. SHE SAID HE SEEMED NICE. HE BROKE UP WITH ME, BUT AT LEAST HE WASN'T AN ARTIST.
MAYBE SHE'S MY *TEACHER* THEN. I'M SO INTIMIDATED WHEN WE TALK, I BARELY REMEMBER *ANYTHING* SHE SAYS. I JUST WANT TO VOMIT MY EMOTIONS ON HER AND HAVE HER *FIX* ME.
JOHNNIE CHRISTMAS, MY FRIEND AND MARGARET'S COLLABORATOR, IS ALWAYS VERY RELAXED AROUND HER AND I'M JEALOUS!
BUT I'M VERY RELAXED AROUND JOHNNIE, SO WE WORK WELL AS A TEAM.
"IT'S LIKE SUMMER CAMP," MARGARET SAYS. I AGREE.

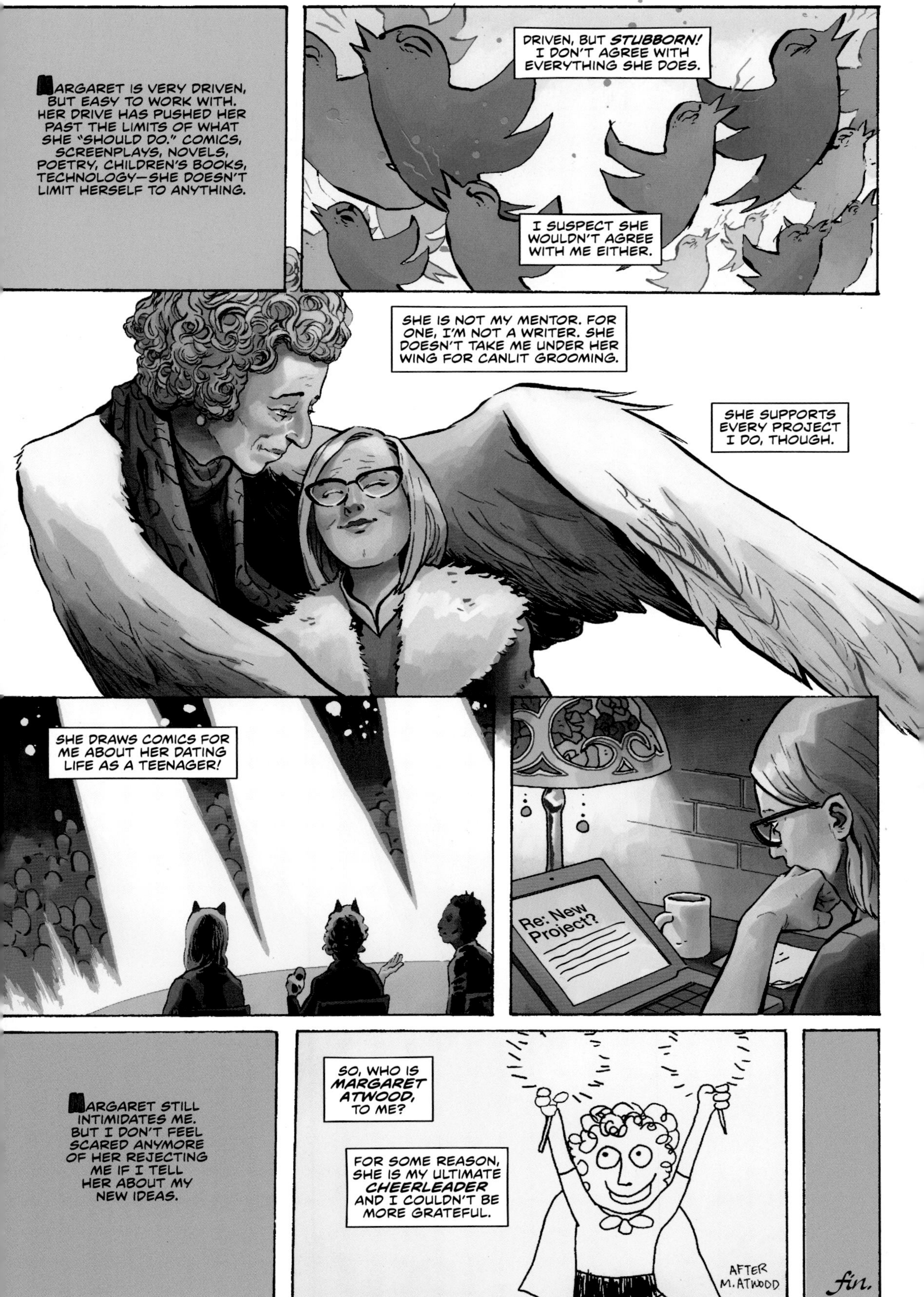
MARGARET IS VERY DRIVEN, BUT EASY TO WORK WITH. HER DRIVE HAS PUSHED HER PAST THE LIMITS OF WHAT SHE "SHOULD DO." COMICS, SCREENPLAYS, NOVELS, POETRY, CHILDREN'S BOOKS, TECHNOLOGY—SHE DOESN'T LIMIT HERSELF TO ANYTHING.
DRIVEN, BUT *STUBBORN!* I DON'T AGREE WITH EVERYTHING SHE DOES.
I SUSPECT SHE WOULDN'T AGREE WITH ME EITHER.
SHE IS NOT MY MENTOR. FOR ONE, I'M NOT A WRITER. SHE DOESN'T TAKE ME UNDER HER WING FOR CANLIT GROOMING.
SHE SUPPORTS EVERY PROJECT I DO, THOUGH.
SHE DRAWS COMICS FOR ME ABOUT HER DATING LIFE AS A TEENAGER!
Re: New Project?
MARGARET STILL INTIMIDATES ME. BUT I DON'T FEEL SCARED ANYMORE OF HER REJECTING ME IF I TELL HER ABOUT MY NEW IDEAS.
SO, WHO IS ***MARGARET ATWOOD,*** TO ME?
FOR SOME REASON, SHE IS MY ULTIMATE ***CHEERLEADER*** AND I COULDN'T BE MORE GRATEFUL.
AFTER M. ATWOOD
fin.

"I was thoroughly fed up with the standard cis narrative about trans people in which we are interesting set dressing — victims of crime or intolerance. There absolutely needed, still needs, to be fiction that centers on trans people."

—Roz Kaveney

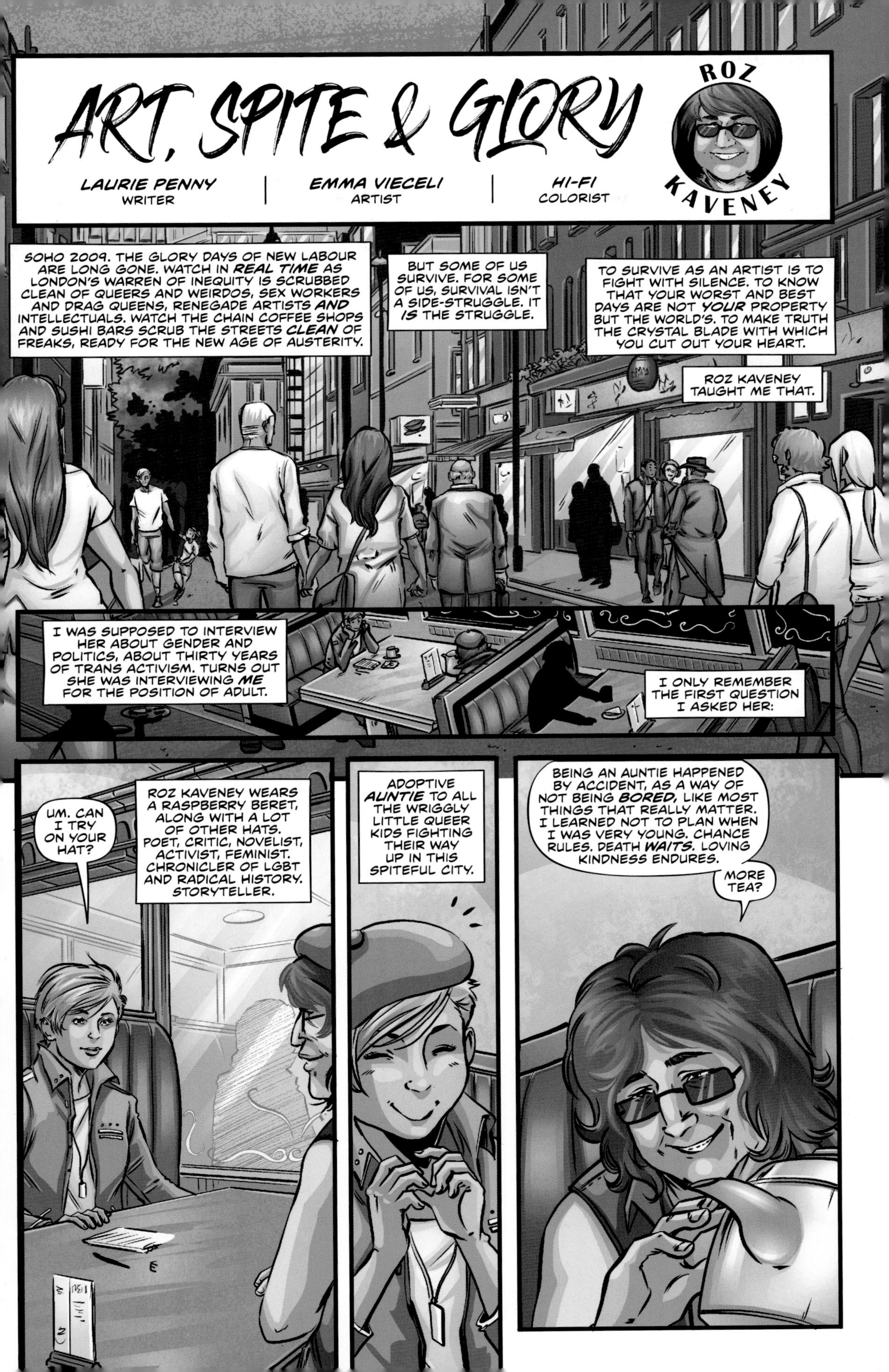

ART, SPITE & GLORY
LAURIE PENNY
WRITER
EMMA VIECELI
ARTIST
HI-FI
COLORIST
ROZ KAVENEY
SOHO 2009. THE GLORY DAYS OF NEW LABOUR ARE LONG GONE. WATCH IN REAL TIME AS LONDON'S WARREN OF INEQUITY IS SCRUBBED CLEAN OF QUEERS AND WEIRDOS, SEX WORKERS AND DRAG QUEENS, RENEGADE ARTISTS AND INTELLECTUALS. WATCH THE CHAIN COFFEE SHOPS AND SUSHI BARS SCRUB THE STREETS CLEAN OF FREAKS, READY FOR THE NEW AGE OF AUSTERITY.
BUT SOME OF US SURVIVE. FOR SOME OF US, SURVIVAL ISN'T A SIDE-STRUGGLE. IT IS THE STRUGGLE.
TO SURVIVE AS AN ARTIST IS TO FIGHT WITH SILENCE. TO KNOW THAT YOUR WORST AND BEST DAYS ARE NOT YOUR PROPERTY BUT THE WORLD'S. TO MAKE TRUTH THE CRYSTAL BLADE WITH WHICH YOU CUT OUT YOUR HEART.
ROZ KAVENEY TAUGHT ME THAT.
I WAS SUPPOSED TO INTERVIEW HER ABOUT GENDER AND POLITICS, ABOUT THIRTY YEARS OF TRANS ACTIVISM. TURNS OUT SHE WAS INTERVIEWING ME FOR THE POSITION OF ADULT.
I ONLY REMEMBER THE FIRST QUESTION I ASKED HER:
UM. CAN I TRY ON YOUR HAT?
ROZ KAVENEY WEARS A RASPBERRY BERET, ALONG WITH A LOT OF OTHER HATS. POET, CRITIC, NOVELIST, ACTIVIST, FEMINIST. CHRONICLER OF LGBT AND RADICAL HISTORY. STORYTELLER.
ADOPTIVE AUNTIE TO ALL THE WRIGGLY LITTLE QUEER KIDS FIGHTING THEIR WAY UP IN THIS SPITEFUL CITY.
BEING AN AUNTIE HAPPENED BY ACCIDENT, AS A WAY OF NOT BEING BORED, LIKE MOST THINGS THAT REALLY MATTER. I LEARNED NOT TO PLAN WHEN I WAS VERY YOUNG. CHANCE RULES. DEATH WAITS. LOVING KINDNESS ENDURES.
MORE TEA?

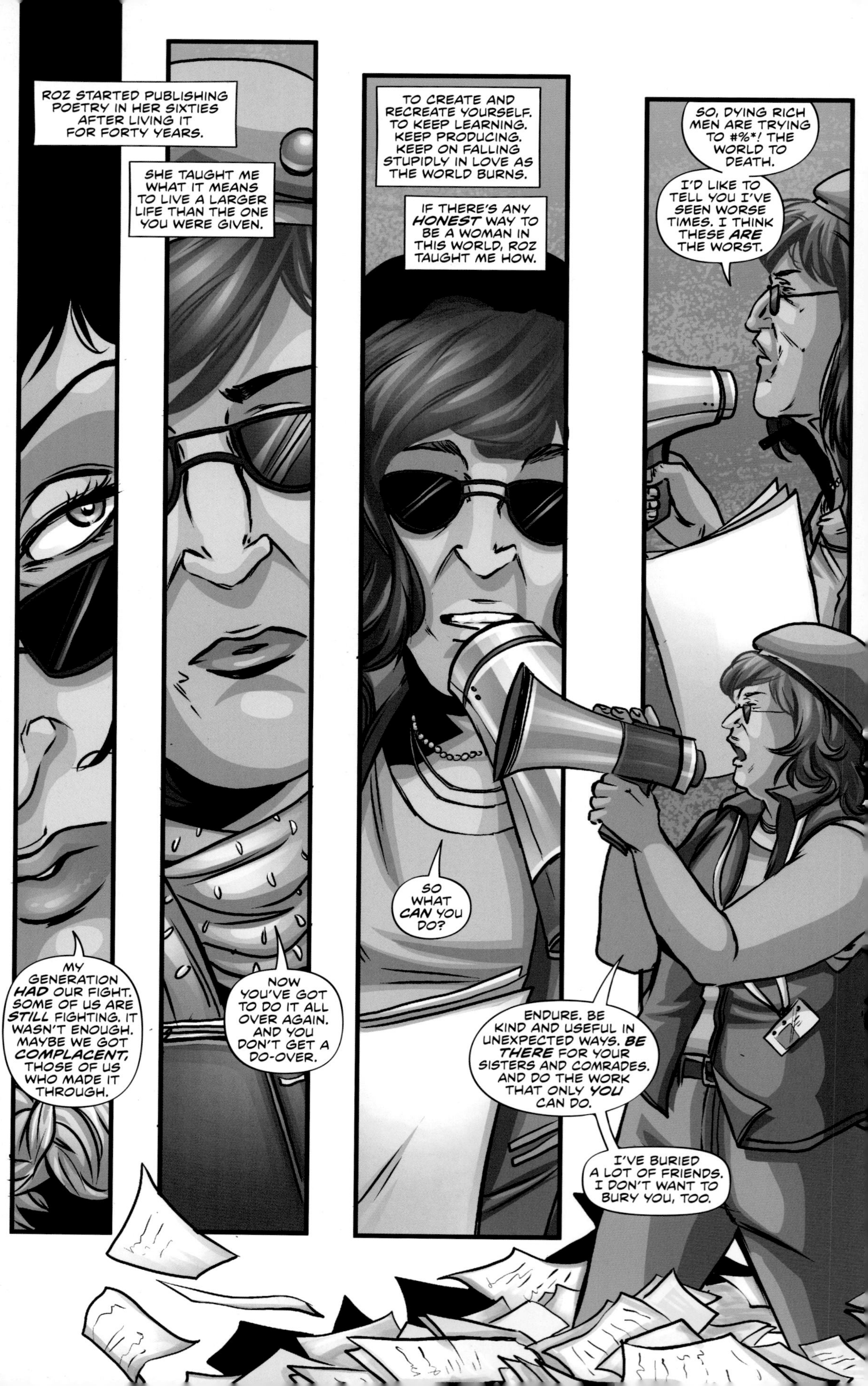
ROZ STARTED PUBLISHING POETRY IN HER SIXTIES AFTER LIVING IT FOR FORTY YEARS.
MY GENERATION **HAD** OUR FIGHT. SOME OF US ARE **STILL** FIGHTING. IT WASN'T ENOUGH. MAYBE WE GOT **COMPLACENT,** THOSE OF US WHO MADE IT THROUGH.
SHE TAUGHT ME WHAT IT MEANS TO LIVE A LARGER LIFE THAN THE ONE YOU WERE GIVEN.
NOW YOU'VE GOT TO DO IT ALL OVER AGAIN. AND YOU DON'T GET A DO-OVER.
TO CREATE AND RECREATE YOURSELF. TO KEEP LEARNING. KEEP PRODUCING. KEEP ON FALLING STUPIDLY IN LOVE AS THE WORLD BURNS.
IF THERE'S ANY **HONEST** WAY TO BE A WOMAN IN THIS WORLD, ROZ TAUGHT ME HOW.
SO WHAT **CAN** YOU DO?
SO, DYING RICH MEN ARE TRYING TO #%*! THE WORLD TO DEATH.
I'D LIKE TO TELL YOU I'VE SEEN WORSE TIMES. I THINK THESE **ARE** THE WORST.
ENDURE. BE KIND AND USEFUL IN UNEXPECTED WAYS. **BE THERE** FOR YOUR SISTERS AND COMRADES. AND DO THE WORK THAT ONLY **YOU** CAN DO.
I'VE BURIED A LOT OF FRIENDS. I DON'T WANT TO BURY YOU, TOO.

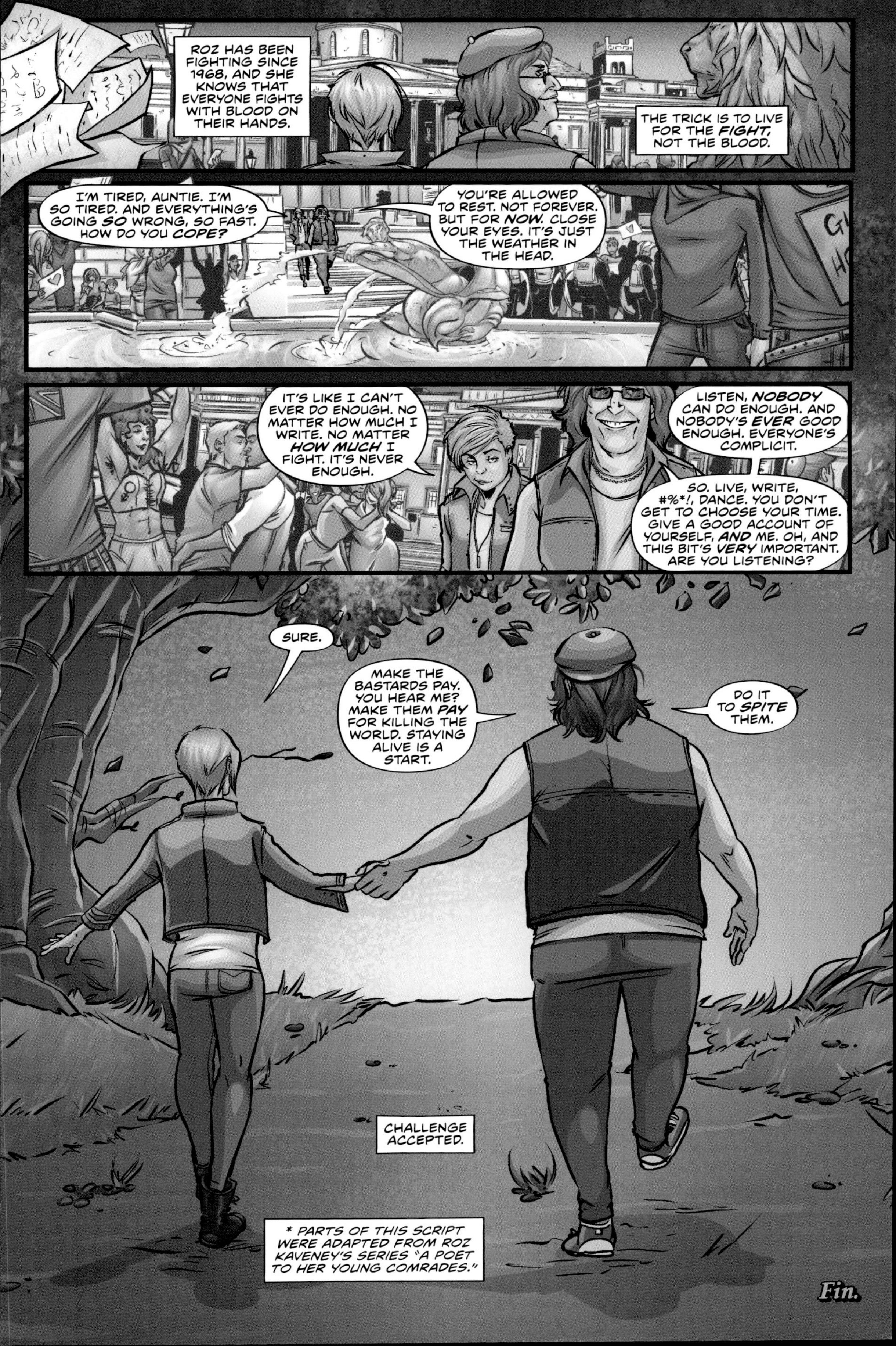

ROZ HAS BEEN FIGHTING SINCE 1968, AND SHE KNOWS THAT EVERYONE FIGHTS WITH BLOOD ON THEIR HANDS.
THE TRICK IS TO LIVE FOR THE *FIGHT,* NOT THE BLOOD.
I'M TIRED, AUNTIE. I'M SO TIRED. AND EVERYTHING'S GOING ***SO*** WRONG, SO FAST. HOW DO YOU ***COPE?***
YOU'RE ALLOWED TO REST. NOT FOREVER. BUT FOR ***NOW.*** CLOSE YOUR EYES. IT'S JUST THE WEATHER IN THE HEAD.
IT'S LIKE I CAN'T EVER DO ENOUGH. NO MATTER HOW MUCH I WRITE. NO MATTER ***HOW MUCH*** I FIGHT. IT'S NEVER ENOUGH.
LISTEN, ***NOBODY*** CAN DO ENOUGH. AND NOBODY'S ***EVER*** GOOD ENOUGH. EVERYONE'S COMPLICIT.
SO. LIVE, WRITE, #%*!, DANCE. YOU DON'T GET TO CHOOSE YOUR TIME. GIVE A GOOD ACCOUNT OF YOURSELF, ***AND*** ME. OH, AND THIS BIT'S ***VERY*** IMPORTANT. ARE YOU LISTENING?
SURE.
MAKE THE BASTARDS PAY. YOU HEAR ME? MAKE THEM ***PAY*** FOR KILLING THE WORLD. STAYING ALIVE IS A START.
DO IT TO ***SPITE*** THEM.
CHALLENGE ACCEPTED.
** PARTS OF THIS SCRIPT WERE ADAPTED FROM ROZ KAVENEY'S SERIES "A POET TO HER YOUNG COMRADES."*
Fin.

"We've got a responsibility to live up to the legacy of those who came before us by doing all that we can to help those who come after us."

—Michelle Obama

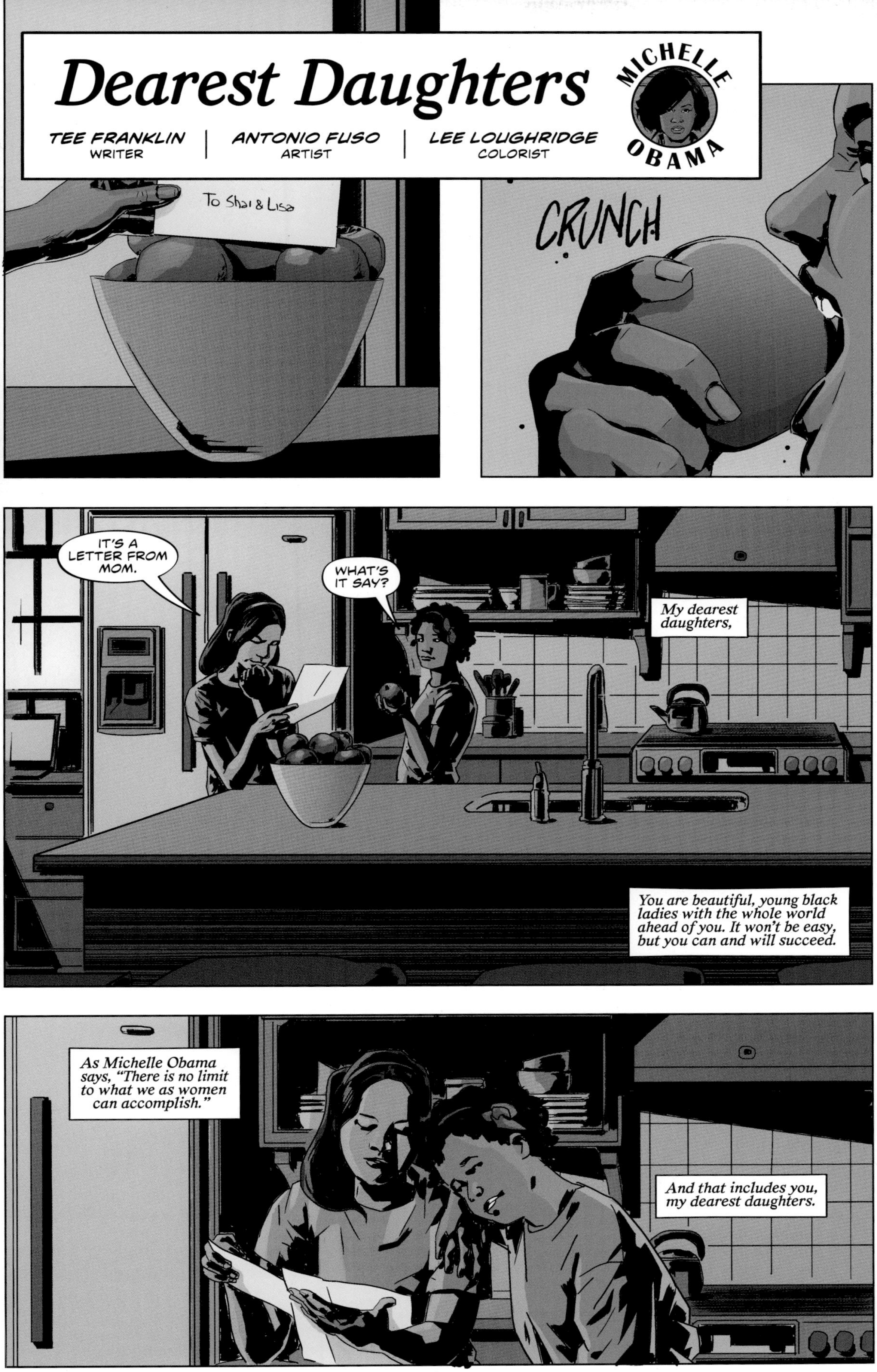
Dearest Daughters
TEE FRANKLIN
WRITER
ANTONIO FUSO
ARTIST
LEE LOUGHRIDGE
COLORIST
MICHELLE OBAMA
To Shai & Lisa
CRUNCH
IT'S A LETTER FROM MOM.
WHAT'S IT SAY?
My dearest daughters,
You are beautiful, young black ladies with the whole world ahead of you. It won't be easy, but you can and will succeed.
As Michelle Obama says, "There is no limit to what we as women can accomplish."
And that includes you, my dearest daughters.

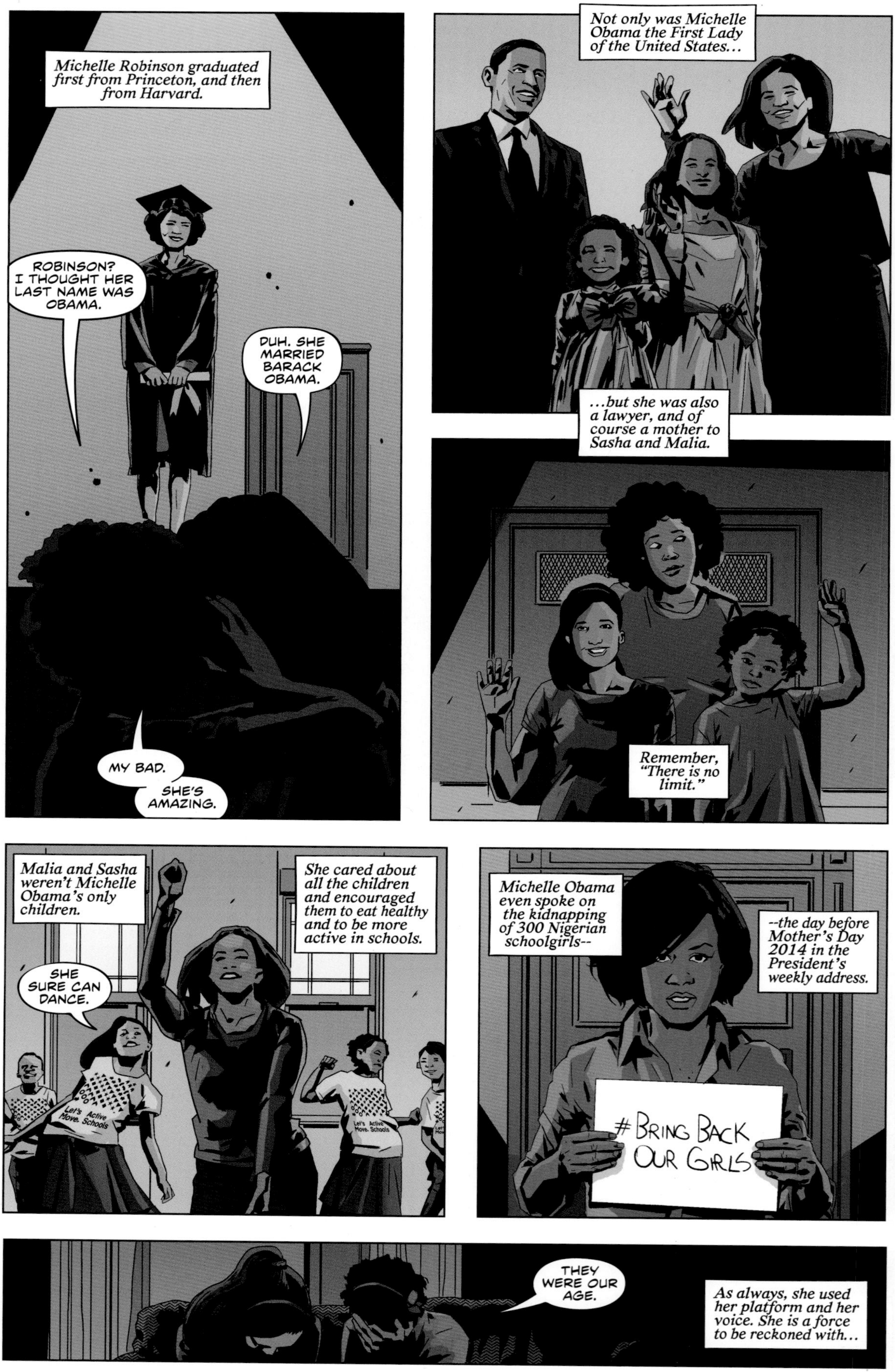
Michelle Robinson graduated first from Princeton, and then from Harvard.
ROBINSON? I THOUGHT HER LAST NAME WAS OBAMA.
DUH. SHE MARRIED BARACK OBAMA.
MY BAD.
SHE'S AMAZING.
Not only was Michelle Obama the First Lady of the United States...
...but she was also a lawyer, and of course a mother to Sasha and Malia.
Remember, "There is no limit."
Malia and Sasha weren't Michelle Obama's only children.
She cared about all the children and encouraged them to eat healthy and to be more active in schools.
SHE SURE CAN DANCE.
Let's Active Move. Schools
Michelle Obama even spoke on the kidnapping of 300 Nigerian schoolgirls--
--the day before Mother's Day 2014 in the President's weekly address.
#BRING BACK OUR GIRLS
THEY WERE OUR AGE.
As always, she used her platform and her voice. She is a force to be reckoned with...

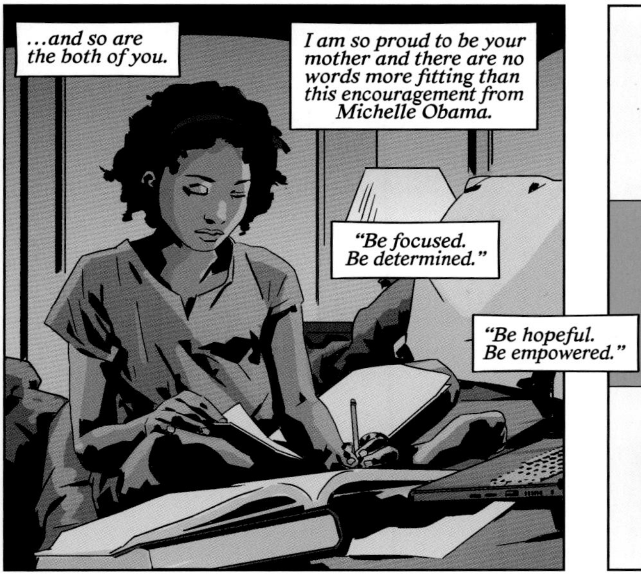
...and so are the both of you.
I am so proud to be your mother and there are no words more fitting than this encouragement from Michelle Obama.
"Be focused. Be determined."
"Be hopeful. Be empowered."

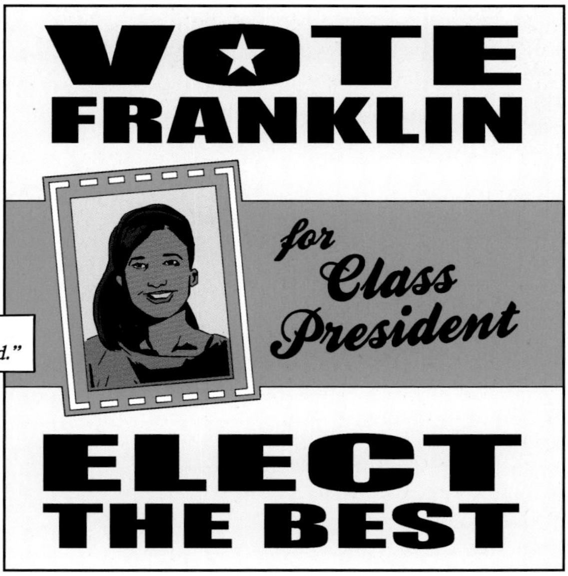
VOTE FRANKLIN
for Class President
ELECT THE BEST

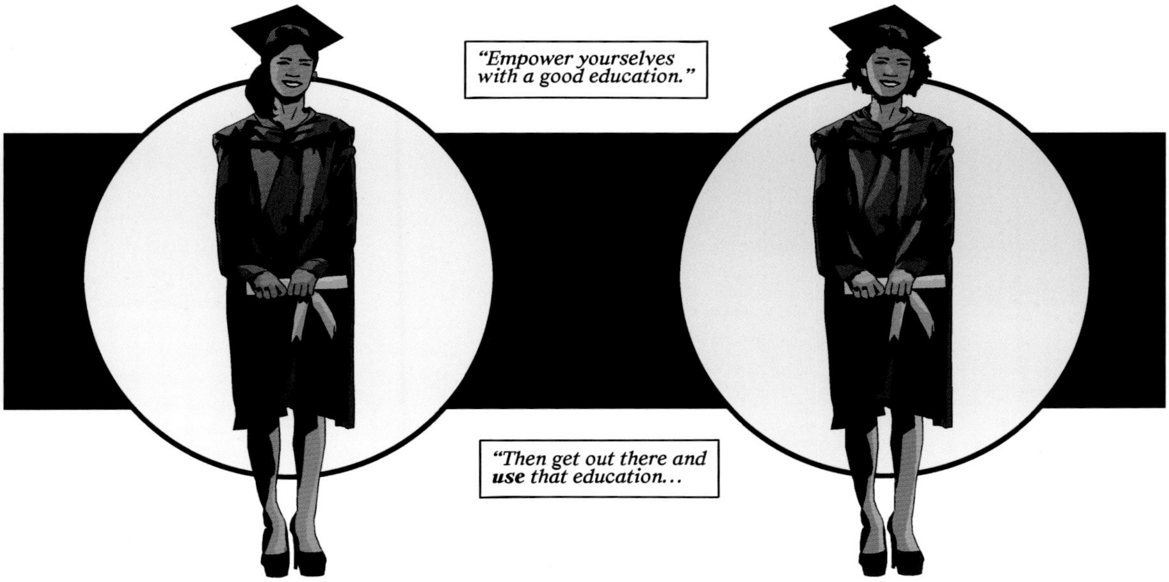
"Empower yourselves with a good education."
"Then get out there and **use** that education...

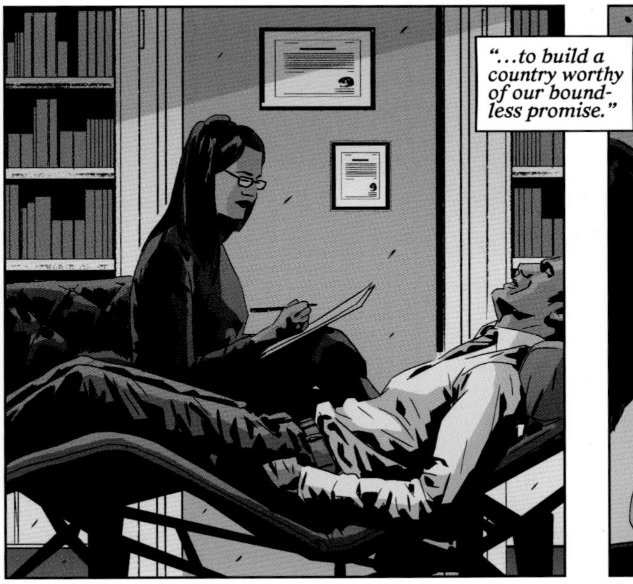
"...to build a country worthy of our boundless promise."

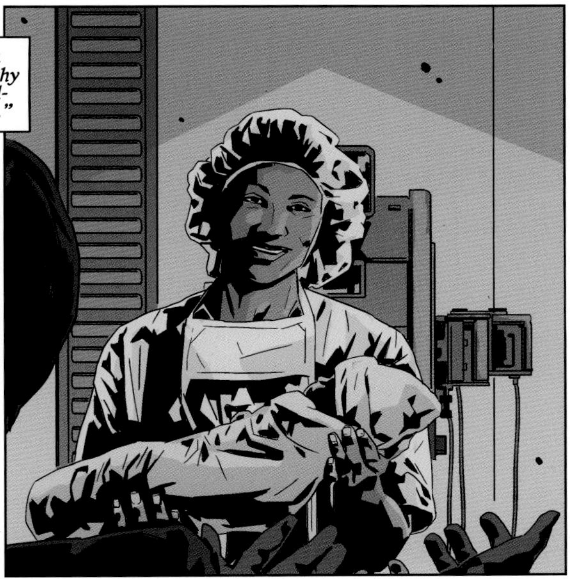

"The world isn't getting any easier. With all these new inventions I believe that people are hurried more and pushed more... The hurried way is not the right way; you need time for everything — time to work, time to play, time to rest."

—Hedy Lamarr

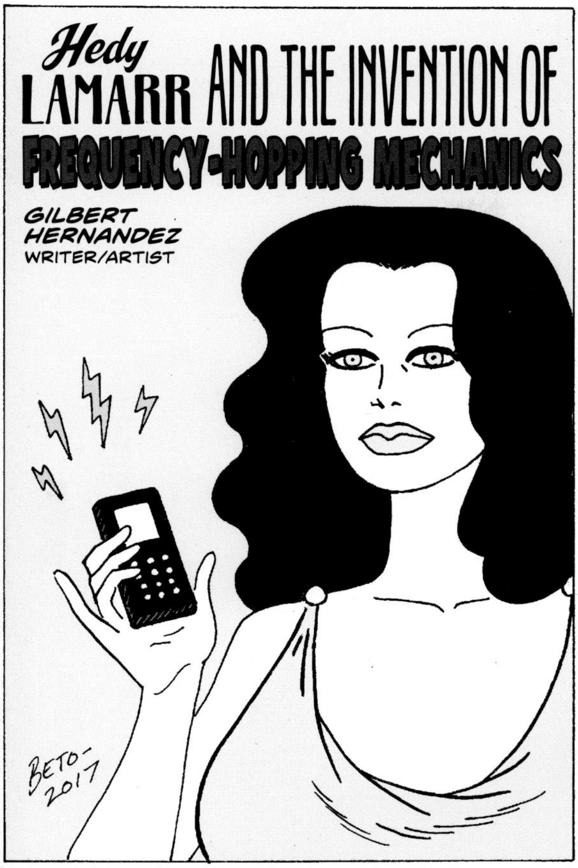
Hedy
LAMARR AND THE INVENTION OF
FREQUENCY-HOPPING MECHANICS
GILBERT
HERNANDEZ
WRITER/ARTIST
BETO-
2017

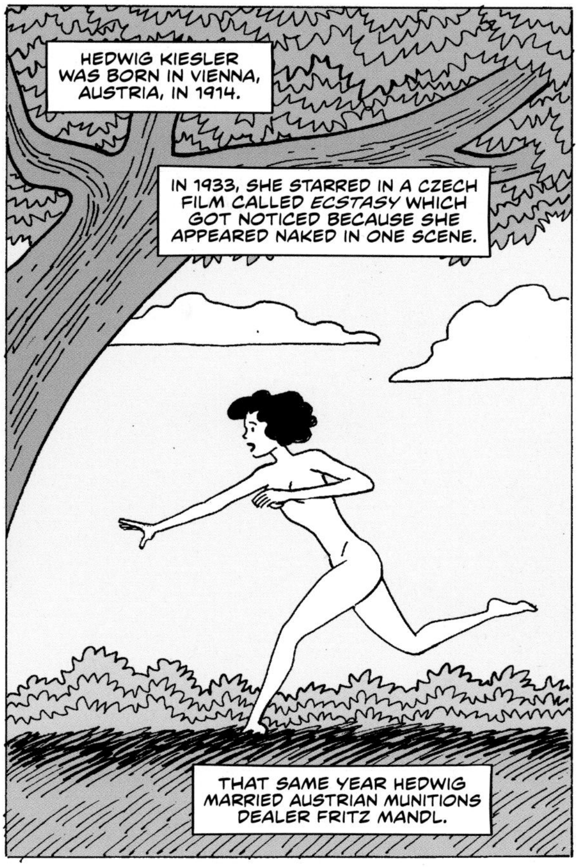
HEDWIG KIESLER WAS BORN IN VIENNA, AUSTRIA, IN 1914.
IN 1933, SHE STARRED IN A CZECH FILM CALLED *ECSTASY* WHICH GOT NOTICED BECAUSE SHE APPEARED NAKED IN ONE SCENE.
THAT SAME YEAR HEDWIG MARRIED AUSTRIAN MUNITIONS DEALER FRITZ MANDL.

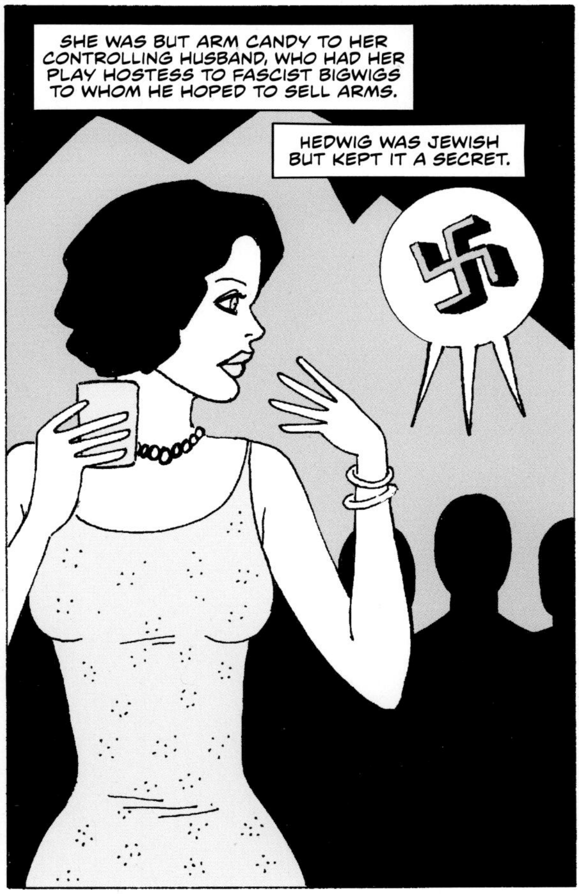
SHE WAS BUT ARM CANDY TO HER CONTROLLING HUSBAND, WHO HAD HER PLAY HOSTESS TO FASCIST BIGWIGS TO WHOM HE HOPED TO SELL ARMS.
HEDWIG WAS JEWISH BUT KEPT IT A SECRET.

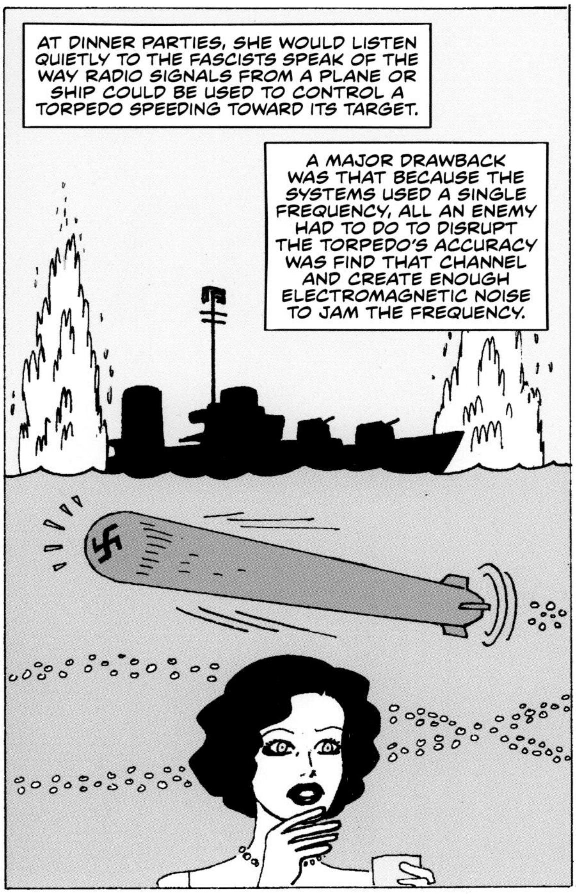
AT DINNER PARTIES, SHE WOULD LISTEN QUIETLY TO THE FASCISTS SPEAK OF THE WAY RADIO SIGNALS FROM A PLANE OR SHIP COULD BE USED TO CONTROL A TORPEDO SPEEDING TOWARD ITS TARGET.
A MAJOR DRAWBACK WAS THAT BECAUSE THE SYSTEMS USED A SINGLE FREQUENCY, ALL AN ENEMY HAD TO DO TO DISRUPT THE TORPEDO'S ACCURACY WAS FIND THAT CHANNEL AND CREATE ENOUGH ELECTROMAGNETIC NOISE TO JAM THE FREQUENCY.

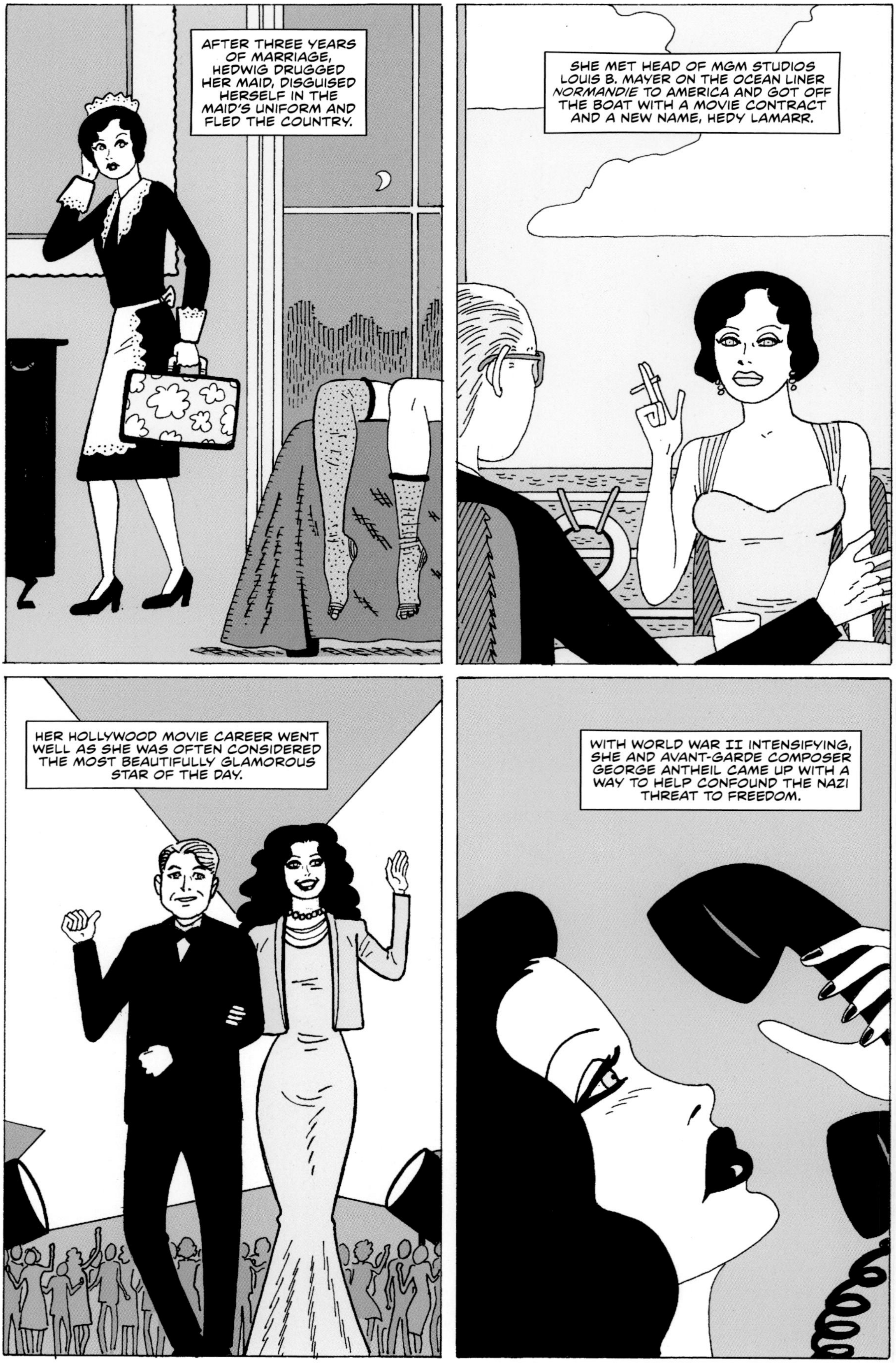
AFTER THREE YEARS OF MARRIAGE, HEDWIG DRUGGED HER MAID, DISGUISED HERSELF IN THE MAID'S UNIFORM AND FLED THE COUNTRY.
SHE MET HEAD OF MGM STUDIOS LOUIS B. MAYER ON THE OCEAN LINER *NORMANDIE* TO AMERICA AND GOT OFF THE BOAT WITH A MOVIE CONTRACT AND A NEW NAME, HEDY LAMARR.
HER HOLLYWOOD MOVIE CAREER WENT WELL AS SHE WAS OFTEN CONSIDERED THE MOST BEAUTIFULLY GLAMOROUS STAR OF THE DAY.
WITH WORLD WAR II INTENSIFYING, SHE AND AVANT-GARDE COMPOSER GEORGE ANTHEIL CAME UP WITH A WAY TO HELP CONFOUND THE NAZI THREAT TO FREEDOM.

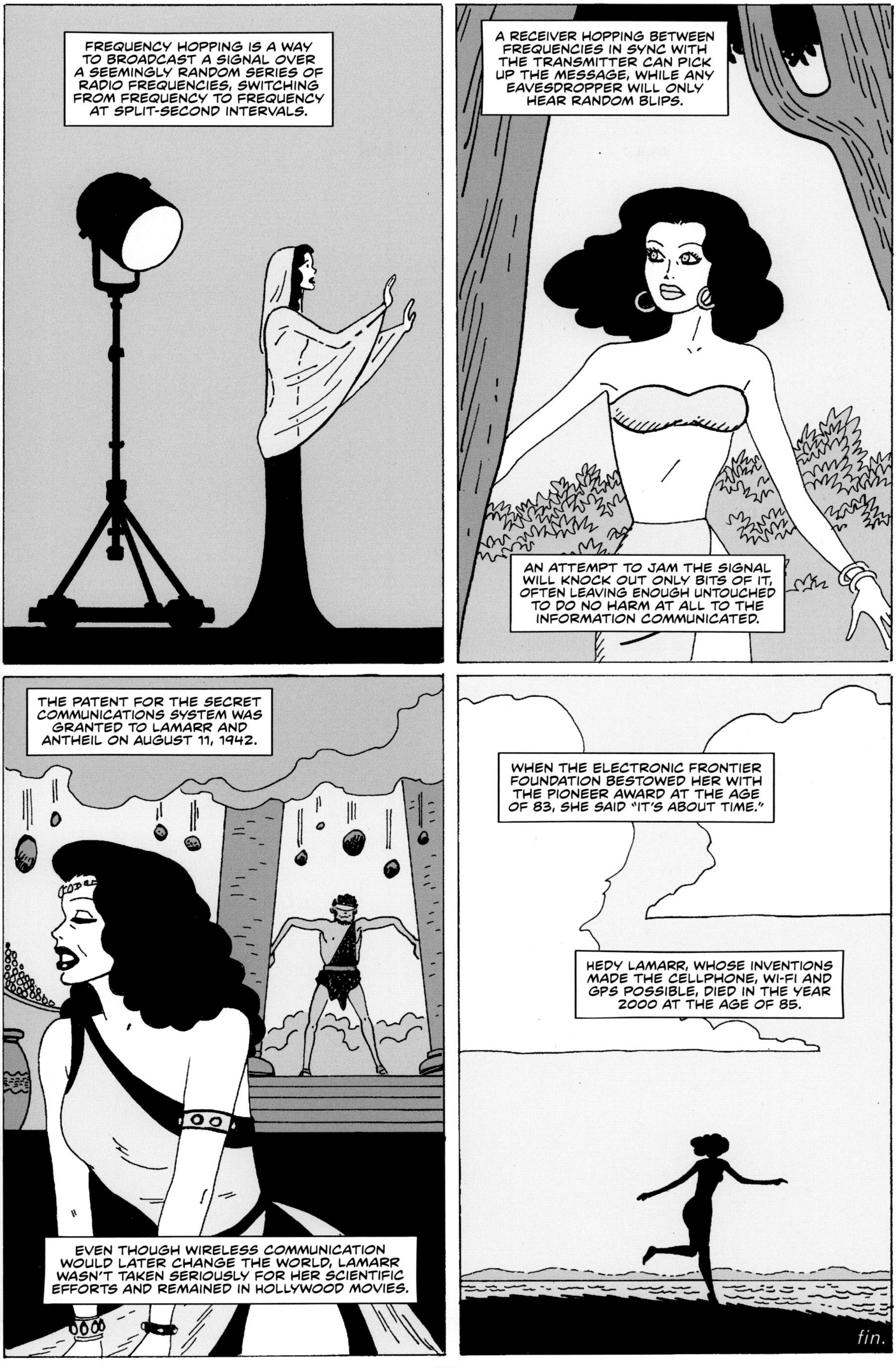
FREQUENCY HOPPING IS A WAY TO BROADCAST A SIGNAL OVER A SEEMINGLY RANDOM SERIES OF RADIO FREQUENCIES, SWITCHING FROM FREQUENCY TO FREQUENCY AT SPLIT-SECOND INTERVALS.
A RECEIVER HOPPING BETWEEN FREQUENCIES IN SYNC WITH THE TRANSMITTER CAN PICK UP THE MESSAGE, WHILE ANY EAVESDROPPER WILL ONLY HEAR RANDOM BLIPS.
AN ATTEMPT TO JAM THE SIGNAL WILL KNOCK OUT ONLY BITS OF IT, OFTEN LEAVING ENOUGH UNTOUCHED TO DO NO HARM AT ALL TO THE INFORMATION COMMUNICATED.
THE PATENT FOR THE SECRET COMMUNICATIONS SYSTEM WAS GRANTED TO LAMARR AND ANTHEIL ON AUGUST 11, 1942.
EVEN THOUGH WIRELESS COMMUNICATION WOULD LATER CHANGE THE WORLD, LAMARR WASN'T TAKEN SERIOUSLY FOR HER SCIENTIFIC EFFORTS AND REMAINED IN HOLLYWOOD MOVIES.
WHEN THE ELECTRONIC FRONTIER FOUNDATION BESTOWED HER WITH THE PIONEER AWARD AT THE AGE OF 83, SHE SAID "IT'S ABOUT TIME."
HEDY LAMARR, WHOSE INVENTIONS MADE THE CELLPHONE, WI-FI AND GPS POSSIBLE, DIED IN THE YEAR 2000 AT THE AGE OF 85.
fin.

"Let children read whatever they want and then talk about it with them. If parents and kids can talk together, we won't have as much censorship because we won't have as much fear."

—Judy Blume

In Blume

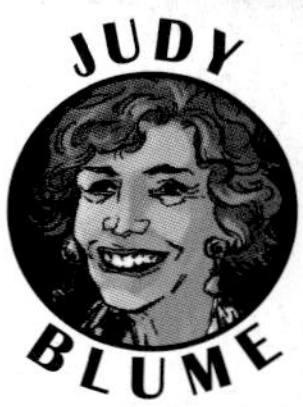
JUDY
BLUME

PAULA SEVENBERGEN WRITER | **CLAIRE ROE** ARTIST | **HI-FI** COLORIST

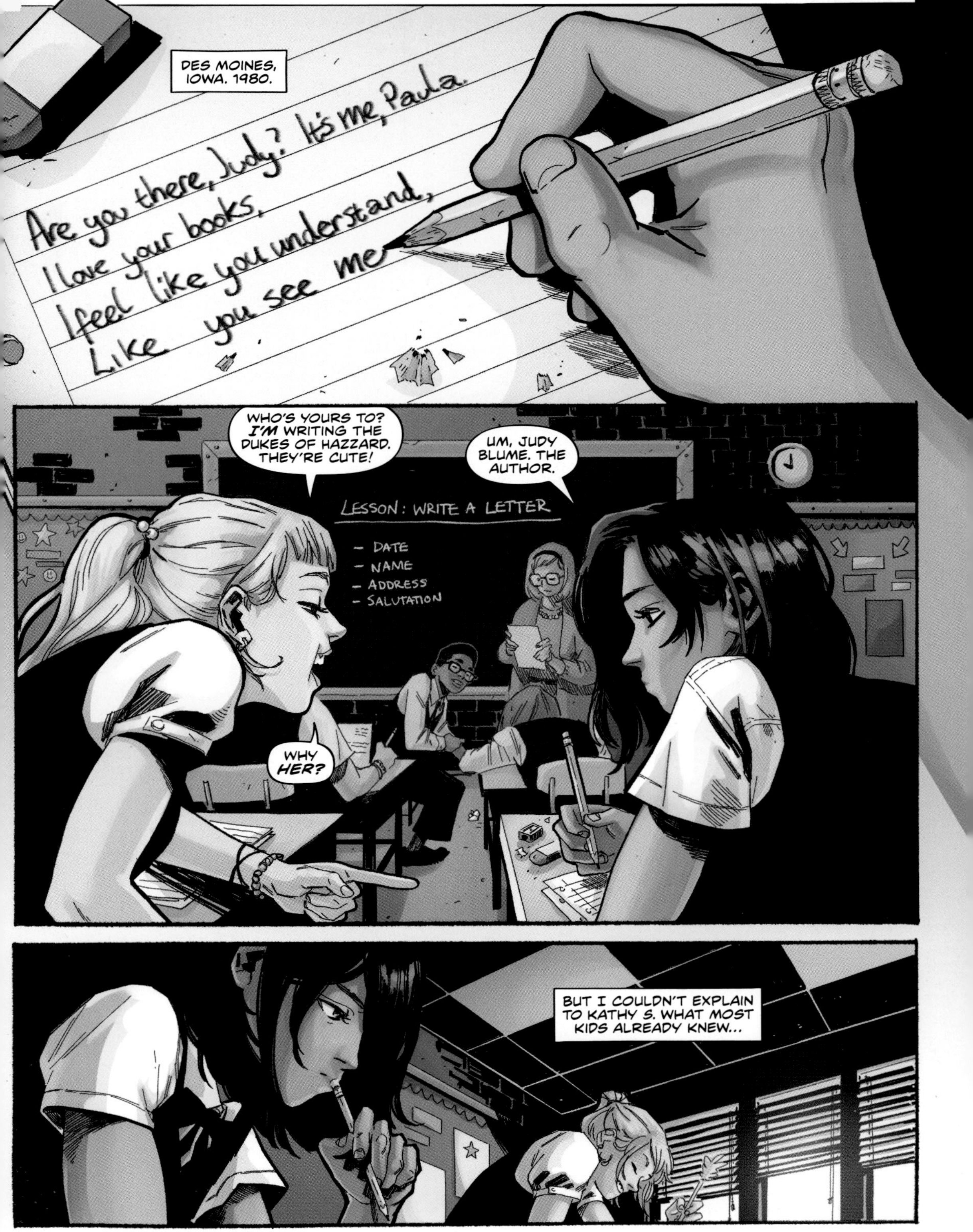
DES MOINES, IOWA. 1980.
Are you there, Judy? It's me, Paula.
I love your books,
I feel like you understand,
Like you see me
WHO'S YOURS TO? *I'M* WRITING THE DUKES OF HAZZARD. THEY'RE CUTE!
UM, JUDY BLUME. THE AUTHOR.
LESSON: WRITE A LETTER
- DATE
- NAME
- ADDRESS
- SALUTATION
WHY *HER*?
BUT I COULDN'T EXPLAIN TO KATHY S. WHAT MOST KIDS ALREADY KNEW...

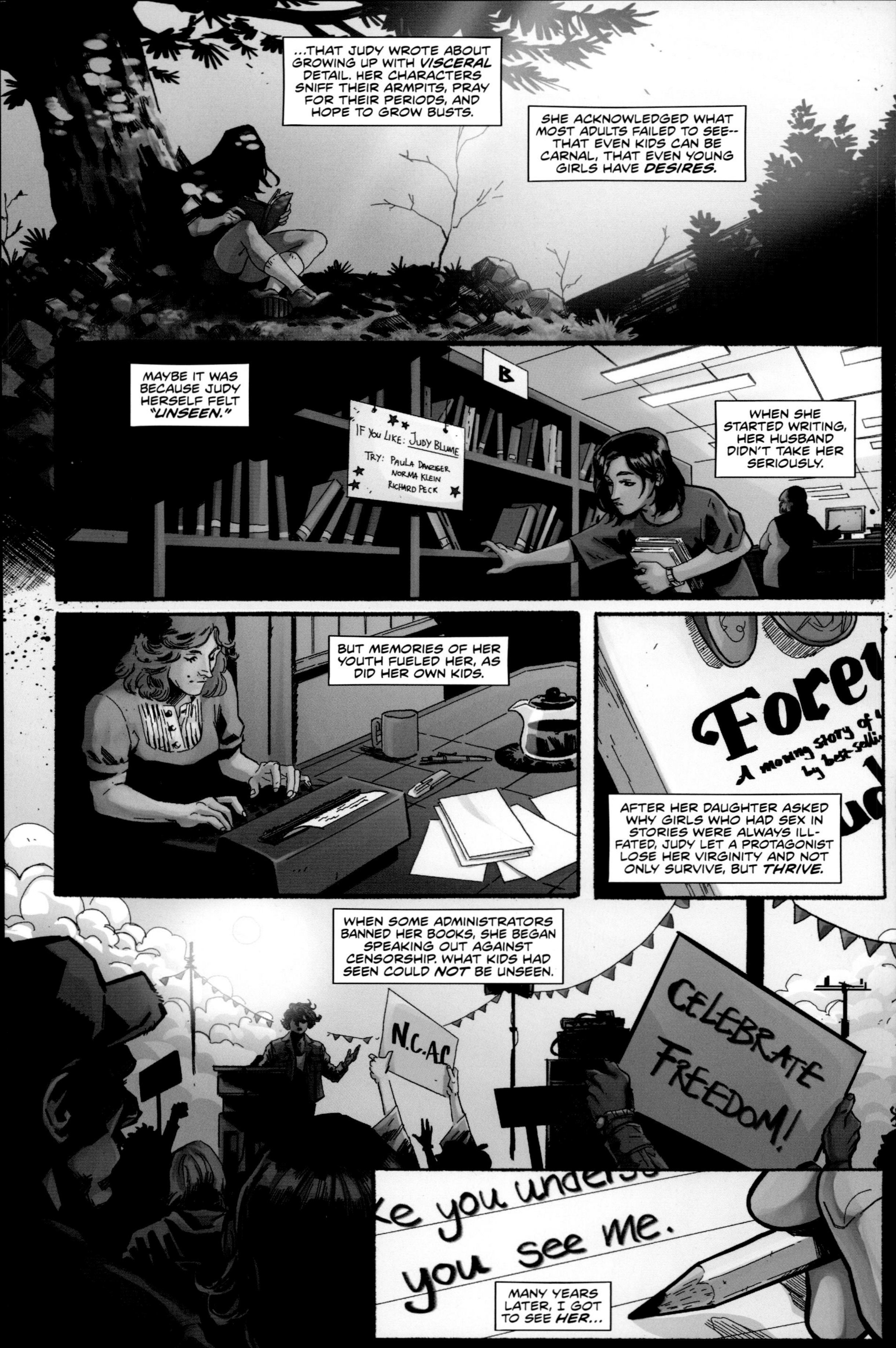

...THAT JUDY WROTE ABOUT GROWING UP WITH *VISCERAL* DETAIL. HER CHARACTERS SNIFF THEIR ARMPITS, PRAY FOR THEIR PERIODS, AND HOPE TO GROW BUSTS.
SHE ACKNOWLEDGED WHAT MOST ADULTS FAILED TO SEE-- THAT EVEN KIDS CAN BE CARNAL, THAT EVEN YOUNG GIRLS HAVE ***DESIRES.***
MAYBE IT WAS BECAUSE JUDY HERSELF FELT ***"UNSEEN."***
B
IF YOU LIKE: JUDY BLUME
TRY: PAULA DANZIGER
NORMA KLEIN
RICHARD PECK
WHEN SHE STARTED WRITING, HER HUSBAND DIDN'T TAKE HER SERIOUSLY.
BUT MEMORIES OF HER YOUTH FUELED HER, AS DID HER OWN KIDS.
AFTER HER DAUGHTER ASKED WHY GIRLS WHO HAD SEX IN STORIES WERE ALWAYS ILL-FATED, JUDY LET A PROTAGONIST LOSE HER VIRGINITY AND NOT ONLY SURVIVE, BUT ***THRIVE.***
WHEN SOME ADMINISTRATORS BANNED HER BOOKS, SHE BEGAN SPEAKING OUT AGAINST CENSORSHIP. WHAT KIDS HAD SEEN COULD ***NOT*** BE UNSEEN.
N.C.A.C.
CELEBRATE FREEDOM!
you see me.
MANY YEARS LATER, I GOT TO SEE ***HER...***

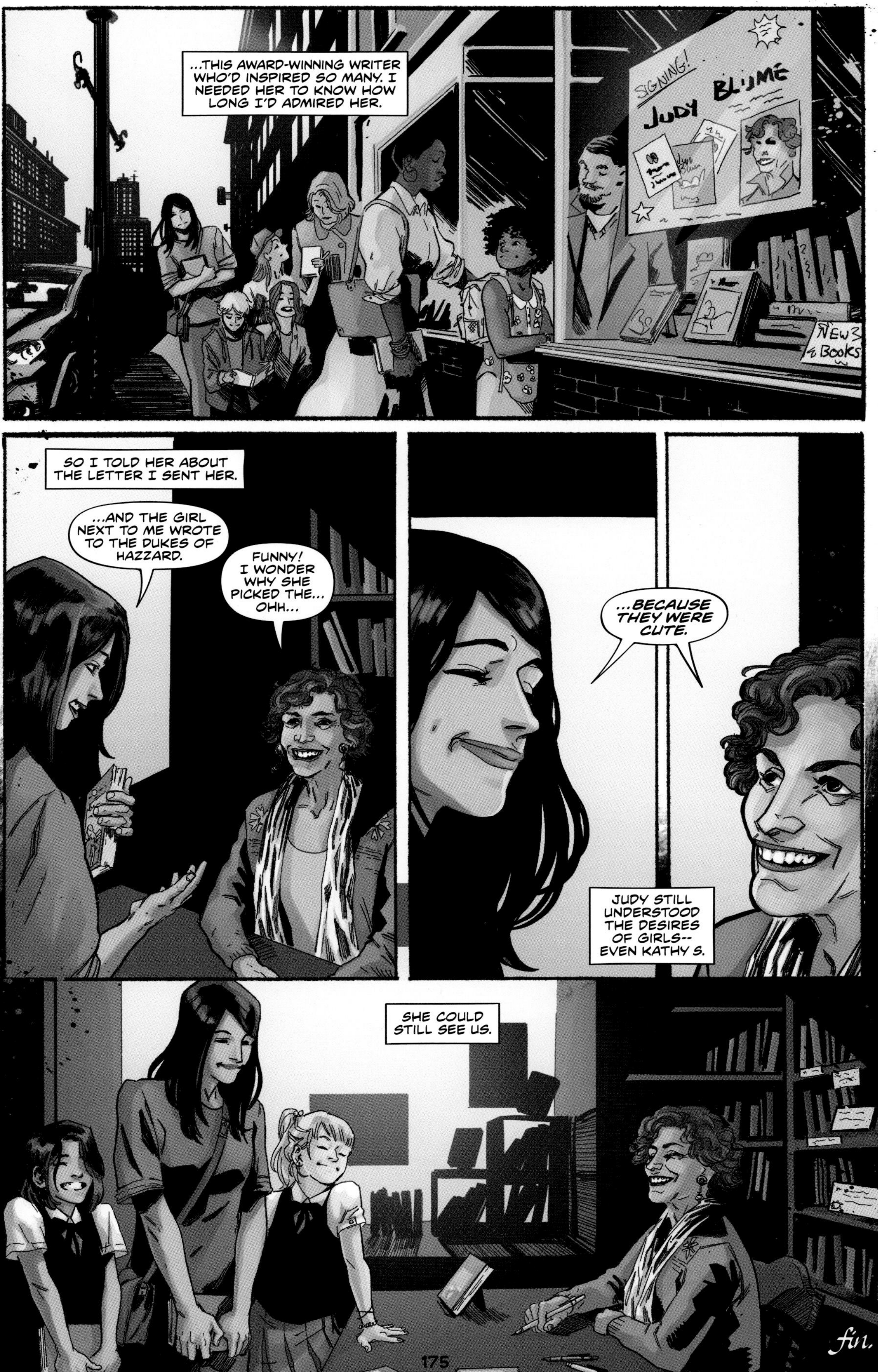
...THIS AWARD-WINNING WRITER WHO'D INSPIRED SO MANY. I NEEDED HER TO KNOW HOW LONG I'D ADMIRED HER.
SIGNING!
JUDY BLUME
NEW BOOKS
SO I TOLD HER ABOUT THE LETTER I SENT HER.
...AND THE GIRL NEXT TO ME WROTE TO THE DUKES OF HAZZARD.
FUNNY! I WONDER WHY SHE PICKED THE... OHH...
...BECAUSE THEY WERE CUTE.
JUDY STILL UNDERSTOOD THE DESIRES OF GIRLS-- EVEN KATHY S.
SHE COULD STILL SEE US.
fin.

"How many lives could be saved? I was to ascertain how many passengers the *Tiger Hill* could feasibly carry. Yet, I knew nothing whatever about ships."

—Ruth Klüger

MISSION "TIGER HILL"

RUTH KLÜGER

BETSY HOULTON WRITER | ***TYLER CROOK*** ARTIST | ***HI-FI*** COLORIST

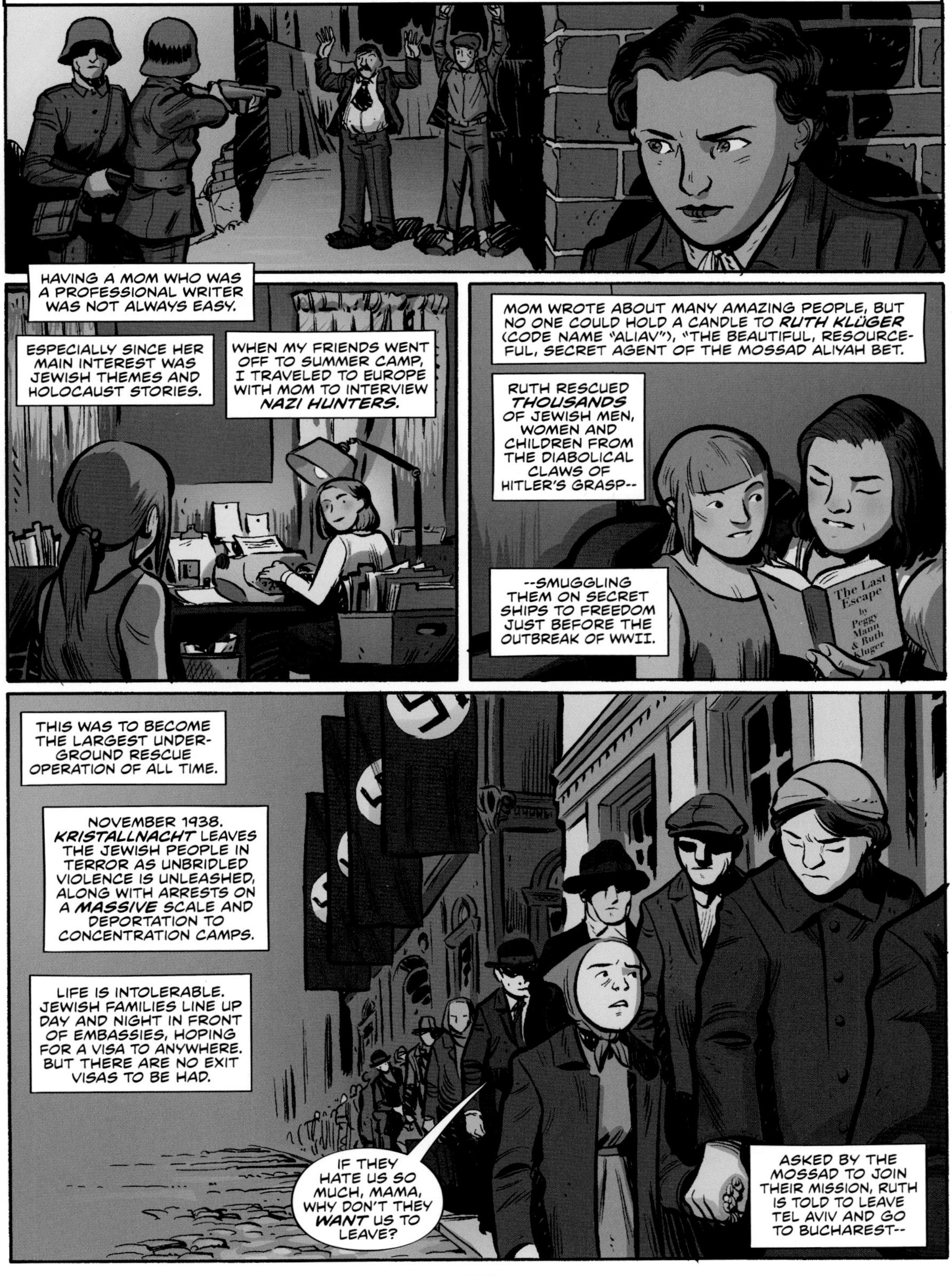
HAVING A MOM WHO WAS A PROFESSIONAL WRITER WAS NOT ALWAYS EASY.
ESPECIALLY SINCE HER MAIN INTEREST WAS JEWISH THEMES AND HOLOCAUST STORIES.
WHEN MY FRIENDS WENT OFF TO SUMMER CAMP, I TRAVELED TO EUROPE WITH MOM TO INTERVIEW NAZI HUNTERS.
MOM WROTE ABOUT MANY AMAZING PEOPLE, BUT NO ONE COULD HOLD A CANDLE TO RUTH KLÜGER (CODE NAME "ALIAV"), "THE BEAUTIFUL, RESOURCEFUL, SECRET AGENT OF THE MOSSAD ALIYAH BET.
RUTH RESCUED THOUSANDS OF JEWISH MEN, WOMEN AND CHILDREN FROM THE DIABOLICAL CLAWS OF HITLER'S GRASP--
The Last Escape by Peggy Mann & Ruth Kluger
--SMUGGLING THEM ON SECRET SHIPS TO FREEDOM JUST BEFORE THE OUTBREAK OF WWII.
THIS WAS TO BECOME THE LARGEST UNDERGROUND RESCUE OPERATION OF ALL TIME.
NOVEMBER 1938. KRISTALLNACHT LEAVES THE JEWISH PEOPLE IN TERROR AS UNBRIDLED VIOLENCE IS UNLEASHED, ALONG WITH ARRESTS ON A MASSIVE SCALE AND DEPORTATION TO CONCENTRATION CAMPS.
LIFE IS INTOLERABLE. JEWISH FAMILIES LINE UP DAY AND NIGHT IN FRONT OF EMBASSIES, HOPING FOR A VISA TO ANYWHERE. BUT THERE ARE NO EXIT VISAS TO BE HAD.
IF THEY HATE US SO MUCH, MAMA, WHY DON'T THEY WANT US TO LEAVE?
ASKED BY THE MOSSAD TO JOIN THEIR MISSION, RUTH IS TOLD TO LEAVE TEL AVIV AND GO TO BUCHAREST--

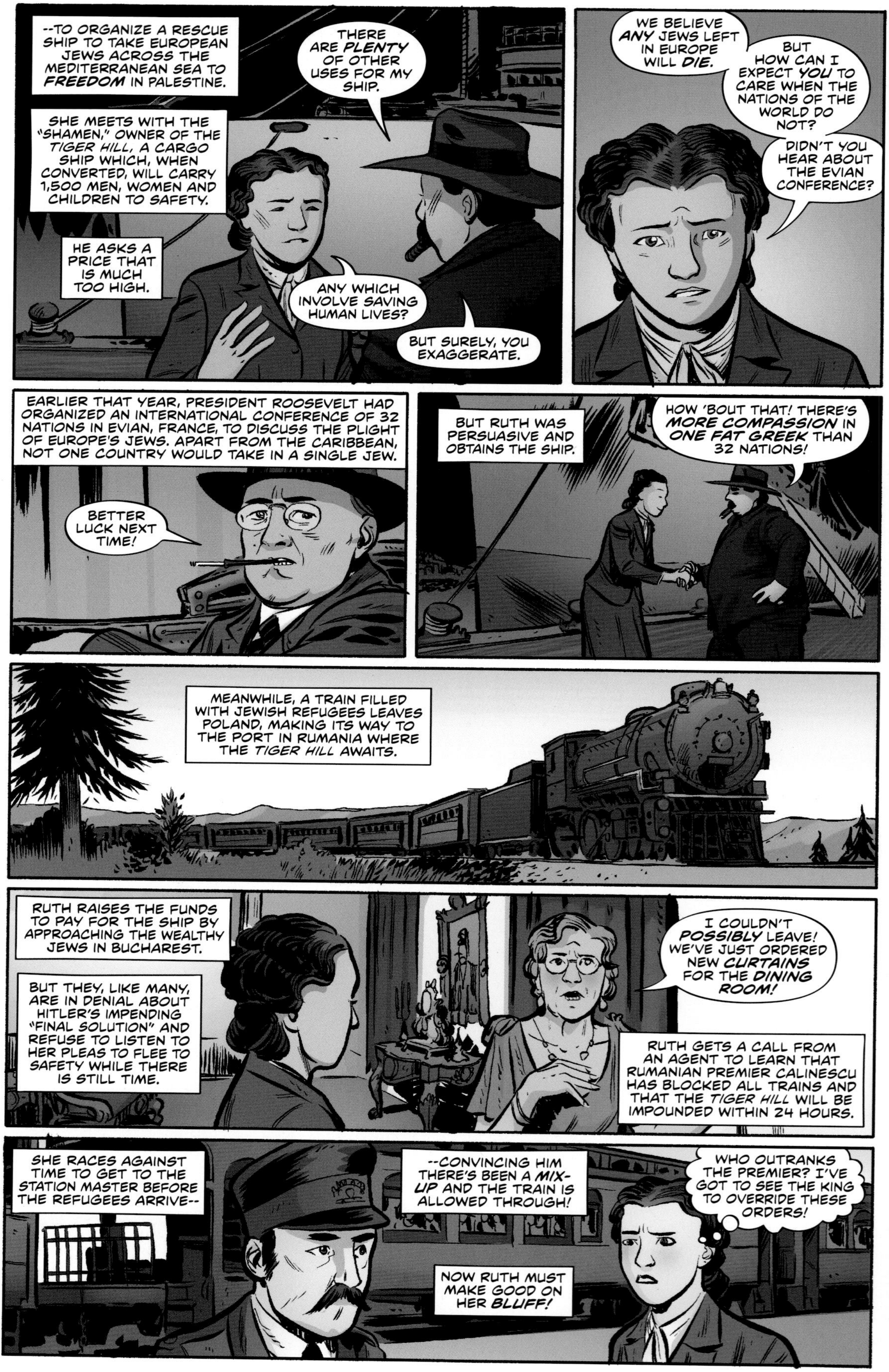
--TO ORGANIZE A RESCUE SHIP TO TAKE EUROPEAN JEWS ACROSS THE MEDITERRANEAN SEA TO FREEDOM IN PALESTINE.
THERE ARE PLENTY OF OTHER USES FOR MY SHIP.
SHE MEETS WITH THE "SHAMEN," OWNER OF THE TIGER HILL, A CARGO SHIP WHICH, WHEN CONVERTED, WILL CARRY 1,500 MEN, WOMEN AND CHILDREN TO SAFETY.
HE ASKS A PRICE THAT IS MUCH TOO HIGH.
ANY WHICH INVOLVE SAVING HUMAN LIVES?
BUT SURELY, YOU EXAGGERATE.
WE BELIEVE ANY JEWS LEFT IN EUROPE WILL DIE.
BUT HOW CAN I EXPECT YOU TO CARE WHEN THE NATIONS OF THE WORLD DO NOT?
DIDN'T YOU HEAR ABOUT THE EVIAN CONFERENCE?
EARLIER THAT YEAR, PRESIDENT ROOSEVELT HAD ORGANIZED AN INTERNATIONAL CONFERENCE OF 32 NATIONS IN EVIAN, FRANCE, TO DISCUSS THE PLIGHT OF EUROPE'S JEWS. APART FROM THE CARIBBEAN, NOT ONE COUNTRY WOULD TAKE IN A SINGLE JEW.
BETTER LUCK NEXT TIME!
BUT RUTH WAS PERSUASIVE AND OBTAINS THE SHIP.
HOW 'BOUT THAT! THERE'S MORE COMPASSION IN ONE FAT GREEK THAN 32 NATIONS!
MEANWHILE, A TRAIN FILLED WITH JEWISH REFUGEES LEAVES POLAND, MAKING ITS WAY TO THE PORT IN RUMANIA WHERE THE TIGER HILL AWAITS.
RUTH RAISES THE FUNDS TO PAY FOR THE SHIP BY APPROACHING THE WEALTHY JEWS IN BUCHAREST.
BUT THEY, LIKE MANY, ARE IN DENIAL ABOUT HITLER'S IMPENDING "FINAL SOLUTION" AND REFUSE TO LISTEN TO HER PLEAS TO FLEE TO SAFETY WHILE THERE IS STILL TIME.
I COULDN'T POSSIBLY LEAVE! WE'VE JUST ORDERED NEW CURTAINS FOR THE DINING ROOM!
RUTH GETS A CALL FROM AN AGENT TO LEARN THAT RUMANIAN PREMIER CALINESCU HAS BLOCKED ALL TRAINS AND THAT THE TIGER HILL WILL BE IMPOUNDED WITHIN 24 HOURS.
SHE RACES AGAINST TIME TO GET TO THE STATION MASTER BEFORE THE REFUGEES ARRIVE--
--CONVINCING HIM THERE'S BEEN A MIX-UP AND THE TRAIN IS ALLOWED THROUGH!
NOW RUTH MUST MAKE GOOD ON HER BLUFF!
WHO OUTRANKS THE PREMIER? I'VE GOT TO SEE THE KING TO OVERRIDE THESE ORDERS!

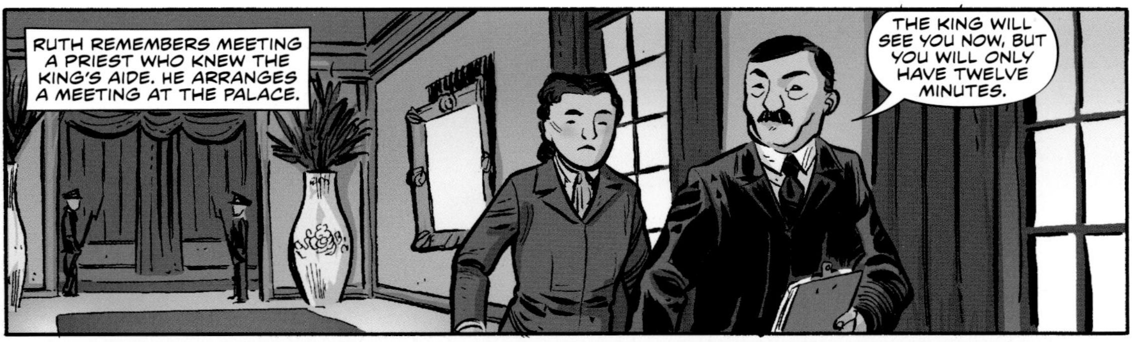
RUTH REMEMBERS MEETING A PRIEST WHO KNEW THE KING'S AIDE. HE ARRANGES A MEETING AT THE PALACE.
THE KING WILL SEE YOU NOW, BUT YOU WILL ONLY HAVE TWELVE MINUTES.

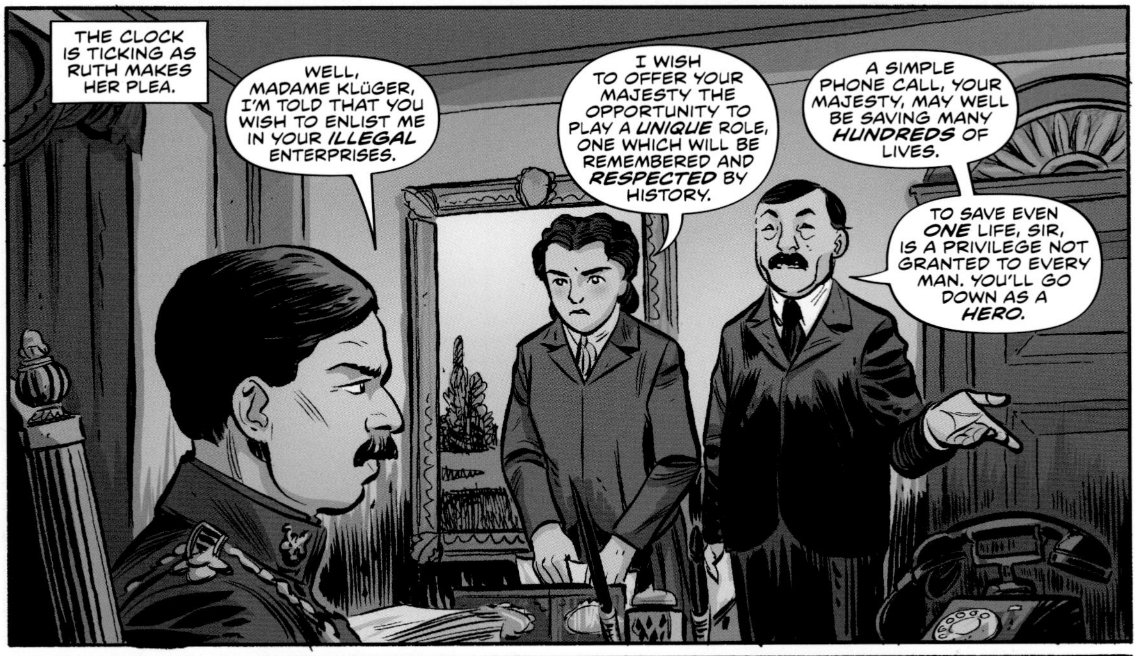
THE CLOCK IS TICKING AS RUTH MAKES HER PLEA.
WELL, MADAME KLÜGER, I'M TOLD THAT YOU WISH TO ENLIST ME IN YOUR *ILLEGAL* ENTERPRISES.
I WISH TO OFFER YOUR MAJESTY THE OPPORTUNITY TO PLAY A *UNIQUE* ROLE, ONE WHICH WILL BE REMEMBERED AND *RESPECTED* BY HISTORY.
A SIMPLE PHONE CALL, YOUR MAJESTY, MAY WELL BE SAVING MANY *HUNDREDS* OF LIVES.
TO SAVE EVEN *ONE* LIFE, SIR, IS A PRIVILEGE NOT GRANTED TO EVERY MAN. YOU'LL GO DOWN AS A *HERO*.

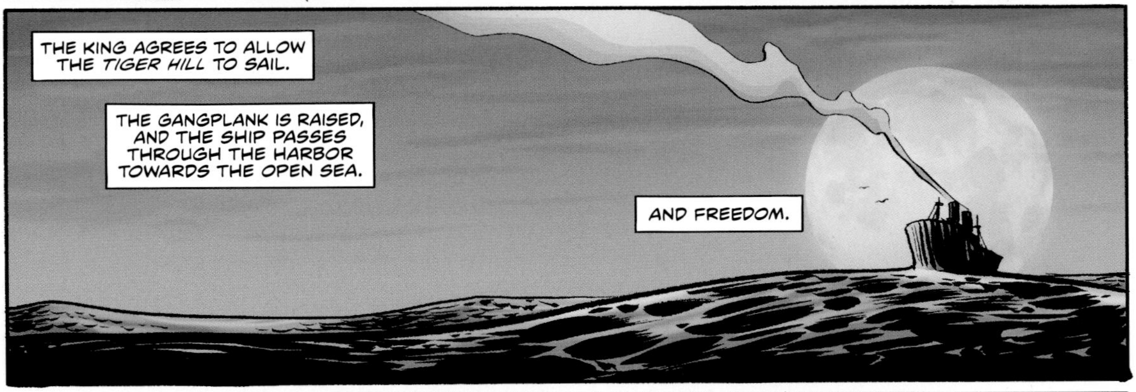
THE KING AGREES TO ALLOW THE *TIGER HILL* TO SAIL.
THE GANGPLANK IS RAISED, AND THE SHIP PASSES THROUGH THE HARBOR TOWARDS THE OPEN SEA.
AND FREEDOM.

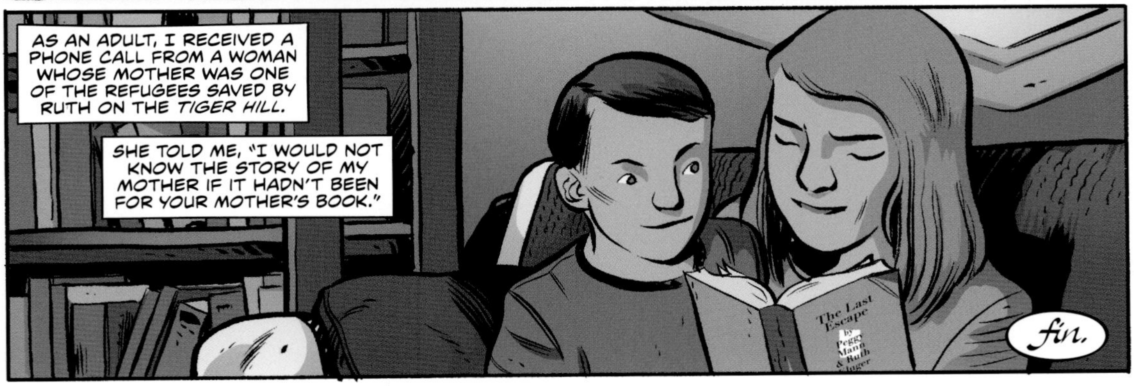
AS AN ADULT, I RECEIVED A PHONE CALL FROM A WOMAN WHOSE MOTHER WAS ONE OF THE REFUGEES SAVED BY RUTH ON THE *TIGER HILL*.
SHE TOLD ME, "I WOULD NOT KNOW THE STORY OF MY MOTHER IF IT HADN'T BEEN FOR YOUR MOTHER'S BOOK."
The Last Escape
fin.

"Archaeology is like a jigsaw puzzle; putting together all the pieces gives you an image of past cultures."
—Kristy Miller

THE REAL INDIANA JONES

KRISTY MILLER

BRIAN MILLER WRITER | **EVA CABRERA** ARTIST | **CLAUDIA AGUIRRE** COLORIST

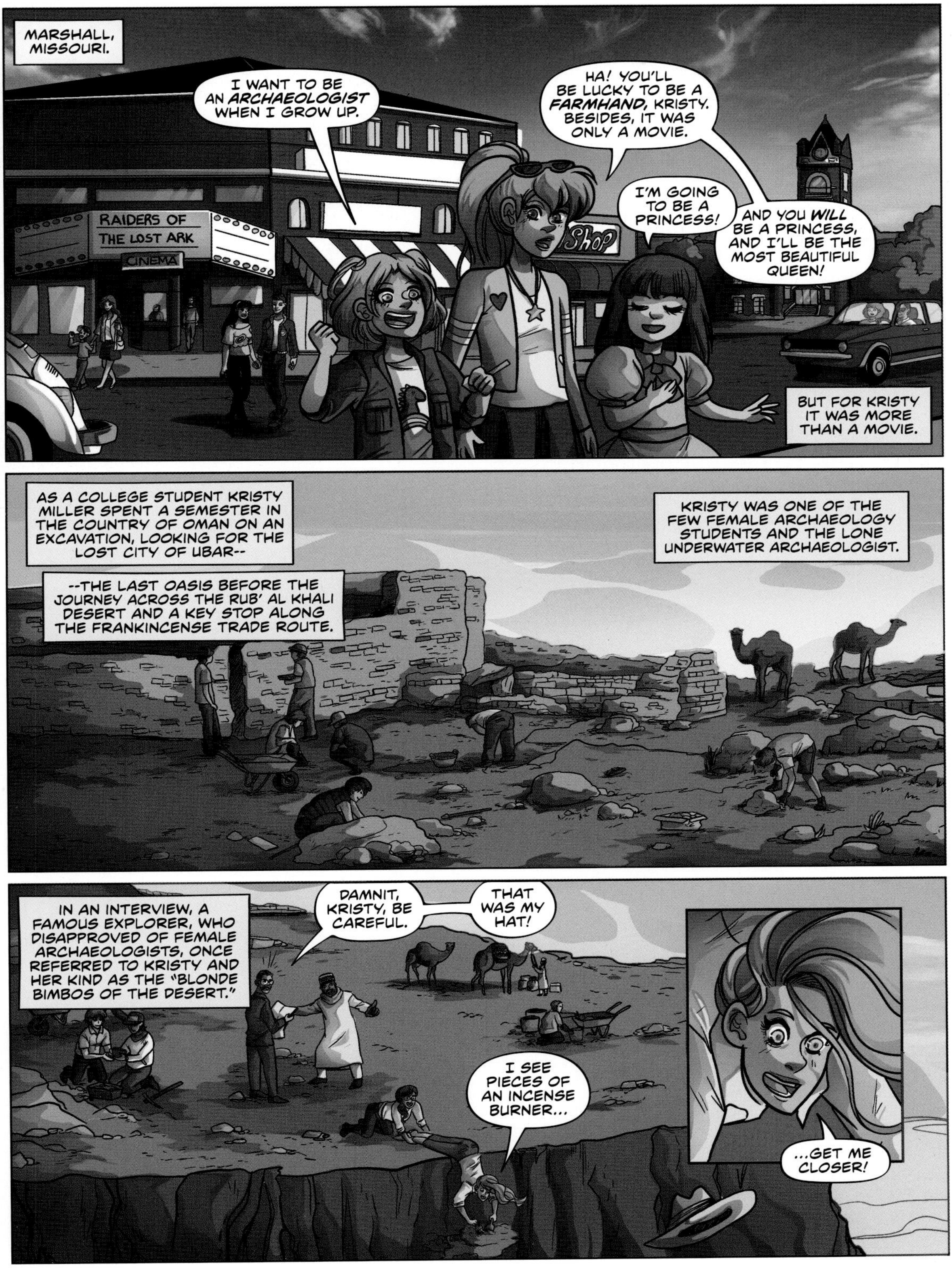
MARSHALL, MISSOURI.
I WANT TO BE AN ARCHAEOLOGIST WHEN I GROW UP.
HA! YOU'LL BE LUCKY TO BE A FARMHAND, KRISTY. BESIDES, IT WAS ONLY A MOVIE.
I'M GOING TO BE A PRINCESS!
AND YOU WILL BE A PRINCESS, AND I'LL BE THE MOST BEAUTIFUL QUEEN!
RAIDERS OF THE LOST ARK
CINEMA
SHOP
BUT FOR KRISTY IT WAS MORE THAN A MOVIE.
AS A COLLEGE STUDENT KRISTY MILLER SPENT A SEMESTER IN THE COUNTRY OF OMAN ON AN EXCAVATION, LOOKING FOR THE LOST CITY OF UBAR--
--THE LAST OASIS BEFORE THE JOURNEY ACROSS THE RUB' AL KHALI DESERT AND A KEY STOP ALONG THE FRANKINCENSE TRADE ROUTE.
KRISTY WAS ONE OF THE FEW FEMALE ARCHAEOLOGY STUDENTS AND THE LONE UNDERWATER ARCHAEOLOGIST.
IN AN INTERVIEW, A FAMOUS EXPLORER, WHO DISAPPROVED OF FEMALE ARCHAEOLOGISTS, ONCE REFERRED TO KRISTY AND HER KIND AS THE "BLONDE BIMBOS OF THE DESERT."
DAMNIT, KRISTY, BE CAREFUL.
THAT WAS MY HAT!
I SEE PIECES OF AN INCENSE BURNER...
...GET ME CLOSER!

SHE LED A TEAM OF DIVERS ON SURVEYS AROUND THE COAST OF OMAN WHERE SHE DISCOVERED ANCIENT POTTERY VESSELS, ANCHORS, AND MORE.*

* SOME OF THE ARTIFACTS SHE DISCOVERED AS A STUDENT ARE NOW ON DISPLAY AT THE LAND OF FRANKINCENSE MUSEUM IN SALALAH, OMAN. – EDITOR'S NOTE

I FOUND REMNANTS OF SHIPPING TRADE.

WHAT'S FOR DINNER?

FRESH LOBSTER!

BE READY FOR CAVE-DIVING AT DAWN.

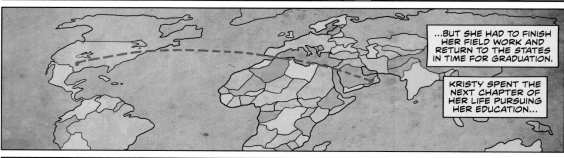

ON LAND, THE SURVEY TEAM CAMPED AMONG MOUNTAIN-SIZED DUNES WITH A NIGHT SKY SO VAST SHE COULD SEE EVERY STAR.

KRISTY FELL IN LOVE WITH THE DESERT...

...BUT SHE HAD TO FINISH HER FIELD WORK AND RETURN TO THE STATES IN TIME FOR GRADUATION.

KRISTY SPENT THE NEXT CHAPTER OF HER LIFE PURSUING HER EDUCATION...

...AND EDUCATING OTHERS. INTRODUCING ARCHAEOLOGICAL PROGRAMS TO MUSEUMS, KRISTY EVEN TRAVELED TO YEMEN--

--TO HELP WITH AN ARCHAEOLOGICAL EXCAVATION.

BUT SHE NEVER FORGOT THE SANDS OF OMAN.

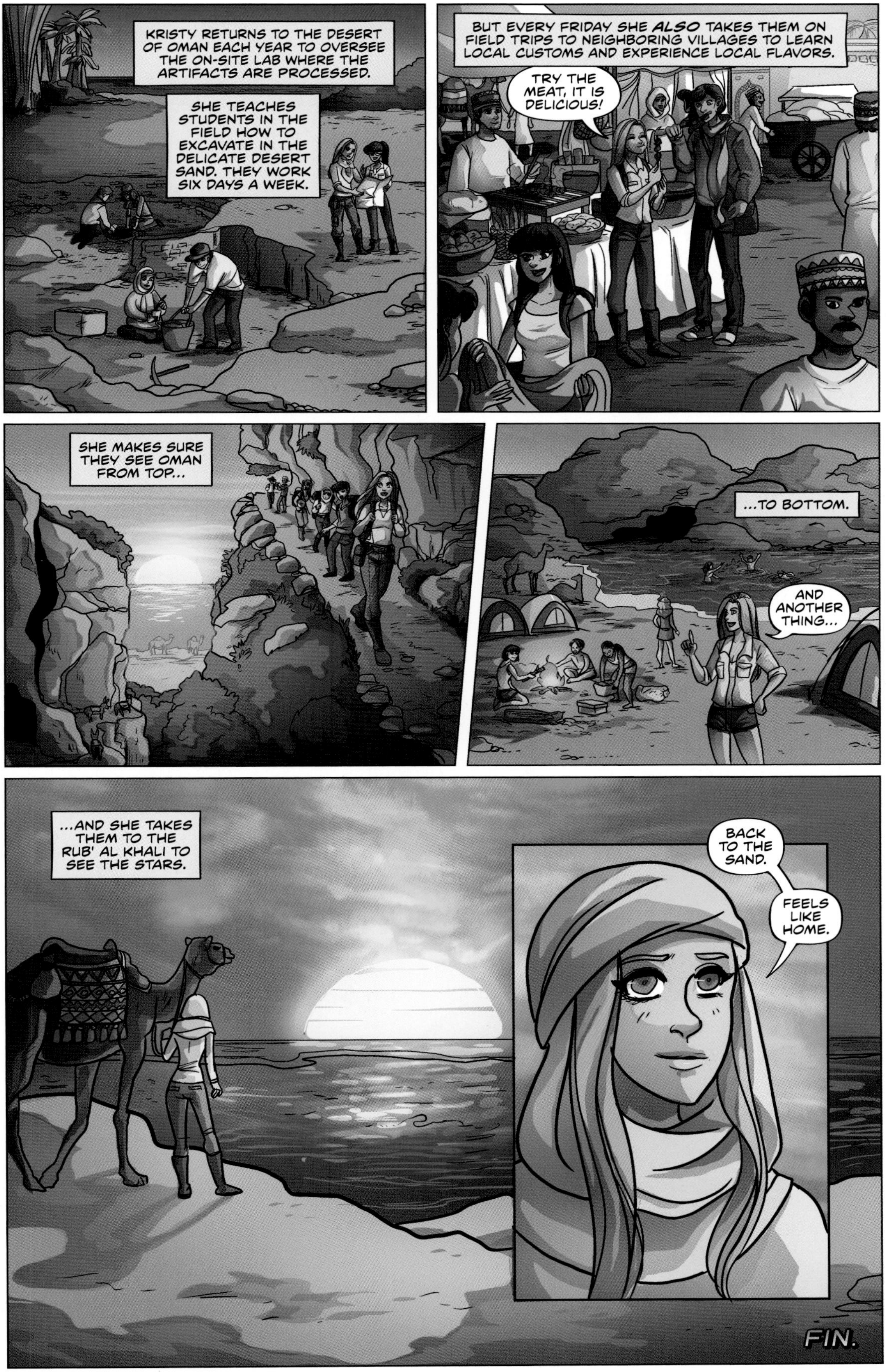
KRISTY RETURNS TO THE DESERT OF OMAN EACH YEAR TO OVERSEE THE ON-SITE LAB WHERE THE ARTIFACTS ARE PROCESSED.
SHE TEACHES STUDENTS IN THE FIELD HOW TO EXCAVATE IN THE DELICATE DESERT SAND. THEY WORK SIX DAYS A WEEK.
BUT EVERY FRIDAY SHE ALSO TAKES THEM ON FIELD TRIPS TO NEIGHBORING VILLAGES TO LEARN LOCAL CUSTOMS AND EXPERIENCE LOCAL FLAVORS.
TRY THE MEAT, IT IS DELICIOUS!
SHE MAKES SURE THEY SEE OMAN FROM TOP...
...TO BOTTOM.
AND ANOTHER THING...
...AND SHE TAKES THEM TO THE RUB' AL KHALI TO SEE THE STARS.
BACK TO THE SAND.
FEELS LIKE HOME.
FIN.

"A good story is a good story. If what I'm writing reaches you, then it reaches you no matter what title is stuck on it."

—Octavia Butler

The Wild Seed

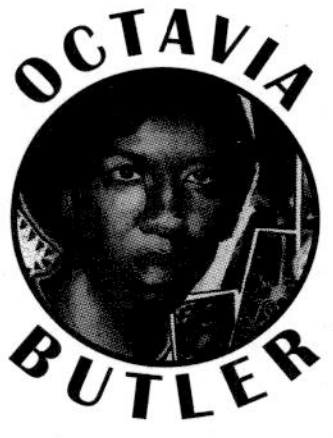
OCTAVIA
BUTLER

CHE GRAYSON
WRITER

JASON SHAWN ALEXANDER
ARTIST

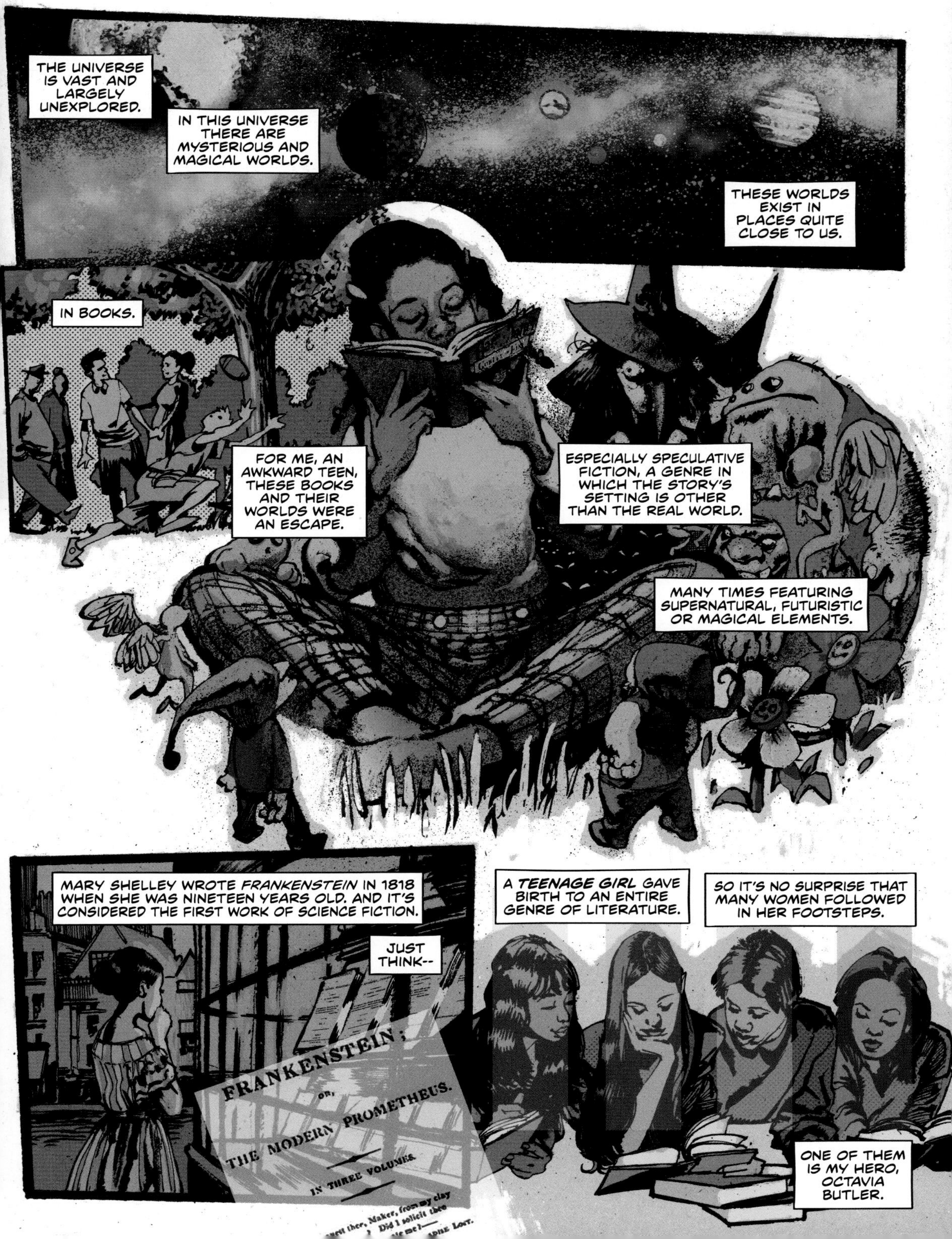
THE UNIVERSE IS VAST AND LARGELY UNEXPLORED.
IN THIS UNIVERSE THERE ARE MYSTERIOUS AND MAGICAL WORLDS.
THESE WORLDS EXIST IN PLACES QUITE CLOSE TO US.
IN BOOKS.
FOR ME, AN AWKWARD TEEN, THESE BOOKS AND THEIR WORLDS WERE AN ESCAPE.
ESPECIALLY SPECULATIVE FICTION, A GENRE IN WHICH THE STORY'S SETTING IS OTHER THAN THE REAL WORLD.
MANY TIMES FEATURING SUPERNATURAL, FUTURISTIC OR MAGICAL ELEMENTS.
MARY SHELLEY WROTE *FRANKENSTEIN* IN 1818 WHEN SHE WAS NINETEEN YEARS OLD. AND IT'S CONSIDERED THE FIRST WORK OF SCIENCE FICTION.
JUST THINK--
FRANKENSTEIN;
OR,
THE MODERN PROMETHEUS.
IN THREE VOLUMES.
A ***TEENAGE GIRL*** GAVE BIRTH TO AN ENTIRE GENRE OF LITERATURE.
SO IT'S NO SURPRISE THAT MANY WOMEN FOLLOWED IN HER FOOTSTEPS.
ONE OF THEM IS MY HERO, OCTAVIA BUTLER.

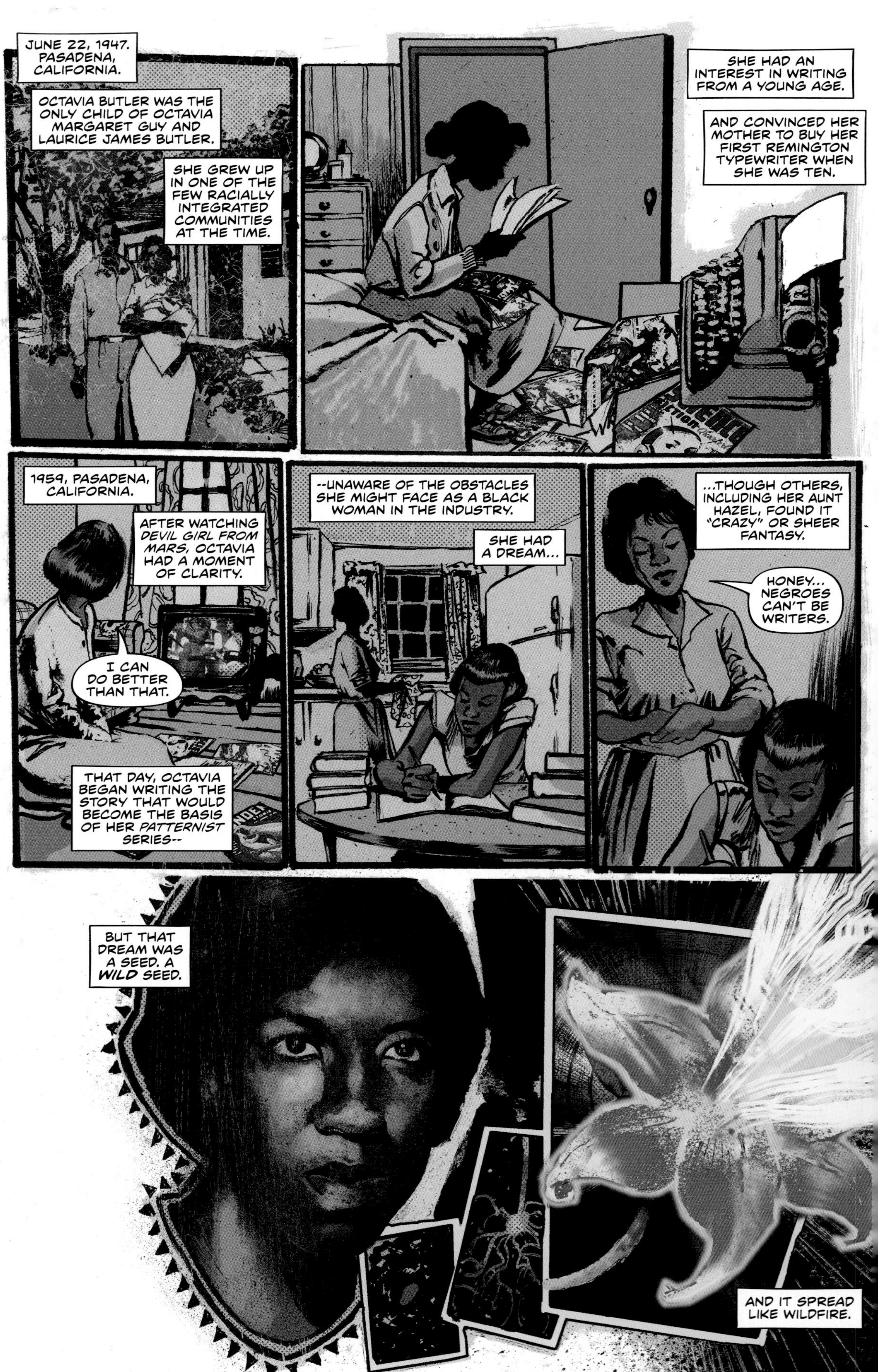
JUNE 22, 1947. PASADENA, CALIFORNIA.
OCTAVIA BUTLER WAS THE ONLY CHILD OF OCTAVIA MARGARET GUY AND LAURICE JAMES BUTLER.
SHE GREW UP IN ONE OF THE FEW RACIALLY INTEGRATED COMMUNITIES AT THE TIME.
SHE HAD AN INTEREST IN WRITING FROM A YOUNG AGE.
AND CONVINCED HER MOTHER TO BUY HER FIRST REMINGTON TYPEWRITER WHEN SHE WAS TEN.
1959, PASADENA, CALIFORNIA.
AFTER WATCHING *DEVIL GIRL FROM MARS*, OCTAVIA HAD A MOMENT OF CLARITY.
I CAN DO BETTER THAN THAT.
THAT DAY, OCTAVIA BEGAN WRITING THE STORY THAT WOULD BECOME THE BASIS OF HER *PATTERNIST* SERIES--
--UNAWARE OF THE OBSTACLES SHE MIGHT FACE AS A BLACK WOMAN IN THE INDUSTRY.
SHE HAD A DREAM...
...THOUGH OTHERS, INCLUDING HER AUNT HAZEL, FOUND IT "CRAZY" OR SHEER FANTASY.
HONEY... NEGROES CAN'T BE WRITERS.
BUT THAT DREAM WAS A SEED. A ***WILD*** SEED.
AND IT SPREAD LIKE WILDFIRE.

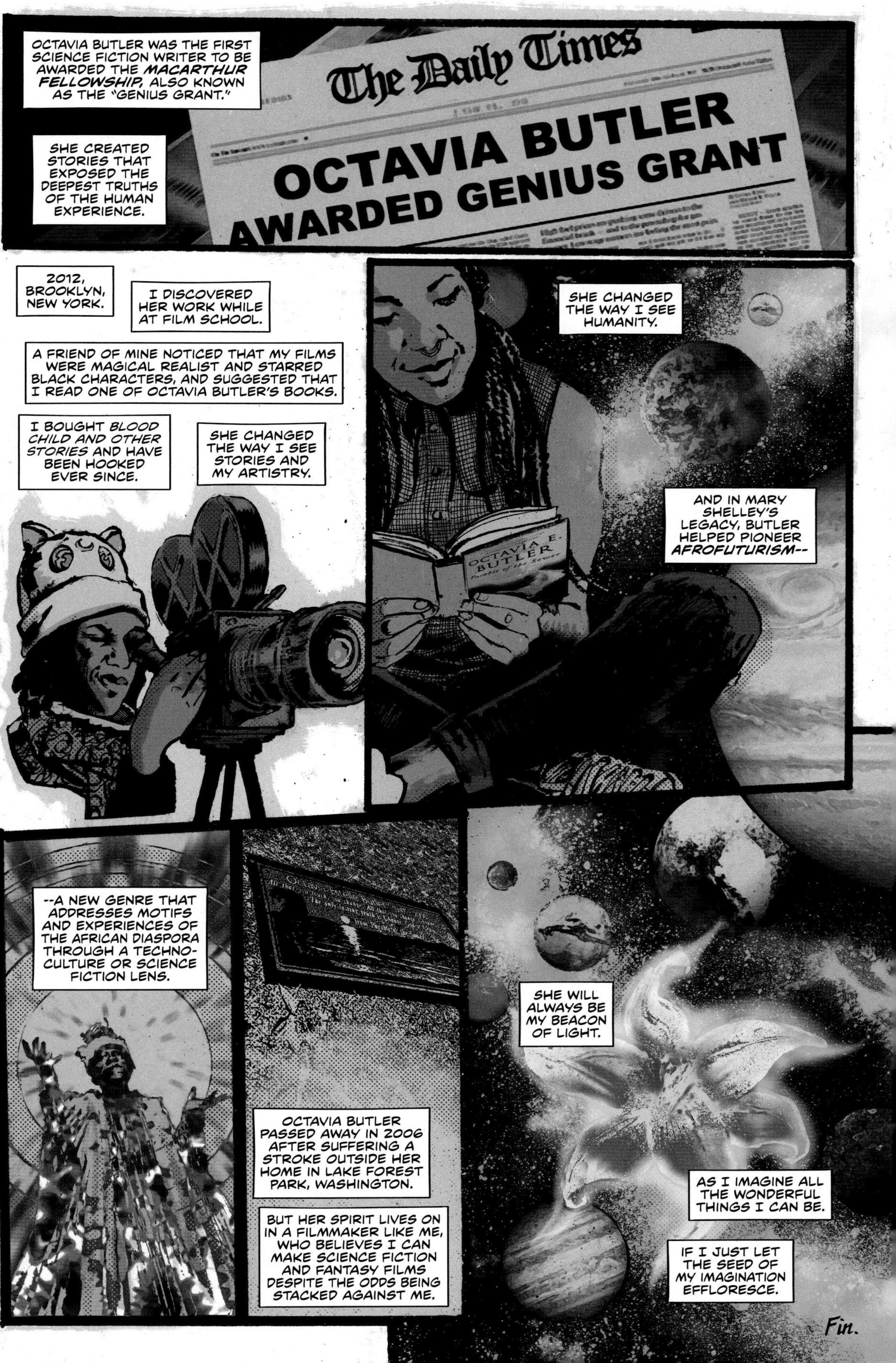
OCTAVIA BUTLER WAS THE FIRST SCIENCE FICTION WRITER TO BE AWARDED THE *MACARTHUR FELLOWSHIP*, ALSO KNOWN AS THE "GENIUS GRANT."
The Daily Times
OCTAVIA BUTLER AWARDED GENIUS GRANT
SHE CREATED STORIES THAT EXPOSED THE DEEPEST TRUTHS OF THE HUMAN EXPERIENCE.
2012, BROOKLYN, NEW YORK.
I DISCOVERED HER WORK WHILE AT FILM SCHOOL.
A FRIEND OF MINE NOTICED THAT MY FILMS WERE MAGICAL REALIST AND STARRED BLACK CHARACTERS, AND SUGGESTED THAT I READ ONE OF OCTAVIA BUTLER'S BOOKS.
I BOUGHT *BLOOD CHILD AND OTHER STORIES* AND HAVE BEEN HOOKED EVER SINCE.
SHE CHANGED THE WAY I SEE STORIES AND MY ARTISTRY.
SHE CHANGED THE WAY I SEE HUMANITY.
OCTAVIA E. BUTLER
Parable of the Sower
AND IN MARY SHELLEY'S LEGACY, BUTLER HELPED PIONEER *AFROFUTURISM*--
--A NEW GENRE THAT ADDRESSES MOTIFS AND EXPERIENCES OF THE AFRICAN DIASPORA THROUGH A TECHNO-CULTURE OR SCIENCE FICTION LENS.
OCTAVIA BUTLER PASSED AWAY IN 2006 AFTER SUFFERING A STROKE OUTSIDE HER HOME IN LAKE FOREST PARK, WASHINGTON.
BUT HER SPIRIT LIVES ON IN A FILMMAKER LIKE ME, WHO BELIEVES I CAN MAKE SCIENCE FICTION AND FANTASY FILMS DESPITE THE ODDS BEING STACKED AGAINST ME.
SHE WILL ALWAYS BE MY BEACON OF LIGHT.
AS I IMAGINE ALL THE WONDERFUL THINGS I CAN BE.
IF I JUST LET THE SEED OF MY IMAGINATION EFFLORESCE.
Fin.

"When the shield failed me, I chose the sword."
—Artemisia Gentileschi

CONVICTION

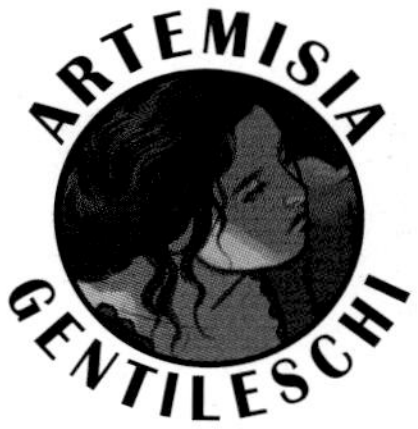
ARTEMISIA GENTILESCHI

MARGUERITE BENNETT
WRITER

JEN BARTEL
ARTIST/COLORIST

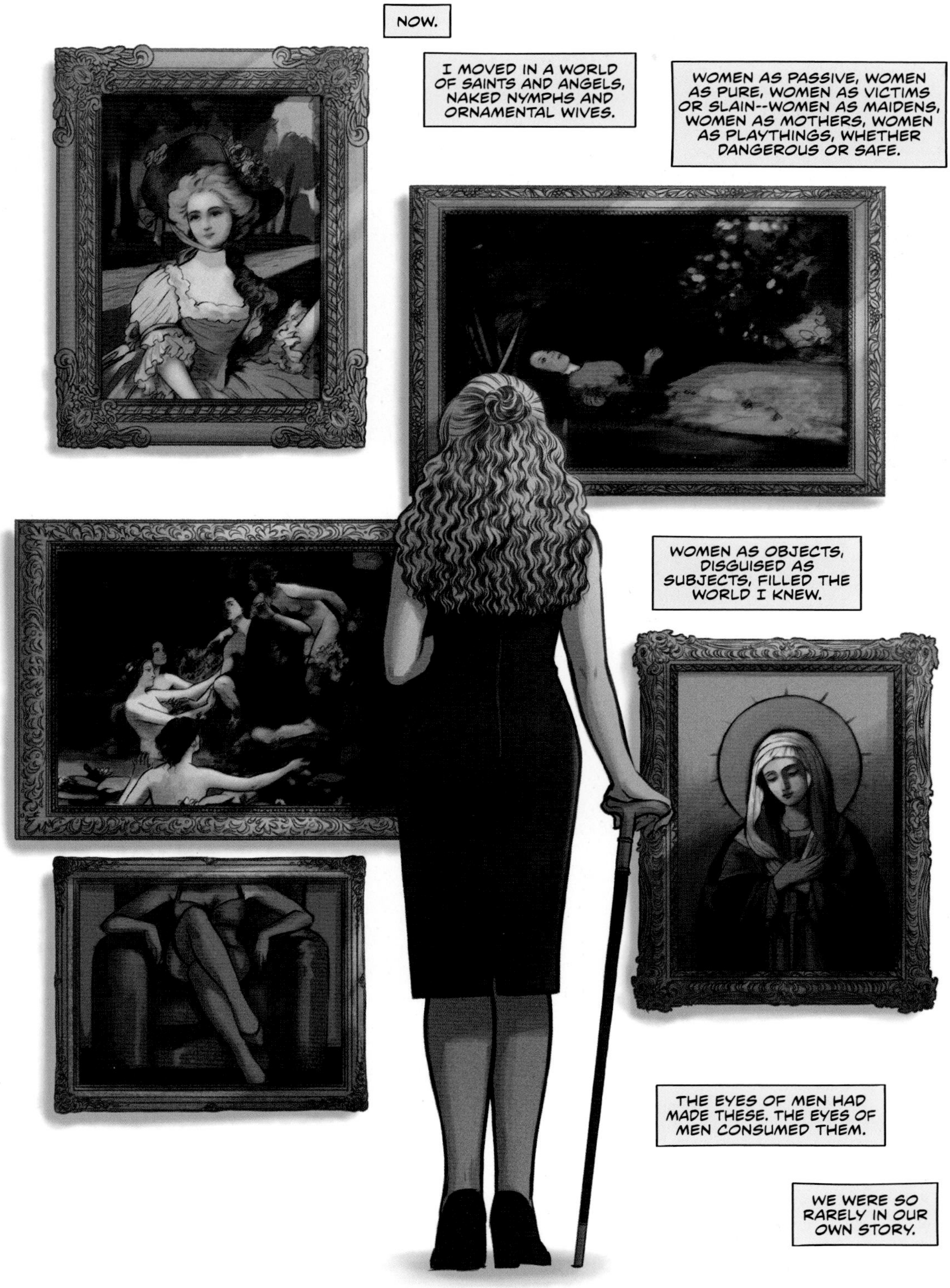
NOW.
I MOVED IN A WORLD OF SAINTS AND ANGELS, NAKED NYMPHS AND ORNAMENTAL WIVES.
WOMEN AS PASSIVE, WOMEN AS PURE, WOMEN AS VICTIMS OR SLAIN--WOMEN AS MAIDENS, WOMEN AS MOTHERS, WOMEN AS PLAYTHINGS, WHETHER DANGEROUS OR SAFE.
WOMEN AS OBJECTS, DISGUISED AS SUBJECTS, FILLED THE WORLD I KNEW.
THE EYES OF MEN HAD MADE THESE. THE EYES OF MEN CONSUMED THEM.
WE WERE SO RARELY IN OUR OWN STORY.

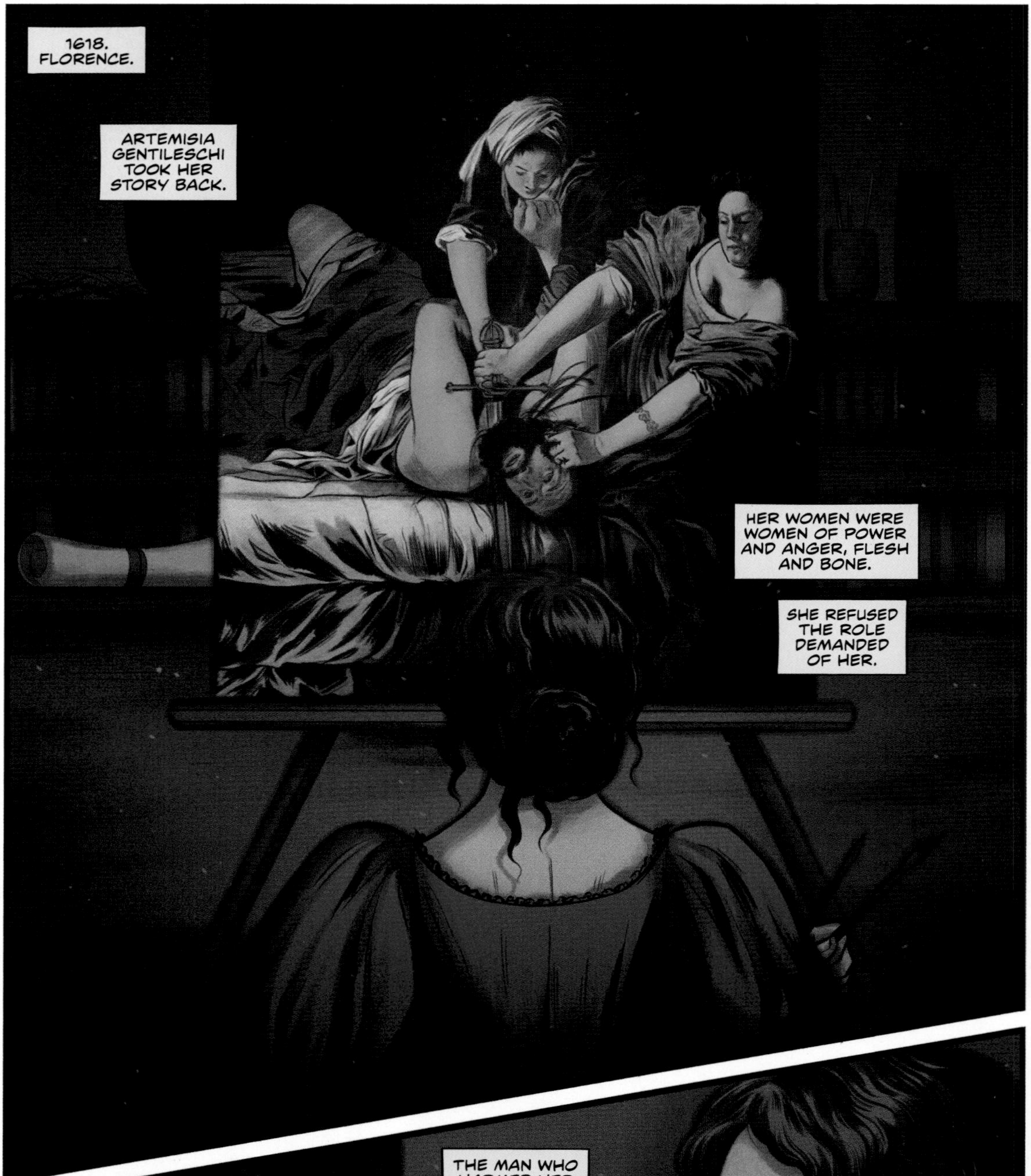
1618.
FLORENCE.
ARTEMISIA GENTILESCHI TOOK HER STORY BACK.
HER WOMEN WERE WOMEN OF POWER AND ANGER, FLESH AND BONE.
SHE REFUSED THE ROLE DEMANDED OF HER.
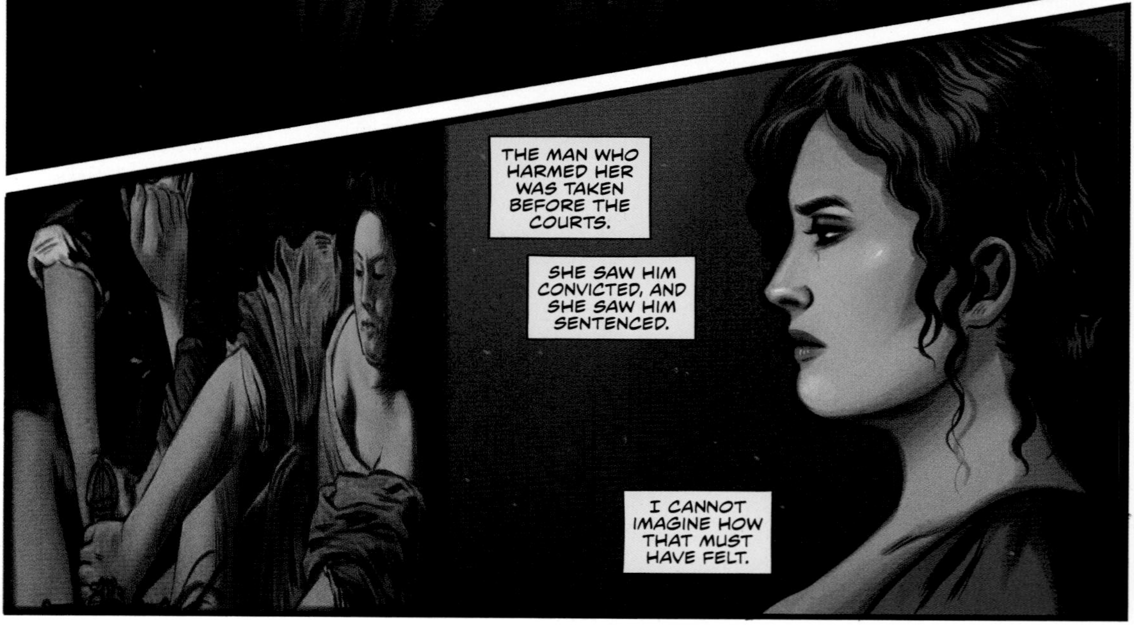
THE MAN WHO HARMED HER WAS TAKEN BEFORE THE COURTS.
SHE SAW HIM CONVICTED, AND SHE SAW HIM SENTENCED.
I CANNOT IMAGINE HOW THAT MUST HAVE FELT.

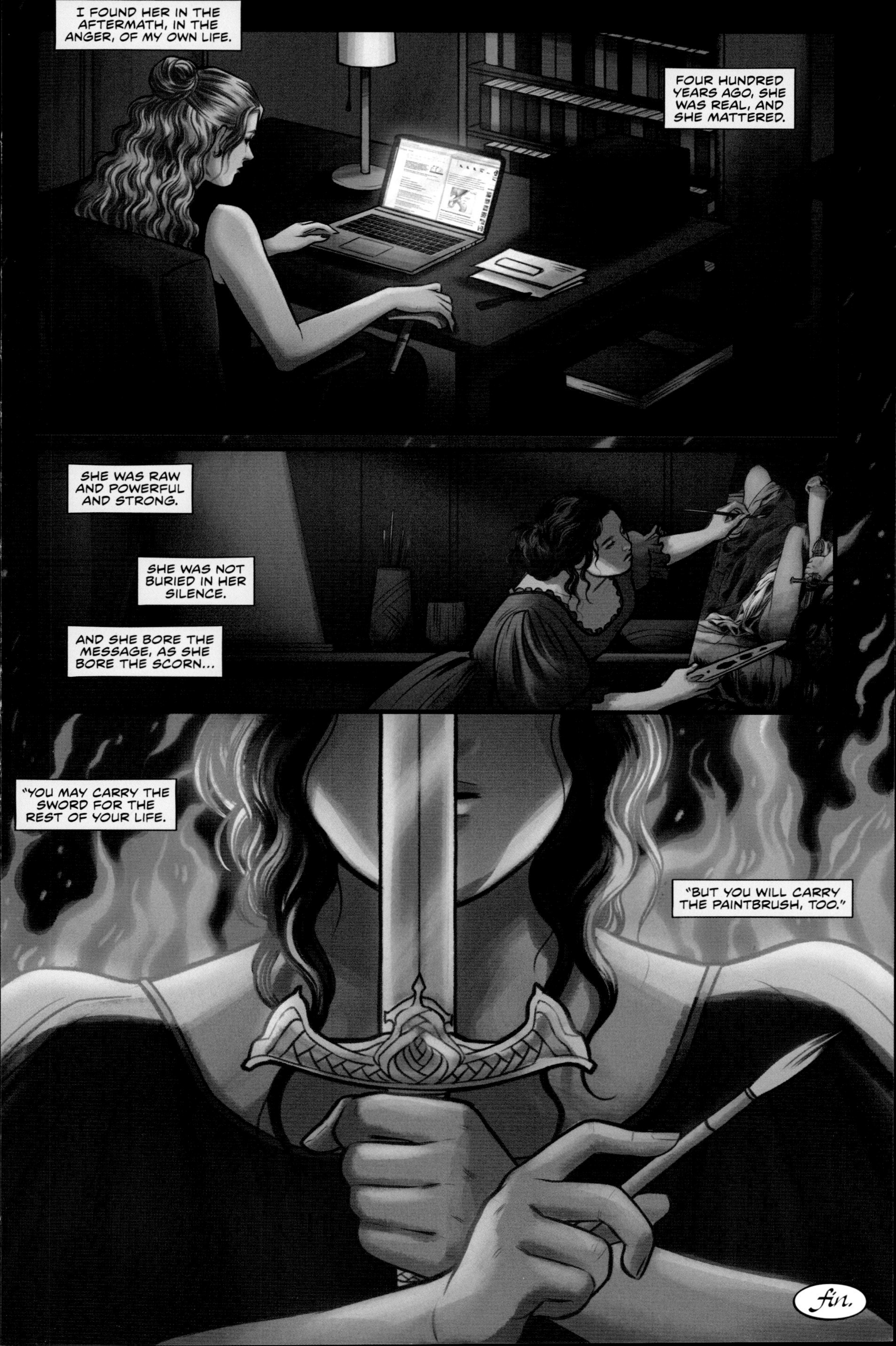
I FOUND HER IN THE AFTERMATH, IN THE ANGER, OF MY OWN LIFE.
FOUR HUNDRED YEARS AGO, SHE WAS REAL, AND SHE MATTERED.
SHE WAS RAW AND POWERFUL AND STRONG.
SHE WAS NOT BURIED IN HER SILENCE.
AND SHE BORE THE MESSAGE, AS SHE BORE THE SCORN...
"YOU MAY CARRY THE SWORD FOR THE REST OF YOUR LIFE.
"BUT YOU WILL CARRY THE PAINTBRUSH, TOO."
fin.

"Go forward bravely. Fear nothing. Trust in God; all will be well."

—Joan of Arc

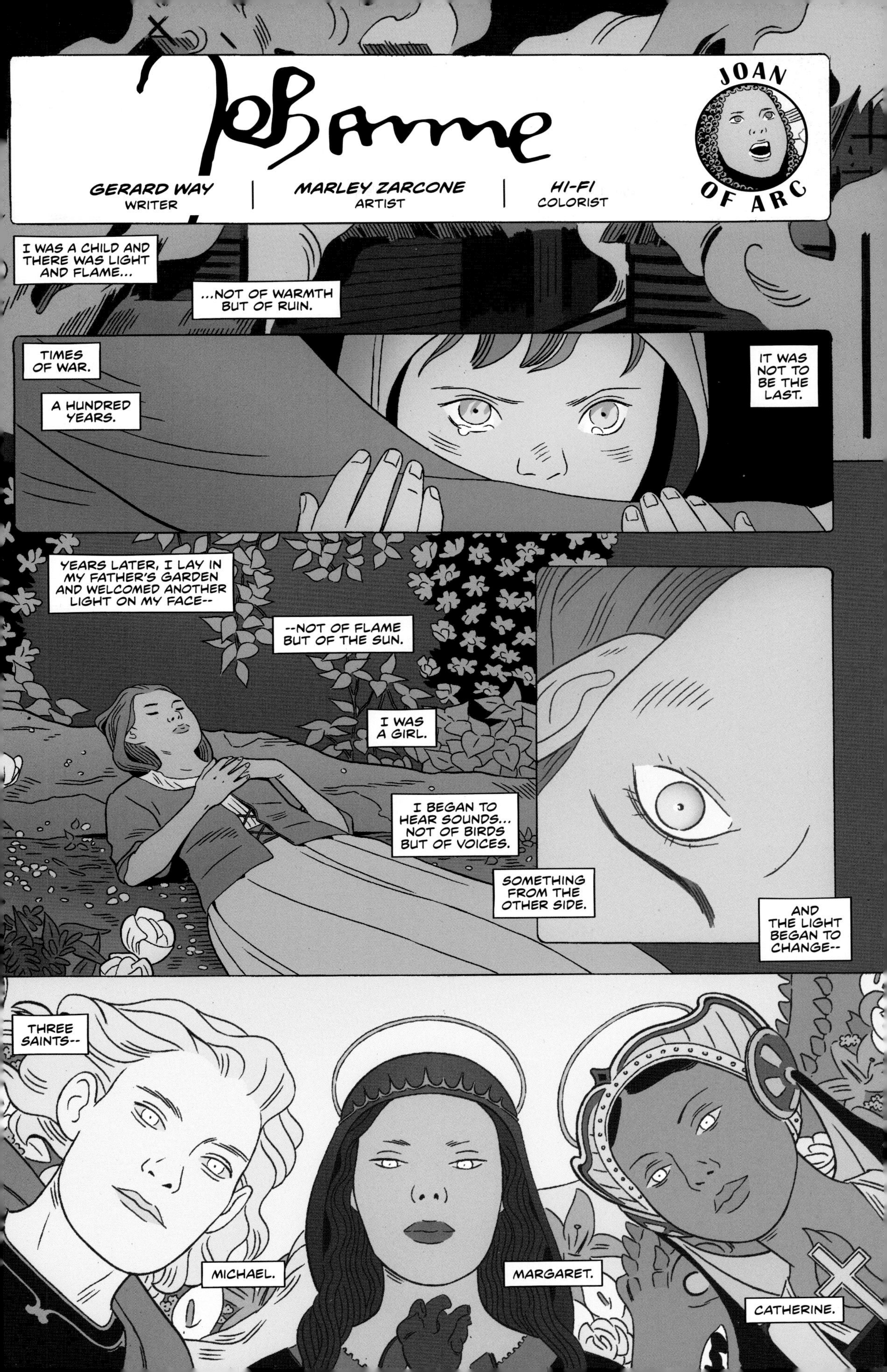
Jehanne
GERARD WAY
WRITER
MARLEY ZARCONE
ARTIST
HI-FI
COLORIST
JOAN OF ARC
I WAS A CHILD AND THERE WAS LIGHT AND FLAME...
...NOT OF WARMTH BUT OF RUIN.
TIMES OF WAR.
A HUNDRED YEARS.
IT WAS NOT TO BE THE LAST.
YEARS LATER, I LAY IN MY FATHER'S GARDEN AND WELCOMED ANOTHER LIGHT ON MY FACE--
--NOT OF FLAME BUT OF THE SUN.
I WAS A GIRL.
I BEGAN TO HEAR SOUNDS... NOT OF BIRDS BUT OF VOICES.
SOMETHING FROM THE OTHER SIDE.
AND THE LIGHT BEGAN TO CHANGE--
THREE SAINTS--
MICHAEL.
MARGARET.
CATHERINE.

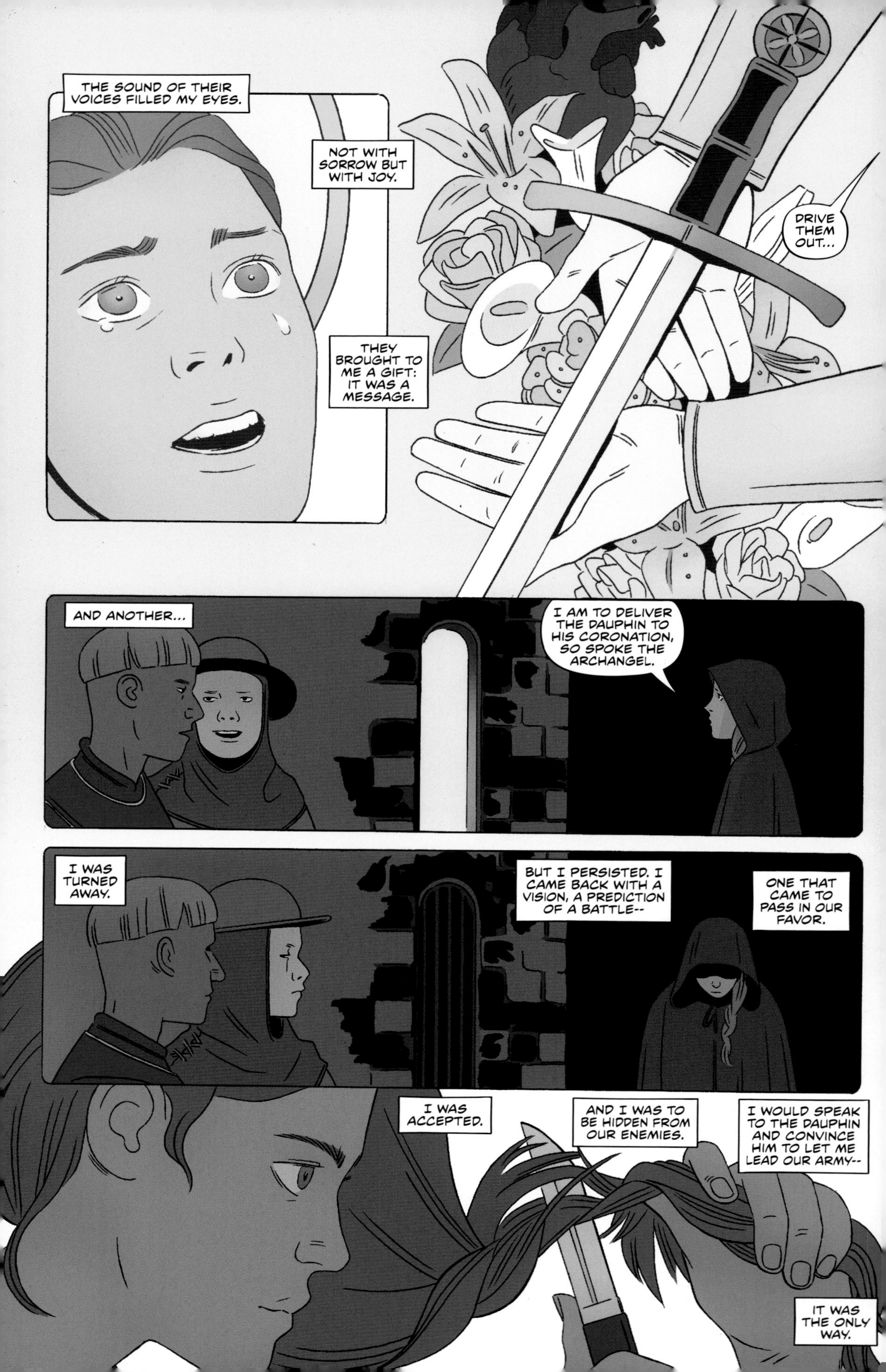
THE SOUND OF THEIR VOICES FILLED MY EYES.
NOT WITH SORROW BUT WITH JOY.
THEY BROUGHT TO ME A GIFT: IT WAS A MESSAGE.
DRIVE THEM OUT...
AND ANOTHER...
I AM TO DELIVER THE DAUPHIN TO HIS CORONATION, SO SPOKE THE ARCHANGEL.
I WAS TURNED AWAY.
BUT I PERSISTED. I CAME BACK WITH A VISION, A PREDICTION OF A BATTLE--
ONE THAT CAME TO PASS IN OUR FAVOR.
I WAS ACCEPTED.
AND I WAS TO BE HIDDEN FROM OUR ENEMIES.
I WOULD SPEAK TO THE DAUPHIN AND CONVINCE HIM TO LET ME LEAD OUR ARMY--
IT WAS THE ONLY WAY.

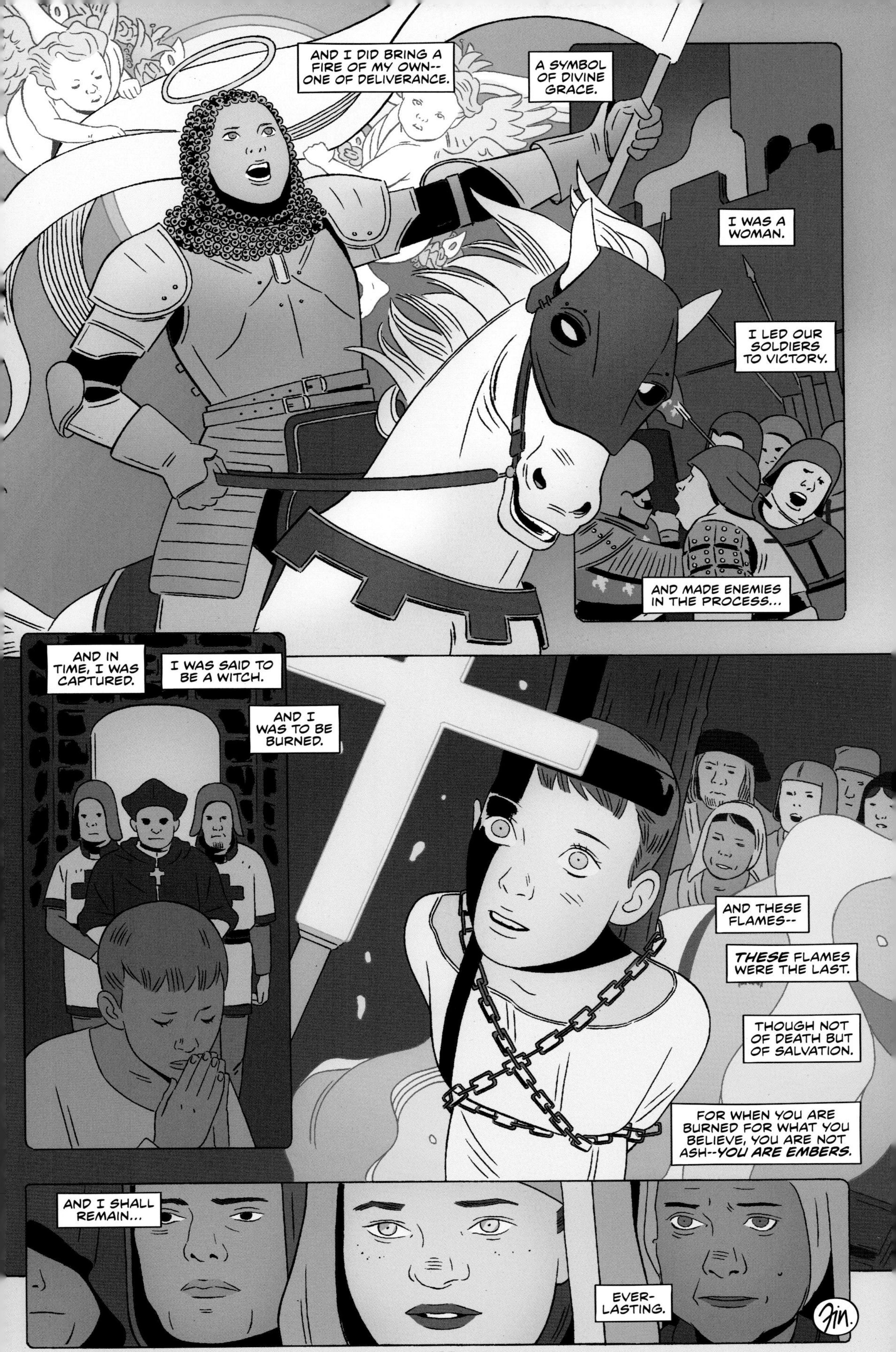

AND I DID BRING A FIRE OF MY OWN-- ONE OF DELIVERANCE.
A SYMBOL OF DIVINE GRACE.
I WAS A WOMAN.
I LED OUR SOLDIERS TO VICTORY.
AND MADE ENEMIES IN THE PROCESS...
AND IN TIME, I WAS CAPTURED.
I WAS SAID TO BE A WITCH.
AND I WAS TO BE BURNED.
AND THESE FLAMES--
THESE FLAMES WERE THE LAST.
THOUGH NOT OF DEATH BUT OF SALVATION.
FOR WHEN YOU ARE BURNED FOR WHAT YOU BELIEVE, YOU ARE NOT ASH--*YOU ARE EMBERS.*
AND I SHALL REMAIN...
EVER-LASTING.
FIN.

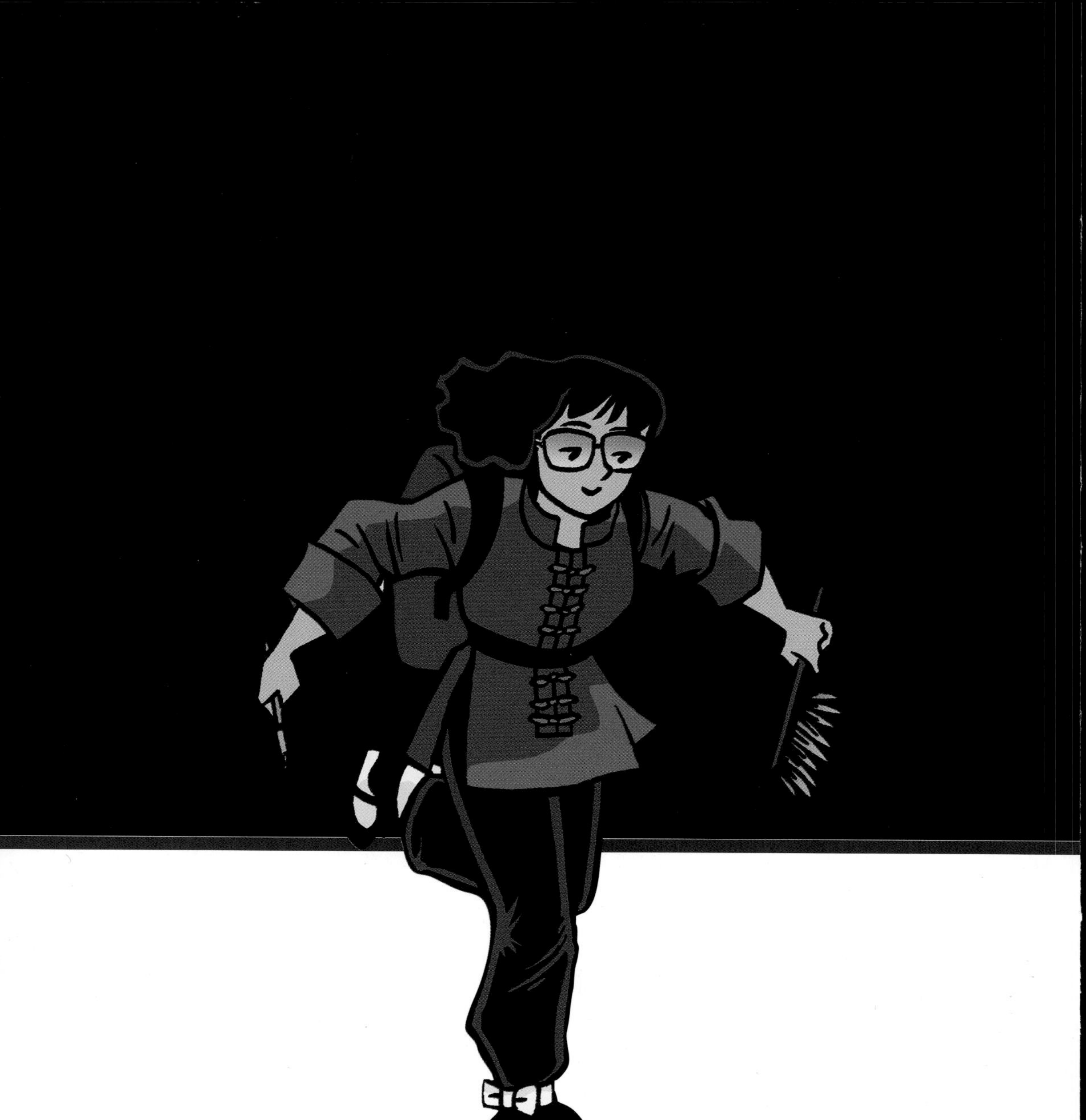

"If people became more gentle in their lives because of my comics, then that would really make me happy. It would be worth all the work and sacrifice in my life so far."

—Rumiko Takahashi

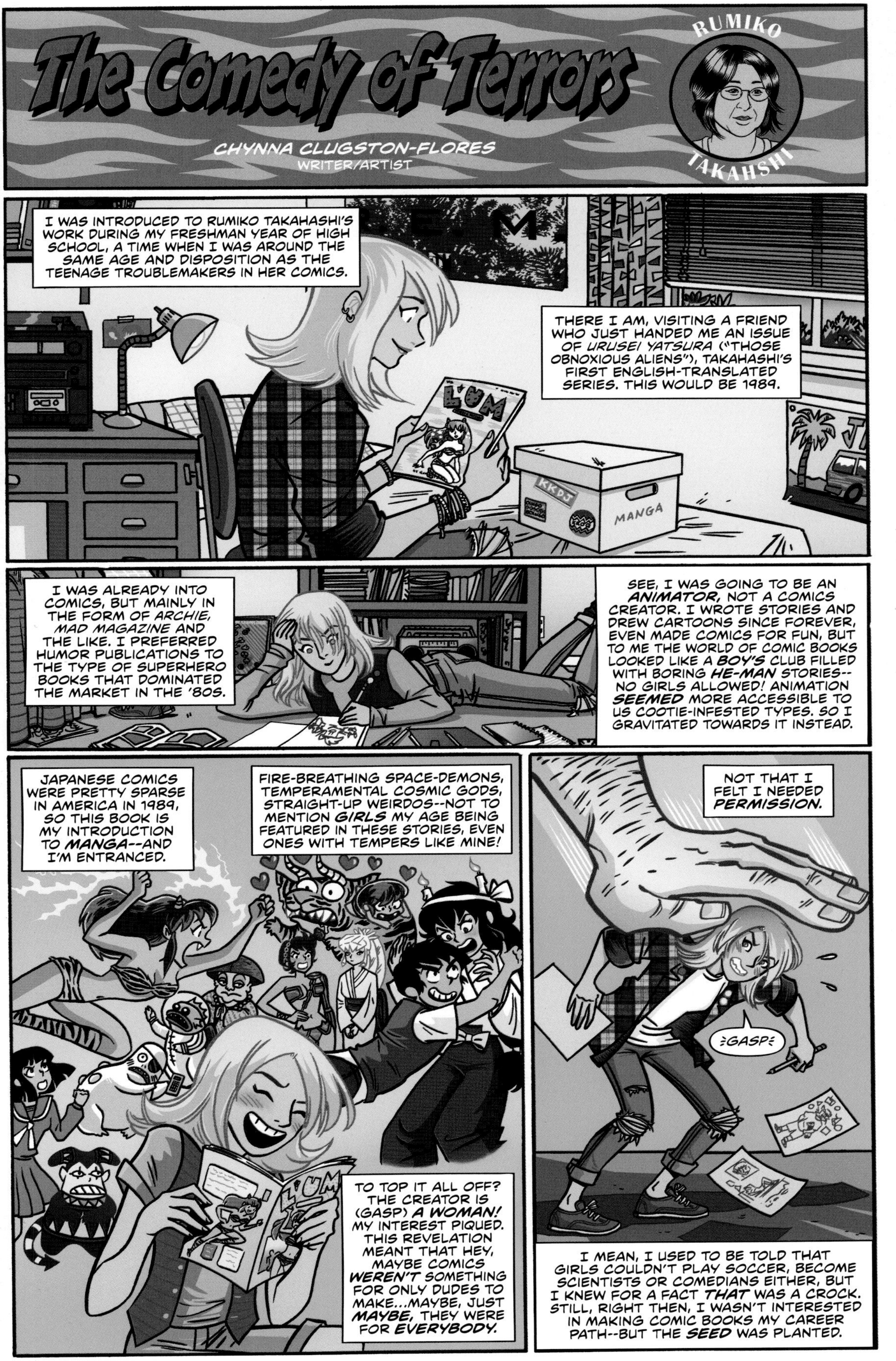
The Comedy of Terrors
RUMIKO TAKAHSHI
CHYNNA CLUGSTON-FLORES
WRITER/ARTIST
I WAS INTRODUCED TO RUMIKO TAKAHASHI'S WORK DURING MY FRESHMAN YEAR OF HIGH SCHOOL, A TIME WHEN I WAS AROUND THE SAME AGE AND DISPOSITION AS THE TEENAGE TROUBLEMAKERS IN HER COMICS.
THERE I AM, VISITING A FRIEND WHO JUST HANDED ME AN ISSUE OF URUSEI YATSURA ("THOSE OBNOXIOUS ALIENS"), TAKAHASHI'S FIRST ENGLISH-TRANSLATED SERIES. THIS WOULD BE 1989.
LUM
MANGA
KKDJ
I WAS ALREADY INTO COMICS, BUT MAINLY IN THE FORM OF ARCHIE, MAD MAGAZINE AND THE LIKE. I PREFERRED HUMOR PUBLICATIONS TO THE TYPE OF SUPERHERO BOOKS THAT DOMINATED THE MARKET IN THE '80S.
SEE, I WAS GOING TO BE AN ANIMATOR, NOT A COMICS CREATOR. I WROTE STORIES AND DREW CARTOONS SINCE FOREVER, EVEN MADE COMICS FOR FUN, BUT TO ME THE WORLD OF COMIC BOOKS LOOKED LIKE A BOY'S CLUB FILLED WITH BORING HE-MAN STORIES--NO GIRLS ALLOWED! ANIMATION SEEMED MORE ACCESSIBLE TO US COOTIE-INFESTED TYPES. SO I GRAVITATED TOWARDS IT INSTEAD.
JAPANESE COMICS WERE PRETTY SPARSE IN AMERICA IN 1989, SO THIS BOOK IS MY INTRODUCTION TO MANGA--AND I'M ENTRANCED.
FIRE-BREATHING SPACE-DEMONS, TEMPERAMENTAL COSMIC GODS, STRAIGHT-UP WEIRDOS--NOT TO MENTION GIRLS MY AGE BEING FEATURED IN THESE STORIES, EVEN ONES WITH TEMPERS LIKE MINE!
TO TOP IT ALL OFF? THE CREATOR IS (GASP) A WOMAN! MY INTEREST PIQUED. THIS REVELATION MEANT THAT HEY, MAYBE COMICS WEREN'T SOMETHING FOR ONLY DUDES TO MAKE...MAYBE, JUST MAYBE, THEY WERE FOR EVERYBODY.
NOT THAT I FELT I NEEDED PERMISSION.
GASP
I MEAN, I USED TO BE TOLD THAT GIRLS COULDN'T PLAY SOCCER, BECOME SCIENTISTS OR COMEDIANS EITHER, BUT I KNEW FOR A FACT THAT WAS A CROCK. STILL, RIGHT THEN, I WASN'T INTERESTED IN MAKING COMIC BOOKS MY CAREER PATH--BUT THE SEED WAS PLANTED.

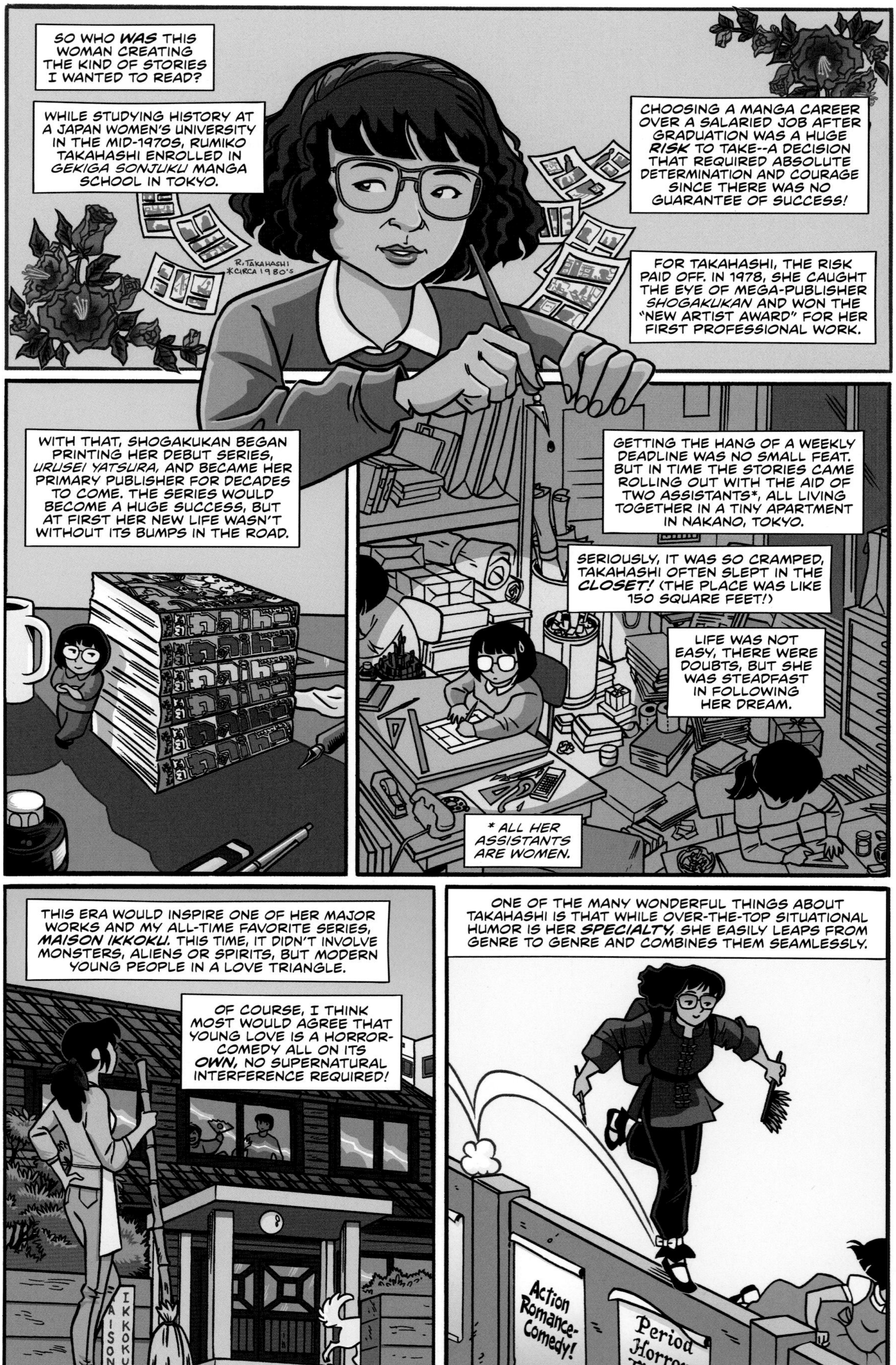
SO WHO *WAS* THIS WOMAN CREATING THE KIND OF STORIES I WANTED TO READ?
WHILE STUDYING HISTORY AT A JAPAN WOMEN'S UNIVERSITY IN THE MID-1970S, RUMIKO TAKAHASHI ENROLLED IN *GEKIGA SONJUKU* MANGA SCHOOL IN TOKYO.
R. TAKAHASHI *CIRCA 1980'S
CHOOSING A MANGA CAREER OVER A SALARIED JOB AFTER GRADUATION WAS A HUGE *RISK* TO TAKE--A DECISION THAT REQUIRED ABSOLUTE DETERMINATION AND COURAGE SINCE THERE WAS NO GUARANTEE OF SUCCESS!
FOR TAKAHASHI, THE RISK PAID OFF. IN 1978, SHE CAUGHT THE EYE OF MEGA-PUBLISHER *SHOGAKUKAN* AND WON THE "NEW ARTIST AWARD" FOR HER FIRST PROFESSIONAL WORK.
WITH THAT, SHOGAKUKAN BEGAN PRINTING HER DEBUT SERIES, *URUSEI YATSURA,* AND BECAME HER PRIMARY PUBLISHER FOR DECADES TO COME. THE SERIES WOULD BECOME A HUGE SUCCESS, BUT AT FIRST HER NEW LIFE WASN'T WITHOUT ITS BUMPS IN THE ROAD.
GETTING THE HANG OF A WEEKLY DEADLINE WAS NO SMALL FEAT. BUT IN TIME THE STORIES CAME ROLLING OUT WITH THE AID OF TWO ASSISTANTS*, ALL LIVING TOGETHER IN A TINY APARTMENT IN NAKANO, TOKYO.
SERIOUSLY, IT WAS SO CRAMPED, TAKAHASHI OFTEN SLEPT IN THE *CLOSET!* (THE PLACE WAS LIKE 150 SQUARE FEET!)
LIFE WAS NOT EASY, THERE WERE DOUBTS, BUT SHE WAS STEADFAST IN FOLLOWING HER DREAM.
* ALL HER ASSISTANTS ARE WOMEN.
THIS ERA WOULD INSPIRE ONE OF HER MAJOR WORKS AND MY ALL-TIME FAVORITE SERIES, ***MAISON IKKOKU.*** THIS TIME, IT DIDN'T INVOLVE MONSTERS, ALIENS OR SPIRITS, BUT MODERN YOUNG PEOPLE IN A LOVE TRIANGLE.
OF COURSE, I THINK MOST WOULD AGREE THAT YOUNG LOVE IS A HORROR-COMEDY ALL ON ITS *OWN,* NO SUPERNATURAL INTERFERENCE REQUIRED!
MAISON IKKOKU
ONE OF THE MANY WONDERFUL THINGS ABOUT TAKAHASHI IS THAT WHILE OVER-THE-TOP SITUATIONAL HUMOR IS HER *SPECIALTY,* SHE EASILY LEAPS FROM GENRE TO GENRE AND COMBINES THEM SEAMLESSLY.
Action Romance-Comedy!
Period Horror

FROM THE BEGINNING OF HER CAREER SHE ALSO WENT AGAINST TYPICAL MANGA *STEREOTYPES* OF THE TIME--HER BRILLIANT CHARACTERIZATION BECAME THE ZENITH OF HER WORLD-RENOWNED TALENT.

WITH SUCH A LARGE, ORIGINAL CAST OF CHARACTERS ALL HER OWN AND UNDENIABLE UNIVERSAL APPEAL, SHE ACHIEVED THE KIND OF CAREER THAT MOST CREATORS COULD ONLY EVER *DREAM* ABOUT.

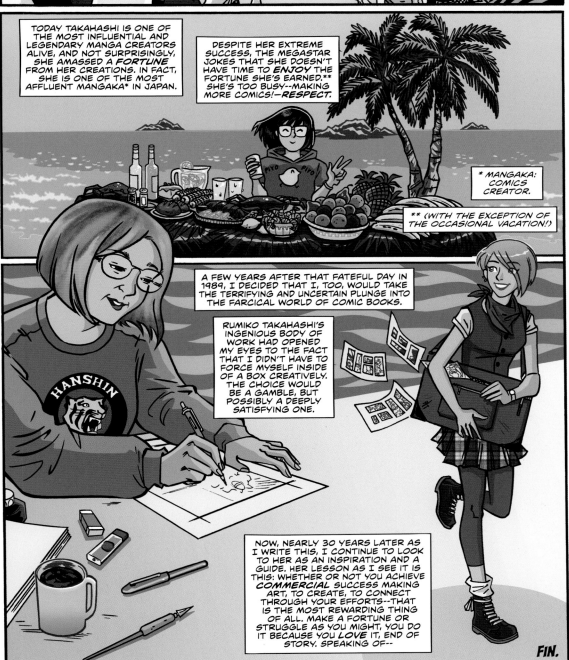

TODAY TAKAHASHI IS ONE OF THE MOST INFLUENTIAL AND LEGENDARY MANGA CREATORS ALIVE, AND NOT SURPRISINGLY, SHE AMASSED A *FORTUNE* FROM HER CREATIONS. IN FACT, SHE IS ONE OF THE MOST AFFLUENT MANGAKA* IN JAPAN.

DESPITE HER EXTREME SUCCESS, THE MEGASTAR JOKES THAT SHE DOESN'T HAVE TIME TO *ENJOY* THE FORTUNE SHE'S EARNED.** SHE'S TOO BUSY--MAKING MORE COMICS!--*RESPECT.*

* MANGAKA: COMICS CREATOR.

** (WITH THE EXCEPTION OF THE OCCASIONAL VACATION!)

A FEW YEARS AFTER THAT FATEFUL DAY IN 1989, I DECIDED THAT I, TOO, WOULD TAKE THE TERRIFYING AND UNCERTAIN PLUNGE INTO THE FARCICAL WORLD OF COMIC BOOKS.

RUMIKO TAKAHASHI'S INGENIOUS BODY OF WORK HAD OPENED MY EYES TO THE FACT THAT I DIDN'T HAVE TO FORCE MYSELF INSIDE OF A BOX CREATIVELY. THE CHOICE WOULD BE A GAMBLE, BUT POSSIBLY A DEEPLY SATISFYING ONE.

NOW, NEARLY 30 YEARS LATER AS I WRITE THIS, I CONTINUE TO LOOK TO HER AS AN INSPIRATION AND A GUIDE. HER LESSON AS I SEE IT IS THIS: WHETHER OR NOT YOU ACHIEVE *COMMERCIAL* SUCCESS MAKING ART, TO CREATE, TO CONNECT THROUGH YOUR EFFORTS--THAT IS THE MOST REWARDING THING OF ALL. MAKE A FORTUNE OR STRUGGLE AS YOU MIGHT, YOU DO IT BECAUSE YOU *LOVE* IT, END OF STORY. SPEAKING OF--

FIN.

"Go out there, have adventures and regret nothing."

—Cindy Whitehead

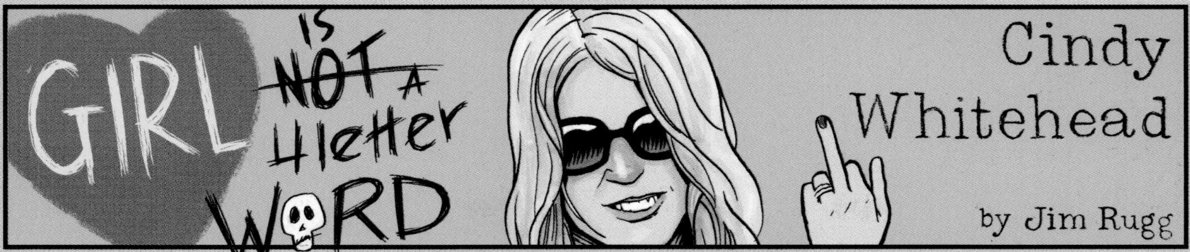
GIRL IS ~~NOT~~ A 4letter WORD
Cindy Whitehead
by Jim Rugg

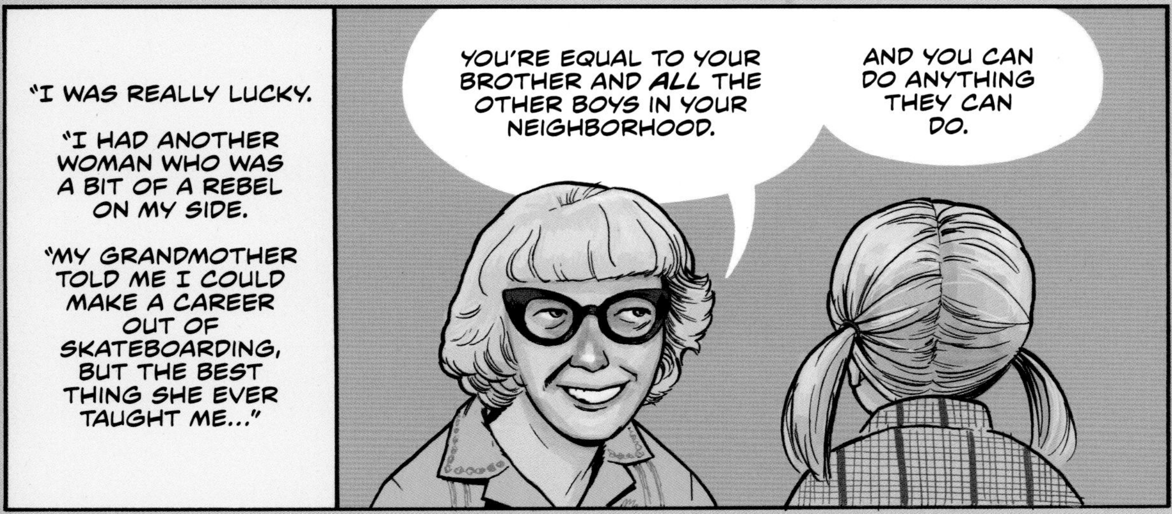
"I WAS REALLY LUCKY.
"I HAD ANOTHER WOMAN WHO WAS A BIT OF A REBEL ON MY SIDE.
"MY GRANDMOTHER TOLD ME I COULD MAKE A CAREER OUT OF SKATEBOARDING, BUT THE BEST THING SHE EVER TAUGHT ME..."
YOU'RE EQUAL TO YOUR BROTHER AND *ALL* THE OTHER BOYS IN YOUR NEIGHBORHOOD.
AND YOU CAN DO ANYTHING THEY CAN DO.

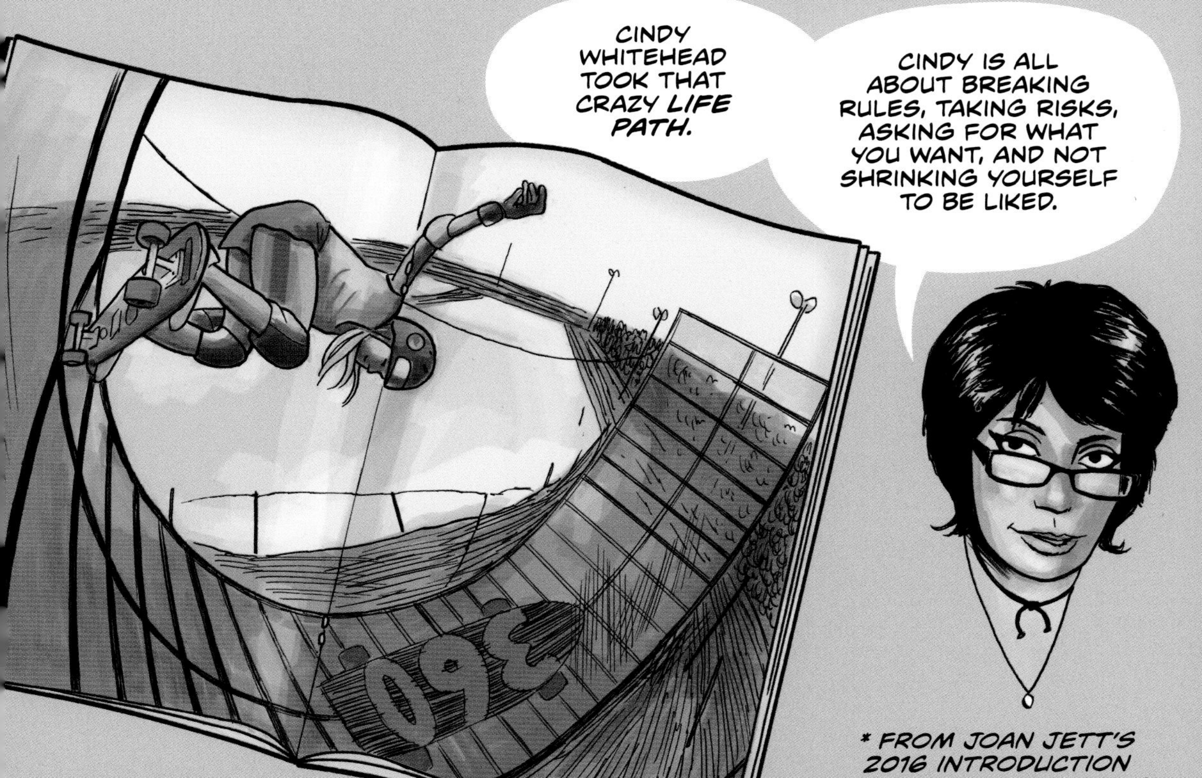
CINDY WHITEHEAD TOOK THAT CRAZY *LIFE PATH.*
CINDY IS ALL ABOUT BREAKING RULES, TAKING RISKS, ASKING FOR WHAT YOU WANT, AND NOT SHRINKING YOURSELF TO BE LIKED.
360
WILD WORLD OF SKATEBOARDING JUNE 1978.
* FROM JOAN JETT'S 2016 INTRODUCTION AT CINDY WHITEHEAD'S SKATEBOARD HALL OF FAME INDUCTION.

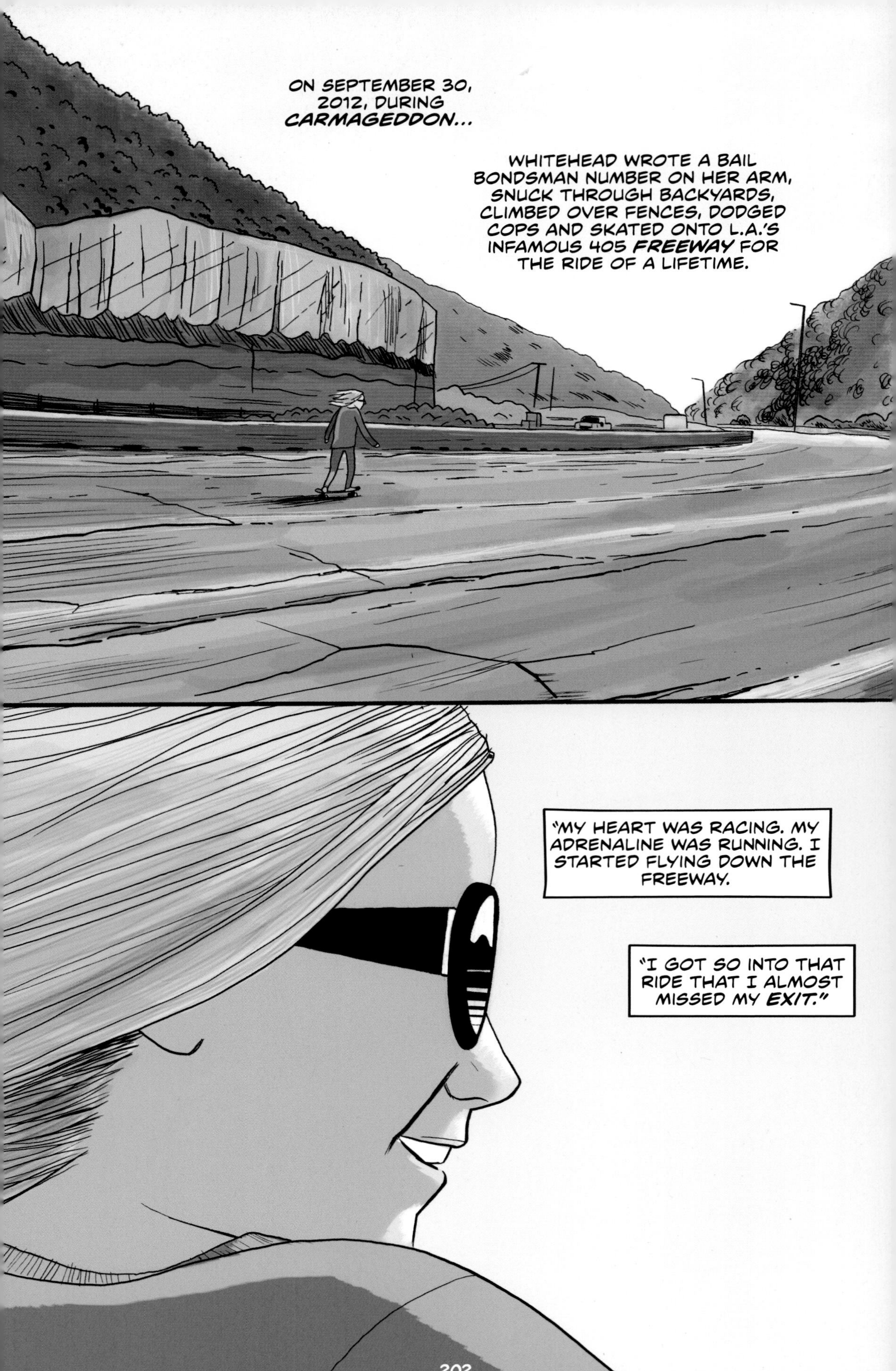

ON SEPTEMBER 30, 2012, DURING *CARMAGEDDON...*
WHITEHEAD WROTE A BAIL BONDSMAN NUMBER ON HER ARM, SNUCK THROUGH BACKYARDS, CLIMBED OVER FENCES, DODGED COPS AND SKATED ONTO L.A.'S INFAMOUS 405 *FREEWAY* FOR THE RIDE OF A LIFETIME.
"MY HEART WAS RACING. MY ADRENALINE WAS RUNNING. I STARTED FLYING DOWN THE FREEWAY.
"I GOT SO INTO THAT RIDE THAT I ALMOST MISSED MY *EXIT*."

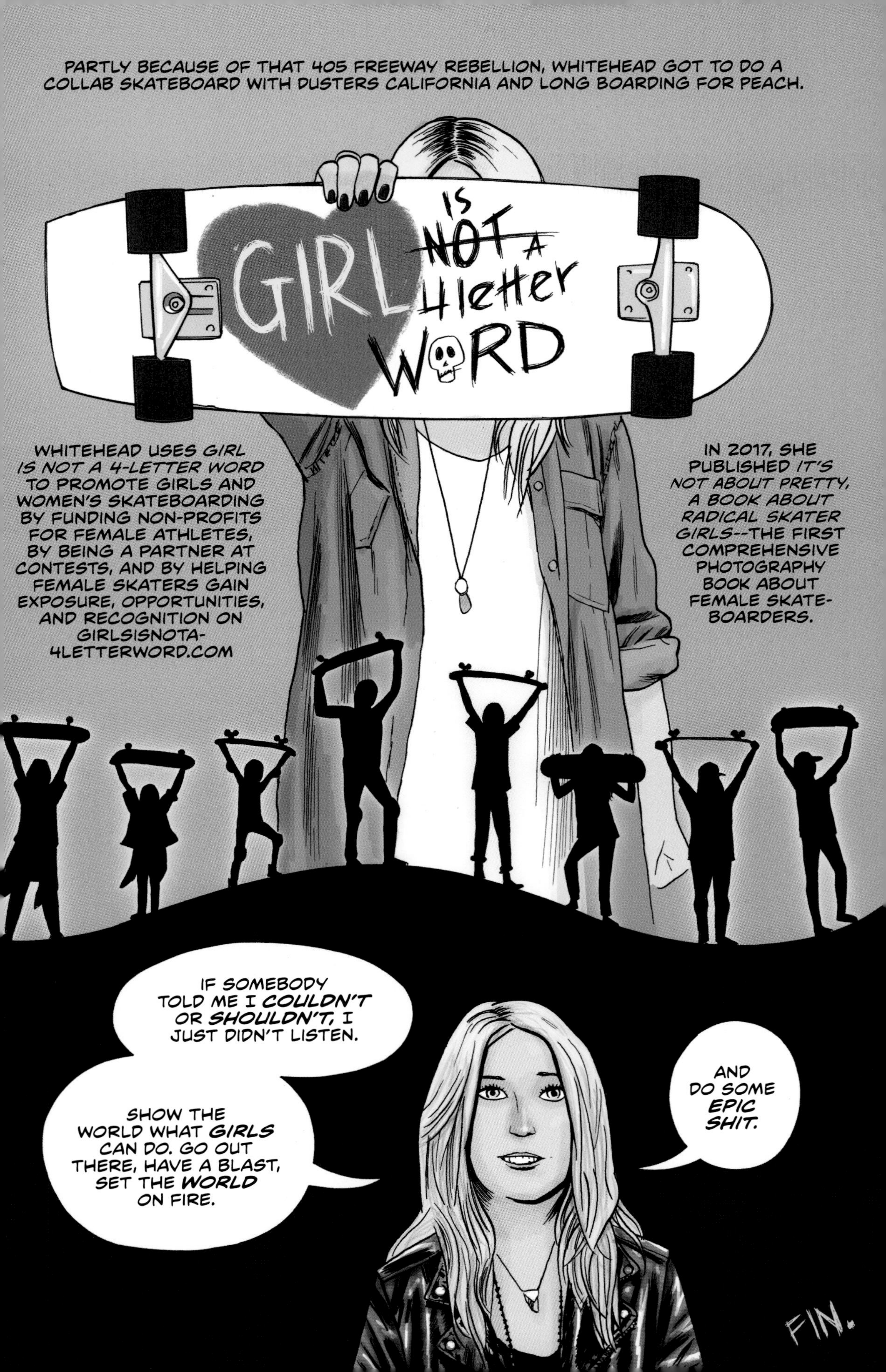
PARTLY BECAUSE OF THAT 405 FREEWAY REBELLION, WHITEHEAD GOT TO DO A COLLAB SKATEBOARD WITH DUSTERS CALIFORNIA AND LONG BOARDING FOR PEACH.
GIRL IS NOT A 4 letter WORD
WHITEHEAD USES GIRL IS NOT A 4-LETTER WORD TO PROMOTE GIRLS AND WOMEN'S SKATEBOARDING BY FUNDING NON-PROFITS FOR FEMALE ATHLETES, BY BEING A PARTNER AT CONTESTS, AND BY HELPING FEMALE SKATERS GAIN EXPOSURE, OPPORTUNITIES, AND RECOGNITION ON GIRLSISNOTA-4LETTERWORD.COM
IN 2017, SHE PUBLISHED IT'S NOT ABOUT PRETTY, A BOOK ABOUT RADICAL SKATER GIRLS--THE FIRST COMPREHENSIVE PHOTOGRAPHY BOOK ABOUT FEMALE SKATE-BOARDERS.
IF SOMEBODY TOLD ME I COULDN'T OR SHOULDN'T, I JUST DIDN'T LISTEN.
SHOW THE WORLD WHAT GIRLS CAN DO. GO OUT THERE, HAVE A BLAST, SET THE WORLD ON FIRE.
AND DO SOME EPIC SHIT.
FIN.

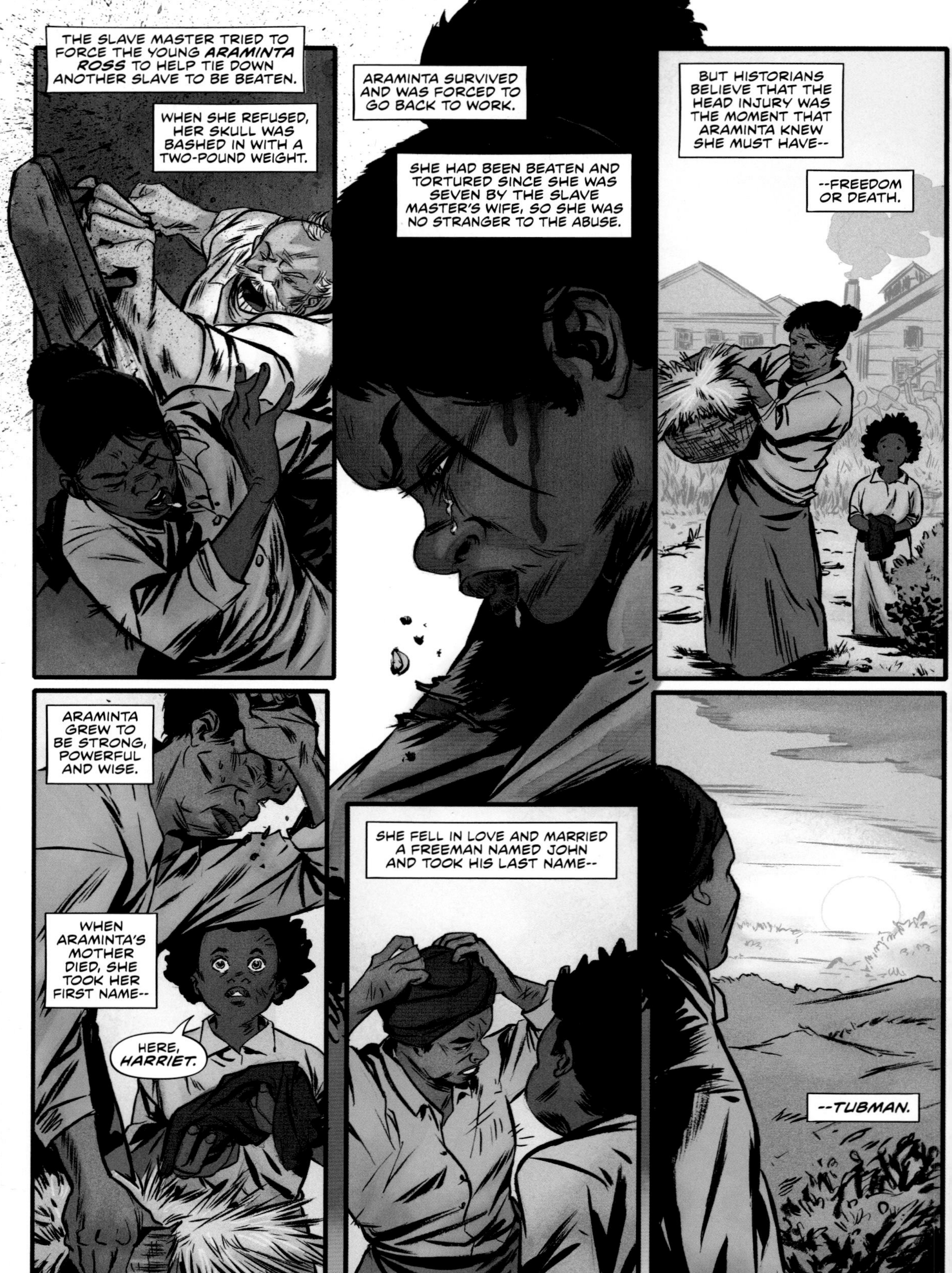

THE SLAVE MASTER TRIED TO FORCE THE YOUNG ARAMINTA ROSS TO HELP TIE DOWN ANOTHER SLAVE TO BE BEATEN.
WHEN SHE REFUSED, HER SKULL WAS BASHED IN WITH A TWO-POUND WEIGHT.
ARAMINTA SURVIVED AND WAS FORCED TO GO BACK TO WORK.
SHE HAD BEEN BEATEN AND TORTURED SINCE SHE WAS SEVEN BY THE SLAVE MASTER'S WIFE, SO SHE WAS NO STRANGER TO THE ABUSE.
BUT HISTORIANS BELIEVE THAT THE HEAD INJURY WAS THE MOMENT THAT ARAMINTA KNEW SHE MUST HAVE--
--FREEDOM OR DEATH.
ARAMINTA GREW TO BE STRONG, POWERFUL AND WISE.
WHEN ARAMINTA'S MOTHER DIED, SHE TOOK HER FIRST NAME--
HERE, HARRIET.
SHE FELL IN LOVE AND MARRIED A FREEMAN NAMED JOHN AND TOOK HIS LAST NAME--
--TUBMAN.

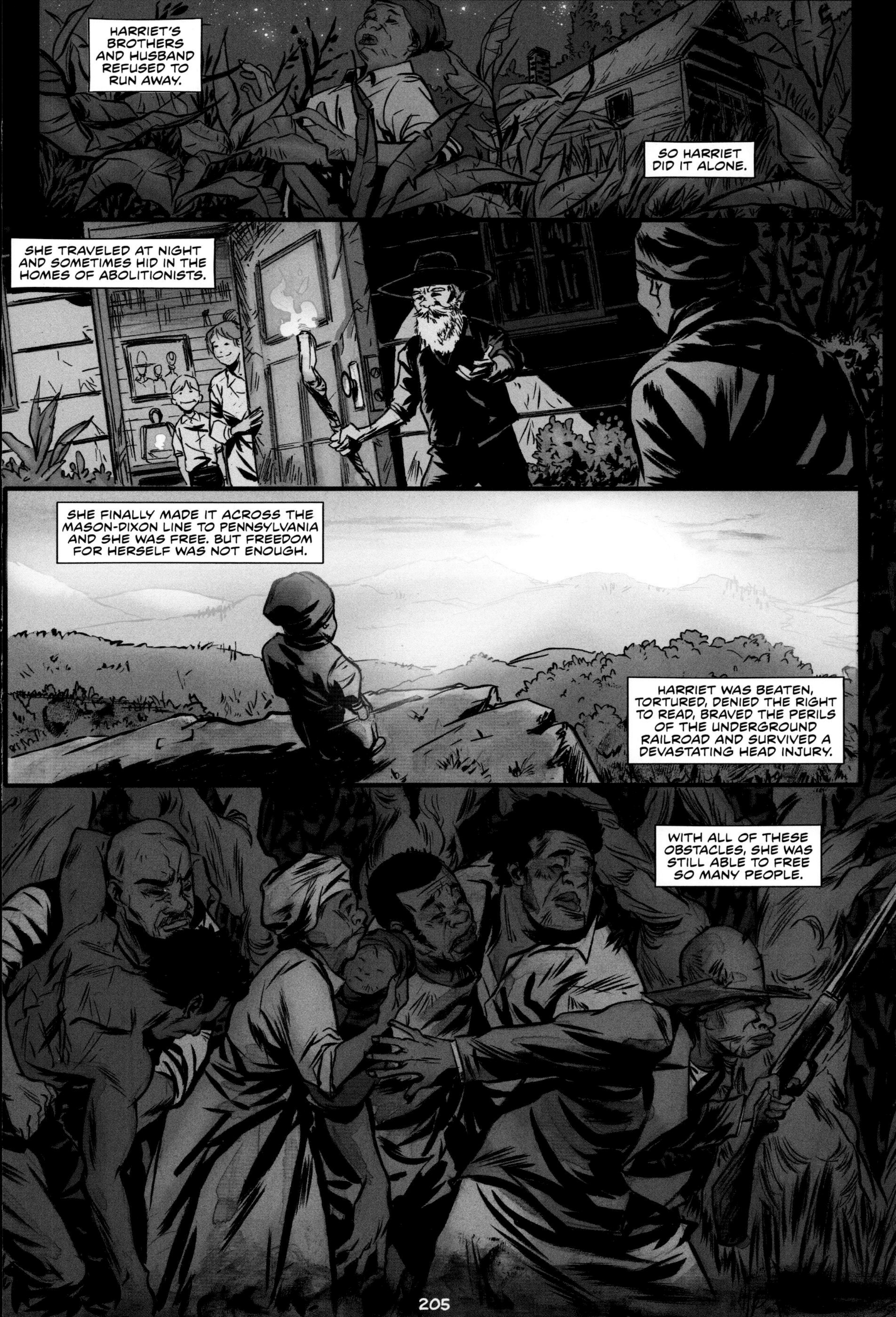
HARRIET'S BROTHERS AND HUSBAND REFUSED TO RUN AWAY.
SO HARRIET DID IT ALONE.
SHE TRAVELED AT NIGHT AND SOMETIMES HID IN THE HOMES OF ABOLITIONISTS.
SHE FINALLY MADE IT ACROSS THE MASON-DIXON LINE TO PENNSYLVANIA AND SHE WAS FREE. BUT FREEDOM FOR HERSELF WAS NOT ENOUGH.
HARRIET WAS BEATEN, TORTURED, DENIED THE RIGHT TO READ, BRAVED THE PERILS OF THE UNDERGROUND RAILROAD AND SURVIVED A DEVASTATING HEAD INJURY.
WITH ALL OF THESE OBSTACLES, SHE WAS STILL ABLE TO FREE SO MANY PEOPLE.

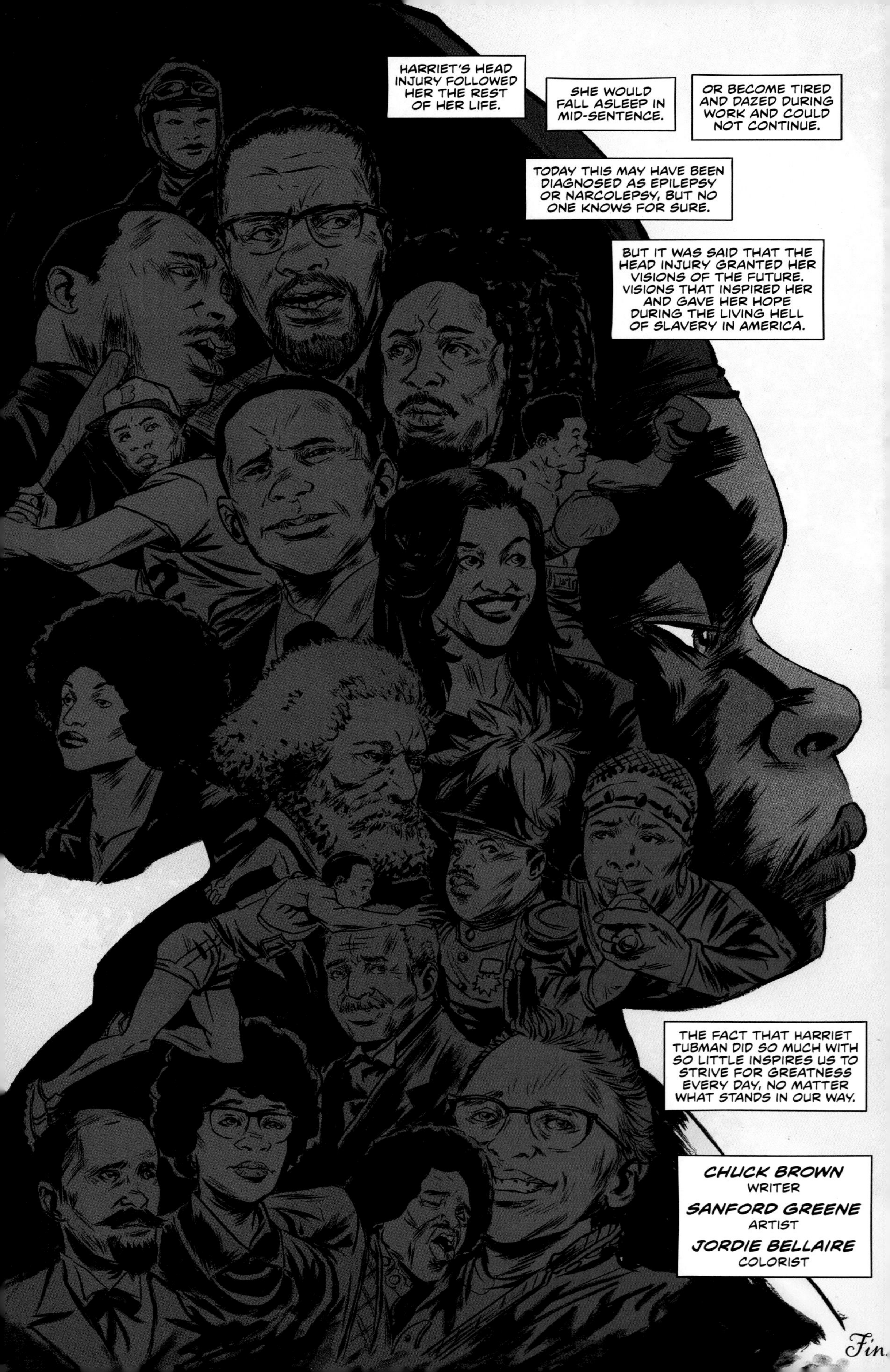
HARRIET'S HEAD INJURY FOLLOWED HER THE REST OF HER LIFE.
SHE WOULD FALL ASLEEP IN MID-SENTENCE.
OR BECOME TIRED AND DAZED DURING WORK AND COULD NOT CONTINUE.
TODAY THIS MAY HAVE BEEN DIAGNOSED AS EPILEPSY OR NARCOLEPSY, BUT NO ONE KNOWS FOR SURE.
BUT IT WAS SAID THAT THE HEAD INJURY GRANTED HER VISIONS OF THE FUTURE. VISIONS THAT INSPIRED HER AND GAVE HER HOPE DURING THE LIVING HELL OF SLAVERY IN AMERICA.
THE FACT THAT HARRIET TUBMAN DID SO MUCH WITH SO LITTLE INSPIRES US TO STRIVE FOR GREATNESS EVERY DAY, NO MATTER WHAT STANDS IN OUR WAY.
CHUCK BROWN
WRITER
SANFORD GREENE
ARTIST
JORDIE BELLAIRE
COLORIST
Fin.

"I had reasoned this out in my mind; there was one of two things I had a right to: liberty or death. If I could not have one, I would have the other; for no man should take me alive; I should fight for my liberty as long as my strength lasted, and when the time came for me to go, the Lord would let them take me."

—Harriet Tubman

BONUS MATERIAL

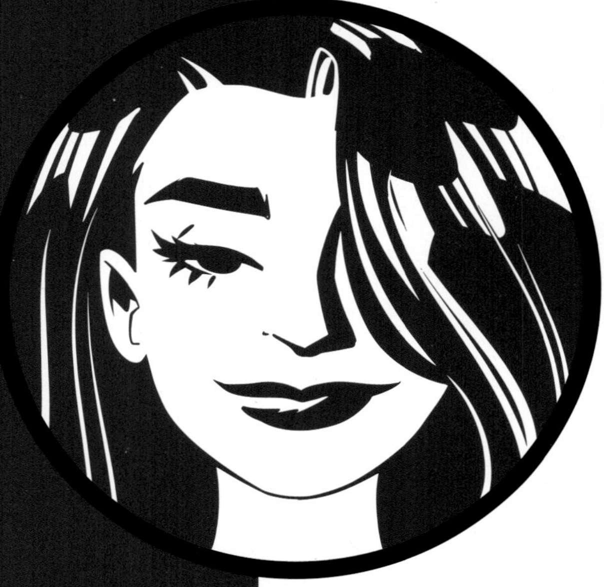

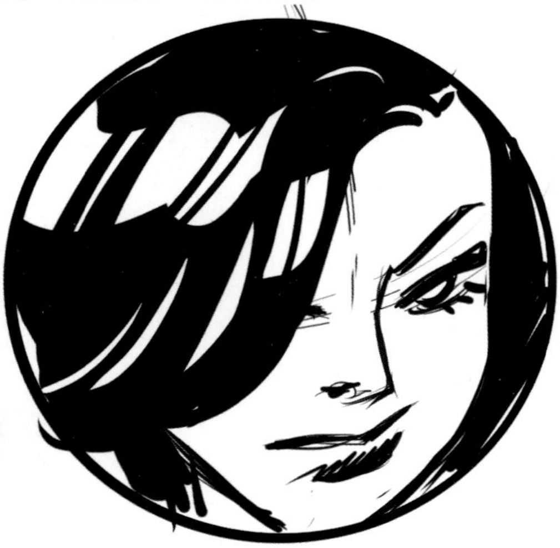

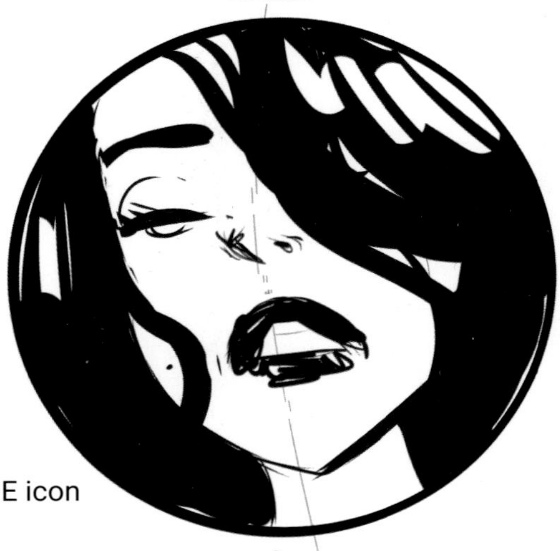

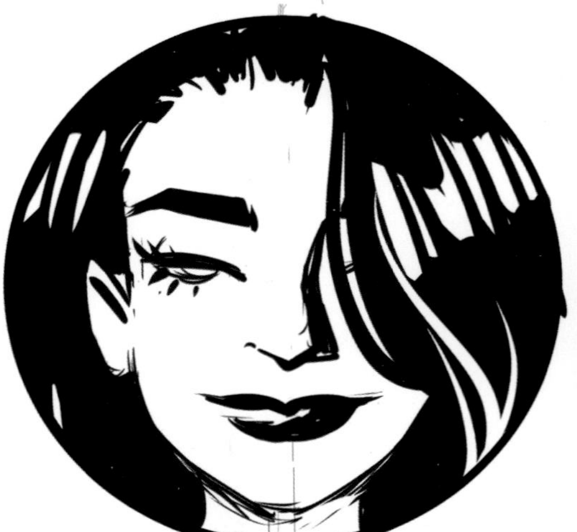

Original FEMME MAGNIFIQUE icon sketches by Elsa Charretier

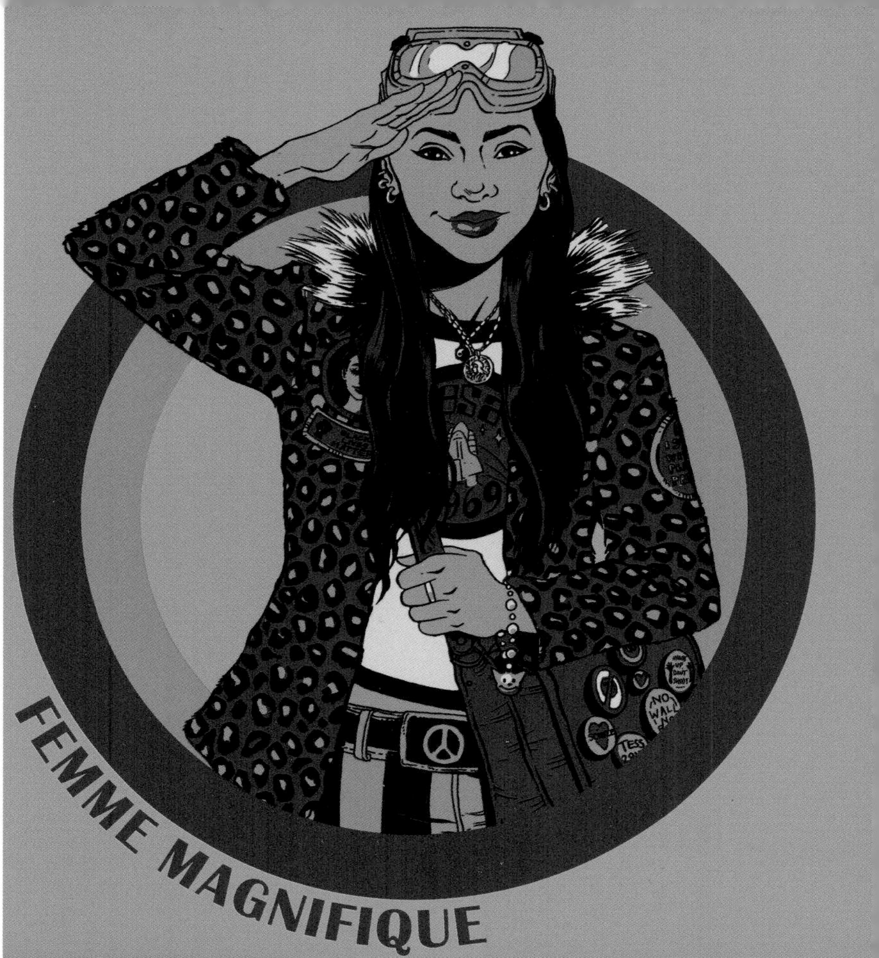
FEMME MAGNIFIQUE

Threadless
T-shirt designs
by Tess Fowler
and Philip Bond

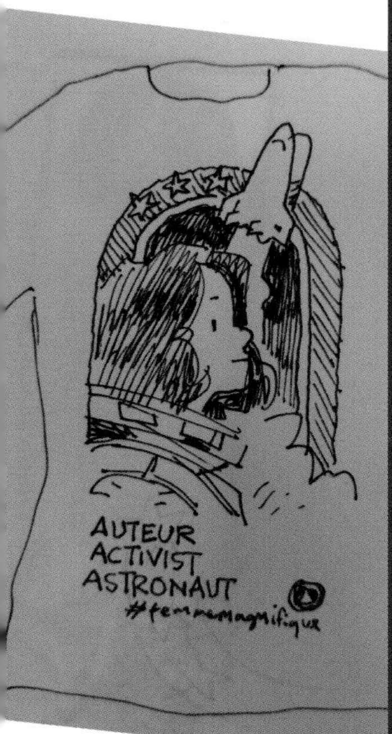
AUTEUR
ACTIVIST
ASTRONAUT
#femmemagnifique

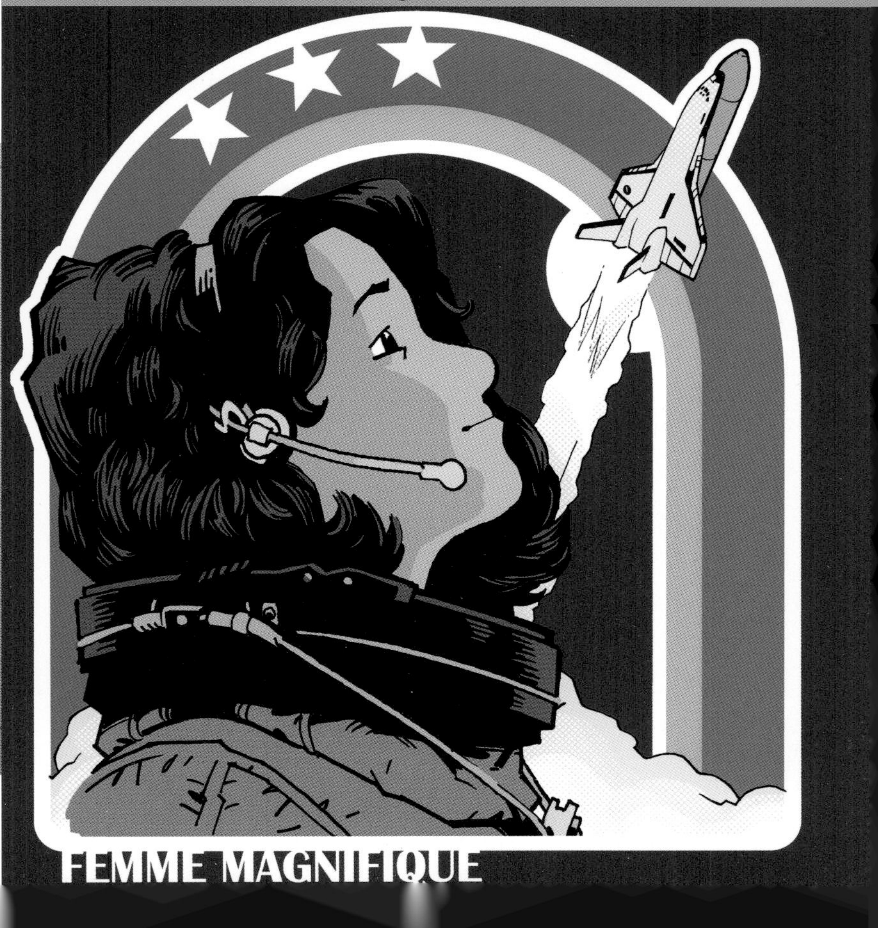
FEMME MAGNIFIQUE

"I'll tell you what freedom is to me: No fear."
—Nina Simone

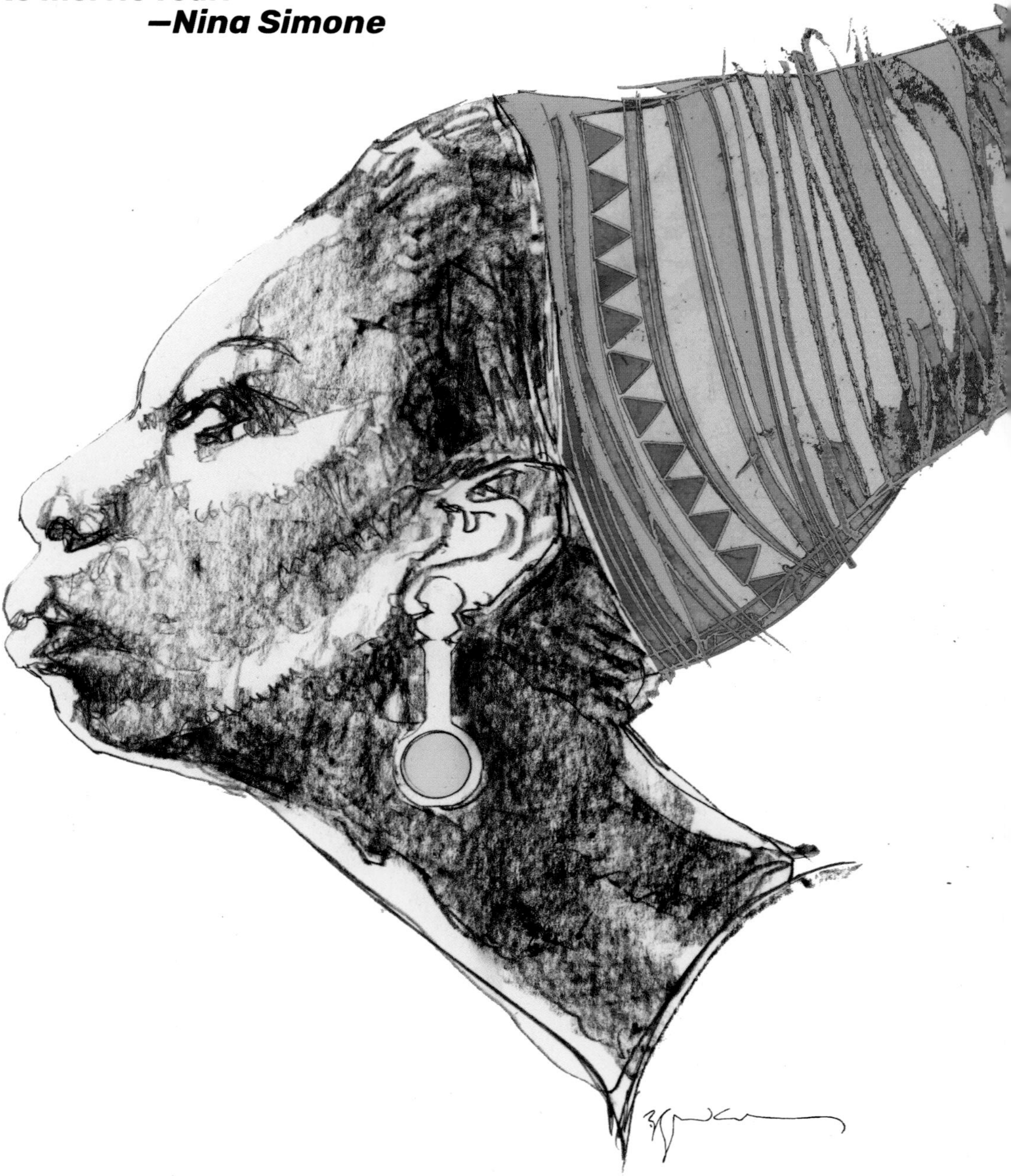

Character studies by Bill Sienkiewicz

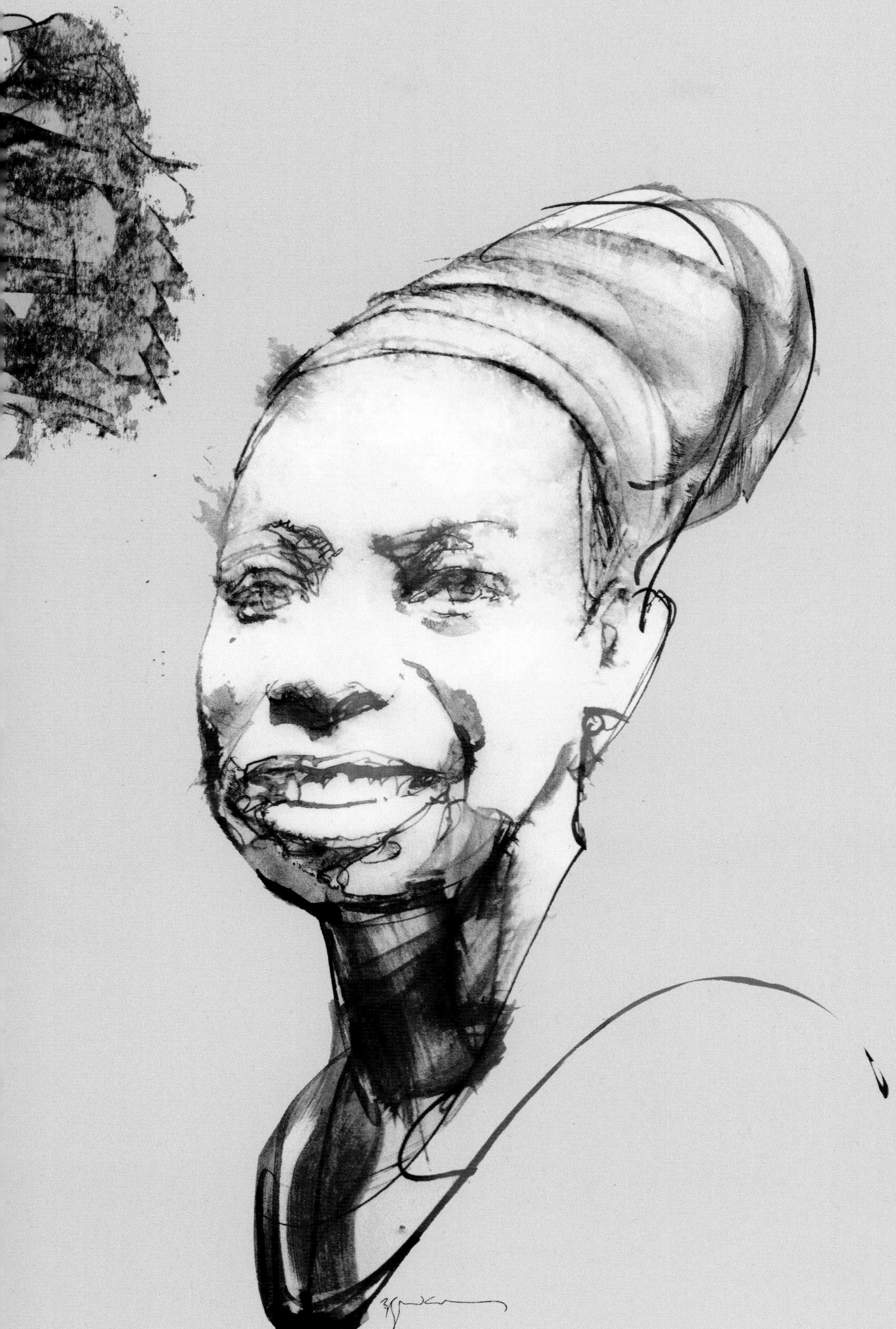

Mary Anning development sketches
by Shawn McManus

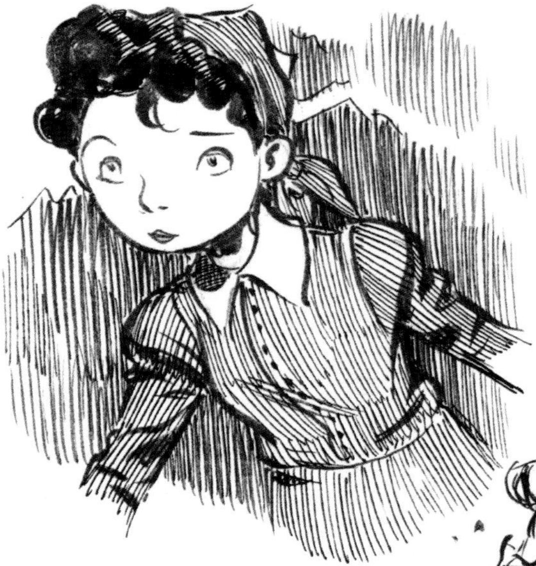

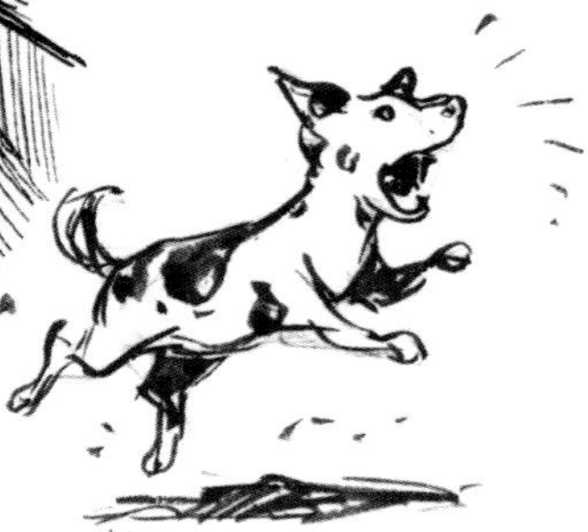

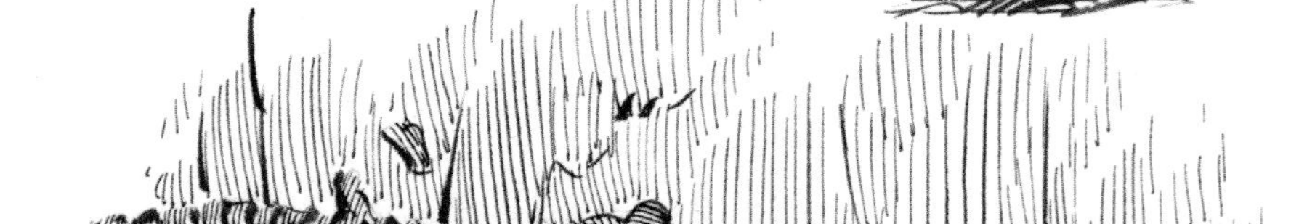

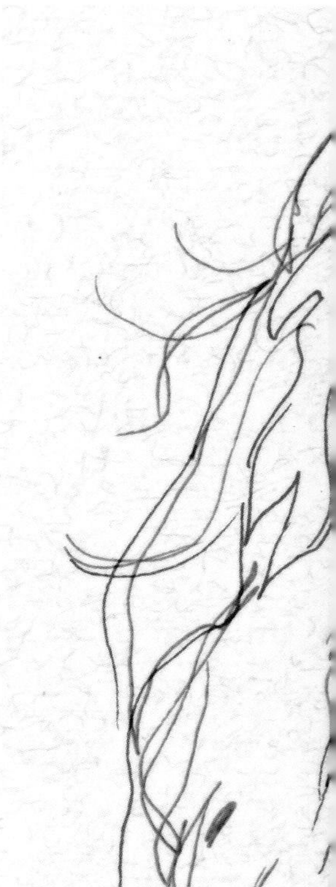
KATE BUSH!

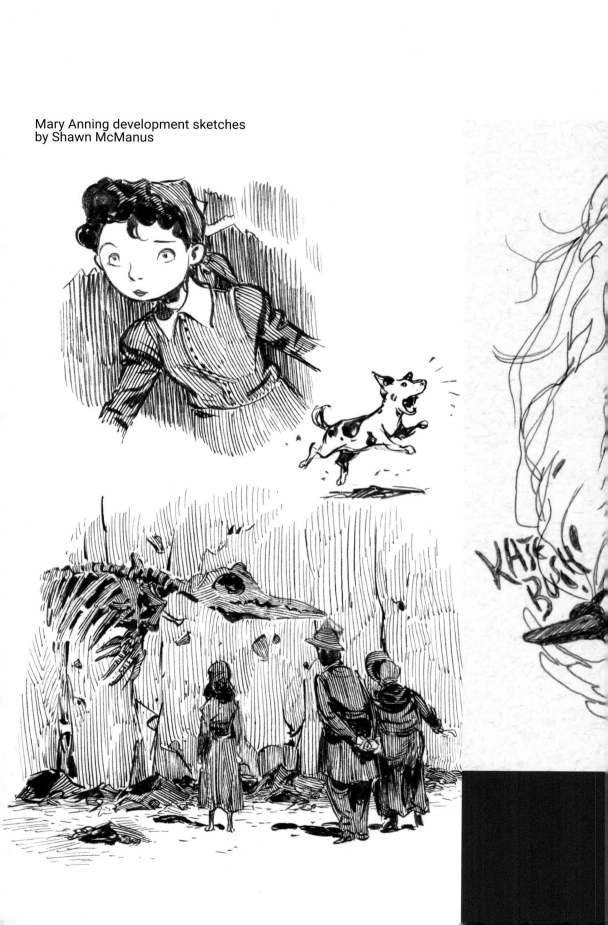

Kate Bush character sketches
by Marguerite Sauvage

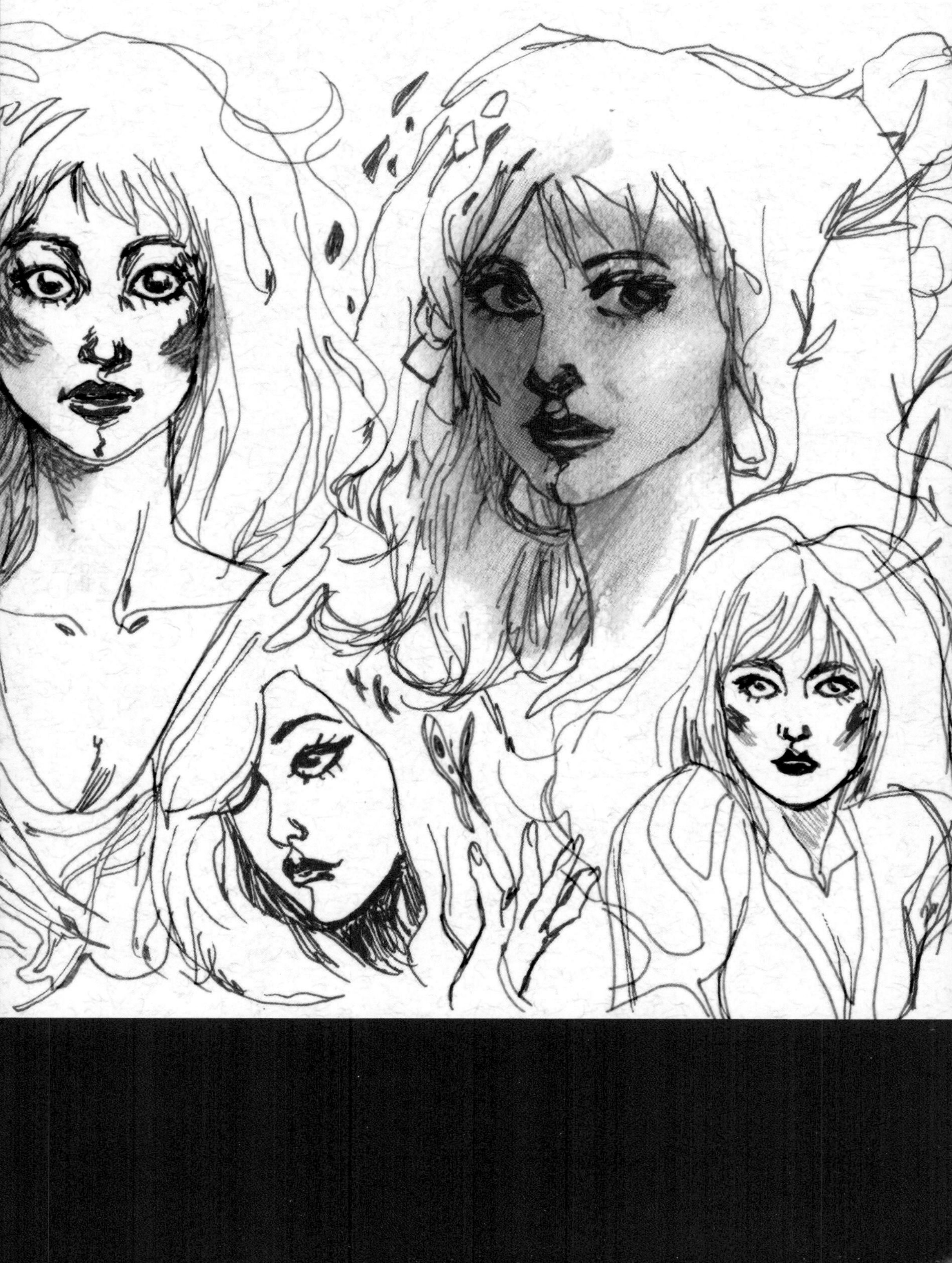

What Does a Feminist Look Like?

by Kristy Miller

Every year, on the campus where I teach in Arizona, during Women's History Month students hand out buttons that say "This is what a feminist looks like!" By the time the end of March rolls around, practically everyone on campus is wearing one. Most of the students don't realize what a powerful image this is until I point it out. Our campus is full of people from all walks of life. We are very diverse, and by wearing those buttons they believe themselves to be feminists. We all look like feminists.

On July 19, 1848 Lucretia Mott and Elizabeth Cady Stanton organized the Seneca Falls Convention. This was the first women's rights convention held in the United States. I think we sometimes forget that the second day of the convention was open to everyone no matter their sex or race. Approximately 40 men attended that convention, some of them also abolitionists (like Frederick Douglass) who were fighting for equality for all people. Men look like feminists.

Seneca Falls led to more and more conventions, and finally in 1920 the 19th Amendment was passed. Women rejoiced in winning only to discover that the right to vote gave them very few additional rights. As so many have learned, voting does not mean equality. World War II gave women a taste of control and freedom because they were needed for jobs they were not normally allowed to pursue. After the war was over, women were encouraged to go back home and let men handle everything. Do we still look like feminists?

Betty Friedan wrote *The Feminine Mystique* in 1963, a groundbreaking and controversial study where she argued that women in the 1950s were pressured into becoming housewives. Friedan argued that women were not given the chance to find their own identities and the idea of a domestic life was a detriment to all women. Friedan's ideas of women finding themselves and their own identities was very powerful and pushed many women back out into the world. However, many people feel *The Feminine Mystique* is very myopic; it ignores the struggles of most women and focuses on middle class, white women. Friedan's book is considered the start of Second Wave Feminism and although she made good points, she needed to cast a wider net. In 1984 bell hooks wrote *From Margin to Center*, a counterpoint to *The Feminine Mystique* in which hooks focused on "intersectionality," or the point where race and gender meet and the struggles caused by both. Feminism looks like different things to different people.

Rebecca Walker is given credit for coining the phrase Third Wave Feminism, when she wrote an article about the Anita Hill case in 1992. Third Wave Feminism branches from hook's ideas of intersection, that ALL women from ALL backgrounds are equal and should be treated as such. Third Wave Feminism is all about diversity. Men and women from all races, sexes, ethnic backgrounds, religions, sexual orientation, and others can all find a comfortable home in the third wave. We are still living in Third Wave Feminism, but some say the Fourth Wave is just around the corner. We may not always agree, but we all look like feminists.

Let us not forget that the Equal Rights Amendment has never passed. Women are still treated unequally at work, at school, at home, in reproductive rights, in religion, in practically all aspects of our lives. Although we make up half the world population we are still considered a minority. As long as there is inequality there will be feminism. We may have "come a long way, baby," but there is still so much further to go. The only way to get true equality for everyone is for everyone to fight for true equality. We must all look like feminists all the time.

Kristy Miller, BA, MA, PhD Candidate
Adjunct Faculty, Anthropology & Women's Studies

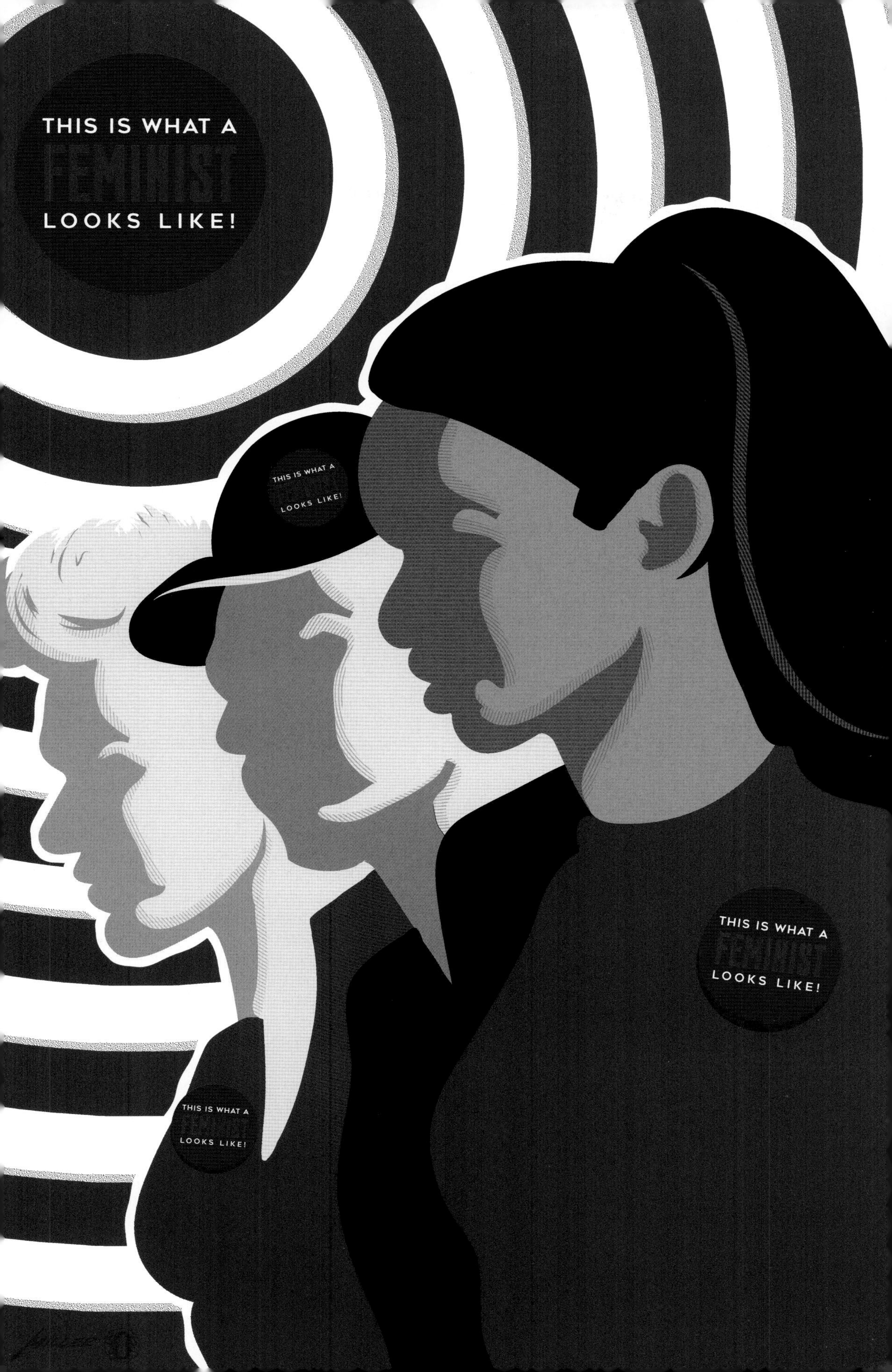
THIS IS WHAT A
FEMINIST
LOOKS LIKE!
THIS IS WHAT A
FEMINIST
LOOKS LIKE!
THIS IS WHAT A
FEMINIST
LOOKS LIKE!
THIS IS WHAT A
FEMINIST
LOOKS LIKE!

Trust the Witch: Why I Love Lydia by Cathi Unsworth

Her face stared up at me from inside the mangled remains of an automobile. Penetrating eyes stared a challenge as her lips curled in a snarl, perfect features on a china-white face framed by a shock of hair the colour of midnight. Beside her, a Goth Clyde to her black-clad Bonnie, a louche Nick Cave unfurled his spidery limbs, eyes narrowed against his cigarette smoke. It was 1981. She was the Queen of Siam and I was a gauche teenage hick with no friends who lived in the middle of a field. Still she spoke to me, direct from New York City to Nowhere in Norfolk, England, with that gaze.

I ripped her out of the NME [New Musical Expression] and put her on my wall.

"For those who don't have a voice, I lend mine. I'm saying the things that need to be said for myself and for other people who are afflicted with the same curse, the curse of being too sensitive to this life."

Over a decade passed. To my own disbelief, this former land girl was now working for the music press in London, a career I wouldn't even have dared dreaming of as I shared those long evenings with John Peel on the radio and the inky face of my heroine gazing down from the bedroom wall. I had got to know her music well, starting with the double death disc *The Agony is the Ecstacy/Drunk on the Pope's Blood* that picture had illustrated. Currently, I intoxicated myself with nightly doses of her *Shotgun Wedding* LP, wherein The Birthday Party's angular guitar genius Rowland S Howard replaced his former lead singer as Clyde, lending his shivering strings to Lydia's tales of Deep South delirium. It was 1993, I was writing the singles column for *Melody Maker*... and what was this beauty?

The Clawfist Singles Club: *Unearthly Delights* by Lydia Lunch.

That face again. This time a back view, looking over her tattooed shoulders, her torso tapering down to a narrow waist and then transmogrifying into a hand, like Thing in *The Addams Family*, scuttling her away. An image created by JK Potter, she later told me, in the garden of The Earl of Lonsdale public house on Portobello Road. My review of this single brought us together for the first time. The Goddess made flesh sat in front of me, her piercing eyes more blue than I could ever have imagined, as she explained the purpose of the heady mantra contained within those black vinyl grooves; the inevitable revenge of Mother Nature against those that had defiled her.

"When you are surrounded by death you either roll into the grave or you dance upon it in a wild dervish – and most of us chose the dance."

Lydia talks in pure prose, I discovered. Every sentence that dropped from those red lips was perfectly crafted as lines in a novel, exquisitely rendered with irresistible humour, wisdom and the devastating ability to cut right to the chase. This is why her spoken word stuns and why her albums feel like great works of *noir* fiction. It's not just her affinity with the music of the marginalized, brutalized and ignored – the jazz echoes, hip-hop hypnosis, swamp witch blues, truck-stop country and Latino grooves that she has fused and used for her ever-mutating soundtracks – it is the precision with which she uses language. Feeding into that, the mediumistic empathy she has for those on the receiving end of violence and injustice, fueled by her infinite rage against the eternal patriarchal war machine of society.

"For some reason as an ultimate survival skill, my instinct for timing is reflected in all my work. It's what drives me, this internal mechanism that, trusting my instinct as I do, tells me when to end a relationship, when to end that drug, when to end that city, when to end that band and when to go on."

Shortly after our first interview, I went to Brighton with my friend Billy Chainsaw to watch Lydia in a club called Do Tongues. As she began her performance, my world went Cinemascope. The room before me stretched into a line running through a black backdrop, which, as it got longer and longer and thinner and thinner, turned from colour into black and white. Within seconds it had become no more than a white ribbon that abruptly pinged into a tiny dot, just like an analogue TV turning itself off. Thinking in that instant that the plug had been pulled on my own life, I passed out on top of the unfortunate Billy. I have never fainted before or since, and this I put down to Lydia's magick – This Night Has Opened My Third Eye.

I saw things differently after that; sought out knowledge with the same kind of thirst I have seen Lydia apply to every aspect of her creativity. Her words shaped very clearly what I felt I should do

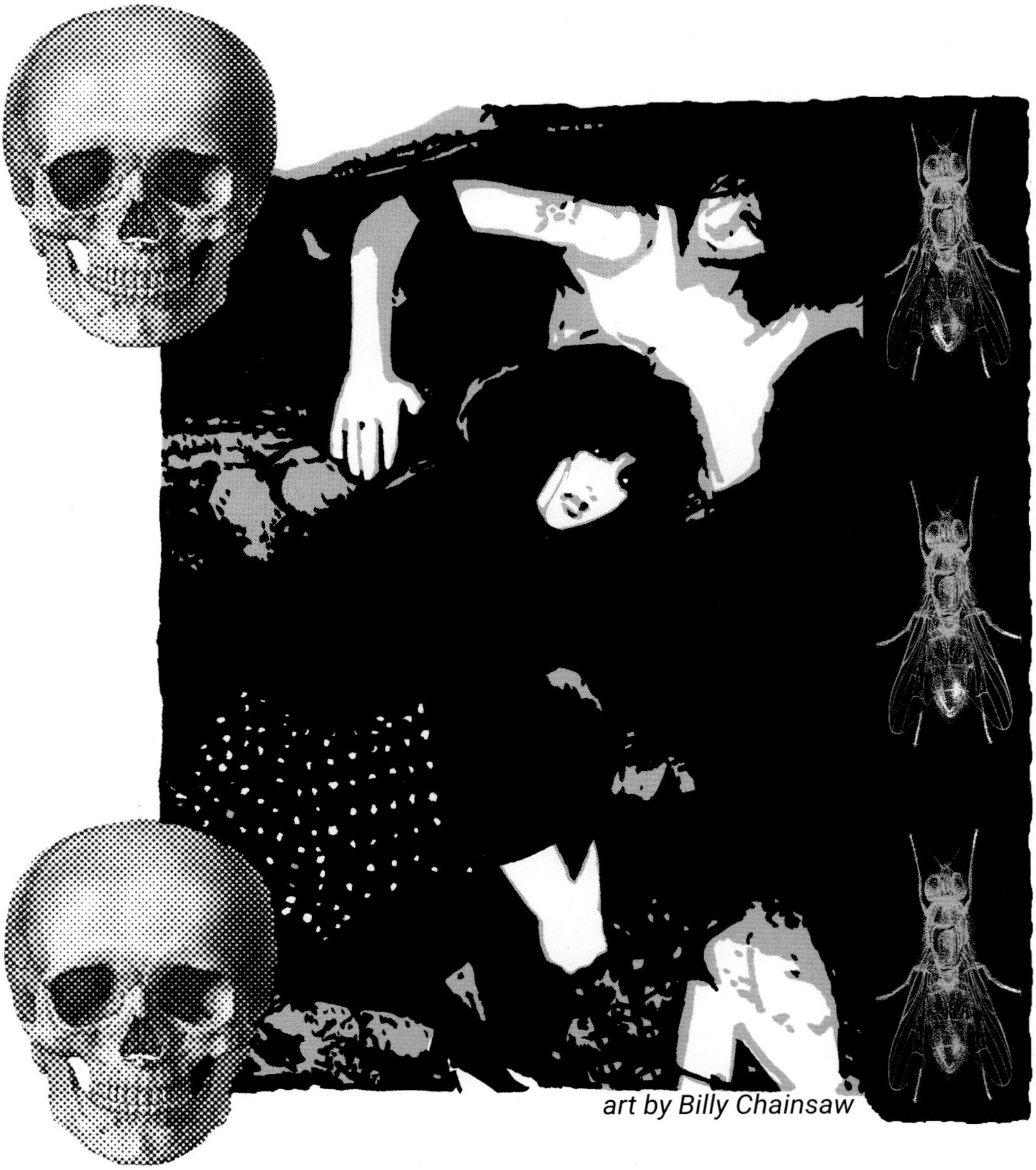

art by Billy Chainsaw

with my own work – become a voice for those who have had theirs taken away, inhabit the shadow realm of the brutalized, the marginalized and the dead, and try to make some kind of valediction for lives left buried in the dirt. The six crime fiction novels I have written since the night I got the Evangelist's Blessing have Lydia's lipstick traces all over them – they are not just a catalogue of inhumanity but of the saving graces of friendship, creativity and love that bring us together and deliver us from the void.

"A point that is within everything I do is that, in times of war – and it's always a time of war – women especially need to seek out more pleasure. Because it's the first thing they steal from us and it's exactly what their fear campaigns intend to steal from us – you never have a moment's peace or pleasure."

Thank you, Lydia.

[Lydia's quotes taken from interviews with the author from 1993-2017]

Afterword by Shelly Bond with art by Lee Garbett

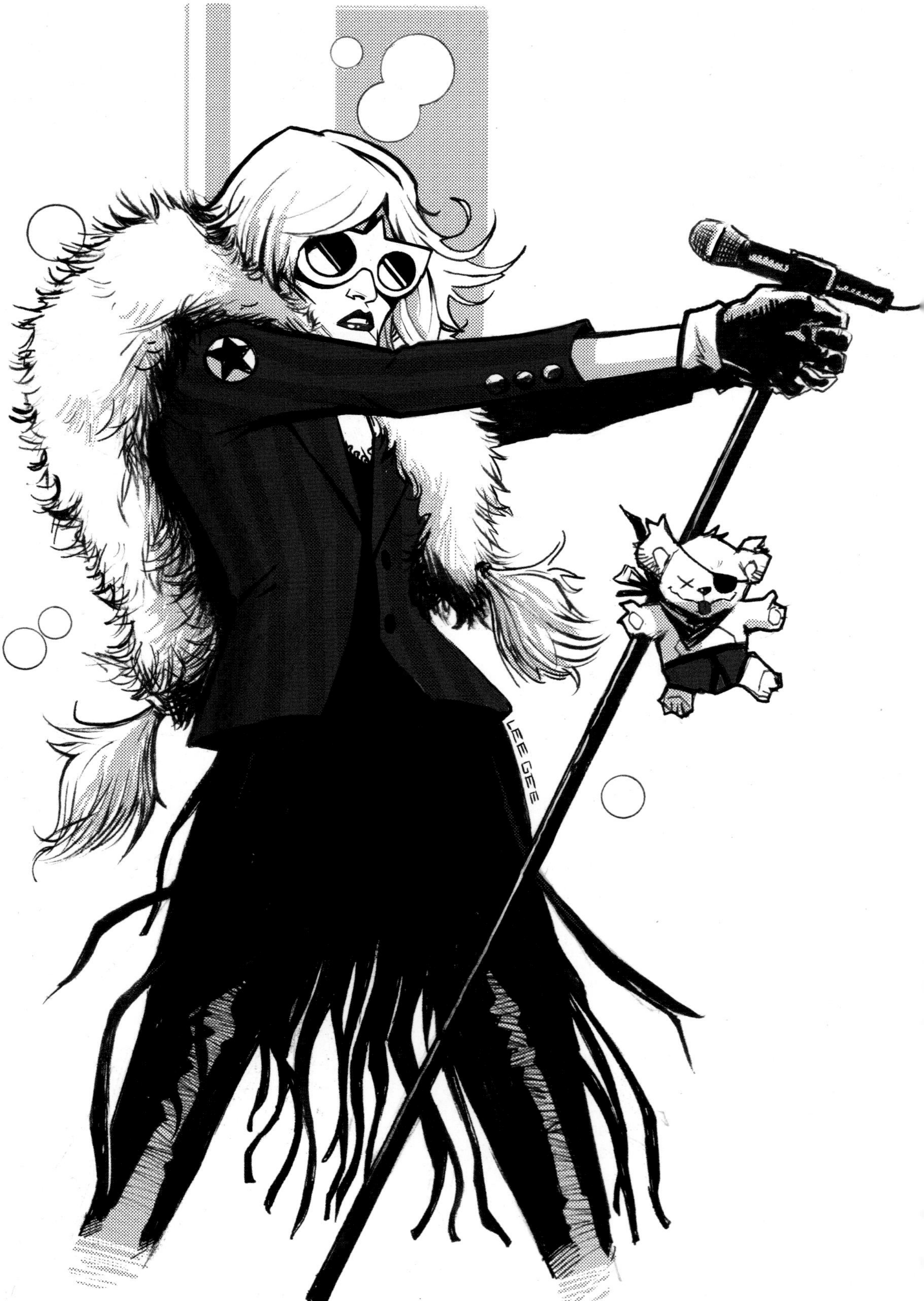
LEE GEE

Full disclosure: I'm a sucker for a great title. My favorite ideas often occur after I drag two disparate words together to see how they look and sound as one titular unit, to determine if they're more memorable together than apart. From there it happens pretty fast or crashes badly, the overwhelming urge to create something from this discordant union and what it connotes, what it can become.

All Femme. No Fluff.

During the summer of 2016 I found myself in between gigs. I spent many hours reading comics and graphic novels at my local library, secretly crafting a new comics imprint. So I added FEMME MAGNIFIQUE to my "titles that should become comics" list. Everything crystallized in early November thanks to two back-to-back events.

Of course the first one is obvious: discovering the outcome of the U.S. Presidential election. My family had just returned from a convention in the U.K. We sleep with the TV on, so while I was enjoying a much-needed slumber I was rudely awakened by what I believed was a *Black Mirror* version of the news. Clearly, it was a missed opportunity for women. And everyone noticed the online vitriol. As a comic book and graphic novel editor for a quarter-century, I felt a tug from my inner Samaritan to contact my storytelling comrades, so we could get over ourselves. But I had some serious jet lag to combat first, which led to the events of the following night.

All Femme. Frontwoman.

I had a solo ticket to finally see Róisín Murphy, my favorite female singer/songwriter, perform live. It was a transcendent electronic music show at L.A.'s legendary El Rey Theatre, an opulent Art Deco ballroom with excellent acoustics. Bowie would have been impressed by Murphy's seamless onstage costume changes. But it was the moment I did a quarter head turn to witness the crush of the enraptured crowd that I knew FEMME MAGNIFIQUE had to happen. If art does anything, it speaks volumes — commands attention. I had to harness the energy to create a body of work to remind ourselves just how far women have come. And precisely where we're going. As in everywhere. And fast.

The following day I reached out to comics colleagues Brian and Kristy Miller of Hi-Fi Colour Design and we agreed to put our skills to good use via Kickstarter and curate FEMME MAGNIFIQUE, a comic book story celebration — of women, dreamers and fierce achievers, glass ceiling crackers, fearless innovators of our history now and forevermore. And of equal importance: a grande dame salute to sequential storytelling as an art form.

All Femme. No Frills.

Great titles go places.

Supreme thanks to the impressive coterie of writers and artists who filled this collection by digging deep and sharing their personal tributes. Every one brought her/his A-game from South Africa to Singapore, from India and Brazil to Greece and to the U.K., Canada and stateside, from coast to coast. Whether I teamed up seasoned professionals (who owed me a favor) with impressive newcomers or cold-called indie auteurs, each of the fifty salutes comes with its own charming backstory. It's been a tremendous privilege to work with all 100+ of you.

It seemed essential that these diverse stories and art styles would need to be grounded by one daring draftsman with fast fingertips. Eternal thanks to letterer Aditya Bidikar, who took on the immense job of placing the words, and the balloons and captions that house them, onto these pages with flair and no fuss.

Special thanks to proofreader Arlene Lo, my longtime favorite expert on grammar and syntax, who is the very definition of *sui generis*. Great thanks to Lillian Laserson, our magnificent legal counsel who was on board from day one. Thanks to Megan Hutchison, whose editorial credit goes beyond Assist to include production artist, designer, ardent Bowie fan and lunch companion on demand.

An abundance of gratitude goes to each Kickstarter backer and reader. Without your support we wouldn't be here. You enabled us to take FEMME MAGNIFIQUE from two disparate words to a final, 4-color execution. Thank you times 1,730.

Finally, I'd be remiss if I didn't thank the two guys who put up with me (and my crazy title theory) and inspire me to live large: my favorite artist/husband/fearless soul mate Philip and our favorite son, Spencer.

I hope you'll continue to promote positivity and equality. Share this book and spread the word. Let's become a global fortress of knowledge and through knowledge, be a force for change.

All Femme. Forward.

Shelly Bond
July 4, 2017
Los Angeles

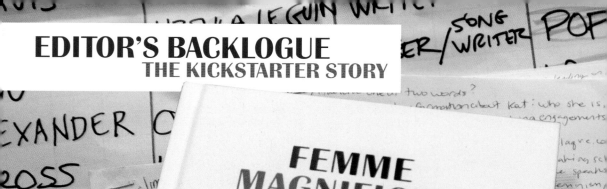

EDITOR'S BACKLOGUE
THE KICKSTARTER STORY

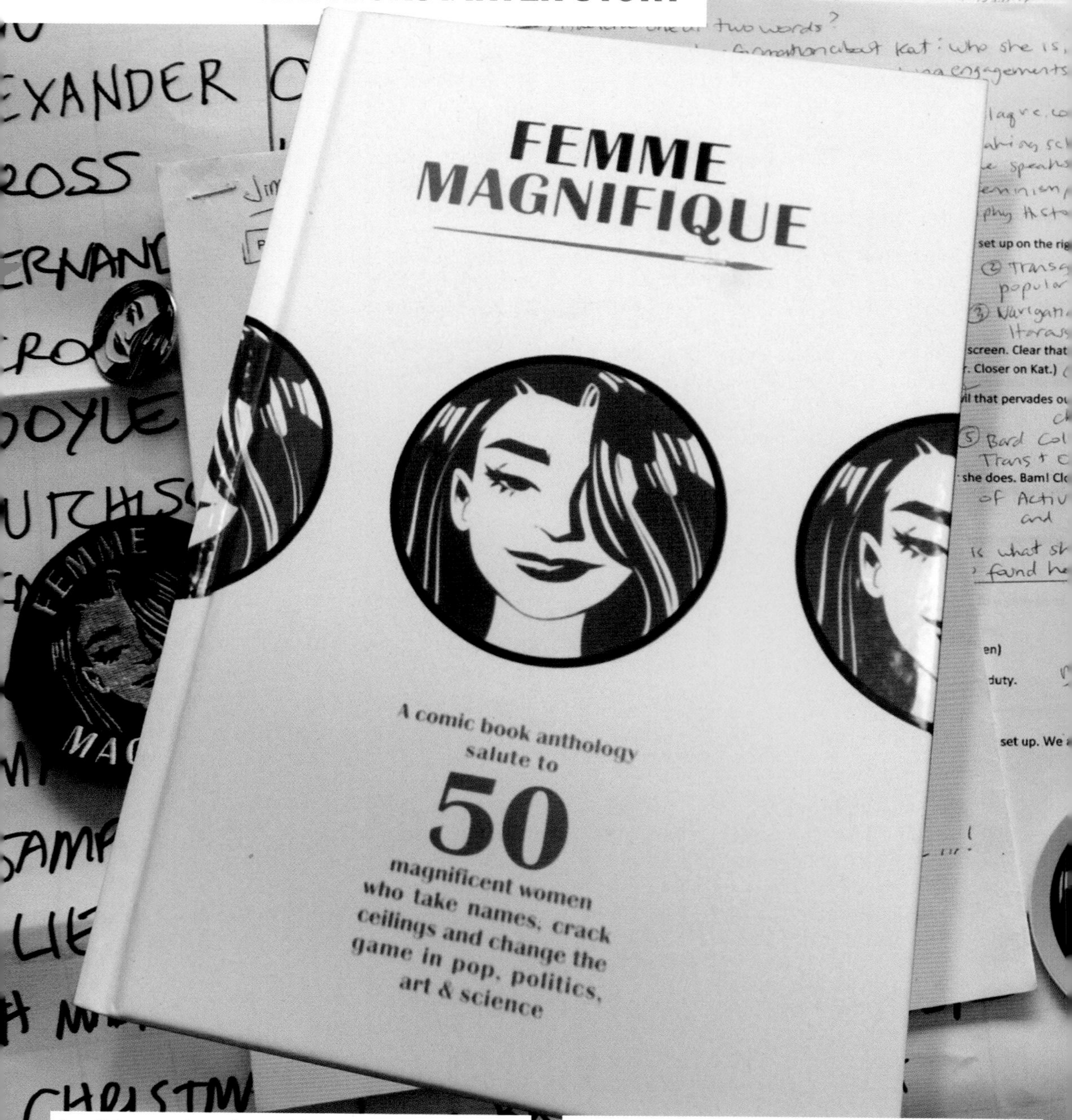
FEMME MAGNIFIQUE
A comic book anthology salute to
50
magnificent women who take names, crack ceilings and change the game in pop, politics, art & science

It all began in a local library, as magnificent ideas often do. (Cue thunderous applause to and for all librarians!). I wanted to raise awareness for equality in general and specifically, the comic book/graphic novel as a storytelling medium.

From the original brief:

"FEMME MAGNIFIQUE! A hardcover comics anthology that celebrates 50 women who take names, crack ceilings and change the game.

A way to serve the greater good: something positive, chock-full of personal short stories to celebrate the mighty, magnificent women (young or old, living or deceased) who have inspired us all.

Each story will contain 3 story/art pages about a woman who personally inspires you.

Put your money where your mouth is and channel your depression / aggression / revulsion / repulsion — to pay it forward for the next gen.

Warning: May crack glass in your cabinet, ceiling, or houses. Read at your own risk.

You up for it?"

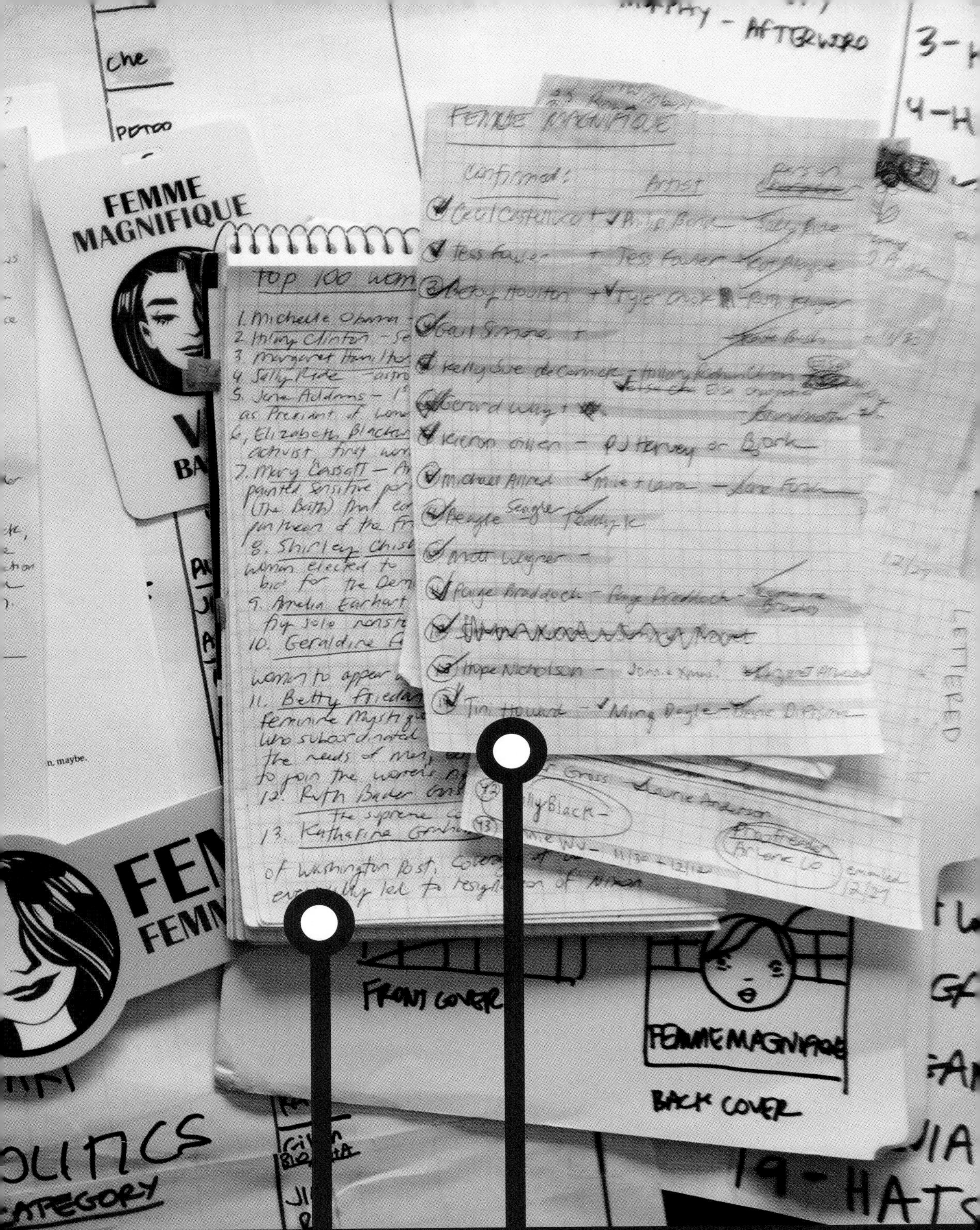
FEMME MAGNIFIQUE
FEMME MAGNIFIQUE
Confirmed:
Artist
FRONT COVER
FEMME MAGNIFIQUE
BACK COVER

List of potential subjects from the early days putting the initial concept together.

I knew that to really resonate as a "call to action," I would need to procure a diverse coterie of writers, artists and subjects — and, above all, make the stories original by making them personal.

Very few writers requested a subject that

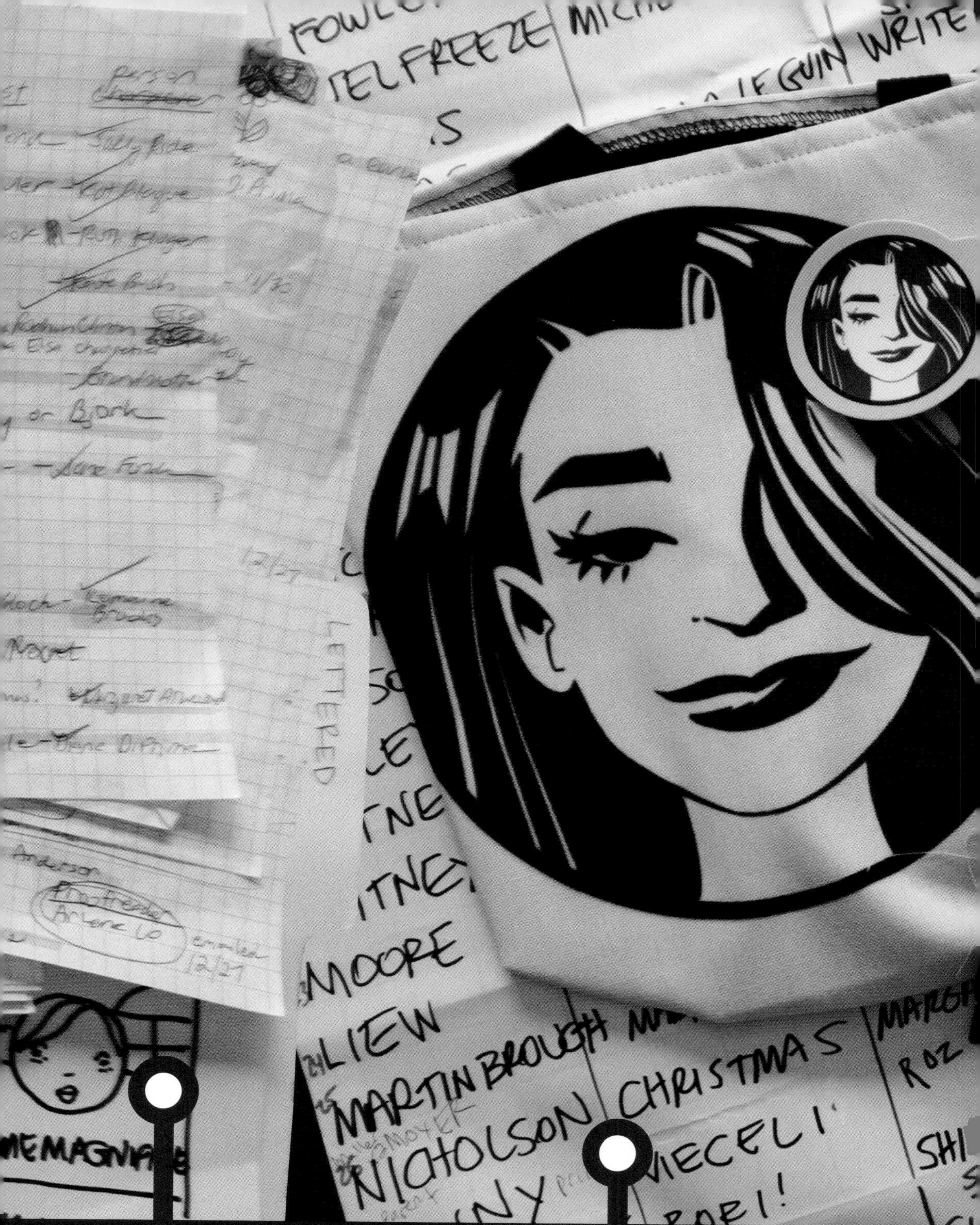
LE GUIN
WRITE
or Bjork
LETTERED
MOORE
LIEW
MARTIN BROUGH
CHRISTMAS
NICHOLSON

Early sketch of the FEMME MAGNIFIQUE icon by yours truly, black Sharpie on 8.5 X 11 manila envelope.

Charts hung in my office to keep a record of the balance of subjects and creative teams.

Note: There is a running theme of writers who salute writers, but that's to be expected.

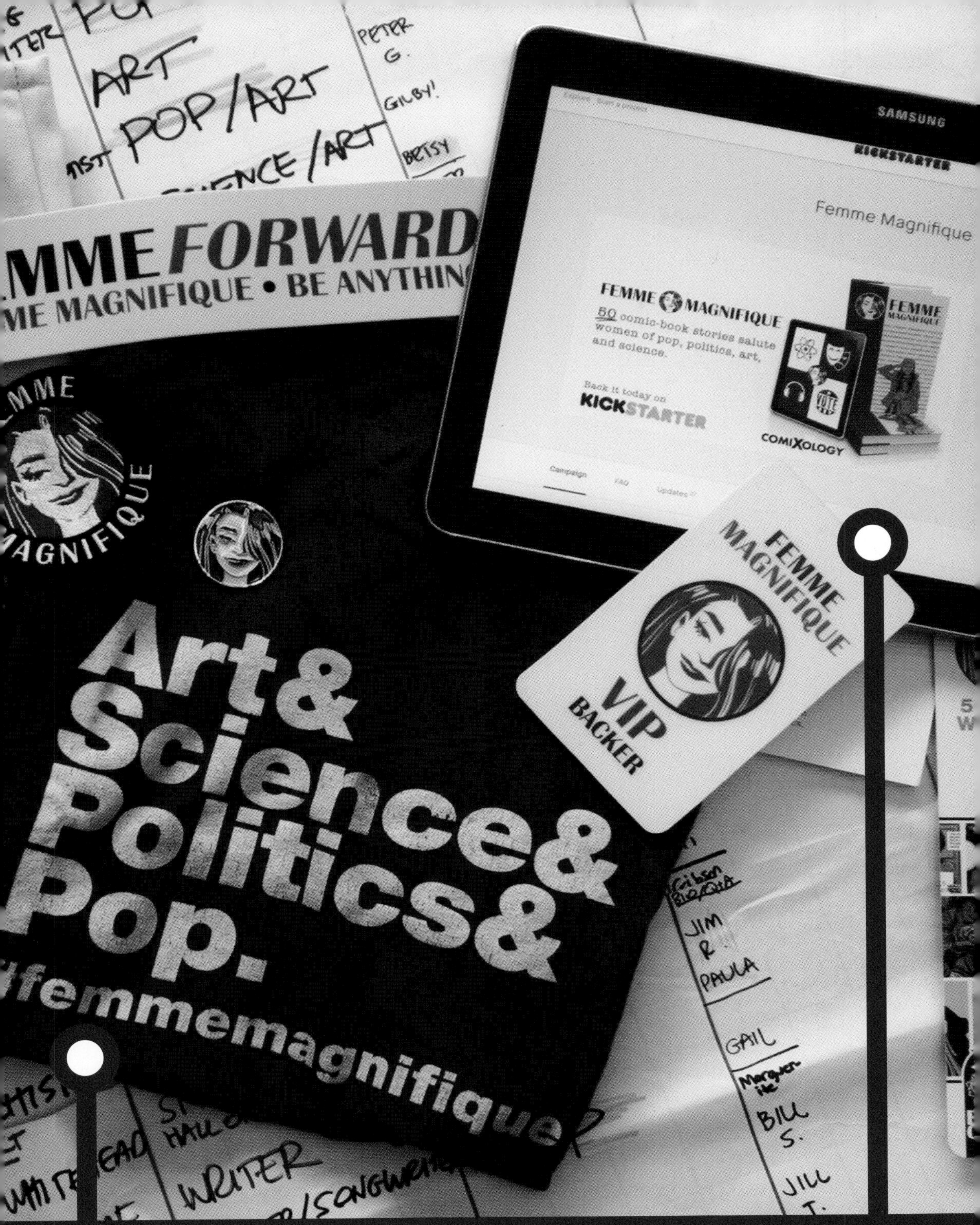
ART
POP/ART
PETER G.
GILBY!
BETSY
SAMSUNG
KICKSTARTER
Femme Magnifique
FEMME MAGNIFIQUE
50 comic-book stories salute women of pop, politics, art, and science.
Back it today on
KICKSTARTER
COMIXOLOGY
Campaign
FAQ
FEMME MAGNIFIQUE
VIP
BACKER
Art&
Science&
Politics&
Pop.
JIM
R
PAULA
GAIL
BILL
S.
JILL
WRITER

Magnificent swag for backer level incentives:

FEMME MAGNIFIQUE bumper sticker, patch, enamel pin, and badge for convention lanyard.

The online store *Threadless* helped us produce T-shirts, tote bags and other goods.

The original campaign on the Kickstarter website.

We had a lofty goal for this collection and reached 10K on our first day, eventually unlocking every level to earn over $96,000 for our generous 1,730 backers.

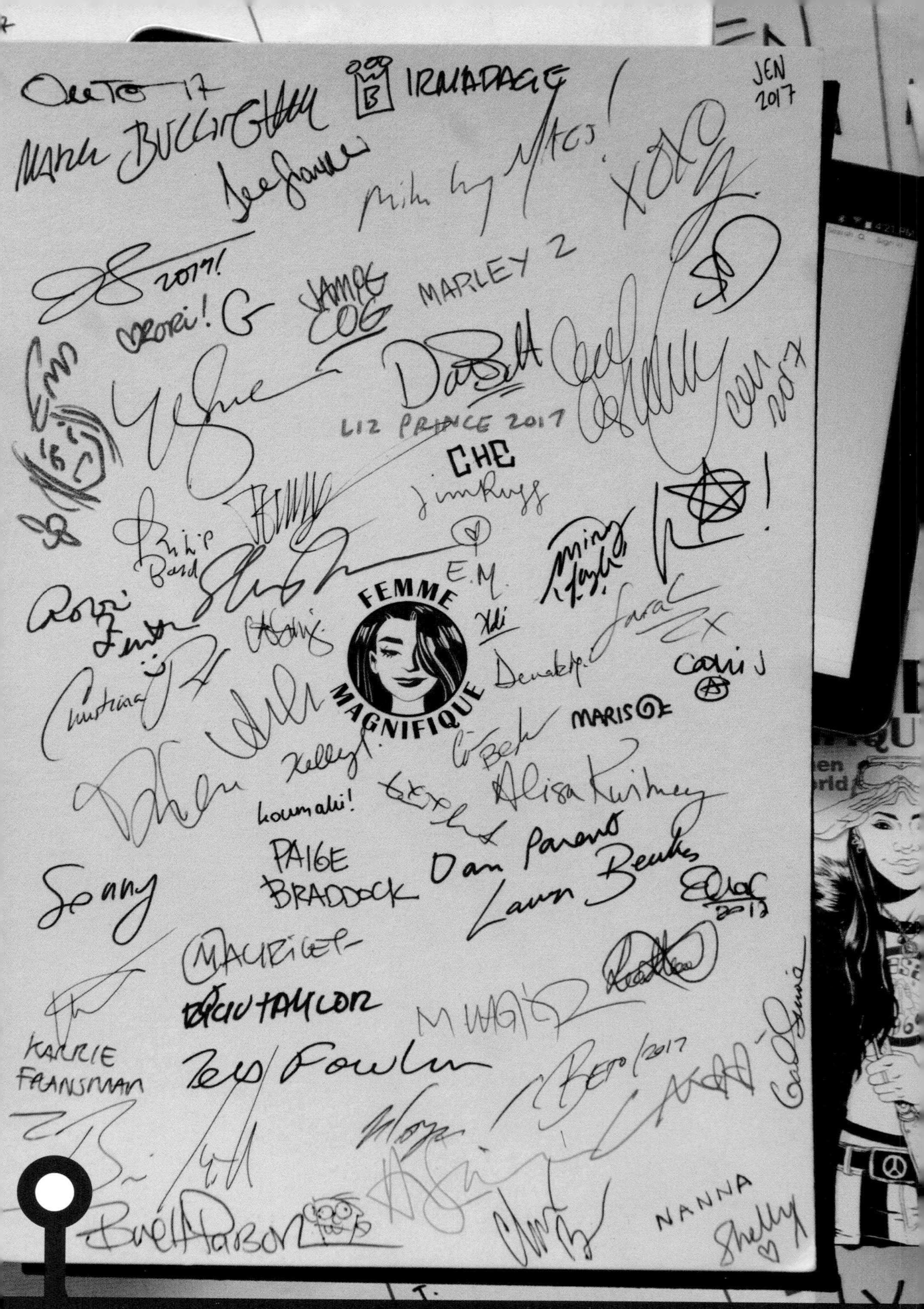
JEN 2017
MARLEY 2
LIZ PRINCE 2017
CHE
FEMME MAGNIFIQUE
PAIGE BRADDOCK
KARRIE FRANSMAN
NANNA

ND THE WORLD IN MANY SIGNATURES

fered 20 signed bookplate editions at a r level of $150.00 per hardcover.

k much effort and coordination on one's part to procure signatures via al Express or at conventions.

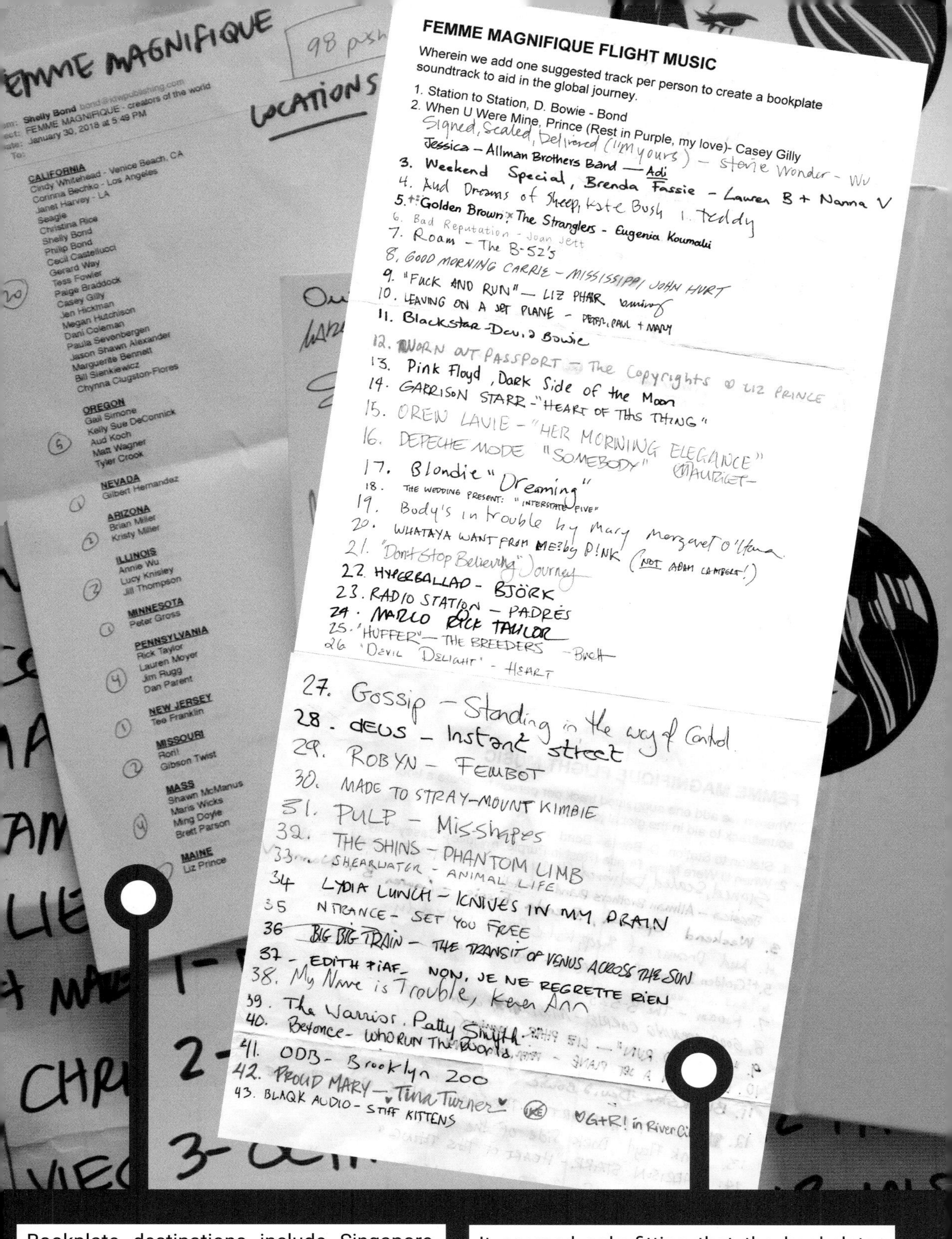
FEMME MAGNIFIQUE
LOCATIONS
CALIFORNIA
Cindy Whitehead - Venice Beach, CA
Corinna Bechko - Los Angeles
Janet Harvey - LA
Seagle
Christina Rice
Shelly Bond
Philip Bond
Cecil Castellucci
Gerard Way
Tess Fowler
Paige Braddock
Casey Gilly
Jen Hickman
Megan Hutchison
Dani Coleman
Paula Sevenbergen
Jason Shawn Alexander
Marguerite Bennett
Bill Sienkiewicz
Chynna Clugston-Flores
OREGON
Gail Simone
Kelly Sue DeConnick
Aud Koch
Matt Wagner
Tyler Crook
NEVADA
Gilbert Hernandez
ARIZONA
Brian Miller
Kristy Miller
ILLINOIS
Annie Wu
Lucy Knisley
Jill Thompson
MINNESOTA
Peter Gross
PENNSYLVANIA
Rick Taylor
Lauren Moyer
Jim Rugg
Dan Parent
NEW JERSEY
Tee Franklin
MISSOURI
Ron!
Gibson Twist
MASS
Shawn McManus
Maris Wicks
Ming Doyle
Brett Parson
MAINE
Liz Prince
FEMME MAGNIFIQUE FLIGHT MUSIC
Wherein we add one suggested track per person to create a bookplate soundtrack to aid in the global journey.
1. Station to Station, D. Bowie - Bond
2. When U Were Mine, Prince (Rest in Purple, my love)- Casey Gilly
Signed, Sealed, Delivered (I'm yours) - Stevie Wonder - Wu
Jessica - Allman Brothers Band - Adi
3. Weekend Special, Brenda Fassie - Lauren B + Nanna V
4. And Dreams of Sheep, Kate Bush - Teddy
5. Golden Brown, The Stranglers - Eugenia Koumaki
6. Bad Reputation - Joan Jett
7. Roam - The B-52's
8. GOOD MORNING CARRIE - MISSISSIPPI JOHN HURT
9. "FUCK AND RUN" - LIZ PHAIR
10. LEAVING ON A JET PLANE - PETER, PAUL + MARY
11. Blackstar - David Bowie
12. WORN OUT PASSPORT - The Copyrights ♡ LIZ PRINCE
13. Pink Floyd, Dark Side of the Moon
14. GARRISON STARR - "HEART OF THIS THING"
15. OREN LAVIE - "HER MORNING ELEGANCE"
16. DEPECHE MODE "SOMEBODY"
17. Blondie "Dreaming"
18. THE WEDDING PRESENT: "INTERSTATE FIVE"
19. Body's in trouble by Mary Margaret O'Hara
20. WHATAYA WANT FROM ME? by P!NK (NOT ADAM LAMBERT!)
21. "Don't Stop Believing" Journey
22. HYPERBALLAD - BJÖRK
23. RADIO STATION - PADRES
24. MARCO RICK TAYLOR
25. "HUFFER" - THE BREEDERS - Brett
26. "DEVIL DELIGHT" - HEART
27. Gossip - Standing in the way of Control
28. dEUS - Instant street
29. ROBYN - FEMBOT
30. MADE TO STRAY - MOUNT KIMBIE
31. PULP - Mis-shapes
32. THE SHINS - PHANTOM LIMB
33. SHEARWATER - ANIMAL LIFE
34. LYDIA LUNCH - KNIVES IN MY BRAIN
35. NTRANCE - SET YOU FREE
36. BIG BIG TRAIN - THE TRANSIT OF VENUS ACROSS THE SUN
37. EDITH PIAF - NON, JE NE REGRETTE RIEN
38. My Name is Trouble, Keren Ann
39. The Warrior, Patty Smyth
40. Beyonce - WHO RUN THE World
41. ODB - Brooklyn Zoo
42. PROUD MARY - Tina Turner
43. BLAQK AUDIO - STIFF KITTENS

Bookplate destinations include Singapore, Brazil, Italy, Greece, South Africa, India, England, Scotland, Ireland, France, Denmark, Canada, Mexico, and the USA.

It seemed only fitting that the bookplates would travel with an inflight playlist on this incredible, globe-spanning journey. Each contributor added a song to the list.

PROCESS

Writer/Artist Jim Rugg suggested pro skateboarder [Cindy] Whitehead as the subject of his story. Since Jim is a [writer] and an artist, he submitted his typed script with his [own] layouts attached. It then went through our rigorous e[ditorial] department (see red pen).

Jim! So excited to meet again as editor to artist — and this time as writer/artist. Let the games begin! ♥ Shelly

PAGE 1

TITLE: Cindy Whitehead, *Girl Is Not a 4 Letter Word* founder, Sports Stylist, Hall of Fame Skateboarder

} Great info.

(You're the first person to remember to include the title area on this page @ the top. #alsoartist

What's the title? Oh, that is the title #genius

1:1

Grandmother talking to young, blonde girl.

A CAPTION: "I was really lucky. I had another woman who was a bit of a rebel on my side. My grandmother told me I could make a career out of skateboarding but the best thing she ever taught me…"

1 GRANDMOTHER: You're equal to your brother and all the other boys in your neighborhood.

2 GRANDMOTHER: And you can do anything that they can do.

1:2

This is a big panel, it is the bottom half of the page. It features an image of Cindy Whitehead's skateboard magazine centerfold (Wild World of Skateboarding, June 1978). The magazine is on the right 2/3rds of the panel. On the left side of the panel is a picture of Joan Jett, from when Whitehead was introduced into the skateboard Hall of Fame.

3 JOAN JETT: Cindy Whitehead took that crazy life path. Cindy is all about breaking rules, taking risks, asking for what you want, and not shrinking yourself to be liked.*

4 CAPTION (footnote under Jett): *From Joan Jett's 2016 introduction at Cindy Whitehead's Skateboard Hall of Fame induction.

5 CAPTION (footnote under the magazine): Wild World of Skateboarding, June 1978

✱ I tend to bold 1-2 words per page for impact. Please change accordingly. This is your cadence, not mine. Unless you like my choices, of course …!

PAGE 2

2:1

Half page panel. Long shot of Cindy skating down the 405.

CAPTION: On September 30, 2012, during Carmageddon...

CAPTION: Whitehead wrote a bail bondsman number on her arm, snuck thru back yards, climbed over fences, dodged cops, and snuck onto L.A.'s infamous 405 freeway for the ride of a lifetime!

Epic shit! Go, Cindy!

Or... delete it because we see it and ... she says it?

2:2

Close up Whitehead's profile. Happy.

CAPTION: "My heart was racing. My adrenaline

CAPTION: "I got so into that ride that I almost m

Is "405 REBELLION for page 1? Just call, Jim.

PAGE 3

3:1
Horizontal panel. The Girl Is Not a 4 Letter Word c
horizontally oriented. The panel is based on an ic
pink space on the left. In that space will be text.

CAPTION (above board): Partly because of that
collab skateboard with Dusters California and L

CAPTION: Whitehead uses Girl is NOT a 4 Le
skateboarding by funding non-profits for femal
helping female skaters gain exposure, opport
girlisnotea4letterword.com

CAPTION: In 2017, she published *It's Not Al*
first comprehensive photography book abou

3:2
Girls with skateboards - homage to the intr

3:3
Cindy Whitehead wearing a cool leather j

4 WHITEHEAD: If somebody told me I cou

5 WHITEHEAD: Show the world what girl
fire.

6 WHITEHEAD: And do some epic shit.

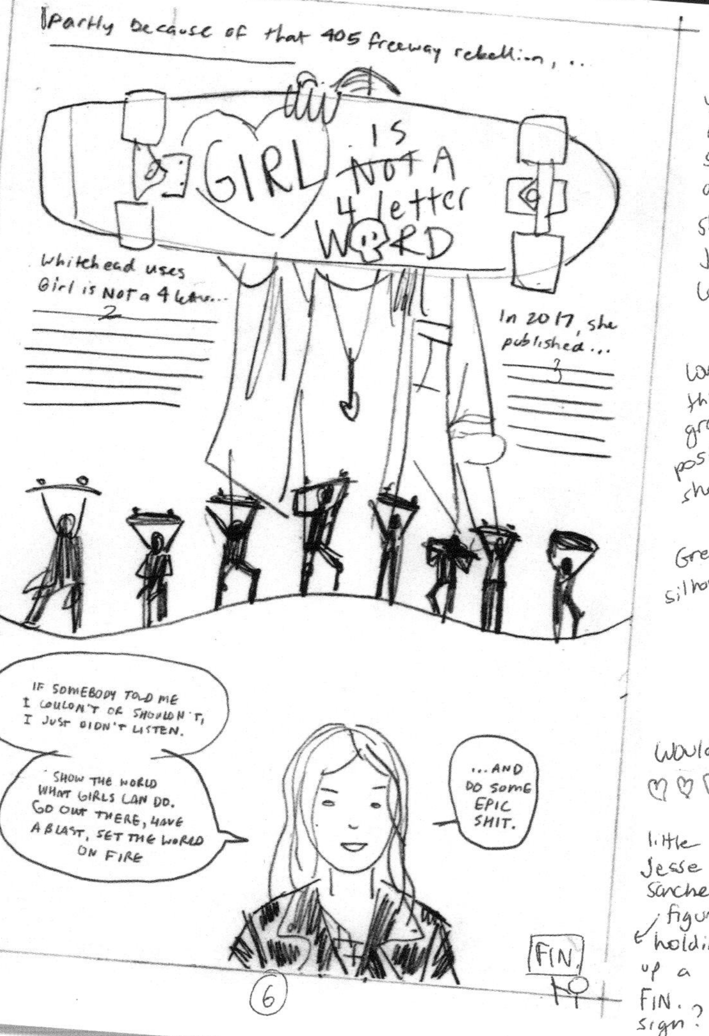

Partly because of that 405 freeway rebellion, ..
GIRL IS NOT A 4 letter WORD
Whitehead uses Girl is Not a 4 letter...
2
In 2017, she published...
3
IF SOMEBODY TOLD ME I COULDN'T OR SHOULDN'T, I JUST DIDN'T LISTEN.
SHOW THE WORLD WHAT GIRLS CAN DO. GO OUT THERE, HAVE A BLAST, SET THE WORLD ON FIRE
...AND DO SOME EPIC SHIT.
FIN.
6

your design skills are showing, Jim! Love it!

Love this grand poster shot!

Great silhouettes!

Would ♡♡♡ little Jesse Sanchez figure holding up a FIN. sign?

FIN.

Cindy ... so psyched about this!

THIS IS EPIC SHIT! AMAZING WORK, JIM! Can I show this edited version to the masses on the Femme Magnifique FB page? ♡ Shelly

5

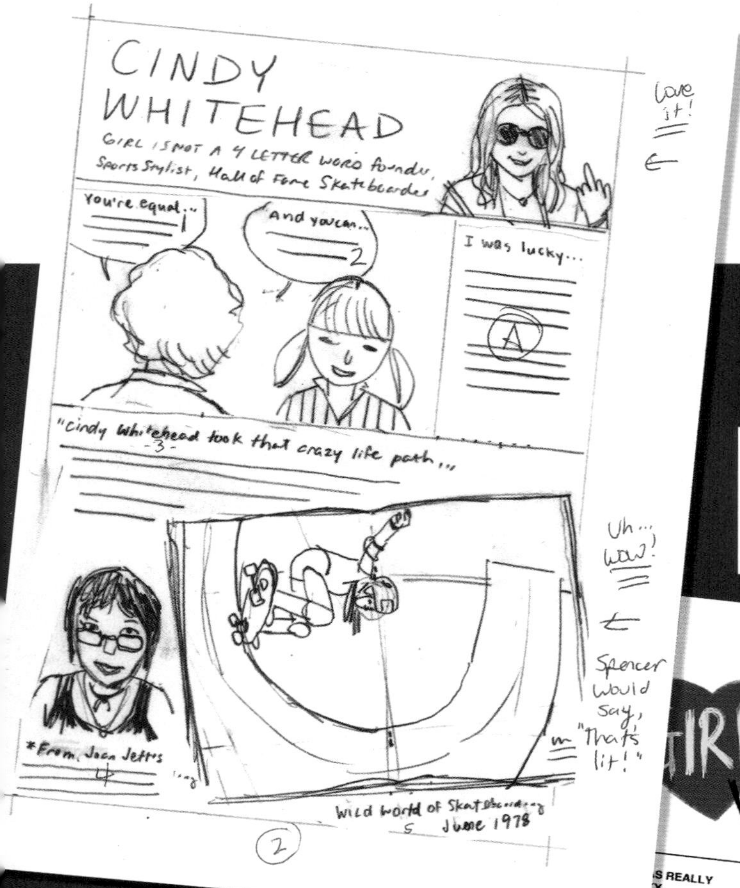
CINDY WHITEHEAD
GIRL IS NOT A 4 LETTER WORD founder, Sports Stylist, Hall of Fame Skateboarder
love it!
You're equal...
And you can...
I was lucky...
A
"Cindy Whitehead took that crazy life path..."
Uh... WOW!
Spencer would say, "That's it!"
*From Joan Jett's
Wild World of Skateboarding June 1978
2

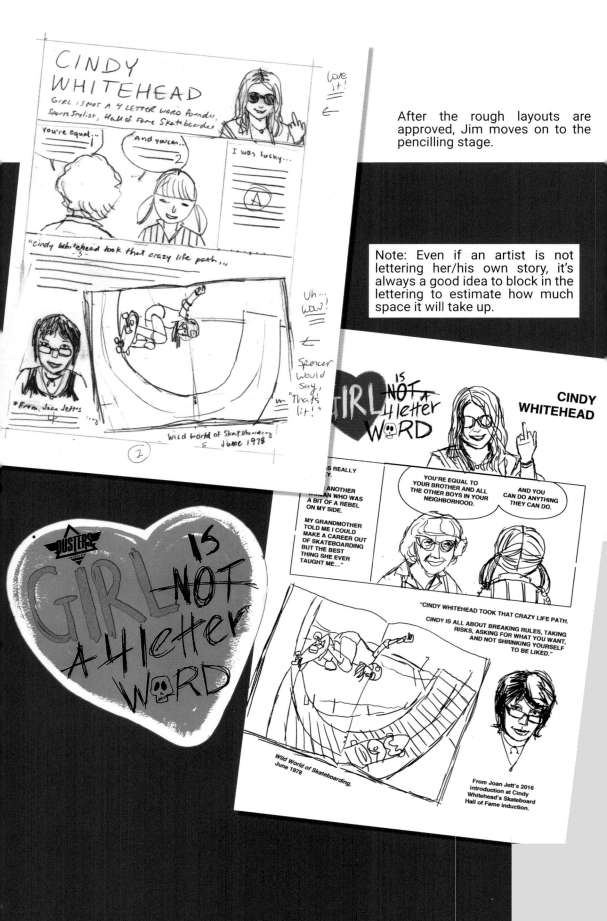

After the rough layouts are approved, Jim moves on to the pencilling stage.

Note: Even if an artist is not lettering her/his own story, it's always a good idea to block in the lettering to estimate how much space it will take up.

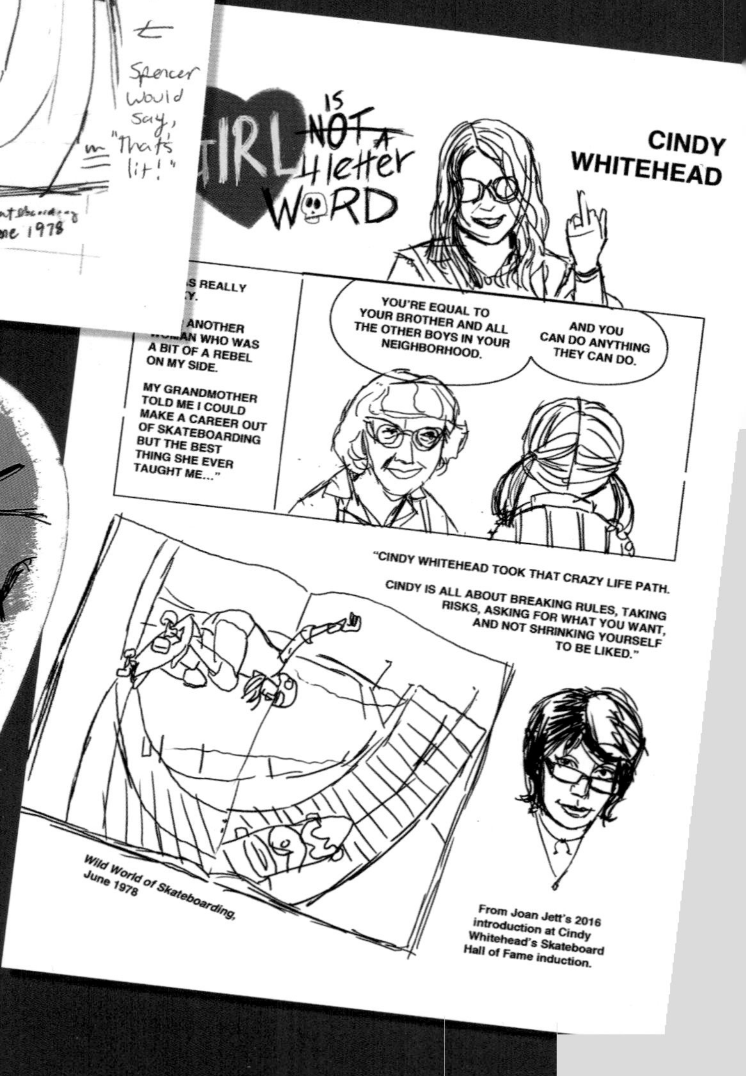
GIRL IS NOT A 4 letter WORD
CINDY WHITEHEAD
A BIT OF A REBEL ON MY SIDE.
MY GRANDMOTHER TOLD ME I COULD MAKE A CAREER OUT OF SKATEBOARDING BUT THE BEST THING SHE EVER TAUGHT ME..."
YOU'RE EQUAL TO YOUR BROTHER AND ALL THE OTHER BOYS IN YOUR NEIGHBORHOOD.
AND YOU CAN DO ANYTHING THEY CAN DO.
"CINDY WHITEHEAD TOOK THAT CRAZY LIFE PATH.
CINDY IS ALL ABOUT BREAKING RULES, TAKING RISKS, ASKING FOR WHAT YOU WANT, AND NOT SHRINKING YOURSELF TO BE LIKED."
Wild World of Skateboarding, June 1978
From Joan Jett's 2016 introduction at Cindy Whitehead's Skateboard Hall of Fame induction.

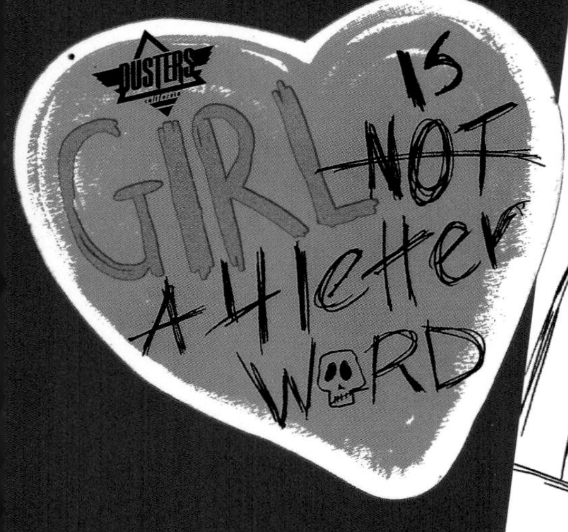
DUSTERS
california
GIRL IS NOT A 4 letter WORD

From pencils to inks and finally color, Jim's story is almost ready for print.

Often a separate colorist works on the inked story. In Jim's case he wanted to do it all himself.

"I was so taken with Jim's salute to Cindy and her infectious enthusiasm for FEMME MAGNIFIQUE I asked her to write the introduction," says Shelly Bond, editor.

Create Your Own

Now's your chance to add to the *Femme Magnifique* canon. We've saved a page in this section so you can create your own short story salute.

Of note: In the original brief that we sent to our talented writers and artists as a call to action, we explained that the emphasis of the *Femme Magnifique* stories is twofold: part nonfiction biopic to educate people about these esteemed women, their unique careers and general awesomeness/bravado. The other part is personal, how you discovered her, what her work means to you, how it can translate to a better future for women.

Utilize the following page layout or create your own and consider a few tips of the trade below from some of our inimitable contributors.

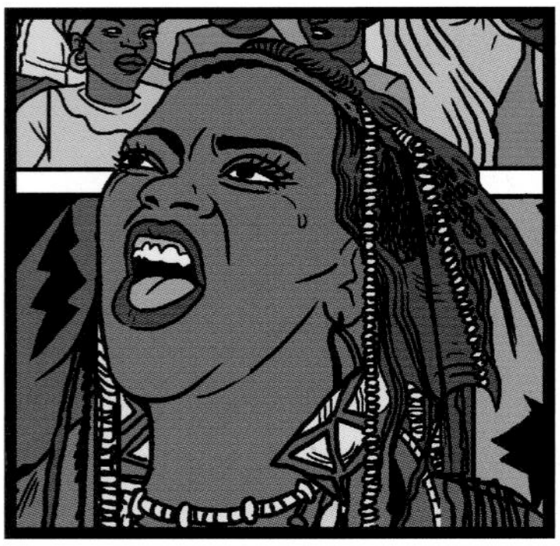

Writer Lauren Beukes

"My number one tip is work with a brilliant artist who knows what they're doing. The art does so much of the work in comics. Clever layout that lets you play with scene jumps and time jumps is the way to go. It's a great exercise in distilling the story into its most elegant and compact form. Be ruthless. Cut anything that's not essential to the story. Pick your key moments. Trust your reader to fill in the gaps — and give them enough context in the words and pictures to be able to do so."

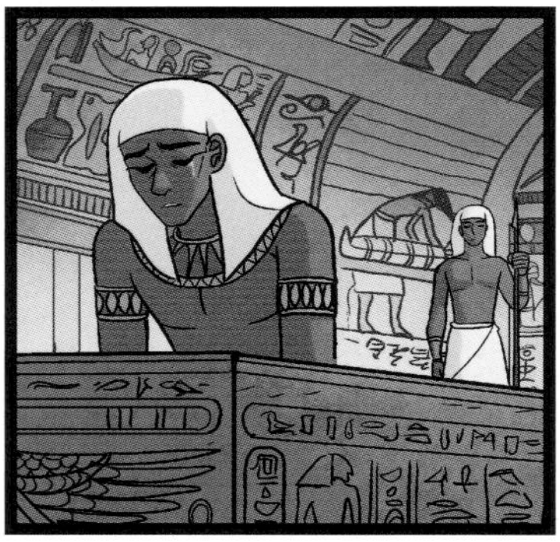

Colorist Brian Miller

"Colorists apply their skills to visual storytelling using light, shadow, and hue. One tip colorists can apply to their work is using a combination of warm and cool values to guide the reader's eye to the important story elements in a panel or page. In this way color emphasizes key story beats so readers won't miss them."

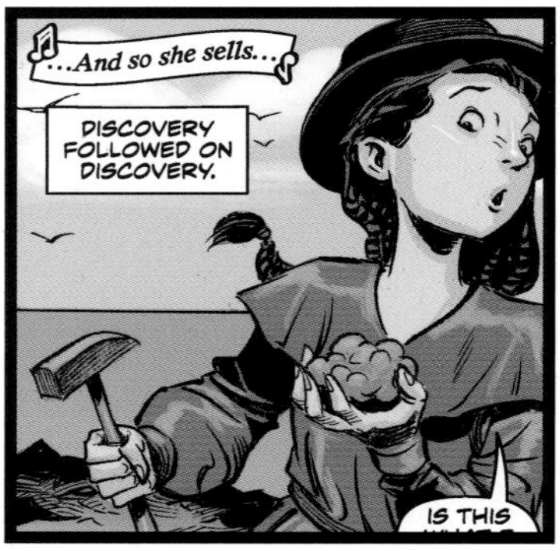
...And so she sells...
DISCOVERY FOLLOWED ON DISCOVERY.
IS THIS

Letterer Aditya Bidikar

"Good lettering is all about storytelling. The font selection and balloon style should suit the genre and tone of the story, and should help to highlight important elements of the art."

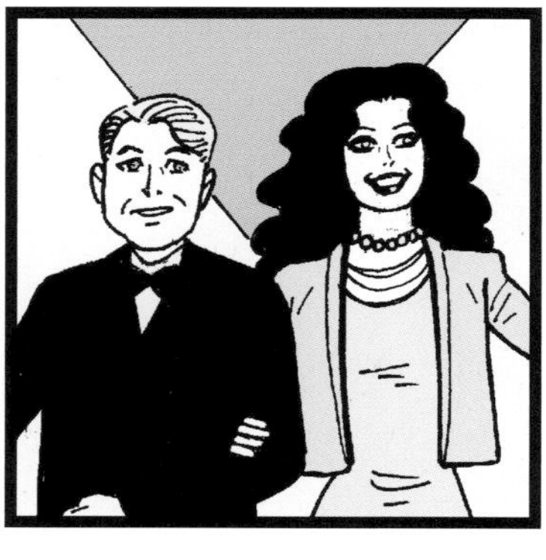

Editor Shelly Bond

"Keep it simple. Comics is about deciding what to say versus what to show. Avoid repetition. Strive for clarity. Consider the three-act structure and be sure to have a beginning, a middle and an end. Make it personal. Tell the story only you can tell."

Bios

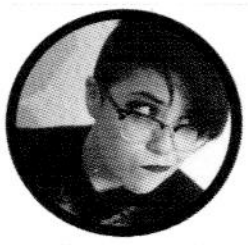

CLAUDIA AGUIRRE
Credits: *Kim & Kim*, *Hotel Dare*
facebook.com/claudiaguirreart
Twitter: @claudiaguirre
Likes: cats & comics
Despises: unnecessary meaness

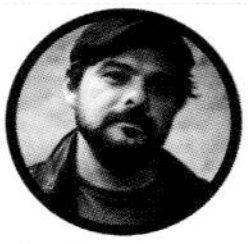

RAFAEL ALBUQUERQUE
Credits: *American Vampire*, *Huck*
rafaelalbuquerque.com
Twitter: @rafaalbuquerque

JASON SHAWN ALEXANDER
Credits: *Spawn*, *Empty Zone*
studiojsa.com
twit and insta: @jasonshawnalex

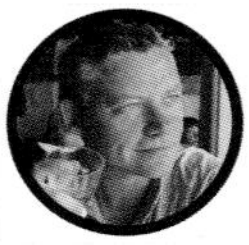

DAVID BARNETT
Credits: *Punks Not Dead*, *Calling Major Tom*
davidmbarnett.com
Twitter: @davidmbarnett
Likes: magpies
Despises: inequality

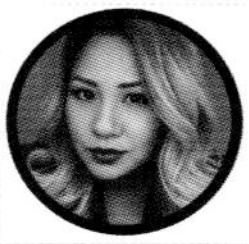

JEN BARTEL
Credits: *Blackbird*, *The Mighty Thor*
jenbartel.com
Twitter: @heyjenbartel
Likes: dogs
Despises: cilantro

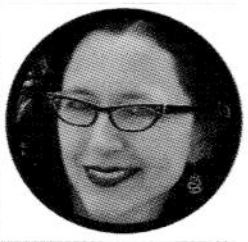

CORINNA BECHKO
Credits: *Dig It: Dinosaurs*, *Green Lantern: Earth One*
corinnabechko.com
Likes: fossils and books
Despises: the patriarchy and olives

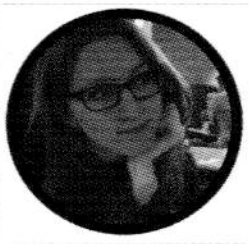

JORDIE BELLAIRE
Credits: writes *Redlands*, *Vision*
Twitter: @whoajordie
Likes: burritos and professionalism
Despises: key lime pie and sexism

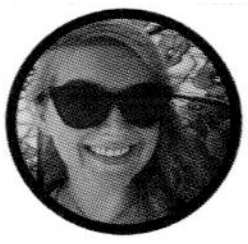

MARGUERITE BENNETT
Credits: *DC Bombshells*, *Animosity*
Twitter: @EvilMarguerite
Likes: audiobooks, animals, women's rights and history.
Despises: when the hot sun wilts her garden

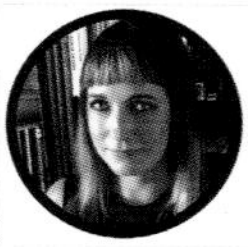

LAUREN BEUKES
Credits: *The Shining Girls*, *Survivors Club*
laurenbeukes.com
Twitter: @laurenbeukes
Likes: social justice
Despises: awful people

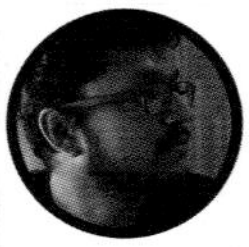

ADITYA BIDIKAR
Credits: *Kid Lobotomy*, *Grafity's Wall*
adityab.net/lettering
Twitter: @adityab
Likes: forest walks, keyboards with satisfying clicks

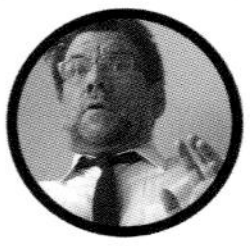

PHILIP BOND
Credits: *CUD: Rich And Strange*, *Kill Your Boyfriend*
philipbond.net Twitter: @pjbond
Likes: my music Despises: your music

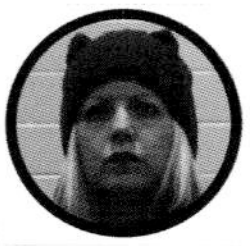

SHELLY BOND
Credits: Editor/Curator, BLACK CROWN
blackcrown.pub
Twitter: @sxbond @blackcrownhq
Likes: red pens, red currant & Courreges red
Despises: tangents

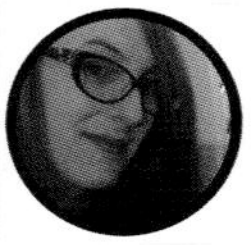

TAMRA BONVILLAIN
Credits: *Doom Patrol*, *Moon Girl*
Twitter: twitter.com/TBonvillain
Likes: salsa
Despises: running out of salsa

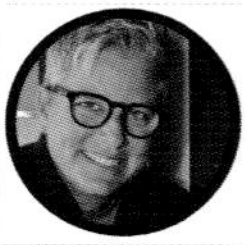

PAIGE BRADDOCK
Credits: *Jane's World*, *Stinky Cecil*
PaigeBraddock.com
Twitter: @PaigeBraddock
Likes: sci-fi movies and cars.
Despises: karaoke

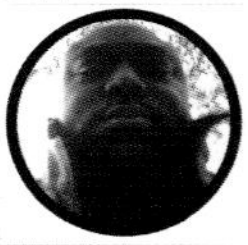

CHUCK BROWN
Credits: *The Punisher*, *Bitter Root*
Twitter: @Cbrown803
Likes: solitude, Chinese food and reruns of The Simpsons
Despises: traffic, awkward silence and flies

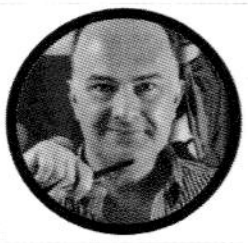

MARK BUCKINGHAM
Credits: *Fables*, *Miracleman*
Facebook: @MarkBuckinghamComicArtist
Likes: prog rock and drawing animals

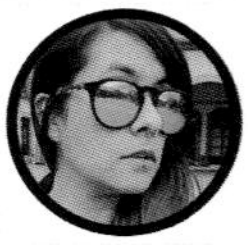

EVA CABRERA
Credits: *Kim & Kim*, *Betty & Veronica Vixens*
behance.net/evacabrera
Twitter: @evacabrera
Likes: books and nature
Despises: loud noises and disorder

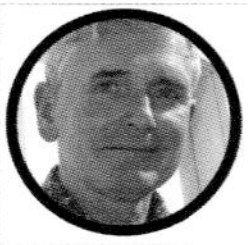

MICHAEL CAREY
Credits: *Lucifer*, *The Girl with All the Gifts* and *The Felix Castor series.*
Twitter: @michaelcarey191
Likes: Indian food
Despises: reality TV

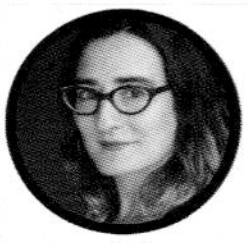

CECIL CASTELLUCCI
Credits: *Shade, the Changing Girl*, *The Plain Janes*
misscecil.com
Twitter: @misscecil
Likes: comets Despises: space junk

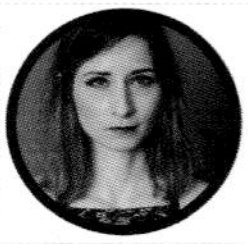

ELSA CHARRETIER
Credits: *The Infinite Loop*, *Star Wars Adventures*
Twitter: @e_charretier
Likes: all things art
Despises: offal

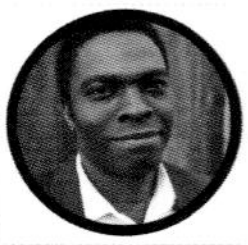

JOHNNIE CHRISTMAS
Credits: *Angel Catbird*, *Firebug*
johnniechristmas.com
Twitter: @j_xmas
Likes: a cool drink at dusk
Despises: apathy

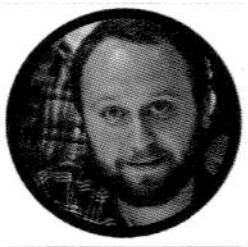

JAMIE COE
Credits: *Shade, the Changing Girl*, *The New Yorker*
Twitter: @jamiecoart

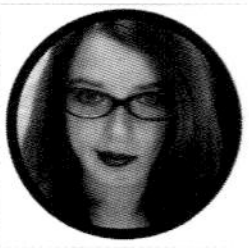

DANI COLEMAN
Credits: *ODY-C*, *Black Jack Ketchum*
daniwritesstuff.com
Twitter: @DirectorDaniC
Likes: owls
Despises: the word "hella"

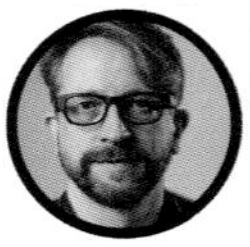

THEDY CORREA
thedycorrea.com
Twitter: @thedycorrea
Likes: poetry, Beat Generation, David Bowie
Despises: racism, prejudice

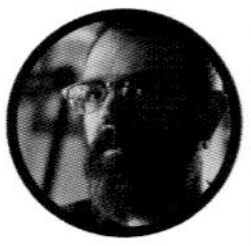

TYLER CROOK
Credits: *Harrow County*, *Petrograd*
mrcrook.com
Twitter: @mrcrook.com
Likes: dogs
Despises: fascism

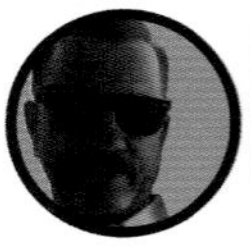

ROB DAVIS
Credits: *The Motherless Oven*, *Black Crown Quarterly: Tales from the Black Crown Pub*
dinlos.blogspot
Twitter: @Robgog

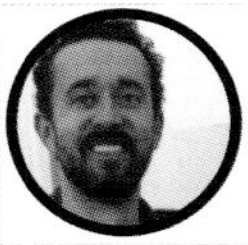

JON DAVIS-HUNT
Credits: *The Wildstorm*, *Clean Room*
jondavis-hunt.com
Twitter: @JonDavisHunt
Likes: comics and video games
Despises: when he can't play video games

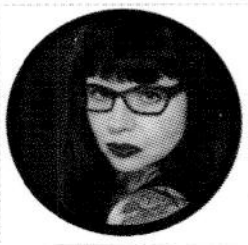

KELLY SUE DeCONNICK
Credits: *Bitch Planet*, *Pretty Deadly*
milkfed.com
Twitter: @kellysue
Likes: heavy metal
Despises: complaining

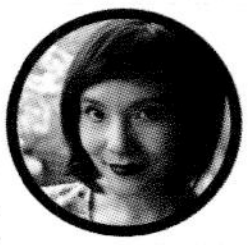

MING DOYLE
Credits: *The Kitchen*, *Constantine: The Hellblazer*
Twitter: @mingdoyle
Likes: Halloween
Despises: most other things

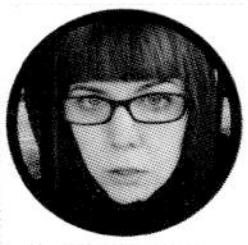

KELLY FITZPATRICK
Credits: *Bitch Planet*, *Shade, the Changing Girl*
kellyfcolors.com Twitter: @wastedwings
Likes: coffee, reading in the bath
Despises: Patriarchal social constructs

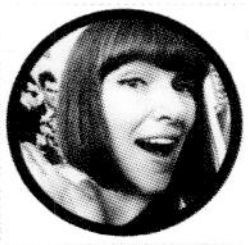

CHYNNA CLUGSTON-FLORES
Credits: *Blue Monday*, *Scooter Girl*
newwavezombie.bigcartel.com
Twitter: @ chynnasyndrome
Likes: time travel
Despises: abandoned exoskeletons

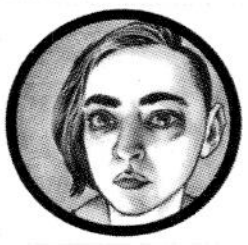

TESS FOWLER
Credits: *Kid Lobotomy*, *infamous C.R.A.F.T.*
Twitter: @TessFowler
tessfowler.storeenvy.com
Likes: *Critical Role*

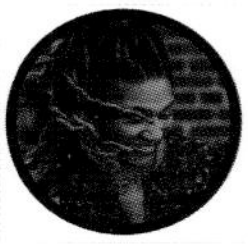

TEE FRANKLIN
Credits: *Bingo Love*, *Jook Joint*
TeeFranklin.com
Twitter: @MizTeeFranklin
Likes: Sleeping, cooking, *Spaceballs*
Despises: Inaccessibility, patriarchy

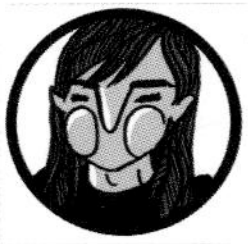

KARRIE FRANSMAN
Credits: *The House that Groaned*, *Death of the Artist*
karriefransman.com
Twitter: @KarrieFransman

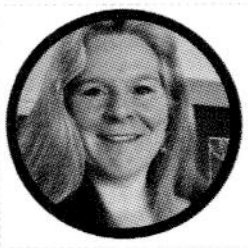

ROBIN FURTH
Credits: *The Bride in Sea-Green Velvet*, *The Dark Tower*
robinfurth.com Twitter: @robinfurth
Likes: visionary art
Despises: the alt-right

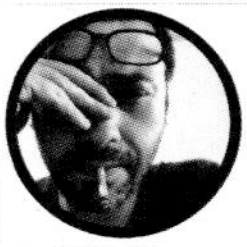

ANTONIO FUSO
Credits: *Clankillers*, *James Bond 007: Service*
antoniofuso.tumblr..com
Twitter: @antonio_fuso
Likes: interior design Despises: clip frames

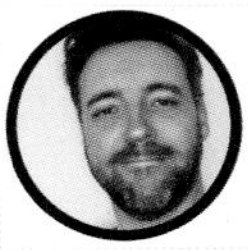

LEE GARBETT
Credits: *Loki: Agent of Asgard*, *Skyward*
leegarbett.com
Twitter: @LeeGarbett
Likes: coffee
Despises: tea

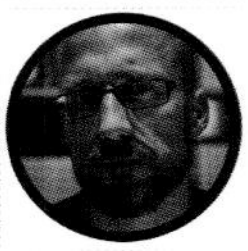

KIERON GILLEN
Credits: *The Wicked + The Divine*, *Phonogram*
kierongillen.com
Twitter: @kierongillen
Likes: rarely Despises: often

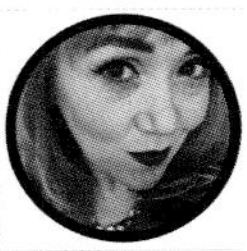

CASEY GILLY
Credits: *Womanthology*, *Mine! Anthology*
Twitter: @RunBarbara
Likes: seances
Despises: misogyny

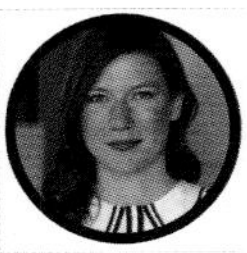

GILLIAN GOERZ
Credits: *Secret Loves of Geek Girls*, *Shirley Bones*
GillianG.com
Twitter: @GillianGDotCom
Likes: friendship Despises: bad listeners

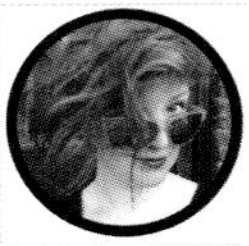

SARAH GORDON
Credits: *Deeds Not Words*, *Queen Rat*
sarah-gordon.com
Twitter: @notsarahgordon
Likes: folk horror, singing along to The B-52's after 2 am Despises: fake strawberry

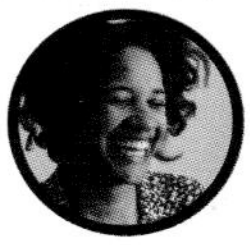

CHE GRAYSON
Credits: *Rigamo*, *Bitch Planet: Triple Feature*
chegrayson.com
Twitter: @cheinwonderland
Likes: Ms. Pacman
Despises: littering

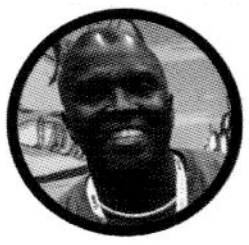

SANDFORD GREENE
Credits: *Bitter Root*, *Rotten Apple*
Twitter: @sanfordgreene
greenestreet.deviantart.com
Likes: sleep
Despises: dishonesty

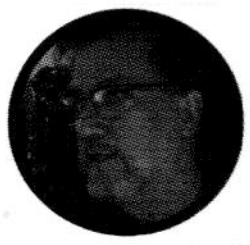

PETER GROSS
Credits: *The Unwritten*, *The Highest House*
petergrossart.com
Twitter: @PeterGrossArt
Likes: finishing deadlines
Despises: It's 2018, do I even have to say...

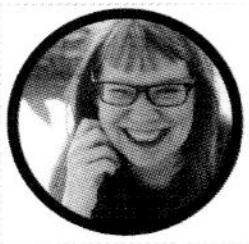

JANET HARVEY
Credits: *Angel City*, *Batman*
janetharvey.com
Twitter: @janetharvey
Likes: Marmite
Despises: breakfast cereal

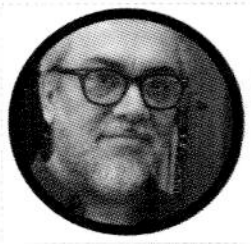

GILBERT HERNANDEZ
Credits: *Love And Rockets*, *Assassinistas*
Twitter: @BetomessGIlbert
Likes: *Little Archie #20*
Despises: roller skating

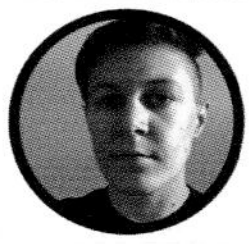

JEN HICKMAN
Credits: *Jem and the Holograms*
umicorms.com
Twitter: @Umicorns
Likes: inks
Despises: charcoal

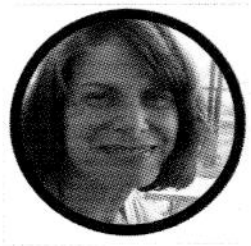

BETSY HOULTON
Credits: *New York Daily News*
Likes: brilliant diplomacy
Despises: guns

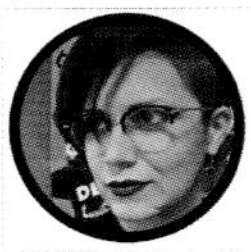

TINI HOWARD
Credits: *Assassinistas*, *Euthanauts*
tinihoward.com
Twitter: @tinihoward
Likes: spiders
Despises: mosquitoes

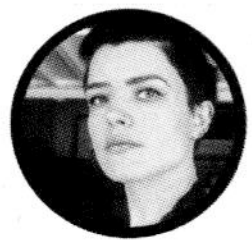

MEGAN HUTCHISON
Credits: *Rockstars*, *Will O' the Wisp*
blackem-art.com
Twitter: @blackem_art
Likes: darkness, bats, graveyards
Despises: stereotypes about Goths

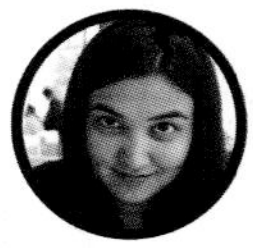

IRMA KNIIVILA
Credits: *Joyride*, *Jane*
irmaillustration.com
Twitter: @kniivila
Likes: gentle-at-heart things

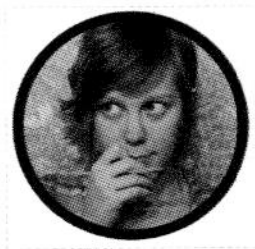

LUCY KNISLEY
Credits: *Relish*, *Something New, Kid Gloves*
LucyKnisley.com
Twitter: @LucyKnisley

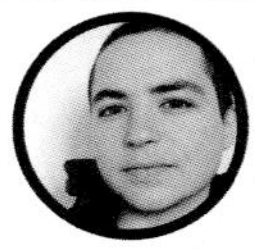

AUD KOCH
Credits: *Ultimates2*, *The Wicked + The Divine*
audkoch.com
Twitter: @audkoch
Likes: blue cheese Despises: marzipan

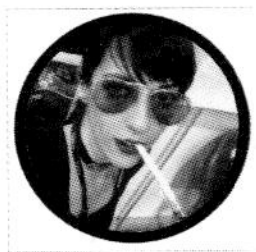

EUGENIA KOUMAKI
Credits: *Womanthology*, *Mine! Anthology*
Twitter: @EugeniaKoumaki
Likes: flamboyant cuttlefish, cheese
Despises: bigotry, sugar crashes

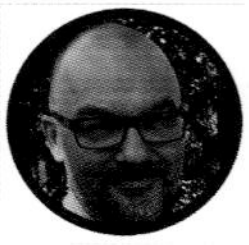

TEDDY KRISTIANSEN
Credits: *It's a Bird, Re(a)d Diary*
teddykristiansenblog.blogspot.dk
Twitter: @TeddyKrist
Likes: books, food, but love my family

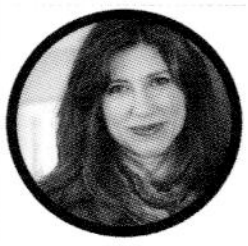

ALISA KWITNEY
Credits: *Mystik U, Cadaver & Queen*
alisakwitney.com
Twitter: @akwitney
Likes: dancing like a frenzied victim of the tarantella

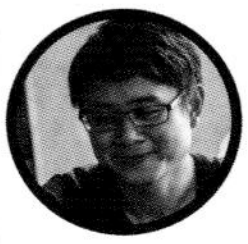

SONNY LIEW
Credits: *The Art of Charlie Chan Hock Chye, Eternity Girl*
sonnyliew.com
Twitter: @sonny_liew

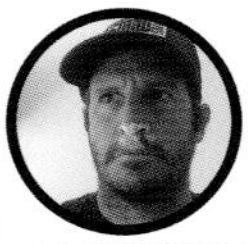

LEE LOUGHRIDGE
Credits: *Fables, Kid Lobotomy Punk Rock Paper Scissors*
Twitter: @leeloughridge
Likes: surfing
Despises: not surfing

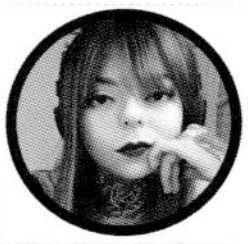

FABI MARQUES
Credits: *designer for Microsoft*
behance.net/fabianamarques
Likes: painting comics and her dog Ramona

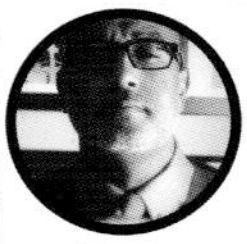

SHAWN MARTINBROUGH
Credits: *Thief of Thieves, How to Draw Noir Comics*
Twitter: @smartinbrough
Likes: positivity
Despises: non-accountability

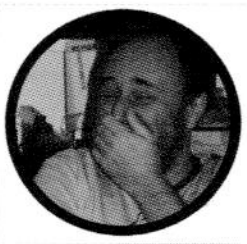

ALAIN MAURICET
Credits: *Harley Quinn and Her Gang of Harleys, Dasterdly and Muttley*
Twitter: @Mauricet34
Likes: Jack Kirby characters based on action figures, toys and statues

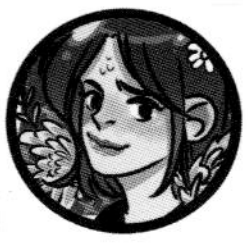

CARA McGEE
Credits: *Dodge City, Over the Garden Wall*
caramcgee.com
Twitter: @ohcarara
Likes: traveling to eat new food
Despises: arguing

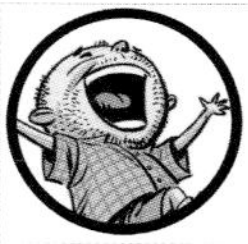

SHAWN McMANUS
Credits: *Fables, The Sandman, House Amok*
shawnmcmanus.net
Instagram @shawndrawscomics
Likes: snowy winters

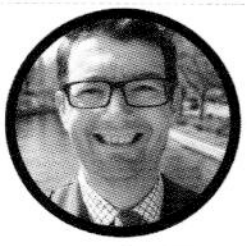

BRIAN MILLER
Credits: *DC Bombshells, Doctor Who*
hifidesign.com
Twitter: @hificolor
Likes: empowerment
Despises: oppression

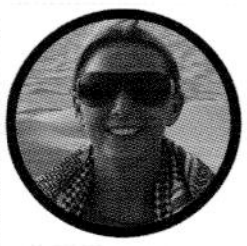

KRISTY MILLER
Credits: *Hi-Fi Color for Comics, Scooby Apocalypse*
hifidesign.com
Twitter: @kristy1az
Likes: a hot desert Despises: snow

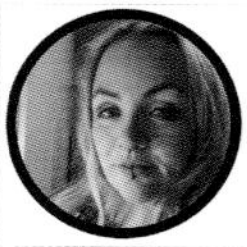

LEAH MOORE
Credits: *Sherlock Holmes:The Vanishing Man, Black Crown Quarterly*
Twitter: @leahmoore
Likes: dive bars
Despises: the Patriarchy

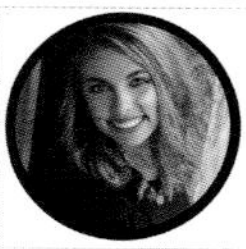

LAUREN MOYER
Credits: Berks Ballet Theatre
Twitter: @laurenmoyer8
Likes: chocolate, ice cream, Pittsburgh
Despises: negative energy, messy rooms

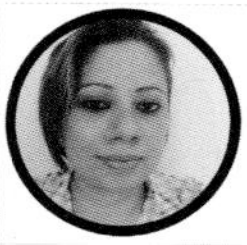

DEVAKI NEOGI
Credits: *The Skeptics, Curb Stomp*
behance.net/devakineogi
Twitter: @DevakiNeogi
Likes: pets, is mother to 3 cats and a dog

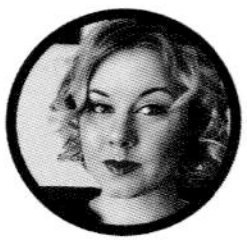

HOPE NICHOLSON
Credits: *The Secret Loves of Geek Girls*
hopenicholson.com
Twitter: @HopeLNicholson
Likes: innovative book spines
Despises: talking about the weather

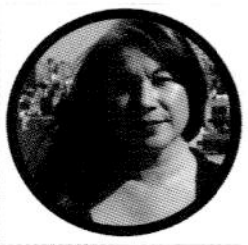

CHRISTINE NORRIE
Credits: *Hopeless Savages, Cheat*
Twitter: @christinenorrie
Likes: food and eating

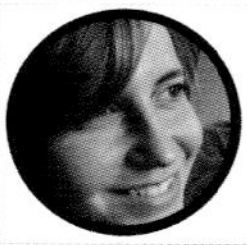

IRMA PAGE
Twitter: @london_nerd
Likes: comic books, good food and wine

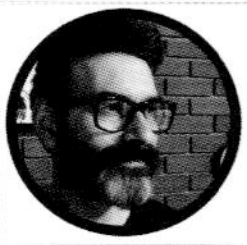

DAN PARENT
Credits: *Archie Meets Batman, Die, Kitty, Die*
danparent.com
Twitter: @parentdaniel

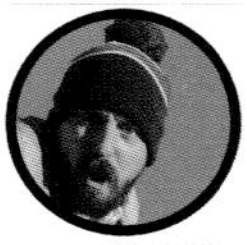

BRETT PARSON
Credits: *The Legend of Tank Girl, New Romancer*
Twitter: @blitzcadet
Likes: being a dad, cartoons, guitar and beer

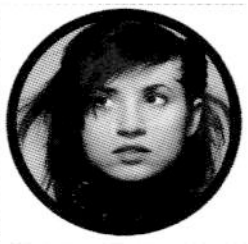

LAURIE PENNY
Credits: *Bitch Doctrine*
Twitter: @PennyRed

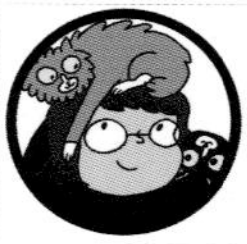

LIZ PRINCE
Credits: *Tomboy, Alone Forever*
lizprincepower.com
Twitter: @comicnrrd
Likes: pinball
Despises: how bad she is at pinball

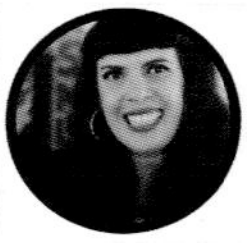

CHRISTINA RICE
Credits: *Ann Dvorak, Hollywood's Forgotten Rebel* christinaricewrites.com
Twitter: @christinarice
Likes: vintage movie posters
Despises: brussels sprouts

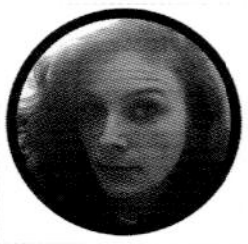

CLAIRE ROE
Credits: *We(l)come Back, Batgirl and the Birds of Prey*
claireroe.com
Twitter: @claireroe
Likes: memes Despises: genji mains

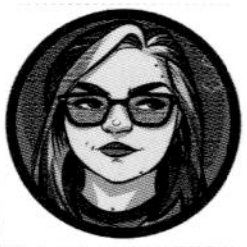

RORI!
Credits: *Tiny Pink Robots, 100 Days, 100 Women*
GiantKittenHead.com
Twitter: @RoriComics
Likes: bears Despises: snares

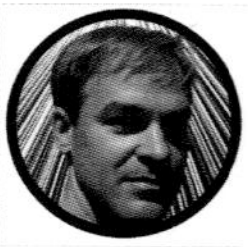

JIM RUGG
Credits: *Street Angel, PLAIN Janes*
jimrugg.com
Twitter: @jimruggart
Likes: ice cream and cats
Despises: noises

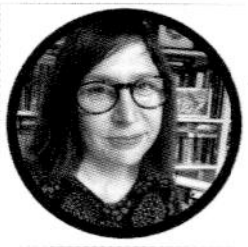

ALISON SAMPSON
Credits: *Hit Girl, Winnebago Graveyard*
alisonsampson.com
Twitter: @alis_samp
Likes: dinner with friends, holidays
Despises: Grappa, Brexit

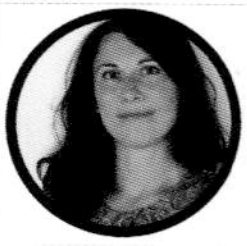

MARGUERITE SAUVAGE
Credits: *DC Bombshells, Faith*
Twitter: @S_Marguerite
Likes: espressos, otters
Despises: certitudes, loud places

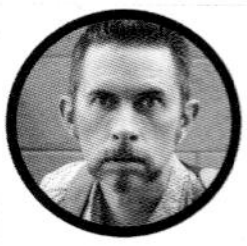

STEVEN T. SEAGLE
Credits: *It's A Bird, Get Naked*
ManOfAction.TV
Twitter: @StevenTSeagle
Likes: drum corps, water

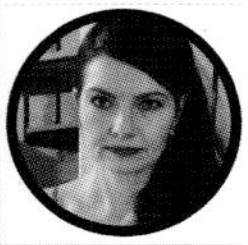

PAULA SEVENBERGEN
Credits: *MAD Magazine, Washington Post*
paula7bergen.com
Twitter: @paula7bergen
Likes: writing
Despises: writing

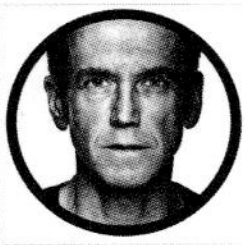

BILL SIENKIEWICZ
Credits: *Elektra Assassin, Stray Toasters*
billsienkiewicz.com
Twitter: @sinKEVitch

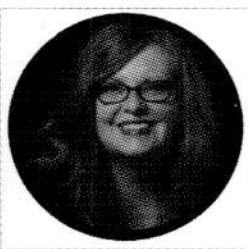

GAIL SIMONE
Credits: *Batgirl, Clean Room*
gailsimone.tumblr.com
Twitter: @gailsimone
Likes: Greyhounds Despises: purposeful ignorance but also Necco Wafers

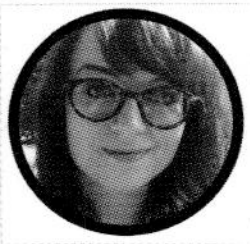

RACHAEL STOTT
Credits: *Doctor Who, Motherlands*
instagram.com/rachael_stott.com
Twitter: @RachaelAtWork

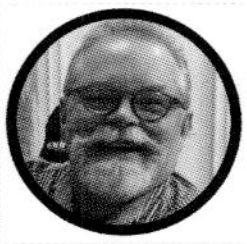

RICK TAYLOR
Credits: *Terminal City, E-Man*
Likes: Chim Chim
Despises: Spritle

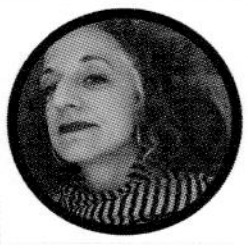

JILL THOMPSON
Credits: *Scary Godmother, The Sandman*
thescarygodmother.com
Twitter:@thejillthompson
Likes: education, equality
Despises: intolerance, apathy

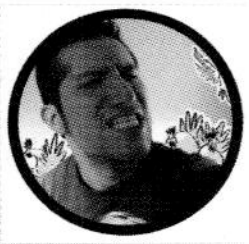

RAUL TREVINO
Credits: *Live Forever*
LiveForeverComic.com
Twitter: @raultrevinoart

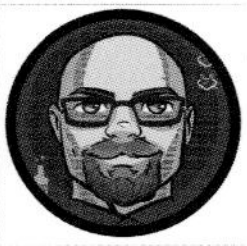

GIBSON TWIST
Credits: *Pictures of You, Our Time in Eden*
picturesofyoucomic.com
Twitter: @GibsonTwist
Likes: a drink with friends
Despises: when it ends

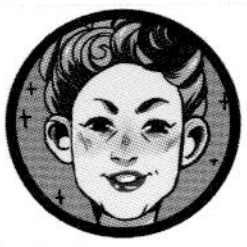

CATHI UNSWORTH
Credits: *The Singer, Weirdo*
cathiunsworth.co.uk
Likes: Lydia Lunch

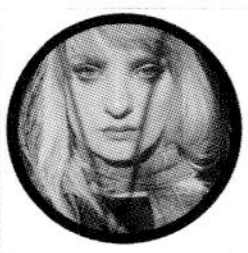

NANNA VENTER
Credits: *Intrepid Astronaut, 1/2 of Bad Form* Podcast
nannaventer.co.za
Twitter: @nannaventer
Likes: punk rock Despises: insincerity

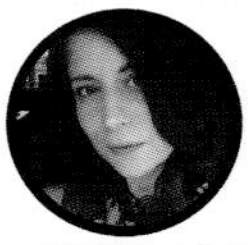

EMMA VIECELI
Credits: *Breaks, Doctor Who*
breakscomic.com
Twitter: @emmavieceli
Likes: board games
Despises: hypocrisy

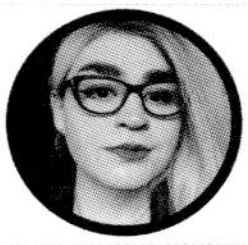

MAGDALENE VISAGGIO
Credits: *Eternity Girl, Kim & Kim*
Twitter: @magsvisaggs
Likes: Star Trek
Despises: video games with linear stories

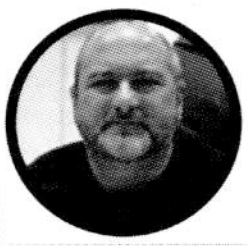

MATT WAGNER
Credits: *Mage: The Hero Denied, Grendel*
mattwagnercomics.com

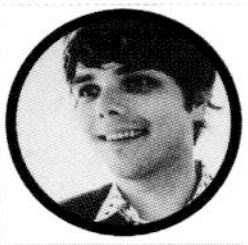

GERARD WAY
Credits: *Doom Patrol, Umbrella Academy*
gerardway.com
Twitter: @gerardway

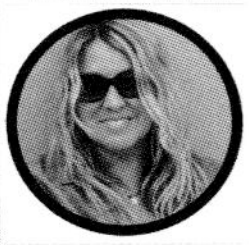

CINDY WHITEHEAD
Credits: OG pro vert skateboarder
girlisnota4letterword.com
Twitter: @GirlisNOTa4LW
Likes: Breaking the rules
Dislikes: Rules

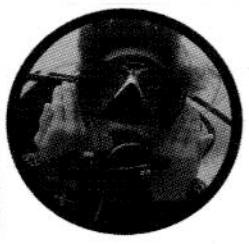

MARIS WICKS
Credits: *Human Body Theater, Coral Reefs: Cities of the Ocean*
mariswicks.com
Twitter: @mariswicks
Likes: water Despises: being dehydrated

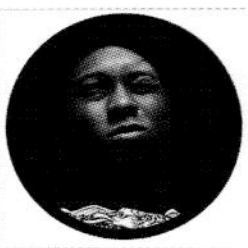

RONALD WIMBERLY
Credits: *Prince of Cats, LAAB*
instagram.com/ronaldwimberly
Twitter: @RaynardFaux

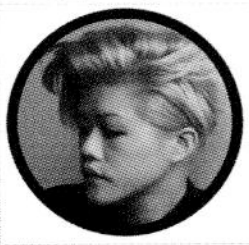

ANNIE WU
Credits: *Dead Guy Fan Club, Black Canary*
anniewuart.com
Twitter: @anniew
Likes: black coffee
Despises: not having black coffee

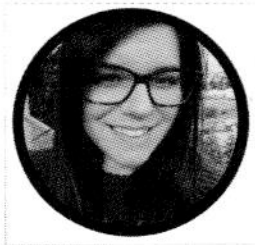

MARLEY ZARCONE
Credits: *Shade, the Changing Girl, Effigy*
instagram.com/kittycoffeekitty
Twitter: @kittycoffee
Likes: cats, coffee and couture

A very special thank-you to the original FEMME MAGNIFIQUE Kickstarter backers.

FEMMEMAGNIFIQUE

"[It brings] new questions about vigilantism, justice, and heroics to the field... Mulligan and Ostertag's creation strikes just the right balance. It's super."
— Cory Doctorow, *Boing Boing*

"Deliberately shatter some stereotypes... with a story about a young woman who is strong in every sense of the word."
— *Entertainment Weekly*

STRONG FEMALE PROTAGONIST
BOOK TWO

BRENNAN LEE MULLIGAN · MOLLY OSTERTAG

Full Color • 336 pages • 6" x 9"
• $24.99 US / $33.99 CAN
• ISBN: 978-0-692-90610-1

© 2018 Molly Ostertag and Brennan Lee Mulligan. All rights reserved.

Top Shelf PRODUCTIONS

"...a truly brilliant, cohesive, curated line of creator-owned comics that will pick up the comics industry, shake it up, and spit it out." — *Comicosity*

kid lobotomy · black crown quarterly · assassinistas · punks not dead · euthanauts · house amok

@blackcrownhq   blackcrown.pub

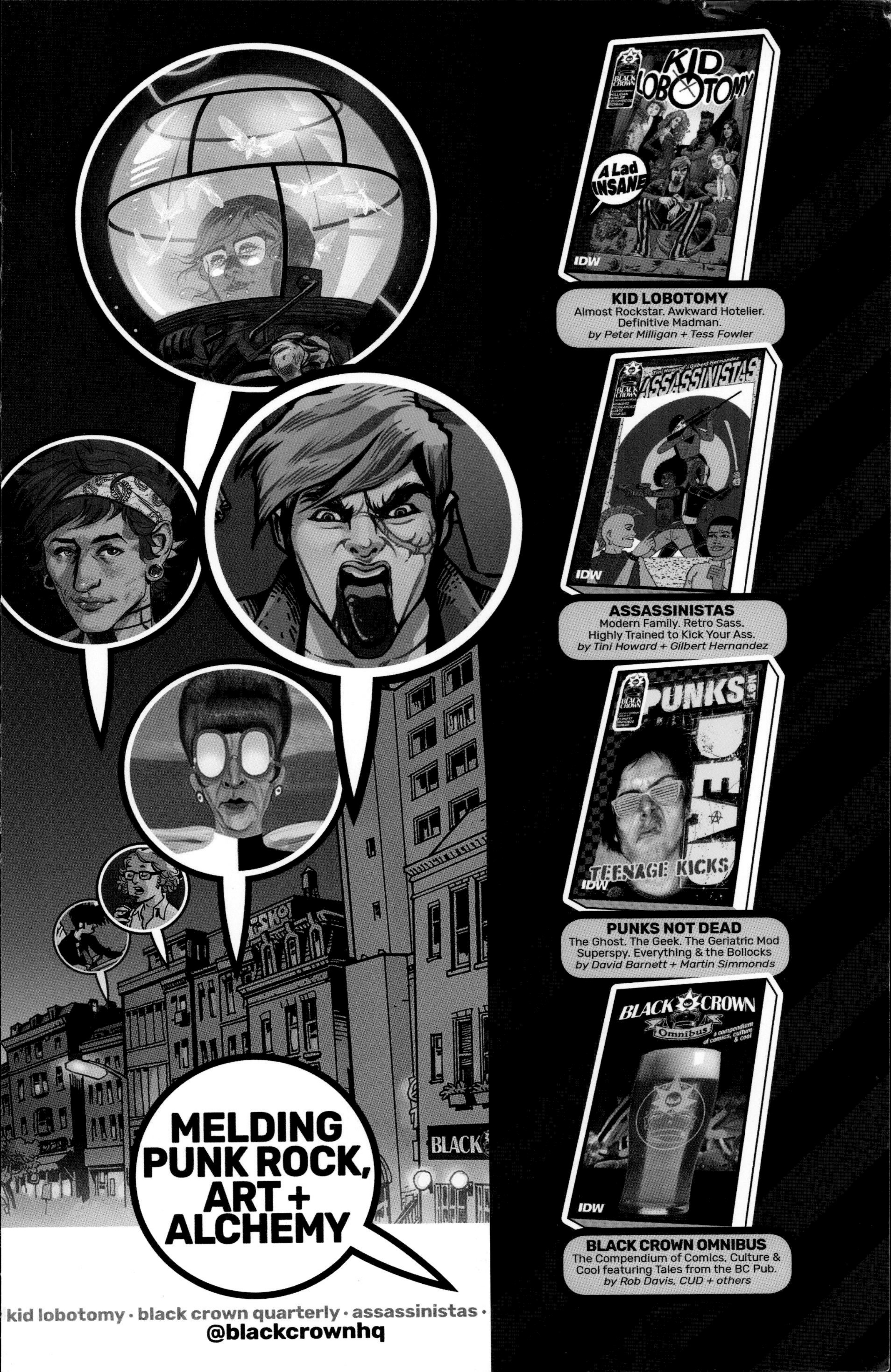
KID LOBOTOMY
A Lad INSANE
IDW
KID LOBOTOMY
Almost Rockstar. Awkward Hotelier. Definitive Madman.
by Peter Milligan + Tess Fowler
ASSASSINISTAS
IDW
ASSASSINISTAS
Modern Family. Retro Sass. Highly Trained to Kick Your Ass.
by Tini Howard + Gilbert Hernandez
PUNKS NOT DEAD
TEENAGE KICKS
IDW
PUNKS NOT DEAD
The Ghost. The Geek. The Geriatric Mod Superspy. Everything & the Bollocks
by David Barnett + Martin Simmonds
BLACK CROWN
Omnibus
a compendium of comics, culture & cool
IDW
BLACK CROWN OMNIBUS
The Compendium of Comics, Culture & Cool featuring Tales from the BC Pub.
by Rob Davis, CUD + others
BLACK
MELDING PUNK ROCK, ART + ALCHEMY
kid lobotomy · black crown quarterly · assassinistas ·
@blackcrownhq

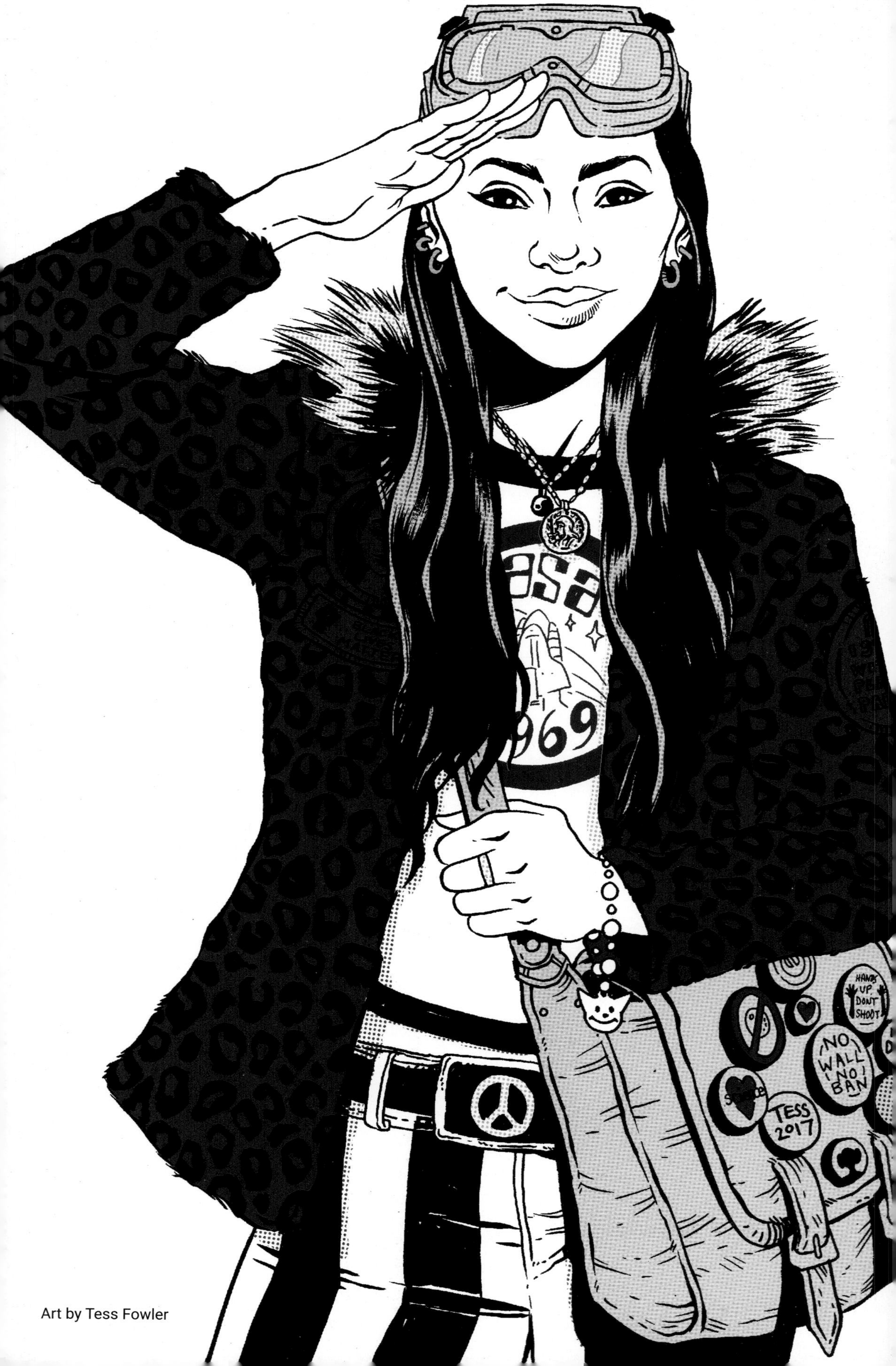
HANDS UP DONT SHOOT
NO WALL NO BAN
TESS 2017

Art by Tess Fowler